October 15–18, 2014
Atlanta, Georgia, USA

I0054761

Association for Computing Machinery

Advancing Computing as a Science & Profession

SIGITE'14

Proceedings of the 15th Annual Conference on
Information Technology Education

RIIT'14

Proceedings of the 3rd Annual Conference on
Research in Information Technology

Sponsored by:
ACM SIGITE

Supported by:
**ORACLE ACADEMY, NetApp, Academic Alliance,
Illinois Institute of Technology**

In cooperation with:
INSTICC

Association for Computing Machinery

Advancing Computing as a Science & Profession

The Association for Computing Machinery
2 Penn Plaza, Suite 701
New York, New York 10121-0701

ISBN: 978-1-4503-2686-5 (Digital)

ISBN: 978-1-4503-3373-3 (Print)

Additional copies may be ordered prepaid from:

ACM Order Department
PO Box 30777
New York, NY 10087-0777, USA

Phone: 1-800-342-6626 (USA and Canada)
+1-212-626-0500 (Global)
Fax: +1-212-944-1318
E-mail: acmhelp@acm.org
Hours of Operation: 8:30 am – 4:30 pm ET

Printed in the USA

Welcome from the Chair

Welcome to Atlanta!! Southern Polytechnic State University (SPSU) is your host institution for our 15th Annual SIGITE and 3rd Annual RIIT conferences. We are located in Marietta, GA – a bit northwest of downtown Atlanta. We hope your stay before, during and after the conference will allow you to see some of our great venues in and around the city.

Close to SPSU you will find Kennesaw Mountain (for those Civil War buffs), and the "General" Train Museum. For those interested in politics and history we have the President Carter Library, Dr. Martin Luther King memorial, Margaret Mitchell house, the Fernbank Museum of Natural History and the Swam House and Historical Center. In downtown Atlanta you can visit such things as the Atlanta Aquarium, CNN Center, Centennial Olympic Park, and the World of Coca-Cola. Cultural venues include the Fox Theater, High Museum, Atlanta Symphony and Center for Puppetry Arts. You can take a 90-minute Trolley tour around Atlanta to see highlights. Zoo Atlanta and Stone Mountain (with the carving of civil war historical figures – President Jefferson Davis, General Robert E. Lee and General Thomas "Stonewall" Jackson) offer full or half-day experiences. And, of course, the Atlanta Falcons may be playing as well.

Our Conference Hotel is the Atlanta Buckhead Marriott Hotel and Conference Center. Buckhead is located a bit northeast of downtown Atlanta. The hotel is also close to MARTA – our mass transit system. We have wonderful restaurants in Buckhead and downtown Atlanta. We have two lovely malls – Lenox Square and Phipps Plaza - close to the hotel. All in all, Atlanta offers you great cultural, culinary and fun activities. We hope you can take advantage of seeing some of these while you are here.

Our program chairs have done a wonderful job of coordinating our papers and workshops for the conference. We have a busy and active schedule. I wish each of you a great conference and exciting time in Atlanta!!

Becky Rutherfoord
Conference Chair

Program Chairs' Welcome

It is with great pleasure that we welcome you to the *15th Annual Conference on Information Technology Education (SIGITE 2014)* and the *3rd Annual Conference on Research in Information Technology (RIIT 2014)*. The theme this year is "Riding the Wave of Change in Information Technology" and the many quality submissions we received allowed us to assemble one of the strongest programs in the history of the conferences. As in past years, the synergies between research and education in information technology are prevalent, and several themes emerged from the accepted submissions. Networking, security, and development remain popular with researchers, and interest in mobile computing, resource measurement and management, capstone courses, and personalization has grown.

The call for participation attracted 111 submissions, 72 of which were submitted to SIGITE and 39 to RIIT. Both numbers represent a larger pool than in recent years, demonstrating that the conferences are of great interest in the community. Ninety-five of the submissions were papers, with 59 papers submitted to SIGITE and 36 papers submitted to RIIT. SIGITE has 27 papers in its program for an acceptance rate of 46% and RIIT has 14 papers for an acceptance rate of 39%. All of the authors presenting should be congratulated on their excellent work.

A conference cannot happen without the help of its reviewers, and this year was no exception. Fifty-five reviewers worked diligently to ensure that every paper had at least three independent reviews. It was a significant effort to produce the 317 reviews that ended up in the system, and we thank the reviewers from the bottom of our heart. New to the conferences this year was a meta review process, in which 13 diligent meta reviewers together examined all reviews for each submission and reconciled those reviews into a coherent message for each author. We hope the meta review process enabled authors to have more substantive feedback on their work, whether it appears in the final program or not.

The conference runs from Thursday to Saturday and each day offers something of interest to attendees. On Thursday our keynote speaker is Dr. Flavio Villanustre, Vice-President of Technology Architecture & Product for LexisNexis and HPCC Systems. The day continues with a workshop on end-user development activities and paper sessions for both SIGITE and RIIT. Thursday concludes with a reception, which we know will be useful for networking with colleagues old and new. Friday introduces a new presentation format, lightning talks on research in progress, at the conferences. There are also paper sessions for SIGITE and RIIT, a poster session in the afternoon and, of course, more opportunities for networking during lunch and the breaks. Saturday offers a three-hour workshop on process-oriented guided inquiry learning (POGIL) as well as a panel on mobile computing courses and some excellent SIGITE papers. We also hope that you stay for the closing session where we will share our plans for SIGITE/RIIT 2015 in Chicago.

We hope you find the conference presentations interesting and thought-provoking, you reconnect with colleagues you know, you find new collaborators, and you submit the work that results to SIGITE or RIIT next year. The excellence you see at SIGITE/RIIT 2014 depends on your energy and effort, and we thank you for letting us be a part of it.

Amber Settle and Terry Steinbach
SIGITE/RIIT 2014 Program Co-chairs
DePaul University, USA

Table of Contents

SIGITE Paper Session 6
Session Chair: Kris Nagel *(Georgia Gwinnett College)*

SIGITE Lightning Talks
Session Chair: Terry Steinbach *(DePaul University)*

SIGITE Paper Session 7
Session Chair: Xing Liu *(Kwantlen Polytechnic University)*

SIGITE Paper Session 8
Session Chair: Bill Paterson *(Mount Royal University)*

SIGITE Posters

SIGITE Paper Session 9
Session Chair: David S. Kerven *(Georgia Gwinnett College)*

SIGITE Workshop 2

SIGITE Panel

SIGITE Paper Session 10
Session Chair: Jim Leone *(Rochester Institute of Technology)*

Keynote Address

SIGITE 2014 Conference Organization

General Chair: Becky Rutherfoord *(Southern Polytechnic State University, USA)*

Assisting Co-Chairs: Lei Li *(Southern Polytechnic State University, USA)*
Susan Van de Ven *(Southern Polytechnic State University, USA)*

Program Co-Chairs: Amber Settle *(DePaul University, USA)*
Terry Steinbach *(DePaul University, USA)*

Logistics Co-Chairs: Jon Preston *(Southern Polytechnic State University, USA)*
Greg Scott *(Southern Polytechnic State University, USA)*

Publicity Co-Chairs: Jack Zheng *(Southern Polytechnic State University, USA)*
Dawn Tatum *(Southern Polytechnic State University, USA)*

Registration Chair: Ashley McClure *(Southern Polytechnic State University, USA)*

Materials Co-Chairs: Marilee McClure *(Southern Polytechnic State University, USA)*
Faith Gonzales *(Southern Polytechnic State University, USA)*
Jasmine Watkins *(Southern Polytechnic State University, USA)*

Meta-reviewers: Joseph J. Ekstrom *(Brigham Young University, USA)*
Rob Friedman *(UW Tacoma, USA)*
Derek L. Hansen *(Brigham Young University, USA)*
Richard Helps *(Brigham Young University, USA)*
Rick Homkes *(Purdue College of Technology, USA)*
Jim Leone *(Rochester Institute of Technology, USA)*
Barry M. Lunt *(Brigham Young University, USA)*
Bonnie MacKellar *(St. John's University, USA)*
Craig S. Miller *(DePaul University, USA)*
Mihaela Sabin *(University of New Hampshire, USA)*
Edward Sobiesk *(United States Military Academy, USA)*

SIGITE RIIT 2014 Sponsor & Supporters

Sponsor:

Supporters:

In cooperation with:

Prospects & Practices for End-User Development Activities in Business Computing Education

Umar Ruhi
Telfer School of Management
University of Ottawa
Ottawa, ON, Canada, K1N 6N5
umar.ruhi@uottawa.ca

ABSTRACT
Many academic courses geared towards improving computer and information literacy (CIL) among non-IT specialists draw upon end-user development (EUD) activities where the end-user assumes a central role in creating or modifying software artefacts. Traditional examples of EUD in educational contexts include exploring and manipulating features and functions in software packages such as spreadsheets & databases, working with simulations, developing websites, utilizing content feeds from a variety of information sources, and creating mashups and widgets with diverse functionality. Although the benefits of improving computing education with EUD practices has been acknowledged in the extant literature, guidelines for the inclusion of EUD-based tasks and tools in academic programs have not been documented in as much detail. The objective of this workshop is to discuss and demonstrate use-cases for EUD based pedagogical components in business computing education, especially so as to meet the objectives set out in model curricula by ACM and AIS.

Categories and Subject Descriptors
K.3.2 [**Computers and Education**]: Computer and Information Science Education

General Terms
Human Factors.

Keywords
End-User Development, EUD, Information Systems, Information Science, Education, Pedagogy, Information Literacy.

1. INTRODUCTION
End-user Development (EUD) can be defined as "a set of methods, techniques, and tools that allow users of software systems, who are acting as non-professional software developers, at some point to create or modify a software artefact" [1]. As a critical trend in personal and enterprise computing [2], EUD continues to gain traction as many interactive software applications are being crafted not by professional software developers but by people with specific domain expertise [3]. Key enablers for EUD include the availability of customizable applications and simplified development toolkits, as well as

SIGITE'14, October 15–18, 2014, Atlanta, Georgia, USA.
ACM 978-1-4503-2686-5/14/10.
http://dx.doi.org/10.1145/2656450.2656490

evolving cloud ecosystems that provide web data services and software functionality through content feeds and application programming interfaces (APIs).

The EUD process has been regarded as a useful learning experience [3, 4] since it facilitates users to gain more control over their computers by engaging in a development process [4, 5]. EUD typically involves a combination of tasks such as parameter customization, workflow specification, curation and integration of content, and modification or assembly of application components.

Many courses offered to non-IT students often include EUD components. Basic examples of such EUD-style activities include experimenting with the extended functionality of productivity software and office-style products such as spreadsheets, database management systems, and word processors. Whether it is working with advanced formulas in a spreadsheet, formulating queries in a database, or customizing macros and stylesheets in a word processor, these skills can play an important role in enhancing computer and information literacy (CIL) of students. Many courses also include web development activities such as web page design and website backend integration. More recently, tools such as mashups have become a popular choice for end-user development (EUD) [6] to facilitate the creation of user-centric applications by re-purposing heterogeneous content or functionality components that already exist elsewhere [7, 8]. These tools have been used across a variety of academic offerings over the past few years, and have been shown to support many positive learning outcomes in educational contexts [9, 10, 11].

2. WORKSHOP OBJECTIVES
The goal of this workshop is to discuss prospects and practices for incorporating end-user development as core activities in academic curricula – specifically geared towards students in business and management programs. The workshop facilitator will present examples of course activities and discuss key lessons from implementation of EUD pedagogical components in various information systems and e-business courses. Furthermore, he will discuss his experiences and views highlighting some of the following:

- alignment of EUD activities with model curricula learning outcomes
- rationale for choice of technologies,
- content and resources for classroom activities, student assignments or group projects,
- student feedback and opinions,
- guidelines for pedagogical implementation,

Workshop participants will be invited to pilot and appraise some of the tasks and tools being presented in the workshop, and to provide their assessments about the efficacy of such activities. Furthermore, the workshop will be conducted in the form of an interactive dialogue in order to foster constructive discussion about key success factors for implementing EUD activities in courses.

It is hoped that this workshop will also serve as a launchpad for pedagogical and research collaboration among colleagues and some of the workshop participants will report on related research work and pedagogical developments at future SIGITE conferences.

3. PRESENTER BIOGRAPHY

Umar Ruhi teaches various undergraduate and graduate level courses in Information Systems, E-Business and Technology Management at the Telfer School of Management, University of Ottawa. In addition to teaching various courses in the BCom and MBA programs, he is a principal professor in the University's Interdisciplinary Graduate Program in E-Business Technologies where he teaches various courses such as Mobile Commerce, Enterprise Social Media Strategy, and Internet Security.

End-User Development (EUD) based learning modules are core components in most of Umar's courses. Activities are designed with the aim to instill a basic practical understanding of technology tools and functional software applications, and to aid students' understanding of theory and concepts introduced in the classroom. Umar believes that EUD tools and tasks provide a useful means to enhance student experience through active experimentation, concrete experiences and reflective observations – learning styles that are at the core of the experiential learning process [12].

4. REFERENCES

[1] Lieberman, H., Paternò, F., Klann, M. and Wulf, V., "End-User Development: An Emerging Paradigm," in Human Computer Interaction Series, H. Lieberman, F. Paternò, M. Klann and V. Wulf, Springer Netherlands, 2006, pp. 1-8.

[2] Lewis, G. A., "Emerging Technologies for Software-Reliant Systems of Systems," Software Engineering Institute, Carnegie Mellon University. Tech. Rep. CMU/SEI-2010-TN-019, 2010.

[3] Paternò, F., "End User Development: Survey of an Emerging Field for Empowering People," ISRN Software Engineering, vol. 2013, 2013.

[4] Paternò, F., "D1.2 Research Agenda: End-User Development: Empowering people to flexibly employ advanced information and communication technology," EUD-Net: End-User Development Network of Excellence, vol. 17, 2003.

[5] Klann, M., "D1.1 Roadmap: End-User Development: Empowering people to flexibly employ advanced information and communication technology," EUD-Net: End-User Development Network of Excellence, vol. 17, 2003.

[6] Cappiello, C., Daniel, F., Matera, M., Picozzi, M. and Weiss, M., "Enabling end user development through mashups: requirements, abstractions and innovation toolkits," in End-User Development, Springer, 2011, pp. 9-24.

[7] Ahmed, S. and Ruhi, U., "Towards a functional taxonomy of enterprise business intelligence mashups," in Informatics and Applications (ICIA), 2013 Second International Conference on, pp. 98-103, 2013.

[8] Ruhi, U. and Choi, D., "Enterprise Mashups for Knowledge Management," in 1st International Conference on Information and Communication Technology Trends (ICICTT), Proceedings of, 2013.

[9] Liu, M., Horton, L., Olmanson, J. and Wang, P., "An exploration of mashups and their potential educational uses," Computers in the Schools, vol. 25, pp. 243-258, 2008.

[10] Ting, H. H. M., "Mash-ups: remixing education?" Access to Knowledge: A Course Journal, vol. 1, 2009.

[11] Bawden, D., "Towards Curriculum 2.0: library/information education for a Web 2.0 world," Library and Information Research, vol. 31, pp. 14-25, 2007.

[12] Kolb, D.A., Boyatzis, R.E. and Mainemelis, C., "Experiential learning theory: Previous research and new directions," Perspectives on Thinking, Learning, and Cognitive Styles, vol. 1, pp. 227-247, 2001.

A Virtualized Testbed with Physical Outlets for Hands-on Computer Networking Education

Mark Schmidt   Florian Heimgaertner   Michael Menth

{mark-thomas.schmidt,florian.heimgaertner,menth}@uni-tuebingen.de
University of Tuebingen, Dept. of Computer Science, Tuebingen, Germany

ABSTRACT

Many computer science curricula include practical courses to undergraduate and graduate students to offer them hands-on networking experience by connecting PCs, switches, and routers in a testbed. Such testbeds are expensive, bulky, energy-intensive, and cause heat problems. Virtualization of PCs and routers on commodity hardware is a solution to those problems. A challenge is to provide physical interfaces for the virtualized components so that students still have the hands-on experience including cabling. In this work, we propose a solution based on inexpensive hardware that can be mounted in a standard 19-inch cabinet. As WiFi adapters, headsets, or additional serial interfaces are needed for advanced experiments, we provide means to connect them as USB devices to virtualized PCs and routers. The system is configured so that students have only access to the virtual machines and their physical interfaces.

Categories and Subject Descriptors

K.3.2 [**Computers and Education**]: Computer and Information Science Education; C.2.3 [**Computer-Communication Networks**]: Network Operations

Keywords

Laboratories; Networking; Virtual Machines; Computer networking education

1. INTRODUCTION

While practical networking courses are not mandatory for most computer science and electrical engineering degrees, they are very popular among students. A major reason for that is the insight that applied networking knowledge may be helpful for their future career but also the fact that interconnecting devices with cables and switches is fun for most

The authors acknowledge the funding by the Deutsche Forschungsgemeinschaft (DFG) under grant ME2727/1-1. The authors alone are responsible for the content of the paper.

students. Such hands-on networking courses were offered at the University of Tuebingen since 2004 based on the concept of Liebeherr and Zarki [15]. The testbeds consisted of 6 PC and 2 routers that can be connected via two unmanaged desktop switches, as well as via a wireless access point and WiFi adapters attached to the PCs. The PCs were connected to a central server through an additional switch. This setup is depicted in Figure 1.

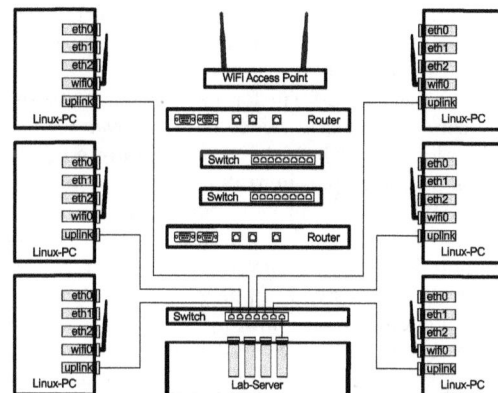

Figure 1: Initial situation. Testbed with physical nodes.

In 2012, a fundamental renewal was necessary, because the testbed hardware was both outdated and degraded. The following conditions had to be taken into account. The networking lab was so successful that the three testbeds, operated in time-sharing mode, were no longer sufficient for the large number of interested students, but our lab had not enough space for more physical testbeds. As no sponsors for hardware could be found and the testbed hardware is expected to be renewed in the future again, the hardware and software expenses should be low. Resources for scientific computing were needed at the same time.

At that time, new advances in hardware support for virtualization of the x86 architecture stipulated academic experiments in our group. As a result, we designed and implemented a testbed setup where the 6 PCs and 2 routers were implemented as virtual machines (VMs) on a commodity server. The Ethernet interfaces of the virtual nodes are connected through the Ethernet ports of the testbed host via a managed switch to a patch panel using Virtual Local Area Network (VLAN) technology. This way, the interfaces of the virtual nodes are physically accessible. Likewise, USB devices can be plugged into a USB hub and mapped to specific virtual machines. In such a testbed, the hands-on experience for students is retained as they can interconnect the physical interfaces of the virtual nodes with real switches and cables or attach USB devices. This is not the case in fully virtualized or emulated environments.

The testbed was shown as a demonstration [23] at SIG-COMM'14. This paper presents the setup in detail.

The paper is structured as follows. Section 2 reviews various approaches for networking lab testbeds. Section 3 describes the testbed architecture and explains solutions to special challenges. Section 4 summarizes this work and draws conclusions.

2. RELATED WORK

As practical networking courses are quite common in computer science and IT education, various designs for labs and testbeds have been published. In this section we provide an overview of different implementation approaches.

In [15] Liebeherr and Zarki describe a hands-on Internet course. The book contains both the syllabus and instructions for setting up a testbed. The testbed consists of 4 physical Linux PCs and 4 Cisco routers. In [3] a testbed design based on 3 PCs, one laptop computer, and two multi-protocol routers is described. In addition, central networking equipment is proposed for management purposes and inter-testbed connectivity.

Emulab [26] is a platform for networking testbeds that allows to connect physical nodes or VMs over virtual networks. Topologies and link characteristics are modelled using VLANs and transparent traffic shaping nodes. In addition, simulated nodes can be integrated into experiments. The authors of [24] describe a similar implementation. To enable remote learning, the physical nodes are connected by configuring VLANs instead of plugging cables.

Other hands-on labs are entirely built on VMs. In [2] a setup is described where 120 PCs and routers run as Xen VMs on a single host and are connected by virtual switches. dVirt [17] is a virtualized BGP router testbed consisting of Xen VMs connected by Open vSwitch. V-Lab [27] is a remote access lab with VMs on a XenServer cluster connected using VLANs.

In [1] a reconfigurable network lab based on VMware is described. Each physical interface can be assigned to at most one VM to provide physical access to Ethernet interfaces of VMs. This approach requires at least as many physical Ethernet interfaces as virtual Ethernet interfaces. As the number of pluggable network interface cards (NICs) per host is limited, this is a severe limitation on the number of virtual interfaces supported by the host. Therefore, we use a different approach which can support more virtual interfaces than the number of Ethernet ports on a host.

3. TESTBED ARCHITECTURE

This section starts with an overview of the testbed and a hardware description. We explain the virtualization platform and the software infrastructure of the networking lab. Finally, we describe our realization of physical access to interfaces of VMs, and present solutions to problems encountered during the actual implementation of our concept.

3.1 Overview

The new testbed provides the same features as the old testbed given in Figure 1. It consists of a "testbed host" and

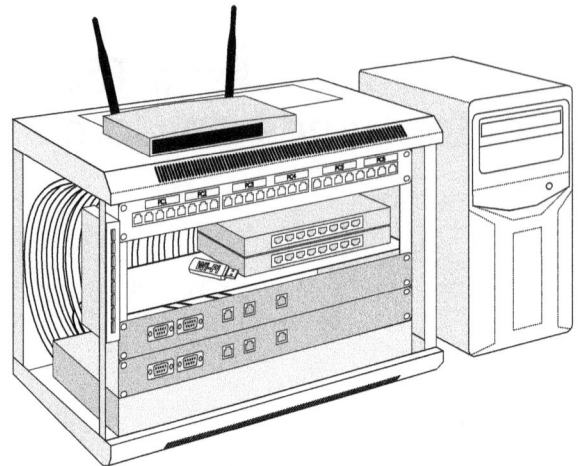

Figure 2: Networking cabinet and testbed host running the virtual nodes.

a cabinet with networking hardware, which are illustrated in Figure 2. The "testbed host" hosts 6 virtualized Linux PCs and 2 routers. The networking hardware is placed in a 6U wall mount cabinet (covers and front door are removed in the figure). At the bottom a managed switch is mounted facing backwards. Above the switch, two front panels carry DB9 and RJ45 outlets for the virtual routers. Unmanaged desktop switches for student exercises and other networking devices are placed on a rack-mount shelf. The topmost rack unit is covered by a labeled patch panel, serving as network outlets for the virtualized PCs. A USB hub is attached to the left mounting post. The WiFi adapters for the PCs are provided as USB devices that can be passed through to the VMs. In the same way physical headsets for voice-over-IP (VoIP) exercises can also be connected. On top of the cabinet, a wireless access point running the OpenWrt embedded Linux distribution is available for experiments involving IEEE 802.11 technology.

An additional "lab server" provides common services (see Section 3.4.2) to all the testbeds.

3.2 Hardware Description

We use commodity server hardware based on the Intel Xeon platform (Xeon E3 Sandy Brigde) for the testbed host. The machine is equipped with 32 GB RAM, RAID-5 disk storage, and an Intel I350-T4 Ethernet adapter. Multiple USB WiFi adapters, two USB/Serial converters, and two USB headsets can be connected through a powered 8 port USB hub.

To provide access to the Ethernet interfaces of the VMs, we use a managed HP Procurve 48 port Ethernet switch in combination with a 24 port patch panel. The students use two unmanaged desktop switches and large quantity of Cat5e twisted pair patch cables to create and modify network topologies in the course of their exercises.

The lab server relies on the same hardware platform as the testbed hosts, but it is equipped with additional Ethernet interfaces so that every testbed can be connected.

3.3 Virtualization Platform

We describe the hardware and software support for the virtualization concept of the testbed host.

3.3.1 Hardware Support for Virtualization

The hardware of the testbed host has to provide support for multiple hardware virtualization features.

Firstly, the CPU has to provide extensions that enable the x86 architecture to be virtualized with hardware support, which is not possible by default. This is necessary as pure software virtualization is very CPU intensive and lacks performance. Those extensions are marketed as VT-x [25] by Intel. Different implementations are available from other CPU manufacturers.

Secondly, an Input/Output Memory Management Unit (IOMMU) is required as we want to pass through physically available hardware, e.g., Ethernet devices, to the VMs. An IOMMU provides features such as translation from virtual device addresses to physical device address, which is needed for remapping of interrupts and DMA. In the case of Intel hardware this feature is summarized as VT-d [7].

As a testbed host does not provide enough PCI slots to plug in four dedicated Ethernet devices per VM, we have to be able to realize more than one virtual Ethernet interface per physically available NIC. Two additional technologies are used to realize and subsequently map these virtual interfaces to VMs. Virtual Machine Device Queues (VMDQ) [8] enable multiple queues per NIC. They are connected by an internal bridge, and implement the packet forwarding to the VMs in hardware. PCI-SIG Single Root I/O Virtualization (SR-IOV) [18] provides an extension of the PCI Express standard that allows multiple so-called virtual functions (VF) on a single physical function (PF). A PF is a full-featured PCI device whereas VFs are lightweight PCI devices that are managed by a PF. Each VF can be individually passed through to a VM. Together with VMDQ, it is possible to provide multiple virtual Ethernet interfaces, each with its own queue, on a single physical device, which is called VT-c [6] for Intel hardware.

3.3.2 Software Support for Virtualization

Software support is required to make the virtualization mechanisms available. The hypervisor used to run the VMs needs support for the extensions described above. Especially, it should be possible to pass through both Ethernet and USB devices to the VMs. Additionally, we need to limit the resources used by each VM so that misconfiguration of a VM by students does not affect the host system.

We use the Kernel-based Virtual Machine (KVM) [10] of Linux as hypervisor on the testbed host for the VMs. The basic idea of KVM is to implement the hypervisor as part of the Linux kernel on the host machine instead of using a dedicated software like Xen. That means, the host kernel has direct access to the hardware and is responsible for regulating VM access to the hardware. However, KVM cannot be used directly as it is realized as a kernel module and does not provide an interface for user interaction. QEMU [19] is the user space software to run the VMs. It is a multipurpose virtualization tool which can emulate various types of hardware such as CPU, hard disk, or network adapters. Additionally, it can use KVM as a backend to benefit from hardware virtualization features of modern x86 CPUs and chipsets. In the presence of hardware support, entire hardware devices like PCI or USB devices can be passed through to a VM.

For improved maintainability a virtualization framework should be used to create, manage and run the VMs, instead of starting QEMU directly. We use the libvirt [21] framework which provides among other tools the command line frontend `virsh` and the graphical tool `virt-manager`. Hardware and resources assigned to a VM are configured using XML files which are convenient to understand and modify for both humans and computers. Furthermore, libvirt allows to add and remove hardware like USB devices at VM runtime. Thereby we can connect WiFi adapters, headsets, or USB/Serial adapters to the VMs.

The VMs can either be accessed by a serial text terminal or graphically using "virt-viewer" which can use VNC or spice [22] to provide the screen of the VM. We prefer spice because of better performance and additional features such as clipboard sharing between testbed host and VM as well as automatic adjustment of screen resolution for the VMs depending on the window size of the viewer.

As we want a Cisco-IOS-like experience for the virtual routers, we do not provide graphical access to them, but only a command line interface. This interface is realized by the `vtysh` shell of the Quagga [20] routing software suite.

3.4 Networking Lab Software Infrastructure

We describe the software support for the testbed host and the VMs and the services provided by the lab server.

3.4.1 Software Support for Testbed Host and VMs

All machines, physical and virtual, are powered by the Ubuntu [4] Linux operating system. The testbed hosts are based on a minimal installation and contain only the software required to run and access the VMs, that means in particular QEMU and libvirt with their dependencies, but also a simple user interface (see Figure 3). The interface provides a menu to start, stop, attach USB devices and access the VMs and a web browser. The VMs run on a default Lubuntu installation, the LXDE (a lightweight desktop environment) flavor of Ubuntu, and are equipped with additional software such as wireshark to monitor traffic or services, which is needed for practical exercises. The virtual routers are also based on a minimal installation and additionally provide the Quagga router suite.

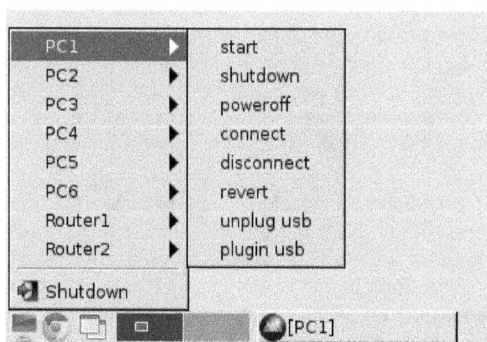

Figure 3: User interface of the testbed host.

To simplify the management of the network interfaces, we decided to rename the network interfaces by the use of udev [11] in a more structured way instead of the new default `biosdevname` [16] based naming scheme. Figure 5(b) shows that the interfaces within the VMs are named according to the traditional scheme, e.g. `eth{0,1,2}`, which provides a better mapping to the physical network outlets. Before a

VF eth$i$ of VM j is passed through to that VM, it is named vm$j$-eth$i$ on the host. The VFs eth$i$ of all VMs are hosted by the same PF which is named vm-eth0.

3.4.2 Services Provided by the Lab Server

The lab server provides several services for the testbed hosts as well as for the VMs, which is shown in Figure 4. In addition to infrastructure services, such as DHCP or DNS and gateway, we also use services for a central account and configuration management.

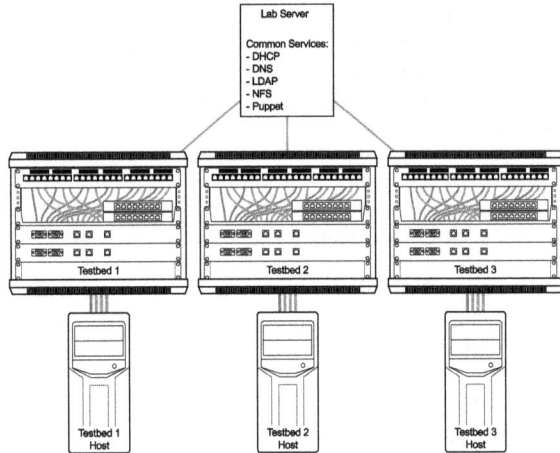

Figure 4: Lab setup with 3 testbeds.

To allow flexible and efficient management of both VMs and testbed hosts, large parts of the system configuration are managed centrally on the lab server. For this purpose we use the puppet [9] configuration management software. Using a declarative domain specific language, the desired configuration of a node can be specified in so-called manifests. This way we manage software packages, services as well as configuration files of testbed hosts and VMs. The puppet "master" is running on the lab server, providing the configuration information. On the testbed hosts and VMs, puppet "agents" are fetching and applying the configurations.

The user accounts for the students are managed using an Lightweight Directory Access Protocol (LDAP) service and their home directories are provided using the Network File System (NFS). That way, the students can log in at any available testbed and have access to their stored data. This is especially useful in the case of testbed maintenance or in the case of hardware problems. In addition to the home directories, we use NFS to provide initial configuration files and scripts for the students to use in the exercises.

Some commands in the exercises, such as starting or stopping a service, require special permissions – they have to be run as the *root* user. This can be achieved using the sudo tool. However, for security reasons, students should not be allowed to execute arbitrary commands as root, but only a restricted set of commands. To realize this, sudo allows to define these permissions for each command for both users and groups. Therefore, students are members of a special student group which has limited root permissions defined in the sudo configuration. As we do not want to manage this configuration by hand on each VM, we also use LDAP to provide these rules for all VMs which requires sudo-ldap, a special version of sudo, on the VMs.

3.5 Providing Physical Access to Virtual Ethernet Interfaces

One of our main goals is to enable students to physically connect VMs with real cables and switches. To that end, physical access to Ethernet interfaces of the VMs is required.

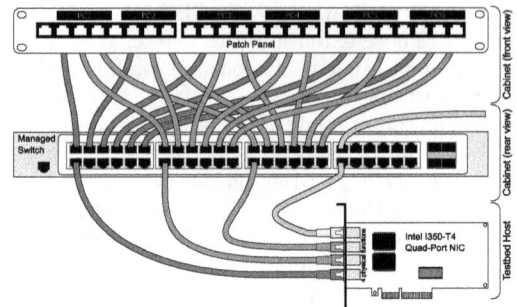

(a) Physical setup; cables for the virtual routers are omitted.

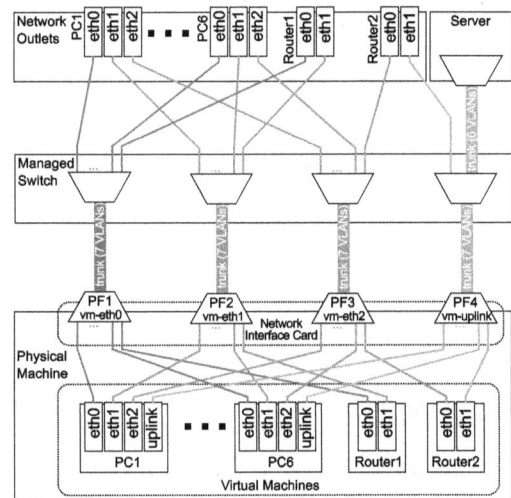

(b) Logical overview.

Figure 5: Providing physical access to Ethernet interfaces of VMs.

Each of the 6 virtual PCs has 4 Ethernet interfaces and each of the 2 virtual routers has 2 Ethernet interfaces. Figure 5(a) illustrates that the Ethernet interfaces of the VMs are multiplexed over an Intel I350 quad-port NIC and demultiplexed by a managed switch. From there, they are connected to a patch panel where physical access to each of them is provided.

Each of the 4 ports on the NIC is implemented as a separate PF providing 7 VFs that represent the Ethernet interfaces of the VMs. As explained in Section 3.3.1, they are logically separate PCI devices that are individually passed through to VMs.

A major challenge is the multiplexing and demultiplexing. Figure 5(b) shows that the VFs eth{0,1,2} and uplink from each VM are multiplexed over one PF (vm-...) of the testbed host. We use VLAN technology for that multiplexing so that the managed switch can easily demultiplex the individual Ethernet interfaces. VLAN is defined by IEEE 802.1Q [13] and allows multiplexing and demultiplexing of several virtual LANs (VLANs) over a common physical link which is then called "trunk" link. To enable multiplexing and demultiplexing, a "tag" is inserted into the header of Ethernet frames indicating the VLAN. In our solution, we use a dedicated VLAN with a unique ID per VF, representing a VM interface. The PFs act as an Ethernet bridge, forwarding data for the VFs as tagged VLANs. The driver on the testbed host configures the PF to transparently add/remove the tags in the Ethernet frames during the transition from/to the VM. The managed VLAN-capable switch also adds/removes the tags while multiplexing/demultiplexing the VLANs from/to the patch panel. As a result, VLAN tags cannot be observed in Ethernet frames neither in VMs nor on the patch panel.

3.6 Attaching USB Devices to VMs

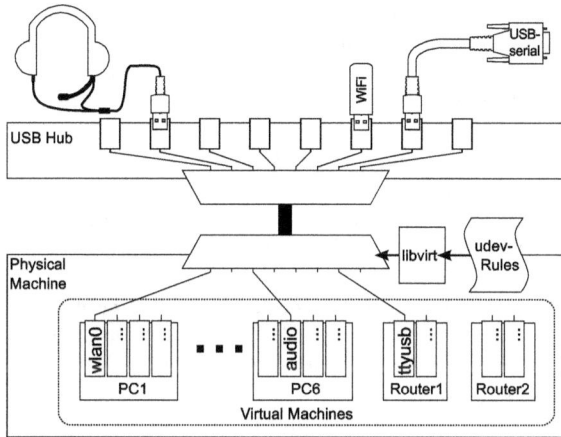

Figure 6: Connecting USB devices to VMs.

As shown in Figure 6, selected USB devices can be plugged into a USB hub that is connected to the testbed host and then be passed through to a VM. In the following, we explain how we configure this passthrough.

USB devices have a unique ID and get an address assigned as soon as they are connected to the bus. We implement a fixed assignment of USB devices to VMs inside a testbed. For selected USB devices the assignment of the IDs to VMs needs to be defined in appropriate udev rules. Flexible assignment of special USB devices to VMs is basically possible but not implemented as not needed.

When a USB device is plugged in, the testbed host gets a udev event containing the address and ID of that USB device. The testbed host matches the ID against a udev rule set that triggers an action. We defined as an action for the IDs of the special USB devices the execution of a shell script that generates a configuration file for libvirt. The user can then trigger the passthrough of the USB device to the VM over the GUI illustrated in Figure 3. The trigger calls libvirt which loads the configuration file and possibly interacts with QEMU to pass the address of the respective USB device through to the appropriate VM. This design allows the special USB devices to be plugged in before the VMs are started.

3.7 Problems and Solutions

During development and testing of the testbed we encountered several problems. We describe some of them and our solutions.

3.7.1 Bridged Virtual Functions

The Intel I350 network adapter provides a feature called *PF Loopback*. This technique is intended to improve network performance by bypassing an external switch in cases where both source and destination are VFs of the same PF. While PF Loopback is a desirable feature for common datacenter applications, it leads to unwanted side effects in the testbed. Under certain configurations, network connectivity between VMs remains available even though the corresponding cables are unplugged.

Version 4.3.0 and below of the Intel NIC driver [5] did not provide an option to disable this behavior without modifying the source code. Since version 5.0.5 the behavior is configurable and can be changed using the `bridge` tool[1] of the iproute [12] package. It can be used to change the bridge mode of the PF to *Virtual Ethernet Port Aggregator* (VEPA) [14] mode, which enforces the desired behavior.

3.7.2 Shared Network Bandwitdh

The bandwidth of a PF is shared by its VFs. This may lead to problems with point-to-point performance measurement. A workaround is to use at most one VF per PF for such experiments. Another solution is to connect the PF to Gbit ports of the switch but to connect the VLANs on patch panels to 100 Mbit ports of the switch. This reduces the p2p bandwidth to at most 100 Mbit/s.

3.7.3 Identification of USB Devices

Some vendors do not respect the purpose of unique serial number fields and use the same ID for all devices in an entire product batch. Therefore, it is not always possible to distinguish plugged USB devices only by their IDs.

To still differentiate them, the specific driver, e.g., an Ethernet driver, for the device has to be loaded on the host. Thereby, USB WiFi adapters can be distinguished by their MAC addresses. However, to use the USB passthrough mechanism and assign the USB device to a specific VM, the driver has to be unloaded on the host again. This can be achieved by special udev rules and scripts.

3.7.4 Virtual Machine Images

Local file system changes made by students should be persistent during exercises and in particular be kept on power cycles. After the completion of an exercise or in case of a major misconfiguration, it should be possible to reset the file system to a default configuration. We describe how we achieve these two goals.

The VM image is stored on the hard disk on a separate volume. It contains the initial file system. Changes to the file system are stored as increments in a special file on another volume. By resetting that file, the original file system is restored.

We implement this method by using LVM2 to create logical volumes (LVs) of the hard disk which are virtual disk partitions. Each VM image is stored in a separate LV; they differentiate only by minor configuration differences. The incremental storage of file system changes is performed by QEMU and commonly known as overlay. The base volume is the so-called backing file and the file with the incremental changes is called image and uses the qcow2 format.

---

[1]tested with version 3.12. The bridge tool was introduced in version 3.5.0, 2012

3.7.5 Serial Network Interface

The serial link between the virtual routers is realized by a PPP connection over a null modem RS-232 serial cable. By default PPP provides flow control for the communication which leads to the effect that packets are queued if the physical link is broken and all packets are sent if the link becomes available again. This effect can be observed with the `ping` command. Packets are not dropped as expected when unplugging the cable. When the cable is plugged in again, large round-trip times can be observed as they include the downtime caused by unplugging the cable. To enforce the desired behavior, it is necessary to explicitly disable flow control in PPP.

4. CONCLUSION

We presented a testbed setup with all PCs and routers virtualized on a single commodity server. The testbed distinguishes from others by the fact that Ethernet and USB interfaces to the virtual machines are accessible on a patch panel and a USB hub, respectively. The implementation combines the advantages of a purely virtualized testbed and an entirely physical testbed. On the one hand, our approach is cost-effective, saves energy and space and causes only little heat, and the testbed host can be reused for scientific computing if not needed for exercises. On the other hand, it retains hands-on experience for students in the sense that they can connect nodes using real switches and cables. The suggested architecture is easily extensible as new devices can be attached to virtual nodes via the USB hub, which allows the integration of new experiments in networking courses.

We successfully operate 6 of these testbeds since January 2013 and gained experience from 3 rounds of successful networking courses since then. The interoperation of the early virtualization-capable versions of the operating system, drivers, as well as other software and hardware was initially rather challenging. However, the software has sufficiently evolved in the meantime so that the operation of the testbed is stable. This experience shows that virtualization of low-cost devices has matured to a degree that they can be plugged together even for non-standard deployment.

5. ACKNOWLEDGEMENTS

The authors thank Wolfgang Braun, Michael Hoefling, Andreas Stockmayer and Sebastian Veith for helping assembling the testbeds, Jakob Herrmann, Cynthia Mills and Andreas Stockmayer for support in executing the networking courses, and the Institut fuer Astronomie und Astrophysik Tuebingen (IAAT) Workshop for manufacturing the front panels of the virtual routers.

6. REFERENCES

[1] S. Abbott-McCune, A. J. Newtson, and B. S. Goda. Developing a Reconfigurable Network Lab. In *ACM SIGITE*, 2008.

[2] C. Avin, M. Borokhovich, and A. Goldfeld. Mastering (Virtual) Networks - A Case Study of Virtualizing Internet Lab. In *International Conference on Computer Supported Education (CSEDU)*, 2009.

[3] C. E. Caicedo and W. Cerroni. Design of a Computer Networking Laboratory for Efficient Manageability and Effective Teaching. In *IEEE Conference on Frontiers in Education*, 2009.

[4] Canonical Ltd. Ubuntu 14.04 LTS (Trusty Tahr). http://releases.ubuntu.com/14.04/, 2014.

[5] Intel Corp. igb Linux Base Driver for Intel Ethernet Network Connection. http://sourceforge.net/projects/e1000/files/igb_stable.

[6] Intel Corp. Intel Virtualization Technology for Connectivity (VT-c), 2012.

[7] Intel Corp. Intel Virtualization Technology for Directed I/O (VT-d) Architecture Specification, 2012.

[8] Intel LAN Access Division. Intel VMDq Technology. Whitepaper, Intel Corp, 2008.

[9] L. Kanies. Puppet: Next-Generation Configuration Management. *The USENIX Magazine*, 31(1), 2006.

[10] A. Kivity et al. kvm: the Linux virtual machine monitor. In *Linux Symposium*, 2007.

[11] G. Kroah-Hartman. udev – A Userspace Implementation of devfs. In *Linux Symposium*, 2003.

[12] A. Kuznetsov and S. Hemminger. iproute2: Utilities for Controlling TCP/IP Networking and Traffic, 2012.

[13] LAN/MAN Standards Committee of the IEEE Computer Society. *IEEE 802.1Q: Virtual Bridged Local Area Networks*, 2003.

[14] LAN/MAN Standards Committee of the IEEE Computer Society. *IEEE 802.1Qbg: Edge Virtual Bridging*, 2012.

[15] J. Liebeherr and M. E. Zarki. *Mastering networks – an internet lab manual.* Pearson Education, 2003.

[16] Narendra K. Consistent Network Device Naming in Linux. Whitepaper, Dell Linux Engineering, 2012.

[17] I. Oprescu, M. Meulle, and P. Owezarski. dVirt: A Virtualized Infrastructure for Experimenting BGP Routing. In *IEEE Conference on Local Computer Networks (LCN)*, 2011.

[18] PCI SIG. Single Root I/O Virtualization and Sharing Specification 1.1, 2010.

[19] QEMU team. QEMU 2. http://wiki.qemu.org/ChangeLog/2.0, 2014.

[20] Quagga team. Quagga Routing Suite. http://www.nongnu.org/quagga/.

[21] Red Hat. libvirt: The Virtualization API. http://libvirt.org, 2012.

[22] Red Hat. SPICE. http://www.spice-space.org/, 2012.

[23] M. Schmidt, F. Heimgaertner, and M. Menth. Demo: A Virtualized Lab Testbed with Physical Network Outlets for Hands-on Computer Networking Education. In *ACM SIGCOMM*, 2014.

[24] S. C. Sivakumar, W. Robertson, M. M. Artimy, and N. Aslam. A Web-Based Remote Interactive Laboratory for Internetworking Education. *IEEE Transactions on Education*, 48(4):586–598, 2005.

[25] R. Uhlig et al. Intel Virtualization Technology. *IEEE Computer*, 38(5):48–56, 2005.

[26] B. White et al. An Integrated Experimental Environment for Distributed Systems and Networks. In *Symposium on Operating Systems Design and Implementation (OSDI)*, 2002.

[27] L. Xu, D. Huang, and W.-T. Tsai. V-Lab: A Cloud-Based Virtual Laboratory Platform for Hands-On Networking Courses. In *Conference on Innovation and Technology in Computer Science Education (ITiCSE)*, 2012.

Teaching a Networking Class for Freshmen: Course Design and Lessons Learned

Yang Wang, Thomas Blum, Margaret McCoey
Dept. of Mathematics and Computer Science
La Salle University
1900 W Olney Ave
Philadelphia, PA 19141
{wang,blum,mccoey}@lasalle.edu

ABSTRACT

In Computer Science/Information Technology (CS/IT), it is challenging to teach a networking class for freshmen students. On one hand, freshmen students have a very limited knowledge base, and the transition process from high school to college education patterns may take a long time (and vary on a individual basis). On the other hand, teaching networking requires the coverage of abstract networking theories and concepts and demands extensive hands-on practice. Consequently, a successful design of the freshmen networking class is vital to ensure the smooth transition and build a solid basis for advanced classes. In this paper, we present our design for teaching a freshmen networking class. Different from literature studies where the major focus is keeping the teaching up with the cutting-edge technologies, we embed the principle of *simple, relevant, and interesting*, with the aim to keep the interests of the freshmen students and to avoid the creation of frustration in their early studies. We also summarize our major design strategies and share feedback from the students and lessons that we learned. The presented design, although dedicated to teaching networks for CS/IT freshmen, can be applied to many other subjects of CS/IT as well as other majors.

Categories and Subject Descriptors

K.3.2 [**Computer and Information Science Education**]: Computing and Network Education

General Terms

Design, Experimentation

Keywords

Network, course design, freshmen

1. INTRODUCTION

One of the most important factors in teaching is "what the learners already know" [1]. It is not only the prior knowledge stored in memory trace that influences learning, but also the learning strategies attained through previous experiences that impact the learning behaviors [2]. Teaching entry level freshmen classes hence faces huge challenges. Freshmen students have a very limited knowledge base to facilitate the learning. Moreover, the transition process from high school to college education is never "seamless" [3] given the learning strategies difference from high school. In particular, teaching networking classes for Computer Science/Information Technology (CS/IT) freshmen poses extra difficulties such as the high-pace of networking technology innovation and the abstractness of networking theories/concepts. Consequently, a successful design of the freshmen networking class is vital to ensure the smooth transition, stimulate students' interests in CS/IT majors, and build a solid basis (i.e., prior knowledge and strategy) for future advanced classes.

In this work, we aim to present our design of a freshmen networking class that addresses the above challenges. In the literature, there is limited work dedicated to the course design for CS/IT freshmen students. A recent work [4] faced similar challenges and designed a course of Computer Forensics for first-year students. There is a more extensive literature on the lab design of a networking class (e.g., [5, 6, 7, 8, 9, 10, 11, 12, 13, 14, 15, 16]). The proposed lab design is either general for supporting multiple networking classes (e.g., [6, 7, 8, 13]) or dedicated to a particular class (e.g., [9, 10] for wireless networking, and [17] for security auditing). Similarly, there are many literature studies on introducing cutting-edge technologies to the classroom (e.g., introduction of virtualization [18, 5, 11, 7, 19], cloud [15], and IP phone [16]). Different from the literature, we seek to propose an overall course design that is *simple, relevant and interesting*, with the aim to stimulate the interests of the freshmen students and to avoid the creation of frustration in their transition period. At the same time, we expect to maintain sufficient depth of the important networking concepts to prepare the students for future study. We also share lessons that we learned in teaching this class, and discuss the feedback from the students. In addition, the major design principles are summarized, and can be transformed to many other subjects in CS/IT as well as other majors.

The rest of this paper is organized as follows. Section 2 presents the background and the major objective of this freshmen networking class. In Section 3, we discuss the major challenges that need to be addressed in the design. We present the major components of the course design in Section 4, and the major principles that we adopt are summarized in Section 5. We share the feedback of students and lessons learned in Section 6. Finally, Section 7 draws conclusions and presents the future work.

2. BACKGROUND AND OBJECTIVES OF THE CLASS

Our university is an urban institution, and the Math and Computer Science Department offers both Computer Science (CS) and Information Technology (IT) majors. Over the past decade, the CS/IT majors constitute a diverse population with over 42% from under-represented ethnic groups (as of Year of 2014). Computer networks, as a common subject for both CS and IT majors, are decoupled into three major classes: 220 Data Communication, 320 Network Administration, and 422 Information Security, where the 220 class offers a general introduction to networking (for freshmen students), and the 320, 422 classes address the adminstration, and security aspects of networking. This breakdown aims to reinforce the learning of networking with gradually increased depth and difficulty. The 220 course also provides background for courses in Client Support and Administrative Scripting (which covers *bash*, *PowerShell* and *Active Directory*). Furthermore, in 220 students are exposed to the *client-server* paradigm which informs them about the differences between client-side scripting and server-side scripting.

Teaching the network class for freshmen can expose various aspects of the core concepts of computer science such as binary number system, algorithms, networking, and programming (e.g., socket programming) to students, hence they can determine their career path early in their study. In addition, compared to other subjects, networking is more closely tied to the daily lives of students, thanks to the popularity of Internet applications. Consequently, it is easier to motivate students and attract their interests to dive into the networking technologies behind those applications.

Our design presented in this paper is dedicated to the 220 class. The major objectives of this course are: (i) Present students with a big picture of networking; (ii) Stimulate the freshmen's interests in CS/IT; (iii) Build a solid basis on key concepts of networking and prepare students for advanced classes.

3. CHALLENGES

In this section, we discuss the major challenges we faced when developing the networking class for freshmen.

As mentioned above, previous knowledge can greatly improve the acquisition and understanding of new knowledge in the human cognitive process. In teaching freshmen courses, the first challenge is the lack of the prior knowledge. Teaching networking demands the support of the knowledge that is covered in diverse topics, as summarized in Table 1. For instance, the binary number system (including the conversion between binary and decimal) is needed for understanding IP addressing, and subnetting. Another example is Finite State Machines (FSMs), which are generally used to describe the mechanism of Internet protocols (e.g., TCP [20]).

Ultimately, the knowledge learned through this class is expected to serve as *prior* knowledge for future advanced networking classes. As a result, despite the abstractness and complexity of networking, we need to cover a sufficient

Table 1: Needed Knowledge Support

Needed Knowledge	Covered in	Used for
Binary System	Discrete Math	IP Address, subnetting
ASCII Code	Programming	App. Layer Protocols
Finite State Machine	Automata	Protocol Description
Graph Algorithm	Algorithm	Routing

set of concepts that present a big picture of networking. At the same time, we need to balance the depth and complexity of the coverage given the student's limited background.

Another concern is that teaching networking should have a hybrid flavor of theory and practice. For instance, it is a common practice to rely on *layering* to organize network protocols. Layering, however, is not a straightforward concept for freshmen due to its abstractness. At the same time, the best strategy for teaching a protocol (e.g., DNS) probably is through hands-on exercises. Given the background of freshmen, we have to make sure that the abstract concepts are accessible, but we also need to make sure that exercises are simple, important, relevant, and interesting.

Overall, given the number of networking protocols and technologies, we face the challenge of identifying a minimum set of important concepts that meets the objective of the course and motivates the interests of freshmen students.

4. COURSE DESIGN

In this section, we present the detailed design of our network class. Given the space limitation, instead of covering all the details, we will focus on the components that mostly reflect our design principles.

4.1 Introduction to Networking

In our design, the introduction serves a critical role. Due to the limited knowledge base and diverse backgrounds of freshmen, we resort to the introduction to prepare them for the rest of the class. Attempting to motivate many aspects of networking, we design the introduction based on a question-oriented manner to answer:

1. What is a network?

2. What is the Internet?

3. How does the Internet identify nodes?

4. How does the Internet transmit messages between nodes?

5. How do you get a connection to the Internet?

6. How fast is your Internet connection?

Note that these questions are selected not only because of their importance, but also because of the relevance to students' daily lives and/or prior knowledge. Specifically, the first question dissects a network into nodes, links, and protocols, which greatly simplifies the introduction of Internet via those components. Furthermore, given that the network consists of nodes and links, it is natural to ask the next two questions. The motivation of the third question is to introduce the concept of IP addressing at an early stage instead of waiting until the Network layer [1]. While explaining IP addresses, we insert a discussion on how numbers and text are represented in computers. The fourth question introduces the concept of packet switching, routers and routing. And the fifth question introduces the ISP and Internet topology. And the last question discusses delays on the Internet. Students are also asked to use command-line tools to explore the answer for the above questions on their own PCs and Smart Phones when applicable. For instance, they are asked to use "tracert" to explore the nodes (i.e., routers) between a source and destination (identified by an IP address), and estimate the total delay between the source and destination.

The introduction ends with the discussion of the Internet protocol stack. As mentioned above, the concept of layering is very abstract for freshmen students. To explain layering, we designed an integrated example by extending the letter exchange example of Transport layer from [20], which is shown in Fig. 1. An integrated example from a daily application can greatly help the students to understand layering by correlating respective concepts as shown in Table 2.

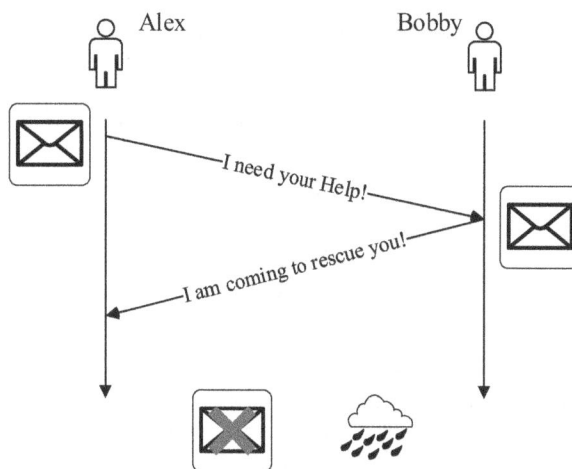

Figure 2: Exercise on Reliable Protocol Design

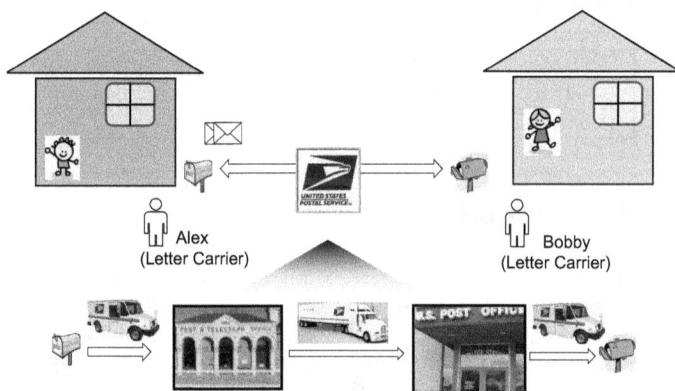

Figure 1: The example incorporates all the layers of the Internet (see Table 2)

Table 2: Layer Analogy

Layer	Analogy
Application Layer	Letter Exchange between Kids
Transport Layer	Letter Carriers: Alex and Bobby
Network Layer	USPS
Link Layer	USPS Shipping Segments

We also designed two exercises on protocol designs. The first one is shown in Fig. 2, where Alex sends a letter to Bobby asking for help. The letter, however, may get caught in rain or be lost on the way, so Bobby will not be able to understand or receive the message. The students are asked to design a reliable protocol to address the problem of letter corruption and/or lost. The motivation of this exercise is to demonstrate the two key components of a reliable protocol: Time-out and Acknowledgement (Negative and Positive). These discussions will serve as *prior* knowledge for

[1] This is motivated by the fact that in a *top-down* approach, we need to refer to IP addresses at Application layer and/or Transport layer (e.g., DNS).

the students as they learn TCP at the Transport layer. The second exercise is to design social rules for a table discussion to ensure everyone can have the chance to speak without interfering with each other as shown in Fig. 3. This exercise is a preparation for MAC protocols at the Link layer. These two exercises together help the students understand what a protocol is and how to design it.

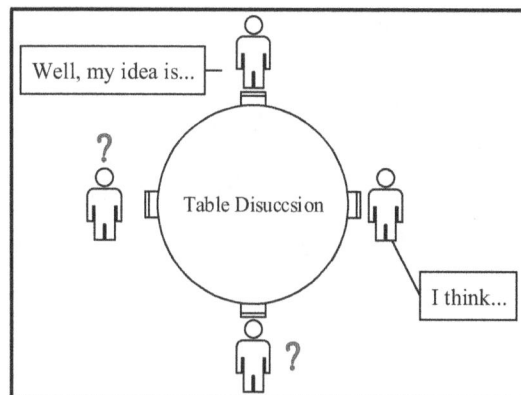

Figure 3: Exercise on Sharing Protocol Design

4.2 Application Layer

We adopt a "top-down" approach [20] since the students have more experience (as well as direct interest) at the Application layer. We focus on a set of most important and relevant protocols that belong to the *client-server* paradigm: HTTP, FTP, SMTP, DHCP, and DNS. A group of labs described in Table 3 were designed to facilitate learning these protocols.

The major principle for selecting the lab software is that it is simple, free, lightweight and requires no installation (due to the privilege management complexity in the student lab). For HTTP, the students are asked to setup an HTTP server working on ports depending on their birth date, and to use three means to access the web server: browser, (command-

Table 3: Application Layer Protocol Coverage and Lab Design

Protocol	Software List
HTTP	HFS (Http File Server)[21], telnet, wireshark
FTP	Xlight[22], wireshark, Filezilla and ftp
DNS	nslookup
DNS	ipconfig/*, host file

line) telnet client, and wireshark. For FTP, students are asked to setup an FTP server at a chosen port, and access the ftp server via three means: web browser (need to specify the port), (command-line) ftp client, and FileZilla [23]. One key concept that we force the students to practice is the connection between port number and process. For DNS, we develop an "nslookup" lab to simulate the DNS query process of a general DNS lookup: root query, the top level DNS server query, and then the authoritative DNS server query. We also designed a lab exercise to use "ipconfig/flushdns", "ipconfig/displaydns", and "host" file to understand the DNS caching and DNS record. All the labs share the same feature of being simple and free of installation while serving the purpose of understanding the key application layer protocols and explaining the *client-server* paradigm.

4.3 Transport Layer

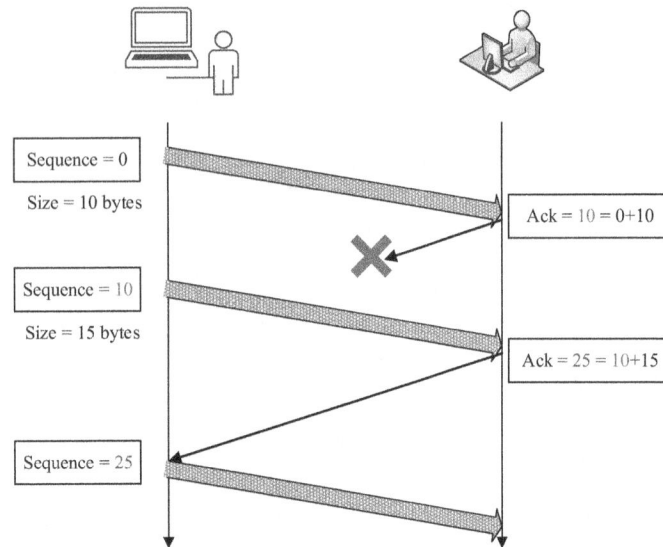

Figure 4: A Scenario of Cumulative Acknowledgement

At the Transport layer, we focus on the UDP protocol and TCP protocol. The UDP lab is based on the analysis of a wireshark trace of DHCP packet, which also serves the purpose of reviewing the DHCP protocol learned in the Application layer. Given the complexity of TCP, we first revisit the reliable protocol design exercise that illustrates the key components of TCP from Fig. 2. Since students lack the background on FSMs, we prepare a case-study that covers all major features of TCP: cumulative acknowledgement, timeout, premature timeout, and sequence number. In each case, we use animations to describe the sequence of

TCP packets to illustrate the major idea (instead of relying on FSMs). An example that explains cumulative acknowledgement is shown in Fig. 4. We designed three labs to strengthen the understanding of UDP and TCP as shown in Table 4.

For both UDP and TCP, we have a lab for wireshark analysis of the packet format of a UDP and TCP segment, which is generally given before the respective lecture on the segment format. We also designed a lab to ask the student to utilize the HTTP server (from a prior lab) to capture HTTP messages and analyze the TCP three-way handshaking process as well as the interaction between acknowledge number and sequence number. To understand the different states of TCP protocol (as well as the stateless feature of UDP), we designed a lab to ask students to observe the TCP/UDP sessions of a computer and monitor all the state updates with *TCPView* [24]. We only touch on the motivation of flow control and congestion control and leave the details for advanced classes.

Table 4: Application Layer Protocol Coverage and Lab Design

Protocol	Software List
UDP/TCP	Wireshark Capture/Packet Format Analysis
TCP	Wireshark, HFS, TCP mechanism Analysis
TCP & UDP	TCPView [24]

4.4 Network Layer

For the Network layer, we cover the following concepts: IP addressing (major focus), subnet, route architecture, and routing algorithm (only a basic understanding). We minimize the time spent on the binary-decimal conversion for subnetting by allowing the use of a scientific calculator application. This approach motivates the use of binary especially for the IT majors who tend to be concrete and pragmatic as opposed to as abstract thinkers. It is worth noting that we designed a lab that asks students to bring their laptops and use assigned switches to construct a small subnet. This setup may be counter-intuitive since a switch is a link layer device. We purposely design this lab due to multiple considerations: (i) Compared to a router, a switch is plug-and-play, which is easy for freshmen students to implement; (ii) Our major focus is to ask students to configure IP addresses and subnet masks to ensure the network connectivity, where a switch-based lab sufficiently serves the purpose. Specifically, students are given two sets of subnet masks, one of which will not allow the given IP addresses to fit within the same subnet. We also ask the students to capture ARP packets in the subnet of the switch-based lab with the aim to pre-load their knowledge on concepts of the Link layer.

4.5 Link Layer

Our major focus on the Link layer include: Medium Access Protocols, MAC address, ARP, Ethernet, and switches. We revisit the table discussion rule exercise from Fig. 3 to examine the motivation of MAC protocols and uncover the general design philosophy. Despite its complexity, ARP is one of most important protocols in the protocol stack. We prepared a lab that asks students to capture link layer frames (when accessing the Internet) in the student lab PC (without router configuration). This exercise is to ensure that the students can dissect the trace to understand the ARP protocol and the role of gateway router in Internet routing.

4.6 Overview of Networking

As important as the introduction, we devote special emphasis to the connection of the Internet protocol layers in the overview. This outcome is achieved with four major components. First, we revisit Fig. 1 to understand the motivation of layering. Second, we use a case study to examine all the protocols that are used when a student accesses the Internet to view the *Youtube* Website, including: HTTP, DNS, DHCP at the Application layer, TCP and UDP (e.g., for DHCP) at the Transport layer, IP at the Network layer, and ARP at the Link layer. Third, we summarize the technical details on how the layers are glued together in Table 5 [2]. Finally, we present a table that summarizes and compares the features of all the layers, including the identifier for the communication entities, the pattern of the communication, example of protocols and devices working in respective layers, as shown in Table 6.

Table 5: Glue between Neighboring Layers

Layers	Glue
Application & Transport	Socket
Transport & Network	*Protocol* field of IP datagram
Network & Link	*Type* field in the link layer frame

5. DESIGN PRINCIPLES

In this section, we summarize the major design principles that we use to address the challenges mentioned above.

Teaching some networking concepts to freshmen is challenging given their limited backgrounds. We adopt multiple strategies to overcome this difficulty: (i) Resort to alternative approaches. For example, in the discussion of TCP protocol, instead of relying on FSMs, we use animations to describe various scenarios to illustrate the mechanism of TCP (e.g., Fig. 4). (ii) Adjust the requirement, where an example is the link-state routing algorithm. Instead of asking for a full understanding of the algorithm (e.g., the complexity of the distribution mechanism), we only require students to have a basic understanding (and expect to revisit the topic after the algorithm class). (iii). Supplement the needed knowledge in the class sessions. For example, we cover the binary number system, and ASCII code in the introduction.

Many networking concepts are very abstract. Our design relies on analogies of daily life to relate to students' prior knowledge. One example is the integrated analogy of the Internet layers as shown in Fig. 1 and Table 2. The exercise on the reliable protocol design and table discussion rules also follow the same strategy.

For important network concepts (that are needed for future classes), we purposely enforce the repetition to ensure that the students remember and understand. For instance, the DHCP protocol is first covered at the Application layer, and revisited in the Transport layer (when UDP is discussed), and further elaborated at the Network layer when IP addresses are discussed.

For challenging topics, we also purposely pre-load students with some related knowledge. For instance, IP address is introduced at the early introduction stage. Exercises are designed to prepare students with ideas about TCP, ARP, and MAC protocols before reaching the detailed discussion in respective chapters.

The final important strategy is to balance the depth and the easiness of the topic. Instead of chasing the cutting-edge technologies [3], we resort to simple to use, simple to install software in the lab to avoid the creation of frustration during the lab exercises. At the same time, we only identify a minimum set of concepts for coverage (without hurting the overall big picture) while leaving some concepts for advanced classes (e.g., NAT, router configuration, flow and congestion control).

6. FEEDBACK AND LESSONS

Over two semesters of following this approach, the evaluations for this course rated it 91.5% (=4.575/5) on average in terms of the overall value that it has contributed to learning (excluding the instructor factor). Over 65% of the surveyed students positively confirmed the value of this class [4], and we list some representative (anonymous) feedback from the students:

1. *"non major and taking the class as an elective it did increase my knowledge of the subject. I do have a general knowledge of the layers of computer communication."*

2. *"Covered a wide range of the subject, while still helping you learn what you needed to."*

3. *"It gives the student an overall understanding of how networking works as well as a basic understanding of how to administrate and manage computer networks."*

4. *"I felt that the class flowed very well. I feel like I have a very good understanding of the course. It was very informative and the content was very relevant."*

5. *"The course really breaks down the layers."*

6. This course gives *"Modern knowledge someone like me should retain in this informational world. Actually knowledge that will help someone get a job."*

In addition, we did receive some negative feedback and observed some issues in the current design, which are listed below.

First, for the TCP trace analysis lab, one can provide a recorded trace, and ask the student to analyze it, or ask the students to capture themselves. In our practice, it seems that the former way suits the freshmen student better. Current browser software create multiple three-way handshaking sessions when accessing a website, leaving a lot of difficulties for freshmen students. In contrast, with a recorded trace, the instructor can provide a better and detailed guide leading to a more uniform and stable solution which the freshmen need.

---

[2]For socket programming, we demonstrate a java-based example.

[3]One such example is virtualization. Virtual machines, particularly virtual networks indeed create a lot of confusion for freshmen, and hence we decided to introduce it later in 320 class.

[4]The other 35% did not leave any comments.

Table 6: Internet Layer Stack and Associated Features Summary

Layer	Identifier	Communication Pattern	Protocol Examples	Device Examples
Application	Port Number	Process to Process	HTTP, FTP, SMTP, DNS	HTTP/FTP Server
Transport	Port Number	Process to Process	TCP, UDP,	N/A
Network	IP Address	Host to Host	IP, ICMP	Routers
Link	MAC Address	Neighbor to Neighbor (adaptor)	MAC protocols (e.g., CSMA), ARP	Switches

Second, our major design was based on Windows platform since the lab computers all have *Windows 7* installed. However, there are a large body of students using *MacBook*, and they face difficulties using the provided software based on virtual machines. We are currently adapting those labs to take both platforms into account.

Third, we designed two protocol design exercises in the introduction stage. The first one is for the preparation of TCP, and the second one is for the MAC protocols. In the teaching, one major issue was that this preparation seems to work well for the TCP protocol (but not for MAC protocols) due to the different time gap between the exercise and respective lecture. Consequently, we are considering moving the second exercise to a later phase of this class.

7. CONCLUSION AND FUTURE WORK

Given the challenges in teaching freshmen, we have presented the major principles and detailed class design for a networking class of freshmen CS/IT majors. The generalized design principles can also be applied to the teaching of other subjects and majors. In the next step, we plan to incorporate the lessons and feedback from students to improve the course design, and extend those strategies in the teaching of other freshmen courses at our university. We want to further follow up on the freshmen students in later classes to reexamine the impact of this class. Moreover, we plan to collect more comparative results on applying alternative approaches (e.g., *bottom-up*) in the networking class, and systematically redesign the high level networking class to ensure that the three networking classes offered at our university, when combined together, can build a solid and strong basis for the career of the CS/IT major students.

8. REFERENCES

[1] D. Ausubel, *Educational Psychology: A Cognitive View.* New York: Holt, Rinehart and Winston, 1968.

[2] T. Matsuka and Y. Sakamoto, "A cognitive model that describes the influence of prior knowledge on concept learning," in *Lecture Notes in Computer Science (LNCS).* Berlin: Springer-Verlag, 2007.

[3] J. E. Sefton, "Reflections on the teaching of freshmen," http://www.csun.edu/afye.

[4] Y. Pan, S. Mishra, B. Yuan, B. Stackpole, and D. Schwartz, "Game-based forensics course for first year students," in *Proceedings of SIGITE'12*, pp. 13–18.

[5] S. Abbott-McCune, A. Newtson, B. S. Goda, and J. Girard, "Developing a reconfigurable network lab," in *Proceedings of SIGITE'08*, pp. 255–258.

[6] M. Casado and N. McKeown, "The virtual network system," in *Proceedings of SIGCSE'05*, pp. 76–80.

[7] J. C. Adams and W. D. Laverell, "Configuring a multi-course lab for system-level projects," in *Proceedings of SIGCSE'05*, pp. 525–529.

[8] J. Gerdes and S. Tilley, "A conceptual overview of the virtual networking laboratory," in *Proceedings of SIGITE'07*, pp. 75–82.

[9] B. Hartpence, "Teaching wireless security for results," in *Proceedings of SIGITE'05*, pp. 89–93.

[10] B. Hartpence and L. Hill, "Wireless cart- an inexpensive education and research platform," in *Proceedings of SIGITE'05*, pp. 79–82.

[11] S. Rigby and M. Dark, "Designing a flexible, multipurpose remote lab for the it curriculum," in *Proceedings of SIGITE'06*, pp. 161–164.

[12] B. Stackpole, "The evolution of a virtualized laboratory environment," in *Proceedings of SIGITE'08*, pp. 243–248.

[13] X. Cao, Y. Wang, A. Caciula, and Y. Wang, "Developing a multifunctional network laboratory for teaching and research," in *Proceedings of SIGITE'09*, pp. 155–160.

[14] S. Cosgrove, "Bringing together a low-cost networking learning environment," in *Proceedings of SIGITE'11*, pp. 101–106.

[15] J. Alexander, A. Dick, J. Hacker, D. Hicks, and M. Stockman, "Building a cloud based systems lab," in *Proceedings of SIGITE'12*, pp. 151–154.

[16] D. Yuan, C. Lewandowski, and J. Zhong, "Developing ip telephony laboratory and curriculum with private cloud computing," in *Proceedings of SIGITE'11*, pp. 107–112.

[17] Y. Pan, "Security auditing course development," in *Proceedings of SIGITE'07*, pp. 259–266.

[18] W. Bullers, S. Burd, and A. Seazzu, "Virtual machines: an idea whose time has returned," in *Proceedings of SIGCSE'06*, pp. 102–106.

[19] B. Stackpole, J. Koppe, T. Haskell, L. Guay, and Y. Pan, "Decentralized virtualization in systems administration education," in *Proceedings of SIGITE'08*, pp. 249–254.

[20] J. F. Kurose and K. W. Ross, *Computer Networking: A Top-Down Approach.* Pearson, 2012.

[21] HFS, "http://www.rejetto.com/hfs/."

[22] Xlight, "http://www.xlightftpd.com/."

[23] FileZilla, "https://filezilla-project.org/."

[24] TcpView.EXE, http://technet.microsoft.com.

FLaSKU - A Classroom Experience with Teaching Computer Networking: Is it useful to others in the field?

Shan Suthaharan
Department of Computer Science
University of North Carolina at Greensboro,
Greensboro, NC, USA
s_suthah@uncg.edu

ABSTRACT

In general, every educator has a classroom experience that he or she wants to share for the benefit of other educators and students in the field. This paper presents a classroom experience with teaching a computer networking course to both undergraduate and graduate students in Information Technology (IT) areas. This course uses conceptualization and summarization techniques coupled with standard teaching methods, such as independent learning, incremental learning, and out-of-class assignments. It also defines two terms: *independent conceptualization* and *dependent conceptualization*, and adopts them with a summarization technique to improve conceptualized computer networking. Two simple examples are presented to illustrate these definitions. The paper also presents a teaching philosophy and a flexible grading policy that help motivate learning over earning a grade.

The experience and knowledge gained from the delivery of a computer networking course over eight years is shared in this paper. Course evaluations were conducted using a departmental questionnaire, peer evaluations, and an independent survey. The course evaluation results of over eight years demonstrate a significant improvement in the overall quality of the course delivery. The methods, results, and findings can deliver benefits to young university educators and students in the IT field.

Categories and Subject Descriptors

K.3.2 [**Computers and Information Science Education**]: Computer science education, Curriculum, Literacy

General Terms

Design, Experimentation, Measurement and Performance

Keywords

Conceptualized learning, incremental learning, independent learning, computer networking

1. INTRODUCTION

Educating information technology students is paramount in today's technologically advanced society. In particular, the delivery of a computer networking course is challenging due to rapidly changing technology, limitations in the usage of technology and industry demands. This paper provides an experience with teaching a computer networking course while addressing these challenges. Conceptualization and summarization techniques in teaching and learning combined with appropriate course structure, course delivery, assessment mechanisms of student work, and a course evaluation plan can help confront these challenges. The conceptualization and summarization have been used in the education arena to address general educational and psychological issues. For example, Friedman and Kass [4] studied the problems associated with how teachers perceive their own teaching competency and how that affects students' learning. They also studied the conceptualization of teacher efficacy, focusing on classroom organization and its effect on students' creativity, motivation, and participation.

In 2003, Manning [6] presented a master's thesis in which both conceptualization and summarization were addressed relating to reading comprehension in disabled students using visual tools in classrooms. Noah et al. [8] used conceptualization and summarization for the semantic annotation and searching of digital images with keyword tagging. They utilized conceptualization to disambiguate terms of keyword texts used for tagging images and summarization to extract knowledge from the surrounding text that provides description of the images. Recently Chubbuck [1] used conceptualization to build a framework that provides informed decisions to educators about the learning ability of students. Most recently, Hsieh et al. [5] utilized conceptualization for developing indicators that help investigate the quality of international mathematics education in different countries, and Mueller et al. [7] utilized it for demonstrating the importance of longhand note taking over laptop note taking. In general, the conceptualization and summarization have been used in the psychology aspects of education, but a detailed study on their contributions to improve computer networking courses is still needed.

This paper presents a Flexible Learning and Sequential Knowledge Update (FLaSKU) technique that can help instructors accomplish their teaching objectives and help students succeed in their learning outcomes. In FLaSKU, an improved version of conceptualization (independent conceptualization and dependent conceptualization) and summarization techniques are explored and combined with an effective teaching philosophy, an independent learning technique, an incremental learning technique, a motivational assessment mechanism of students' work, and a course evaluation plan and improvement strategy. The results and findings from eight years of course evaluations are also presented.

2. COURSE STRUCTURE

Structuring the course so the instructor and students can achieve their teaching and learning goals successfully is a highly thoughtful, resource-intensive, and time-consuming task. Tools such as the teaching philosophy, course outline, course objectives, student learning outcomes, assessment mechanisms, and grading policies, can help achieve these goals.

2.1 Teaching Philosophy

The author devised a teaching philosophy from his 30 years of teaching experience. It reflects the instructor's beliefs on teaching and learning, and how those beliefs could be integrated into the course structure and course delivery. A strong teaching philosophy is one of the key factors that help motivate both the instructor and students to be engaged in teaching and learning. A well-structured, meaningful, and feasible teaching philosophy was developed, adopted, and practiced strictly throughout the course. It reflected a genuine commitment and effort from the instructor, thus motivating the students. It helped promote students' own commitments and engagement in the course. The following teaching philosophy was developed and adopted in the computer networking course: SUCCESSFUL.

- (S)tudious: Teaching must be studious. The commitments and efforts of the instructor can stimulate the same level of commitments and efforts among students. They must be presented to students.

- (U)ltimate: Teaching must be ultimate. The perfection in teaching materials contributes to this philosophy. The course materials must be current, simple, challenging, and interactive. This is one of the contributors that encourage student participation.

- (C)reative: Teaching must be creative. Interesting examples keep students engaged in learning new knowledge and developing skills to achieve more than what they think is possible.

- (C)omplete: Teaching must be complete. Completeness in the networking course comes from the integration of the instructor's own research findings. The research techniques and deliverables must be incorporated in the delivery of instruction.

- (E)ffective: Teaching must be effective. The instructor provides a friendly and comfortable atmosphere to students during the delivery of instruction in classroom, as well as during one-on-one advising in the office. Effective teaching is another contributor that helps motivate student participation.

- (S)uperior: Teaching must be superior. This describes the genuine interest to deliver advanced knowledge. Difficult theories are simplified in the course with real world examples and applications. Superior teaching helps students visualize and understand theories and concepts.

- (S)trong: Teaching must be strong. The instructor must display leadership qualities and bring energy and enthusiasm to the classroom to motivate students and increase their interest in the subject.

- (F)ruitful: Teaching must be fruitful. When students' opinions are well received and respected, fruitfulness is achieved in class. Additionally, students' opinions and comments must be used as a mechanism to improve both course materials and mode of instruction.

- (U)seful: Teaching must be useful. Well-structured, modern tools with state-of-the-art, technology-based resources should be used in the delivery of instruction, focusing on encouraging students toward lifelong learning. Lifelong learning is an important requirement for rapidly advancing fields like computer networking.

- (L)uminous: Teaching must be luminous. The course must give brightness to students. The instructor must update knowledge through professional training, learn the latest advancements in the field, and transform this knowledge to students.

The keyword "SUCCESSFUL" imprinted the success in students' minds at the early stage of the course. As students saw a bright future, they engaged in the course and participated in class activities. The successful interaction in this course was reported in the peer evaluation. Class visits by professional peers, one of the effective course evaluation mechanisms used, stated: "...lecture was an example of good interaction between the instructor and the students..." and "...the interaction style and student engagements and accessible levels to students ...".

2.2 Course Objectives

The main objective of the course was to educate students in computer networking, including hardware and software components of computer networks, and their organization and operations. In particular, the conceptualization and summarization aspects of computer networking, hop-to-hop mechanisms, host-to-host mechanisms, process-to-process mechanisms, and network simulator modeling were covered in the course. Another objective was to adopt a variety of teaching models, such as classroom instruction, independent learning, incremental learning, and out-of-class assignments in the structure and delivery of the course.

2.3 Course Outline

The course outline was sketched to include five sections: the conceptualization and summarization, hop-to-hop mechanisms, host-to-host mechanisms, process-to-process mechanisms, and simulator modeling so students can conceptualize the transmission of a packet over a network. Hence, the book chapters intended to be covered were grouped into five parts:

- **Conceptualization and summarization**: Communications, Standards and protocols. Network models.

- **Hop-to-hop mechanisms**: Data and signals. Digital transmission. Bandwidth utilization. Transmission media and switching. Error detection and correction.

- **Host-to-host mechanisms**: Data link control and Multiple Access. Wired LAN and connecting LANs. Logical addressing and Internet protocol. Address mapping, error reporting and multicasting. Routing of IP packets and packet switching.

- **Process-to-process mechanisms**: Congestion control and QoS. Network applications such as Email, telnet, and file transfer protocols (ftp and tftp).

- **Simulator Modeling**: Network programming - simulation of computer networking concepts.

The course outline with course objectives, learning outcomes, prerequisite requirements, required textbooks and materials, grading policies, and instructor information was made available to students during the first week of classes and posted on the course website. The textbooks used for this course in different semesters were: Comer [2], Peterson and Davie [9], Forouzan [3], and Tanenbaum [10]. The last two textbooks were used in recent years.

2.4 Learning Outcomes

Learning outcomes were designed to specify what networking theory and applications students would familiarize and learn from the activities incorporated in the course and played an important role in the evaluation component of the course. The following learning outcomes were developed and announced to students during the first week of classes:

- Ability to identify different types of data communication networks and different applications of computer communication networks;

- Ability to implement seven layer computer network architecture and their corresponding protocols;

- Ability to solve problems related to inter-networking and TCP/IP protocols;

- Ability to understand and apply the packet-switched networks and routing strategies;

- Ability to recognize and implement various ways of enforcing flow control, error detection, and error correction in practice;

- Ability to integrate networking concepts and build computer network simulators.

These learning outcome are measurable and helped design questions in the assignments, class tests, and the final examination that adopted incremental learning and independent learning.

2.5 Assessment Mechanism

Assessment mechanism included three assignments, three class tests, and a final exam. The assignments were designed to support incremental learning and independent learning. The class tests had two sections: multiple choice questions and essay questions. In general, there were about 15 multiple choice questions and 3 essay questions in each test. They carried 40% and 60% weights toward the total grade of each test. Students were asked to answer all 15 multiple choice questions and 2 out of 3 essay questions. The final exam followed the same style, but there were 32 multiple

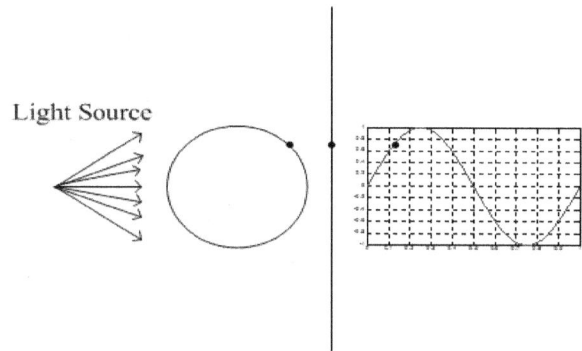

Figure 1: Ant example to conceptualize $f = 1/T$.

choice questions and 4 essay questions. Students were asked to answer all multiple choice questions and 2 out of 4 essay questions. The essay questions in the final exam have more parts or sub questions than the class tests. Students needed the entire 3 hours to complete the final exam. Note that the class tests were 1 hour and 15 minutes long. To support students' success in the class tests and the exam, sample tests and a sample exam were provided for practice.

2.6 Grading Policy

The grading policy encourages learning more than earning a grade. Students earn grades through the demonstration of flexible learning and sequential knowledge updates. This course is an upper division course, and was attended by both undergraduate and graduate students. Therefore, the grading policies were different for undergraduate and graduate students. For undergraduate students, the scores were: Assignment 1: 5%; Test 1: 10%; Assignment 2: 15%; Test 2: 10%; Assignment 3: 15%; Test 3: 10%; and Final Exam: 35%. Graduate students were required to do a mini project thus their scores were: Assignment 1: 5%; Test 1: 10%; Assignment 2: 10%; Test 2: 10%; Assignment 3: 10%; Test 3: 10%; Project: 20%; and Final Exam: 25%.

To support the flexible learning and sequential knowledge updates, this grading policy was relaxed at the end of the semester. If the final assignment score was higher than the previous assignment scores, the final assignment score replaced the other two. Similarly if the final exam score was the highest, then it replaced the class tests grades. The assignments and the tests were designed to be cumulative so students were rewarded for knowing all topics covered in the course and demonstrating networking skills at the end of the semester.

3. COURSE DELIVERY

Course delivery included conceptualization, summarization, independent learning, incremental learning, and out-of-class assignments. These teaching mechanisms were adopted to ensure the actions described for each instrument of the teaching philosophy, "SUCCESSFUL", were emphasized and followed throughout the course delivery.

3.1 Summarization

Summarization uses visual aids to help the instructor teach the course and help students learn the topics. The key to computer networking is the transmission of packets from a source host to a destination host and the processes that

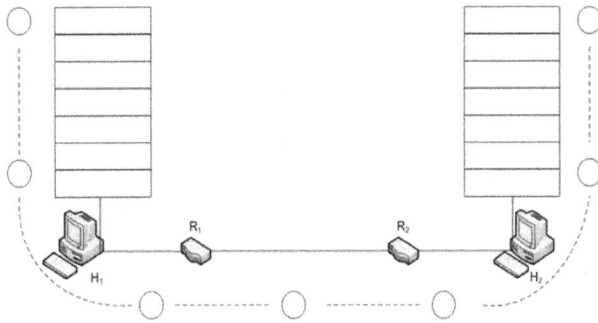

Figure 2: Conceptual model for assignment 1.

packets undergo during their transmission through the intermediate network environment. Based on this, three phases of learning computer networks using the three figures (Figure 2 to 4) were taught to the students in the first week of classes. Students were required to use them as summarization to conceptualize the network model throughout the course.

3.2 Conceptualization

Conceptualization has been addressed in the education research, but its contribution to successful teaching and learning of computer networking has not been reported in the education arena. In the delivery of computer networking course, both textbooks and simulators play important roles. However, they directly address the hardware and software components and theory behind those tools. The concepts behind the techniques that form the network theory are not addressed to a level that the teaching and learning can be successful. The conceptualized learning helps students to understand difficult topics instantly and recall the topics later as needed without realizing the memorization. The goal of conceptualization developed in teaching our computer networking course is to help students understand and learn difficult techniques that are important to computer networking. One of the objectives of conceptualization is to develop simple examples (numerical or visual) for the networking concepts that form the network theory. These examples were grouped in two classes: *Independent Conceptualization* (IC) and *Dependent Conceptualization* (DC). IC helps students understand the concepts by using examples not directly related to the topic, whereas DC helps understand the concepts by using examples that are directly related to the topic. Two examples are presented below: Ant and Bubble Examples.

3.2.1 Independent Conceptualization

Ant Example. Figure 1 describes the Ant example which focuses on the signal representation that plays a major role in the physical layer protocols. It illustrates the relationship between the two main elements of a signal: Frequency (f) and Period (T), and thus helps students understand the meaning of high frequency. This example (i.e., Figure 1) uses a light source to create a shadow, a ring for ant to travel, an Ant to create sine waves for signals, a screen to show the shadow movement, and a paper for students to draw an imaginary sine wave. Students were told that the ant was a smart ant, and it would listen to you. You tell

the ant to travel in a consistent speed and complete 1 cycle in 1 second. While ant travels on the ring, the shadow on the wall moves up and down. As the shadow moves, students had to draw its reflection on the paper using a pencil or pen. This effect is shown in Figure 1. Now the students were asked to tell the ant to double the speed (but maintain consistent speed) and draw the sine wave. They were able to see two sine waves in 1 second. Hence, they were able to see the relationship between f and T. Then the students were asked to tell the ant to increase the speed to 1 million cycles per second and observe the effect. Now they were able to define the term High Frequency.

3.2.2 Dependent Conceptualization

Bubble Example. Figures 2 and 3 show the Bubble examples. The summarization in Figure 1 helped students conceptualize the transmission of a network packet (protocol) from source to destination via a simple link with two routers. With the understanding of this simple conceptualized model, the students were able to construct a large network virtually with a combination of many such simple links and conceptualize the transmission of a packet over a large network like the Internet (as shown in Figure 3). When the packet (i.e., the bubble) travels through the network, its transformation by the network theory was explained thoroughly at each step, then students had to implement that as part of the assignment. However, due to time limitations, students had to implement only some of the networking concepts. This example helped students to understand the topics of the networking course and stay abreast with the instructions and course requirements.

3.3 Independent Learning

Independent learning required students to independently learn certain sections designated by the instructor. This model was applied in the computer networking course, which helped students prepare and face the lifelong learning demand of the IT industry. IT graduates are required to update their knowledge frequently, while employed, by learning on their own from resources like textbooks and the Internet. The independent learning gave students a ground to train themselves to face such a demand.

3.4 Incremental Learning

Incremental learning is a technique that helps students observe connections between topics and motivates them to be enthusiastically engaged in the subject. To adopt incremental learning, the topic covered in a class was connected with the topics covered in the previous class, and that connection was clearly highlighted for the students. In addition, at the end of each class, students were informed of the topics that would be covered in the next class. The class tests were also designed to support the incremental learning by testing 20% of the previously tested topics in a test.

3.5 Out-of-class Assignments

Out-of-class assignments, in contrast to the instructor-led laboratory sessions, provided students a mode of flexible learning to work on their own time while accessing tutors, computer labs, and other classmates. In the out-of-class assignments, students had the opportunity to build a network simulator and learn the concepts of network protocols through visualization of packet transfer at various steps in

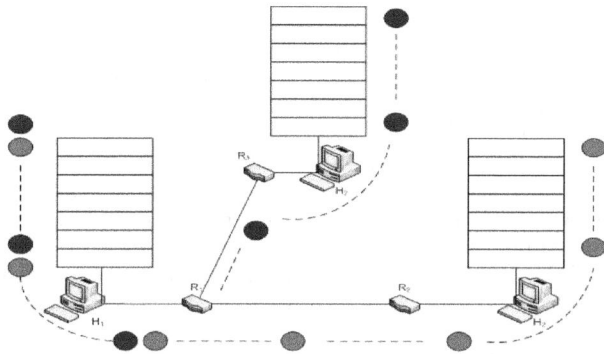

Figure 3: Conceptual model for assignment 2.

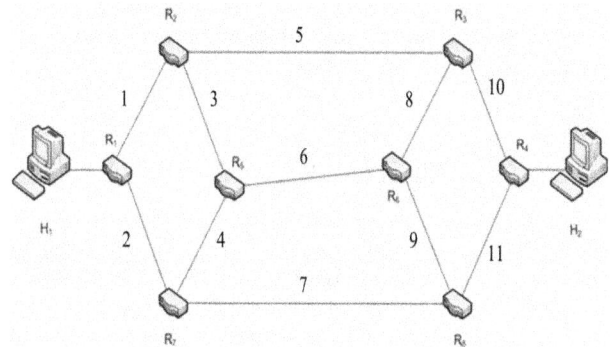

Figure 4: Conceptual model for assignment 3.

a computer network. There were three out-of-class assignments designed to support incremental learning. Students had to demonstrate the network protocols they learned conceptually in the classroom or through independent learning. The goals of these assignments were: (i) understanding of the encoding, decoding, and modulation approaches; (ii) understanding of the error detection and correction techniques; and (iii) understanding of routing algorithms together with the shortest path algorithm called Dijkstra algorithm. End of these three assignments, students had to present an animated system (simulator) that simulates and illustrates some of the important protocols of TCP/IP-based computer networks. Each assignment stated its own network protocols so the students would develop a complete system by the end of the semester. Their simulator had to process and demonstrate the transmission of a message (long enough to show the intended protocols) from a source host to a destination host via a collection of routers with user interaction. The simulator had to incorporate the network diagrams presented in Figures 2, 3, and 4. Figure 2 illustrates a simple host-to-host transformation of a packet (bubble) with the locations where the students had to show the content of the packet and its transformations. Figure 3 shows two packets and there routing locations. Once again, students had to show the transformation of the packets at various locations. Figure 4 shows the network configuration (network graph is from [10]) with a set of random weights to demonstrate the influence of the Dijkstra algorithm to packet routing. All three assignments were posted during the first week of classes, the conceptualization and summarization of the figures were explained, and students were asked to familiarize themselves with these models, use them for learning concepts, and apply them in the simulator.

4. COURSE EVALUATION

Course evaluation is carried out using three different instruments: departmental questionnaire, peer evaluation, and an independent survey.

4.1 Departmental Questionnaire

A departmental questionnaire, used as the first evaluation tool, was circulated to students during the last few weeks of classes. This questionnaire allowed students to rate the course and provide comments. This questionnaire consisted of 16 questions to improve the course at different areas. The following areas were improved based on this evaluation: revision of teaching philosophy, balance of course workload,

quality of instruction, adequacy of resources, quality of students, and effectiveness of teaching methods.

4.2 Peer Evaluation

The second tool used for course evaluation was the observations and comments provided by senior faculty members. In this process, senior faculty members visited the classroom and observed the teaching. The department provides a form for this peer evaluation. Senior faculty members completed the form based on their observations and provided feedback for improvements. Some areas were improved based on this evaluation: organization of materials, delivery of materials, teaching strategies, and contents of the materials.

4.3 Independent Survey

An independent survey was implemented outside the classroom based on students' availability. When students meet with the instructor, their opinions on the strengths and weaknesses of the course were noted and instantaneous improvements were integrated. This process helped both current and future students. Other evaluation strategies can only help future students, thus current students miss the benefits of improvements based on their own contributions. Therefore, the independent survey was considered a preferred mechanism. In addition, independent comments received from colleagues, staff, and other students were also considered for course improvements.

4.4 Course Improvement

Course improvement was carried out based on student evaluations, peer evaluations and independent surveys. These evaluations helped incorporate student-developed simulators in the course. Initially, the course was taught without any simulator, and students only learned the theory of networking. However, the evaluations indicated that students wanted to see the effect of computer networking in motion. Hence, the network simulator called NS-2 [11]was adopted subsequently. Although students enjoyed the animation part of NS-2, they had difficulties in understanding the functionalities of the software itself. This feedback led the instructor to select OPNET IT Guru (an academic version of OPNET) [12] for simulating various concepts of computer networking. However, students found that the use of this software was not challenging. They didn't see the connection between the concepts they learned and the simulation. As a result, the idea of student-developed simulators was proposed in

Table 1: Final step classification accuracies

Type	Y1	Y2	Y3	Y4	Y5	Y6	Y7	Y8
Worst	5.0	5.0	5.0	5.0	5.0	5.0	5.0	5.0
Actual	1.8	1.9	1.6	1.4	1.5	1.7	1.4	1.3
Best	1.0	1.0	1.0	1.0	1.0	1.0	1.0	1.0

which the students had to develop modules and integrate them into a full package. It provided significant success in both teaching and learning computer networking. One problem still remains how to accommodate all the requirements within one semester. Hence, the next level of improvement is to develop a framework for students, and students can add modules to this framework.

5. RESULTS

Results obtained from the course evaluations are presented in Table I and Figure 5. Table I shows 8 years (Y1, Y2, ... Y8) of results; in each year 3 scores are shown. The first score, 5.0, represents the worst score, the second score shows the actual scores for the course, and the third score shows the best score. On average, the course evaluation shows 1.4, which is closer to the best score 1.0. This indicates satisfactory responses from the students for the overall course. Similarly, Figure 5 shows the actual scores received for the course are closer to the perfect score of 1 throughout. However, there are local variations in the course, while the trend of the curve approaches the best score of 1.0. The local fluctuations are somewhat reflective of the simulation softwares, such as NS-2 and OPNET used for the assignments. The last two years, the student-developed simulator assignments were used. This indicates the students like to implement concepts and understand the theory with an animated simulator of their own.

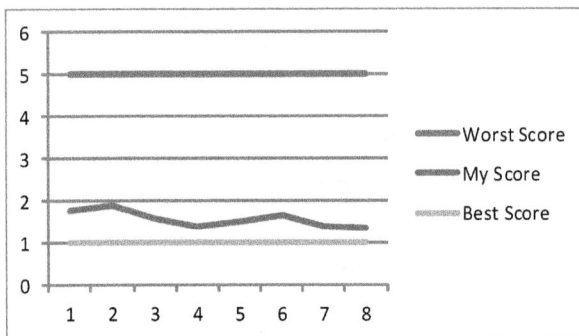

Figure 5: Course evaluation results.

6. CONCLUSION

The experience shows conceptualization and summarization coupled with the general teaching methodologies are effective mechanisms for improving teaching and learning a computer networking course when the class is a mix of undergraduate and graduate students. The examples with independent conceptualization and dependent conceptualization are added techniques that can support the goal of effective teaching and learning. The grading that encourages flexible learning and sequential knowledge updates can

help motivate students' focus on learning more than earning a grade.

In this experience, students preferred to build simulators themselves by integrating concepts than simply using the off-the-shelf simulators. Additionally, the teaching methodology used the knowledge gained and reported, and the findings may be useful to young computer networking educators to adopt and deliver the course successfully, or revise based on their own experience. The framework proposed and practiced for more than 10 years is named FLaSKU (Flexible Learning and Sequential Knowledge Update) in this paper. FLaSKU will be adopted and evaluated for other courses (i.e., Is FLaSKU useful to others in the field?).

7. ACKNOWLEDGMENT

The author thanks the System Administrator Mr Richard Cheek for his tireless support and advice in hardware resources and fixing networking problems.

8. REFERENCES

[1] S. M. Chubbuck. "Individual and structural orientations in socially just teaching: Conceptualization, implementation, and collaborative effort." Journal of Teacher Education, vol. 61, no. 3, pp. 197-210, 2010.

[2] D. E. Comer. *Computer Networks and Internets*. Pearson Education, Inc., 2009.

[3] B. A. Forouzan. *Data Communications and Networking*. McGraw-Hill Education, 2006.

[4] I. A. Friedman, and E. Kass. "Teacher self-efficacy: A classroom-organization conceptualization." Teaching and Teacher Education, vol. 18, no. 6, pp. 675-686, 2002.

[5] F. J. Hsieh, C. K. Law, H. Y. Shy, T. Y. Wang, C. J. Hsieh, and S. J. Tang. "A Conceptualization of Indicators for Mathematics Teacher Education Quality for International Studies. In International Perspectives on Teacher Knowledge, Beliefs and Opportunities to Learn." Springer Netherlands, pp. 457-482, 2014.

[6] C. M. Manning. "Improving reading comprehension through visual tools." Division of Graduate Studies, Division of Teacher Education. Masters dissertation. Eastern Nazarene College. 2003.

[7] P. A. Mueller, and D. M. Oppenheimer. "The Pen Is Mightier Than the Keyboard: Advantages of Longhand Over Laptop Note Taking." Psychological science, 0956797614524581, 2014.

[8] S. A. Noah, D. A. Ali, A. C. Alhadi, and J. M. Kassim. "Going beyond the surrounding text to semantically annotate and search digital images." In Intelligent Information and Database Systems, Springer Berlin Heidelberg, pp. 169-179, 2010.

[9] L. L. Peterson and B. S. Davie. *Computer Networks: A Systems Approach*. Elsevier, Inc. 2007.

[10] A. S. Tanenbaum. *Computer Networks*. Prentice-Hall, Englewood Cliffs, 1987.

[11] The Network Simulator - NS-2. Available online at http://www.isi.edu/nsnam/ns/.

[12] OPNET IT Guru (Academic Edition). Available online at http://www.opnet.com/university_program/itguru_academic_edition/.

Analysis of Source Code Snapshot Granularity Levels

Arto Vihavainen and Matti Luukkainen
University of Helsinki
Department of Computer Science
Helsinki, Finland
{ avihavai, mluukkai }@cs.helsinki.fi

Petri Ihantola
Aalto University
Department of Computer Science and Eng.
Helsinki, Finland
petri.ihantola@aalto.fi

ABSTRACT

Systems that record students' programming process have become increasingly popular during the last decade. The granularity of stored data varies across these systems and ranges from storing the final state, e.g. a solution, to storing fine-grained event streams, e.g. every key-press made while working on a task. Researchers that study such data make assumptions based on the granularity. If no fine-grained data exists, the baseline assumption is that a student proceeds in a linear fashion from one recorded state to the next. In this work, we analyze three different granularities of data; (1) submissions, (2) snapshots (i.e. save, compile, run, test events), and (3) keystroke-events. Our study provides insight on the quantity of lost data when storing data at a specific granularity and shows how the lost data varies depending on previous programming experience and the programming assignment type.

Categories and Subject Descriptors

K.3.1 [**Computers and Education**]: Computer Uses in Education—*Computer-assisted instruction (CAI), Distance learning*; K.3.2 [**Computers and Education**]: Computer and Information Science Education—*Computer science education*

Keywords

data collection; programming education; programming process; programming snapshots; source code; source code snapshots; source code submissions; fine-grained data analysis

1. INTRODUCTION

Systems that assess and record students' solutions to programming assignments have existed for decades [5]. While at first, these systems were used mainly for automated assessment and they recorded only students' final submissions, systems that gather more than the end result have started to emerge. More modern systems typically involve students

SIGITE'14, October 15–18, 2014, Atlanta, Georgia, USA.
Copyright 2014 ACM 978-1-4503-2686-5/14/10 ...$15.00.
http://dx.doi.org/10.1145/2656450.2656473.

having a software component on their machine, and typically capture snapshots from students' progress, either using a defined interval, or when students perform an action such as saving their current work [13].

A growing body of research that uses the programming process rather than the final submissions exists [4]. To provide a few examples, Allevato and Edwards found out that weaker students, when editing their programs, often deleted larger code blocks (e.g. entire methods) and then possibly rewrote those from scratch [1], while multiple authors, led by Jadud's work [6], have created data-driven approaches for finding factors that contribute to students' success with the goal of predicting student outcomes or detecting at-risk students [6, 10, 17, 20]. Another use of such data is the identification of challenging concepts or assignments, which can then be refined to help students succeed [11], and the use of hint systems, which analyze the source code and provide hints based on the students' situation [7].

The benefit of data-driven approaches that look at how students solve programming errors [6, 20] or how they schedule their time and whether they pay attention to code quality [17] is that they are directly based on programming behavior of a student and therefore can directly reflect changes in their learning and skills over time. Moreover, as the data is recorded from the students' normal learning activity – programming – instead of additional or external tests, there is no overhead for administering e.g. aptitude tests [21].

Overall, students' programming process and behavior is recorded in at least one of the following granularity levels. *Submission-level* data is gathered by the assessment system whenever a student submits her source code for evaluation. *Snapshot-level* data can be gathered either using specific time-intervals, or e.g. whenever the students save, run, or test the programs that they are currently working on. Finally, one can record every source code change that the student makes, which provides a *Keystroke-level* view to source code changes. Additional information can be gathered e.g. by recording other events within the used programming environment [9] and by using additional gadgets to monitor the programmer herself [2, 16].

Gathering keystroke-level data can be rationalized from multiple viewpoints. For example, the big deletes observed by Allevato and Edwards are easier to observe from detailed data than from subsequent snapshots. Open programming courses also often have noncompleters (i.e. shoppers, dabblers or auditors [3]) who may work on programming tasks, but do not submit their solutions. Keystroke-level data may provide insight on the activities of these lurkers. Finally, and most importantly, when analyzing programming process based on submissions or snapshots, one follows Occam's razor and assumes that students take the most direct path between subsequent states. What is lost are the possible detours that are taken; even if the students would follow the most direct paths, no information on the order in which new elements are introduced to the code is retained.

2. RESEARCH QUESTIONS AND METHODOLOGY

In this study, we investigate how much data is lost when programming process is stored using different granularities. More specifically, we compare three approaches for saving students' work; submissions, snapshots and keystrokes. In addition, we look at factors that affect the amount of lost data. Our research questions are as follows;

1. How much snapshot-level data is lost when storing submissions but not snapshots or keystroke-level events?

2. How much keystroke-level data is lost when storing snapshots but not keystroke-level events?

3. What factors affect the amount of data lost?

To answer research questions one and two, the data is analyzed quantitatively to identify (1) the number of snapshots and keystroke-events that are lost when storing submissions or snapshots respectively, (2) the changes between subsequent snapshots and how much of that data is lost when storing submissions, (3) the amount of compilation errors that are lost in different granularities, and (4) the amount of unique source code states that are lost when storing submissions. As no assumptions of normality of the data is made, reported means are medians, and paired difference testing is done using the Wilcoxon rank sum test.

To answer research question three, the data is augmented with details on the students' programming background, which have been gathered using an online survey. This data is investigated to determine if students' previous programming experience affects the results of questions one and two. Our study also also seeks to determine whether the amount of lost data changes during the course, and considers different types of programming assignments.

2.1 Course

The data used in this study comes from a six-week introductory programming course that was offered by the University of Helsinki during Spring 2014. No previous programming experience was expected from the participants, and the course was open and free to anyone willing to participate (including participants not admitted to the University of Helsinki; this opportunity was organized as a massive open online course (MOOC) in programming, see [18] for details of a previous implementation). Half of the course was devoted to learning elementary procedural programming (input, output, conditional statements, loops, methods, and working with lists), while the latter part was an introduction to object-oriented programming; the workload of the course for the University of Helsinki students was 5 ECTS (European Credit Transfer and Accumulation System) points.

During the course, the participants work on 106 programming exercises, some of which contain multiple tasks that provide step-by-step guidance. In total, the course has 193 tasks

	min	max	mean	median	std. dev. (σ)
all participants (n=1166)					
points	1	193	110.7	122.5	75.3
programming experience = Y (n=264)					
points	1	193	136.9	183	67.0
age	15	76	30.6	28	12.0
programming experience = N (n=297)					
points	1	193	111.0	121	74.9
age	12	66	27.9	25	9.8

Table 1: Study participant details

that are distributed over the six week duration. From the start of the course, the participants program using NetBeans IDE for which they download the Test My Code -plugin [19]. The plugin is used to download the course exercises, to provide textual feedback as the participants are working on the exercises, and to run tests and to submit the assignments for grading. The tests can be run locally in the student's machine, which means that submitting the exercise is often done after locally run tests pass. While it is typical that all tests are available locally, some 15% of the exercises have hidden tests that are only run on the assessment server. For this study, we used a newer version of the Test My Code -plugin that gathered keystroke-level data in addition to the submission- and snapshot-level data.

The source code data was augmented with information on event time, change size, information on compilation success or failure for each of the data entries.

2.2 Participants

The data contains snapshots from 1166 participants that participated in the course during Spring 2014. Every participant agreed on the use of their programming data for research purposes.

All participants were asked to fill in a voluntary background survey. From the 1166 participants, 561 provided information on their programming background and age; participant details are shown in Table 1. From the participants that answered the survey, the youngest ones are 12, while the oldest ones are 76 years old. From the participants, 297 have no previous programming experience, while 264 have at least some programming experience. In this study, when using the term all participants, we mean all 1166 participants, while when discussing participants with programming background or no programming background, the 264 or 297 participants are meant respectively.

3. RESULTS AND ANALYSIS

The descriptive statistics of the data are presented in Section 3.1. Section 3.2 provides the data needed to answer research questions 1 and 3 – how many snapshots are related to each submission and how some background factors affect this ratio. Section 3.3 provides data needed to answer research question 2, and finally, Section 3.4 provides additional insights to research questions 1 and 2 by investigating the amount of lost data from the perspective of source code states and their compilation statistics.

3.1 Overview of the Data

During the six week course, the 1166 participants made 93231 submissions, 1.3 million snapshots (save, run, test), and

event type	count	% of category
Submit project	93231	100%
Save project	524898	40.5%
Run and save project	572238	44.2%
Execute tests on project	198897	15.3%
Text insert	27940882	74.8%
Text delete	9062214	24.3%
Text paste	326993	0.9%

Table 2: Snapshot data statistics.

tries	all	%	exp = Y	%	exp = N	%
1	73939	79.3	20186	83.7	19370	76.8
2-5	15141	16.2	3296	13.7	4658	18.5
6-10	2842	3.1	418	1.7	868	3.4
11-	1309	1.4	204	0.9	326	1.3

Table 3: Amount of submission tries per exercise aggregated over all exercises.

37 million events (text insert, text remove, text paste). Table 2 describes the overall amount of different types of snapshots in the data set; the two most common reasons for the snapshots are running the application in the IDE (44.2%) and saving the project (40.5%), while the remaining snapshots were from testing the application locally (15.3%). When considering the keystroke-level events, the most common event was inserting text (74.8%), while 24.3% of the events were text removes. Less than 1 percentage were paste-events. However, as the length of pastes is typically longer than one character these numbers do not directly reflect the amount of text pasted into the codebase.

The majority of the students do not submit each exercise more than once. Table 3 contains statistics on the amount of submissions aggregated over all exercises. While participants with no previous programming experience submit each program once in 76.8% of the cases, the participants with previous programming experience submit each program once in 83.7% of the cases. In practice, the participants with previous programming experience are likely to get their exercises correct on the first submission more often than the participants with no previous experience. The total amount of submissions attempted two to five times is roughly one fifth from the amount of submissions attempted only once.

3.2 Snapshots and Submissions

Here, we consider the snapshots per submission ratio and how previous programming experience affects this ratio. The cases where a learner worked on an assignments but did not submit it have been filtered out from the analysis. In total there were 2599 user-assignment pairs that were never submitted. In these, 674 unique users created on average 12.7 snapshots (σ=26.8) to assignments they did not submit even once. Median and median absolute deviation were 5 and 5.9 snapshots, respectively. Only 7 students worked on the assignments but did not try to submit any of them.

Table 4 contains weekly statistics on the amount of submissions, snapshots and their ratio per users, grouped by programming experience. The amount of snapshots per submission is statistically significantly different during the first four weeks, after which the behavior of the groups with previous programming experience and no previous programming

are more similar. On average, if storing only submissions, 6.28 snapshots are lost for each submission from participants that have previous programming experience, while when considering participants with no previous programming experience, on average eight snapshots are lost for each submission. The amount varies during each week and as larger assignments are introduced during the later weeks, more data is lost.

Assignment Type

When considering the effect of the type of the exercise, we investigate two exercises from the first week of the course. In one of the exercises, the participants need to create an application that determines whether the input provided by an user represents a leap year or not, while in another exercise, the participants use an existing API to guide a robot in pushing an arbitrarily placed crate to a specified area. Both exercises are typically considered challenging by the students, and are positioned at the end of the first week. There are two major differences between the exercises; (1) the scale of the leap year exercise is smaller, and (2) the robot exercise provides students a visualization that provides a step-by-step view on the robot movements.

For the leap year assignment, the median snapshots per submission for students with previous programming is five, while for students with no previous experience the median is seven. A Wilcoxon rank sum test revealed that the difference is statistically significant ($p < .01$). For the robot assignment, the median snapshots per submission for students with previous programming experience is 17.8, while for students with no previous experience the median is 23. However, when performing a Wilcoxon rank sum test, while a marginal difference exists, there is no statistically significant difference between the two populations ($p = .08$). Thus, more data is lost from novice programmers than from programmers with some experience. The results of the Wilcoxon rank sum test can be interpreted so that the visualization support helps the participants with no previous programming experience to bridge the gap between the two populations, or that mathematical concepts needed in the leap year divide the two populations better than an assignment with visual support.

3.3 Keystrokes and Snapshots

On average, participants with previous programming experience spend 29.0 keylevel-events per snapshot, while the participants with no previous programming experience spend 30.2 keylevel-events per snapshots. That is, the participants with previous programming experience spend on average 1.2 keylevel-events less for each snapshot than the participants without programming experience. Two possible explanations exist; one rarely writes programs without making any mistakes during the process, and students without previous background perform more errors, while another possible explanation is that participants with existing programming background utilize shorter variable names and other descriptors. This analysis, however, is out of the scope of this article.

When considering the differences between subsequent snapshots and the actual keylevel-events, multiple sidesteps are taken by both the participants with previous programming experience and the participants with no previous programming experience.

week	n		snapshots/user		submissions/user		ratio/user		
	exp=Y	exp=N	exp=Y	exp=N	exp=Y	exp=N	exp=Y	exp=N	Wilcox (p)
1	256	294	110±49	134±73	23±1.5	23±1.5	4.6±1.9	6.0±3.0	1.381e-10
2	227	224	116±70	161±85	18±1.5	18±3.0	6.3±3.1	8.7±4.5	3.673e-07
3	208	195	125±63	195±153	29±1.5	29±3.0	4.4±2.0	5.4±2.1	6.668e-05
4	176	160	115±49	134±47	14±1.5	14±1.5	7.8±3.4	9.1±4.2	0.01142
5	158	144	127±70	143±73	10±0	10.5±1.5	11.7±6.7	12.2±7.8	0.2973
6	147	136	216±128	212±112	15±3.0	14.5±3.7	14±7.7	14.6±8.6	0.5516
1-6	264	297	604±529	641±606	104±30	85±61	6.28±3.23	8±3.91	0.0003

Table 4: Does programming experience affect snapshot count, submission count and snapshots per submission? Medians and median absolute deviations are reported. Wilcoxon rank sum test is used to compare the two populations. P-values are reported.

event type	all	exp = Y	exp = N
Submission	99.2%	99.5%	99.0%
Snapshot	92.1%	93.2%	91.2%
Keylevel, 5	44.4%	42.9%	48.9%
Keylevel, all	25.7%	27.5%	25.2%

Table 5: Compilation statistics

week	all	exp = Y	exp = N
Week 1	47.2%	51.5 %	45.4%
Week 2	48.4%	55.2 %	45.9%
Week 3	39.5%	44.6 %	37.4%
Week 4	45.5%	51.4 %	44.3%
Week 5	44.8%	49.9 %	44.5%
Week 6	42.3%	44.7 %	40.9%

Table 6: Compilation statistics for keylevel-events separated by weeks, events that have 5 or more seconds from the last event are taken into account.

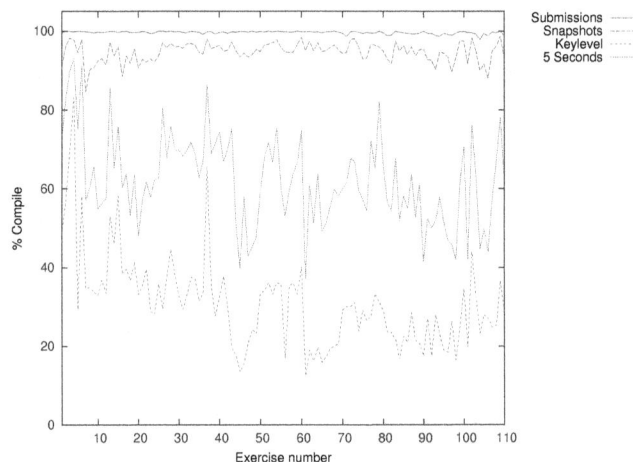

Figure 1: Compilation success percentages over all exercises with four different granularities. The topmost line indicates the compilation successes for submission, the next row snapshots, then keylevel-events with 5 second window, and finally all keylevel-events.

3.4 Compilation Statistics and Source Code States

The events are considered from two additional viewpoints. One is the compilation errors in the data, and another is the different source code states. Occurrence of compilation errors and the error message types are used to identify at risk students [6, 20], while source code states can be used to determine pathways that students can follow when stuck [7].

Table 5 shows the percentage of the submission types that compile for each participant group. While over 90% of submissions and snapshots compile for all groups, the keylevel data has been split into two parts. The row "Keylevel, 5" contains all keylevel entries that have been preceded by at least a 5 second break from typing, while the row "Keylevel, all" contains data from all keylevel events. In all cases, over 25% of the events compile for all groups. The distinction between the two separate keylevel groups was motivated by the fact that the "Keylevel, all"-group contains errors also from moments when participants are typing variable names etc.

Aggregated weekly compilation statistics are shown in Table 6; the statistics use the minimum 5 seconds window, meaning that the students have had a small pause from typing. Figure 1 displays the compilation statistics using four different granularities over the whole course. Both snapshots and submissions compile in majority of the cases, while the keylevel-events compile less frequently.

Next, we consider the different states in the sources. To calculate the different states, comments and whitespaces in the source codes are discarded from the data, but the syntax is retained unaltered. While researchers can reduce the search space by e.g. investigating the abstract syntax tree representation of the source code, we consider parse trees; this takes the variable names into account as they can be used to gain additional insight into how students follow good programming practices (including meaningful naming of variables).

To achieve a perspective on the number of parse tree states available with different granularities, we consider two separate assignments. The first assignment is a simple assignment, where the student has to modify variable values to create the correct output, while the other is the robot assignment that was also analyzed in Section 3.2, where the participant has to utilize a given API to guide a robot in pushing a crate to a loading area.

For the simple assignment, where the participants need to effectively change the values of existing variables, 51 distinct submissions exist from 1057 participants, while a total of 245 different states are stored from snapshots. The inclusion of every keylevel-event increases the amount of different states to 2726, which is reduced to 405 when considering only states that are present after the participant has taken a 5 second pause from typing. On the other hand, for the robot exercise, 1127 different parse trees exist from 850 participants, while there are 18404 different snapshot parse trees. If all keylevel-events are considered, there are a total of 128641 different program states. The number is reduced to 24463 when we include only keylevel-events for which the state is available after a 5 second wait. This suggests that the more complex the assignment is, the more states there are that the students can explore, and thus, more data is lost if data is stored at a coarser granularity.

4. DISCUSSION AND RELATED WORK

The dataset comes from a course that provides plenty of exercises for the students. As is common for courses that are available for anyone, not every participant in the course did every exercise. However, on average, the participants did over one half of the available tasks. Half of the course participants provided background details, and from them, one half worked until the last week of the course.

The programming environment used in the course provides standard functionality such as syntax highlighting and continuous code compilation with error checking. This can be one of the factors that explain the low amount of compilation errors in the snapshots and submissions when compared to those reported in the literature (see e.g. [15, 8]). In addition, the relatively high percentage of first submissions without additional submissions is likely partially influenced by the Test My Code-plugin, which provided ready made tests for the assignments.

The goal of this work has been to compare different log-levels that have been used to describe students' programming process. The use of fine-grained log data provides interesting opportunities. Events such as large deletes as pointed out by Allevato and Edwards [1] are easier to detect. To provide another example, Werner et al. [22] have aimed at using low-level log data to answer questions such as "Can logging data reveal the conditions under which students notice and use key features of an initial programming environment? Do students recognize problem patterns and try creative solutions or do they keep repeating the same ineffective strategies? Do students' strategies vary, depending on whether they are working on a closed-ended or open-ended task? Are student actions related to the sophistication of the games they produce?" Our work, presented in this article, takes first steps to understanding how low this low-level log data needs to be by providing an answer to the question "How much data is lost between different log-level granularities". Moreover, the key-level data displayed students that worked on assignments but did not submit anything. Indeed, in our data set, over 1000 student-exercise pairs with snapshots and key-level data but no submissions existed.

One may think that the amount of data stored is not worth the space. In the dataset that we were provided, the raw submissions, that were compressed using multiple-levels in a flat-file format, took a little over one gigabyte of space in total. When considering courses with hundreds of thousands of participants, the dataset could take up to hundred gigabytes, which in the light of modern hardware is little – most courses also do not have as many assignments as the one from which our dataset came from. The preprocessing of the data (compilation, creating parse trees, calculating snapshot differences) was performed on a cluster using 64 cores, and it took approximately 8 hours. While the compilation process was optimized by modifying the Java compiler input and output so that everything was done in memory, plenty of room for optimization remains; for our purposes the speed was sufficient.

While we did not find comparable work where the the amount of data lost when using different granularities was compared, plenty of work on utilizing snapshots of different granularities exist. Many of the platforms doing fine grained logging and related research in this field are surveyed by Helminen et al. [4]. With regard to what kinds of data should be stored, Stephens-Martinez et al. have asked instructors teaching massive open online courses, what data helps them to understand their class. Although the answers varied a lot, quantitative data that can be used to characterize students' actions was often raised up [14]. Snapshots from the programming process are clearly such data.

5. CONCLUSIONS AND FUTURE WORK

In this study, we have considered the amount of data lost when utilizing different storage granularity levels. While our results indicate that one should record students' programming process and store the data using a fine granularity, we have also shown that the amount of steps lost when using a coarser granularity depends on both the programming assignment and previous programming experience.

The data showed that about half of the students did also work on assignments that they never submitted to the assessment server, and that some students also worked on the assignments after submission. If only submissions are stored, no trace of such work is recorded, and the students that struggle on an assignment but never submit it are never seen.

Statistically significant differences were found in the amounts of work that the participants with existing programming background and the participants with no existing programming background needed to reach the programming assignment goals. The differences were visible in both submissions and snapshots up to the last weeks in the course, where the behavior of the participants was more alike. It is possible that the participants had learned to better work in the environment that they were placed in, that the participants that had less motivation and were less dispositioned towards learning had dropped out, or that the effect of the larger programming assignments that are more visible towards the end of the course diminishes the effect of programming experience, or a combination of the previous.

When considering the differences between subsequent snapshots and keylevel-events, multiple sidesteps are taken by both the participants with previous programming experience and the participants with no previous programming experience. The differences between participant backgrounds were more visible in traditional programming assignments, such as the "create an application that determines whether the inputted number is a leap year", while the differences between the participant groups were more subtle in programming assignments where participants had additional support in form of visualization. This finding is in line with existing research on the use of visualization software in teaching programming, which suggests that visualization components increase interaction [12].

While in this study we have shed light on the types of factors that affect the amount of lost data, in the future we will continue the study with a larger dataset. We will especially focus on the time usage and the program completeness to determine their effect, and are including various predictors such as the Jadud's EQ [6] to provide additional viewpoints from which the differences in participant populations can be considered. Future work will also determine and answer research questions that cannot be answered without sufficiently fine-grained data.

6. REFERENCES

[1] A. Allevato and S. H. Edwards. Discovering patterns in student activity on programming assignments. In *2010 ASEE Southeastern Section Annual Conference and Meeting*, 2010.

[2] T. Busjahn, C. Schulte, B. Sharif, Simon, A. Begel, M. Hansen, R. Bednarik, P. Orlov, P. Ihantola, G. Shchekotova, and M. Antropova. Eye tracking in computing education. In *Proceedings of the Tenth Annual Conference on International Computing Education Research*, ICER '14, pages 3–10, New York, NY, USA, 2014. ACM.

[3] J. DeBoer, A. D. Ho, G. S. Stump, and L. Breslow. Changing "course": Reconceptualizing educational variables for massive open online courses. *Educational Researcher*, 2014.

[4] J. Helminen, P. Ihantola, and V. Karavirta. Recording and analyzing in-browser programming sessions. In *Proc. of the 13th Koli Calling International Conference on Computing Education Research*, Koli Calling '13, pages 13–22, New York, NY, USA, 2013. ACM.

[5] P. Ihantola, T. Ahoniemi, V. Karavirta, and O. Seppälä. Review of recent systems for automatic assessment of programming assignments. In *Proceedings of the 10th Koli Calling International Conference on Computing Education Research*, pages 86–93. ACM, 2010.

[6] M. C. Jadud. Methods and tools for exploring novice compilation behaviour. In *Proc. Int. Workshop on Computing Education Research*, ICER '06, pages 73–84, 2006.

[7] W. Jin, T. Barnes, J. Stamper, M. Eagle, M. Johnson, and L. Lehmann. Program representation for automatic hint generation for a data-driven novice programming tutor. In S. Cerri, W. Clancey, G. Papadourakis, and K. Panourgia, editors, *Intelligent Tutoring Systems*, volume 7315 of *Lecture Notes in Computer Science*, pages 304–309. Springer Berlin Heidelberg, 2012.

[8] J. Kasurinen and U. Nikula. Estimating programming knowledge with bayesian knowledge tracing. *SIGCSE Bull.*, 41(3):313–317, July 2009.

[9] J. McKeogh and C. Exton. Eclipse plug-in to monitor the programmer behaviour. In *Proc. of the 2004 OOPSLA Workshop on Eclipse Technology eXchange*, eclipse '04, pages 93–97, New York, NY, USA, 2004. ACM.

[10] M. M. T. Rodrigo, R. S. Baker, M. C. Jadud, A. C. M. Amarra, T. Dy, M. B. V. Espejo-Lahoz, S. A. L. Lim, S. A. Pascua, J. O. Sugay, and E. S. Tabanao. Affective and behavioral predictors of novice programmer achievement. *ACM SIGCSE Bull.*, 41(3):156–160, 2009.

[11] S. C. Shaffer and M. B. Rosson. Increasing student success by modifying course delivery based on student submission data. *ACM Inroads*, 4(4):81–86, Dec. 2013.

[12] J. Sorva, V. Karavirta, and L. Malmi. A review of generic program visualization systems for introductory programming education. *Trans. Comput. Educ.*, 13(4):15:1–15:64, Nov. 2013.

[13] J. Spacco, D. Hovemeyer, W. Pugh, F. Emad, J. K. Hollingsworth, and N. Padua-Perez. Experiences with marmoset: Designing and using an advanced submission and testing system for programming courses. *SIGCSE Bull.*, 38(3):13–17, June 2006.

[14] K. Stephens-Martinez, M. A. Hearst, and A. Fox. Monitoring moocs: Which information sources do instructors value? In *Proc. of the First ACM Conference on Learning @ Scale Conference*, L@S '14, pages 79–88, New York, NY, USA, 2014. ACM.

[15] E. S. Tabanao, M. M. T. Rodrigo, and M. C. Jadud. Predicting at-risk novice java programmers through the analysis of online protocols. In *Proceedings of the Seventh International Workshop on Computing Education Research*, ICER '11, pages 85–92, New York, NY, USA, 2011. ACM.

[16] R. Turner, M. Falcone, B. Sharif, and A. Lazar. An eye-tracking study assessing the comprehension of c++ and python source code. In *Proc. of the Symposium on Eye Tracking Research and Applications*, ETRA '14, pages 231–234, New York, NY, USA, 2014. ACM.

[17] A. Vihavainen. Predicting students' performance in an introductory programming course using data from students' own programming process. In *Proc. 13th Int. Conference on Advanced Learning Technologies*, ICALT '13, pages 498–499, 2013.

[18] A. Vihavainen, M. Luukkainen, and J. Kurhila. Multi-faceted support for MOOC in programming. In *Proceedings of the 13th Annual Conference on Information Technology Education*, SIGITE '12, pages 171–176, New York, NY, USA, 2012. ACM.

[19] A. Vihavainen, T. Vikberg, M. Luukkainen, and M. Pärtel. Scaffolding students' learning using Test My Code. In *Proc. of the 18th ACM Conf. on Innovation and Technology in Computer Science Education*, ITiCSE '13, pages 117–122, 2013.

[20] C. Watson, F. Li, and J. Godwin. Predicting performance in an introductory programming course by logging and analyzing student programming behavior. In *Proc. 13th Int. Conference on Advanced Learning Technologies*, ICALT '13, pages 319–323, 2013.

[21] C. Watson, F. W. Li, and J. L. Godwin. No tests required: Comparing traditional and dynamic predictors of programming success. In *Proceedings of the 45th ACM Technical Symposium on Computer Science Education*, SIGCSE '14, pages 469–474, New York, NY, USA, 2014. ACM.

[22] L. Werner, C. McDowell, and J. Denner. Middle school students using alice: What can we learn from logging data? In *Proceeding of the 44th ACM Technical Symposium on Computer Science Education*, SIGCSE '13, pages 507–512, New York, NY, USA, 2013. ACM.

An Analysis of Team Performance in High School Programming Contests

Stoney Jackson, Heidi J. C. Ellis, Robert Crouse
Western New England University
1215 Wilbraham Rd.
Springfield, MA USA
001-413-782-1748
hjackson@wne.edu, ellis@wne.edu, rcrouse@wne.edu

ABSTRACT

Programming contests are used by educational institutions as a way to attract high school students to computing degrees. While there has been some analysis of the artifacts and process of programming contests including complexity of algorithms and the impact of teamwork strategies on team success, there has been little work investigating the impact of programming language and team submission pattern on team performance. This paper presents the results of an analysis of five years of contest results for the Western New England University high school programming contest. The analysis looks at the frequency of submissions, types of errors that occurred, and languages used by winning teams. Results appear to indicate that Python and Java have the highest success rate and that the most frequent type of error is incorrect output.

Categories and Subject Descriptors

K.3.2 [**Computers and Education**]: Computer and Information Science Education – *Computer Science Education*.

General Terms

Human Factors

Keywords

Programming contest, high school.

1. INTRODUCTION

Programming contests have been held for high school students as early as the 1970's [1] and have grown in popularity since the 1980's [2]. Many such early contests grew out of Math Olympiads.

The most common reason for colleges and universities to host high school programming contests is as an outreach and recruitment tool [1-3] to draw students into computing degree programs. Some schools have a scholarship program associated with the contest [1] or concurrent workshops for high school teachers [3]. In addition to outreach, such contests generate

excitement about computing and create positive advertising for the host institutions.

Many high school contests mirror the ACM Collegiate Contest where teams of students work on a problem set within a defined time period and winners are judged by the correctness of the program results and speed. However, there are also colleges and universities that host other computing-related competitions for high school students. Henderson [4] describes the Indiana Student Software Awards Competition (ISSAC) which encourages students who have developed a software project either on their own or for a class to submit a project for judging. Winners are awarded scholarships and plaques.

Sherrell [5] reports on a high school competition that emphasizes software development over coding. The contest is carried out over several weeks as teams work to develop a software project. Results are judged on the quality of the development artifacts in addition to the functionality of the code

Bowring [6] describes a similar approach that uses a single-day competition. The College of Charleston's competition also emphasizes the quality of software process over programming. Students are provided with a working skeleton of code and a set of requirements that they must implement. Students must present their working code in addition to documentation and test cases. Judging is based on how well the code meets the requirements, and the readability of the code and artifacts.

While there has been some analysis of the artifacts and process of collegiate programming contests such as the complexity of algorithms [7], the impact of teamwork strategies on team success [8], and how to make contests more gender-neutral [9], there has been little work investigating the impact of programming language and team submission pattern on team performance.

This paper presents the results of an analysis of five years of contest results from the Western New England University high school programming contest. Historically, the contest has been sponsored by Microsoft who provides prizes in the form of software and books. The analysis looks at the frequency of submissions, types of errors that occurred, and languages used by winning teams.

2. THE STUDY

The first high school programming contest was held at Western New England University in spring 1984 [10]. Since that time, the contest has been run annually with between 14 and 26 teams competing. The competition is held during the University's spring break which is a school-day for most local high schools. The competition itself mirrors the ACM Collegiate Competition in that it is four hours long and students work in a timed fashion on a pre-determined set of problems. Faculty members at Western New England University create the problems and also serve as judges during the contest.

High Schools are allowed to have multiple teams participate in the contest and there are between three and four members per team. During the years 2007-2011 teams were allowed to use Java, C++, Visual Basic 6, QBasic, and Visual Basic.Net. Python was added in 2012. During the time of the study, Java was used for the AP exam.

It should be noted that a total of 14 different schools participated in the contest from 2007 through 2013. Five of the schools attended all five contests, consistently accounting for over half of the teams in attendance. Another school attended four of the five contests. The coaches of these six teams have remained consistent throughout the contests and, for the most part, the coaches of the remaining teams have also remained the same.

This study reviews data from the results of competitions in years 2007, 2008, 2010, 2012, and 2013. This study looks only at student submission information gathered from the programming contest shell. We were unable to collect information on the types of classes that were being taught in the high schools, the programming languages used, or the longevity of the teachers with the exception that the coaches of the teams most consistently attending the contest remained the same during the years of the study. In addition, the data for years 2009 and 2011 were lost and the programming languages used in the contests changed over time. Lastly, additional error messages were added after the 2007 contest. However, even given these confounding factors, some interesting observations about the impact of programming language and submission pattern on team performance can be made.

A home-grown programming shell was used during the competition to manage submissions. When a team submits a solution to a problem, the solution is automatically executed against a set of test data provided by the faculty member responsible for developing the question. This test data is different than the test data provided in the problem description. The faculty member who is judging the result then assigns a result code based on the result of the execution. Result codes include:

- **Program Correct** – program executes as expected with all test data
- **Incomplete Output or No Output** – program produces partial correct or no output
- **Incorrect Output** – program produces incorrect output for one or more test cases
- **Run-Time Error** – program throws a run-time error
- **Incorrect Output Format** – program is producing the correct values, but not in the correct format
- **Syntax/Compilation Error** – syntax or compilation error
- **Max Execution Time Exceeded** – program timed out
- **Submission Solution for Wrong Problem** – program appears to have been submitted for a problem other than the one the submission indicated
- **Invalid Program Extension** – program has an unrecognized extension (e.g., txt)

It should be noted that the goal is for the judges to provide feedback that will aid students as opposed to strictly identifying the problem. This introduces some subjectivity into the judging. For example, the case where the output is incomplete and only part of the output is displayed could be viewed as either "incomplete output", "runtime error", or "wrong format" (assuming that some output is visible that is correct but not in the correct format). However, since 2007, the same faculty members have been serving as judges and therefore there is consistency in the judge pool.

This study arose from a curiosity about the impact of programming language on team success within high school programming contests. Below we describe the data, and outline our study questions.

2.1 Overview of Data

A summary of the five years of data that were collected is shown in Table 1 below. There were a total of 802 program submissions by student teams across all five years. The number of teams varied somewhat. The average number of submissions per team varied from a low of 6.59 to a high of 11.4 per team with an overall average of 9.56 submissions per team. The *Python* column indicates the years when Python was included in the set of programming languages supported.

Table 1. Contest data summary

Year	Schools	Teams	Submissions	Python
2007	8	17	112	No
2008	11	21	220	No
2010	8	16	146	No
2012	8	15	153	Yes
2013	9	15	171	Yes
Total	44	84	802	

2.2 Study Questions

The main motivation for our study was to determine if there were patterns in language and submissions of high school programming teams. In particular we were interested in whether language or submission pattern impacted team success. We focused on three main questions:

Q1. Does the programming language used impact team performance/ranking? We wanted to know if teams tended to be more successful when using one programming language over another.

Q2. What is the impact of programming language on the number and types of submission results? It would be of interest to see if there are more submissions and/or more successful submissions for a particular programming language. Do certain programming languages result in a larger number of one kind of error?

Q3. Does the number of submissions per team impact team performance/ranking? This question looks at the submission pattern of teams to determine if teams who make more submissions are more likely to rank higher.

3. RESULTS

Before discussing the results pertaining to the three research questions, we present some general results that are of interest. Table 2 shows the distribution of the various different submission results across error types. It is interesting to note that only some 20% of submissions were correct. Therefore, a student team may expect to have, on average, one in five submissions be correct. One other obvious result is that almost 60% of submissions result in logic errors (Incorrect Output/No Output and Run Time Error), a not unexpected result.

Table 2. Submission results

Result	%
Incomplete or no output	2.99
Incorrect output	44.89
Incorrect output format	7.89
Invalid program extension	1.37
Max. execution time exceeded	2.37
Program correct	19.95
Run time error	15.59
Submission for wrong problem	0.87
Syntax/compilation error	3.99

It should also be noted that the Syntax/Compile Errors could be the result of switching environments for testing student programs. Students may possibly have linked to a library that they were not allowed to use or be using different versions of a language, resulting in different outcomes from their programs when run in the judging shell.

Figure 1 below shows the percentage of teams that used each programming language. We have separated the years 2007, 2008, and 2010, pre-Python, from the post-Python years of 2012 and 2013 in order to show the impact of adding Python to the contest.

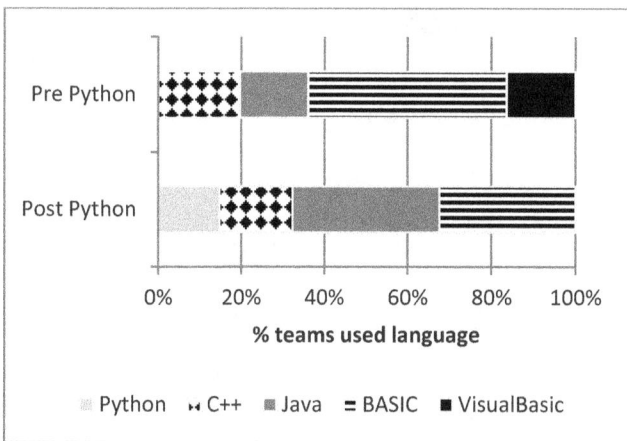

Figure 1. Language use

In observing Figure 1, it is interesting to note that BASIC and VisualBasic make up over half of the entries in the pre-Python era. This may be a reflection of the fact that many high schools were still using these languages to introduce students to computing during that time. It is also interesting to note that in the post-Python years, Python was used by some 18% of teams, but Java became much more widely used, going from approximately 10% pre-Python to approximately 30% post-Python. VisualBasic disappeared in the post-Python years.

3.1 Q1 - Programming Language vs. Rank

The answer to the question of whether programming language impacts team performance is one that may be of interest to many high school programming teachers. Figure 2 below shows a comparison of team rank versus programming language used. We have again separated the information into Pre-Python years (2007, 2008, 2010) and Post-Python (2012, 2013). In order to better

understand patterns, team ranks were grouped by threes. (Team ranks were based on placement in the programming contest. It should be noted that the number of teams in the programming contests varied resulting in an uneven number of teams per rank. Ranks 1 through 15 had 15 teams within a range while ranks between 16 through 18 had six teams, and ranks 19 through 21 had three.)

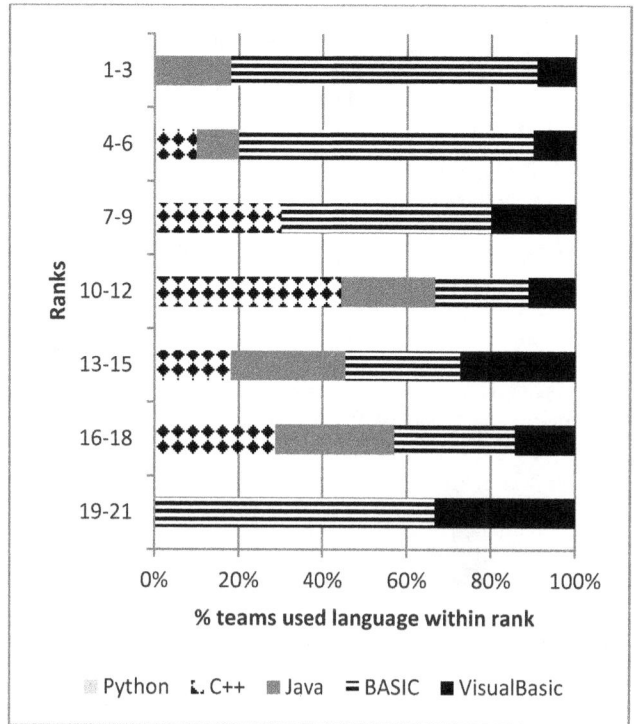

Figure 2a. Language use by rank – pre-Python

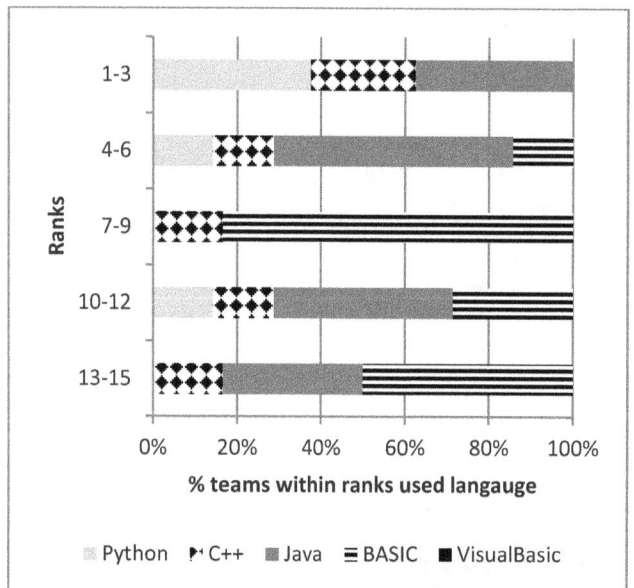

Figure 2b. Language use by rank – post-Python

One of the most striking observations that occurs when comparing Figure 2a and Figure 2b is the clear shift away from BASIC and VisualBasic after the adoption of Python. There is a similar shift towards the use of Java Post-Python. It is also interesting to note that the use of BASIC and VisualBasic is lower for the higher performing teams. When Python was introduced to the contest in 2012, the use of BASIC and VisualBasic combined went from 76% of submissions pre-Python to 38% of submissions post-Python.

3.2 Q2 - Programming Language vs Submission Results

The second study question investigates the impact of programming language on the number and types of submission results. An understanding of the types of errors that occur for a particular language could allow teachers and coaches to better support student learning by concentrating on the issues that result in a certain type of error.

One key question is that of whether programming language impacts team success. Figure 3 below shows the percentage of submissions that are successful (Program Correct) for each language. It is interesting to note that Python appears to have the highest success rate, followed closely by Java. This indicates that teams using Java and Python had relatively fewer incorrect submissions before obtaining a correct submission than teams using other languages. This could improve the efficiency of team performance as students would spend less time submitting incorrect programs and waiting for results.

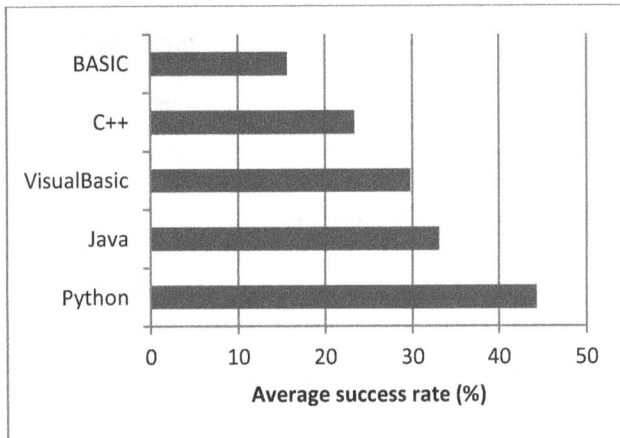

Figure 3. Average team success rate by language

Figure 4 below combines the success rate shown in Figure 3 above with the percentage of teams using each programming language (both pre- and post-Python). A couple of obvious observations result from viewing this figure. First, although a large number of submissions were in BASIC, this does not appear to translate into a high success rate. Second, Python has a very high success rate when compared to its' relatively low usage. Java also has a higher success rate than usage rate, although not as marked as Python. This figure appears to suggest that coding in Java and Python would tend to lead to greater success. However, it could also be that the students who are more proficient in coding are taught Python and Java while the less proficient students are using BASIC and VisualBasic. Figure 4 also seems to show a shift away from BASIC and VisualBasic and towards Python and Java.

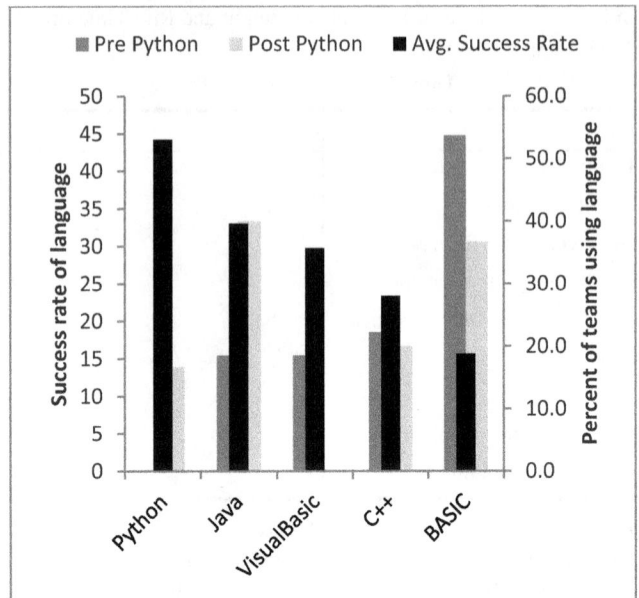

Figure 4. Language use and average success rate

In addition to looking at how programming languages impact team success, it is also interesting to look at the patterns of error results based on programming language as shown in Figure 5. Note that the error types of *Submission solution for wrong problem* and *invalid program extension* were omitted in Figure 5 in order to provide a clearer picture of the errors related directly to the programming language itself.

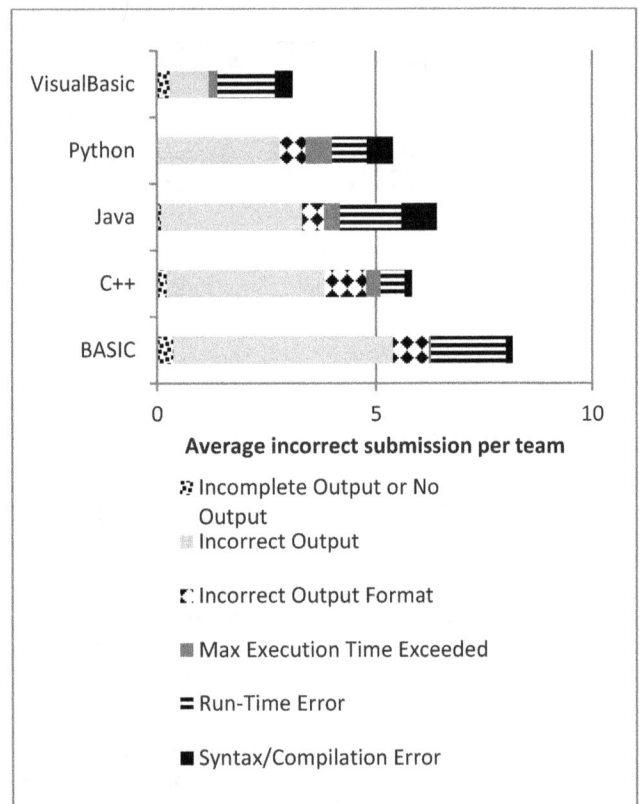

Figure 5. Average incorrect submissions per team

One major observation that can be made from observing Figure 5 is that the majority of all errors are related to incorrect output.

BASIC is especially prone to this type of error while VisualBasic seems less prone. This is not an unexpected result, but also highlights the need for students to pay careful attention to their test cases and corresponding output.

It is interesting to note that while Python and Java have the highest success rate, they also have the highest numbers of syntax errors. It is also interesting that C++ does not seem to suffer that problem. This is somewhat unexpected as C++ and Java have similar syntax and it would be reasonable to expect that they had similar syntax error rates. C++ does seem to be the most likely language to have an Incorrect Output Format error. This may be related to the complex approach to formatting numbers in C++.

Interestingly, Python is the most likely language to result in a Max Execution Time Exceeded. The reason for this is unclear.

3.3 Q3 - Rank vs. Number of Submissions

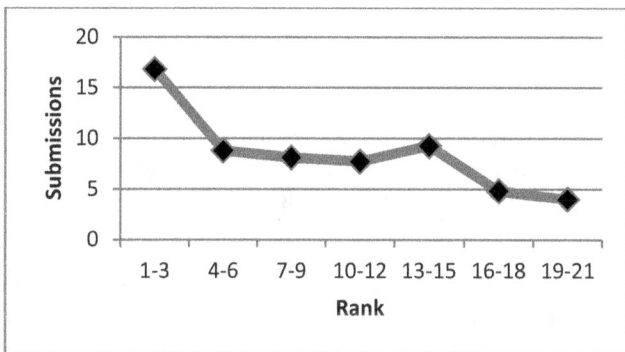

Figure 6a. Average submissions per team by rank

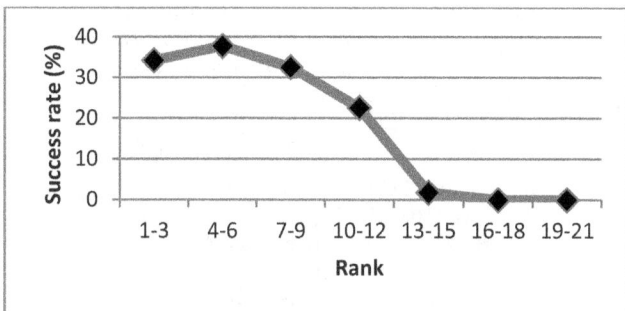

Figure 6b. Average team success rate by rank

The third research question focuses on the impact of the submission pattern on team performance. Figure 6 contains two graphs that show the average number of submissions per team and the success rate by team. As in section 3.1, team ranks were grouped by threes.

These two charts tell an interesting story. The average number of submissions by team decreases as team rank gets worse. The average number of submissions by the top three teams is approximately seven more than the next team grouping. This may suggest that the top teams are using feedback from the judging to guide their development. This appears to give them an edge over the team group 4-6 which has a higher success rate, although the difference is small. These results may suggest that there is some benefit to be gained by submitting a larger number of code tries.

The results shown in Figure 6a are counter to a common perception that poorer performing students tend to blindly submit code in the hopes that it will work. Instead, it appears that teams

that are less proficient are submitting fewer programs and the programs that they do submit are less frequently correct as shown in Figure 6b.

3.4 Confounding Factors
As mentioned in Section 1, this is not a formal study as there are many factors that could potentially impact the results. The number of teams per contest and the number of students per team varied. The programming languages used during the timespan of the study varied as Python was added in 2012. In addition, we are missing data for the years 2009 and 2011.

The subjectivity of judges when assigning error codes to the results introduces another variation into the study. In addition, different high schools teach different programming languages and different level courses. It is therefore difficult to tell the exact impact of programming language as not all high schools teach all languages. Another issue is that the Max Execution Time Exceeded error was added after the 2007 contest.

4. OBSERVATIONS
Based on the results of this study, we can make several interesting observations about programming team success with respect to programming language and submissions. While the top teams used BASIC, Java and Python successfully, the use of VisualBasic went up as team ranking went down. This could suggest either that the less experienced students have not yet been exposed to Java or Python, or that the less experienced students are attracted to what appears to be an easier language, but what turns out to be a less effective language for programming contests.

The comparison of language usage and success rate would suggest that Python would be a better language to use and that the use of BASIC isn't recommended. BASIC was the most widely used language, but by far had the lowest success rate based on average number of submissions. Java and Python both had better success rates than their rate of usage might suggest. This result might suggest that high school instructors migrate to Python and/or Java and shun BASIC. As we have only two years of data with students using Python, it will be interesting to see if increased use of Python increases the rate of successful submissions.

The investigation into types of errors indicates that the majority of student errors are related to output errors which are most likely logic errors, a reasonable result. Having students carefully check output may improve contest performance.

There are still a relatively large number of run time errors across most languages. These errors should be obvious to students and submitting programs with these errors wastes time. Highlighting this to students might improve their performance.

Not unexpectedly, the better teams were more efficient in their submission behavior. It was interesting to note that the teams that ranked 3-5 were slightly more efficient in their submissions and had a higher success rate, yet these teams had lower performance than the top teams. This may indicate that there is some benefit to submitting a "mostly correct" program over taking the time to ensure that a program is completely correct.

It should be noted that programming contests are artificial environments. Some of the factors that lead to success in this environment are not necessarily those that lead to good coding practice. For instance, the teams ranked 4-6 have a higher success rate than the higher ranked teams. This may indicate that these students spend more time on their programs ensuring correctness before submitting, a behavior that is desirable in industry.

5. CONCLUSION

In this study we observed the following:

1. Teams that rank higher in recent contests tend not to use VisualBasic and C++. Instead they preferred BASIC, Java, and Python, showing a shift away from VisualBasic towards Python and Java.
2. Python and Java had relatively high success rates, and yet were not used by a majority of teams. Conversely, nearly half the teams used BASIC, the language with the worst success rate.
3. There are differences in the types of error results that different languages tended to receive. Observation of these differences could improve team efficiency by identifying the types of errors students should watch for.
4. Higher ranking teams tend to have a higher success rate, and low ranking teams tend to submit fewer programs.

However, we must be careful about what conclusions we draw from these observations. For example (1) and (2) may be explained as one language being more effective in programming contests than another, or it may be reflection of a student's level of education at a school that teaches one language before another.

Although we may not be able to draw hard conclusions about causality, we do believe that educators can use this information to help guide their efforts. For example, when training teams for contests, one might consider using a language that enjoys a higher success rate like Java or Python. Or similarly, help students focus on identifying, removing, or entirely avoiding errors that are common for particular languages.

In the future we would like to perform an in-depth analysis of the actual code that was submitted with each submission, classifying more precisely different types of errors. We hope that this analysis will give a clearer picture of common types of errors students make in programming contests, and/or the types of errors that each language is more prone to.

We would also like to further investigate the frequency between submissions, successful and unsuccessful, to learn what that might tell us about different languages and team performance.

We have only two years of data on the use of Python, however, the data in this study seams to show that it has great potential, at least for use in programming contests. We will continue to monitor and track its use in programming contests.

6. ACKNOWLEDGMENTS

Our thanks to Dr. Leh-Sheng Tang who ran the Western New England University High School Programming Contest for many years. Without his support, this analysis would have been impossible.

7. REFERENCES

[1] Doug Myers, D., Null, L. 1986. Design and implementation of a programming contest for high school students. IN *SIGCSE Bull.* 18, 1 (Feb. 1986), 307-312. DOI=10.1145/953055.5705 http://doi.acm.org/10.1145/953055.5705

[2] Struble, G. 1991. Experience hosting a high-school level programming contest. *SIGCSE Bull.* 23, 2 (May 1991), 36-38. DOI=10.1145/122106.122114 http://doi.acm.org/10.1145/122106.122114

[3] Chow, B. and Zhang, V. 2009. CASCON high school programming competition 2009. In *Proceedings of the 2009 Conference of the Center for Advanced Studies on Collaborative Research* (CASCON '09), Patrick Martin, Anatol W. Kark, and Darlene Stewart (Eds.). IBM Corp., Riverton, NJ, USA, 361-361. DOI=10.1145/1723028.1723108 http://dx.doi.org/10.1145/1723028.1723108

[4] Henderson, P.B. 2003. ISSAC: Indiana student software awards competition. *SIGCSE Bull.* 35, 1 (Jan. 2003), 332-335. DOI=10.1145/792548.612000 http://doi.acm.org/10.1145/792548.612000

[5] Sherrell, L. and McCauley, L. 2004. A programming competition for high school students emphasizing process. In *Proceedings of the 2nd annual conference on Mid-south college computing* (MSCCC '04). Mid-South College Computing Conference, Little Rock, Arkansas, United States, 173-182.

[6] Bowring, J.F. 2008. A new paradigm for programming competitions. *SIGCSE Bull.* 40, 1 (Mar. 2008), 87-91. DOI=10.1145/1352322.1352166 http://doi.acm.org/10.1145/1352322.1352166

[7] Forisek, M. 2009. The Difficulty of Programming Contests Increases. In *Proceedings of the 4th International Conference on Informatics in Secondary Schools - Evolution and Perspectives: Teaching Fundamentals Concepts of Informatics* (ISSEP '10), Springer-Verlag, Berlin, Heidelberg, 72-85. DOI=10.1007/978-3-642-11376-5_8 http://dx.doi.org/10.1007/978-3-642-11376-5_8

[8] Amraii, S.A. 2007. Observations on teamwork strategies in the ACM international collegiate programming contest. *Crossroads* 14, 1, Article 9 (Dec. 2007), 9 pages. DOI=10.1145/1349332.1349341 http://doi.acm.org/10.1145/1349332.1349341

[9] Fisher, M. and Cox, A. 2006. Gender and programming contests: mitigating exclusionary practices. *Informatics in education* 5, 1 (Jan. 2006), 47-62.

[10] Carabetta, J.R. 1987. The planning and procedures associated with the Western New England College Winter Invitational High school Programming contest. *SIGCSE Bull.* 19, 2 (Jun. 1987), 29-35. DOI=10.1145/24728.24735 http://doi.acm.org/10.1145/24728.24735

Automatically Detectable Indicators of Programming Assignment Difficulty

Petri Ihantola
Aalto University
Department of Computer
Science and Engineering
Helsinki, Finland
petri.ihantola@aalto.fi

Juha Sorva
Aalto University
Department of Computer
Science and Engineering
Helsinki, Finland
juha.sorva@aalto.fi

Arto Vihavainen
University of Helsinki
Department of Computer
Science
Helsinki, Finland
avihavai@cs.helsinki.fi

ABSTRACT

The difficulty of learning tasks is a major factor in learning, as is the feedback given to students. Even automatic feedback should ideally be influenced by student-dependent factors such as task difficulty. We report on a preliminary exploration of such indicators of programming assignment difficulty that can be automatically detected for each student from source code snapshots of the student's evolving code. Using a combination of different metrics emerged as a promising approach. In the future, our results may help provide students with personalized automatic feedback.

Categories and Subject Descriptors

D.2.8 [**Software Engineering**]: Metrics—*complexity measures, performance measures*; K.3.2 [**Computers and Education**]: Computer and Information Science Education—*Computer science education*

Keywords

automated assessment; programming assignments; assignment difficulty; personalized feedback

1. INTRODUCTION

In typical CS and IT curricula, introductory programming courses are among the first that students take. The rest of the curricula build on the skills learned in those courses, and indeed success in introductory courses affects whether students' continue with their studies or not [7]. It is not surprising that ways to improve introductory-level programming education has been under study for decades [21, 29].

Some decades ago, programming was a skill needed by a select few. It was often learned and taught in an *ad hoc* fashion, as educators often sought to replicate the ways in which they had themselves happened to learn to program, and there was no pressure to educate large numbers of graduates. From the 1980s onwards, programming has become increasingly mainstream, to the point that some countries have included programming education in primary school (e.g. [9]). At the same time, the practices and tools used to teach programming have evolved; these include novice-friendly programming environments [16] and microworlds [10], languages for beginners [20, 24], and program visualization tools [26], among others. Nevertheless, this evolution is arguably lagging behind the demand for more programmers and better programming pedagogy.

Pedagogical approaches to programming have been proposed in which students in read code and study many worked examples [17, 18]; software tools have also been designed to support activities such as code-reading and multiple-choice questions that help develop knowledge of important concepts. Such activities can be very useful in a complementary role, but if the goal is to learn to write programs, the pedagogy should be aligned with that goal [4] and must eventually include activities in which the students practice writing programs. In a university course or similar formal learning context, this means that the pedagogy needs to include *programming assignments*.

As with any form of practice, two key aspects of a programming assignments are feedback and student motivation. These aspects are connected, as good feedback can not only help the learner with the topic of the assignment but also increase the learner's motivation. Poor feedback, on the other hand, can make a learner less inclined to persist with a programming task or an entire course.

Feedback can be partially or fully automatic [28, 14]. Automatic assessment systems and intelligent tutoring systems bring benefits such as easy accessibility and low cost per student, which makes them particularly attractive in large classes with hundreds or thousands of students — and even more so in the context of modern massive online courses. The downside of many automatic solutions is that they fall short of a human tutor in terms of quality of feedback. A part of this problem is that the feedback provided by automatic systems is usually not personalized to take the learner and the learner's present knowledge into account. In order to provide better automatic feedback, we need to be able to judge how the individual learner (or group) relates to the assignment at hand. For instance, do they find it difficult? Trivial? Helpful? Ideally, a reasonably reliable estimate of such factors could be elicited automatically.

SIGITE'14, October 15–18, 2014, Atlanta, Georgia, USA.
Copyright 2014 ACM 978-1-4503-2686-5/14/10 ...$15.00.
http://dx.doi.org/10.1145/2656450.2656476.

2. RESEARCH QUESTION

This article presents a study which is a preliminary exploration of factors that may influence the difficulty of programming assignments and metrics for automatically assessing those factors. More specifically, we explore the research question: *How do a learner's programming background and automatically analyzable programming behavior relate to the perceived difficulty of different programming assignments?*

The work is motivated by the current state of automated assessment systems for programming assignments: We believe that an appropriate next step in the automated assessment of programming assignments is the ability to provide feedback that is adjusted to fit particular students' needs and struggles. One aspect of this development is that feedback should be adjusted to match students' perceptions of assignment difficulty. Ideally, such feedback could be provided without constantly prompting students to assess the difficulty of the various assignments they work on.

The remainder of this article is organized as follows. First, we review the related literature in Section 3 below. Sections 4 and 5 outline our research methodology and present our empirical results and related discussion. Section 6 discusses some limitations of our work and possibilities for expanding on this exploratory study; Section 7 concludes the article.

3. RELATED WORK

Related work is explored through four themes. We start with theories of learning as we discuss the relationship between task difficulty, practice and motivation, which leads to the second theme of feedback. This in turn brings us to the third theme: software for automatic assessment. Finally, we consider those empirical studies within computing education research which resemble ours in that they have measured students' difficulties with programming assignments.

3.1 Task difficulty and practice

Expertise is not innate. It commonly grows through *deliberate practice*, that is, effortful activity whose purpose is to optimize improvement [11]. The importance of deliberate practice is reflected in programming courses around the world, which are designed around assignments that afford students with the opportunity to practice their programming skills on increasingly complex tasks.

Practice can be more or less effective. Ideally, the difficulty of an assignment matches the learner's existing knowledge and skills so that the learner is challenged to make use of their full cognitive capacity but is not overwhelmed by *cognitive load* [22]. Although the ideal is difficult to meet, not least because learners' prior knowledge varies, teachers may consider their students' expected learning trajectories and sequence assignments accordingly. Models of instructional design have been proposed to support these endeavors (e.g., the 4C/ID model [27]). The design and sequencing of assignments may be viewed as a form of *scaffolding* that aids the learner to make progress within their *zone of proximal development* [31] as they practice on tasks that they could not do without the help of the scaffolding.

Task difficulty impacts students' motivation in several ways. For instance, as per expectancy–value theories of motivation [2], assignments that are too easy are likely to have low perceived utility, while hard ones have a higher cost of completion, which reduces motivation unless they have been carefully designed to sustain interest. Excessive difficulty also contributes towards poor *self-efficacy* [3], which hampers further learning.

Another form of scaffolding that impacts motivation is the feedback that learners receive.

3.2 Feedback and motivation

Hattie and Timperley [12] argue that three main roles of feedback are to help a learner understand 1) the goals of learning, 2) the learner's own progress towards those goals, and 3) the activities that are needed to make better progress. For present purposes, the second role—the progress made by the learner—is the most salient.

A teacher or educational environment can help a student reflect on their progress by providing feedback that relates the student's performance to a particular goal or subgoal. Constructive feedback can improve self-efficacy. Constructive does not always imply positive, however, and feedback on progress should take into account the student's background and prior performance as well as the difficulty of the task. A beginner completing a difficult task should be applauded, but as Borich and Tombari argue on the basis of the literature, teachers who "show surprise at [students'] success, give excessive unsolicited help, or lavishly praise success on easy tasks are telling students that they lack ability" [5]. Such feedback can be detrimental to self-efficacy and motivation. Inappropriate feedback may also quickly cause students to learn to distrust the feedback-giving teacher or environment. The matter is, of course, complicated by the fact that an activity is not equally challenging to all learners.

3.3 Automatic feedback

An on-campus lab with an instructor and a small number of students is a setting that is well-suited to good, individualized feedback [8]. When such labs are not an option, or as a supplementary measure to them, feedback may be worked into course materials and programming assignments, which can be delivered online.

There is a robust field of research that seeks to improve the automatic assessment of students' solutions to programming problems [14]. Typically, automatic feedback is provided after students' take an action such as submitting a solution for assessment; the feedback often consists of information on the correctness of the solution and perhaps some additional information about observed deficiencies. The feedback may also praise the student for getting a good score or exhort them to make an improved attempt.

Two weaknesses of the typical approach discussed above are: 1) The feedback is "passive", as it is only presented when the student requests it, e.g., by submitting a solution, instead of being proactively offered, say, when the student is experiencing difficulty. 2) Feedback messages are based on the features of the submitted solution only, and are not influenced by other relevant factors such as the student's background or the difficulty of the task for the particular student. For instance, an experienced student may receive excessive accolades for a trivial assignment, which then undermines any praise received for more challenging ones.

3.4 Programming assignment difficulty

In this subsection, we briefly review some work similar to ours, that is, projects whose purpose has been to evaluate the difficulty of programming tasks.

Alvarez and Scott studied the relationship between the student-estimated difficulty of programming assignments and a number of metrics [1]. They used a survey that asked students to estimate difficulty twice, first after initially familiarizing themselves with an assignment and again after finishing it. The highest correlations to estimated difficulty were found using code metrics such as lines of code and the amount of control flow statements within the code.

Several threads of research exist that have utilized data recorded from the students' programming process. Although these studies generally have not focused on assignment difficulty, some of them have explored related phenomena. For instance, Jadud [15] proposed a formula for quantifying compilation errors, which has been used to identify students' course and assignment outcomes. In another study, Rodrigo and Baker [25] sought to identify students that are frustrated using both log data as well as observations from external observers. It is plausible that compilation errors and frustration do correlate positively with difficulty.

Another approach could be to estimate the cognitive load of students: cognitive load depends on both the intrinsic difficulty of a learning task and the prior knowledge that students bring to it. One way to estimate cognitive load is to use a suitable questionnaire. This approach, which is being explored in a programming context by Morrison et al. [19], has the benefit of using validated instruments and a solid theoretical basis, but since it requires a survey with multiple items, it is not suitable for our purposes. Another method also based on cognitive load is featured in a recent pilot study [6], in which the concept of "thrashing" was operationalized by measuring mouse clicks in an IDE; thrashing was taken to be an indication of (excessive) cognitive load. The results of the study demonstrated that different programming languages lead to different patterns of thrashing, which may be indicative of differences in difficulty.

In the present study, we seek to explore new metrics for automatically identifying which programming assignments different students find difficult. Our intention is to take one step closer to providing better, individualized, motivating automatic feedback that takes into account not only the student's program but also task difficulty as experienced by the particular student.

4. DATA AND METHODS

The data used in this study comes from an open online programming course offered by the University of Helsinki during Spring 2014. It is a six-week Java course in which students are taught procedural programming for the first three weeks and object-oriented programming for the second three-week period. The course is taught using an assignment-intensive teaching style, where majority of the work is done within a programming environment. Details of the course have been previously published in [30].

After each assignment, students could provide numeric feedback on the difficulty of the assignment. The difficulty was given on a scale from 1 to 5, where one stands for "easy" and five for "hard". In addition, the programming environment used in the course stored key-level snapshot data, that is, each key-press by a student while working on a programming assignment was recorded. None of the questions were mandatory, and students could turn off the key-level snapshot data gathering at will. At the beginning of the course,

the participants were asked to provide details on their programming experience.

The data set used in this study contains information on 417 students. This is after we included only students who had provided details on their programming background, provided feedback on assignment difficulty on at least three occasions, and kept the key-level snapshot recording enabled. Overall, the included students submitted 31255 solutions to assignments and provided details on the difficulty of an assignment 11161 times. That is, in about 36% of the submissions, the participant also provided feedback on the assignment difficulty.

The snapshot data was processed to include a time stamp as well as information on compilation state, i.e., whether the source code in each snapshot compiles. This data was aggregated to provide information on the process that each student took to solve an assignment. More specifically, for each assignment that a student works on, we aggregated details on (1) the time spent on the assignment, (2) the number of keystrokes made, (3) the percentage of keystrokes and time in a non-compiling state, (4) the number of lines of code, and (5) the number of control-flow elements in the program (e.g. *if, else, while, for, return*). By "time spent on the assignment" we mean the overall time spent modified with by truncating any pause of over five minutes between keystrokes to only five minutes. The number of keystrokes and the percentage of time/keystrokes in a non-compiling state are also potential indicators of struggling to make progress; if a student spends more time in a state where the code does not compile, or takes more steps than others while solving the problem, the assignment may seem more difficult overall. Line and control-flow element counts measure code complexity, and have previously been observed to be decent indicators of perceived difficulty [1].

We used quantitative analysis to identify factors that explain programming assignment difficulty. Correlations between the students' perceived difficulty and factors were computed using the R statistics package [23].

5. RESULTS AND DISCUSSION

This section describes our results in three parts. First, we discuss the effect of programming experience on perceived assignment difficulty. Then, we consider the relationships between perceived difficulty and individual factors: time, number of keystrokes, compilation state, lines of code, and the number of control-flow elements. Finally, we look at combining the various factors.

5.1 Programming Experience

In order to evaluate the effect of prior programming experience, the students were split in two groups on the basis of on their background. Of the participants, 230 reported no previous programming experience, while 187 described at least some experience with programming. Figure 1 displays the average perceived difficulty of each assignment for the groups, as well as a combined metric for all participants. As a Shapiro-Francia test revealed that the populations do not follow a normal distribution, a Wilcoxon signed-rank test was used as the paired difference test to measure whether the population means differ.

For the population with at least some existing programming experience, the median difficulty of the assignments is 1.735, while for the population with no previous program-

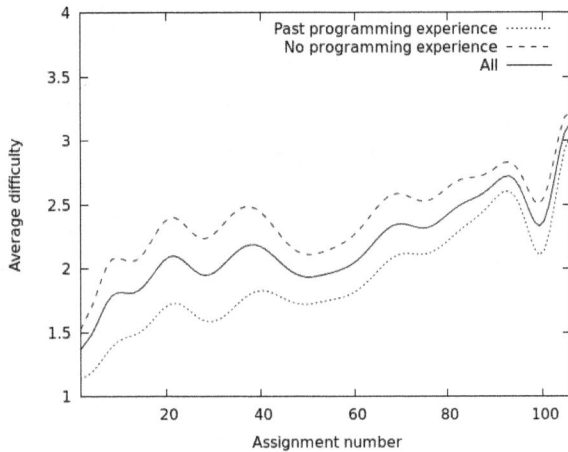

Figure 1: The means of students' estimates of the difficulty of the assignments. The curves have been smoothed for ease of viewing.

Table 1: Correlation coefficients between perceived assignment difficulty and various metrics, grouped by assignment type (math-oriented vs. open-ended vs. visually supported). Correlations marked with an asterisk are statistically significant ($p < 0.01$).

Factor	All	Math	Open	Vis
All participants				
Time	.49*	.48*	.30*	.48*
Number of keystrokes	.44*	.42*	.27*	.39*
% states not compiling	.16*	.10	.03	.33*
% time not compiling	.03	.09	.11	.20*
Lines of code	.36*	.27*	.24*	.26*
Control-flow elements	.35*	.26*	.22*	.38*
Programming experience				
Time	.54*	.45*	.36*	.45*
Number of keystrokes	.50*	.47*	.35*	.37*
% states not compiling	.15*	.10	.04	.27*
% time not compiling	.01	.11	.02	.13
Lines of code	.44*	.34*	.33*	.34*
Control-flow elements	.43*	.30*	.19	.36*
No programming experience				
Time	.46*	.48*	.25*	.53*
Number of keystrokes	.40*	.38*	.22*	.45*
% states not compiling	.16*	.10	.03	.36*
% time not compiling	.03	.08	.22	.20*
Lines of code	.33*	.25*	.18*	.23*
Control-flow elements	.31*	.25*	.25*	.45*

ming experience, the median difficulty of the assignments is 2.375. The populations are statistically different ($p < 0.01$), and thus there is, as one would expect, a difference in how the two populations perceive the difficulty of the assignments. However, as can be observed from Figure 1, the between-group difference in mean perceived difficulty diminishes towards the end of the six-week course. This trend suggests that the course taught skills that the more experienced students already had to some extent, and that the beginners partially caught up with the more experienced students.

5.2 Individual factors

Initially, an analysis was carried out to determine the correlations between difficulty and various other factors, each of which was considered separately. These factors were: time, number of keystrokes, proportions of keystrokes and time in a non-compiling states, lines of code, and count of control-flow elements. Table 1 displays these correlations for all participants as well as beginners and experienced students separately. For each factor, the table shows four values: one for all assignments, one for mathematically oriented assignments, one for open-ended assignments, and one for assignments with visual elements such as a given GUI that helps evaluate one's progress.

While a majority of the observed correlations are statistically significant, the correlation values are mostly medium-sized ($0.3 < r < 0.5$). In only two of the cases, the individual factors show a high correlation with difficulty ($r > 0.5$); both factors being time. The pattern of correlations appears to be largely similar for students with and without prior programming experience.

The correlations that we found between perceived difficulty and the number of lines of code as well as the number of control-flow elements were lower than the corresponding results reported earlier by Alvarez and Scott [1]. In their study, lines of code and control-flow elements had the highest correlations with perceived difficulty, whereas in our data, time on task and the number of keystrokes had somewhat higher correlations.

As Table 1 further shows, in most cases we found only low, largely insignificant correlations between perceived dif-

ficulty and the factors related to compilation status. The assignments with visual programming support constitute an exception to this trend, as a low-to-medium positive correlation was observed in these assignments.

5.3 Combined factors

In the previous section, we considered individual indicators of assignment difficulty one at a time. To get an initial understanding of how these factors interact in the data set at our disposal, we applied a recursive partitioning to construct a decision tree of assignment difficulty. The model is based on the metrics presented in the previous section.

The model was built using the ctree implementation of R^1. This method guarantees that the size of the tree is appropriate so that no pruning or cross-validation is necessary. A general description of the method is provided by Hothorn et al. [13].

The resulting decision tree is depicted in Figure 2. At each end node (leaf), a range of difficulty values is shown. This is the range of all the assessments of difficulty by students whose development snapshots matched the decision nodes leading to the end node. As can be seen from the figure, the tree is dominated by the amount of time that the student spent on the assignment. Although program size, complexity, and the degree to which the student maintained their program in a compilable state had an effect, students generally reported time-consuming exercises to be difficult.

6. LIMITATIONS AND FUTURE WORK

Our data comes from a particular programming course taught in a particular way in a Nordic country with a rather homogeneous population and high quality of education. Our results may be context-dependent. Indeed, as a part of the

---

[1] http://www.inside-r.org/packages/cran/party/docs/ctree

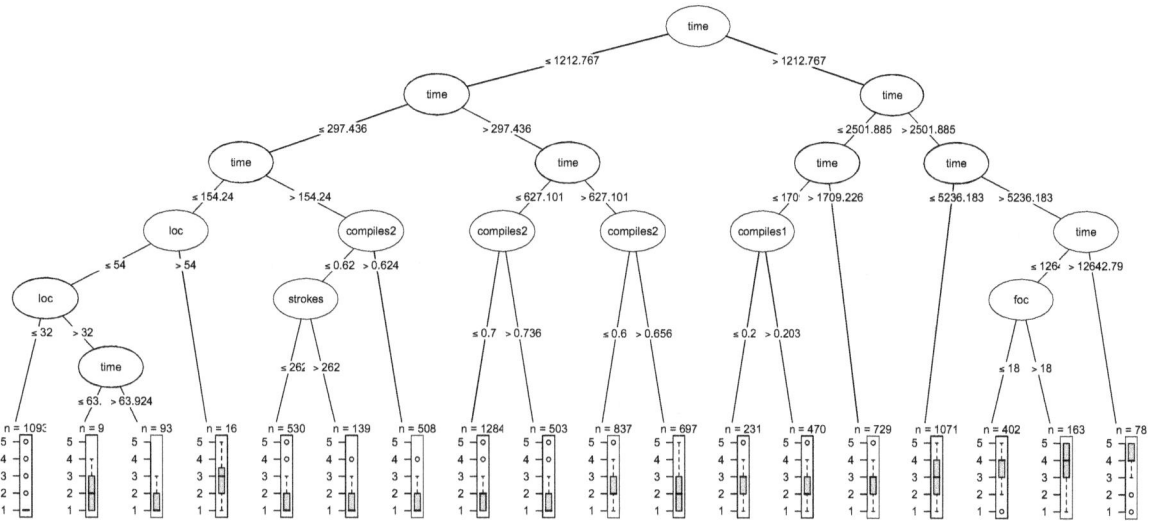

Figure 2: A decision tree of assignment difficulty constructed using recursive partitioning. *Loc* stands for lines of code and *foc* for flow-of-control count. *Compiles1* and *compiles2* stand for the proportion of compiling states and the proportion of time during which a program compiles, respectively.

present work, we re-examined the factors such as lines of code and number of control-flow elements that had the highest correlations with difficulty as reported by Alvarez and Scott [1], and while our work confirms that these metrics correlate positively with perceived difficulty, we found lower correlations for these factors than the other study. This difference in results suggests that the phenomena we have studied are at least in part, and perhaps quite significantly, dependent on context. Although a decision tree such as the one in Figure 2 may be useful in tailoring feedback in a particular context, other contexts need to be addressed separately. Future work may explore different programming courses, introductory or otherwise, and determine the extent to which our findings are transferable.

Our study draws on students' subjective assessments of difficulty. However, different students may have different interpretations of what "difficult" means. As pointed out in Section 5.3, much of "assignment difficulty" can be explained by the time it takes from students to do the assignment; similarly, Alvarez and Scott [1] reported that the size of the program was an important factor. A challenge in research such as ours, and one that we have not addressed in the present work, is teasing apart difficulty and workload, or at least determining the extent to which the distinction between the two is important for providing good feedback. The decision tree approach used above would easily accommodate additional variables, if necessary.

Another limitation is that although each assignment received a difficulty rating from at least 60 different students, providing the ratings was voluntary and we cannot rule out the possibility of an inherent self-selection bias. It is possible that the students that provided ratings are different from other students.

In this work, we split students in two groups on the basis of their prior programming experience. Future work could replace this simple model with a more fine-grained one so as to explore the variation among the experienced students.

To enable a critical examination of our results and facilitate follow-up studies, we have published our data set at http://bit.ly/1oZnEKG.

7. CONCLUSIONS

In this article, we have explored factors that relate to the perceived difficulty of programming assignments. The factors, excluding past programming experience, can be automatically detected from a stream of programming events—or keystrokes—that are performed within a programming environment. Our analysis suggests that the time spent on an assignment and the amount of programming events both have a medium to high correlation with perceived difficulty. Barely any correlation was found between perceived difficulty and the number of states that fail to compile or the length of time that the student's program is in a non-compiling state.

Although automatic feedback remains a far cry from what a good human tutor can provide, many students do not have convenient access to good human tutors, and any advance in automatic feedback is welcome. Our results show that metrics related to perceived difficulty can be automatically extracted from data that describes students' programming process. Automatic feedback systems can be adjusted to take task difficulty into account, which may improve the quality of feedback.

We conclude this article with some observations about the use of key-level data of student behavior. As a basis for assessing difficulty, this data has the benefit that it can be collected *in situ* and makes it possible to provide early, proactive feedback that the student does not need to explicitly request by submitting an assignment. An additional benefit, whose implications for automatic feedback may be explored in future work, is that such data provides details about students' programming process. Since, as Hattie and Timperley put it, "feedback is effective when it consists of information about progress, and/or about how to proceed" [12], key-level data has the potential to further enhance feedback.

8. REFERENCES

[1] A. Alvarez and T. A. Scott. Using student surveys in determining the difficulty of programming assignments. *J. Comput. Sci. Coll.*, 26(2):157–163, Dec. 2010.

[2] E. M. Anderman and H. Dawson. Learning with motivation. Routledge, 2011.

[3] A. Bandura. Self-efficacy: Toward a unifying theory of behavioral change. *Psych. Review*, 84(2):191, 1977.

[4] J. Biggs and C. Tang. *Teaching for Quality Learning at University*. McGraw-Hill, 3rd edition, 2007.

[5] G. D. Borich and M. L. Tombari. *Educational Psychology: A Contemporary Approach*. Longman Publishing/Addison Wesley, 2nd edition, 1997.

[6] S. Buist. Extending an IDE to support input device logging of programmers during the activity of user-interface programming: Analysing cognitive load. Bachelor of Science dissertation, The University of Bath, 2014.

[7] A. Christopher Strenta, R. Elliott, R. Adair, M. Matier, and J. Scott. Choosing and leaving science in highly selective institutions. *Research in Higher Education*, 35(5):513–547, 1994.

[8] M. Clancy, N. Titterton, C. Ryan, J. Slotta, and M. Linn. New roles for students, instructors, and computers in a lab-based introductory programming course. In *Proceedings of the 34th SIGCSE Technical Symposium on Computer Science Education*, SIGCSE '03, pages 132–136, New York, NY, USA, 2003. ACM.

[9] Computing At School. Computing at school web site. http://www.computingatschool.org.uk/, n.d.

[10] S. Cooper, W. Dann, and R. Pausch. Alice: A 3-D tool for introductory programming concepts. *J. Comput. Sci. Coll.*, 15(5):107–116, Apr. 2000.

[11] K. A. Ericsson, R. T. Krampe, and C. Tesch-Römer. The role of deliberate practice in the acquisition of expert performance. *Psych. Review*, 100(3):363, 1993.

[12] J. Hattie and H. Timperley. The power of feedback. *Review of Educational Research*, 77(1):81–112, 2007.

[13] T. Hothorn, K. Hornik, and A. Zeileis. Unbiased recursive partitioning: A conditional inference framework. *Journal of Computational and Graphical Statistics*, 15(3):651–674, 2006.

[14] P. Ihantola, T. Ahoniemi, V. Karavirta, and O. Seppälä. Review of recent systems for automatic assessment of programming assignments. In *Proceedings of the 10th Koli Calling International Conference on Computing Education Research*, Koli Calling '10, pages 86–93. ACM, 2010.

[15] M. C. Jadud. Methods and tools for exploring novice compilation behaviour. In *Proceedings of the Second International Workshop on Computing Education Research*, ICER '06, pages 73–84. ACM, 2006.

[16] M. Kölling, B. Quig, A. Patterson, and J. Rosenberg. The BlueJ system and its pedagogy. *Computer Science Education*, 13(4):249–268, 2003.

[17] M. C. Linn and M. J. Clancy. The case for case studies of programming problems. *Communications of the ACM*, 35(3):121–132, March 1992.

[18] R. Lister. Concrete and other neo-Piagetian forms of reasoning in the novice programmer. In J. Hamer and M. de Raadt, editors, *Proceedings of the 13th Australasian Conference on Computing Education (ACE '11)*, volume 114 of *CRPIT*, pages 9–18, Perth, Australia, 2011. Australian Computer Society.

[19] B. B. Morrison, B. Dorn, and M. Guzdial. Measuring cognitive load in introductory CS: Adaptation of an instrument. In *Proceedings of the Tenth Annual Conference on International Computing Education Research*, ICER '14, pages 131–138, New York, NY, USA, 2014. ACM.

[20] S. Papert. *Teaching Children Thinking (LOGO Memo)*. Massachusetts Institute of Technology, A.I. Laboratory, 1971.

[21] A. Pears, S. Seidman, L. Malmi, L. Mannila, E. Adams, J. Bennedsen, M. Devlin, and J. Paterson. A survey of literature on the teaching of introductory programming. In *ITiCSE Working Group Reports*, ITiCSE-WGR '07, pages 204–223, New York, NY, USA, 2007. ACM.

[22] J. L. Plass, R. Moreno, and R. Brünken, editors. *Cognitive Load Theory*. Cambridge Univ. Press, 2010.

[23] R Core Team. *R: A Language and Environment for Statistical Computing*. R Foundation for Statistical Computing, Vienna, Austria, 2014.

[24] M. Resnick, J. Maloney, A. Monroy-Hernández, N. Rusk, E. Eastmond, K. Brennan, A. Millner, E. Rosenbaum, J. Silver, B. Silverman, and Y. Kafai. Scratch: Programming for all. *Commun. ACM*, 52(11):60–67, Nov. 2009.

[25] M. M. T. Rodrigo and R. S. Baker. Coarse-grained detection of student frustration in an introductory programming course. In *Proceedings of the Fifth International Workshop on Computing Education Research*, ICER '09, pages 75–80, New York, NY, USA, 2009. ACM.

[26] J. Sorva, V. Karavirta, and L. Malmi. A review of generic program visualization systems for introductory programming education. *ACM Transactions on Computing Education*, 13(4):15:1–15:64, Nov. 2013.

[27] J. J. G. van Merriënboer and P. A. Kirschner. *Ten Steps to Complex Learning: A Systematic Approach to Four-Component Instructional Design*. Lawrence Erlbaum, 2007.

[28] K. VanLehn. The relative effectiveness of human tutoring, intelligent tutoring systems, and other tutoring systems. *Educational Psychologist*, 46(4):197–221, 2011.

[29] A. Vihavainen, J. Airaksinen, and C. Watson. A systematic review of approaches for teaching introductory programming and their influence on success. In *Proceedings of the Tenth Annual Conference on International Computing Education Research*, ICER '14, pages 19–26, New York, NY, USA, 2014. ACM.

[30] A. Vihavainen, M. Luukkainen, and J. Kurhila. Multi-faceted support for MOOC in programming. In *Proceedings of the 13th Annual Conference on Information Technology Education*, SIGITE '12, pages 171–176, New York, NY, USA, 2012. ACM.

[31] L. S. Vygotsky. *Mind in Society: The Development of Higher Psychological Processes*. Harvard University Press, 1978.

Enhancing the Comprehension of Network Sniffing Attack in Information Security Education using a Hands-on Lab Approach

Zouheir Trabelsi
College of Information Technology
UAE University, UAE
Trabelsi@uaeu.ac.ae

ABSTRACT

Sniffing attack is a common network attack and a fundamental topic to information security education. The sniffing attack is usually used by malicious users to spy network traffic, and to collect confidential and sensitive information. With the objective of enhancing information security education, this paper discusses what fundamental security concepts and hands-on skills the students need to know and acquire about network sniffing attack, respectively. The learning objective of the discussed hands-on lab exercises is to teach students how to practically sniff network traffic in an isolated network laboratory environment and detect hosts preforming sniffing activities. The paper does so in the hope that it will encourage the teaching of sniffing attack topic when offering courses on network security, using a hands-on approach. The paper discusses also the implications of the offered hands-on lab exercises on the students' performance and learning outcomes.

Categories and Subject Descriptors

[C.2] Computer-Communication Networks
[K.3.2] Computer and Information Science Education

General Terms

Security.

Keywords

Information security curriculum; Network sniffing attack; Promiscuous mode detection; Ethical hacking; Learning outcomes.

1. INTRODUCTION

Information security programs offer courses that cover various security fields, including mainly network security, cryptography, database and distributed systems security, software security, computer forensics, biometrics, operating systems security, and ethical and legal issues in computer security. A security course on intrusion detection and network attacks requires extensive hands-on experience to fully develop the students' knowledge base. The network security field covers typically network packet filtering, firewalls, network traffic analysis, network attacks, VPN, intrusion detection and prevention, and network attacks topics. All these security topics are included in NSTISSI 4011 [11] and CNSSI 4013 [5], which are required by the USA National Security Agency to certify an institution as a National Center of Academic Excellence in Information Assurance Education (CAE/IAE).

Nowadays, the field of academic security education is dominated by hands-on lab exercises on defensive techniques. However, there is growing interest in offensive techniques, which were originally developed by hackers [2, 6, 7, 8, 14, 15, 19]. Teaching ethical hacking techniques is becoming a necessary component of information security curriculum as it yields better security professionals than other curricula teaching defensive techniques alone. Among common attack techniques taught in a course on intrusion detection and prevention, is network sniffing attack which is an easy attack to perform but it can be a very harmful attack since it allows malicious users to easily steal confidential data, passwords and anyone's privacy.

On the other hand, information security courses commonly require both the preparation of regular lectures to teach students the fundamental security concepts, and the development of hands-on laboratory exercises. The courseware should be designed in a way that the laboratory exercises bring to students effective operational experiences on the use and implementation of security techniques and solutions. It is important to mention that nowadays the need to use a practice and application oriented approach in information security education is paramount [3]. In fact, a security education curriculum that does not give the students the opportunity to experiment in practice with security techniques cannot prepare them to be able to protect efficiently the confidentiality, integrity, and availability of computer systems and assets.

With the objective of enhancing information security education, this paper discusses what fundamental concepts and hands-on skills the students need to know and acquire about network traffic sniffing attack, respectively. Throughout the paper, students will learn how to sniff and spy network users as well as a common defense technique used to detect malicious network sniffing hosts. The discussed educational contents in this paper can be offered to students during security courses mainly on offensive techniques and intrusion detection, and are designed to accompany and compliment any existing academic press text. On the other hand, the paper discusses the implications of the offered hands-on lab exercises on the students' performance and learning outcomes.

The paper is organized as follows: Section 2 includes a brief understanding of network traffic sniffing attack. Section 3 describes the implementation of a hands-on lab exercise about a common sniffing attack detection technique. Section 4 discusses sniffing attack detection in wireless network. Section 5 discusses the learning implications of introducing hands-on lab exercises on sniffing attack. Section 6 discusses some ethical concerns emerged when teaching ethical hacking techniques. Finally, Section 7 concludes the paper.

2. NETWORK TRAFFIC SNIFFING

Sniffing attack is among various types of attacks on LAN networks. It is an easy attack to perform and can be very harmful. Network traffic sniffing allows malicious users to easily steal confidential data, passwords and anyone's privacy. Since many basic services, such as FTP, Telnet and email

(SMTP/POP3), may send passwords and data in clear text, malicious users can easily spy networks' users, by analyzing the contents of the corresponding captured network traffic. For other services, a decryption programs may be needed to pull passwords out of data streams. All unprotected network traffic can be vulnerable to sniffing attacks.

Network traffic sniffing can be simply done by downloading a free sniffer program from the Internet. In addition, in a switched LAN network, sniffing attack requires that the sniffing host should either be connected to a SPAN port (known also as Monitoring port) on the network's switch or use a technique, such as Man-in-the-Middle attack (MiM) [16], to redirect the target network traffic. This is because switched LAN networks do not broadcast the exchanged network traffic. However, in broadcast LAN networks, such as wireless networks, there is no need to redirect traffic to the sniffing host or to connect the sniffing host to a SPAN port, since the network traffic is broadcasted to all network's hosts.

Sniffer tools are programs that allow a host to capture and display the contents of packets that pass through the host's Network Interface Card (NIC), also known as the Network adapter, even if they are not destined to the host. This sniffing activity can be done by putting the host's NIC card into a mode called "Promiscuous mode". This mode allows the NIC card to blindly receive any packet, not just packets intended for it, on the Ethernet network without checking its destination MAC address at all, and pass it to the system kernel. Hence, packets that are not supposed to arrive to the sniffing host are no longer blocked by the host's NIC card. By default, NIC cards are set to a mode called "Normal mode". When a host's NIC card is in the normal mode, it captures only packets destined to the host, using a filtering mechanism, known as the NIC's hardware filter. That is, the host's NIC card accepts only packets whose destination MAC addresses are set to the host NIC card's MAC address. In fact, NIC cards are represented by a 6-bytes hardware address (Ethernet MAC address). The cards' manufacturers assign a unique MAC address for each card, such that each MAC address is unique in the whole world. All communications on an Ethernet network are based on this unicast hardware MAC address. However, a NIC card can set up additional hardware filters in order to receive different kinds of packets. In the normal mode, the NIC card filters packets based on the hardware filter that has been set up. The following are a list of possible additional hardware filters:

➤ *Broadcast*: This filter allows the NIC card to receive broadcast packets that have a destination MAC address set to "*FF:FF:FF:FF:FF:FF*".
➤ *Multicast*: This filter allows the NIC card to receive all packets which are specifically configured to arrive at some multicast group addresses. Only packets from the hardware multicast addresses registered beforehand in the multicast list can be received by the NIC card. Multicast packets have a destination MAC address set to "*01:00:5E:xx:xx:xx*".
➤ *All Multicast*: This filter allows the NIC card to receive all multicast packets that have their group bit set to "*01:xx:xx:xx:xx:xx*".

Many sniffer programs support passwords monitoring through standard application protocols, such as Ace Password Sniffer tool [1], Figure 1.

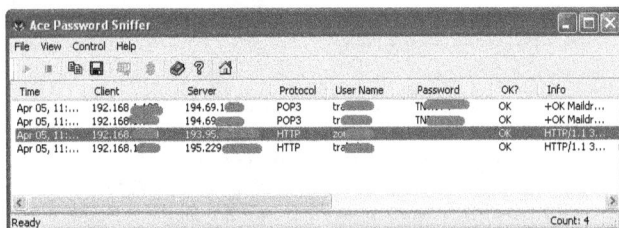

Figure 1. Password sniffing using Ace Password Sniffer.

3. HANDS-ON LAB EXERICE ON SNIFFING HOST DETECTION

The sniffing attack on a network is usually difficult to detect, since it does not interfere with the network traffic at all. In practice, the detection of sniffing hosts in LAN networks consists into detecting the hosts with NIC cards running in promiscuous mode. In fact, network hosts with NIC cards running in promiscuous mode can be considered as suspicious hosts. It is important to mention that some programs, once installed in a host, may set the host's NIC card to the promiscuous mode without having the intention to perform malicious sniffing activities. In addition, the host's user is unaware of the fact that his/her host's NIC card has been set to the promiscuous mode by the installed program. Such a host will be identified as a suspicious host since its NIC card is running in promiscuous mode. In such a case, it is up to the network administrator to take the appropriate actions.

The following subsections discuss a hands-on lab exercise about the implementation of a common promiscuous mode detection technique.

3.1 Detection Technique Description

When a NIC card is running in promiscuous mode, packets that are supposed to be filtered by the NIC card's hardware filter are now passed to the system kernel. Therefore, if we configure an ARP request packet such that it does not have broadcast MAC address as the destination MAC address in the packet's Ethernet header, send it to a suspicious host on the network and discover that the host responds to it, then we can conclude that the host is running in promiscuous mode.

Hence, this detection technique consists into checking whether or not a suspicious host responds to trap ARP request packets that are not supposed to be treated by the suspicious host. Since a sniffing host receives packets that are not targeting to it, it may make mistakes such as responding to an ARP request packet, which originally is supposed to be filtered by the host NIC's hardware filter. Therefore, the detection is performed by checking the ARP response packets that are received after sending ARP request packets to suspicious hosts.

As an example, the trap ARP request packet's destination MAC address is set to a MAC address that does not exist, such as "00-00-00-00-00-01". When the NIC card is running in normal mode, the trap ARP packet is considered to be "to other host" packet, and it is refused by the NIC card's hardware filter. However, when the NIC card is running in promiscuous mode, its hardware filter is disabled. Then, the trap ARP request packet will be able to pass to the system kernel. The system kernel assumes that the packet arrives because it has been allowed by the NIC card's hardware filter, and consequently a response packet should be generated. However, this is not true. There exists some sort of additional software filter in the system kernel, called the software filter. After the hardware filter, packets are actually filtered again by the software filter of the system kernel. Therefore, when a NIC card is running in normal mode, both the hardware and software filters are enabled. However, when the NIC card is running in promiscuous mode, the hardware filter is disabled, but the system kernel's software filter remains enabled. The types of filters performed by the software filter depend on the OS's kernel.

3.2 Tests

The objective of the tests, conducted in [17], is to identify the filtering mechanisms used by the software filters of several common OSs' kernels. For each OS kernel, the tests consist into identifying the special MAC addresses that can be used by trap ARP packets to detect the NIC cards running in promiscuous mode. If an ARP response is received as a result of the test ARP request packet, then the special destination MAC address included in the ARP request packet can be used to identify the

NIC cards running in promiscuous mode. The following list includes the main special MAC addresses used in the tests:

- *FF:FF:FF:FF:FF:FE (Br47), FF:FF:00:00:00:00 (Br16), and FF:00:00:00:00:00 (Br8):* These are fake broadcast MAC addresses. They are used to verify whether or not the software filter checks all bits of a given MAC address to classify it as a broadcast MAC address.

The tests results showed that the tested OS kernel's software filters do not properly filter several types of MAC addresses, mainly Br47 and Br16 addresses. As expected, all tested kernels responded only to the broadcast MAC address (Br) when the NIC card is running in normal mode. However, when the NIC card is running in promiscuous mode, the tests results are OS dependent. That is:

➢ In the case of Windows 8, Windows 7, Windows Vista, Mac OS 10.7.3, Ubuntu 8.10, Red Hat Enterprise 7.2, and FreeBSD 5.0, their system kernels responded to all fake broadcast MAC addresses (Br47, Br16 and Br8). Therefore, the foregoing MAC addresses can be used to identify the NIC cards running in promiscuous mode.
➢ In the case of Windows XP and Windows Server 2003, their system kernels responded only to the fake broadcast MAC addresses Br47 and Br16. Hence, the software filters determine the broadcast MAC address by checking only the first two bytes. Therefore, the addresses Br47 and Br16 can be used to identify whether or not a NIC card is running in promiscuous mode.

Consequently, based on the above tests results, the fake broadcast MAC addresses Br47 and Br16 can be used to identify the NIC card running in promiscuous mode, for all tested OSs (Figure 2).

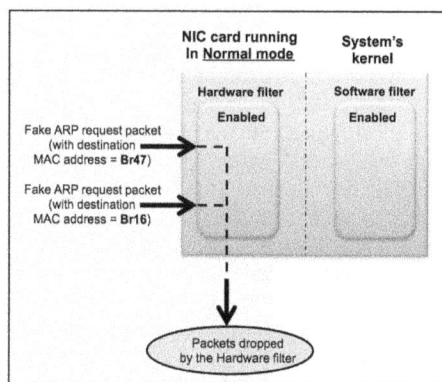

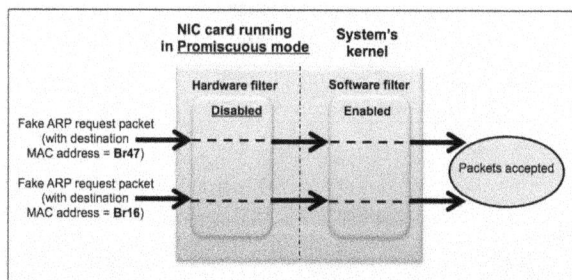

Figure 2. NIC card normal mode vs. promiscuous mode.

3.3 Promiscuous Mode Detection Tools

A number of ready-to-use promiscuous detection tools are available, such as PMD [12], PromiScan [13], Nmap [10], and NetScanTools Pro [9]. The tools are used to find out the hosts whose NIC cards are running in promiscuous mode, in a LAN network. Most of these tools are based on the above described promiscuous mode detection technique.

3.4 Lab Exercise Implementation

The learning objective of the lab exercise is for students to learn how to detect the NIC cards running in promiscuous mode by implementing the above described detection technique. Practically, the lab exercise objective is to allow students to learn how to generate manually trap ARP request packets to identify the NIC cards running in promiscuous mode in a LAN network.

3.4.1 Network Architecture
The network architecture used in the lab exercise is shown in Figure 3. The two hosts A and B are assigned static IP addresses and are connected to a switch.

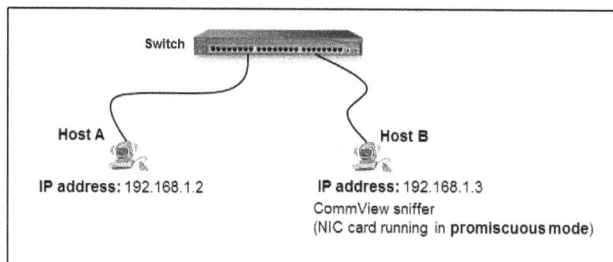

Figure 3. Network architecture.

3.4.2 Hands-on Lab Exercise's Steps
The following steps are used to implement the lab exercise:
- Step 1: Run Host B's NIC card in promiscuous mode
- Step 2: Generate trap ARP request packets
- Step 3: Analyze the ARP response packets

3.4.2.1 Step 1: Run Host B's NIC Card in Promiscuous Mode
Install CommView sniffer tool [4] (or any available sniffer tool) at Host B so that its NIC card runs in promiscuous mode.

3.4.2.2 Step 2: Generate Trap ARP Request Packets
From Host A, tests are conducted to identify whether or not Host B's NIC card is running in promiscuous mode. Hence, Host A will proceed to send a number of trap ARP request packets to Host B, using the fake broadcast MAC addresses Br47 and Br16. The trap ARP request packets will look like:

ARP header	
• Operation code	1 (for ARP request)
• Source IP address	IP address of Host A
• Source MAC address	MAC address of Host A
• Destination IP address	**IP address of Host B**
• Destination MAC address	00:00:00:00:00:00
Ethernet header:	
• Source MAC address	MAC address of Host A
• **Destination MAC address**	**Br47 or Br16**
• Ethernet Type	0x0806 for ARP message

Using any packet builder tool, the above trap ARP requests can be easily built. CommView Visual Packet Builder [4] provides a very friendly GUI interface to build ARP packets. Figures 4 is a screenshot showing the content of an example of a trap ARP request packet with the destination MAC address set to the fake MAC address Br47 in the Ethernet header.

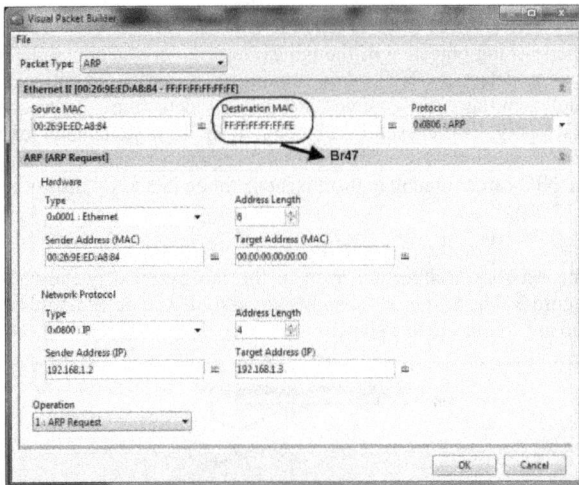

Figure 4. Fake ARP request packet with destination MAC address Br47.

3.4.2.3 Step 3: Analyze the ARP Response Packets

Host A uses CommView sniffer to collect any ARP reply packets generated by Host B after receiving the trap ARP request packets. Figure 5 is a screenshot of CommView sniffer showing the contents of the generated trap ARP request packet with the destination MAC address Br47. Figure 6 shows clearly that an ARP reply packet has been received from Host B after sending the foregoing trap ARP request packet.

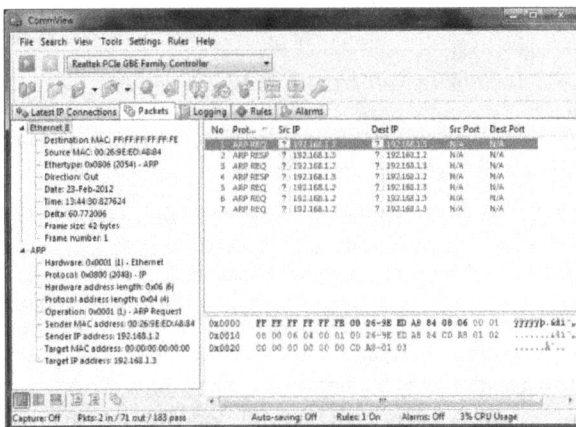

Figure 5. Trap ARP request packet with the destination MAC address Br47.

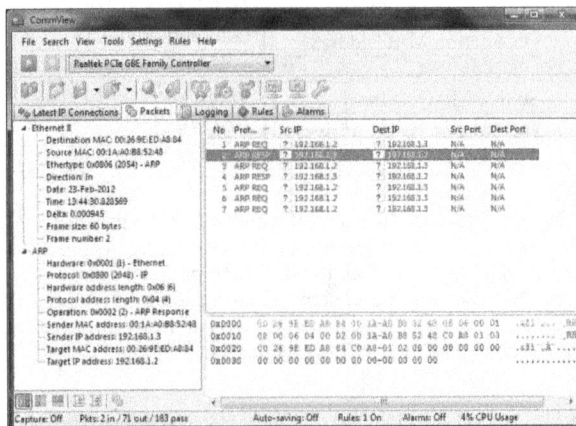

Figure 6. ARP reply packet received from Host B after sending the trap ARP request packet.

Consequently, Host B's system kernel responded to the fake broadcast MAC addresses Br47. Hence, it can be concluded that Host B's NIC card is running in promiscuous mode.

4. MONITORING MODE IN WIRELESS NETWORK

In the case of wireless 802.11 traffic, there are many frames that are not picked up in promiscuous mode. In order to detect all packets, even those that are not associated with an access point or ad-hoc network, the wireless NIC card should runs in a mode called "Monitor mode". In fact, wireless cards can operate in six modes, namely: Master (acting as an access point), Managed (client, also known as station), Ad-hoc, Mesh, Repeater, and Monitor mode.

In wireless networks, promiscuous mode can be used for packet sniffing. However, wireless NIC card can be set to the monitor mode which allows packets to be captured without having to associate with an access point or ad-hoc network first. Monitor mode only applies to wireless networks, while promiscuous mode can be used on both wired and wireless networks. Users can use monitor mode for malicious purpose, such as collecting traffic for WEP cracking.

Depending on the wireless NIC card's driver, its firmware, and its chip set's features, usually the wireless NIC card is unable to transmit in monitor mode and is restricted to a single wireless channel. Also, in monitor mode, the NIC card does not check to see if the cyclic redundancy check (CRC) values are correct for packets captured, so some captured packets may be corrupted.

The detection of wireless NIC cards running in monitor mode is a challenge that is different than the challenge of the detection of NIC cards running in promiscuous mode. The difficulty comes from the fact that when configured in monitor mode, the wireless card stops transmitting data. Traditional, detection techniques uses usually rely on the use of trap packets to identify NIC cards running in promiscuous mode. However, when a wireless card does not transmit data, it becomes consequently difficult to detect whether or not it is sniffing the network.

5. STUDENTS' PERFORMANCE AND FEEDBACKS

This section is concerned with the implication of using a hands-on approach while teaching network sniffing attack on the students' grading performance. Three assessment tools are used, namely a quiz, two midterm exam's problems, and a lab report. The quiz and midterm exam's problems assessment tools have been used to evaluate the students' comprehension of the taught security concepts relative to sniffing attack and promiscuous mode detection techniques. However, the lab report assessment tool has been used to evaluate the students' hands-on skills on sniffing attack and promiscuous mode detection techniques implementation. Table 1 shows the student's average grades for the quiz, the midterm exam's problems, and the lab report.

Table 1. Student performance before and after introducing the hands-on lab exercise on sniffing attack

	Quiz (/ 100)	Midterm exam's problem #1 (/ 20)	Midterm exam's problem #2 (/ 20)	Lab report (/ 100)
2008/2009	68	12	13	No lab exercise was offered
2009/2010	66	10	11	No lab exercise was offered
2010/2011	76	15	16	85
2011/2012	80	14	17	84
2012/2013	79	16	15	88

It is clear that after introducing the discussed security concepts and hands-on lab exercises, during the academic year 2010/2011, the students' grading performances relative to the sniffing attack topic improved. This is mainly due to the fact that the offered hands-on lab exercises allowed students to better anatomize the sniffing attack and assimilate the concepts learned from the lecture. The students have learned better with the hands-on lab exercises, which had a positive effect on their performance. For example, in case of the quiz, the average student grade improved by 15% from 66 to 76 and maintained the improvement for the following two academic years.

On the other hand, Table 2 shows the results of an anonymous questionnaire that was administered to 110 students enrolled in our information security program and who participated in the offered hands-on lab exercises on sniffing attack. The objective of the questionnaire is to collect the students' feedbacks regarding the hands-on lab exercises. The results of the questionnaire showed that more than 85% of all students who answered the questionnaire believed the offered exercises to be useful and helped them better understand the underlying theoretical concepts associated with the experimented sniffing attack.

Table 2. Students' feedbacks on the offered hands-on lab exercises

Questions	Students' Responses
Do you think the lab exercises are easy to follow and straightforward?	82% (Strongly agree) 10% (Agree) 5% (Neutral) 3% (Disagree)
Do you feel you better anatomize the attacks and assimilate the concepts learned from the lectures after performing the lab exercises?	85% (Strongly agree) 13% (Agree) 1% (Neutral) 1% (Disagree)
Do you feel you understand hackers' thinking ways and the ways in which security systems fails better after performing the lab exercises?	84% (Strongly agree) 7% (Agree) 5% (Neutral) 4% (Disagree)
How likely are you to recommend the lab exercises to others?	86% (Strongly agree) 11% (Agree) 2% (Neutral) 1% (Disagree)
Would you like to see similar lab exercises offered in all information security classes?	87% (Strongly agree) 8% (Agree) 4% (Neutral) 1% (Disagree)
Lab exercises helped me to learn how to apply security principles and tools in practice.	80% (Strongly agree) 10% (Agree) 4% (Neutral) 6% (Disagree)

The questionnaire also revealed that 87% of the students were interested in similar exercises in other information security classes, and 86% would strongly recommend the lab exercises to other students. Hence, the questionnaire results supports the fact that the offered offensive hands-on lab exercises had a positive impact on the students' performance and consequently would contribute to achieve the overall course learning outcomes. In fact, the hands-on lab exercises allowed students to better anatomize and assimilate the sniffing attack concepts learned from the lecture.

6. ETHICAL CONCERNS

Students who have acquired hands-on skills on sniffing attack may attempt to use their attack skills in an irresponsible, inappropriate and illegal manner to perform malicious activities. Consequently, such students may represent a serious threat in the academia environment. Practically, these students may attempt to sniff their university network traffic for collecting confidential and sensitive information about the network's users and use them for further malicious activities, such as accessing the users' mailboxes or university systems, such as the Blackboard system.

The hands-on lab exercise on sniffing attack has been offered in our intrusion detection and response course (SECB 455) for the last few years. A major ethical concern has been identified while analyzing the log files of the intrusion detection systems (IDSs) installed in the university network segments. The collected data in the log files showed clearly a significant increase (200% to 650%) in the average number of sniffing hosts detected by the university's IDSs during the few days following the hands-on lab exercise practice. This is due to the fact that students always attempt to experiment the learned sniffing technique outside the isolated network laboratory environment.

On the other hand, a student survey has been conducted to probe the students' behavior after executing the sniffing attack lab exercise. The survey results showed that most of the students acknowledged that they have tried the learned sniffing attack outside the isolated network laboratory environment. The results of the questionnaire showed that about 88% of all students who answered the questionnaire tried to sniff the University network. The questionnaire also revealed that 70% of the students have the faculty members as their main target users while sniffing the University network.

This is a dilemma when offering hands-on lab exercises on offensive techniques. Hence, adding ethical hacking techniques to the curriculum raises a variety of legal issues. Some students will certainly use their offensive hands-on skills in inappropriate and sometimes illegal ways. In addition, schools and educators may be held liable for the actions of their students. Hence, students may threaten their careers, hurt others, and put their institution's entire information security program at risk.

It is clear that there are a number of problems with teaching ethical hacking techniques. However, there are many steps [18] that schools and educators can take to reduce their liabilities, to prevent student's misconduct, and to help students to not misbehave and be responsible. The steps can contribute to improve the chances of having a successful and problem free information security programs that teach offensive techniques.

7. CONCLUSION

It is necessary that information security students anatomize offensive techniques to truly understand how to defend networks and computer systems, and strengthen their security skills. Using a hands-on approach, this paper discussed what fundamental security concepts and hands-on skills the students need to know and acquire about network sniffing attack, as well as how to detect sniffing hosts. The security educational content presented in this paper is designed to be used as a part of an undergraduate or graduate-level security course on intrusion detection and ethical hacking techniques, and is intended to allow students to better comprehend the sniffing attack in an isolated network laboratory environment. As a consequence of using a hands-on teaching approach, students' grading performance relative to the sniffing attack topic has been improved significantly. Moreover, it is expected that the hands-on lab exercises discussed in this paper will contribute to improve the achievement level of course learning outcomes. Even thought, there are ethical concerns as a result of exposing students to dangerous hacking techniques, this ethical concerns are dwarfed by the need for knowledgeable, competent, and, above all, experienced information security professionals.

8. REFERENCES

[1] Ace Password Sniffer tool. http://www.effetech.com/aps.

[2] Brutus, S., Shubina, A., and Locasto. M. 2010. Teaching principles of the hacker curriculum to undergraduates. *In the Procceedings of the 41st ACM Technical Symposium on Computer Science Education.* 2010, Milwaukee, WI, USA, 122-126.

[3] Chen, L., and Lin, C. 2007. Combining theory with practice in information security education. *In Proceedings of the 11th Colloquium for Information Systems Security Education.* 2007, Boston, MA, USA, 28-35.

[4] CommView Packet Analyzer tool. http://www.tamos.com.

[5] CNSS. 2004. National Information Assurance Standard for System Administrators (SAs). *Committee on National Security Systems.* March 2004.

[6] Cook, T., Conti, G., and Raymond, D. 2012. When good Ninjas turn bad: Preventing your students from becoming the threat. *In the Procceedings of the 16th Colloquim for Informaion System Security Education.* 2012, Lake Buena Vista, Florida, USA, 61-67.

[7] Ledin, G. 2011. The growing harm of not teaching malware. *Communications of the ACM,* 54(2), 2011, 32-34.

[8] Logan, P., and Clarkson, A. 2005. Teaching students to hack: Curriculum issues in information security. *In the Procceedings of the 36th SIGCSE Technical Symposium on Computer Science.* ACM SIGCSE. 2005. St. Louis, MO, USA, 157-161.

[9] NetScanTools Pro tool. http://www.netscantools.com.

[10] Nmap tool. http://www.nmap.org.

[11] NSTISS. 1994. National Training Standard for Information Systems Security (InfoSec) Professionals. NSTISS. June 20 1994.

[12] PMD tool. http://webteca.altervista.org/index.htm.

[13] PromiScan tool. http://www.securityfriday.com.

[14] Trabelsi, Z., and Alketbi, L. 2013. Using network packet generators and Snort rules for teaching Denail of Service Attacks", *In the Proceedings of the 18th ACM Conference on Innovation and Technology in Computer Science Education.* ITiCSE'13. 2013, Canterbury, UK, 285-290.

[15] Trabelsi, Z. 2011. Hands-on lab exercises implementation of DoS and MiM attacks using ARP cache poisoning. *In the Proceedings of the Information Security Curriculum Development Conference.* 2011, Kennesaw, GA, USA, 74-83.

[16] Trabelsi, Z., and Shuaib, K. 2008. A novel Man-in-the-Middle intrusion detection scheme for switched LANs. *International Journal of Computers and Application* (202), 2008.3.202-2195.

[17] Trabelsi, Z., Hayawi, K., Al Braiki, A., and Mathew, S. S. 2013. Network attacks and defenses: A hands-on approach. *CRC Press,* 2013.

[18] Trabelsi, Z., and Ibrahim, W. 2013. A Hands-on Approach for Teaching Denial of Service Attacks: A Case Study, *Journal of Information Technology Education: Innovations in Practice (JITE:IIP).* Volume 12, 2013, 299-319.

[19] Yuan, D., and Zhong, J. 2008. A lab implementation of TCP SYN flood attack and defense. *In the Procceedings of the 9th ACM SIGITE Conference on Information Technology Education.* 2008, Cincinnati, OH, USA, 57-58.

Bottleneck Analysis with NetKit: Teaching Information Security with Hands-on Labs

Svetlana Peltsverger
Southern Polytechnic State University
speltsve@spsu.edu

Chi Zhang
Southern Polytechnic State University
chizhang@spsu.edu

ABSTRACT

In this paper, we describe our experience with developing a bottleneck analysis lab with a virtual network emulation environment NetKit. This lab is one of a series of online information security labs that provides students practical experiment opportunities at low cost and little effort. A few new real-world hands-on exercises with NetKit are introduced in this paper. We introduce the NetKit lab setup, outline major sections of the lab, illustrate lab instructions, and report the lab feedback. The hands-on labs can significantly help facilitating students' understanding of the concepts and challenges of computer networks and network security.

Categories and Subject Descriptors

C.2.3 [**Network Operations**]

General Terms

Security

Keywords

Information security education, information security labs, bottleneck analysis, NetKit.

1. INTRODUCTION

Information security continues to grow in importance as cyber-attacks are increasingly becoming the primary threat against the United States [4]. Cyber security and privacy concerns dominate headlines. Information security professionals are greatly needed to protect networked operations and information assets. There is an increasing demand from the industry and the students for more experience in information security [3]. Lab ware and hands-on exercises are considered an essential component in information security courses [13–15].

As both of our undergraduate and graduate programs in Information Technology as well as the graduate and undergraduate certificate programs are offered entirely online, one of the continuing challenges facing the programs is to develop and support the hands-on exercises for online students, who do not have physical access to on-campus lab facilities and in some cases have difficulties accessing lab virtual machines. To solve the problem, we investigated the online-based and open-source-based information security tools, exercises and resources. They are easy to implement and cost effective (mostly free), which makes it

easier and more accessible for online students and all students in general.

This paper outlines our experience with a network emulation environment, namely virtual network NetKit that allows building a network from virtual devices. We also discuss how we plan to use it in a security lab to teach traffic monitor, network bottleneck analysis, and network performance improvement.

2. BACKGROUND

Bottleneck is a point of congestion in a system. Bottlenecks are caused by simultaneous access to shared resources [6]. Network bottleneck happens when there is not enough network bandwidth available to ensure that all data packets in the network can reach their destination in a timely fashion. In general, bottlenecks are present in "every software system and are inevitable" [6].

"Very often, organizations think that they've outgrown their network, without considering that the real problem is that it's a bottleneck," that is causing the problem [5]. There are many reasons why network users might have problems with the network performance [2]:

- Delayed data retrieval due to inefficient storage placement strategy
- Overloaded network: placing to many devices/appliances on the network
- Improper network segmentation
- Misconfigured devices or poorly written applications that produce unnecessary traffic
- Not defining Service Level Objectives for applications
- Security issues (e.g. spam, zombie systems)
- Loss of network integrity
- Generating too much network management traffic.

The bottleneck is often due to the lack of proactive network administration [9]. How do we detect and avoid network bottlenecks? The general practice suggest we capture the traffic, analyze the system's bandwidth usage, detect network congestion, and identify what changes to be performed or which resources are needed in order to ensure sufficient bandwidth capacity.

In the era of virtualization, virtual networking plays an important role. It can be used in production use or testing use in which emulation of functionalities can be tested before deployment or be used in evaluation of what-if scenarios. Thus labs leveraging virtual machines or the virtual hands-on labs have become one of the key education resources in many fields including computer networking and information security education [10, 14].

Understanding computer networks and identifying possible network security issues without performing practical experiments is difficult. However, setting up a networking lab can be very expensive. Netkit is an environment for setting up and performing networking experiences at low cost and with little effort [11, 12]. It allows us to create virtual network devices, such as routers, switches, and computers that can be interconnected to form a network on a PC.

The Netkit official website offers ready-to-use virtual laboratories that focus on specific networking topics such as NAT (Network Address Translation), DNS (Domain Name System), OSPF (Open Shortest Path First), among others [8]. The instructions on the website cover downloading a lab and starting necessary services. We found that these labs are good exercises yet do not provide students with real-world scenarios. The unique approach in our newly developed labs is reconfiguration of an existing network to meet new business requirements. Example labs include enabling Internet connection on the network PCs and installing traffic monitoring software or enabling RIP (Routing Information Protocol) on a network with static routes.

The following sections describe the lab setups and the experiments as an initial exploration of a security lab intended for our information security courses.

3. DESCRIPTION OF THE LAB USING NETKIT

3.1 Lab Objectives and Support Materials

The NetKit-based lab is designed for the students to learn how to set up a virtual network, capture the traffic and analyze the system performance. The objectives of the lab are:

- build virtual networks using NetKit
- monitor ARP (Address Resolution Protocol) traffic
- enable RIP (Routing Information Protocol)
- analyze network bottlenecks
- make recommendations to improve network performance

The following online support materials are provided for students to be familiar with the virtual environment NetKit, and the concepts and best practices of network performance analysis.

- NetKit is a network emulation environment that allows building a network from virtual devices. Documentation is available at http://wiki.netkit.org/netkit-labs/netkit_introduction/netkit-introduction.pdf
- Resolving Network Bottlenecks http://technet.microsoft.com/en-us/library/cc938651.asp
- Uncover Your 10 Most Painful Performance Bottlenecks http://www.serverwatch.com/trends/article.php/3912821/Uncover-Your-10-Most-Painful-Performance-Bottlenecks.htm

3.2 Pre-Lab

To ensure students understand the concepts in depth, a pre-lab is designed on the topics of network quality and performance bottleneck. Reading materials and video demonstrations are provided.

3.2.1 Network Quality

Students are instructed to read "Keep Users Happy by Avoiding Network Traffic Bottlenecks" by Brad Hale [7] and watch a video demonstration of a Real-Time Bandwidth Monitor (RTBM) tool.

The goal of the network management is to achieve 100% network availability. The bandwidth should be effectively available. All services should be reliable and available.

The ways to improve network availability include:

- add redundant hardware
- add redundant communication path
- rerouting traffic
- implement systems for end-to-end provisioning of a service
- monitor performance trend analysis
- use alarm correlation capabilities (identification of the root cause)

3.2.2 Performance Bottleneck

Students need to be able to differentiate different types of bottlenecks. They are instructed to start the analysis of the network bottlenecks but to exclude other application bottlenecks:

- CPU bursts
- Memory shortage
- Storage access time
- Network and system outdated or damaged hardware
- Application design
- Malware

To resolve network bottlenecks, students need to:

- Use adapters with the highest bandwidth and support task offloading capabilities
- Minimize broadcasts
- Divide network into multiple subnets/segments/VLANS

A short fill-in-blank quiz is then provided for the students to self-test their knowledge covered in the pre-lab.

3.3 Lab Instructions

The lab instructions consist of four parts: installation instructions, using NetKit, ARP Cache, and bottleneck analysis. Lab instructions include the step-by-step instructions and a variety of screenshots to demonstrate the processes. An answer sheet is the last step for the students to report their lab results and reflections on their lab experience.

3.3.1 Part I Installation Instructions

The first five steps of the instructions for setting up VM players are listed below as an example:

1. Download and install VM player from http://www.vmware.com/products/player/
2. Create new directory and call it Netkit.
3. Go to http://releases.ubuntu.com/14.04/ and download 32 bit ubuntu-14.04-desktop-i386.iso file. Save the iso file in the directory that you created in #2.
4. Start VM Player, choose Create a New Virtual machine
5. Locate installer ubuntu-14.04-desktop-i386.iso file and click Next.

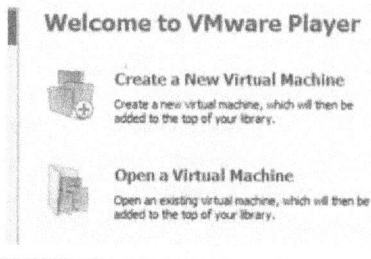

Figure 1. VM Player Setup.

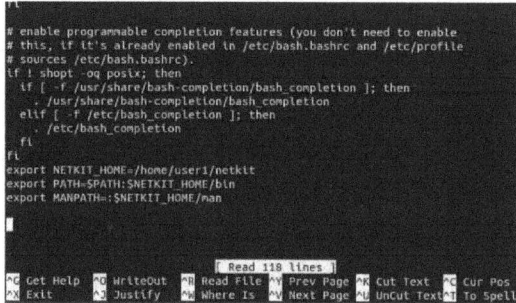

Figure 2. Configuration of Shell.

3.3.2 Using NetKit

Detailed instructions are provided for the configuration of NetKit. Example instructions and screenshots are shown below:

- …
- In one of the PC1's xterm windows run the following commands to install traffic monitoring software bmon

  su

  apt-get install bmon

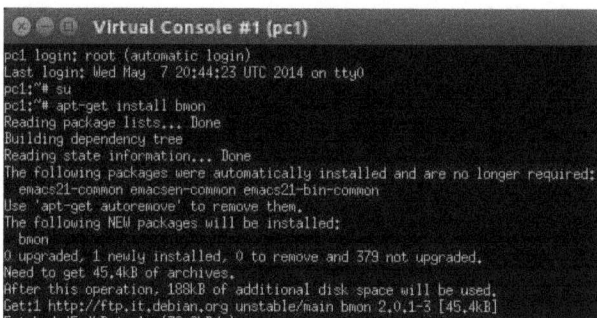

Figure 3. Configuration of Virtual Console #1.

3.3.3 ARP Cache

Address Resolution Protocol (ARP) is a very important part of IP networking. ARP is a dynamic resolution protocol and used to convert an IP address to a physical machine address that is recognized in the local network. The general solution to the efficiency issues with dynamic resolution is to employ caching which reduces network traffic to ensure that the resolution of commonly-used addresses is fast [1].

The ARP lab and configuration files were adopted from the official NetKit site. Students download the lab and then modify network layout and configuration. The network topology is first illustrated for the students:

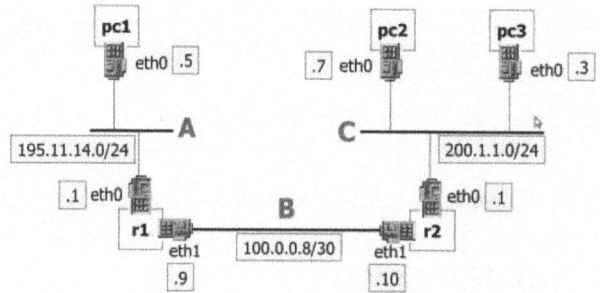

Figure 4. The Network Topology for the ARP Lab.

The instructions are followed to let students experiment with the message routing and traffic generating. Questions are embedded in the lab instructions for students to stick to the lab procedure. For example:

- What route will message from PC2 to PC1 will take? Do not generate any traffic yet.
  - List all devices in the route and explain why this route:
  - ARP cache router 1:
  - ARP cache router 2:
- Generate traffic from PC2 to PC1. Check the route and ARP cache on both virtual PCs.
  - What command did you use:
  - ARP cache router 1:
  - ARP cache router 2:

The ARP lab intends to give students a practical experience with the route manipulation and observation.

3.3.4 Bottleneck Analysis

Students modify ARP lab in this section. They will add RIP routing and the internet access to the network and install iperf tool that can create TCP/UDP data streams and measure the throughput of a network. Demonstration on client machine after APR change is shown in Figure 5.

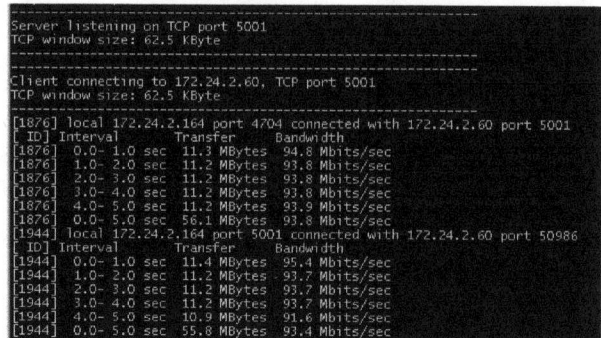

Figure 5. Demonstration on Client Machine after ARP Change.

3.4 Lab Report

As the last step of the entire lab, students are asked to fill out the lab report with the questions specifically for each part of the lab. Sample questions for the part of "Using NetKit" include:

- What is the NetKit command to start a single guest VM?
- What is the NetKit command(s) to stop and delete lab files?

- What is the purpose of netkit.conf file?
- What difficulties did you have while completing Part II Using NetKit section of the lab and how did you resolve them?

For the last two parts of the lab, students are asked to report and explain their observations in the ARP Cache section and in the bottleneck analysis section of the lab. Lab feedback with regard to the lab difficulties and learning experience is also collected in the lab report.

4. LAB FEEDBACK

The NetKit lab was used as the first lab in "network security" lab series. To help answer students' questions and share information, a discussion board "help with labs" was set up in the course management system Desire2Learn. The lab had to be redesigned on the fly because of an early indication that students have difficulties with Linux cli. When the questions about Linux were posted and no replies received from fellow students, the instructor modified the lab to include Linux tutorial and a small Linux command pre-lab. The problem was resolved and it was praised by the students as shown in their feedback: "Ubuntu Linux commands were inserted later in the lab and that solved much conflict."

Collected feedback is very positive indicating that most of the students liked the hands-on nature of the lab and the idea of a network in a box.

"Using Netkit to build our network was a great hands-on approach in taking what I had learned in theory from my previous Networking course and applying the practices here."

"It is very informative and gives a hands-on experience to a topic that I have only been able to cover theoretically."

"I think the NetKit tool is interesting. I am excited to dive deeper into its capabilities."

"I liked tracking the network traffic between the routers and PCs by viewing the ARP cache and configuring the router by using the quagga program."

"The router configuration part of the lab was the most interesting part. Learning how to manipulate multiple machines via command line is something that I had never done before."

Other labs following the first NetKit lab may include network intrusion detection and network forensics. We plan to develop more NetKit labs and test them in our networking and information security courses in the near future, and collect student and instructor feedback to make necessary improvements.

5. CONCLUSION

This paper discusses our experience of developing a computer networking lab with an open source virtual environment NetKit, as part of our effort to develop a series of online hands-on labs for our information security courses. The investigation and development of the series of labs intends to help online students as well as other universities and colleges that may have limited resources to offer lab facilities and technical support to information security and assurance classes.

The complete series of labs will provide students with information security problems and case studies, encourage them to apply the concepts learned in the lectures to the cases and lab exercises, and leverage the lab environment to enhance student learning in information security.

In addition to working on the labs, students will be encouraged to contribute to further research to improve the labs. They will be involved in investigating and pilot-testing other security tools and techniques in an online environment. This will help build student's hands-on, research and problem solving skills.

Besides, the investigation and development of the labs will help faculty strengthen their expertise in information security & assurance and provide relevant content and updated applications for students to see the value of their learning. The labs are developed modularly and offer faculty to implement the topics of their choice to many courses. The "ready-to-adopt" model of the labs will help save resources for enhancing learning and teaching experience and meeting the training needs of the emerging workforce.

6. ACKNOWLEDGMENTS

This work is partially supported by the 2014 Southern Polytechnic State University STEM mini grant.

7. REFERENCES

[1] Address Resolution Protocol: 2014. *http://technet.microsoft.com/en-us/library/cc940021.aspx.* Accessed: 2014-06-07.

[2] Chappell, L.A. 2012. *Wireshark Network Analysis: The Official Wireshark Certified Network Analyst Study Guide.* podbooks.com, LLC.

[3] Cyber-attacks increase leads to jobs boom: *http://www.bbc.com/news/business-26647795.* Accessed: 2014-06-07.

[4] FBI: Cyber-attacks surpassing terrorism as major domestic threat: *http://rt.com/usa/fbi-cyber-attack-threat-739/.* Accessed: 2014-06-07.

[5] Fixing Your Network's Five Worst Bottlenecks: 2005. *http://www.networkcomputing.com/data-networking-management/fixing-your-networks-five-worst-bottlene/229614929.* Accessed: 2014-06-07.

[6] Identify Bottlenecks: 2014. *http://msdn.microsoft.com/en-us/library/ms190994.aspx.* Accessed: 2014-08-13.

[7] Keep Users Happy by Avoiding Network Traffic Bottlenecks: 2012. *http://www.lovemytool.com/blog/2012/10/keep-users-happy-by-avoiding-network-traffic-bottlenecks-by-brad-hale.html.* Accessed: 2014-06-07.

[8] Labs Official - Netkit Wiki: *http://wiki.netkit.org/index.php/Labs_Official.* Accessed: 2014-08-13.

[9] Limoncelli, T.A., Hogan, C.J. and Chalup, S.R. 2007. *The Practice of System and Network Administration.* Pearson Education.

[10] Moreira Gurgel, P.H., Barbosa, E.F. and Castelo Branco, K.R.L.J. 2013. Teaching computer networks: A practical approach using virtualization tools. *2013 IEEE Frontiers in Education Conference* (Oct. 2013), 1021–1026.

[11] Netkit Wiki: 2014. *http://wiki.netkit.org/index.php/Main_Page.* Accessed: 2014-06-07.

[12] Pizzonia, M. and Rimondini, M. 2014. Netkit: network emulation for education. *Software: Practice and Experience.* (May 2014), n/a–n/a.

[13] Weiss, R., Locasto, M.E., Mache, J., Taylor, B. and Hawthorne, E. 2013. Teaching Security Using Hands-on Exercises (Abstract Only). *Proceeding of the 44th ACM Technical Symposium on Computer Science Education* (New York, NY, USA, 2013), 754–754.

[14] Wu, D., Fulmer, J. and Johnson, S. 2014. Teaching Information Security with Virtual Laboratories. *Innovative Practices in Teaching Information Sciences and Technology*. J.M. Carroll, ed. Springer International Publishing. 179–192.

[15] Yuan, X., Williams, K., Yu, H., Chu, B.-T., Rorrer, A., Yang, L., Winters, K. and Kizza, J. 2014. Developing Faculty Expertise in Information Assurance through Case Studies and Hands-On Experiences. *2014 47th Hawaii International Conference on System Sciences (HICSS)* (Jan. 2014), 4938–4945.

Curricular and Performance Measurement Challenges in Cloud Environments

Bruce Hartpence
IST Department, RIT
152 Lomb Memorial Drive
Rochester, New York 14623
585-475-7938
bhhics@rit.edu

ABSTRACT

As more applications move to the cloud, the operation and performance of the cloud comes under greater scrutiny. In addition, educational programs incorporate more desktop and server virtualization. In trying to understand and work with this architecture, it is important to understand not only the structural change but the impact on performance metrics as well. Traditional tools used to measure performance and capacity of these connections may not take into account the cloud infrastructure itself or the behavior of these increasingly software based systems. This paper explores the mechanisms typically used for evaluating typical connections established for coursework and the issues associated measurement in this environment.

Categories and Subject Descriptors:

C.4Performance of Systems
K.3 Computers and Education

General Terms

Measurement, Performance

Keywords

Networking, Cloud, Curriculum Design

1. INTRODUCTION

Cloud computing is not emerging – it has emerged. With an astonishing adoption rate for servers and storage, organizations place a vast amount of data in either private or public electronic repositories. Users now access this data over connections that are not controlled by one entity as there may be several Internet Service Providers (ISPs) between the client and the computing resources.
In addition, host services such as Voice over IP (VoIP) offered at a lower total cost of ownership when compared to maintaining infrastructure encourage organizations to adopt cloud based or off-site services.

SIGITE'14, October 15–18, 2014, Atlanta, Georgia, USA.

http://dx.doi.org/10.1145/2656450.2656471

Educational programs respond by adopting this same type of architecture as they attempt to address desktop and server virtualization.

The number of providers offering cloud computing platforms is growing. The benefits of deploying company assets within public or private clouds are difficult to deny. Infrastructure as a Service, Software as a Service and Platform as a Service (IaaS, Saas, and PaaS respectively) are joined by storage and the proliferation of other hosted services. Today, instead of asking whether or not these services should be adopted, organizations and individuals now ask what features and performance they can expect from the provider they choose.

We now have the need to understand more about the performance metrics one can expect from these platforms. Coursework must add virtualization topics but also take into consideration the impact on virtualizing these services. For example, classes studying network services such as the Dynamic Host Configuration Protocol (DHCP) must address the virtualization of the DHCP server but also the difference in performance because the server is virtualized. Figure 1 depicts a simple topology in which virtual resources are deployed. The topology of the cloud infrastructure on the right is typically unknown to us but can have a dramatic effect on performance.

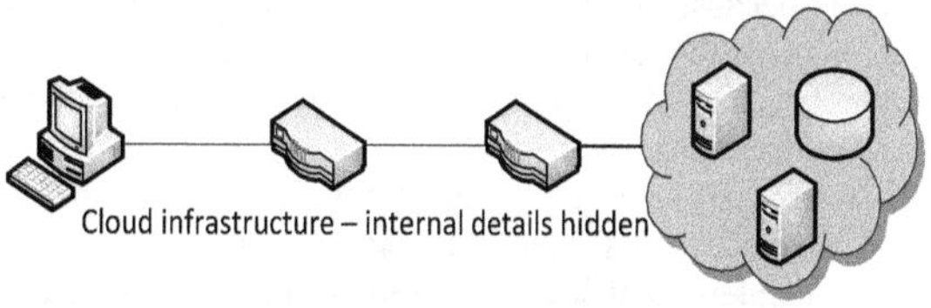

Figure 1 – Topology details hidden

While there are several critical aspects of performance, this paper examines the network performance measurement techniques commonly deployed, and specifically, that these techniques may not accurately represent the actual value of the measured parameters. Thus, the desire to better understand latency, response time, throughput, packet loss, processing capability, etc. of connections, cloud endpoints and how they work moves to the fore. In the next three sections we will discuss some of the common methods of evaluation connectivity and the changes as a result of virtualization and cloud architectures. This will be followed by an examination of the impact of these changes.

2. MEASURING PERFORMANCE
2.1 How, What, Tools

How do we measure performance? Applications tend to determine what measurements might be important. For example, in VoIP the values of latency, packet loss and jitter are critical as they directly impact call quality. However, as the need to transfer large amounts of data are added, questions regarding the capacity of the links, utilization and congestion must be added to the list of measurements needed to accurately gauge the performance of a connection.

Some of these parameters are straight-forward to measure. The pathway can be determined by tools such as tracert (traceroute) and once the path is determined we can use either the response times from tracert or another tool such as ping, yaz or pathload. [1]

This last collection of tools, along with popular packages such as iperf (jperf) [2] and netperf [3] can provide additional insight into connection characteristics because a client and server can be installed on either end of the connection. Thus, data controller by the researcher can be transmitted over the link in question. But even with this level of input, some items such as congestion and total link capacity are very difficult to measure although a number of tools have attempted to interpret results from packets injected into the path [4].

2.2 Virtualization

The tools mentioned previously are favorites of just about any networking/communication program. Students should understand both their use and how they work. Each of these tools uses different techniques to measure the various parameters. Common approaches include the installation of software on both ends of the link to transmit/receive traffic, adjusting time to live in IP packets causing the hops along to path to respond or sending a certain number of packets/data per unit time. These work well when each hop along the path can be identified and perhaps be coaxed into a response. But there are times when these techniques have difficulty or fail entirely. One example is with Network Address Translation or NAT. This is because the inbound path is often prevented which eliminates much of the telemetry from the test. NAT is used here as an example because of its ubiquitous nature and prevalence in Hypervisor connections. That is, virtualized nodes are be deployed using either bridged, host-only or NAT type connections between the virtual machine (VM) and the physical network. Figure 2 depicts the adapters that can be used within VirtualBox and VMWare products use the same types.

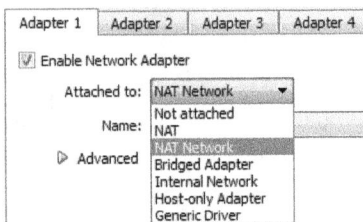

Figure 2 – Virtual Adapter Types

Virtualization presents another environment that is potentially problematic for measurement because some measure of the path *includes the virtual environment itself*.

The problem(s) for education programs is twofold; understanding the actual path and developing test that accurately report the data because in a cloud (public or private) a percentage of the performance is based not on the physical path but the physical path plus the virtualized environment.

In a very straight-forward example, a host uses ping to send icmp echo request messages to a distant node. Both Windows and Linux operating systems can be used are they provide maximum, minimum and average round trip times as well as packet loss numbers. The topology can be seen in Figure 3. In the first test, the devices are not virtualized.

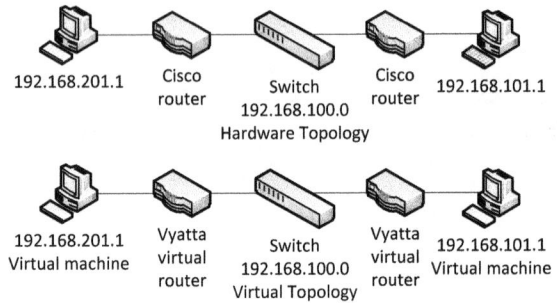

Figure 3 – Test Topology

In a second test, the same host issues the ping command to the exact same destination but this time, the command is run from a virtual machine. Care was taken to ensure that the size of the packets and duration of the test were the same. After running the test several times we see that the virtual machine average round trip times are slightly higher. This means that on average, it takes longer for the icmp echo requests issued from the virtual machine to reach their destination as receive a response than the icmp echo requests issues from the host OS. The results if the test can be seen in Table 1.

Table 1 – ping results

Topology	Max	Min	Ave
Hardware	1ms	<1ms	<1ms
Virtual	1.7ms	<1ms	1.3ms

Even on this small topology, shifting to a virtualized infrastructure in which the routers and hosts are virtual machines results in a 30% increase in latency on average. To what can we attribute this difference? The obvious answer is that there is an extra step necessary when sending traffic from the virtual machine. Packets travel first from the guest operating system and then to the host operating system.

Running the virtual machine also requires resources; resources that cannot be redirected to handle packet processing in the event of larger traffic loads. The network configuration of the virtual machine can impact on processing. The network interfaces typically operate in either bridged, network address translation (NAT) or isolated modes.

Thus, the interface must also be negotiated prior to transmission. This configuration can also have an impact on the path itself. In the case where the tools used to measure the connection rely on a response from interfaces along the path, the path used by the virtual machine is actually longer than that path of the host operating system. Said another way, the vertices and edges in the physical path are a subset of the vertices in the path that includes the physical connections and the virtual architecture. A basic question we might ask when constructing laboratory activities designed to explore server performance is whether we have addressed all that is required to understand the connections?

Another common tool that can be used to illustrate the difference is tracert. This test topology is shown in Figure 4.

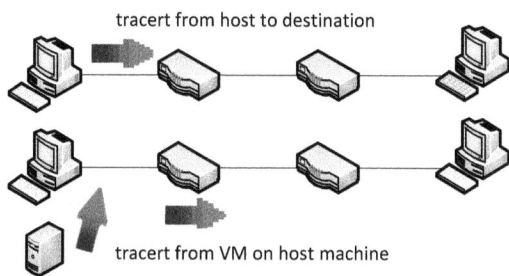

Figure 4 – Test Topology

Using the time to live (TTL) field, tracert causes the near side router interfaces to respond because they will decrement the TTL field to 0 of the ICMP packet sent from the host. This results in an ICMP time exceeded message from that router interface. As the test moves on, the TTL field is increased in order to learn the next hop in the path and so on. In comparing the results, it can be seen that the first hop from the host OS is the default gateway or router of the host. However from the perspective of the guest OS, the first hop is the outside NAT interface on the host or virtual router. Using the topology described earlier we can run another test based on tracert and these results are depicted in Table 2.

Table 2 – traceroute results

Hardware Topology	Return 1	Return 2	Return 3
Hop 1	<1ms	<1ms	<1ms
Hop 2	1ms	1ms	1ms
Hop 3	<1ms	<1ms	<1ms
Virtual Topology	Return 1	Return 2	Return 3
Hop 1	2.6/.4ms	2.3/.2ms	2.2/.2ms
Hop 2	2.2/1.1ms	2.2/1ms	2.1/1.3ms
Hop 3	7.4/2.2ms	7.4/2.2ms	7.3/2.1ms

Table 2 includes the high and low values for the hardware and virtual topologies. Like the ping test results we can see that there is a dramatic difference in the performance of the two systems even though the topology is the same size. In this case, the latency on the virtual topology was more than twice that of the physical topology.

2.3 Cloud Computing Architectures

It is clear that the use of virtual machines, and the associated network configuration, has an impact on the measurement of the path and the performance data for the connection. It is increasingly common to utilize virtual machines for servers. For educational institutions, the progression is often from desktop virtualization to some version of cloud infrastructure either private or in the public space. This was the case at RIT and this progression is documented in [6][7].

With public and private cloud infrastructures, the provider grants the user a virtual machine for a particular purpose. Combing this idea with desktop virtualization means that there is the potential for a virtual machine to be resident on both ends of the connection, doubling the distortion in the performance data.

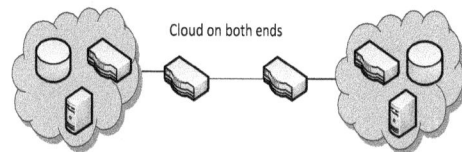

Figure 5 – Cloud to cloud hidden details

Further examination into the structures used reveals that the cloud architecture includes not only virtual machines used as servers and client machines, but virtual routers and switches as well. Virtual switches are an integral component and virtual routers such as Vyatta [5] are often added to extend the non-physical network in order to provide connectivity for virtual machines. Therefore we must also examine the complexity of the virtual network. In fact, when delivering a networking education, an increasing portion must be allocated to virtual networking and network support of virtualized/cloud environments.

2.3 Cloud Resources

While the benchmarking of traditional and dedicated routers is well documented, the same cannot be said of virtual routers. A virtual machine is typically allocated resources from the host machine and these resources are based on the estimated demand of the virtual machine. For example, Windows machines are generally allocated greater memory and storage space than comparable Linux distributions. The virtual router performance is directly related to the amount of memory spared for the network demand, number of interfaces, etc. In the analysis of the performance data there are a number of questions that should be asked before be satisfied with the results.

- Can the virtual router be evaluated in the same way as a dedicated router chassis?
- Do the resources allocated impact the measurements?
- Is the lack of application specific hardware a hindrance?

Another potential area for concern is whether or not the resources given to the virtual machines are consistent. For example, a virtual router may receive a different amount of memory in one instance than in another. When comparing virtual machines resident on disparate providers the memory provided may also be different. While some companies advertise this information, others may not.

3. IMPACT

In order to determine the potential impact of the virtualized architecture on the experimental data, the reason and goal for the test must be evaluated;

- Was the goal of the test to determine performance metrics for the path itself or were the endpoints to be included?
- Are distinctions being made between the cloud provider and the service provider architectures?
- How many providers are involved?

There are cases in which the difference is not significant. For example, if the goal is to measure the end to end (client and server) performance values then the values for the parameters measured can be accepted at face value. Provider A provides a service level of X and Provider B has a service level of Y. But even if this is the case, it is important to note that the differences will be based on several variables and that many of these may have less to do with the path than the provider architecture.

If, when comparing two providers, the virtualization environment is constructed in the same way and the client side configuration is consistent this may also lead us to believe that the metrics are sound. However, any differences in the virtualized topology and resources will result in measurements that are not representative of the actual path.

If the goal was to test service to the various cloud provider servers from a collection of client sites, clear differences will emerge. A conclusion, assuming such things as time of day and network utilization are relatively consistent, might be that these differences are a function of path differences. But as we have seen, it is possible that the variations are more a function of the virtualization environment resources rather than the physical lines and network devices used in the topology.

4. MEASUREMENT

The task of measurement then becomes to not simply run a battery of tests between the source and destination, but to truly understand the components deployed in the path and any cloud architecture used. If possible, where differences in resources are found, effort might be made to change the resources allocated in order to remove or minimize these variables.

Once the playing field has been leveled, differences in the results revealed from the comparison should be tracked back to the main cause. It is possible that there are as of yet undiscovered differences between the systems. Examples might include limitations on TCP window size or fragmentation for IP packets. Tools must be used that can accurately measure each component along the way or ascertain how these components affect the performance. Only when this is done can we compare results between tests run on separate systems with any certainty.

5. FUTURE WORK

Congestion measurement continues to be a rich field because the values are difficult to measure and present a moving target. An extension of this work will be to provide greater and wider measurements in the cloud computing architecture. This may allow models for establishing performance data that is truly representative of the full connection in a virtualized space and an understanding of how each component challenge can be addressed.

As more work in done in the area of separating the control and data planes, especially in the area of software defined networks [8], the need to update curriculum and study the changes in performance increases. Metrics affecting connectivity and server installations will be very rich and interesting areas of study.

6. CONCLUSION

This paper has examined the measurement of network performance in the presence of virtualized or cloud infrastructures and the potential impact this has on educational programs. The basic problems examined include understanding the nature of the path and what may be encountered when trying to measure the behavior of the connection. It is clear, even from small topologies, that cloud or virtualized topologies can negatively impact performance metrics. The physical path and the path plus virtualized environment differ quite a bit and this difference is growing. While access to endpoints is sometimes the same, this is not always the case. Thus measurements cannot always be interpreted as they once were. Educational programs must ensure that they not only adopt the topics and laboratory exercises covering virtualized environments, but the techniques to understand the architectural differences.

7. REFERENCES

[1] Sommers J., Barford P., Willinger W., *Laboratory-based Calibration of Available Bandwidth Estimation Tools*, Microprocessors & Microsystems, V.31 N.4, 2007.
[2] http://iperf.fr/
[3] http://www.netperf.org/netperf/NetperfPage.html
[4] Ningning, Hu, et al, *Locating Internet Bottlenecks: Algorithms, Measurements, and Implications*, SIGCOM '04.
[5] http://www.vyatta.com/
[6] Johnson, D., et al, "Designing, Constructing and Implementing a Low-Cost Virtualization Cluster for Education", EISTA 2013.
[7] Stackpole, B., et al, "Natural Selection in Virtual Environments", EISTA 2013.
[8] Masoud Moshref, Minlan Yu, Ramesh Govindan, "Resource/Accuracy Tradeoffs in Software Defined Measurement", HotSDN 2013.

Capstone Experience – Achieving Success with an Undergraduate Research Group in Speech

Dr. Michael Jonas
University of New Hampshire at
Manchester
400 Commercial Street
Manchester, NH 03101
603-641-4352
michael.jonas@unh.edu

ABSTRACT

We present an experience paper describing progress made with a Capstone course in Computer Information Systems (CIS) at the University of New Hampshire (UNH) at Manchester that was transformed into an undergraduate research group. When initially created four years ago, the aim of the course was to help students develop sound problem solving skills in information technology by exposing them to a real world research project. We used Automatic Speech Recognition as the field of research, a complex and challenging technology that has a very appealing, hands-on nature where students can see applicable results of their work. UNH Manchester is a commuter college, representing a non-traditional educational setting. Many students work day jobs and thus have limited amount of time they can focus on school. The goal of this project is to pique student interest in science to help further their education beyond the undergraduate experience.

Categories and Subject Descriptors

K.3.2 [**Computers and Education**]: Computer and Information Science Education – *computer science education and curriculum.*

General Terms

Experimentation.

Keywords

Capstone, research, speech recognition.

1. INTRODUCTION

For the past four years, the one semester Capstone course in Computer Information Systems (CIS) at UNH Manchester, has offered students a faculty-guided project in speech recognition. The course was designed as a group research project, infusing both an element of collaboration as well as internal competition. Integrating an active research agenda in speech helped self-guide the direction of the project, since there is no better motivation than to apply learning skills to solve real problems.

The spring course has also spawned a summer program, called the Summer Speech Academy, which allows students to continue their work, earning additional credits for summer independent study work. Seniors, short a few credits of graduating, participate during the summer and with the skills learned in the spring, are able to continue their work. The summer program is presently being expanded to include high school students, creating mentorship opportunities for graduating seniors before they leave.

1.1 First Year

In its first year, the goal of the course was to set up processes that would enable a group of students to not only learn how to develop robust speech models, but to document those activities and capture any tools that were developed so that future classes would not have to begin from scratch. A potential pitfall in formulating the Capstone course as a research group would be if each spring semester, students would re-create the work of the past year, spending little time advancing the research topic. It was therefore vital to the success of the course that students in subsequent years would not only learn the system infrastructure quickly but also how speech worked. The latter was problematic since speech, being a complex task, requires considerable effort for students to learn. Though the inaugural course went better than expected [1][2][3], it was unclear if this would translate successfully going forth. This paper describes how the course has transformed.

2. SPEECH RECOGNITION

The primary hurdle in the Capstone course is learning about the complexity of speech recognition and the infrastructure needed to manage it. The project uses the open source Sphinx Speech Recognition Toolkit as its system [4] and the 250 hour Switchboard corpus for its data. We present a cursory description of the speech recognition process and a brief introduction to its theory. For more in depth knowledge, see these references [5][6].

Speech recognition is the process of converting a spoken conversation into text. The audio is first converted to phonemes, then mapped to words via a dictionary, and finally pieced together to form the sentence of what was said. We thus need to recognize phonemes, and for this we use a mathematically representation known as a Hidden Markov Model (HMM).

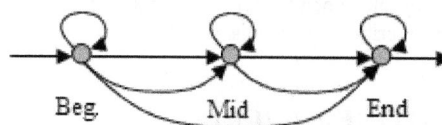

Fig 1: A 3 state HMM

The HMM is used to account for each phoneme and deal with its many forms of variability, including pronunciation, dialect, accent and duration [7]. It represents our acoustic model, transitioning from beginning to end as it aligns its states to the best possible sequence of features of the audio signal. In practice, many inaccurate alignments are found, with the optimal match depending on the overall alignment of the entire audio signal to a set of phonemes.

2.1 Training and Decoding

Speech recognition requires a training process where an iterative approach builds our set of acoustic models (i.e. our HMM's). Once built, these models can then be used on new data to decode an answer.

Building acoustic models uses audio data and a set of associated text utterances. We use a training process that aligns our HMM representation of phonemes to our text utterances using numeric features extracted from the audio stream. Since our utterances are expanded via the dictionary of phonetic spellings to a sequence of phonemes, we simply work to optimally align all features to their respective phonetic models [8].

Decoding is a simpler step whose task is to align a set of features from audio input to a set of possible models. However, there are no text utterances to guide which models to use; therefore every combination of models is possible. There are efficient alignment techniques to make this work in real time and this task only requires the models that were built in training. Decoding is therefore a much more straightforward and easier to understand task [9].

3. LEARNING ENVIRONMENT

In addition to the complexity of the research topic, what adds to the difficulty of the course is the environment which our students find themselves in. UNH Manchester is the urban campus of UNH, with a total of 900 undergraduate students. UNH Manchester is a non-residential commuter college with a more diverse student population when compared to students from the main campus. A majority of the students receive financial aid and their average age is 23, a few years above the traditional college student age.

The majority of UNH Manchester students work approximately 20 or more hours per week. Full-time students, on average, carry a course load of 16 credit hours (i.e. with most classes being 4 credit hours, that's 4 classes total). Students can take a maximum of 20 credit hours during the semester although it is rare for students to do so.

3.1 Constraints

Being a commuter college, the format of many classes fall into a single weekly class running for 3 hours. A constraint on students is how they manage time. Since a majority of students work at least 20 hours a week, between and around classes, it is important to keep that in mind when developing a class that challenges students to learn differently. Mentoring by both faculty and peers becomes a key element to alleviate potential problems students face and is a critical mechanism that is heavily promoted to students.

4. CAPSTONE EXPERIENCE

The Capstone project is now in its fourth year. Additionally, a more loosely defined summer project exists that has since morphed into the Summer Speech Academy, allowing for continuation of the work. The initial goal of the Capstone course has been for students to fine-tune the Sphinx speech system and develop a world-class baseline using the 250 hour Switchboard corpus. Once achieved, research can steer towards improving the technology and making real-world contributions to the field of speech recognition.

Because speech is a data intensive tasks, a major amount of student work focuses on organizing large sets of data, developing tools to automate tasks and integrating complex systems needed for Sphinx to function properly, all on a set of servers hosting the project. Although one could conclude that speech recognition is better suited for computer science, this indeed is a perfect match for information technology.

4.1 Documentation

One of the most crucial elements in successfully transferring knowledge between multiple years of a course is to develop a robust means of documenting what students have done. Not only should the outcomes be captured, but also the process with all its pitfalls, stumbles and restarts. Creating and maintaining such a repository was a critical component of the Capstone course and making it easy for students would insure future success of the project.

4.1.1 MediaWiki

It was decided early in the project to use MediaWiki, an open source wiki platform, as the central repository for all documented information. The use of a wiki based collaborative approach has been investigated as a platform for engaging students in active learning [10][11] and has been successfully applied within our curriculum [12][13]. A wiki page is easily maintained and for intellectual property issues, hosting a local MediaWiki server was deemed safer than using online services whose rights-to-use licensing could impact potential discoveries. It creates a seamless environment where students can share their ideas with ease and do so without fear of either losing work or corrupting information, as all changes are recorded and tracked within its framework.

The wiki page was divided into sections that captured process and accumulated project artifacts. The process section took the form of personal logs where students reflected on their journey through the semester and project documentation detailing how the work proceeded. The artifacts sections collected information that conveyed current state of the project and kept an experiment log detailing methods and results used to improve system performance.

4.1.2 Student Logs

One integral element of the project was for students to keep weekly logs of their work. Because of the relatively short amount of time students had to exchange information over a 16 week semester, a model was devised that forced students to make log entries on 4 different days of the week. MediaWiki's tracking feature made enforcing this process easy as it keeps a history of all changes and when they were made. With students knowing this, it was a natural incentive to follow the guidelines to avoid receiving any point penalties. Students could choose when they did their work and 2 of those days could simply be an entry stating that they read other students logs. Even if students gamed the systems, having them access the page and sign in at least forced them to engage in logging and overall helped improve communication among project members.

4.1.3 Project Artifacts

The project documentation consisted of a proposal that each class had to create in the first few weeks of the semester, highlighting planned tasks and creating a rough schedule for the rest of the semester, a somewhat difficult task since there were many unknowns. Each year this task became easier as the previous proposals helped give context to what was expected. At the end of the semester the class had to write a final report detailing successes and failures and, if applicable, presenting results. Both the proposal and final report were collaborative, group-written documents and made easier by use of a wiki page, which lends itself well to that type of task.

The information section captured the current state of the project. This included details regarding the current Sphinx configuration, the collection of hardware platforms to run on, the variety of operating systems supported and any auxiliary tools used. A comprehensive description of the data set was also created as well as step by step instructions on how to apply this set to building acoustic speech models. These instructions saw yearly revisions that were continuously fine-tuned as student understanding of the modeling process improved.

4.1.4 Experimentation

An important element to the project was a log for recording experiments to track progress of any improvements in baseline numbers. These experiments were initially used by students to gain insights into how the speech process worked and eventually morphed into more tangible ones to improve performance. As students worked with larger and larger amounts of data it was important to keep track of each attempt and document it clearly. This was one of the more difficult aspects for students to accept.

One of the most fundamental tenants of research is to be able to recreate results. The best way to do this is to keep accurate records of what was done and how it was achieved. Though students became eager to create and run many experiments, the documentation part lagged behind, so much so that the faculty advisor needed to call out individual students for sloppy work. Many instances of undocumented experiments existed and, regardless of the results achieved, were meaningless in the overall scheme of the project if the manner in which these results were attained was not accurately captured.

As the number of experiments increased, especially in the fourth year, it became important to fix this shortcoming. An improvement to the process was to tie the MediaWiki page that tracked experiments to the actual experiment environment. Ideally, a script would be written that, when setting up an experimental run, would add an entry into the experiment log and force the user to enter some critical information. Even if incomplete, at least a basic outline of the experiment would exist. At present this is still an ongoing task and students in the summer program are working on this integration.

4.2 Organization

At the start of each semester, students were organized into 5 topic groups: data, experiment, modeling, system and tools. These groups represented the primary areas that students focused their initial month of class on. What students soon discovered was that regardless of which group they belonged to, the most important thing was to understand how the speech system worked, both from a usage point of view as well as from a scientific point of view. In other words, students had to learn how to run the Sphinx speech system and understand what it meant to train acoustic models, how it related to the data and how to interpret results.

Dividing students into small groups gave them not only direction but also started forming bonds and added opportunity for leadership roles to form. In the initial month of class, each topic group had to learn what past groups had done, devise a plan for the semester and add their part to the project proposal. The primary goal of the class was two fold: update and revise the system infrastructure, if needed, and continue building a world-class baseline using the Switchboard data corpus. The latter required more input from the faculty advisor.

Once a successful baseline is achieved, this will enable the research project to move forward and investigate more tangible contributions to the field of speech. It would also add opportunity to apply a well trained system to solve real world problem for actual clients.

4.2.1 Boot Camp and Competition

Having students understand how to approach building a world-class baseline required a bit more direction. In the second month, the class was again divided into 4 new groups in what was called Speech Boot Camp. Each group contained members from the 5 respective topic groups and would share the identical task of having every student complete a training and decoding run on a small subset of the data in order to learn how the entire process worked. The idea was that the new groups had experts from each of the topic groups and information exchange could flow more easily. This was better said than done as not everyone brought expertise to their new group since it took some students time to get fully involved in class activities.

This boot camp phase was given a two week time frame and upon completion, new groupings were formed again, this time by splitting the class in half and forming two competing teams. Each team was populated randomly with equal representation of members from the original topic groups, again to promote the exchange of expertise. This final phase would add a competitive element to the project as both teams had the same task, train as much data in a month and achieve the best decoding result possible. The team with the best result could spend the final two weeks of class fine tuning the system while the losing team had to take lead in writing the project report.

Since the report grade was shared by the entire class, even the winning team had to contribute to the report since they had a stake in it. So winning the competition did not remove half the class from this important task. However, it was left to the losing team to organize the writing and resources needed for the report and take leadership in finalizing it.

4.2.2 Adding a Twist

In the course's fourth iteration a twist was added to the competition phase, due in part at the perceived inequality of the two teams. One team felt confident it had a winning strategy while the other had leadership issues and became bogged down in internal politics. A trade was proposed midway through the month-long competition. If either team wanted a trade, then each team could protect one individual and choose a member of the other team.

This trade had a tremendous impact as the struggling team got to pick a needed resource and lost one of its disgruntled members. In the course of a few minutes both teams were invigorated and the final two weeks went down to the wire. It also added a fun, fantasy-football-like element to the class and gave hope to half the students that, at one point, felt destined to lose, so much so that some had already started writing the final project report. Adding this type of intrigue was a positive step and helped move the project forward.

4.3 Motivation

Although speech recognition is an exciting and dynamic research field, that alone was not enough to automatically engage students in it. To motivate students to not only individually learn challenging topics, but help each other, a grading rubric was devised that would promote collaboration and peer support. Only 15% of a student's grade was based on individual accomplishment (i.e. personal log entries). Another 35% was based on shared work which included both the project proposal and its final report. The final 50% added both incentive and yielded a good deal of stress as it encompassed anonymous peer reviews.

4.3.1 Peer Reviews

In order to be successful in the class, students needed to work well with others and demonstrate a contribution to the project. A peer review process was the equivalent to a final exam and students were made aware of its impact to their grade. This process happened during the final day of class and students were given uniform evaluation sheets that required them to select each student they were scoring, give a score and add a handwritten narrative in defense of that score. Depending on class size, a minimum number of evaluations were needed for each student, with any shortfalls being considered a failing grade. With a normal class size ranging from mid teens to about 20 students, the minimum number was 7 evaluation scores. This meant that, to do well in the class, each student had to impact the project and demonstrate that impact to more than a few handfuls of students. Engaging others, creating good lines of communication and especially showing interest in the work were critical elements.

To mitigate any personal issues, the faculty advisor guaranteed fairness by investigating any low scores, or if a student didn't receive enough evaluations, made a determination as to why that was the case. For any outliers or low scores, artifacts could demonstrate a case for the student so that a judgment call could be made on whether the score was unfair. An additional element that helped were student self evaluations. If a student and their fellow class mates all gave similar grades then that student's evaluation was pretty straightforward. As it turned out, it was rare that a detailed investigation was needed. Students that were struggling readily reflected that on their own and it was easily verifiable through their log entries and tracing of artifacts, which for weaker students was somewhat sparse.

4.4 Observations

With four years of experience with the Capstone course it has shown itself to be a surprising success. Initial expectations were that some progress would be made but in all likelihood changes needed to be added in order to guarantee more continuity. Most prominent was the idea of making Capstone into a year long, two semester course to allow enough time for its goals to be accomplished. Having both semesters would give students a full 9 months to investigate speech and give more time for stumbles, restarts and failures. Although perhaps an ideal solution, in practice, adding a second semester is somewhat problematic as it would be difficult to fit into the current curriculum for CIS majors.

4.4.1 Class Size

After the first year, class size has not fluctuated much and has ranged between 15 and 20 students. Anything larger than that would likely hinder productivity, requiring multiple sections to be held which would add complexity to the project. As it stands, with our program's growth in number of majors expected to soon rise near 100, it will fall in line with next phase of the Capstone course when project groups will form to focus on specific areas in speech. This then should alleviate any potential bottlenecks caused by having too large a group focusing on the same task.

Another option is to apply this undergraduate research group project to other topics aside from speech. That requires an active research agenda from additional faculty in a predominantly teaching oriented environment. The hope is that the success of this model will spur on faculty involvement and excite colleagues about the potential of seeing their own research effort advanced by a group of undergraduate students.

4.4.2 Progress

Each year the Capstone course continues to progress and its pace quickens. In its second year, students took two-thirds of the semester to catch up to the previous year's class and then proceeded to move the needle forward. The third year saw a similar result but slightly sooner, at the half-way mark of the semester. This past year, the fourth year, after barely a month into the semester, at about the one-third mark of the course, students were continuing where the previous class had ended. This left almost 10 weeks for students to run experiments to fine tune the system. With computing resources tied to the size of the data set and some experimental runs taking almost a week to complete, the extra time was critical to improve system performance and increase the likelihood for success.

Keeping track of student progression is one of the fundamental responsibilities a faculty advisor has to any Capstone project, be it an internal group project or an individualized industry-based one. As the course has transformed, expectations of students has gone up, not because of demand by the faculty advisor, but because success breeds its own internal competition. In its fourth year there was a real fear that some students might fail the course as those leading the project had little patience with students that did not commit themselves to the work. As a required major course, a C- or better needed to be earned. The faculty advisor's responsibility thus required helping some students find ways to improve their performance.

At the half way mark of the semester, anonymous feedback was sought for students deemed to be struggling. This occurred through offline conversations with various group leaders and gave a good indication of how students were doing. Some students were surprised to find that the feedback they got was not positive and after some consternation re-focused their effort. This feedback system was invaluable to those students and at the end of the semester everyone passed the class.

4.4.3 Leadership

With the format of the class relatively stable it has been interesting to observe how students end up in leadership roles. Each semester a set of students emerge to lead the entire project and it is not clear from the onset who those students will be. Clearly, some students find speech an engaging field and dive into the topic, learning all they can. With some success achieved, confidence builds into leadership and sometimes a surprising set of students take on that role.

Predominately the modeling group tended to get the strongest students as it was hyped as both the hardest and most critical task and commonly yielded many of the group leaders. Additionally, since building acoustic models (i.e. training the system) is at the heart of speech recognition, students from the modeling group were also forced into becoming leaders of the boot camp groups as the purpose of those groups was to learn about modeling and so other students naturally looked to these students for guidance.

Leadership definitely comes to the forefront during the final month when each half of the class competes for the best possible results. The strongest students not only took on responsibility but also realized that, with limited time, resources, and an overwhelming amount of work, reaching out to their weaker classmates was an integral part to a team's success. This also provided opportunity for struggling students to demonstrate their ability and impress others which in turn helped their final evaluation. Although the winning team did not have to take lead role in the final report, consensus was that getting a better result was more driven by desire to solve the problem than to get out of additional work. For the winning team not to be responsible for the final report was merely icing on the cake.

5. CONCLUSION

After four years of running the Capstone course as an undergraduate research project, a few things have become clear. With a good documentation mechanism, the artifacts that students create and capture and the processes they record become an invaluable resource for future classes. Although the amount of information grows steadily each year, it does not add to the time it takes for that information to be disseminated. This is primarily due to the fact that each new class tends to only look back to the previous year and use that distilled information as its guide.

Additionally, since the project captures both process and artifacts, the latter tends to take the form of improving and revising what already exists. Though student logs, which recorded process, are also important resources, they tend to be looked at as a secondary source, especially during the start of the semester when students quickly get bogged down in details that they still don't understand.

This project provides many learning moments for students. As is inevitably the case with real world projects, students tend to view the approach of previous years as sloppy, badly documented and lament at how incomplete the information that has been presented to them is. All the while, however, the same thing occurs with the present class and the faculty advisor can only urge students to be more diligent about documentation while observing in bemusement, realizing that it is not a primary concern of most students. This is something that needs be improved though it is a difficult topic to solve.

Since the purpose of the Capstone course is to be a real-world project, to incentivize the capture of that process and properly record its artifacts has to be formulated in a real world manner. Students don't get paid and only need to get past one marker, their final grade, whereas an employee at a company needs to not only worry about their immediate year-end review, but their extended future with the company. This may not be something that can be fully addressed and since progress on the research project has been surprisingly good, it is not deemed critical to the health of the ongoing Capstone course.

6. MOVING FORWARD

Creating a world-class baseline is not a trivial task as it requires tuning a complex system. Sphinx has many parameters that need to be adjusted to a respective data set to achieve optimal performance. In addition, the Switchboard corpus, with 250 hours of recorded audio data and thousands of sentences does not fit with what the Sphinx system is looking for without extensive cleanup. This requires not only understanding what the data is, but how to transform it into a workable set for model building and proceeding to write utilities that make those changes. It is primarily an iterative approach where, with large amounts of data, each iteration is not done in a trivial amount of time. To reach the world-class baseline marker requires some out-of-the-box thinking and perhaps some additional, out-of-domain data and is why it is considered a difficult research task.

6.1 Future Plans

It is expected that the project will soon enter a new, exciting phase. Once the infrastructure is in place and a robust baseline of the 250 hour Switchboard corpus has been created in Sphinx, more cutting edge work can be addressed. The sense is that a sound baseline may be attained either after the summer program or with one more iteration of the Capstone course, and after that, focus can shift to making technology changes to Sphinx itself and add to the science of speech recognition. At that juncture we expect the format of the Capstone course to change into smaller group projects where each group focuses on a specific technology to improve. Speech is a wonderfully complex field with many areas that one can focus on including the acoustic modeling process, signal processing, feature extraction, language modeling, and a host of others.

6.1.1 Applied Domains

Opportunity at this stage also presents the possibility of applying a well trained speech system to applications in various domains. The summer program has demonstrated how such small, focused project may manifest themselves. One summer project currently is creating an internal call routing application that will add a voice activated directory assistant to the college's phone system. A past project had students studying a massively parallel approach to improve model building and resulted in a student poster presentation at a regional computing conference [14].

Other such applied projects could be supported by the vast number of high tech companies surrounding the college. This would transform part of the Capstone project into an internal consulting shop with real-world clients, adding yet another twist to the internal project model that this Capstone experience has focused on. As a side benefit, it would expose students to local industry and increase their employment opportunities after graduation.

Either a pure research approach or the application of speech to a problem domain yields flexibility for the future of the Capstone course and will align well with the growth of both the CIS major and the computing department that houses it. All the while, it will also continue to move the research agenda of the faculty advisor forward, considered a bonus in the teaching focus environment of UNH Manchester.

6.1.2 Research Experience for Undergraduates

An important component of the Capstone experience is the addition of an intensive summer program that applies the work done during the semester and moves it to individualized speech focused research projects for a cohort of undergraduate students. Specifically, the aim is to attract community college students in the area that might not otherwise continue their education. With strong working relationships already in place with many of the area community colleges, and the opportunity to extend our reach, the expectation is to develop such a program and integrate it into the existing summer model. This would expand into a fulltime, two month experience that immerses students in as close to a real world research group as is possible in an undergraduate academic setting.

The National Science Foundation's Research Experience for Undergraduates (NSF-REU) supports such a program, providing stipends and housing support during summer for up to two months to a group of students. The purpose of the program is to engage undergraduate students in research to interest them in graduate work. Our aim is to enhance the experience by not only exposing undergraduates to the possibility of graduate school but enticing community college students to continue their undergraduate careers so that they are able to apply to those graduate programs.

The plan, if the program is funded, is to move this project forward under the umbrella of the Summer Speech Academy. We are presently in the application phase and if successful, hope to recruit students and start in the summer of 2015. Once in place, this program could then tie back into the Capstone course by enabling students during the spring semester to continue unfinished summer projects. This would be the final piece to truly create continuity to allow students the maximum opportunity to successfully pursue a research agenda in speech recognition at UNH Manchester.

7. ONLINE RESOURCE
The current state of the Capstone experience for the speech project can be found online at the link below. This MediaWiki site is the active site that the project uses in both the spring and summer terms.

http://foss.unh.edu/projects/index.php/Speech:Home

The site provides three top level links that allow for navigation to the various sections that were discussed earlier in part 4.1 of this paper.

- Semesters – points to student weekly personal logs as well as project plan and final report tied to each semester
- Information – points to current state of the system with instructional links on how to run the training and decoding jobs
- Experiments – the primary resource that captures experimental work detailing results and discussions of how they were attained.

8. ACKNOWLEDGMENTS
I want to thank my fellow colleagues for helping with this course. I'm extremely grateful to all my students over the past four years who struggled to grasp the difficult concepts of speech recognition in a hectic and challenging environment that is UNH Manchester.

9. REFERENCES
[1] Jonas, M., Capstone Experience – Lessons from an Undergraduate Research Group in Speech at UNH Manchester. in *Proceedings of the 2011 conference on Information Technology Education*, (West Point, NY, 2011) ACM, Pages 275-280.

[2] Jonas, M., Capstone Experience: Engaging Students in Speech Processing to excite them about STEM. in *Journal of Computing Sciences in Colleges*, (Springfield, MA, 2011) faculty poster, Volume 26 Issue 6, June 2011, Pages 180-181.

[3] Jonas, M., Capstone Experience at UNH Manchester: Student Guided Mentoring for an Undergraduate Research, Group in Speech. CUR pre-conference symposium at ISSOTL 2012, faculty poster, Hamilton, Ontario, October 2012

[4] *CMU Sphinx - Speech Recognition Toolkit,* Carnegie Mellon University, School of Computer Science, Pittsburgh, PA. http://www.speech.cs.cmu.edu

[5] Rabiner, L. R. and Juang B. H., Fundamentals of Speech Recognition. Prentice Hall, Englewood Cliffs, N.J, 1993.

[6] Jelinek, F., Statistical Methods for Speech Recognition, MIT Press, Cambridge, MA, 1997.

[7] Huang, X. D., Ariki, Y. and Jack, M., Hidden Markov Models for Speech Recognition. Edinburgh University Press, 1990.

[8] Brown, P. F., The Acoustic Modeling Problem in Automatic Speech Recognition. Ph.D. thesis, Carnegie Mellon University, 1987.

[9] Viterbi, A. J., Error Bounds for Convolutional Codes and an Asymptotically Optimum Decoding Algorithm. IEEE Transactions on Information Theory, IT-13, pp 260-67, 1967

[10] Peters, V. and Slotta, J., Analyzing Student Collaborations in a Wiki-Based Science Curriculum. in *Proceedings of the 9th International Conference of the Learning Sciences*, (Chicago, IL, 2010), Volume 2, Pages 119-120.

[11] Forte, A. and Brukman, A., Constructing Text: Wiki as a Toolkit for (Collaborative?) Learning. in *Proceedings of the 2007 international symposium on Wikis*, (Montreal, Canada, 2007), ACM, Pages 31-42.

[12] Jonas, M., Group Note Taking in MediaWiki, a Collaborative Approach. in *Proceeding of the 14th annual ACM SIGITE conference on Information Technology Education*, Orlando, FL, ACM, Pages 131-132.

[13] Jonas, M., A Student Generated Wiki Based Online Textbook: a Flipped Approach. in *Proceedings of Society for Information Technology & Teacher Education International Conference 2014* (Jacksonville, FL 2014), AACE, Pages 1267-1272.

[14] McCarthy, T., Meehan, D., Johnson, C., and Surprenant, F., Massive Parallel Acoustic Training in Speech using the SETI Model. student poster in CCSCNE-2014, Providence, RI, April 2014.

The Evolution of Information Technology Capstone Projects into Research Projects

Susan Chard
Whitireia Polytechnic
Porirua
New Zealand
+64 4 2373100
Sue.Chard@whitireia.ac.nz

Brenda Lloyd
Whitireia Polytechnic
Porirua
New Zealand
+64 4 2373100
Brenda.Lloyd@whitireia.ac.nz

ABSTRACT
In this paper, we present the motivation and process followed to extend our undergraduate Information Technology programmes to include postgraduate and masters programmes. The undergraduate degree included a capstone project which had gradually evolved to include research projects. This highlighted a growing need in our local industry for graduates with research skills in Information Technologies to keep pace with the rapid rate of change in Information Technologies.

Categories and Subject Descriptors
K.3.2 [**Computer and Information Science Education**]: Computer Science Education, Curriculum

General Terms
Theory.

Keywords
Industry, Research, Information Technology Projects, Capstone Projects.

1. INTRODUCTION
Polytechnics in New Zealand have a history of offering qualifications to prepare students to join the Information Technology workforce. These qualifications focus on two primary skillsets, the first is skills for Software Developers and the second is skills for Systems and Network Administrators. The IT degree programmes offered by New Zealand Polytechnics generally include a capstone project, this is usually a group project to create an IT artefact for an external industry organization. The capstone projects are supervised by a member of the faculty. Over the last seven years a trend has emerged in these projects at our Polytechnic, a growing proportion of the projects undertaken have had a research focus. During this time capstone projects have investigated a wide range of topics including: issues associated with the processing of laser scanner generated point cloud images, the efficacy of different automatic code converters, and the evaluation of methods for the forensic reconstruction of websites.

To address this need we have developed postgraduate IT programmes enabling a growing range of projects to be undertaken to produce graduates with the applied IT research skills needed by our local industry. The postgraduate programmes in IT include three different research projects, this means that there are now four different types of applied IT projects available within the programmes. This allows a variety of different types of research projects to be undertaken by students at the polytechnic, with a minimal outlay of resources by the individual industry partners. It also gives the students the ability to undertake different levels and types of research projects to complete either an undergraduate or a postgraduate qualification.

2. BACKGROUND
Lloyd and Chard [1] reported an analysis of capstone projects completed between 2007 and 2012 at our Polytechnic. This study used the following definitions for the categories identified:

- Non Research: is a project that has been developed before using the same or similar tools.
- Research: a totally new concept and has not been attempted before, these were often proofs of concept with an element requiring evaluation of the outcome
- Part research: combination of both for example proof of concept then develop using familiar tools.

Analysis of the capstone projects offered to students during this time found that (23) 41% were applied research projects; (17) 30.4% of the projects were categorized as part research and (16) 28.6% were non research.

The undergraduate degree programme, which includes the capstone project, by nature does not include instruction on the processes used to carry out research. As the capstone projects evolved towards becoming research projects, the gap between the skills gained by the students during their degree study and the skills needed to complete the project has become wider and the level of support required from the supervisors has increased dramatically. The undergraduate study has not been preparing the students adequately to carry out the research projects as there is no formal introduction to research methodologies integrated into the course.

Chin [2] identified that there were many IT research projects being conducted in partnerships between academics and industry and the important role that this collaboration has in education informing teaching. The rapid changes in IT bring new technologies, new domains for technology to be applied in, and new ways of doing things. The research informs both practice and teaching when it is conducted in collaborative partnerships with industry.

3. DEVELOPING NEW PROGRAMMES

To address the issue of research capability for students engaging in industry projects, new postgraduate programmes have been developed. The new programmes that have been developed include a 60 credit Postgraduate Certificate in Information Technology (PGCertIT), a 120 credit Postgraduate Diploma in Information Technology (PGDipIT) and a 180 credit Master of Information Technology (MIT). These qualifications are polytechnic qualifications, which in New Zealand are defined as "applied qualifications". The applied nature of the qualifications differentiates them from the New Zealand University qualifications. The applied nature of the qualifications is attractive to industry and ensures that the graduates are in demand as the graduates are perceived as work ready [3].

These new postgraduate programmes are aligned with the New Zealand Government Tertiary Education Strategy [4] which emphasizes the need to produce high quality research, and develop the skills and knowledge to meet labor market demand, and the labor market reports indicating the types of roles required by New Zealand employers.

The Tertiary Education Commission's 2010-2015 strategy [4] states that we expect the tertiary education system to:

- provide New Zealanders of all backgrounds with opportunities to gain world-class skills and knowledge

- raise the skills and knowledge of the current and future workforce to meet labor market demand and social needs

- produce high quality research to build on New Zealand's knowledge base, respond to the needs of the economy and address environmental and social challenges

- enable Māori to enjoy education success as Māori.

A review of the current labor market in New Zealand was conducted to identify the areas of IT most in demand by industry. This review was used to assist in determining the topics for the papers offered in the new programmes.

The New Zealand Labour Department predicts that by 2015 the need for knowledge professionals in the IT sector will not be met by the combination of New Zealand graduates and employees from overseas and identifies long term skill shortages in the following areas: Project Manager, Business Analyst, Systems Analyst, Multimedia Analyst, Web Developer, Analyst Programmer, Software Developer, Software Engineer, Software Tester, Software and Applications Programmer, Database Administrator, Security Specialist, Systems Administrator, Computer Network and Systems Engineer, Network Administrator, Network Analyst, Quality Assurance Engineer, Support Engineer, Systems Test Engineer, Network Engineer, Customer Support Officer [5].

Absolute IT is a specialist recruitment company operating across New Zealand solely in the ICT market. Absolute IT's January 2014 Employer Insight Report [6] based on a survey of more than 500 ICT employers throughout New Zealand, showed that 75% of respondents planned to hire new staff in 2014, with 38% citing new projects as the main reason and the second highest reason cited was increased demand for IT from the business. The top skills "in hot demand" were business analysis, Software Development and project management. Skills that employers expect to see on the future "hot list" were cloud, business analysis, mobile application development, and business intelligence. AbsoluteIT's June 2013 Remuneration Report [7], based on a survey of more than 27,500 ICT professionals throughout New Zealand, showed that the "top 25" jobs (in order by median salary) were: Architect, IT Manager, Software Architect, Project Manager, Consultant (ERP/Supply), Consultant (BI/CRM), Consultant, IT Security, Business Analyst, DBA Database Developer, Sales Exec/Account Manager, Software Analyst Programmer, Systems Integrator, Systems Analyst, Software Developer, WAN/Telecommunications, Network Engineer, Testing and QA, Systems Administrator, Technical Writer/Documenter, Data Record Manager, Network Administrator, Trainer, Web/multimedia Developer, Web/multimedia Designer.

Robert Walters Global Salary Survey [8] produced similar results to those obtained by AbsoluteIT. Their New Zealand report noted that business analysts with business process re-engineering were in extremely high demand in 2012 and predicted a shortage of available job seekers in 2013 and an increase in demand for business intelligence and data analysis. Their Wellington report noted increased demand in 2012 for business analysts, project managers, developers, solutions and enterprise architects and predicted that business analysts, project managers and experienced developers were likely to be highly sought after in 2013.

A comparison of industry needs was compared with existing Masters degrees in New Zealand. Industry need was identified from job advertisements on New Zealand job seeker websites Seek and TradeMe. This was compared with trends identified from publications like Computerworld, Communications of the ACM and IEEE Computing, and with the content of existing master's degrees offered in Auckland and Wellington. This identified gaps in the following areas: Business Analysis, Infrastructure, Mobile Applications, Systems Integration, Testing and Quality Assurance.

4. DESIGN OF PROGRAMMES

The postgraduate qualifications were designed after taking into account the data summarized above and NZQA's definitions and requirements for postgraduate certificates and postgraduate diplomas and master's degrees [9], which have recently been amended to allow for 180 credit master's degrees. The Polytechnic offers a 120 credit Post Graduate Diploma, a 60 credit Postgraduate Certificate and a 180 credit Master of Information Technology with two pathways; one involving a 45 credit applied research project and the other involving a 90 credit thesis. Students who wish to undertake more level 8 electives in order to advance their careers as IT professionals take the first pathway, whereas those wishing to undertake more substantial research as preparation for roles as researchers or tertiary teachers take the second pathway.

The new postgraduate programmes include the following papers to introduce students to research and prepare them to undertake a research project. One compulsory paper introduces students to research in IT covering an introduction to the subject area, research methods that are commonly used and a general introduction to the literature. This paper is studied by all postgraduate students in their first semester. The second paper steps the students through the process of creating a research proposal, defining the question conducting a literature review, identifying the research methods and planning the research. This paper also introduces the process for ethics approval.

There are three research papers in the post graduate programmes. The first is a level 8 research report which is a 30 credit paper, completed in one semester. This can be taken as part of any of the three postgraduate programmes. The second is a 45 credit level 9 research project, this is an applied research project and the third is a 90 credit Thesis. Masters students may take either the 45 research project or the Thesis with the rest of the Masters credits gained through taught papers. Students undertaking either of the 45 credit research project or 90 credit Thesis must complete the research proposal paper first.

The development of the postgraduate programmes included defining research in the context of IT. A review of the literature identified the following definitions of research in IT. ACM defines five sub-disciplines of computing: Computer Science, Computer Engineering, Information Systems, Information Technology, and Software Engineering [10].

The ACM IT2008 Model Curriculum [11] the field of Information Technology is defined as follows: Information Technology in its broadest sense encompasses all aspects of computing technology. IT, as an academic discipline, is concerned with issues related to advocating for users and meeting their needs within an organizational and societal context through the selection, creation, application, integration and administration of computing technologies. The pillars of IT include programming, networking, human-computer interaction, databases, and web systems, built on a foundation of knowledge of the fundamentals of IT. Overarching the entire foundation and pillars are information assurance and security, and professionalism. An IT graduate would able to select, create or assist to create, apply, integrate, and administer the solution within the application context.

5. DEFINING THE RESEARCH PAPERS

The Given this definitions of Information technology as an academic discipline, what sort of will be undertaken in the Postgraduate Diploma and Master of Information Technology? A review of the information on the IT Thesis Analysis Project website [12] combined with Zilora's paper on the changing nature of IT as an Academic Discipline [13] an understanding based on a wide ranging research project into current IT Postgraduate courses globally identified that IT theses generally took the form of:

• Evaluation of [technology] for [purpose]

• What is the value of an IT application and how do you measure that value

• What is the cost of an IT application and how do you measure that cost

• Overarching: What are the cost/effects of an IT application and how do you measure that value

Potentially the Polytechnic MIT Research Theses will follow methodologies such as: Design science for theory building and testing; Evaluation; Case studies of IT in a context; Action research for evaluating an IT artefact or framework; Quantitative evaluation of IT performance; Defining and testing measures.

Examples of research questions currently being investigated as appropriate in this masters are; Evaluation of wireless networking in a wildlife sanctuary for the purposes of scientific data collection; Wireless systems in disaster recovery situations: a measurement model and application; Evaluation of tools for data visualization using parallel processing models; Business connectivity, a study of flexible secure data delivery in the insurance sector; Analysis tool for scrubbing oil deposits: development and field test of a mobile application tool (image analysis)

In addition Cole and Ekstrom's analysis of IT Research Theses showed the following pattern of topics [14]:

DEV: Development, building, implementation, integration indicating delivery of a system into a context.

ED: These theses came in two flavors, those that were focused on concept learning and those that were actually the application of IT to an educational setting.

IAS: Information Assurance, Security, and Forensics

PROJ: Project management and applications of IT to Project Management

TECH: Technology evaluation and testing. "Comparison" and "evaluation" seem to be the most common indicator terms.

The programmes started in 2013 and are now two thirds of the way through the second year of delivery. Since the programmes started in 2013 there have been fourteen level 8 research report projects and three level 9 Thesis research projects either underway or completed. In addition, fifteen level 7 capstone projects have been completed. To date no 45 credit research projects have been undertaken. Analysis of titles to date show that

DEV: 10 research reports, 12 capstone projects

ED: 2 Master's Thesis.

IAS: 0

PROJ: 1 Master's Thesis

TECH: 4 Research report 3 Capstone projects

Many of our projects are initiated by requests from our Local Industry. The working criteria we have used to decide which project type a proposal belongs in is based on the current understanding of a technology and the understanding of the situation it is being applied to. If the technology is well understood, if the problem domain is well understood, and the technology has been used in the same or very similar situations before, it is definitely not a research project to build a solution for the client, and this could form a capstone project, where the students will either source an available product and install it or build a new solution for the client. However if the technology is not well understood or the problem domain is not well understood then this is most likely to be a Master's Thesis with a research question in the form of: Evaluation of [technology] for [purpose]. If the project is to look at the impact of a technology or the effectiveness of a technology, scale of the evaluation would determines which of the three research projects, level 8 research report, 45 credit research project or 90 credit research thesis will be used for the investigation.

Level 9 thesis (90 Credits), evaluation of application of new or emerging technology and / or investigation of problem domain which is new or not well understood

Level 9 research project (45 credits), evaluation of new or emerging technology

Level 8 research report (30 Credits), evaluation of new or emerging technology for purpose

Level 7 capstone project (45 Credits), development of IT solution for purpose.

6. CONCLUSION

Information Technology develops at a very fast pace and although industry would like to take advantage of new and emerging technologies, they often do not have the expertise, time or resources to conduct the necessary investigation and research into new technologies. Collaborative projects with Academia and industry in the form of capstone and applied research projects are a proven method of informing course development while enabling industry to investigate new technologies and problem domains. The development of postgraduate courses to meet the growing IT research needs of local industry will enable this collaboration to grow benefiting both parties. This paper has presented the rationale behind the development of postgraduate courses and presented classifications to assist in the identification of suitable projects for the four different IT project courses offered in our polytechnic. Further research is required to validate these classifications of research project type, research topic type, research methodologies, and research form from the pattern of thesis titles. It will also be interesting to conduct follow up research on the outcomes of the projects for students and industry.

7. REFERENCES

[1] Lloyd, B. and Chard, S. M. Interaction between Industry research and academic projects. In Proceedings of the New Zealand Association for Cooperative Education 2014 Conference Proceedings (Christchurch, 2014)

[2] Chin, K. L. and Chang, E. A sustainable ICT education ontology. IEEE, City, 2011.

[3] Lloyd, B. and Chard, S. M. Who Wins with Capstone Industry IT Projects? , City, 2013.

[4] New Zealand Ministry of Education Tertiary Education Strategy 2010 - 2015. 2010.

[5] Immigration New Zealand Long-term Skill Shortage List. 2014.

[6] AbsoluteIT Employer Insight Report. City, 2014.

[7] AbsoluteIT. Remuneration Report. 2013.

[8] Robert Walters. Global Salary Survey. 2013.

[9] NZQA Master's Degree. City, 2014.

[10] SIGITE IT Discipline. City, 2014.

[11] IT 2008: Curriculum Guidelines for Undergraduate Degree Programs in Information Technology., Association for Computing Machinery (ACM) and IEEE Computer Society, 2008.

[12] Cole, C. and Ekstrom, J. J. Research in Information Technology - Thesis Collection Project (2010).

[13] Zilora, S. J., Bogaard, D. S. and Leone, J. The changing face of information technology. ACM, City, 2013.

[14] Cole, C. and Ekstrom, J. J. The IT thesis project: a slow beginning. ACM, City, 2010.

Student Initiated Capstone Projects

Alan Fedoruk
Dept. of Computer Science &
Information Systems
Mount Royal University
Calgary, AB
afedoruk@mtroyal.ca

Mingwei Gong
Dept. of Computer Science &
Information Systems
Mount Royal University
Calgary, AB
mgong@mtroyal.ca

Michael McCarthy
Dept. of Computer Science &
Information Systems
Mount Royal University
Calgary, AB
mmcca772@mtroyal.ca

ABSTRACT

Capstone projects/courses, in which students undertake a significant project under supervision, have been offered in many computing programs In this paper, we present our experience for the senior project course as offered by the BCIS program at Mount Royal University, which provides an environment for students to successfully complete a capstone experience. This senior project capstone is a student initiated, single semester, individual, open ended project. We include the motivation for and the advantages of this approach as well as details of an exemplar project. The exemplar project shows student initiated projects foster student interest and motivation and enable projects with depth and breadth to be completed.

Categories and Subject Descriptors

K.3.2 [Computers and Education]: Computer & Information Science Education – information systems education.

Keywords

Information technology education: computer science education: capstone experience.

1. INTRODUCTION

Capstone projects are a fixture in IT and CS degrees. The ACM 2008 IT Model Curriculum [1] includes "the integrative capstone experience" as a key component of the senior IT curriculum. The purpose of a capstone project is to give students the experience of applying the skills and knowledge they have acquired in a real, substantial, challenging project environment. While the value of a capstone experience is well accepted, how to deliver it is still open to some discussion.

At Mount Royal University (MRU) we offer a project course that fills a senior computing option course in the Bachelor of Computer Information Systems (BCIS) degree program [2]. As a capstone experience it differs from most offerings in that it is student initiated and features a single student working with one or more faculty on open-ended projects. We argue that a capstone of this type provides interest, and hence motivation for the student, the integration of skills, a realistic environment, meets the learning outcomes, and is therefore a solid and successful capstone experience. To support this we give details of one such project that began with a student wanting to collect all of the lyrics for a particular band and ended with building a web crawler, and a data warehouse.

2. THE CAPSTONE EXPERIENCE

With the need for and the value of the capstone experience established, how should it be offered? Clear et al [3] ask a series of questions that can be used to classify the various instances of the capstone course. The variables include: goals of the course, types of projects, deliverables, prerequisites and preparation, assessment and supervision. In the literature, common ways of offering a capstone appear to be: projects assigned by the instructor [4,5,6], span two semesters and have multiple teams of students supervised by one faculty member.

One of the challenges for running a capstone course or courses is finding suitable projects. There are several approaches to this. A simulated client where the instructor or other instructors act as the clients, real clients, or as part of an ongoing faculty research or development project [7]. All of these have advantages and weaknesses. Simulated clients allow tight control and allow the projects to be tailored exactly to the desired learning outcomes but these types of projects are not real and students know this. A real project with a real client is exactly what the capstone should be about, but finding a steady supply of suitable projects is not easy. Projects must be the right size, involve the right level of complexity and take place near or on campus. MRU includes several other courses (Systems Analysis, Information Systems Organization) that involve groups of students working with real clients. While these courses are very successful, it gets more and more difficult to find projects. Client needs are not endless and since there is a time and resource commitment from the clients, project fatigue can set in. Ongoing faculty research projects offer a good venue for student capstones. There is almost always more work that could be done, and the size and scope can be varied as desired, but for an applied software engineering, or IT student these types of projects may not be optimal.

Service learning projects are a way to have students working on meaningful projects. In the case of [13] students are tasked with developing software for nonprofit organizations.

Many authors have identified that having a meaningful, relevant project is key to student interest and motivation [4,6,8]. Meaning and relevance are of course, in the eye of the student beholder. Students seem to want to work on projects that are impactful, that can aid society [7]. Finding these types of projects seems to point the project selection process toward real life projects.

Another key consideration for projects is also whether the projects is open or closed. A closed project is one that has a defined end point. Classroom assignments or simulated client projects would normally fall into this category. Some real life projects can be closed but most real client projects or research projects are open.

3. THE SENIOR PROJECT COURSE AT MRU

MRU has a relatively new Bachelor Of Information Systems (BCIS) degree, the first students were admitted in 2009, based on the ACM IT model curriculum [1]. The capstone course, *Senior Project*, was added in 2013. The idea was to provide a venue and resources for motivated and capable and students to work on a project that interested them and to allow them to earn course credit for it.

The BCIS degree evolved from a Bachelor Of Applied Computer Information Systems and Business degree and the applied gene is still strong in the BCIS. At the same time that the BCIS was being deployed Mount Royal College was also being transformed into Mount Royal University and the institutional emphasis on research was increasing. The senior project course had to be flexible enough for students to carry out applied projects such as the implementation of a killer app they dreamed up or more formal experimental research projects.

There are a large number of variables that can be used to classify a capstone project instance. The framework of questions given in [3] gives an excellent method for categorizing the various offerings. The MRU BCIS senior project course can be categorized by the following.

- **Goals of the course**. The objective of the senior project is to provide a venue for students to integrate and apply the skills they have learned to a project with meaning for them. For students considering graduate studies a senior project would give them a taste of the graduate student experience and the possibility of a publication.
- **Types of projects**. Suitable projects may vary greatly. In the time that the senior project has been offered there have been development of a web crawler (described below), data mining projects, development of a commercial product, and exploration of parallel programming using graphics processing units (GPU). Most projects come from student initiatives but some come from faculty suggestions. All projects are open ended.
- **Deliverables**. Students are expected to produce a plan, a final report and present their findings to the department (faculty and students).
- **Prerequisites and preparation.** The senior project is restricted to students in their final year who have achieved a given minimum GPA (3.0). The course is optional. It fills one of 4-6 senior computer courses required for the degree.
- **Grading and assessment.** Supervisor determined.
- **Supervision.** Students will be supervised by one or more faculty members.

The availability of the course is advertised to students and if they are interested they are directed to seek out a faculty member to work with. Faculty can also approach students or let students know of an available project. Students and faculty are urged get the relationship established early and to do some preliminary work to set the topic and scope of the project before the semester starts, if possible, so that the semester time can be used to best effect.

The deliverables are a conference style presentation by the student and a final report. The format of either deliverable is not highly specified. It is left up to the faculty members to determine an appropriate format for the work at hand. All students are expected to formulate a clear goal for the project, create a project plan and do some form of literature review. Publication of results is not required, but is certainly encouraged, particularly for students wishing to go on to graduate studies. Meeting times and other mid-term deliverables are up to the students and faculty to negotiate.

A key distinguishing feature of the MRU BCIS project is that students work independently, not in teams. (A group project proposal would not be rejected out of hand but so far all projects have been independent.) Throughout the BCIS program students have been participating in group projects. In the 11 required computer courses in the degree, fully half have a group project component. The BCIS also requires 4 core and 3-5 optional business courses, almost all of which require group project work. The objectives that group work covers, teamwork skills etc. are well covered in the core curriculum. The senior project is an opportunity for a student to focus on their own work.

Overall the project course is very flexible and intended to enable rather than restrict the student. It is an optional course with student choosing their own project so they are highly motivated. Students work independently so they need to develop their project management skills. Faculty supervisors ensure that the project has sufficient scope to integrate skills from all areas of the curriculum.

4. THE BR PROJECT

To show how the MRU *Senior Project* course meets the objectives of a capstone course this section describes a particular project completed in the Fall of 2013.

This project is the child of a love of the music of Bad Religion [9], thus the name BR project (BRP), and new found computer skills. The student was interested in collecting the lyrics, available from many WWW lyrics sites, for all of the Bad Religion songs, but the band has been active since 1979 and has produced more than 20 albums so manually collecting lyrics would be tedious. After about two and one half years of study in the BCIS program the student had completed several programming classes, a web development class, a database class and a networking class and realized that rather than cut-pasting the lyrics he wanted, he could write a program to automatically grab lyrics. With the informal help of the faculty network specialist, one of co-authors, the student began writing a web crawler.

Initial attempts quickly revealed some flaws in the design of the web crawler and posed some interesting ethical questions. Once he had a working crawler and pointed it at a likely lyrics site, he was blocked by the site administrators. A cat and mouse game ensued with the student running the crawler from different locations and changing the operation, slowing it down mainly, to make it less obtrusive. This raised the questions of, is what he is doing legal and even if it is strictly legal, is it ethical? [12]

Realizing that the information gleaned from the lyrics site should really go into a database the student enlisted the help of another faculty member, the database specialist to advise on the creation of the database.

When the senior project course became available the faculty suggested that the student continue work on the project, improving the initial efforts and in so doing, get a course credit. The project was supervised by two faculty, a network specialist and a database specialist.

The goals of the project were:

- Make the crawler more robust.
- Make the crawler more intelligent, able to crawl not just the one web site.
- Improve the database design. Move the data collected into a data warehouse for better reporting and further analysis.
- Build a testing environment consisting of an in house lyrics site. (To avoid the ethical, legal issues).

In total six components were identified for the BR project:

1. Design and planning
2. Web and database server set up
3. Lyrics test Web application implementation
4. Topical crawler implementation
5. Data warehouse implementation
6. Testing

4.1 Planning and Design

The BR project consisted of multiple deliverables, from setting up servers to implementing databases to programming a crawler and a test website. Along with these various tasks, there were time constraints attached to the project. There was a four-month time frame where some of that time was set aside for initial planning and organization of ideas that would be used to complete the objectives in the project. This consisted of making decisions on necessary applications, programming languages to be used, and designing a conceptual representation of the applications. All parts of the project had their own initial requirements and goals to achieve, which could be easily altered throughout the project if needed. Also, the project had a sense of looseness in the beginning to see where the research would lead as the crawler progressed and challenges arose. Most design features, especially when it came to conceptual drawings of the crawler, web application, and databases were mostly derived immediately before implementation began for that part.

4.2 Server Set Up

Once the initial planning phase was complete, the administrative steps of setting up a web server with a database server capabilities was the next obvious deliverable. Thus, the web server would be ready for deploying a web application and data for that site. Since the project's main objective is not directly on the implementation of web and database servers and, as mentioned earlier, limited time constraints were a key factor in the project, the use of third party tools were obtained. Mount Royal University, with its affiliates, provided a domain, http://nmserver.csis.mtroyal.ca, and hosting services to manage the server. The hosting service came with tools for managing web files, and a MySQL database management system (DBMS). For instance, the hosting service used 'phpMyAdmin' to import, create, or use any other database commands (DDL, DML, DCL, etc) with a very simple and user-friendly interface. Using the university's tools that are available took a minimal learning curve, and saved a tremendous amount of time that was better focused on the crawler research.

Also, for the student to have full control of the web server would allow tests and results of crawler to be more accurate by eliminating unknown variables with server side effects. In other words, the student would have a better testing ground, when not having to worry about server side network issues while debugging the issues with the crawler. If network issues arise, for example

loss of connectivity, the issue can be promptly defined without possible increased lengthened debugging times. Also, the crawler will not cause any unsuspecting web servers unwanted traffic.

4.3 Lyrics Test Website

Testing a crawler on any random web server, especially where the crawler is making multiple requests, can cause major annoyances for the unfortunate web administrators. For this reason, the BR project crawler needed one or more web sites to go up against while testing. For testing purposes, the student implemented a lyrics test site for the application to crawl.

The test site is based on data collected from a music lyrics site. Once the data was collected, the data could then be stored in the main site's MySQL database and used accordingly. PHP server side scripting language was chosen to implement the site. This simple and loosely typed language was chosen mainly due to the fact that it interfaces seamlessly with Apache web server and MySQL, the ease of integration into HTML static scripts, and the fact that PHP is cross-platform.

Before commencing with the implementation, design plans were drawn to have a conceptual view of the displays and the functionalities of the site. Some of the main functionalities of the site included:

- Pages: index.php, bands.php, artist.php, and lyrics.php
- All pages extract data from MySQL database through PHP
- Random band and lyric functions that display appropriate hyperlinks
- External hyperlinks added for crawler testing purposes
- Downloadable file hyperlinks added for crawler testing purposes
- Alphabet Navigation bar for linking to bands.php that displays data according to letter chosen by user. ('#' for bands that do not start with a letter)
- Search Engine: searches by band, album, or lyric name and will display all results in all three categories in a pop up window. User is able to do more searches within pop up window if needed. The search window is implemented using the integration of JavaScript, Ajax, and PHP
- Lyrics database currently holds 77 bands, 291 albums, and 3215 song lyrics

4.4 Topical Web Crawler

To solve previous crawler issues such as lack of flexibility of crawling various sites and multiple topics, the BRP crawler is designed and implemented with a more modular design and generic framework [11]. Along with the high robustness, the crawler is able to extract data as specific and detailed as the user desires. All functionalities can be conceptually viewed within three key modules. First, the crawler/search engine can be executed on any site desired. Secondly, the speed/crawl time module assists the crawler with network issues and added artificial intelligence. Along with these modules, the last key area is the data processing, which consists of functions that save and load data collected from the search engine.

The BR project crawler is implemented in the Java programming language, which has a vast API Library. The crawler requires the interaction with networking and MySQL server components..

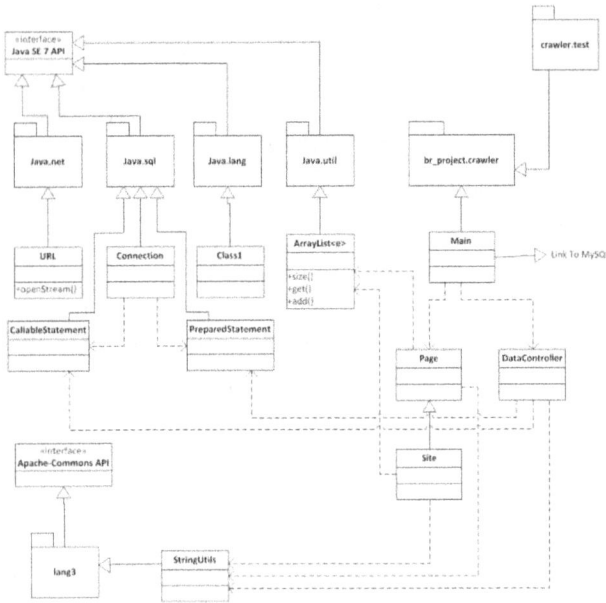

br_project: Crawler Application
Class Structure UML
Diagram

Figure 1. Class Structure UML Diagram

Figure 1 shows, via a UML diagram, how the BRP interacts with the Java API.

The crawler provides three ways to store the data collected. Firstly, the crawler has the capability to save a Page or a Site object so it can be retrieved at a later date. Since web sites can have one page or over 300 pages, like SAE Lyrics (the test site) to ensure there was sufficient memory set aside for collecting hundreds of Java objects, the maximum JVM memory heap was configured to 1GB, where the default is set to 64MB. The objects are stored in a directory within the programs bundle. The second way to save any data collected is to have the program to write the Page's HTML to a text file, if the user desires. The third way, and most desirable, was storing the data in a MySQL database. One benefit of storing the collected data in this database is that the user can crawl an entire site or a single page one day, and then again on another date and track if there are any changes in the html.

4.5 Lyrics Data Warehouse

To show how the crawler's collection of data can be useful, the student used the data collected from the SAE Lyrics site to show an example of a data warehouse approach of further data analysis. Once the warehouse was implemented and data loaded, the data can then be analyzed to learn new ideas from the data that Internet users are displaying.

The data warehouse was implemented using the STAR Schema to develop the tables, with the lyric being the center or fact table, and 4 other tables being the dimension tables. The process of ETL[1] was used in entering the properly formatted data into the warehouse. This process consisted of extracting pertinent data from the SAE Lyrics database tables, configuring data to appropriate data types used in warehouse tables, then loading the

_____
[1] ETL: Extract, Transform, Load – process used in cleaning transforming and populating appropriate data for data warehousing

data to the appropriate warehouse tables. This was all implemented using SQL functions for the completion of the properly formatted warehouse.

4.6 Testing and Results

A crucial component of the project from start to finish was the continuous role of testing. This occurred in all aspects of the project. In using an agile environment for the project promotes the process of iterative and incremental development [10]. Having frequent incremental tests gave the student the ability to change components of the project based on the outcome of the test results [14]. This involved significant white box testing of all PHP scripts, Java modules and functions across to find as many possible errors with most conditional paths as possible. Further testing with a black box approach was also used to examine the output of modules to ensure agreeable results. The implementation consisted of test areas for both the SAE Lyrics web application and the crawler. As for the web application, the use of a local web server was used to create and style the site and implement and test all PHP functions before they were deployed to the public server (nmserver.csis.mtroyal.ca). The crawler test area consisted of test modules (unit tests) to resolve any errors or undesirable outcomes.

The BRP had to do with building an application and to see what sort of data can be collected. When the crawler scraped Lyrics, all internal pages and external links are stored into the crawler's database. To get an idea of how much data is stored in a lyrics site, statistics by the crawler are summarized in Table 1:

Table 1. Web Crawler Statistic Results

Number of pages:	5977
Time to crawl entire site	37 minutes
Number of bands	77
Number of albums	291
Number of song lyrics	3215

5. OUTCOMES OF THE PROJECT

From the description above we can see that the BR Project met the objectives of the capstone experience. The student was able to integrate a wide range of technical and soft skills, struggle with ethical issues and ultimately created a product of interest.

The project involved systems analysis and design, programming, database design and programming, data warehouse and data mining, web design and development, networking, system administration, testing and ethics. The project required skills and knowledge from at least 10 of the 12 core courses in the MRU BCIS degree. This is a remarkable integration and synthesis of skills. Of particular note was the need to create an abstract version of the web crawler, a valuable high level skill, not normally needed in closed projects.

As shown in section 4, this project had a simple, straight-forward goal, but the realization of that goal was a broad, realistic and challenging project.

A project of this kind requires considerable planning and organization, even without the extra burden of having multiple students working on the project. As the project progressed new avenues for exploration opened up and the student needed to determine if there was time and resources to expand the scope.

Having two faculty members supervising the student was a mixed blessing. Two faculty members, from different areas, provided more breadth and more varied advice and guidance, but as always, more administration.

The ethical issues that the project raised are of particular interest. In the early stages the student was quite concerned that he was "doing something wrong". This led to an investigation of the legality and ethicality of crawling the web and the intellectual property issues that were raised. The student was able to compare this to the more academic discussion of intellectual property rights, net neutrality that took place in the required Computers and Society course.

6. CONCLUSION

We have argued that the senior project course, as offered by the BCIS program at MRU, provides an environment for students to successfully complete a capstone experience. This senior project capstone is a student initiated, single semester, individual, open ended project.

As the exemplar project shows, student initiated projects foster student interest and motivation and enable projects with depth and breadth to be completed.

An individual project, rather than group, allows students to focus on the project, keeping their interests, rather than focusing on group management issues. Working one on one (or one to many) with a faculty member fosters a deeper working relationship, than if one faculty member supervised many students.

In an environment with a large number of students and few faculty this model may be difficult to implement. Not all students will come with a suitable project in mind. Even when students do have a project idea it often needs to be modified to ensure sufficient breadth and depth. Faculty workload is often such that a faculty to student ratio of one to one or one to many is not practical.

Overall, the MRU BCIS senior project is still young, but it appears to be an effective way of offering a capstone experience to students.

7. REFERENCES

[1] Barry M. Lunt (Chair), Joseph J. Ekstrom, Sandra Gorka, Gregory Hislop, Reza Kamali, Eydie Lawson, Richard LeBlanc, Jacob Miller, Han Reichgelt. 2008. Information Technology 2008: Curriculum Guidelines for Undergraduate Degree Programs in Information Technology Association for Computing Machinery (ACM) IEEE Computer Society. www.acm.org/education/curricula/IT2008 Curriculum.pdf

[2] MRU BCIS Program http://www.mtroyal.ca/ProgramsCourses/FacultiesSchoolsCentres/ScienceTechnology/Programs/BachelorofComputerInformationSystems/index.htm

[3] Tony Clear, Michael Goldweber, Frank H. Young, Paul M. Leidig, and Kirk Scott. 2001. Resources for instructors of capstone courses in computing. In *Working group reports from ITiCSE on Innovation and technology in computer science education*(ITiCSE-WGR '01). ACM, New York, NY, USA, 93-113. DOI=10.1145/572133.572135. http://doi.acm.org/10.1145/572133.572135

[4] James Parrish, Jr., Janet Bailey, and Bradley Jensen. 2010. Using the imagine cup SDI as the foundation for computer science capstone projects. In *Proceedings of the 41st ACM technical symposium on Computer science education* (SIGCSE '10). ACM, New York, NY, USA, 68-71. DOI=10.1145/1734263.1734289. http://doi.acm.org/10.1145/1734263.1734289

[5] Michael Jonas. 2011. Capstone experience: lessons from an undergraduate research group in speech at UNH Manchester. In *Proceedings of the 2011 conference on Information technology education* (SIGITE '11). ACM, New York, NY, USA, 275-280. DOI=10.1145/2047594.2047665. http://doi.acm.org/10.1145/2047594.2047665

[6] Debra L. Smarkusky, Stanley J. Stancavage, Ryan E. Eagan, Preston E. Propert, Raymond F. Plociniak, and Andrew M. Nichols. 2011. Physics in motion: an interdisciplinary project. In *Proceedings of the 2011 conference on Information technology education* (SIGITE '11). ACM, New York, NY, USA, 33-38. DOI=10.1145/2047594.2047602. http://doi.acm.org/10.1145/2047594.2047602

[7] Sriram Mohan, Stephen Chenoweth, and Shawn Bohner. 2012. Towards a better capstone experience. In *Proceedings of the 43rd ACM technical symposium on Computer Science Education*(SIGCSE '12). ACM, New York, NY, USA, 111-116. DOI=10.1145/2157136.2157173. http://doi.acm.org/10.1145/2157136.2157173

[8] Lucas Layman, Laurie Williams, and Kelli Slaten. 2007. Note to self: make assignments meaningful. In *Proceedings of the 38th SIGCSE technical symposium on Computer science education*(SIGCSE '07). ACM, New York, NY, USA, 459-463. DOI=10.1145/1227310.1227466 http://doi.acm.org/10.1145/1227310.1227466.

[9] Bad Religion http://en.wikipedia.org/wiki/Bad_Religion

[10] Cockburn, A., Highsmith, J., 2001. Agile Software Development: The People Factor. Computer, 34(11), p131-133, DOI: 10.1109/2.963450.

[11] Filippo Menczer, Gautam Pant, and Padmini Srinivasan. 2004. Topical web crawlers: Evaluating adaptive algorithms. *ACM Trans. Internet Technol.* 4, 4 (November 2004), 378-419. DOI=10.1145/1031114.1031117 http://doi.acm.org/10.1145/1031114.1031117.

[12] Yang Sun, Isaac G. Councill, and C. Lee Giles. 2010. The Ethicality of Web Crawlers. In *Proceedings of the 2010 IEEE/WIC/ACM International Conference on Web Intelligence and Intelligent Agent Technology - Volume 01* (WI-IAT '10), Vol. 1. IEEE Computer Society, Washington, DC, USA, 668-675. DOI=10.1109/WI-IAT.2010.316 http://dx.doi.org/10.1109/WI-IAT.2010.316

[13] Aaron Bloomfield, Mark Sherriff, and Kara Williams. 2014. A service learning practicum capstone. In *Proceedings of the 45th ACM technical symposium on Computer science education*(SIGCSE '14). ACM, New York, NY, USA, 265-270. DOI=10.1145/2538862.2538974 http://doi.acm.org/10.1145/2538862.2538974

[14] Glenford Myers, Corey Sandler, Tom Badgett. 2011. The Art of Software Testing, 3rd Edition.

The Critical Role of Profiles in Social E-Learning Design

Lei Shi
Department of Computer Science,
University of Warwick
CV4 7AL, Coventry, United Kingdom
+44 (0)24 765 73797
lei.shi@dcs.warwick.ac.uk

Alexandra I. Cristea
Department of Computer Science,
University of Warwick
CV4 7AL, Coventry, United Kingdom
+44 (0)24 765 73774
acristea@dcs.warwick.ac.uk

Suncica Hadzidedic
Department of Computer Science,
University of Warwick
CV4 7AL, Coventry, United Kingdom
+44 (0)24 765 73797
s.hadzidedic@warwick.ac.uk

ABSTRACT

Evidence points to the fact that the integration of *Social Networking Sites (SNS) features*, into e-learning environments has been highly accepted by students, because of its benefits of improving the learning experience. Yet, not enough attention has been paid to what role learners' *profiles* play in the use of social e-learning environments, which does not match the importance of *profiles* in SNS. This paper presents how *profiles* are implemented in the second version of Topolor, a *social personalised adaptive e-learning environment (SPAEE)*, and learners' perceived acceptance of the design and the implementation. To complement the findings, a case study is conducted to analyse the *profile-related* features in Topolor, which illustrates a generally high level of learner acceptance of these features. The analysis is finally concluded to suggest future research directions, in order to further analyse and improve these features.

Categories and Subject Descriptors

K.3.1 [**Computers and Education**]: Computer Uses in Education – *Collaborative learning*.

H.5.3 [**Information Interfaces and Presentation**]: Group and Organization Interfaces – *Web-based interaction*.

Keywords

Social E-Learning; Curriculum; Web-based Learning; Evaluation

1. INTRODUCTION

Social Networking Sites (SNS) are web-based services that allow users to construct public or semi-public *profiles* within a bounded system, articulate a list of other users with whom they share a connection, and view and traverse their list of connections and those made by others within the system [13]. Diverse technical features have been implemented in SNS, but the backbone is always based on profiles for self-presenting, and the visible connections among users within the system. As a central component of SNS, the profile a user is constructing is the staging of oneself for a particular audience or a particular task [19], which influences SNS-based relationships and interactions among users.

Learning is intrinsically a social endeavour [37]. The social facets of learning have been described in various theoretical frameworks to explain how people learn [9]. A growing number of researchers have been working on facilitating e-learning environments by introducing a social dimension [31]. For instance, there is a great deal of research on social interaction tools for e-learning [22, 34], learning behaviour analysis [33] and open social student modelling [23]. The in-progress results have indicated that users tend to be more motivated towards contributing to creating effective learning environment and enriching learning experiences in SNS-based e-learning [9]. Yet, further research needs to be performed to find the appropriate balance of features necessary in such environments.

While social interaction features drew on SNS have become widely accepted and heavily embedded in e-learning systems [8, 26], not enough attention has been paid to what role learners' *profiles* play in the use of social e-learning environments, which does not match the importance of *profiles* in SNS. This study, therefore, aims to fill this void by investigating learners' perceived acceptance of the use of *profile-related* features in a social personalised adaptive e-learning environment (SPAEE). Firstly, we introduce the second version of Topolor, a prototype of SPAEE, focusing on those *profile-related* features. We then present the pedagogical aspects of the design and implementation, and an experimental case study on the evaluation of the *profile-related* features. Finally, we draw the conclusion and suggest future research directions and further improvements.

2. RELATED WORK

Connectivism argues that learning is the process of building networks of information, contacts, and resources that are applied to real problems [11]. Connectivist learning builds and maintains networked connections between people, digital artefacts, and content those are current and flexible enough to be applied to existing and emergent problems [2]. Connectivist pedagogy emphasises that learners are benefited from social activities such as sharing, comments and the insights of other past and current learners' contributions and the knowledge relevant to the learning goals [2]. One of the essential characteristics of connectivist pedagogy is the need to gain high levels of skills using personal learning networks that provide ubiquitous access to infinite resources including learning materials and learning peers; the other one is the focus on the creation of information and knowledge resources [1]. In addition, information overload (IO) is frequently reported as one of the main problems that learners encounter in e-learning, yet connectivism assumes that although information is plentiful, it is not necessary to memorise or even understand everything, but to have the capacity to find, filter and apply knowledge when and where it is needed [1].

These studies suggest the necessity of designing intelligent social e-learning that support learners to build and maintain personal learning resource networks with the help of smart tools for creating and accessing knowledge and connecting to their learning peers, in an adaptive manner. Efficient and effective connectivist learning needs learners' capability of publishing, sharing, finding, filtering, sorting, commenting, rating and so on, of the learning resources in the connected networks. These competencies demand high-usability tools, while on the other hand, these tools need to be adaptive and adaptable in order to cater for learners' personal needs, including their learning goals, knowledge background, preferences, skill levels of using such tools and so on.

In parallel with the research on learning environment that makes use of connectivist pedagogy, adaptive educational hypermedia (AEH) [3] systems, as another branch of educational platform research, focus on utilising adaptive hypermedia [4] techniques to tailor learning according to individual needs. Adaptation involves the definition and continual maintenance of a user model. AEH systems use such a user model to decide how to personalise an e-learning environment, taking into account aspects such as learning goals, background knowledge and preferences [20]. Moreover, an AEH system continually refines the user model according to the learner's interactions within the system. These intelligent properties of AEH systems, on the one hand, optimise the knowledge network to support adaptive and personalised learning content and learning path, and on the other hand, optimise the tools to access the connected knowledge network so as to provide context-aware user interfaces and interaction methods [21].

Drawing lessons from both connectivist learning and AEH, social personalised adaptive e-learning environments (SPAEE) [24] have been proposed as novel SNS-based learning environments offering creative opportunities for improving learning experience. Several studies on the granularity of social interactions and how it can be supported by adaptations have been conducted, towards the ultimate goal of rich learning experience, such as system architecture design [30], usage of the social interaction toolset [29], and learning behaviour patterns analysis [35]. The discussions and results from these studies have shown learners' high interest and high satisfaction in using such learning environments as well as the further directions to improve them. For instance, Shi, *et al*. have proposed three 'light gamification' mechanisms [32] to reduce the 'side effect' brought by the wide access to social interaction features, such as learners' abuse of such features for unrelated chatting, which might lower the learning efficiency. Building on this, the research reported in this paper describes a novel investigation of the critical role that learners' *profiles* play in SPAEE, which has not been addressed almost at all by the existing research.

3. TOPOLOR – A SPAEE PROTOTYPE

Topolor is a social personalised adaptive personalised e-learning environment (SPAEE) prototype developed at the University of Warwick. It is implemented based on the requirement analysis studies [27], and built on Yii Framework (yiiframework.com) and Bootstrap (getbootstrap.com). The first version of Topolor was launched in November 2012, and has been used as an online learning environment for MSc level students at the University of Warwick. It has been evaluated from various perspectives [25]. Based on these prior evaluation results, the second version of Topolor has been designed and implemented. In the following sub-sections, first, we briefly introduce main features of the second version of Topolor, and then we present more details about the *profile-related* features.

3.1 Overview of the 2nd Version of Topolor

Comparing with the first version, the second version of Topolor has more powerful tools for asking, sharing and filtering learning content as well as social interactions. As shown in Figure 1 (a), it has finer categories especially for sharing (Figure 1 (1)), i.e., a text (Figure 1 (1.2)), an image (Figure 1 (1.3)), a quote (Figure 1 (1.4)), a link (Figure 1 (1.5)), an audio (Figure 1 (1.6)) and a video (Figure 1 (1.7)), while in the first version, learners can only share a 'learning status' in a text format. Learners can specify related topics when they share a learning resource (Figure 1 (1.2) – (1.7)) or ask a question (Figure 1 (1.1)). It has also finer filters (Figure 1 (2)), i.e., only showing questions (Figure 1 (2.2)), learning resources (Figure 1 (2.3)), learning activities (Figure 1 (2.4)), those the learner bookmarked (Figure 1 (2.5)), those the learner participated (Figure 2 (2.6)), those the learner shared (Figure 1 (2.7)) and those are featured (Figure 1 (2.8)), while in the first version, learning resources, e.g., can only be filtered by their tags. In such way, the recommendations of learning resources and peers are more personalised and have more effective adaptability.

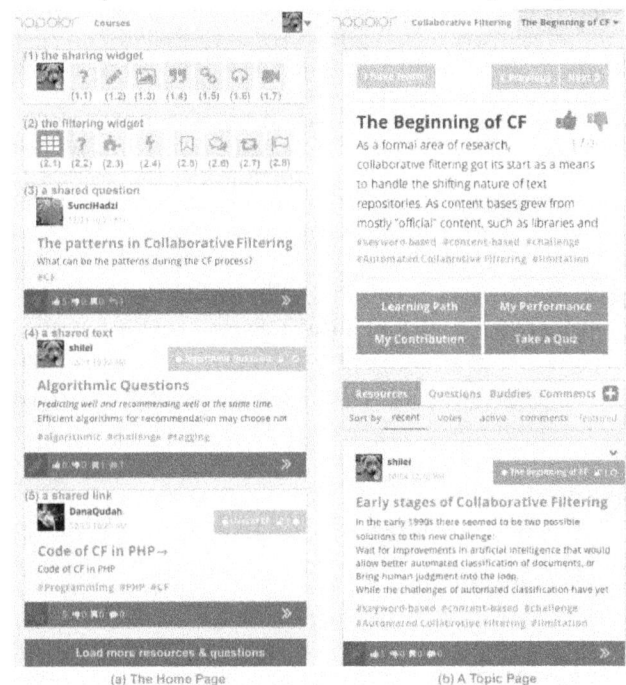

Figure. 1 User Interface: (a) The Home Page (b) A Topic Page

Another difference is in the topic page, as shown in Figure 1 (b). The second version of Topolor provides graphical and interactive pop-up views of learner performance and contribution, supported by the newly introduced open social student modelling [28] component. The interactive visualisation of performance and contribution allows learners to operate multi-context comparisons (i.e., in the context of a specific course or a specific topic) and as multi-group comparisons (i.e., compare to another learner, top 20% learners, or all other learners). It also provides various lists of related entities such as resources, questions, learning peers and comments, and various sorters and filters, such as showing the questions sorted by votes to more deeply analyse social navigation support mechanisms with finer adaptivity and adaptability.

3.2 The Profile-Related Features

One of the major milestone-updates in the second version of Topolor, which is the focus of this paper, is that it provides profile pages as another information and interaction 'hub'. This leads to various new features including social interaction and user model visualisation. In the following, we sketch up the main *profile-related* features.

There are several ways of accessing the learners' profiles. As shown in Figure 2, for instance, by clicking on a learner's avatar on the home page, a pop-up view appears, with some statistics of learning status, the shortcuts to send a message and to go to the learner's profile page (Figure 2 (a)). In a shared question or learning resource page, the webpage will be directed to the author's (learner's) profile page, by clicking on his avatar or name in the author information panel (Figure 2 (b)). In any page, a learner can always go to his own profile page, by clicking on 'My Profile' in the dropdown menu (appears when clicking on his avatar on the top menu bar) (Figure 2 (c)). On a profile page, there is a set of options for a learner to interact with the profile page's owner such as commenting on his/her activity logs, liking a question s/he asked, bookmarking a video s/he shared.

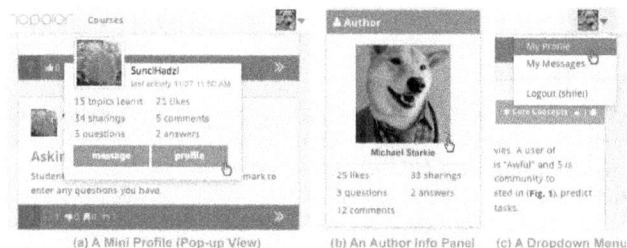

Figure 2. (a) A pop-up view of mini profile in the Home Page; (b) an author information panel in a shared learning resource page; (c) the dropdown menu in the top menu bar.

Learners' user models are visualised in various ways. Figure 3 (a) shows a profile page presented in a smart phone client-side, presenting the information about the profile's owner, such as the resources recently shared, the questions recently asked, the questions recently answered, the topics currently learning, the topics recently learnt and so on. By clicking on the button 'PK.' ('Player Killer', naming convention taken from games), a pop-up view shows (Figure 3 (c)), comparing the performance and contribution between its current viewer and the profile page owner. Figure 3 (b) shows the *Activities* sub-view in a profile page, presenting the actions the profile's owner performed, which other learners can 'like' and comment on. This can capture learner motivation by arousing competitive instincts [16].

4. PEDAGOGICAL CONSIDERATIONS

Both technical and pedagogical aspects determine the success of the e-learning implementations. Pedagogy is "the knowledge and skills that practitioners of the profession of teaching employ in performing their duties of facilitating desired learning in others", as defined by Dunkin [12]. The pedagogy in e-learning incorporates this definition but goes beyond it, taking into consideration the instructional strategies for real-time learning resources personalisation and access adaptivity and adaptability.

4.1 Social Constructivism

E-learning systems can support and improve highly effective interactions between learners based on social constructivist learning theory [15], which argues that learners can begin to grasp concepts and knowledge on their own, with the help from learning peers who are more advanced in understanding those concepts. On a profile page (Figure 3 (a)), learners can communicate instantly with one another, and contribute to discussions in-groups. For

example, a learner can click on the button 'send a message', and then a pop-up view will show up, so that s/he can write to the profile's owner. S/he can also discuss with the profile owner about the questions that the profile owner posted before. These features are able to foster collaborative learning that enables learners to acquire a deeper knowledge as well as experience a higher level of motivation [17].

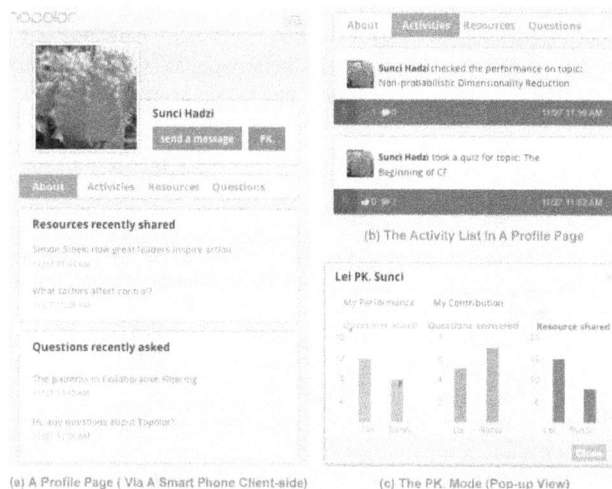

Figure 3. (a) a profile page shown in a smart phone client-side; (b) the activity list in a profile page; (c) a pop-up view for the visualised comparison of performance and contribution.

4.2 Competitive Learning

Competitive learning can lead to a greater engagement of learners by arousing their competitive instincts [16], thereby capturing learners' interest and increasing motivation, satisfaction and fun [5]. Many studies have been investigating the effects of competitive forms of learning, and indicated the benefits, such as the increase in performance, enjoyment, and motivation [14]. In Topolor, a profile page (Figure 3 (a)) enables a learner to check the comparison of performance and contribution between oneself and the profile owner (Figure 3 (c)), in order to compete with each other. Besides, competition is a common element of games, and the use of games to promote effective learning has been widely studied [7]. To take advantage of competitive learning, Topolor has also gamified some elements of user interface. For instance, in a profile page (Figure 3 (a)), when a learner click on the button 'PK.' (a typical label element in games), a comparison panel pop-ups, the bar charts appear with a growing animation (Figure 3 (c)).

4.3 Self-Regulated Learning

Self-regulated learning is a self-directive process where learners transform their mental abilities such as self-generated thoughts, feelings and behaviours oriented towards attaining goals into academic skills [38]. Topolor supports a learner to be aware of her strengths, weakness, limitations and opportunities, by providing statistics of learning status such as the number of topics learnt, line chart of the quiz/test score trend, doughnut chart and bar chats of comparison with learning peers, tree chart of topic completion rate in a course and so on. With these functionalities, learners are able to monitor and evaluate their own behaviours in terms of learning goals and achievement, so as to increase effectiveness, satisfaction, and motivation to continue learning.

4.4 Adaptive Learning

Adaptive learning uses techniques to interpret the activities of learners on the basis of domain-specific models, infers learner needs out of the interpreted activities, represents the needs in associated models appropriately, and acts upon the available knowledge on the learners and the subject matter at hand, in order to dynamically facilitate the learning process [18]. While the implementation of pedagogical theories of social constructivism, competitive learning and self-regulated learning have the potential to improve the learning experience, adaptive learning undoubtedly has the ability to enhance this potential. For example, it supports peer recommendation (for a learner to discuss with the most suitable peers); it can recommend adaptive tasks, when a learner finds her/his weakness and limitations via comparison with other peers' performance. A personalised e-learning environment with adaptive learning resources can more easily raise learners' interest, and therefore improve the learning experience.

5. A CASE STUDY

The second version of Topolor is being evaluated from various perspectives such as motivation mechanisms, gamification, adaptation strategies and social interaction influences. To isolate research variables, this paper focuses exclusively on studying the *profile-related features*, based on a case study of the usage of those features, with a survey that investigates learners' perceived acceptance of the design and the implementation of those features. This case study was comprised of three consecutive phases: 1) the experiment of using Topolor, 2) the questionnaire survey about users' perceived *usefulness* and *ease of use*, and 3) the analysis of the questionnaire results and some qualitative feedback from the learners. In the following, we detail the methodology and the experiment process, and report on the results.

5.1 Instruments and Measurements

Learners' perception on technology is among the determining factors for successful e-learning environments. Technology acceptance model (TAM) [10] incorporating learners' perception on the technology's *usefulness* and *ease of use* has the ability to investigate learners' intention to use a system as a result of a group of perceived qualities, hence interpreting learners' desired outcomes and motivation. Learning environments that are useful and easy to use are expected to facilitate learner satisfaction and engagement [36]. Therefore, for the initial evaluation, this paper reports on the results of learners' perceived *usefulness* and *ease of use* of the *profile-related* features, analysed using a survey instrument. The survey questionnaire includes a set of 23 questions, each of which applies a five Likert scale from 1 to 5 to evaluate selected features' *usefulness* and *ease of use* separately.

5.2 Experiment and Survey

The experiment was carried out with the help of fifteen students from the Department of Computer Science at the University of Warwick, who were registered for a fourth year MSc level module 'Dynamic Web-Based Systems', and a lecturer who was leading this module. The students were asked to learn a lesson on 'Collaborative Filtering' using the second version of Topolor, as well as ensuring to familiarize themselves with the *profile-related* features. The experiment was divided into four stages: two time-controlled one-hour learning stages, during which the students sat in the same classroom, one none time-controlled learning stage between the two time-controlled learning stages, during which the students accessed the system at a preferred time and location, and finally the survey stage, in which a coordinator led the students going through an optional questionnaire question by question, in order to make sure all the students knew clearly which question referred to which feature. (The latter was done as in our

experience, when students are faced with very long questionnaires, with similar questions about different features, they may forget which one exactly is targeted.) Students were clearly told that their participation in the survey questionnaire (answering or not answering questions, or which answers they chose) had no impact on their results of the module. From the fifteen students, ten of them submitted the optional questionnaire.

The questions were asked in a table format, as shown (partially) in Table 1, where for *usefulness*: *1* representing *very useless* to *5* representing *very useful*; and for *ease of use*: *1* representing *very hard to use* to 5 representing *very easy to use*.

Table 1. A sample of questions

	Features	Usefulness					Ease of Use				
...	...	1	2	3	4	5	1	2	3	4	5
13	Checking my performance	1	2	3	4	5	1	2	3	4	5
14	Checking my contribution	1	2	3	4	5	1	2	3	4	5
...	...	1	2	3	4	5	1	2	3	4	5

5.3 Results

Table 2 presents the results of the *usefulness* and *ease of use* of each of the *profile-related* features from the questionnaire. For *usefulness*, the means of the summative results rank between 3.60 and 4.70, and their standard deviations range between 0.42 and 0.99; for *ease of use*, the means of the overall results rank between 4.10 and 4.70, and their standard deviations are between 0.48 and 0.82. All the means are greater than 3 (the neutral response), suggesting students' attitudes to be generally positive. We discuss these results in more detail in section 6.

Cronbach's alpha is adopted to measure the reliability of the test. According to Carmines, a *Cronbach's Alpha* of 0.8 is considered as highly reliable [6]. The values of *Cronbach's Alpha* for each of the questions are shown in Table 3. The values for both *usefulness* and *ease of use* are considerably larger than 0.8, suggesting a high level of reliability of the results.

6. DISCUSSION

In addition to the questionnaire survey results collected from the students, we also received some qualitative feedback on the *profile-related* features from both students and the lecturer. The general feedback was consistent with the quantitative results, but the responses also contained some specific suggestions for further improvement for some evaluated features that ranked relatively lower (whilst above average, i.e., mean $\geq$ 3) in terms of *usefulness* and *ease of use*. Due to the space limitation, this section focuses on the quantitative results from the questionnaire survey, but some qualitative feedback is discussed when appropriate.

Overall, the results show that 91.3% (21 out of 23) of the *profile-related* features have been rated by the students as *useful*, and 100% (all the 23) as *easy to use* (i.e., average mean $\geq$ 4). Consistently with the questionnaire, qualitative feedback included a description of the *profile-related* features, as "it is very useful to compare what I have done to what others have done". Another student said, "There are lots of different ways to interact with the user when I am on his profile page". Besides, the lecturer complimented on the 'alterative paths' to access the same material. In the following, the discussions focus on the highest and the lowest rated features of the two categories, i.e., *social interaction* and *user model visualisation*, separately.

Table 2. Usefulness and ease of use of profile-related features

Features		Usefulness		Ease of Use	
Social Interaction Features					
		Mean	SD	Mean	SD
01	Answering a question	4.00	0.67	4.43	0.68
02	Bookmarking a question	4.30	0.68	4.30	0.68
03	Bookmarking a resource	4.60	0.52	4.60	0.52
04	Checking my messages	4.60	0.52	4.40	0.70
05	Commenting on activity logs	4.20	0.92	4.40	0.52
06	Liking / disliking a question	4.10	0.74	4.40	0.52
07	Liking / disliking a resource	4.30	0.48	4.60	0.52
08	Liking an activity log entry	4.10	0.99	4.30	0.68
09	Replying to a message	4.50	0.71	4.20	0.63
10	Messaging on a profile page	4.40	0.70	4.30	0.82
11	Messaging on a message page	4.50	0.53	4.40	0.52
12	Commenting on a resource	3.90	0.74	4.40	0.70
User Model Visualisation Features					
		Mean	SD	Mean	SD
13	Checking my contribution	4.30	0.68	4.70	0.48
14	Checking my performance	4.60	0.52	4.70	0.48
15	Checking my statistic data	4.70	0.48	4.30	0.48
16	Listing the activity log	3.60	0.97	4.50	0.53
17	Listing courses I am learning	4.60	0.70	4.40	0.52
18	Listing topics I am learning	4.60	0.70	4.20	0.63
19	Listing the topics I learned	4.50	0.71	4.40	0.70
20	Listing questions I answered	4.40	0.70	4.30	0.48
21	Listing questions I asked	4.70	0.48	4.40	0.52
22	Listing resources I shared	4.60	0.52	4.40	0.52
23	Comparing me with others	4.20	0.42	4.10	0.74

Table 3. Cronbach's Alpha (Reliability Statistics)

	Cronbach's Alpha	Std. Alpha	Number of items
Usefulness	.926	.935	23
Ease of use	.970	.972	23

6.1 Social Interaction

As shown in table 2, in the category of social interaction, the *usefulness* of feature (03) *bookmarking a resource* and feature (04) *checking my messages* were ranked the highest (both mean = 4.6). Similar responses were found from the qualitative feedback, where the students mentioned the necessity of collecting and arranging the learning materials they were interested in, as well as communicating with each other. In terms of *ease of use*, the highest rated features including (03) *bookmarking a resource* and (07) *liking / disliking a resource,* were both scored as mean = 4.6, and the lowest rated feature is (09) *replying to a message*, scored as mean = 4.2. All the features categorised as social interaction were marked as easy to use (mean ≥ 4), indicating high-perceived acceptance of these features from *ease of use* point of view.

However, the *usefulness* of feature (12) *writing a comment on a resource* was ranked the lowest (mean = 3.9, whilst still above average i.e. mean = 3) among the features categorised as social interaction. It is conjectured that, for one thing, before the students started learning the lesson 'Collaborative Filtering' using Topolor, the lecturer had already posted at least one resource (either a text, an image, a link, a quote, an audio or a video) for each topic of the lesson (a lesson consists of several tree-structured topics), and these resources were all high-quality learning content, which might make the students think that their complement would be unnecessary. For another, Topolor provides mutual-rating mechanisms, e.g., learners can rate (like or dislike) each other's questions, answers and comments, aiming at improving the quality of UGC i.e. user generated content, but on the other hand, it might cause that the students to feel less confident in creating content including writing a comment. Hence, it is necessary to seek mechanisms for keeping the balance between producing more content and maintaining its high-quality.

6.2 User Model Visualisation

Table 2 also shows that the *usefulness* of feature (15) *checking my statistic data* and feature (21) *listing the questions I recently asked* were both ranked the highest (mean = 4.7) among all the user model visualisation features. This result is further supported by the qualitative feedbacks. For instance, one student explicitly said it was *very useful* to see the overview of what learners had been doing. Similarly to those social interaction features, all the user model visualisation features were rated as *easy to use* i.e. mean ≥ 4, which allows us to conclude high-perceived acceptance of these features from the point of view of *ease of use*.

The rating for (16) *listing the activity log* was, whilst high, the lowest (mean = 3.6) with regards to its *usefulness*. The possible reason is that, as shown in Figure 3 (b), although the activity log demonstrates which topic it is related to, it does not provide further suggestions for what a learner should do accordingly. Therefore, it might be better if an activity log provides a button or a link to click on, as a recommended action to perform.

7. Conclusions and Future Work

This study investigates the critical role that profiles play in social e-learning by investigating learners' perceived acceptance of the design and the implementation of the *profile-related* features in a prototype of social personalised adaptive e-learning environment (SPAEE), the second version of Topolor. We have described the main updated features of Topolor, focusing on those *profile-related* ones. Besides the technical aspects, we have also explained the pedagogical considerations, which reveal some design principles for profiles in social e-learning. An initial case study has then been presented for reporting on the evaluation results of the *profile-related* features' *usefulness* and *ease of use* from end-user point of view, which illustrates a generally high level of learner acceptance of the design and the implementation.

The main limitation of this pilot investigation is the low number of participants, although the *Cronbach's Alpha* suggests a high level of reliability of the results. However, the second version of Topolor has already been opened to the public (http://www.topolor.com), thus a larger cohort of users are expected in the near future, providing opportunities for collecting feedback, usage data and suggestions for follow-up studies. In addition to the larger-scale investigation, several other perspectives of evaluation are on our agenda such as if users feel in control in their interactions with *profile-related* features, how *profile pages* lead learners to access various recommended learning resources and to communicate with their learning peers and so on, for further improvements.

8. REFERENCES

[1] Anderson, T. and Dron, J. 2012. Learning Technology through Three Generations of Technology Enhanced Distance Education Pedagogy. *European J. of open, distance and e-learning*. (2012).

[2] Anderson, T. and Dron, J. 2010. Three generations of distance education pedagogy. *The Intl. Review of Research in Open and Distance Learning*. 12, 3 (Nov. 2010), 80–97.

[3] Brusilovsky, P. 2004. Adaptive educational hypermedia: From generation to generation. *Proc. of 4th Hellenic Conf. on Info. and Comm. Tech. in Edu.* (2004), 19–33.

[4] Brusilovsky, P. 2001. Adaptive hypermedia. *User modeling and user-adapted interaction*. 11, 1-2 (2001), 87–110.

[5] Burguillo, J.C. 2010. Using game theory and competition-based learning to stimulate student motivation and performance. *Comp. & Edu.* 55, 2 (2010), 566–575.

[6] Carmines, E.G. and Zeller, R.A. 1979. *Reliability and validity assessment*. Sage.

[7] Connolly, T.M. et al. 2012. A systematic literature review of empirical evidence on computer games and serious games. *Comp. & Education*. 59, 2 (2012), 661–686.

[8] Cristea, A.I. and Ghali, F. 2011. Towards adaptation in e-learning 2.0. *New Review of Hypermedia and Multimedia*. 17, 2 (2011), 199–238.

[9] Dabbagh, N. and Kitsantas, A. 2012. Personal Learning Environments, social media, and self-regulated learning: A natural formula for connecting formal and informal learning. *The Internet and higher edu*. 15, 1 (2012), 3–8.

[10] Davis, F.D. 1989. Perceived usefulness, perceived ease of use, and user acceptance of information technology. *MIS quarterly*. (1989), 319–340.

[11] Downes, S. 2008. Places to go: Connectivism & connective knowledge. *Innovate: J. of Online Edu*. 5, 1 (2008).

[12] Dunkin, M.J. Introduction to section 4: Classroom processes. *Oxford, Great Britain: Pergamon*. 313–326.

[13] Ellison, N.B. and others 2007. Social network sites: Definition, history, and scholarship. *J. of Comp.-Mediated Comm*. 13, 1 (2007), 210–230.

[14] Fu, F.-L. et al. 2009. An investigation of coopetitive pedagogic design for knowledge creation in Web-based learning. *Comp. & Education*. 53, 3 (2009), 550–562.

[15] Herrington, J. and Oliver, R. 2000. An instructional design framework for authentic learning environments. *Edu. Tech. research and development*. 48, 3 (2000), 23–48.

[16] Johnson, R.T. et al. 1986. Comparison of computer-assisted cooperative, competitive, and individualistic learning. *American Edu. Research J*. 23, 3 (1986), 382–392.

[17] Moreno, L. et al. 2007. Applying a constructivist and collaborative methodological approach in engineering education. *Comp. & Education*. 49, 3 (2007), 891–915.

[18] Paramythis, A. and Loidl-Reisinger, S. 2003. Adaptive learning environments and e-learning standards. *Proc. of the 2nd European Conf. on e-Learning* (2003), 369–379.

[19] Richter, A. and Koch, M. 2008. Functions of social networking services. *Proc. Intl. Conf. on the Design of Coop. Sys.* (2008), 87–98.

[20] Rosmalen, P.V. et al. 2006. Authoring a full life cycle model in standards-based, adaptive e-learning. *J. of Edu. Tech. & Society*. 9, 1 (2006).

[21] Shi, L. et al. 2013. A social personalized adaptive e-learning environment: a case study in Topolor. *IADIS Intl. J. on WWW/Internet*. 11, 3 (2013), 13–34.

[22] Shi, L. et al. 2012. Apply the We! Design methodology in E-learning 2.0 system design: a pilot study. *2012 Imperial College Computing Student Workshop* (2012), 123–128.

[23] Shi, L. et al. 2014. Contextual Gamification of Social Interaction – Towards Increasing Motivation in Social E-learning. *Advances in Web-Based Learning – ICWL 2014*. Springer International Publishing. 116–122.

[24] Shi, L. et al. 2013. Designing Social Personalized Adaptive e-Learning. *Proc. of the 18th ACM Conf. on Innovation and Tech. in Comp. Sci. Edu.* (2013), 341–341.

[25] Shi, L. et al. 2013. Evaluating System Functionality in Social Personalized Adaptive E-Learning Systems. *Scaling up Learning for Sustained Impact*. 633–634.

[26] Shi, L. et al. 2013. Evaluation of Social Interaction Features in Topolor-A Social Personalized Adaptive E-Learning System. *Proc. of the 13th IEEE Intl. Conf. on Advanced Learning Technologies* (2013), 15–18.

[27] Shi, L. et al. 2012. Exploring participatory design for SNS-based AEH systems. *Proc. of IADIS Intl. Conf. on WWW/internet* (2012), 242–249.

[28] Shi, L. et al. 2014. Multifaceted Open Social Learner Modelling. *Advances in Web-Based Learning – ICWL 2014*. Springer International Publishing. 32–42.

[29] Shi, L. et al. 2013. Social e-learning in topolor: a case study. *Proc. of the 7th IADIS Conf. e-Learning* (2013), 57–64.

[30] Shi, L. et al. 2013. Social Personalized Adaptive E-Learning Environment: Topolor - Implementation and Evaluation. *Artificial Intelligence in Education*. 708–711.

[31] Shi, L. et al. Students as Customers: Participatory Design for Adaptive Web 3.0. *Evolution of the Internet in the Business Sector: Web 1.0 to Web 3.0*. IGI Global.

[32] Shi, L. et al. 2013. To build light gamification upon social interactions: requirement analysis for the next version of Topolor. *Proc. of the 6th York Doctoral Symp. on Comp. Sci. and Elec.* (2013), 63–67

[33] Shi, L. et al. 2013. Towards Understanding Learning Behavior Patterns in Social Adaptive Personalized E-Learning Systems. *Proc. of The 19th Americas Conf. on Info. Sys.* (2013), 1–10.

[34] Shi, L. and Cristea, A.I. Designing visualisation and interaction for social e-learning: a case study in Topolor 2. *The 9th EU Conf. on Tech. Enhanced Learning* 526–529.

[35] Shi, L. and Cristea, A.I. 2013. Investigating the impact of social interactions in adaptive E-Learning by learning behaviour analysis. *Proc. of Sixth York Doctoral Symp. on Comp. Sci. and Elec.* (2013), 88.

[36] Shin, N. 2006. Online learner's "flow" experience: an empirical study. *British J. of Edu. Tech*. 37, 5 (2006), 705–720.

[37] Wenger, E. 2000. Communities of practice and social learning systems. *Organization*. 7, 2 (2000), 225–246.

[38] Zimmerman, B.J. 2002. Becoming a self-regulated learner: An overview. *Theory into practice*. 41, 2 (2002), 64–70.

Improving Student Success through Personalization and Customization

Richard Halstead Nussloch
Southern Polytechnic State
University
1100 S Marietta Parkway
Marietta, GA 30060
+1 678 915 5509
rhalstea@spsu.edu

Jon Preston
Southern Polytechnic State
University
1100 S Marietta Parkway
Marietta, GA 30060
+1 678 915 4982
jpreston@spsu.edu

Han Reichgelt
University of South Florida
St Petersburg
140 Seventh Avenue, South
St Petersburg, FL 33701
+1 727 873 4324
reichgelt@usfsp.edu

ABSTRACT

Personalizing and customizing competency-based material to students has the promise of greatly improving student success. In this paper, we present some of the initial work we have done to creating a competency-based program in computing, and some of the issues we have identified in doing so, along with some proposed solutions.

Categories and Subject Descriptors

K.3.2 [**Computer and Information Science Education**]

General Terms: Experimentation, Human Factors.

Keywords: Education, Competency-Based Programs.

1. INTRODUCTION

There is increasing pressure on improving retention, progression, and graduation rates for students. For example, many states are moving to a performance based formula for distribution of state funds to public universities under which an institution's state contribution is no longer exclusively determined based on the number of students it enrolls, but rather on the progress students make towards graduation.

At the same time, many institutions are seeing significant shifts in their student populations, with a declining numbers of traditional students, and a growing percentage of non-traditional adult learners.

It is also clear that for many students, and in particular, the non-traditional adult population, the standard approach to curriculum design and delivery in which all students are asked to master the same material at the same pace, is not appropriate. What is called for is what one might call personalized and customized programs in the form of competency based programs.

This paper describes some of the progress we have made towards creating competency based programs in computing. We also

identify some of the difficulties we have encountered, and propose some preliminary solutions.

2. BACKGROUND

Learning appears to be a constant, natural and automatic activity that is an attribute of the human species. Indeed, Mayer [4, page 141] states that "learning is an active process in which the learner strives to make sense of the presented material." Following the widely accepted framework of modeling human learning and cognition as information processing, Mayer sketches the architecture of the human information processor (HIP) and argues that learners attend to some of the information they are presented on one of two sensory channels (hearing and vision), and then build and organize an internal (mental or cognitive) representation or model of a subset of the attended-to information. Learning occurs when the newly formed representations from the learning materials are integrated with representations storing existing knowledge. For example, if a lower-division computing student has already learned about one-dimensional arrays and forms a mental representation of a one-dimensional array as a contiguous block of bytes (storage), then he or she might easily learn a two-dimensional array through narrating a graphic showing how the two-dimensional array is a contiguous block of contiguous blocks of storage, i.e., a contiguous block of one-dimensional arrays.

Mayer argues that the aim of education is to have learners attain a *meaningful* learning outcome, where the knowledge learned in the module can be transferred and applied in problem solving. The rest of the time the learning outcomes involve *rote* learning, in which facts and concepts are learned so that they can be accurately stated or recognized, but not applied to a problem or transferred to a similar situation. Mayer points out the obvious that the third possible outcome--the *no learning outcome*-- is the result to be avoided. So, continuing with our example of learning about a two-dimensional array, a possible desired meaningful learning outcome is to transfer the knowledge of accessing a specific one-dimensional array element by its subscript to the concept of using two subscripts (row and column) to access a specific two-dimensional array element. At a lower level of rote learning, the learner will be able to state or recognize that arrays are contiguous blocks of storage, and can be one- or two-dimensional. For learners and teachers alike, meaningful learning is the most effective and desirable of the three possible learning outcomes.

It follows that it is imperative that learning material is designed and presented so that learners can quickly "see" and "understand" what is going on, what is important to remember and how it fits with what they already know. Given that different learners may have different prior mental representations, it also follows that the most effective way to instill new skills and knowledge in learners may not be the same for all learners, and that there is a need for personalized education.

Personalized education and learning has enjoyed a long history, including being embraced by prominent educators such as Bloom [11], Gardner [2] and Keller [3]. Historically it has meant that curriculum is designed by educators to account for differences in students. During the delivery of the curriculum, instructors then choose a path that is customized to each student's needs in the moment. In personalization, students have choices. For example, in Keller's approach, students choose the pace at which they proceeded through the material.

More recently, *personalization* in education has taken on a technological connotation as does its cousin, *customization*. Following Nielsen [4], we define *personalization* in education as where educational design and technology aims to provide individualized instructional content to the learner based on a model of the learner's specific needs. For personalization to be successful teachers (or teaching agents) must maintain a detailed model for each learner that includes current learning outcome progress status, elements of the learner's preferred style, e.g., visual versus auditory, possible reasonable next steps in the curriculum, etc. The closely related *customization* in education is personalization under learner control, e.g., students create their own path through the material to be mastered; since we see customization as a type of personalization, we will use *personalization* to refer to both.

Current educational literature draws many equivalencies between personalized education and *competency-based* education. In fact, the U.S. Department of Education has equated them in recent news posting on ed.gov [10]. The claim is that competency based programs leads to better student engagement as each student can choose the material that is most relevant to their own needs. Moreover, the higher level of student engagement, the fact that students can master the material at their own pace, and the fact that there are multiple paths to graduation are likely to lead to better student outcomes.

While the promise of improved student success through personalization and customization is not new, it is the advances in educational technology that make it possible to start implementing competency-based, personalized programs of study. The new technologies, such as game engines (e.g., [9]), now only make it possible to create pedagogical material quickly, they also make it possible to analyze the effectiveness of educational material on student learning and to develop learning agents that can learn to personalize content for their clients, while simultaneously providing a basis to give clients insight into the decisions and actions of their agents ([7]). A final element that has made personalized and customized competency based program development feasible is the decision by the federal government to make federal financial aid available to students enrolled in such programs [see e.g http://chronicle.com/blogs/wiredcampus/u-s-education-department-gives-a-boost-to-competency-based-education/43439].

There have been prior attempts at building competency-based programs. Examples that come to mind are a host of programs offered at Western Governors University (http://www.wgu.edu/), the undergraduate degree in business at Southern New Hampshire University (http://www.snhu.edu/ps/bs_business_admin.asp) or the so-called Flex Option at the University of Wisconsin System (http://flex.wisconsin.edu/). However, as far as we have been able to determine, the competencies covered in the various modules in these programs are at the level of a course learning outcome. In other words, they are at a relatively coarse level of granularity. The competency-based approach that we are describing below is at a much finer level of granularity, with competencies being at the level that would normally be cover in a single lecture, or part thereof.

3. LEARNING OBJECTS

In our efforts to build a competency based program in computing, we have re-analyzed a number of standard computing courses in terms of learning objects. Each learning object corresponds to a competency one wants students to master (at a very fine level of granularity), and consists of a pre-test, covering the material one needs to have mastered in order to be able to successfully master the competency covered in the learning object, a post-test to assess whether the learner has mastered the material, and a range of pedagogical material (videos, texts, simulations, etc) to enable the learner to master the competency. In general, we include different types of pedagogical materials to reflect the fact that different learners have different learning styles and/or preferences, and to allow them to choose the learning material that they consider most appropriate.

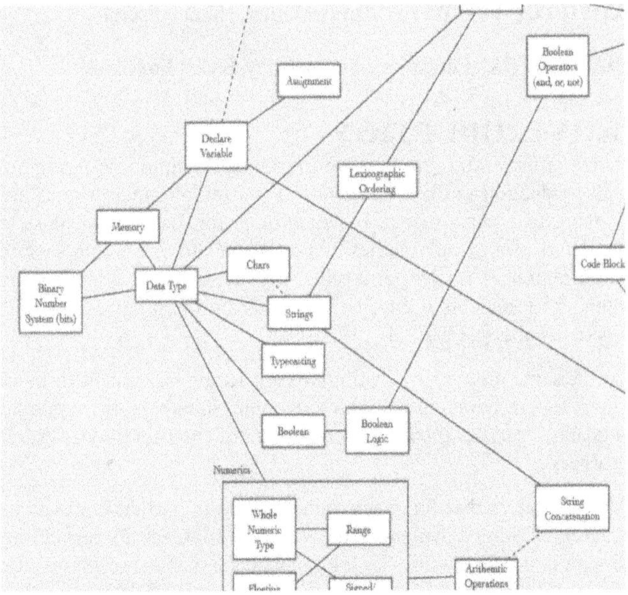

Figure 1: Part of the programming 1/2 learning object graph

Since the pre-test of one learning object is often the post-test of another learning object, one can obviously structure the learning objects in a directed graph. Figure 1 shows a section of the learning object graph we created for programming 1 and 2.

Perhaps not surprisingly, it quickly became clear that there are certain topics that re-occur in different places in a curriculum. Thus, when we analyzed topics within three major Computer Science courses (CS1, CS2, and Data Structures) in relationship to each other, it became clear early on that some of the topics overlap. For example, OOP and File I/O are covered in both CS1 and CS2. Moreover, there are topics, such as Scope/Visibility,

Functions, Parameters, Repetition, and 1-dimensional arrays are covered in all three courses. This is to be expected and appropriate given that some topics are introduced in one course and then examined in more depth in a later course, but we believe this overlap of topics among courses affords an important opportunity to improve the efficiency in how content is delivered in computing courses.

In an historical computing education model, topics are presented and students are required to demonstrate some level of competency for each topic. If a student takes good notes, retains the textbook, or has after-course access to online material, the student can review and reuse the learning objects/material from earlier courses later in their academic careers. But this presumes continued access beyond the course. In our proposed model, content is not only accessible (see section 4), but the content is reused between courses. For example, the OOP content presented in CS1 could be reused in CS2 (given the overlap seen in the following figure). Of course, the learning objects for any topic could be scaled in depth/difficulty to ensure they are presented at the appropriate level for each course; for example, the OOP learning object in CS1 might contain the introductory material, and this same learning object in CS2 might contain the introductory material (again) and more advanced material. In this way, courses can leverage this overlap in topics by reusing content in a positive, learner-centric manner.

An added benefit of this approach is the increased efficiency in which learning objects can be re-used between different computing disciplines. For example, both Computer Science and Information Technology programs require coverage of Operating Systems. However, whereas both computing disciplines require essentially the same coverage of the fundamentals of OS, the more advanced topics covered in OS will differ between the two disciplines. For example, a CS OS course will probably provide a greater coverage of for example deadlock avoidance mechanisms, but little coverage of admin shell scripts, update automation, and virtualization, where the opposite is probably true for an IT OS course. If we continue to organize curricula around courses, it is not straightforward to obtain the efficiencies that could be had if we could teach the common material only once to all CS and IT, rather than twice in two separate OS courses aimed at the different majors.

A final advantage of the competency based approach is more subtle. Most courses cover multiple competencies, and a particular grade in a course can cover a multitude of possibilities. For example, a student can earn a B when they have mastered all competencies in the course, albeit at a minimal level, or when they have fully mastered most competencies in the course but utterly failed to master some. If the course in which the student has earned a B is a prerequisite for a later course, we face two equally bad options in the second case. We can either pass the student and potentially set up the student for failure in the later course if it turns out that the competencies the student has not mastered are crucial for success in the later course; or we can fail the student, in which case we may require him or her to re-cover material that they have already mastered. We of course avoid the situation if we ask students to master each competency separately, and prove their mastery in the post-test. This clearly is an argument for the thesis that personalized and customized competency based programs are likely to lead to better student learning.

4. ISSUES AND POSSIBLE SOLUTIONS

Currently programs are organized around sets of courses, rather than as sets of learning objects, and many of the processes universities are heavily dependent on this way of organizing programs.

One example concerns finances: We currently start students per credit hour. If we allow students to assess different learning objects and to do so at different rates, then charging per credit hour no longer makes sense. Fortunately, this issue has been resolved by the University of Wisconsin flexible option (http://flex.wisconsin.edu/). The UW flexible option is a competency based set of programs. Its business model is essentially a subscription model, where students pay a flat rate for partial access to some of the material (essentially, a course but referred to as a "competency set"), or an obviously higher flat rate for access to all learning objects. Given that we strongly believe that students benefit from continuous access to the learning objects that they have already mastered (see above), we would argue that even if students opt for partial access, they should retain access to the material they have already mastered.

A related issue is how to calculate faculty workloads. Workloads are typically expressed in terms of credit hours taught, with possibly some recognition for teaching high enrollment courses. Again, if we move away from a course and credit hour based design of curricula, we need to rethink faculty workload policies. One obvious solution would be to measure faculty workloads in terms of the number of learning objects they are responsible for.

A related issue is to how to track student progress towards degree completion. Again, this is straightforward if we adopt a course based approach to program design: We simply record the courses that a student has completed, and graduate the student when he or she has completed the required courses. If we replace a limited number of courses by a large number of competency-based learning objects, it becomes harder to track progress. However, we believe that we can rely on techniques developed by the developers of large adventure games, such as Skyrim, in which players complete a series of quests, often in whatever order they choose. When a player saves a game, the system records which quests the player has completed. It will be obvious how we can use these techniques to track progress in our network of learning objects.

A further issue concerns transfer students. It is relatively straightforward to deal with students who transfer from a traditional course-based program into a competency-based program: We can simply record that they have completed the learning objects related to the competencies covered in a course that the student transfers in. The less straightforward case is to deal with students who transfer out of a competency-based program into a traditional course-based program. It seems that the best solution is to chunk up learning objects into the equivalence of courses (the "competency set" notion used in the University of Wisconsin flexible option) and to grant a student credit for the course if they have completed all the learning objects in question.

Allowing students to proceed with their learning at different rates (through our proposed subscription model) introduces some interesting problems to overcome. Specifically, if students are progressing with their learning at different rates, then they will need to demonstrate mastery and be assessed on different topics at different times of the year. We can no longer rely upon fixed term lengths and lock-step progress with final exams at the end of each term. While a challenge to overcome, this problem is a result of a very positive, flexible approach in allowing students to proceed at a learning rate appropriate to each individual. We draw upon two prior domains of experience that offer possible solutions to this customized assessment challenge:

1) Our university has hosted nearly a dozen game development events over the past six years. These "game jam" weekends involve impromptu teams coming together for 48 hours to rapidly prototype and develop small software solutions (games) under intentional constraint. The motivation is to emphasize quick, rapid prototyping and iterative design in such a way that even in "failed" teams, the cost is minimized to the 48 hour timeframe. The "jam" concept has proven quite fruitful internationally in recent years ([1],[6],[8]). At these events, participants range in skill from novice freshmen to advanced seniors. We encourage teams to form early on during the event such that skill levels are balanced and everyone has a role to play on each team. This has resulted in peer mentoring among the participants and a maturation of students' learning through the events.

2) One of the authors of this paper has a son who participates in a karate studio. We note that students in the karate studio enter and leave the studio and progress at different levels; the studio instructors focus their instruction and mentoring at appropriate levels on a per-student basis. One student might take three months to progress from one belt level to the next belt level, whereas another student might make the same belt progress in six months; these different rates of progress could be a result of physical limitations or given the different time commitments each student has. This situation is similar to the advancement and constraints that our university students have.

We propose that a school offering our flexible approach to learning could host a few events each year (similar to our past game jam weekends and martial arts studios) where students at various levels along their learning path could join other students on varied-skill teams. Each student would have specific goals to demonstrate proficiency appropriate to their progress level in the curriculum, and teams would be defined such that each student could contribute and demonstrate their individual contributions.

Such "critical milestone" events could be offered in person to ensure appropriate depth of assessment. Of course, if a student could not attend one of these milestone assessment events, then the student could just attend the next one offered and make progress in their studies appropriate to their level of commitment and mastery.

Another issue is that anecdotal evidence indicates that when successful, personalized learners exhibit more discipline and maturity. This has been made apparent to us in team projects done in our MSIT (Masters of Science in Information Technology). The students' favorite delivery mode for this degree is completely online, as most of our MSIT students live or work hours from our campus. We have observed that our online students will form self-directed cohorts and take courses together through their tenure in the program. By doing so, they can do team projects with their chosen cohort and reduce uncertainty and risk. This is an activity that customizes their learning and we see it as a sign of the increased maturity and discipline of graduate students. It suggests that for personalized learning to be effective, students require increased maturity and discipline, especially with regards to working on a team.

5. CONCLUSION

This paper describes our initial efforts at creating a competency based program in computing. One of our programs that is close to being built as a competency-based program is our graduate transition certificate in computer science, a program that is taken by students who are interested in our MS program in computer science but who do not have an undergraduate degree in computer science. The program offers courses in computer architecture and organization, data bases, data structures, discrete structures, operating systems, and programming. Clearly, these are topics at least some of which are likely to be included in most undergraduate programs in computing, and many of the competencies that students acquire as they progress through this program are also covered in our various undergraduate programs. We have discovered that building the learning objects is relatively straightforward and that we can control the set of learning objects a student has access to through the selective release mechanisms that most learning management systems now make available.

The harder aspects have been the various administrative issues mentioned in section 4. However, we are convinced that the competency based personalized and customized approach to program design has so many advantages in terms of student success that we are determined to continue our work in this area.

6. REFERENCES

[1] Arya, A., Chastine, J., Fowler, A., Preston, J., An International Study on Learning and Process Choices in the Global Game Jam, *International Journal of Games-Based Learning.* 2014.

[2] Gardner, H. (2006). *Multiple Intelligences: New Horizons 2nd Edition*. New York: Basic Books.

[3] Keller, F. S. (1968). Goodbye teacher... *Journal of Applied Behavior Analysis* 1, 79-89

[4] Mayer, R.E. (2009). *Multimedia Learning 2nd Edition*. New York: Cambridge University Press.

[5] Neilsen, J. (1998). Personalization is Over-Rated. Retrieved on 2 June 2014 from http://www.nngroup.com/articles/personalization-is-over-rated/

[6] Preston, J., Chastine, J., O'Donnell, C., Tseng, T., and MacIntyre, B., Game Jams: Community, Motivations, and Learning among Jammers, *International Journal of Games-Based Learning*, number 2, vol 3. July 2012.

[7] Ringle, M.L. and Halstead-Nussloch, R. (1989) Shaping user input: a strategy for natural language dialogue design. *Interacting with computers.* 1(3), 227-244.

[8] Shin, K., Kaneko, K., Matsui, Y., Mikami, K., Nagaku, M., Nakabayashi, T., et al., Localizing global game jam: Designing game development for collaborative learning in the social context. In A. Nijholt, T., Romão, & D. Reidsma, (Eds.) Lecture Notes in Computer Science (pp. 117-132), 7624. Berlin, Germany: Springer. 2012.

[9] Unity Technologies (2014). Unity 3D Gaming Engine. Retrieved on 2 June 2014 from http://unity3d.com/

[10] U.S. Department of Education News Item (2014). Competency-Based Learning or Personalized Learning. Retrieved on 2 June 2014 from http://www.ed.gov/oii-news/competency-based-learning-or-personalized-learning

[11] Wikipedia article on Bloom's Taxonomy (2014). Retrieved on 2 June 2014 from http://en.wikipedia.org/wiki/Bloom's_taxonomy.

A Methodology for Personalized Competency-based Learning in Undergraduate Courses

Ioulia Rytikova
George Mason University
4400 University Dr. MSN 1G8
Fairfax, VA 22030, USA
Tel. 703-993-6134
irytikov@gmu.edu

Mihai Boicu
George Mason University
4400 University Dr. MSN 6B3
Fairfax, VA 22030, USA
Tel. 703-993-1591
mboicu@gmu.edu

ABSTRACT

In this paper, we describe a methodology for integrating personalized competency-based learning in a group of correlated courses in typical undergraduate education settings. The personalization is provided both in terms of content and learning pace. The material is organized in hierarchical modules based on the competencies desired to be achieved, containing both presentation materials and various type of tests. The methodology was integrated in several database and programming courses and its preliminary evaluation shows significant improvement in student grades.

Categories and Subject Descriptors

K.3.1 [**Computer Uses in Education**]: Computer-assisted instruction (CAI); Computer-managed instruction (CMI); Distance learning

K.3.2 [**Computer and Information Science Education**]: Computer science education; Curriculum; Information systems education; Self-assessment

General Terms

Management, Measurement, Performance, Design, Experimentation, Human Factors, Standardization

Keywords

Personalized learning, competency-based learning, databases education;

1. INTRODUCTION

In recent years, many educators all over the world have been participating in a wide variety of research initiatives trying to develop and implement new innovative learning environments to maximize the effectiveness of both teaching and learning models used in higher education ([7], [8], [10], [5], [6], [3], [9]). Today more than ever personalization becomes a critical component in any learning environment, personalized learning being identified by the US National Academy of Engineering as one of the 14 Grand Challenges for Engineering for the 21st Century [20]. Our

SIGITE'14, October 15-18 2014, Atlanta, Georgia, USA.
Copyright © 2014 ACM 978-1-4503-2686-5/14/10...$15.00.
http://dx.doi.org/10.1145/2656450.2656463

teaching experience and existing research show that personalized learning and mentoring is the most effective method in student learning, helping not only a less proficient student significantly improve and cover his/her gaps, but also a talented student further immerse in advanced academic topics ([17], [23], [30]). While personalized learning can be delivered with individual students (e.g. independent research courses) or with very small class sizes, it becomes increasingly difficult as the class size increases. Moreover, the classical setting of college education is oriented toward group teaching rather than personalized teaching ([11], [19]), and the courses' objectives and content are predefined based on a 'typical' student, and will generally not be significantly changed based on the current class composition ([1], [22]). An efficient extension of personalized learning to larger classes in the current settings will require many of the personalization tasks to be performed automatically. Particularly, one of the key elements that require thorough examination is the capacity of creating a student model by understanding the current student competency in the subject matter in order to select and provide tailored educational content. However, the current college level assessment methods focus on obtaining general overall assessment for a course and rarely allow easy breakdown to elementary competencies to the point where they are clear and transparent ([33] p. 60). If identified, such competencies, when mastered, will effectively assist students in building the foundational knowledge of the material discussed in the course [13]. This step becomes critical in courses where students have to integrate knowledge across multiple theoretical concepts and apply it to solve challenging problems. Illustrative examples of such courses taught at the undergraduate level include introductory and advanced programing and database courses, as they assist students in developing critical thinking and complex problem solving skills and demonstrate how rigorous academic content can be applied in a real-world environment. In undergraduate education, such courses serve mostly second- and third-year students. Among them, it is not uncommon to see students who transferred from another institution, such as a community college. Moreover, the level of preparation of students in a class differs significantly and requires a substantial effort from the teacher's perspective to bring both the entire class and each individual to a successful completion of a course. In this paper, we discuss a general methodology of how to implement a personalized competency-based approach in current college settings by using available out-of-the-box systems. Elements of this methodology were applied in various courses at George Mason University. Moreover, preliminary results show that this methodology improved significantly students' performance in an undergraduate database course.

2. METHODOLOGY

2.1 Personalized Competency-based Learning Platform

Personalization of learning is a topic that attracts increasing interest among educators as it embraces promising ideas of creating innovative learning environments to meet the needs of the new generation of learners [[12], [2], [34], [31]]. Among those there are specific requirements that challenge the dominant design of educational systems ([32]). Particularly, learners today want to be in charge of their learning process and its implementation. Research confirms that today it is expected that students are actively involved in creating their own learning environments which combine both formal and informal elements of learning and, ultimately, develop an educational ecosystem where learning becomes an inevitable component of their every day lives. The role of an instructor in this setting shifts from being just the provider of the learning materials to being the mentor who helps students achieve their full potential by effectively facilitating a wide variety of learning resources combined with personalized teaching strategies. An important aspect of this approach requires a simple, straightforward method to assess and confirm the students' readiness to progress to the next level in their learning process. Our research demonstrates that this problem is well addressed through the competency-based methodology implemented in the proposed personalized learning environment.

Figure 1 briefly describes the envisioned process of providing personalized competency-based learning in college settings. The implementation of the methodology starts with the development of a unified curriculum repository containing the learning materials organized into a hierarchy of topics and mapped with their corresponding competencies along with their assessment methods. These are types of *learning objects*. As will be described below, particular attention was devoted to the level of granularity in the process of identifying competencies for each topic. Most undergraduate courses have pre-requisites and it is not very uncommon for an instructor to start a course with a review of the fundamental concepts covered in a pre-requisite course or to request the students to review such material on their own. The repository provides basic building blocks in the form of "ready-to-use" learning objects targeting specific competencies, thus

allowing an easy initial course creation and configuration at the beginning of a semester. In addition, as a class progresses through a semester, the repository supports instructors willing to dynamically extend the course in order to address the specific needs of either individuals or the entire class in the case that certain expectations are exceeded or, on the contrary, not met. This creates a unique opportunity for this repository to be used at the departmental level.

Each student enrolled in the course will have his/her own personalized guided experience. The materials will be made available dynamically as the student proves his/her competence in the required pre-requisites by performing available proficiency assessments. Periodically, by analyzing the performance of the students in the course through a data analysis module, topics and competencies that need to be improved will be identified and both supplementary topic presentation materials and diversified assessment questions will be provided to the student. These results will be also used for the curriculum revision of the course and the enhancement of the repository.

The proposed methodology effectively supports both instructors and students as it offers a high degree of flexibility in terms of the course organization and delivery (from the instructor's perspective) and the course progression (from the student's point of view).

2.2 Developing the Curriculum Repository

The proposed curriculum repository is designed to be developed as an open-source, community-driven collection of learning materials on topics generally covered in college database and programming courses, commonly offered at the undergraduate level. Such repositories are often viewed as dynamic collections of various learning materials, available to support educators in their effort to create effective learning environments for students ([21], [2], [15], [18]). They also serve as communication tools for students and experts giving them the opportunity to exchange their ideas and collaborate on the related topics in a given domain ([14], [24]).

Since the repository is intended to be used for several undergraduate database and programming courses when it is fully deployed, granularity becomes the key focus as it defines and determines the reusability of the learning materials and flexibility of the curriculum development process ([4], [28]). Before being added to the repository, a new topic is sub-divided into a set of sub-topics where each represents one basic, elementary theoretical question. When defining a sub-topic, the ultimate goal is to represent the material in the simplest format possible eliminating the need for further subdivision. For each topic, this might require a different level of granularity as demonstrated in Table 1, however, it can be dynamically refined later, based on the "as-needed" approach and the feedback obtained from the data analysis module. Once the desired level of granularity is

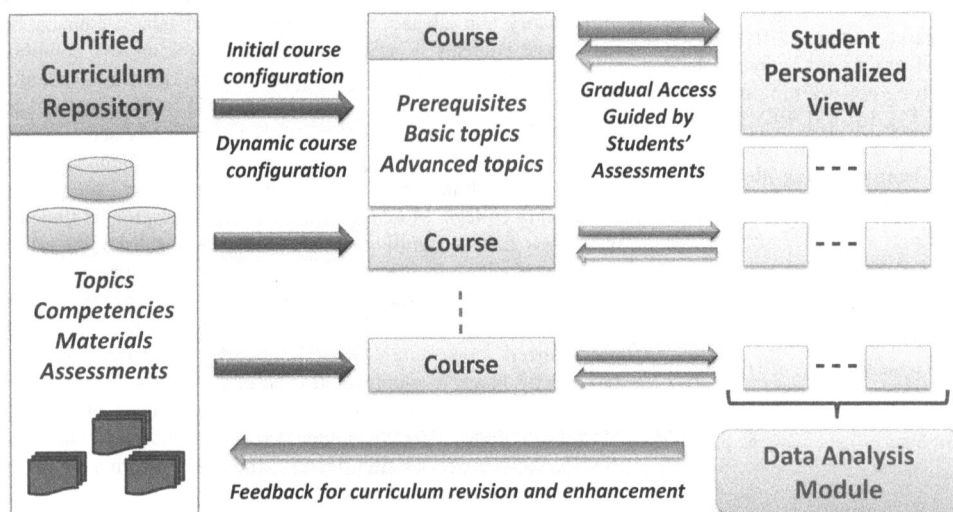

Figure 1: Overview of personalized learning process

achieved, a sub-topic is mapped with its required competencies, available learning materials and assessment methods. This constitutes a new learning object added to the unified repository.

For consistency, we require the topics to be formulated as noun phrases. Also, semantically, the sub-topic relationship is constructed based on "is part of" relationship, and not "is type of" relationship. This allows the topics to be naturally grouped together, generating a hierarchical structure. For example, in the type of hierarchy "1NF *is type of* normal form" but we represented "1NF *is part of* database normalization" relationship in our hierarchy of subtopics.

Topic	Level 1	Level 2
Database normalization	1NF	Repeating groups
	2NF	
	3NF	
	Higher-level forms	BCNF, 4NF, 5NF, DKNF
	Denormalization	

Table 1. Example of the granulation levels of a single topic

The repository is designed to be built using available semantic technology, more precisely Semantic MediaWiki ([25]) or similar technology (e.g. [29]). It offers a good trade-off between free text and complete formal text and provides social support for the learning environment ([16]). It offers a flexible way to include

Topic: Connectivity
Definition: The connectivity of a relationship in ERM describes the classification of the relation between entities A and B based on how many instances of A can be related to an instance of B and how many instances of B can be related to an instance of A. There are three main types of connections: one-to-one, one-to-many and many-to-many relationships.
Competencies:
• Identify relationship connectivity between two entities
• Represent many-to-many relationships using bridges
Related topics... Resources... Used in courses... Comments...

• [[has related competency::Identify relationship connectivity between two entities]]

Figure 2: Sample page in the curriculum repository

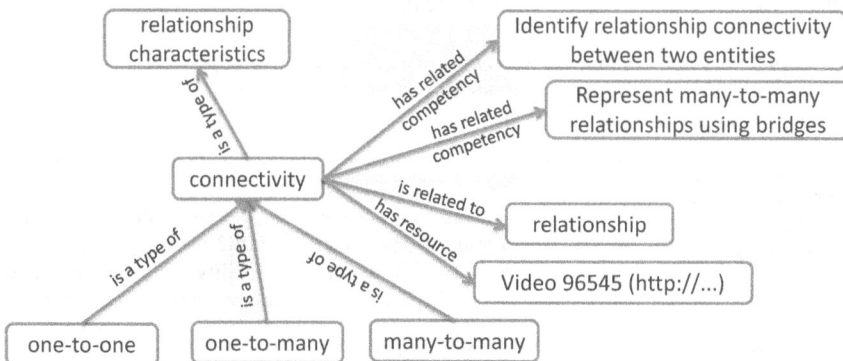

Figure 3: Semantic network corresponding to a text fragment

and structure the repository. Moreover, it allows semantic templates in order to facilitate the organization and elicitation of the information from the development community ([26]). Also, the resulting semantic structure can be easily exported in OWL/RDF that will allow future automatic semantic processing ([27]). While the resulting wiki will be publicly available, in order to maintain the quality of the presented material, the contributors will need to register, have expertise in teaching the subject matter and must be affiliated with an educational institution.

Figure 2 shows a sample text in a semantic wiki and at the bottom how the text is semantically annotated:

The definition of the curriculum repository is further simplified through the use of templates for the main elements (e.g. topics, competencies, resources, comments). Based on such description a semantic network (ontology) might be generated.

Figure 3 graphically illustrates the corresponding semantic network to the free text description above.

3. EXPERIMENT

3.1 Course Organization

Over the past year, some elements of the proposed methodology were implemented in several database and programming courses at the Applied Information Technology (AIT) department at George Mason University. When the preliminary results were received and analyzed, the methodology was fully implemented in one of the undergraduate database courses - IT 314: Database Management - offered to third and fourth-year students. One of the main reasons this course was selected was because it provided an excellent framework for testing and verifying the effectiveness of the proposed methodology. IT 314 is the second database course offered to the AIT students. As a pre-requisite for this course, students are required to complete an introductory course on relational databases with a grade of C or above. Since over 70% of the AIT program consists of transfer students, mostly from Northern Virginia Community Colleges, the population of students taking IT 314 is very heterogeneous. The level of students' preparation in a single class varies significantly as many students complete the required pre-requisite introductory database course prior to coming to AIT, often a few semesters before taking IT 314. In addition, individuals coming into the classroom with a background in programming fundamentals, which is considered a difficult topic for many students, find the semester easier to manage. All together, it creates a challenging classroom environment for the IT 314 instructors trying to accomplish very demanding course objectives.

To help instructors overcome these issues, IT 314 was redesigned using the personalized competency-based modular approach. When implemented, the course provided access to a wide variety of technology enhanced teaching and learning tools, which helped create a customized learning experience for each student throughout the entire course.

The development process started with organizing the learning materials into a hierarchy of topics/sub-topics and mapping them with their corresponding competencies along with the learning tasks and assessment methods. First, all topics were grouped into three categories: Review, Fundamentals, and Advanced. Then, topics were grouped into logical units to be later represented in a single module. Each module has the same standardized structure and consists of several learning objects that students go through progressively. Each learning object represents a single competence. The proposed course organization is presented in Figure 4.

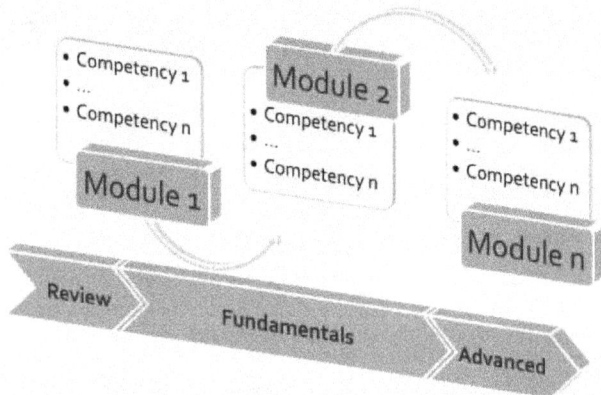

Figure 4: Course organization

Every learning object contains a wide variety of learning resources that include but are not limited to textbooks, videos, presentations, Internet resources selected by the instructor, and surveys, and gives students an opportunity to choose learning materials that work best for his/her learning style. After studying the material for a given sub-topic and before moving on to the next learning object or to more advanced learning tasks that require students to integrate knowledge from multiple concepts, students complete a competency quiz. We experimented with various settings and concluded that an unlimited number of repetitions on each quiz with the best score recorded promote a higher level of student engagement as many students spend more time on each learning object trying to achieve a perfect score. However, this will require a significantly bigger set of test questions in order to avoid solution memorization. Additionally, students were required to receive a grade of 75 or above on each competency quiz to move on to the next learning object. The module ends with a complex learning task that checks students' comprehension of the entire topic. A progressive completion of every activity in each learning object helps students build the required foundation for a given module. On top of that, each module gives students an opportunity to work on optional advanced activities. This approach creates both an active learning experience and a personalized course completion for each student in class helping not only a less proficient student significantly improve and cover his/her gaps, but also a talented student further immerse in advanced academic topics.

When teaching a class, the instructor first starts with presenting new material through a discussion on the database concepts covered in the given module. Then, students continue building required fundamental skills and work collaboratively on practice problems either face-to-face or through a discussion board. Working both individually and together, students exchange their ideas and develop a solution with one another. Next, students work individually to complete required activities available in the learning modules specifically designed to meet their individual needs and to help them achieve every competence for the given module.

The proposed approach stimulates individual active learning and supports dynamic collaboration between the students. Thus, it results in a significant increase in the engagement and the level of preparation of each student in class as demonstrated through the experiment results discussed later on.

The LMS selected for this project was the Blackboard system (http://www.blackboard.com) that allows a satisfactory typical course instruction and offers some support for providing personalized course delivery. Developed learning objects were added to the curriculum repository for further re-use and/or enhancement in the following semesters or other related courses.

3.2 Experiment Set Up

The experiment was conducted in Spring 2013 and Fall 2013 and included all students taking IT 314: Database Management during that time frame. There were eighty-two students participating in the experiment: forty students in Spring 2013 and forty-two students in Fall 2013. Both on-line and in-class sections were offered for each semester. The course was delivered via the Blackboard system. All sections in a particular semester were taught using the same instructional approach and format, designed, implemented and provided by the course coordinators. It included the same syllabus, textbook, videos, schedule of classes, tests, quizzes, homework assignments, practice problems, discussions and extra-credit activities. Graders followed the same grading policy and grading scale for every assignment in all sections.

For the Fall 2013 semester, the course was re-developed using the proposed methodology.

To evaluate the effectiveness of the implemented methodology, tests' scores for the two groups of the IT 314 students were compared. For analysis purposes, the following two groups of students were identified:

- **Control Group:** Students enrolled in IT 314 in Spring 2013 academic year (before the proposed approach was implemented).
- **Treatment Group:** Students enrolled in IT 314 in Fall 2013 academic year (after the proposed approach was implemented).

Students' scores for Test 1 for both groups were collected and compared to identify if there is a significant improvement in students scores.

In both semesters Test 1 was delivered in the same format and included two parts equally weighted. Part 1 consisted of 100 multiple-choice and true-false questions to test a student's ability to understand foundational concepts. Part 2 included several real-world problems to test a student's ability to synthesize and effectively apply knowledge across multiple database concepts.

Neither format nor test questions were modified in Fall 2013. Test 1 was conducted in a secure setting where students were closely monitored by both the instructor and TA.

3.3 Experiment Results

To compare the performance by study groups, a one-way analysis of variance (ANOVA) with a 95% confidence level was used for the statistical analysis of collected data (see below).

ANOVA results for overall students' scores for Test 1 for both groups are presented in Table 2, for Part 1 in Table 3, and for Part 2 in Table 4.

Based on the preliminary results presented in Table 2, there is a statistically significant improvement in overall students' performance at the 95% confidence level (p-value = 0.04379). On average, students' grades on Test 1 improved by more than half a letter grade.

Analysis of Variance (One-Way)

Summary						
Groups	Sample size	Sum	Mean	Variance		
Spring 2013 Test 1: Total	42	2,979.	70.92857	154.79965		
Fall 2013 Test 1: Total	40	3,076.5	76.9125	195.88317		
ANOVA						
Source of Variation	SS	df	MS	F	p-level	F crit
Between Groups	733.61505	1	733.61505	4.19621	0.04379	2.76931
Within Groups	13,986.22946	80	174.82787			
Total	14,719.84451	81				

Table 2: ANOVA results for Test 1 (both Part 1 and Part 2)

Analysis of Variance (One-Way)

Summary						
Groups	Sample size	Sum	Mean	Variance		
Spring 2013 Test 1: Part 1	42	2,968.	70.66667	121.88618		
Fall 2013 Test 1: Part 1	40	3,046.	76.15	90.74615		
ANOVA						
Source of Variation	SS	df	MS	F	p-level	F crit
Between Groups	616.00569	1	616.00569	5.77296	0.01859	2.76931
Within Groups	8,536.43333	80	106.70542			
Total	9,152.43902	81				

Table 3: ANOVA results for Test 1: Part 1

Analysis of Variance (One-Way)

Summary						
Groups	Sample size	Sum	Mean	Variance		
Spring 2013 Test 1: Part 2	42	2,990.	71.19048	252.3043		
Fall 2013 Test 1: Part 2	40	3,107.	77.675	404.68654		
ANOVA						
Source of Variation	SS	df	MS	F	p-level	F crit
Between Groups	861.49271	1	861.49271	2.63784	0.10828	2.76931
Within Groups	26,127.25119	80	326.59064			
Total	26,988.7439	81				

Table 4: ANOVA results for Test 1: Part 2

To further analyze the results of the proposed methodology, we compared students' grades for Part 1 and Part 2 separately to see which part contributed more to the students' improvement on Test 1. Part 1 included multiple-choice and true-false questions and Part 2 asked students to integrate and apply learned concepts to solve several real-world problems.

Preliminary results for Part 1, presented in Table 3, also indicate a statistically significant improvement in students' performance at the 95% confidence level (p-value = 0.01859). Variances obtained

for each group demonstrate a smaller spread of values for students' grades on Part 1 in Fall 2013 (Fall 2013 variance = 90.74615 vs. Spring 2013 variance = 121.88618).

Preliminary results for Part 2, presented in Table 4, do not indicate a statistically significant improvement in students' performance at the 95% confidence level (p-value = 0.10828). Variances obtained for each group demonstrate a larger spread of values for students' grades on Part 2 in Fall 2013 (Fall 2013 variance = 404.68654 vs. Spring 2013 variance = 252.3043). This was expected because the learning materials tested in Part 2 were not significantly changed between the two semesters.

4. CONCLUSION AND FUTURE WORK

In this study we have discussed a general methodology for the implementation of an personalized competency-based approach in the current college settings. We demonstrated how this approach could be applied in an undergraduate database course. We carried out a preliminary evaluation of the proposed methodology and compared students' performance before and after the proposed approach was implemented in one database course. The results of the analysis indicate a statistically significant improvement in overall students' performance. While our findings demonstrate a significant improvement in students' knowledge acquisition in regards to the theoretical database concepts, they also indicated slower progress in the students' ability to synthesize and effectively apply knowledge across multiple database concepts to solve complex problems.

We will continue to explore how the proposed methodology can be further enhanced to better assist students in developing critical thinking and complex problem solving skills. We will investigate how active, collaborative, technology-enhanced teaching and learning techniques can be combined with the curriculum personalization to create a unique, innovative learning experience for each student in class.

Another direction would be to further develop the unified curriculum repository by making it available online and by creating the community of contributors. With the support of other passionate educators in this group, we hope to intensify our efforts in building the most effective learning environments for students, helping them reach their fullest potential and succeed.

Also we are investigating alternative learning management systems that will allow an easier and more natural support both for personalized learning but also for the organization of the learning materials in modules linked to competencies. Most of the current systems are organizing the learning modules based on defined courses with little flexibility in the dynamic reuse of the modules.

This will allow us to further extend the repository and to apply this methodology to all database courses in the near future and then to extend to the programming courses in the department. We consider, based on the preliminary results obtained, that this methodology is easily adaptable to all information technology programs.

5. REFERENCES

[1] Anderson, T. Ed. 2008. *The theory and practice of online learning.* Athabasca University Press.

[2] Attwell, G. (2007). Personal Learning Environments-the future of eLearning?.*eLearning Papers*, *2*(1), 1-8.

[3] Barr, R. B., & Tagg, J. 1995. From teaching to learning - A new paradigm for undergraduate education. *Change: The magazine of higher learning*, *27*(6), 12-26.

[4] Bargiela, A., & Pedrycz, W. (2003). *Granular computing: an introduction*. Springer.

[5] Beetham, H., and Sharpe, R. Eds. 2013. *Rethinking pedagogy for a digital age: Designing for 21st century learning*. Routledge.

[6] Brophy, J. E. 2013. *Motivating students to learn*. Routledge.

[7] Brown, A. L., and Cocking, R. R. 2000. *How people learn* (pp. 285-348). J. D. Bransford Ed. Washington, DC: National Academy Press.

[8] Candy, P., Crebert, G., and O'leary, J. 1994. Developing lifelong learners through undergraduate education.

[9] Carnevale, A. P., Smith, N., and Melton, M. 2011. STEM: Science, Technology, Engineering and Math. *Washington, DC: Georgetown University Center on Education and the Workforce*.

[10] Chickering, A. W., and Gamson, Z. F. 1987. Seven principles for good practice in undergraduate education. *AAHE bulletin*, *3*, 7.

[11] Christensen, C. M., Horn, M. B., and Johnson, C. W. 2008. *Disrupting class: How disruptive innovation will change the way the world learns* (Vol. 98). New York: McGraw-Hill.

[12] Dolog, P., Henze, N., Nejdl, W., & Sintek, M. (2004, May). Personalization in distributed e-learning environments. In *Proceedings of the 13th international World Wide Web conference on Alternate track papers & posters* (pp. 170-179). ACM.

[13] Draganidis, F., & Mentzas, G. (2006). Competency based management: a review of systems and approaches. *Information Management & Computer Security*, *14*(1), 51-64.

[14] Froyd, J. E. 2008. White paper on promising practices in undergraduate STEM education. *Commissioned paper for the Evidence on Promising Practices in Undergraduate Science, Technology, Engineering, and Mathematics (STEM) Education Project, The National Academies Board on Science Education*.

[15] Hill, J. R., & Hannafin, M. J. (2001). Teaching and learning in digital environments: The resurgence of resource-based learning. *Educational Technology Research and Development*, *49*(3), 37-52.

[16] Jonassen, D. H. (1999). Designing constructivist learning environments. *Instructional design theories and models: A new paradigm of instructional theory*, *2*, 215-239.

[17] Kadijevich, D. M., Angeli, C., & Schulte, C. 2013. Improving Computer Science Education. Routledge.

[18] Land, S. M., & Hannafin, M. J. (2000). Student-centered learning environments. *Theoretical foundations of learning environments*, 1-23.

[19] McLoughlin, C., and Lee, M. J. 2010. Personalized and self regulated learning in the Web 2.0 era: International exemplars of innovative pedagogy using social software. *Australasian Journal of Educational Technology*, *26*(1), 28-43.

[20] National Academy of Engineering (NAE). 2012. Advance personalized learning. Instruction can be individualized based on learning styles, speeds, and interests to make learning more reliable. http://www.engineeringchallenges.org/cms/8996/9127.aspx.

[21] Piccoli, G., Ahmad, R., & Ives, B. (2001). Web-based virtual learning environments: A research framework and a preliminary assessment of effectiveness in basic IT skills training. *MIS quarterly*, 401-426.

[22] Schaefer, D., Utschig, T., and Visco D. 2012. A Proposed Teaching and Learning Curriculum for COMPLEETE Based on Current National Trends. In *Proceedings of 2012 Frontiers in Education Conference*.

[23] Sclater, N. 2008. Web 2.0, personal learning environments, and the future of learning management systems. *Research Bulletin*, 13, 2008-2009.

[24] Siddique, Z., Panchal, J., Schaefer, D., Haroon, S., Allen, J. K., & Mistree, F. (2012). Competencies for Innovating in the 21st Century. In *ASME International Conference on Design Education*.

[25] SMW (2013a) Introduction to Semantic MediaWiki. Available online at: http://www.semantic-mediawiki.org/wiki/Help:Introduction_to_Semantic_Media Wiki. Accessed on: July 1st, 2013.

[26] SMW (2013b) Help: Semantic templates. Available online at: http://www.semantic-mediawiki.org/wiki/Help:Semantic_templates. Accessed on: July 1st, 2013.

[27] SMW (2013c) Help: RDF export. Available online at: http://www.semantic-mediawiki.org/wiki/Help:RDF_export. Accessed on: July 1st, 2013.

[28] Thompson, K. V., Chmielewski, J., Gaines, M. S., Hrycyna, C. A., & LaCourse, W. R. (2013). Competency-based reforms of the undergraduate biology curriculum: integrating the physical and biological sciences. *CBE-Life Sciences Education*, *12*(2), 162-169.

[29] TikiWiki (2013) Tiki Feature Checklist. Available online at: http://info.tikiwiki.org/Tiki+Feature+Checklist. Accessed on: July 1st, 2013.

[30] Twigg, C. A. 2003. Models for online learning. *Educause Review*, 28-38.

[31] Van Harmelen, M. (2006, July). Personal Learning Environments. In *ICALT*(Vol. 6, pp. 815-816).

[32] Wilson, S., Liber, O., Johnson, M., Beauvoir, P., Sharples, P., & Milligan, C. (2009). Personal Learning Environments: Challenging the dominant design of educational systems. *Journal of e-Learning and Knowledge Society-English Version*, *3*(2).

[33] Wolf, A. 1995. *Competence-based assessment*. Buckingham: Open University Press.

[34] Zhang, D., Zhao, J. L., Zhou, L., & Nunamaker Jr, J. F. (2004). Can e-learning replace classroom learning?. *Communications of the ACM*, *47*(5), 75-79.

Answering the Question "Where can I work after I graduate?"

Sandra Gorka
Pennsylvania College of Technology
One College Avenue
Williamsport, PA 17701
+1 (570) 326-3761
sgorka@pct.edu

Jacob Miller
Pennsylvania College of Technology
One College Avenue
Williamsport, PA 17701
+1 (570) 326-3761
jmiller3@pct.edu

ABSTRACT
All of us have been confronted with the question "Where can I work when I graduate?" We all have various answers to provide. This paper discusses the efforts of the authors to put together a visual display to answer this question. The display has become a significant resource for recruiting both for the college and the employers it serves.

Categories and Subject Descriptors
K.3.0 [Computing Milieux]: Computers and Education, General
K.3.2 [Computers and Education]: Computer and Information Science Education

General Terms
Human Factors

Keywords
Information Technology, recruitment

1. INTRODUCTION
For virtually any major or program, knowledge of future employment opportunities is a powerful recruiting tool for the program [1]. While leading tours of the information technology labs, the authors noticed one question that students and parents always ask: "Where can I work after I graduate?" In the past, the answer has always been a quick summary of the places recent graduates (who shared their plans) are employed. The answer was often lacking as it failed to indicate the proper breadth of opportunities afforded our graduates.

In an effort to better answer this question, the authors obtained permission to utilize a newly installed display case that is located near our information technology labs. The display case was filled with SWAG and other small items that represent the companies at which our graduates and current students are employed.

2. COLLECTING SWAG
SWAG was obtained from current students with employment plans as well as from graduates. Current upperclassman planning to graduate within the year were informed of our desire to build the display and many rose to the occasion and provided SWAG as they accepted job offers.

In fall 2013, Pennsylvania College of Technology celebrated 50 years of computing programs offered at the college. As part of this celebration, the Alumni Association invited graduates back to campus for a reunion that included a day of talks and tours. As faculty members helping to coordinate the effort, the authors contacted alumni planning to attend the event and requested they consider participating in the display.

Display items include practical SWAG such as coffee mugs, water bottles, pens, and T shirts. It also includes promotional type items like Frisbees, paperweights, iconic figurines, and medallions with logos.

To show the various segments served by the IT industry, corporate logos are also collected on printed displays. The logos are grouped by industry segments such as banking and finance, healthcare, telecommunications, government, etc.

3. CONCLUSION
Now when perspective students and their parents ask the question, the answer includes a stop at the display case. Although the answer is similar in nature, the display case provides a strong visual message that shows our graduates are employed within many sectors of the marketplace. Parents, in particular, are often found lingering at the display case after the tour has moved on. New prospects do not always understand what the display case represents, but we often see currently enrolled students studying the contents of the case. Most recently it has started to become a directory our students consult when seeking employment or internships.

4. ACKNOWLEDGMENTS
Our thanks to the students, graduates and employers who provided SWAG to fill the display case.

5. REFERENCES
[1] Sullivan, J. (September 20, 2010). The Future of College Recruiting Will be Dominated by Market Research (Part 1 of 2). Retrieved from http://www.ere.net/2010/09/20/the-future-of-college-recruiting-will-be-dominated-by-market-research-part-1-of-2/

Industry Partnerships to Support Computer Science High School Teachers' Pedagogical Content Knowledge

Aleata Hubbard
WestEd
400 Seaport Court, Ste 222
Redwood City, CA 9406-2767
+1 (650) 381-6443
ahubbar@wested.org

Yvonne Kao
WestEd
400 Seaport Court, Ste 222
Redwood City, CA 9406-2767
+1 (650) 381-6404
ykao@wested.org

ABSTRACT

There is a critical need for computer scientists in the new digital age, a need that is not being met largely due to a lack of qualified computing teachers in K-12. In this project, we explore a three-year, on-the-job teacher preparation program (TEALS) that pairs high school educators with computing professionals to teach introductory computing courses. We are currently conducting a mixed-methods study to explore the change in teachers' pedagogical content knowledge within this professional development model.

Categories and Subject Descriptors

K.3.2 [**Computers and Education**]: Computer and Information Science Education – *computer science education, information systems education.*

Keywords

Pedagogical Content Knowledge; Secondary Education; Computer Science Education; Teacher Professional Development; Education Industry Partnership

1. INTRODUCTION

A major barrier to increasing the number of qualified K-12 computer science teachers in the US is that few avenues exist for pre-service and in-service teachers to train in computer science pedagogy. A large body of research has identified the critical types of knowledge needed for effective teaching, including knowledge of the subject, educational aims, and connections to other disciplines. Shulman [2] introduced the idea of pedagogical content knowledge (PCK) as the intersection between content knowledge and general pedagogical knowledge. PCK includes, for example, knowledge of teaching strategies that incorporate appropriate conceptual representations to address learner difficulties and how elements of the content can be arranged for better teaching. Teacher performance on PCK assessments in other fields (e.g., mathematics) correlates with student learning gains [1]. The state of research knowledge about computer science PCK (CSPCK) is not nearly as well developed as the

knowledge of PCK in other domains. To contribute to the research knowledge base about CSPCK, we are conducting an in-depth study of how CSPCK develops in novice computer science teachers and identifying important elements of quality K-12 computer science teacher preparation.

TEALS is a non-profit whose mission is to prepare high school computer science teachers. This 3-year program recruits high-tech professionals to volunteer as part-time computer science teachers. These volunteers co-teach with high school teachers to help them develop the capacity to lead introductory computer science courses. TEALS is working in over 70 schools across 12 states.

Developing CSPCK is a 3-year project to (a) study computer science teacher preparation in the context of TEALS and (b) develop a theoretical framework and preliminary assessment for CSPCK. We are collecting quantitative data on a large sample of TEALS team members and triangulating the results with in-depth case studies of a sub-sample of participants. This combination of methodologies will enable us to reliably measure teacher knowledge change around computer science and student thinking and its relationship to student outcomes. The project is currently in its first year and we are piloting our CSPCK assessment items and case study protocols with teachers and volunteers in the TEALS 2014 cohort.

2. ACKNOWLEDGMENTS

This work is supported by the National Science Foundation under Grant No. 1348866. Any opinions, findings, and conclusions or recommendations expressed in this material are those of the author(s) and do not necessarily reflect the views of the National Science Foundation

3. REFERENCES

[1] Hill, H., Rowan, B., and Ball, D. 2005. Effects of teachers' mathematical knowledge for teaching on student achievement. *American Educational Research Journal*, 42, 2 (Jun. 2005), 371-406. DOI= http://aer.sagepub.com/cgi/doi/10.3102/00028312042002371

[2] Shulman, L. S. 1986. Those who understand: Knowledge growth in teaching. *Educational Researcher*. 15, 2 (Feb. 1986), 4-14. DOI= http://edr.sagepub.com/cgi/doi/10.3102/0013189X015002004.

SIGITE'14, October 15–18, 2014, Atlanta, Georgia, USA.
ACM 978-1-4503-2686-5/14/10.
http://dx.doi.org/10.1145/2656450.2656481

Streamlining Courses for the Web Development Concentration of an IT Bachelor Degree Program

Xing Liu
Kwantlen Polytechnic University
12666 – 72 Avenue
Surrey, BC, Canada
xing.liu@kpu.ca

ABSTRACT

This talk introduces the curriculum of the web concentration of a bachelor of information technology degree that is structured to cover the most important aspects of web design and web development.

Categories and Subject Descriptors

K.3.2 [**Computers and Education**]: Computer and Information Science Education – *Curriculum.*

General Terms

Design

Keywords

Curriculum design; web application development

Web designer and developer has become a computer occupation according to the Canadian Information and Communications Technology Council (ICTC-CTIC) (code C075) and the U.S. Bureau of Labor (code 15-1134). ICTC-CTIC has predicted that Canada will experience constant "skills shortage" in web development up to 2016. In the US, demand for web developers is estimated to increase by 20% with around 50,000 jobs by 2022. On the other hand, research has suggested that a multi-course stream in web development in a computer science curriculum would be beneficial to students [1].

The author's institution has developed a web concentration for its bachelor of information technology degree in order to provide students with in-depth and well-rounded training in web design and web development, and prepare them for employment in the IT departments of various organizations, web design and development companies, as well as for self-employment.

The key courses of the web concentration are shown in Figure 1. Apart from the foundation and liberal education courses, there are eight key courses for students in the web concentration. The curriculum of the Concentration includes web fundamentals in the first year (one course). The course aims to teach web basics such as Internet and World Wide Web, web browsers, web servers, domain names and URLs, and web hosting. The course also discusses HTML, Cascading Style Sheets (CSS) and JavaScript in detail, followed by an overview of web design basics, basic web page layout guidelines, and basic usability concepts. The object-oriented programming course and data structures course are taught in the second year. They are very similar to common object-oriented programming and data structure courses in standard computer science curricula, except with less theoretical analyses. The third year covers more advanced web programming and development as well as web multimedia. Currently the advanced web programming course teaches PHP and MySQL. The web multimedia course teaches digital multimedia basics and their applications in web development, including techniques to incorporate digital multimedia in web pages. In the fourth year, there are three web-related courses: web security, human factors and web design. The web security course examines various potential attacks that may be applied on web applications, ranging from client side to data stores and back-end components. The human factors and HCI (human computer interaction) course primarily deals with cognitive factors in user interface design and examines usability issues in detail. The web design course provides in-depth discussions on web design such as color selection, layout design, usability design, and web implementation by applying advanced HTML and CSS techniques.

Year 4	Web Security	Human Factors and HCI	Web Design
Year 3	Advanced Web Programming	Web Multimedia	
Year 2	Object Oriented Programming	Data structures	
Year 1	Web Fundamentals		

Figure 1: Curriculum for the Web concentration

The web-related courses in the curriculum have had a full run from the first year to the fourth year. Feedback from stake-holders indicates that the design of the curriculum has prepared students for real-world web application development jobs.

REFERENCES

[1] Connolly, R. 2011. Awakening Rip Van Winkle: modernizing the computer science web curriculum. In *Proceedings of the 16th annual joint conference on Innovation and technology in computer education (ITiCSE'11).* Darmstadt, Germany. June 27–29, 2011. 18-22.

SIGITE'14, October 15–18, 2014, Atlanta, Georgia, USA.
ACM 978-1-4503-2686-5/14/10.
http://dx.doi.org/10.1145/2656450.2656480

What Is The Next Big Thing? Fulbright's Half-Life Theory

Ron Fulbright
University of South Carolina Upstate
800 University Way
Spartanburg, SC 29303
(864)503-5683
rfulbright@uscupstate.edu

ABSTRACT

My great-grandparents lived one-half of their lives without electricity. My grandparents lived one-half of their lives without a telephone. My parents lived one-half of their lives without a television. I lived one-half of my life without a computer. Today, we could not imagine life without any of these wonderful innovations. What is it that the current college-age generation will live one-half of their lives without? Whatever it is will come about in around 2020-2025 and will change the way we live, work, and/or recreate, and make billions of dollars. But, it won't be anything we know and love and use today. But, based on past experience, the foundation technology of "the next big thing" is just now in research labs.

Categories and Subject Descriptors

K.4.m [**Computers and Society Miscellaneous**]

General Terms

Management, Human Factors, Legal Aspects.

1. INTRODUCTION

For over a century, each generation has witnessed the advent and mass adoption of technologies we now view as indispensible to our daily lives. At some point in their lives, members of each generation did not have the "must-have" technology available. We ask ourselves what technology the current college-age student is going to adopt mid-way through their lives that will in the future be considered indispensable? We assume a person lives 80 years making the midpoint around age 40. Current college students are about 20 years in age, so have about 20 years to go before reaching their "half-life" point. Can we imagine what technology is likely to be the hot, in-demand thing 20 years from now and make some predictions?

2. THE TECHNOLOGICAL LIFECYCLE

All technologies go through a lifecycle. At some point they are just ideas, then research projects, then new products, then mainstream products, only to eventually become outdated. Study of the evolution of technological systems shows it takes roughly 20 years for a technology to go from the research phase to the mass market phase where millions adopt and use it.

SIGITE'14, October 15–18, 2014, Atlanta, Georgia, USA.
ACM 978-1-4503-2686-5/14/10.
http://dx.doi.org/10.1145/2656450.2661044

(It is difficult to pin such numbers down precisely. All numbers here should be considered estimates.) Therefore, "the next big thing" 20 years from now should be just a research topic currently. This means nothing we are currently using, including Facebook, smartphones, and the Internet will be "the next big thing" 20 years from now. A technology adopted by the masses 20 years from now (2034) should be in prototypical form in 5-10 years (2019-2024). So what kind of technologies are in the research stage now that might generate the must-have technology for the college-age generation?

3. CURRENT RESEARCH TOPICS

Listed here are several emerging technologies. Successful, life-changing products are typically the confluence of several technologies so several of these may combine and may be combined with something we can't even imagine today.

Personalized medicine and healthcare services delivery- In 20 years, we may hardly ever physically go to a doctor's office and we will receive medication and treatments personally designed for us and our ailment. Our body's condition will be continuously monitored and analyzed. Cancers will be detected before tumors.

Artificial body parts- heart, pancreas, ears, eyes, kidneys, fingers, toes, hands, feet, legs, and arm will be common place

Telepresence, holograms, VR glasses- concert and sporting events, like the World Cup, with virtual attendance of 1 billion or more per event by virtue of immersive virtual reality

3D printing- primitive currently, think Star Trek-like replicators

Flexible electronics- credit card sized smart phones expandable to full-sized desktop computer-sized devices or anywhere in between

"Doclets"-paper-sized displays/tablets you can place across your desk to handle multiple documents (not just one computer screen)

UAVs- pervasive use of unmanned aerial vehicles for monitoring, sensing, police, delivery, etc.

Quantum computing- computers solving currently intractable problems, 1,000,000 times faster, new kinds of Big Data analysis

Automated vehicles- driverless vehicles, freight, public transportation, new age "cruise control" for personal vehicles

Digital friends- (e.g. the movie *Her*), people having relationships with artificial entities possessing rich and varied personalities

New energy- locally-owned modular energy units

Nanotechnology- affecting nearly every area of technology

Device-less communication- just talk, ambient computing technology delivers the message –no devices needed

Learning Within a Professional Environment: Shared Ownership of an HFOSS Project

Heidi J. C. Ellis
Stoney Jackson
Western New England University
ellis@wne.edu; stoney.jackson@wne.edu

Darci Burdge
Lori Postner
Nassau Community College
darci.burdge@ncc.edu; lori.postner@ncc.edu

Gregory W. Hislop
Drexel University
011-215-895-2179
hislop@drexel.edu

Joanmarie Diggs
Igalia, S.L.
Spain
jdiggs@igalia.com

ABSTRACT

This paper describes student learning within the environment of an HFOSS project that is jointly shared between the GNOME Accessibility Team and three academic institutions. This effort differs from many project-based learning efforts in that the project is shared between the academic participants and the HFOSS community. By involving students in an HFOSS project, learning is started via apprenticeship which allows students to learn from professionals while preparing them for their professional life. Learning within the community of an ongoing FOSS project guides students in the first steps towards understanding the importance of life-long learning as well as providing an initial understanding of the ways in which such learning occurs. The results of a student survey and observations of student reflection papers are discussed.

Categories and Subject Descriptors

K.3.2 [**Computers and Education**]: Computer and Information Science Education – *computer science education.*

General Terms

Human Factors

Keywords

Humanitarian Free and Open Source Software; Student Projects

1. INTRODUCTION

The Curriculum Guidelines for Undergraduate Degree Programs including those for Information Technology [1] and Computer Science [2] emphasize the need for students to obtain experience working on a project of substantial size. Experience with such projects provides students with an understanding of working in a team, project management, professionalism, and exposure to the issues involved in developing a complex, sizeable project.

Student projects can be broadly categorized into three general categories. Some student projects are collaborations with industry [3,4] where an industry partner operates as the client for the project and provides technical information and sometimes oversight. The advantages of this type of project include close academic alignment with the industry partner, potential for professional feedback, and the possibility of future employment for students. The main disadvantage is that all work products typically belong to the industry partner and cannot belong to a visible portfolio of student work. A second category is using a home-grown project where the class, department, or institution develops a project for a client either within or outside of the academic institution [5,6]. Advantages are ease of instructor management of the project and flexibility of allowing students to choose a project to their liking. Disadvantages include possible issues with managing clients and fulfilling client expectations as well as lack of a professional community to interact with the students. The last category is working on a Free and Open Source Software (FOSS) project [7-9]. Students either join an active project or modify an open source project that is no longer being developed. Advantages include easy accessibility of artifacts, access to a diverse professional community and the ability for students to create an online professional portfolio. Disadvantages include dependence on the unpredictable schedule of a FOSS project and the learning curve for FOSS culture and tools.

The FOSS-based form of a student project that is addressed in this paper differs from the industry and home-grown project approaches in two ways. In most of the industry-based and home-grown project experiences, students are typically only exposed to a subset of the activities and artifacts of the project. Involvement in a FOSS project exposes students to the entire spectrum of activities and project deliverables that span a project. Second, in the industry-based and home-grown project approaches, students are only occasionally involved with professionals related to the project (other than the instructor). In the approach discussed in this paper, students are immersed in the project and the community where they interact frequently with professionals working on the project. It is this broad exposure to project artifacts and the professional community that provide the foundation for student life-long learning.

SIGITE'14, October 15–18, 2014, Atlanta, GA, USA.
Copyright is held by the owner/author(s). Publication rights licensed to ACM.
ACM 978-1-4503-2686-5/14/10…$15.00.
http://dx.doi.org/10.1145/2656450.2656468

This paper reports on a unique approach where students are involved in a FOSS project that is jointly shared between the GNOME Accessibility Team and originally three and now one academic institution. The paper describes the project and presents evidence of student learning from activities thus far.

2. BACKGROUND

Participating in professional practice is a widely used educational model that spans the construction trades (apprenticeship), nursing and medicine (clinical practices), education (student teaching, post-doctoral research), law (clerkships) and more. These forms of learning via participation are characterized by students interacting with and gaining knowledge from more experienced practitioners.

Student involvement in FOSS projects has been increasingly adopted by education due to the opportunities for students to gain professional experience with a real-world project [7-10]. In addition to the benefits of ease of access to artifacts including code, low cost, and openness to participation by volunteers, FOSS projects provide students with a distributed professional community within which to learn. This combination of available artifacts, accessible professional community, and the wide array of communication mechanisms available on the Internet today support a form of virtual apprenticeship. Students gain professional experience in large, complex, real-world environments that cannot be reproduced in traditional classrooms.

Communities of practice [11], is a common model used to describe how FOSS projects operate and has been suggested as a relevant theoretical base for computing education research [12]. In the communities of practice model, a group is engaged to complete a common goal. Students participating in a FOSS project are practicing a cognitive apprenticeship form of community of practice [13]. In this apprenticeship, learning is based on the experts of the FOSS community who are "masters of the craft".

Meisner [14] has identified advantages to learning within a community including a wider range of learning resources and a support system that contains experts with a variety of backgrounds. In the GNU/Linux project, Davis and Jabeen [15] identified a positive correlation between participation in community and perceived learning. Glott [16] discovered that student involvement in FOSS communities can support a wide variety of learning including professional skills, patents and licensing, management skills, coding skills and more. FOSS projects have the additional advantage of supporting a wide range of learning approaches including problem-based learning, collaborative learning, active learning and more [17].

The form of apprenticeship utilized in a FOSS project is typically legitimate peripheral participation (LPP) [11]. LPP is the process by which students gain entry to the FOSS project and progress towards becoming contributing members [18]. In LPP, neophytes are gradually introduced to the community starting with observing and listening, progressing through small interactions to larger interactions when the student becomes a full community member.

3. THE PROJECT

This section describes the MouseTrap project and the collaborative effort between academic institutions and the GNOME Accessibility Team that is developing the software. MouseTrap is an application to aid users with disabilities who cannot easily use a hardware mouse. MouseTrap uses a web cam to track the user's forehead and moves the cursor on screen mirroring the user's head movement.

The academic partners in the project are two faculty members each from Nassau Community College, Western New England University (WNE), and Drexel University. These faculty members have anywhere from one to seven years of experience involving students in humanitarian FOSS (HFOSS) projects. This effort is part of an ongoing research study into student and faculty learning via student participation in HFOSS [9, 19].

MouseTrap was started in 2008 as a Google Summer of Code project. MouseTrap was primarily developed by a single person with help from another three developers. It was actively developed until spring of 2010 when the primary maintainer of the code stopped contributing to the project.

In fall 2012, Joanmarie Diggs, co-team lead of the GNOME Accessibility Team and member of GNOME Foundation Board of Directors, approached the three academic partners with the idea to share ownership of the project. Joanmarie Diggs proposed the GNOME Outreach Program for Professors which intends to get faculty up to speed on FOSS culture and tools by giving academic institutions responsibility for GNOME projects. Each of the three academic institutions involved identified one to three students who were interested in working on the MouseTrap project.

Between the time that development stopped in 2010 and resumed again in 2013, the technologies upon which MouseTrap depends evolved and new versions of Python, OpenCV and GNOME were released. These changes created a steep learning curve for the development team as they had to understand multiple versions of each technology and their interdependencies in order to make Mousetrap current. Summer 2013 efforts focused on planning and preparing for the necessary upgrades to be undertaken by students in a fall 2013 Software Engineering course.

The management of the MouseTrap project is shared between the academic institutions and the GNOME Accessibility Team with Western New England University taking the lead. Within the project, the faculty, students, and HFOSS community serve different roles. The GNOME Accessibility Team serves as a resource and guiding hand for the project. They provide students and faculty with the overall direction for the project as well as aiding in code understanding, professional interactions, technical knowledge, understanding of FOSS culture, and knowledge of community practice. Faculty members have a leadership and mentoring role. Faculty are responsible for conducting meetings, guiding planning decisions, overseeing process, directing students to resources, and connecting students with members of the HFOSS community. Students have a developer/researcher role and investigate technologies, analyze the system, identify issues, and write code and documentation.

At the time of this writing, MouseTrap is still under development with WNE being the most active institution. Key progress has been made on several fronts. Given that MouseTrap had not been actively developed in three years, many of the technologies used had changed (Python, OpenCV, etc.). Given the state of the existing code, we decided that a redesign was necessary rather than simply upgrading the existing code. We now have the skeleton of a new design in place and MouseTrap has been ported Python 3. The Python 3 bindings for the OpenCV libraries have just been released and the next step is to incorporate these into MouseTrap. MouseTrap has also been ported to GNOME 3.

4. STUDENT LEARNING

When the collaboration to develop MouseTrap was formed, students were hired to work on the project. Students started by downloading and installing the project and creating instructions for doing so. Students then went on to test the application and to start to document issues to be fixed. Concurrently, both faculty and students were learning FOSS culture and tools. By the summer of 2013, faculty and students had a basic understanding of the project sufficient to support continual development. While a great deal of learning occurred during this time, we did not have instruments to measure this learning.

MouseTrap was first used in the classroom during the fall 2013 term in a 15 week, senior-level course at Western New England University with six students. The course covers the main software development phases of requirements, design, implementation, test, and maintenance. The course was organized around the MouseTrap project with 60% of the course grade based on project deliverables and 40% on homework.

Students were introduced to the project and to the GNOME Accessibility Team in the first week of class. The IRC channels for the GNOME Accessibility Team and MouseTrap were open during class meetings. As questions about the project arose during class, those questions would frequently be posed to the community on the spot using IRC. The first homework required students to follow the instructions to download and install MouseTrap and to report back on problems and how to fix them.

As the course progressed, students wrote a requirements document that was formally reviewed in class and then the document was revised based on the results of the review. A similar process was used for the design specification. These documents are posted on the GNOME MouseTrap wiki. Some of the project deliverables used templates of IEEE Specifications (e.g., IEEE Std 830-1998) and were submitted as Word documents. The homeworks supported the deliverables in some manner. For instance, one homework divided up the reviewed and revised requirements among all students in the class and each student was responsible for posting their portion of the requirements to the GNOME MouseTrap wiki.

As part of the course, students attended the GNOME Summit held in Montreal October 12-14, 2013. The Summit is a hackfest for GNOME developers and contributors with the goal of pushing GNOME and its applications forward. Students worked with Joanmarie Diggs and other GNOME developers on MouseTrap and other projects. Karen Sandler, the GNOME Foundation's executive director, gave students a tutorial on licenses. Students returned from this trip incredibly excited about FOSS and MouseTrap and related many stories about professional interactions and lessons learned. Many commented that the GNOME Summit was the highlight of the term.

Two main sources were used to ascertain student self-reported learning within the course. The first approach was to survey students before and after the course. This survey is part of a larger NSF-funded study of student opinion of involvement in HFOSS [9]. The second approach was to examine student reflection papers written at the end of the course for evidence of learning. These papers asked students to reflect on their learning within the course and in particular about the difference between their learning in the HFOSS project versus a more traditional classroom environment. These approaches to understanding student learning are discussed below.

4.1 Survey

The survey used to ascertain student opinion of involvement in an HFOSS project asked for some student background information as well as eliciting student opinion of three aspects of the impact of student participation in HFOSS:

1. Impact on student attitude towards computing
2. Perceived student learning related to application development
3. Impact on selection of major and career plans

All six students completed both the pre and post surveys.

Opinions on the three aspects of student participation were elicited using 5-point Likert scale sections in the survey. The response values were "strongly disagree", "disagree", "neutral", "agree", and "strongly agree". "Don't know" and "Not applicable" options were also provided. Examples of each of the three types of items are shown in Table 1 below:

Table 1. Sample items for three aspects of HFOSS survey

Attitude	Application Development	Major and Career
Working on an HFOSS project gives me a better appreciation for the usefulness of computing.	I can list the steps in the software process we used in HFOSS project.	The subject matter of this HFOSS project is highly relevant to my future career plans.

In order to gain some insight into the survey results, the responses were converted to an ordinal number from one to five with one representing the "strongly disagree" response and the five representing the "strongly agree" response. Due to the small number of participants, only general observations can be made about the results, but some interesting results were observed.

One aspect of investigation is to look at the average responses for the post-course survey as this provides some insight into student opinion at the end of the course. One interesting observation is that the average post-survey response to every Likert item was above the neutral rating. This provides evidence that students are generally positively impacted by participation in an HFOSS project. It is also interesting to note that five items (out of nine) in the area of attitude towards computing had an average score greater than 4.0 as shown in Table 2.

Table 2. Attitude items - average post-course score > 4.0

Item	Avg
Working on an HFOSS project gives me a better appreciation for the usefulness of computing.	4.5
I have a greater awareness of the potential for computing to benefit society due to working on an HFOSS project.	4.8
Working with an HFOSS community to develop a project has increased my interest in computing.	4.3
Working on an HFOSS project increases my interest in computing.	4.3
Participating in an HFOSS project made me more comfortable with computing.	4.3

These results appear to indicate that on average, students more than "agreed" that working on an HFOSS project had a positive impact on their attitude towards computing. Of particular interest is that five students indicated that they "strongly agreed" and one student indicated that they "agreed" that they gained a better understanding of the potential for computing to benefit society based on their experience working on an HFOSS project.

When considering learning about application development, five items (out of 12) had an average score greater than 4.0 as shown in Table 3. It is interesting to note that three of these five items are related to the professional aspects of application development as opposed to the technical aspects. This appears support the fact that student learning within a community is effective.

Table3. App. dev. items - average post-course score > 4.0

Item	Avg
I can use a software process to develop an HFOSS project.	4.4
I am sure that I can actively participate in an HFOSS community to develop a software project.	4.2
I can use all tools and techniques employed in my HFOSS project.	4.2
I can participate in an HFOSS development team's interactions.	4.3
Participation in an HFOSS project has improved my understanding of how to behave like a computing professional.	4.3

Of the seven items relating to major and career section, only two received an average score above 4.0, shown in Table 4. More items may not have been observed as above 4.0 due to the nature of the item. For instance, one item states: "Participation in an HFOSS project has caused me to consider computing as a major or minor" but since the students surveyed were seniors, they were already committed to the Computer Science major.

Table 4. Major/career items - average post-course score > 4.0

Item	Avg
Participation in an HFOSS project has positively reinforced my decision to make computing my major.	4.2
Overall, I am very satisfied with my learning in the HFOSS project.	4.3

It is also of interest to look at the change between student opinions before the course and after the course. The data set is too small for a 2-tailed t-test to be meaningful. However, a simple observation of the difference between the pre-course and post-course survey averages provides some interesting observations. Of particular interest is that the change from pre-course average to post-course average happens in both a positive (post-course average is higher than pre-course average) and in a negative (post-course average is lower than pre-course average) direction.

Table 5. Items with negative difference < -0.5

Area	Item	Avg
Attitude	I wanted to work on an HFOSS project because I want to help the people who would benefit from the software.	-0.67
Attitude	Working on an HFOSS project increased my confidence in my computing ability.	-0.70
Application Development	I am confident that I can maintain an HFOSS project.	-0.58

The following paragraphs explain changes greater than 0.5 in the positive or negative direction. Three items negatively changed when comparing pre- and post-course surveys. Table 5 shows these items including their general survey area. The negative shift in the item pertaining to the confidence in computing ability may be due to the fact that this is the first time that students have been exposed to a sizeable, complex project and are gaining a better understanding of the scope of computing.

There were eight items that showed a positive change from pre- to post- survey averages (see Table 6). One interesting observation is that seven of the eight items were in the area of application development. It appears that students felt that they gained knowledge about application development from participating in an HFOSS project. The first five items that showed a large difference align with earlier results [9] that indicate a significant positive difference (p <= 0.1) between pre-course and post-course surveys. The one area that differs from previous work is the positive change in the item related to understanding how to behave like a computing professional. The earlier work shows a significant negative difference between pre- and post-course averages. One possible reason for the increase shown with this group of students is the higher degree of interaction with the HFOSS community which may be due to the sharing of the project between the GNOME Accessibility Team and the academic institutions. It is also of interest to note that students had a marked positive change in their opinion of their experience-level with HFOSS.

Table 6. Items with positive difference > 0.5

Area	Item	Avg
Application Development	I can list the steps in the software process we used in HFOSS project.	0.60
Application Development	I can use a software process to develop an HFOSS project.	0.73
Application Development	I can describe the impact of project complexity on the approaches used to develop software.	0.58
Application Development	I can describe the impact of project size on the approaches used to develop software.	0.63
Application Development	I can describe the drawbacks and benefits of OSS to society.	1.0
Application Development	I can use all tools and techniques employed in my HFOSS project.	0.83
Application Development	Participation in an HFOSS project has improved my understanding of how to behave like a computing professional.	1.33
Major/Career	I have a high level of experience in the HFOSS subject matter.	1.17

4.2 Analysis of Reflection Papers

In addition to the surveys, students wrote papers at the end of the term that required them to reflect on their learning experiences, and in particular to comment on the difference of learning within a traditional classroom and their learning within an HFOSS project. The 1500-word reflection paper required students to reflect and report on experiences in "Climbing the Contributor Mountain." Chapter 2 of the Practical Open Source Exploration text [20] describes the path that a typical person new to open source software takes to learning within the FOSS environment. Students were asked to directly address:

- How did classroom learning help in climbing the contributor mountain?
- How did involvement in the FOSS community contribute to learning outside of the classroom?

These papers were analyzed for evidence of student learning within the community. Specifically, the papers were examined for evidence that supported five aspects of student learning. The first three aspects are the three main aspects covered by the Likert sections of the survey:

1. Attitude: Impact on student attitude towards computing
2. Learning about application development: Perceived student learning related to development of applications
3. Career: Impact on selection of major and career plans

In reviewing the papers, two additional aspects became apparent as impacting student learning within an HFOSS project:

4. Community: Impact of community on learning
5. Difference in Learning: Perceived difference in learning as compared to the traditional classroom

Table 7 summarizes the results of examining six student reflection papers for evidence of the impact of student learning within a FOSS environment. The number of comments related to learning about application development and the differences in learning styles are likely a direct response to the structure of the assignment. It is interesting to note that there were nine observed comments from all six students about the community which was not a direct focus of the assignment.

Table 7. Aspects of learning and frequency in papers

Aspect	Total # Comments	% Student Papers
Attitude	9	100%
Learning about Application Dev.	12	100%
Career	6	50%
Community	9	100%
Difference in Learning	20	100%

Comments related to their attitude towards computing appear to indicate that they enjoyed contributing to a FOSS project and that they found the experience rewarding. Comments included:

- "I think that after learning about all of the benefits of Free Open Source Software it is hard for anybody to resist wanting to get involved, the learning curve is steep but extremely rewarding."
- "This unique endeavor has shown me that I enjoy contributing to projects that many people will benefit from and/or help with for a common goal."

The aspect of learning about application development received the largest number of comments which covered learning of professional issues as well as of tools and approaches. Comments included:

- "CS 490 also taught me practical tools such as cost estimation for programming."
- "Also, for the first time, we were able to get an understanding of who the customers were, and why we were working on this project."

Comments about the impact of participation on their career hopes included several comments about attending the GNOME Summit. Based on comments, students appeared to gain an understanding of professionalism as well as confidence in their abilities:

- "... the feeling of professionalism that the [GNOME] summit gave me was a greatly welcomed taste of what the future has in store for me."
- "Going to the conference [GNOME Summit] gave our class a lot more confidence, especially me, that we can be of more help than we originally thought."

The aspect of community was one that all students mentioned had an impact on learning. This aspect was not a direct focus of the reflection paper and it is interesting that students identified it as impacting their learning. Student comments indicate that they found the community helpful and supportive in their learning:

- "I found if you check your ego at the door, and do your best to provide useful, beneficial contributions the community will appreciate your work and push you in the correct direction."
- "It was moments like this when it felt like we were no longer simply students on our way to becoming developers or software engineers, but that we were members of this community of people and that like everyone else we were at the summit to put our time and effort towards creating a program."

Student impressions of the difference in their learning within an HFOSS project appear to indicate that involvement in a sizeable project and community provided some understanding of the need for life-long learning:

- "This experience has been invaluable and will change how I continue to learn as a Software Engineer throughout my career."
- "Rather than coming off like a lecture of different tools and skills, it felt more like a more experienced co-worker giving advice and tools-of-the-trade to a newcomer."

4.3 Observations

While six is too small a sample size from which to draw concrete conclusions, some interesting trends can be observed from examination of the survey responses and reflection papers. One of the most striking observations is that students felt that they gained a great deal of knowledge about application development as supported by both survey results and examination of reflection papers. This result in itself is not surprising. However, the actual learning appeared to go far beyond the topics covered within the course and included a better understanding of professional issues such as communication and teamwork. Students felt that they gained real-world experience and knowledge of how to navigate in the professional world. They are better prepared to enter an industry position that involves project development.

Another interesting result is that students appear to enjoy learning within a community of professionals. Working within such a community increases interest in computing and motivation to continue in computing as evidenced by the very positive comments about the GNOME Accessibility Team and the GNOME Summit. Students felt that the community was supportive, non-judgmental and helped them learn. Student comments reflected an appreciation for their fellow developers within the community and for the encouraging environment that allowed them to explore and learn in the manner that they preferred. One student commented: "Not many people can say they got help from big contributors to GNOME and it was probably one of the coolest experiences I've had in my field."

Lastly, it appears that involvement in an HFOSS project changed not only what students learned, but how they learned. They appear to have gained understanding of the need for life-long learning as well as discernment about how this type of learning differs from classroom learning. One student commented: "This experience has been invaluable and will change how I continue to learn as a Software Engineer throughout my career." And a second said: "Learning from the open source community was different than classroom learning, as we were directed to investigate the problem in a different approach then typical classroom styles."

5. THE FUTURE

The MouseTrap project is under active development. The focus of the effort is to get MouseTrap working with the most recent version of the OpenCV libraries. Once that has been accomplished, additional features will be added such as allowing the user to select the facial feature to be tracked.

Plans for utilizing Mousetrap in academia include involving a greater number of students in the project. Students in introductory classes could help in testing the application and Information Technology students could be utilized to test and document how MouseTrap can be downloaded and installed on a variety of Linux platforms.

Lastly, the GNOME Accessibility Team has several other projects in need of development. It is hoped that additional academic institutions will partner with GNOME to develop these projects in the future.

6. ACKNOWLEDGMENTS

This material is based on work supported by the National Science Foundation under Grant Nos. - DUE-1225708, DUE-1225738, and DUE-1225688. Any opinions, findings and conclusions or recommendations expressed in this material are those of the author(s) and do not necessarily reflect the views of the National Science Foundation (NSF).

7. REFERENCES

[1] Information Technology 2008, Curriculum Guidelines for Undergraduate Degree Programs in Information Technology. ACM. Available at: http://www.acm.org//education/curricula/IT2008%20Curriculum.pdf

[2] ACM/IEEE-CS Joint Task Force on Computing Curricula. Computer Science Curricula 2013. ACM Press and IEEE Computer Society Press. December 2014.

[3] Bolinger, J.; Yackovich, K.; Ramnath, R.; Ramanathan, J.; Soundarajan, N 2010. From Student to Teacher: Transforming Industry Sponsored Student Projects into Relevant, Engaging, and Practical Curricular Materials, *Proc. Transforming Engineering Education: Creating Interdisciplinary Skills for Complex Global Environments, 2010 IEEE,* 1-21.

[4] Knudson, D.; Radermacher, A., 2011. Updating CS capstone projects to incorporate new agile methodologies used in industry, *24th IEEE-CS Conf. on Software Engineering Education and Training, 2011.*444-448.

[5] Longstreet, C.S.; Cooper, K., 2013. Experience report: A sustainable serious educational game capstone project, *Conf. on Computer Games: AI, Animation, Mobile, Interactive Multimedia, Educational & Serious Game,* ,217-221.

[6] Katz, E.P., 2010. Software Engineering Practicum Course Experience, *23rd IEEE Conf. on Software Engineering Education and Training,* 2010, 169-172.

[7] Marmorstein, R. 2011. Open Source Contribution as an Effective Software Engineering Class Project, *Proceedings of the 16th Annual Joint Conference on Innovation and Technology in Computer Science Education,* 268-272.

[8] Ellis, H.J.C., Hislop, G.W., Chua, M., and Dziallas, S., 2011. How to Involve Students in FOSS Projects, *The 2011 Frontiers in Education Conference,* T1H-1,T1H-6 .

[9] Ellis, H.J.C., Hislop, G.W., Rodriguez, J.S., and Morelli, R.A. 2012. Student Software Engineering Learning via Participation in Humanitarian FOSS Projects *119th Association for Engineering Education Annual Conference and Exposition.*

[10] Ludi, S. 2011. The benefits and challenges of using educational game projects in an undergraduate software engineering course, *Proceedings of the 1st International Workshop on Games and Software Engineering,* 13-16.

[11] Lave, J. and Wenger, E. 1991. *Situated learning: Legitimate peripheral participation.* Cambridge, Cambridge University Press. 1991.

[12] Fincher, S., and Tenenberg, J. 2006. Using theory to inform capacity-building: Bootstrapping communities of practice in computer science education, *Journal of Engineering Education,* 95 (4), 265-278.

[13] Collins, A. 2006. "Cognitive Apprenticeship, *Chapter in Cambridge Handbook of the Learning Sciences, Series:* Cambridge Handbooks in Psychology, 47-61.

[14] Meiszner, A., Glott, R., and Sowe, S.K. 2008. Free / Libre Open Source Software (FLOSS) Communities as an Example of Successful Open Participatory Learning Ecosystems , *UPGRADE* IX (3) 62-68.

[15] Davis, D., and Jabeen, I. 2011. Legitimate peripheral participation in the GNU/Linux community, http://misterdavis.org/foss_survey/presentation_of_findings/Davis_Jabeen_LPP_Linux_current.pdf

[16] Glott, R., Andreas, M., Sulayman, K., et al. 2007. Report to FLOSSCom - Using the Principles of Informal Learning Environments of FLOSS Communities to Improve ICT Supported Formal Education: Phase 1 - Analysis of the Informal Learning Environment of FLOSS (Free/Libre Open Source Software) Communities, http://www.scribd.com/doc/1949795/Report-on-the-learning-environment-of-Free-Libre-Open-Source-Software-FLOSS-communities Retrieved 1/8/12.

[17] Weller, M., Meizsner, A., Sowe, S.K. and Karoulis, 2008. "A Report to FLOSSCom - Using the Principles of Informal Learning Environments of FLOSS Communities to Improve ICT Supported Formal Education: Phase 2 - Report on the effectiveness of a FLOSS-like learning community in formal educational settings, http://citeseerx.ist.psu.edu/viewdoc/download?doi=10.1.1.145.4225&rep=rep1&type=pdf

[18] Ye, Y. and Kishida, K., 2003. Toward an Understanding of the Motivation of Open Source Software Developers, *25th International Conference on Software Engineering ,* 419-429.

[19] Ellis, H.J.C., Jackson, S., Burdge, D., Hislop, G.W., and Diggs, J. 2013. Developing HFOSS Projects Using Integrated Teams Across Levels and Institutions, *14th Annual Conference in Information Technology Education.*

[20] "Practical Open Source Software Exploration" Available at: http://teachingopensource.org/index.php/Textbook_Release_0.8. 2012.

Research Skills for Software Engineering Undergraduates in Dutch Universities of Applied Sciences

Mortaza S. Bargh
Creating 010
Rotterdam University of
Applied Sciences, The Netherlands
m.shoae.bargh@hr.nl

Annette van Rooij-Peiman
CMI institute
Rotterdam University of
Applied Sciences, The Netherlands
a.c.van.rooij-peiman@hr.nl

Leo Remijn
CMI institute
Rotterdam University of
Applied Sciences, The Netherlands
l.n.m.remijn@hr.nl

Sunil Choenni
Creating 010
Rotterdam University of
Applied Sciences, The Netherlands
r.choenni@hr.nl

ABSTRACT

Undergraduate students who seek a bachelor degree in Dutch universities of applied sciences are supposed to learn also research skills so that they can provide innovative solutions to real problems of the society and businesses in their future careers. Current education and textbooks on research skills are not tuned well to software engineering disciplines. This paper describes our vision about the scope and model of the research suitable for software engineering disciplines in Dutch universities of applied sciences. Based on literature study we identify a number of research models that are commonly used in computer science. Through reviewing a number of graduation reports in our university, we further identify which of the research models are most suitable for the (graduation) projects of software engineering disciplines and also investigate their shortcomings with respect to the desired research skills. Our study reveals that the approach of most graduation works is close to the implementation-based (also called build-based or proof by example based) research model. In order to be considered as a realization of sound applied research, however, most of theses graduation works need to be improved on a number of aspects such as problem context definition, system/prototype evaluation, and critical literature study.

Categories and Subject Descriptors

K.3.2 [**Computers and Education**]: Computer and Information Science Education – *curriculum, computer science education*

Keywords

Applied science; education; research skills; software engineering; undergraduates

1. INTRODUCTION

In The Netherlands there are two types of universities: Dutch universities of applied sciences and Dutch scientific universities.

SIGITE'14, October 15–18, 2014, Atlanta, GA, USA.
Copyright © 2014 ACM 978-1-4503-2686-5/14/10...$15.00
http://dx.doi.org/10.1145/2656450.2656477

These universities provide higher-level vocational education and highly specialized (and scientific) education, respectively. There are 38 universities of applied sciences in the Netherlands currently, which are responsible for educating about two-thirds of the country's higher education students [18]. These applied universities deliver mainly bachelor level education in a vast variety of disciplines and prepare their graduates for professions with a hands on experience mentality. In recent years these applied universities have aimed at embedding research skills in their curricula in an attempt to prepare their graduates for the rising dynamicity and volatility that we witness in various professions and expertise areas. The dynamicity and volatility stem from the fast pace of innovations occurring in areas such as Information and Computer Technology (ICT).

Mastering research skills is considered important and necessary for the graduates of Dutch universities of applied sciences nowadays. These graduates will be future experts and practitioners who are supposed to act as knowledge-oriented professionals. In the field of ICT, such professionals should translate and transform scientific results to practical applications within various application domains like healthcare, logistics and transport, education, wellbeing and (business) administration. The objective is to equip these professionals with a set of tools and skills so that they can independently consume computer science knowledge and produce useful and useable solutions that address real problems of individuals and organizations. In this way they directly contribute to innovations in ICT (application) fields.

Following the trend at Dutch universities of applies sciences, the board of Rotterdam University of Applied Sciences (RUAS), for example, has envisioned educating its bachelor students on research skills along the following directions [11]: *having a researcher attitude and mentality* where the student works methodically, interprets relevant data, reflects critically (on, for example, the objectives, assumptions, context, approach and results), forms own opinions and draws conclusions; *having an entrepreneurial attitude and mentality* where the student is problem-oriented and result-driven and tries to find practical solutions for real problems; *being multidisciplinary*, where the student has an eye on a broader context and reflects on the bigger picture than of own work; and *being communicative*, where the student conveys the solutions and the corresponding argumentations to the public and experts. Similar objectives are envisioned within other Dutch universities of applied sciences.

There is, however, a gap between the envisioned generic research skills (mentioned above) and the desired research skills that are applicable for the computer and software engineering graduates at the bachelor level. Within RUAS there are three disciplines concerned with software engineering, namely: Informatics (INF) for application related software development, Media Technology (MT) for Human Computer Interaction related software development, and Technical Informatics (TI) for infrastructure related software development. In regard to the envisioned and desired research skills, the current curricula of these disciplines do not nurture adequately the education of research skills and some individuals – ranging from lecturers, students, coaches at associated companies and organizations – unjustifiably and ironically get an impression that these ambitions do not match with or even contradict the way that software engineering disciplines and professions work. Therefore it has become a challenge to motivate these individuals to pursue and educate the research skills mentioned.

One of the reasons behind the existing gap is lack of classical books on the research methodologies and skills needed in the field of computer science and software engineering. Although the existing college books cover a broad spectrum of research skills, for example [3] [4] [15] [10], we have not found a textbook suitable for our target group. Lack of such classical books, in turn, stems from or is related to the fact that computer science and software engineering are relatively new disciplines where research methods are less known compared to those of other disciplines. Also the research in these fields has a volatile and dynamic nature as a result of coping with continuous and rapid developments occurring in ICT fields.

In this contribution we intend to translate the vision of RUAS board into the domain(s) of the software engineering disciplines and move one step towards embedding the required research skills and topics in the curricula of these disciplines. Specifically, the research questions that we would like to address hereto are:
- What does mean research for software engineering disciplines at the bachelor level in universities of applied sciences?
- Which research models are relevant for software engineering disciplines?
- What changes and adaptions are needed to the current approaches of the TI, INF and MT disciplines to enhance the ongoing practices to the level desired?

More specifically, we would like to identify the gaps between how teaching and applying research skills are practiced currently and how they should be practiced in order to prepare RUAS students for finding practical and innovative solutions for real problems. For example, we have to know the shortcomings of the current approaches that students use in executing their assignments with respect to applying the relevant research skills. Hereto it is imperative first to define the set of the research models relevant for software engineering disciplines. Answering these questions will ultimately enable us to develop a scheme for embedding the desired research skills seamlessly in the corresponding curricula. This contribution, which pioneers on its topic in The Netherlands, aims at encouraging the stakeholders (i.e., lecturers, educational staff, students and industry partners) to improve the ways of teaching, learning and applying the research skills within software engineering disciplines.

The paper is organized as follows. Section 2 provides some preliminary information about our research methodology, a generic definition of research and the common research models used in computer science. Our vision of research for software engineering education is described in Section 3. Section 4 presents our analysis of research skill status in INF, MT and TI disciplines, identifies the shortcomings, and elaborates upon improvement aspects. Finally Section 5 draws some conclusions and outlines a number of directions for future work.

2. PRELIMINARIES

2.1 Methodology

This paper is the result of a participatory research, mainly to develop a vision for improving the software engineering education at RUAS. We formed a workgroup consisting of 3 educators who conferred with about 10 other educators from the above-mentioned disciplines in different occasions (including one brainstorming session and three workshops). The workgroup met weekly to brainstorm and share experience about the issues and the (provisionary) solution directions. Through these brainstorming sessions and workshops we took a bottom up approach to elucidate and elicit the tacit knowledge of the practitioners (i.e., carried out a participatory research).

In between these meetings, the workgroup members conducted literature study to learn from the best practices and the state of the art. This study led to identifying 6 generic research models used in computer science and software engineering (see Subsection 2.3). Subsequently we systematically reviewed 60 reports of bachelor graduation projects (see Section 4). We used the reports of the graduation projects, as they are the most comprehensive and representative projects carried out within their curricula. We developed a protocol to review these reports (to be described in Subsection 4.1), whereby we classified the graduation reports according to the identified generic research models. Subsequently we identified the existing shortcomings from the viewpoint of how well the students applied the corresponding research models. Knowing these shortcomings led us to come up with some measures to complement the current approaches so that they accommodate and nurture the desired research skills (see Subsections 4.2).

2.2 Definitions

According to Ellis and Levy [5] research is the process of collecting and analyzing new information/data in order to enhance the body of knowledge, i.e., to create identifiable new knowledge, in an applicable domain. Similarly, Archer [2] considers research as a systematic enquiry in order to produce communicable knowledge. In other words, research is done according to a plan (i.e., being systematic) to find answers to some questions (i.e., being inquiry based). The result of research should be understandable to an audience (i.e., being communicable) and be more than mere information (i.e., being knowledge).

When the acquired information is new for an entity (a person or an organization) but is already known in the literature of that domain, the process is not considered research [8]. In order to determine whether an endeavor is research one has to ask the following questions according to [2]: (1) "Was the activity directed towards the acquisition of knowledge?" (2) "Was it systematically conducted?" (3) "Were the findings explicit?" (4) Was the record of the activity transparent and replicable? (5) "Were the data employed, and the outcome arrived at, validated in appropriate ways?" (6) "Were the findings knowledge rather than information?" (7) "Was the knowledge transmissible to others?" By virtue of the definition of research, see [5], we believe that the term "knowledge" mentioned in question 6 is "new knowledge, in an applicable domain" [5]. If the answers of all these questions are yes, then the corresponding activity is considered as research [2].

2.3 Research Models

For our study it is crucial to shed light on the ways that research is carried out is computer science. Here we enlist a number of typical research models used within various computer science disciplines, without intending to be exhaustive. Our aim is to build a taxonomy, from which one can derive the research methods/ approaches that are most relevant for software engineering disciplines. We should remind that there are papers like [14] and [7] that present more detailed categorizations of the research methods used in computer science. Our list presented below, summarized mainly from [1] and [9], provides a simple, relevant and to the point categorization based on the feedback that we have received from our colleagues and students. Note that the research models to be mentioned are not exhaustive nor are they mutually exclusive (i.e., a research in computer science may rely on a combination of these models).

Formal-based: Here the researcher develops a mathematical model of the artifact (i.e., software implementation) to be created. Subsequently, mathematical proofs, also called formal methods, are used to verify the properties of the artifact. These properties include time complexity, space complexity, correctness of an algorithm, and the validity of a hypothesis given some evidence.

Model-based: Here the researcher defines an abstract model for a real entity/system. The objective of the modeling is to reduce the complexity of the system under study, while keeping the components and component interactions within the model representative to allow a qualitative or quantitative description of the system properties. The researcher can use the model to carry out experiments (i.e., simulations) to reach a better understanding of the system in a cost effective way.

Empirical-based: Here the researcher follows a specific sequence of steps/stages: hypothesis generation (to define or identify the ideas that the research will test), method identification (to determine the techniques that will be used to establish the hypothesis), result compilation (through execution of the method), and conclusion drawing (to support or reject the hypothesis).

Observational-based: Here the researcher is compelled to observe the operation and use of an artifact within its intended working environment rather than explicitly asking users about the performance of the artifacts. It is similar to the empirical model, however, here the researcher approaches the context of work with an open mind and without any hypothesis to prove or disprove.

Implementation-based: Here the researcher realizes a software system as an example of existing a generic class of solutions. This type of research demonstrates the feasibility of the solution. Often achieving a solution requires conducting iterative refinements based on testing and evaluation. In turn, the testing and evaluation techniques can be for example empirical-based or formal-based.

Process-based: This model is concerned with the study and understanding of activities/processes that involve humans to accomplish tasks in computer science (e.g., studying the ways that humans build and use computer systems). The research in this area aims at discovering proven designs, repeated patterns, or recurring strategies, which can be codified in various procedural ways such as best-practice guidelines, pattern languages, application frameworks, process models, and development tools.

3. VISION ON RESEARCH
3.1 Motivations

The advantages of mastering research skills for software engineering graduates at the bachelor level include: Not reinventing the wheel (this is achieved through investigating the sate of the art works before and during devising any solution intended to solve a practical problem), keeping pace and coping with the fast technological advancements that we witness in the ICT field nowadays (the skills learnt once-upon-a-time, i.e., those learnt through education or experience, may become obsolete in a time window of a few years, costing someone's job and an enterprise's business if no new expertise/skill is acquired), learning about and adapting to the real demands and needs of customers and clients (this requires having a wider view than just focusing on technological aspects, i.e., being multi-disciplinary, as ICT integrates with the fabrics of other disciplines more than ever), continuous learning and improving own and organization's expertise (through learning from other's knowledge); and making innovations in fast cycles (through effectively sharing knowledge with peers or colleagues and learning from others).

3.2 Scope and Boundaries

Engineering is defined as "the branch of science and technology concerned with the design, building, and use of engines, machines, and structures" [13]. A software engineer designs, implements, deploys, and administrates a software-based system and enhances the system to a desired solution to address a real problem. Thus engineering coincides with applicability.

Within our study we should first clarify the relation between research and engineering. Due to the relation between engineering and science (see the definition above), there is clearly a relation between engineering and research in its traditional definition (see Section 2.1). Both engineering and research are concerned with addressing problems and hereto they usually carry out iterative refinements of the solution and research. There are, however, also some differences between engineering and research. Engineering may have no or minimum relation to research when for example an engineer works as a pure practitioner doing routine assignments. A precondition for an engineering task to be considered as research is the engineered artifact to be new or to have some new features. Then the resulting artifact can become a means of gaining new knowledge/insight within a given domain or body of knowledge. Research, on the other hand, may have no (or minimum) applicability. For example, fundamental research, usually carried out by scientific universities, is not assessed by or concerned with applicability of the expected outcomes.

To characterize research, Stokes [17] made a distinction between *generalizability* and *applicability*. The general perception of research until the late 20th century was that research is either applied, i.e., has an application but delivers no new insight, or fundamental, i.e., delivers a new insight but has no application [12]. This view was considered too simplistic according to Stokes [17] who believes fundamental research is highly generalized but applied research can be both generic and specific, as illustrated in the front vertical plane (consisting of the green boxes) in Figure 1. The plane implies that applied research can generate also general insight, as shown by the example of Pasteur as a pioneer at the upper-right quadrant. The lower-right quadrant, exemplified by Edison as a pioneer in such approaches, represents research-based practices that strive for excellence and innovation through doing research to solve a specific/real problem. The box with Bohr as an example pioneer represents fundamental research in the quadrant.

We extend here the abovementioned quadrant from [17] with another dimension of 'research' to define a space consisting of three dimensions *research*, *generalizability* and *applicability* for characterizing research and engineering relations (see Figure 1). Let's consider the case where there is no or minimum research involved, as illustrated in the back vertical plane (consisting of the gray boxes) in Figure 1. When a student graduates from an applied university, he/she is able to carry out some routine tasks because he/she has learnt about the required skills during his/her education (e.g., doing straightforward assignments that require programming skills of Java). When such a practitioner year-after-year does similar assignments he/she obtains some experience-based tacit knowledge about his profession (e.g., Java programming). Gaining such a generalization skill occurs gradually with a rather slow pace and has been a norm in vocational endeavors throughout the years (e.g., leaning family business from parents and learning jobs skills from masters). The initial and gained knowledge is illustrated by a gray box and dashed gray box, respectively, in Figure 1.

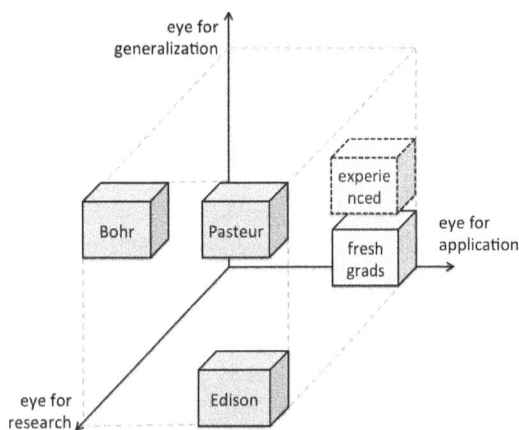

Figure 1: A three-dimensional model, characterizing research and engineering/practice.

To identify the scope of the research within applied universities we first recall Archer's discussion about the research through action for creative practitioners (e.g., artists and designers) [2]. These practitioners claim that what they ordinarily do is research because their outputs, like artworks or design products, constitutes new knowledge. We believe that engineers may belong to this set of practitioners because engineers develop artifacts that, in addition to solving real-problems, may deliver some (new) knowledge (see the implementation-based research-model mentioned in Section 2). Archer [2] distinguishes between 3 cases in regard to research and practice, namely: Research for the purposes of practice, research through practice, and research about practice. In research for the purposes of practice an investigation is conducted through a systematic enquiry to contribute to a practitioner activity like making a software artifact. When the objective hereto is to create communicable new knowledge, then the investigation can be called research. However, in situation where it is sufficient just to show that the outcome is satisfactory, without being concerned about how well the research was done or without evaluating the results obtained the investigation is considered as either "option research" at best or no research at worst (merely being speculation or exploration) by professional scholars and researchers. In research through practice a systematic enquiry is conducted through the medium of the artifact/product (e.g. a software prototype) or the practical action. The product or action is meant for devising or testing new

ideas, information, forms or procedures and generating communicable knowledge. In some circumstances constructing something (like in engineering) or enacting a calculated action (like in action research) is the best or the only way to clarify a proposition/principle or to prescribe a material/process. These situations arise in, for example, engineering, medicine, agriculture, education and business. In research about practice a research is carried out about, for example, the history of the practice, the analysis and criticism of the output of the practice, the relation of the practice to people and society, etc. Archer [2] argues that such studies about practice can be considered as research studies if they employ the methods and principles of the-class to which they belong.

Inspired by Archer's categorization [2], we distinguish the following research levels in relation to the practical endeavors (e.g., making a software prototype) that are devised by the students of applied universities: (1) Practical endeavors to come up with a satisfactory result, without using a systematic research enquiry. We call these as No Research (NR). (2) Practical endeavors to come up with a satisfactory result, using a semi-systematic research enquiry (i.e., with conducting some aspects of research like literature study to choose options or evaluating the results obtained). This can be with or without generalization. We call these practices as Weak-sense Research (WR). (3) Practical endeavors through using a systematic research enquiry as characterized in Section 2. This can be with or without generalization. We call these endeavors as Strict-sense Research (SR). Furthermore, we emphasize that the practical endeavor carried out by a practitioner may lead to a new solution or feature, resulting in new insight and knowledge within a body of knowledge. In other words we have two types of outcomes: (a) A solution, solution feature, insight or knowledge that is already known in the body of knowledge, but it is new for the context of the use (e.g., for a company's specific need). (b) A solution, solution feature, insight and knowledge that is new for the body of knowledge in accordance with the definition of research given in Section 2. When a systematic research is applied to achieve outcomes (a) and (b), we can characterize the corresponding endeavors as WR and SR following the research levels defined.

Considering the ambition of applied universities to educate research skills to their undergraduate studies, one can recognize the research level 2 (i.e., WR) as the research suitable for students of software engineering in applied universities. Note that we regard this research as WR solely because the outcome of this research is of type-a (i.e., in being new for the context of use/application). The other aspects of a systematic research should be in place. Scientific universities in The Netherlands, however, aim at type-b outcomes and carry out SR. As such, both scientific universities and applied universities use the same research methodologies, however, their products differ: the former focuses on creating new knowledge while the latter focuses on creating working solutions for real and practical problems. Note that the term "weak" above describes the 'research aspect' and does not imply anything about the 'quality / the added value of the solution delivered (i.e., it does not describe the practicality of the work).

In light of the insight mentioned above, we introduced an intermediary vertical plane in Figure 2 (consisting of the yellow boxes) to represent Weak-sense Research. The intermediary vertical plane represents the research level sought by Dutch universities of applied sciences and the boxes thereon are marked by "WR 2:a", indicating that it Weak-sense Research only because its outcome is of type-a, i.e., delivering new solutions for a given usage context. Note that the right vertical plane in Figure 2 (consisting of boxes marked by 1, 2:a, and 3:b) represents the scope of engineering within the 3D-space defined.

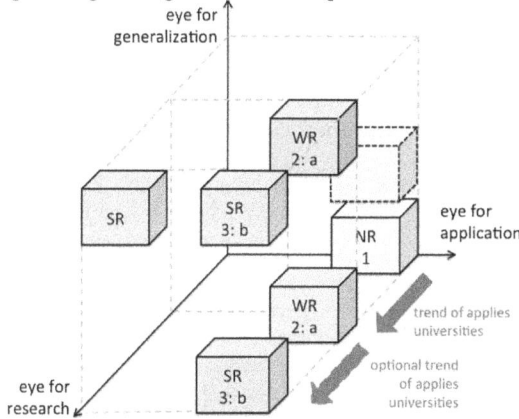

Figure 2: The 3D-model and the trend for research in Dutch universities of applied sciences at the bachelor level.

3.3 Desired Level

Concerning research skills, one needs to fulfill the requirements of the Bachelor level, without being too ambitious to aim at the higher level of Master. There is still a lot of debate going on about what the desired level of research skills for bachelor graduates should be, compared to the level of the research skills required for the graduates of scientific universities (i.e., for the holders of Master of Science degrees).

The European Union has issued a qualification framework, the so-called European Qualification Framework (EQF) [6], whereby all levels of education within Europe can be compared. For the Bachelor level, the EQF requires obtaining "advanced skills, demonstrating mastery and innovation, required *to solve complex and unpredictable problems in a specialized field of work or study*" [6]. For the Master level, however, the EQF requires "specialized problem-solving skills required in research and/or innovation in order *to develop new knowledge and procedures and to integrate knowledge from different fields*" [6]. As seen from these EQF requirements, problems solving skills are relevant for both Master and Bachelor graduates. To this end, therefore, mastering the research skills finds its relevancy for both Master and Bachelor level graduates because research methodologies are devised and used for problem solving for many centuries.

The difference between the problem solving skills (thus research skills) required by EQF for Master and Bachelor levels clearly pertains to the type of the product/output that these graduates deliver. According to the EQF requirements, the product of the graduates with a Bachelor degree is a solution in "a specialized field of work" [6] and that of the graduates with a Master degree is "to develop new knowledge" [6]), while both aiming at real problems and applying (new) solutions in the problem domain. Therefore, our vision for educating research skills in applied universities, described in the previous sections, agrees with the EQF requirements.

4. GRADUATION REPORTS REVIEW

This section presents the result of our analysis of the graduation reports of the students that were graduated in 2012 and 2013 within the INF, MT, and TI disciplines.

4.1 Review Protocol

In Section 2.3 we identified 6 research models that are used in computer science from literature. These research models, in turn, encompass the specific methods (e.g., literature study, case study, user study, etc.). As research in universities of applied sciences and the research in scientific universities only differ in the outcome, we concluded that the identified set of research models is applicable and relevant for the students of universities of applied sciences to define the research processes and methods.

As baseline we would like to know which of the research models are (more) applicable to the typical assignments of INF, MT, and TI software engineering disciplines. For these typical assignments we have chosen the INF, MT, and TI graduation projects carried out in recent years. The motivations for choosing these graduation projects are: They are defined and executed based on the curriculum profiles and guidelines of these disciplines [16] and, as such, they represent the corresponding education profiles, they are the most comprehensive practical works that these students carry out during their education, and they should (ideally) be executed according to the most relevant and appropriate research methods as required by the guidelines of RUAS board.

For the baseline study we classified these graduation assignments to the identified research models. Our objective is to see which research model is most relevant for each of these disciplines. Knowing the relevant class(es) enables us primarily to shed light on the research methodologies that can be used in each of these disciplines. Moreover, we can hereby identify the existing shortcomings in exercising the corresponding research model(s). Based on literature study and conferring with peers, we used the following research models for our classification of the graduation reports: formal-based (M1), model-based (M2), empirical-based (M3), observational-based (M4), implementation-based (M5), implementation-based for influencing experience and/or behavior (M6), process-based (M7) and any other model than those mentioned above (M8). In order to have a more representative set of classes we defined research model M6 as a variant of model M5 to cover the current scope and direction of the MT discipline. Class M8 was defined to control whether this taxonomy covers the space of all assignments.

We used the following protocol to classify the reports: Per discipline we chose 20 graduation reports for review and classification from the last two years (i.e., 2012 and 2013). Thus we studied 60 graduation reports in total. Two members of the workgroup reviewed every paper. Per report we (1) read the introduction to evaluate the problem statement and the research questions, (2) browsed through the report to identify the closest research method, asses the quality of the analyses of the problem context and existing solutions (and if relevant, assessed the validity/grounding of the design choices made and the quality of the evaluation of the results obtained), (3) read the conclusions to evaluate the quality of the reflection on the results achieved and of the answers to the research questions.

4.2 Results and Discussion

The result of our classification of the graduate reports for the three disciplines is presented in Table 1. We see that the implementation-based research-model (sum of classes M5 and M6) is the closest one for the assignments of TI (90%), INF (76%) and MT (77%). These figures imply that the majority of these graduation assignments should closely follow the research method(s) used in the implementation-based research-model in order to enhance their research-related qualities. For enhancing the research quality of the majority of software engineering graduation project we need to identify the existing shortcomings of these assignments with respect to this research model.

Table 1: Result of our classification of the graduation reports of the three technical disciplines.

%	M1	M2	M3	M4	M5	M6	M7	M8
MT	–	–	7	13	13	64	3	–
INF	–	–	14	–	58	18	10	–
TI	–	–	6	4	90	–	–	–

Our review of the old graduation reports and also the experience of our colleagues reveal that the way that our technical oriented students used to carry their graduation works adhered to a process model consisting of design and implementation stages. The input to the assignment was a number of requirements, often determined by the company coach who envisioned how the expected software (or software-hardware) system (component) to be developed. The output of this process model was often a prototype with no or minor evaluation of its performance and functionality. This traditional process model is depicted in Figure 3. In this figure the height of each block conveys the amount of work put in the corresponding stage of the process.

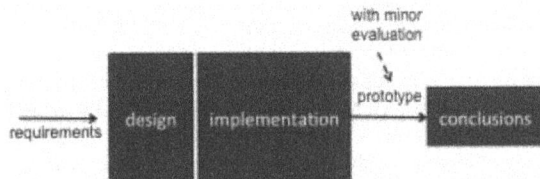

Figure 3: Illustration of the old work process for graduation assignments.

Based on our analysis of (the shortcomings of) the existing graduation reports, we envision the research model of Figure 4 to be appropriate to capture and encompass the implementation based research model that is applicable for majority of the (graduation) assignments of the software engineering disciplines. The model represents the typical development lifecycles of an information system, i.e., analysis, advise, design, implement, and manage, according to [16]. As such, the model resembles the implementation-based research-model directly. One can also show that the model is compatible with the advise-based and service-management-based types of assignments [16]. Showing this compatibility, however, is out of our scope in this paper.

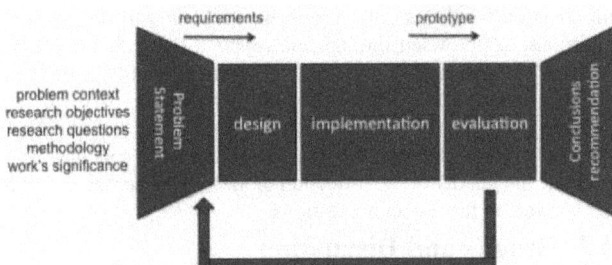

Figure 4: Illustration of the envisioned work process for graduation assignments.

Comparing the old and envisioned models in Figure 3 and Figure 4 reveals the shortcomings (i.e., improvement aspects) of the way that previous assignments were used to be carried out. This comparison emphasizes the importance of project initiation

stage, evaluation stage and conclusion/recommendation stage. The student should start with an initial analysis and investigation of the problem context and understanding the motivations behind the assignment (analysis of the current situation). The student should also investigate the existence of a real problem and the importance/relevancy of the sought solution in its bigger context (in overall system architecture and/or society) in the early stage. This investigation enables the student to define the corresponding research objectives and research questions properly. The design and implementation stages should aim at achieving the objectives (most often, realizing an artifact properly) by examining possible options and making decisions based on some (predefined) criteria.

The evaluation of the achieved results (e.g., a software prototype) is an integral part of the process, which is concerned with validation, verification and test of the artifact realized. The evaluation can be done often in quantitative ways or sometimes in qualitative ways. More generally stated, one can deploy any subset of the formal-based, model-based, empirical based, and observational based research models for the evaluation stage. This evaluation can also be considered as an analysis stage after the prototyping and it usually follows/completes the implementation-based approach. The result of the evaluation may reveal the need for revisiting the assumptions, re-design or reimplementation of the prototype. This is shown with a feedback line in Figure 4, emphasizing the iterative aspect of the whole process. Multiple iterations are common particularly in those designs where human factors are dominant and determinant. Finally, the conclusion process involves a reflection on the obtained results in illustrating the degree to which the research questions are addressed during the work and which lessons are learnt. This concerns also production of some (new) knowledge gained through the whole exercise, possibly with an eye on generalization of the results. The conclusion phase provides also an insight for future directions system-wise, business-wise, etc.

In summary, concerning the analyzed graduation reports, we identify the following improvement aspects: The evaluation (test, verification and/or validation) is often weakly done, the problem context is not well studied, the problem statement is not adjusted to the work carried out (or the question that was solved), the problems and the solutions are often not positioned in a larger context such as society, business and/or overall system architecture, the literature study is often done at a micro level (e.g., what the design options are per component), not at a meta-level (i.e., positioning own work as a whole with respect to similar works to learn from those), and embedding multi-disciplinary aspects in the graduation work is limited (the last one, we suspect, seems inevitable considering the limited timeframe available for executing such projects).

One of the objectives of applied universities is to teach student multi-disciplinary research and communication skills. In the model depicted in Figure 4 we showed this aspect schematically in the form of a funnel in the problem statement and conclusion components. Here the student needs to position his/her work in a larger and wider context (e.g., through investigating the problem context and providing advice across disciplines). We admit that this is a limited exercise for developing multidisciplinary skills, imposed due to limited duration of graduation projects. We believe that there should be some other courses, where students get enough opportunity to carry out such multidisciplinary works in collaborative teams. Communication skills, related to effective communication with professionals and nonprofessionals, become relevant when writing graduation reports and presenting the results.

The extent of the implementation stage (e.g., amount and complexity of the software code written) varies per discipline. It may be the main focus of the work (e.g., in those software engineering assignments that aim at creating new ICT artifacts) or may be of minor focus (e.g., in those assignments that aim at studying the existing ICT artifacts in their (new) settings). In some HCI projects, for example, implementing a mockup prototype might be enough to prove/demonstrate the idea behind. This variation of implementation-depth depends also on the research model chosen. For example, in observational model one can use (or reconfigure) an existing system and study its usability.

Classical research methods like literature study, user study, descriptive research, comparative research, explorative research, evaluative research, explanative research, desktop research, field study, lab research, quantitative research, qualitative research, … can be relevant and applicable in each stage of the model depicted in Figure 4. Depending on the discipline, these methods can be relevant to these stages in a varied extension. For example, user studies are particularly relevant in the begin stage to derive system requirements and in the evaluation stage to evaluate/validate the system functionality and/or performance. We will not elaborate on defining the research methods appropriate for a specific research.

5. CONCLUSIONS

Mastering research skills is crucial for the graduates of universities of applied sciences nowadays because these skills will enable the graduates to become knowledge-oriented professionals. In this contribution we sketched our vision on what research means within universities of applied science, particularly for software engineering disciplines, at the bachelor level. The main conclusion of this study is that while scientific universities and applied universities produce different outcomes – the former focus on creating new knowledge while the latter focus on creating working solutions for problems – both use the same research methodologies. Based on our analysis of the existing graduation reports we identified the implementation-based research to be the most appropriate research model for majority of assignments and projects in software engineering disciplines. Based on and compared to our envisioned research model, we identified the shortcomings of the current practices, specially those in the project initiation phase (to investigate and define the context of the problem), evaluation phase (to evaluate and reflect on the results achieved) and conclusion/recommendation phase (to capture the main outcomes and the lessons learnt, and to define future directions).

Research skills and competences improve with practice. For students to get better at research, we see the necessity of embedding instances of such practices within the curricula next to classic and theoretical courses. These instances can be accommodated within explicit courses on research skills as well as those courses that touch upon research skills implicitly. We are currently busy with adapting the curricula of our software engineering disciplines to properly accommodate these software skills explicitly and implicitly. It seems also necessary to establish some connections among these explicit and implicit courses in order to motivate students and make them aware of the fact that research isn't something far from their reality and that it is indeed something related to and part of their study and future work.

6. REFERENCES

[1] Amaral, J.N., et al.. About computing science research methodology. Available: http://webdocs.cs.ualberta.ca/~c603/readings/research-methods.pdf.

[2] Archer, B. 1995. The nature of research. *Co-Design Journal*, 2, 11.

[3] Baarda, D.B., and Goede, M.P.M. de. 2006. *Basisboek Methoden en Technieken* (in Dutch), 4th edition, Groningen: Noordhoff Uitgevers.

[4] Delnooz, P.V.A. 2010. *Creatieve Actie Methodologie* (in Dutch). Boom Lemma Uitgevers.

[5] Ellis, T.J. and Levy, Y. 2008. Framework of problem based research: a guide for novice researchers on the development of a research-worthy problem. *Information Science: the International Journal of an Emerging Trans-discipline*, 11.

[6] European Qualifications. 2008. *The European Qualifications Framework for Lifelong Learning leaflet*. Available: http://ec.europa.eu/eqf/home_en.htm.

[7] Glass, R. L., Ramesh, V., Vessey, I. (2004). An analysis of research in computing disciplines. *Communications of the ACM*, 47(6), 89-94.

[8] Hart, C. 1998. *Doing a Literature Review: Releasing the Social Science Research Imagination*. Sage Publications, UK

[9] Johnson, C. 2014. What is research in computing science? http://www.dcs.gla.ac.uk/~johnson/teaching/research_skills/research.html.

[10] Oates, B.J. 2012. *Researching Information Systems and Computing*. SAGE publications, London, UK

[11] O&K document. 2013. De HR-visie op eindniveau: onderzoek op zijn Rotterdams (in Dutch). Ver. 1.0, February.

[12] Offermann, P., et al. 2009. Outline of a Design Science Research Process. *In Proc. of the 4th International Conference on Design Science Research in Information Systems and Technology*, ACM, 7.

[13] Oxford, 2013. *Oxford Dictionaries*. Available http://www.oxforddictionaries.com/definition/english/engineering?q=engineering

[14] Ramesh, V., Glass, R. L. and Vessey, I. 2004. Research in computer science: an empirical study. *Journal of systems and software*, 70, 1, 165-176.

[15] Saunders, M., Lewis, P. and Thornhill, A. 2008. *Methoden en Technieken van Onderzoek* (in Dutch). The 4th edition, Amsterdam: Pearson Education Benelux.

[16] Schagen, J.D, van der Kwaak, W., Leenstra, E., Smit, W. and Vonken, F. 2010. *HBO-I Bachelor of ICT Domain Description*. HBO-I foundation, Amsterdam, the NL.

[17] Stokes, D.E. 1997. *Pasteurs Quadrant: Basic Science and Technological Innovation*. Brookings Institution Press

[18] Vereniging Hogescholen (Applied Universities Union). *Over Hogescholen (About Applied Universities)*. Available: http://www.vereniginghogescholen.nl/hogescholen/over-hogescholen

Meaningful Assessment

Geoff Stoker, Jean Blair, and Edward Sobiesk

United States Military Academy

West Point, New York 10996 USA

geoffrey.stoker@usma.edu, jean.blair@usma.edu, edward.sobiesk@usma.edu

ABSTRACT

Assessment of student learning outcomes is a key process used in education to both evaluate students' level of achievement and to identify opportunities for continuous improvement. The most prevalent technique for analyzing data collected from direct assessment methods is to distill the data to a single measure of central tendency, typically the arithmetic mean. Despite well known awareness and understanding of the limitations of the arithmetic mean, it is still commonly used because it is easy to calculate from the readily available data and is familiar to most educators. This paper argues that use of arithmetic mean alone is a poor assessment practice, and an alternate evaluation technique is presented in detail. To illustrate our conceptual arguments, a case study involving the assessment of an intermediate, college-level information technology course is presented. For the evaluation of an outcome in this course, assessment of student performance for the embedded indicators of that outcome are shown using both the commonly used arithmetic mean and what we believe to be a better, more meaningful assessment technique that places individual student performance data points into categories using an Individual Indicator Metric and then evaluates the group's overall performance based on the distribution of these student performances across the categories using a Group Indicator Metric. The paper's concluding section briefly addresses integrating indirect (subjective) evidence, combining all data source evaluations to evaluate an outcome, identifying and acting on opportunities for improvement, and reassessing changes. The central theme of the paper is that the veracity of assessment can be significantly improved with minimal extra effort.

Categories and Subject Descriptors

K.3.2 [**Computer and Information Science Education**]: Accreditation, Self-assessment.

General Terms

Management, Measurement, Standardization

Keywords

Assessment, Continuous Improvement, Outcome Evaluation, Performance Indicators, Individual Indicator Metric, Group Indicator Metric

1. INTRODUCTION

Assessment of student learning outcomes is a key process used in education to both evaluate students' level of achievement and to identify opportunities for continuous improvement. Many educators and programs, however, struggle to make this often mandated activity a valued part of their curriculum evolution. Perhaps the greatest impediment to meaningful outcome assessment, whether it be at the course, program, or institution level, is that the most prevalent technique for analyzing collected data from direct assessment is to only use the data's arithmetic mean. Despite the well known limitations of the arithmetic mean [1-2], it is still commonly used because it is easy to calculate from the readily available data and most educators are very comfortable with it, so it briefs well and is often easily accepted as a valid form of evaluation.

In this paper, we argue that techniques other than the arithmetic mean alone should be used for assessment of student performance and one such technique is presented in detail. In order to illustrate our ideas and techniques, we present a case study of the assessment of a desired outcome for an intermediate, college-level Information Technology course. Using student performance data from course embedded indicators, we directly compare an evaluation of student performance using the arithmetic mean against an evaluation using a technique that places individual student performance data points into categories using an Individual Indicator Metric and then evaluates the group's overall performance based on the distribution across the categories using a Group Indicator Metric. Detailed descriptions are included for each step in our suggested technique. We conclude by highlighting other best practices that should be a part of outcome evaluation and identification of opportunities for improvement.

The benefits of our techniques are: (1) with minimal additional effort there is significant increase in the value of the assessment and (2) the techniques can be applied at multiple levels including course, program, and institution.

2. CASE STUDY BACKGROUND

The course being assessed in this paper is *IT305: Theory and Practice of Military Information Technology Systems*. Each semester, about 365 students who are not majoring in an engineering discipline take this course during their junior year, resulting in about 700-750 students annually.

IT305's major purpose is to significantly contribute to accomplishment of the Information Technology portion of our institution's Science, Technology, Engineering, and Mathematics (STEM) Goal. Specifically, IT305 enables students to achieve the sub-goal that "Graduates can *understand and use information technology appropriately, adaptively, and securely*." The Information Technology sub-goal is one of five sub-goals supporting our institution-level STEM goal. It corresponds directly to the IT Goal described in the United States Military Academy publication "Educating Future Army Officers for a Changing World." In order to articulate the knowledge and skills needed to achieve the institution's Information Technology sub-goal, IT305 has adopted the following course outcomes:

1. Understand the underlying physical and mathematical concepts relevant to IT.
2. Comprehend how IT systems function.
3. Effectively employ IT systems.
4. Apply IT to solve problems and make decisions.
5. Account for legal, ethical, and security issues involved with IT.

Evaluation of Outcome 4 provides the case study for the remainder of this paper.

3. ASSESSMENT USING THE MEAN

This section illustrates an evaluation of IT305 Outcome 4, *Apply IT to solve problems and make decisions*, using the commonly applied arithmetic mean technique.

Table 1 describes the 21 embedded indicators from IT305 that support Outcome 4. Note that these include midterm examination questions, student projects, and final examination questions.

Table 1. The Embedded Indicators used to evaluate IT305. These consist of projects, homeworks, and examination questions.

Code	Embedded Indicator
WEB	Individual Web Site Project
1Q1	Cyber Intellectual Property Rights Test Question
1Q2	Data Acquisition Test Question
1Q3	Moore's Law Test Question
1Q4	XHTML/CSS Test Question
DB	Group Database Project
NET	Network Design Homework
2Q1	Network Concepts Test Question
2Q2	Database Design Test Question
2Q3	Network Design Test Question
2Q4	Database Implementation Test Question
IS	Group Information System Project
TQ1	Cyber Intellectual Property Rights Final Question
TQ2	Moore's Law Final Question
TQ3	Data Acquisition Final Question
TQ4	XHTML/CSS Final Question
TQ5	Database Design Final Question
TQ6	Database Implementation Final Question
TQ7	Active Web Pages Final Question
TQ8	Information Assurance Final Question
TQ9	Network Design Final Question

The general arithmetic mean technique first calculates an average student performance for each of the 21 embedded indicators and then uses a rubric for evaluating the group's performance as a whole for each indicator. The rubric we use for this illustration is: exceeds expectations -- an average of 90% or greater for an indicator (i.e. the overall average for the 365 students on a given exam question is >= 90%); meets expectations -- an average under 90% and greater than or equal to 75%, below expectations -- an average under 75%. Based on this methodology, Figure 1 displays the manner in which student performance on these indicators would be presented and evaluated. The red columns identify indicators for which the semester's average was below expectations, the green columns identify those indicators for which expectations were met, and yellow columns identify those indicators for which expectations were exceeded (the *gold standard*, so to speak).

As can be seen from the results in Figure 1, this technique leads to a very favorable evaluation as only two of the 21 indicators did not at least satisfactorily meet our standard (the network design question on midterm examination 2 (70.0% course average) and the database implementation question on midterm examination 2 (73.6% course average). Overall, under this traditional metric, we would have confidently declared that our students were achieving our outcome, and it would have been difficult to identify weak areas and significant opportunities for improvement.

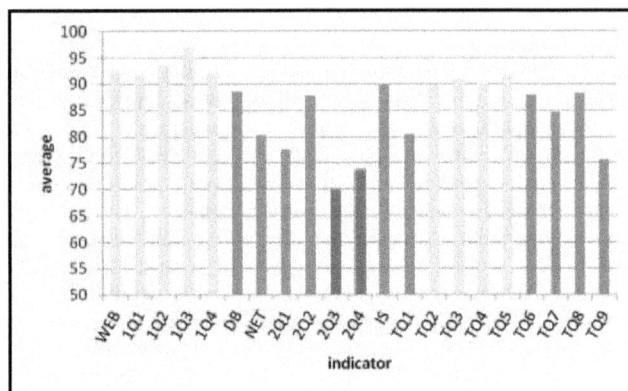

Figure 1. IT305 Outcome 4 embedded indicators evaluated using the traditional method based on the overall average performance. Red bars mean the class average did not meet course expectations, green bars met expectations, and yellow bars exceeded expectations.

4. A BETTER ASSESSMENT METHOD

Based on our desire to get greater granularity in our evaluations and to better identify opportunities to improve our course, we made the following straight-forward changes to our evaluation method.

4.1 Individual Indicator Metric

A key component of improving assessment is creation of a metric that is used to evaluate every instance of student performance for a given embedded indicator. We call such a metric an Individual Indicator Metric. Instead of simply using each student's numerical score/grade (which is typically expressed as a percentage between 0-100), our new methodology uses a metric to evaluate each embedded indicator data point (each student performance on the embedded indicator) in the entire data set. We advocate a rubric for which every individual student performance is identified as being in one of four possible categories. The four general rubric categories are shown in Figure 2.

The student's performance:

    Category 1 -- Completely failed to meet the standard

    Category 2 -- Just barely failed to meet the standard

    Category 3 -- Met the standard

    Category 4 -- Exceeded the standard

Figure 2. Individual Indicator Metric Categories. Each student's performance on an embedded indicator event is placed into one of four categories.

We believe it is important to have two Individual Indicator Metric categories for which a student does not meet the standard. Our experience has shown that if you only have one unsatisfactory category, then many faculty evaluators will be hesitant to place both completely unsatisfactory performances and those who just barely missed the standard into the same category. Having two categories also allows for a more refined evaluation of the group as a whole, which is discussed in greater detail in Section 4.2.

An important aspect of Individual Indicator Metric technique is to document in writing, preferably before the embedded indicator event is graded, what performance standards constitute each of the four categories. To increase efficiency, we also suggest setting up the grading schemes such that any performance that received a grade below 65% corresponded to "completely failed to meet the standard," a performance that "just barely failed to meet the standard" received a grade below 73% but equal to or above 65%, a performance that "met the standard" received a grade below 90% but equal to or above 73%, and a performance that "exceeded the standard" received a grade of 90% or above. With this grading scheme in place, it then takes minimal extra effort to apply an Individual Indicator Metric to every student performance for the given embedded indicator. Figure 3 shows an example of an Individual Indicator Metric for a database design question.

---

1. Completely failed to meet standard – Implementation of the design would meet few of the problem specifications:
- Identifies some tables of the database design
- Identifies most of the fields within the database tables
- Identifies some primary keys for the tables
- Identifies some relationships between tables
- Associates some multiplicities to the relationships identified
- Identifies some foreign keys

2. Just barely failed to meet standard – Implementation of the design would meet some of the problem specifications:
- Identifies main tables of the database design
- Identifies most of the fields of the database tables
- Identifies a primary key for each table
- Identifies relationships between tables
- Associates multiplicities to the relationships identified
- Identifies some kind of foreign key for relationships

3. Met standard – Implementation of the design would meet most of the problem specifications:
- Correctly identifies main tables of the database design
- Correctly identifies most of the fields of the database tables
- Correctly identifies a primary key for each table
- Correctly identifies relationships between tables
- Associates multiplicities to the relationships identified
- Correctly identifies some kind of foreign key for each relationship

4. Exceeded standard – Implementation of the design would meet all of the problem specifications:
- Correctly identifies all tables of the database design
- Correctly identifies all fields of the database tables
- Correctly identifies the primary key for each table, including those that are comprised of multiple fields
- Correctly identifies all relationships between tables
- Correctly identifies the multiplicities of the relationships
- Correctly identifies all foreign keys for each relationship

---

Figure 3. An example of an Individual Indicator Metric for a database design question. We recommend constructing these prior to grading and aligning the Individual Indicator Metric with grading standards to improve efficiency.

Note that by documenting the metric in writing, it allows for both repeatability/verification of a current evaluation and consistency of future evaluations of the same situation, thus establishing credible longitudinal information.

Creating and documenting a metric for evaluating each student's individual performance, however, is not sufficient. For the evaluation of the group of students as a whole, in place of using a single number (i.e. the overall average for the 365 students), our methodology employees a Group Indicator Metric, which is described in Section 4.2.

4.2 Group Indicator Metric

Once the Individual Indicator Metric in Figure 3 is applied to each student's individual performance, one must then decide whether the performance of the group as a whole meets one's goal. Our goal for the performance of the group, which we call the Group Indicator Metric, is presented in Figure 4. Performance levels of 80% and 5% are our choices, and other values could be used based on an organization's goals and requirements.

Group Indicator Metric

At least 80% of the student performances must meet the standard (category 3 or 4) with not more than 5% of the student performances completely failing to meet the standard (category 1).

Figure 4. Group Indicator Metric (our goal for the group).

Having evaluated an embedded indicator data set with an Individual Indicator Metric, the Group Indicator Metric now truly allows for identifying the level of attainment for an embedded indicator, ensuring that a single mean doesn't hide less than desirable results.

As an illustration of this point, Figure 5 shows the results of taking the exact same data whose averages were depicted in Figure 1 and using the metric from Figure 2 to categorize individual student performance for each embedded indicator and then using the metric from Figure 4 to evaluate group performance for each indicator.

Clearly, the use of the individual and group indicator metrics from Figures 2 & 4 are a higher standard, but far more importantly, the use of these metrics provides significantly more information and insights about where weaknesses exist and what areas are opportunities for improvement. Without these new techniques, the weaknesses would often go undetected.

4.3 Comparing Results

Before proceeding to a discussion of evaluating the outcome, it is worth specifically pointing out the differences between the embedded indicator evaluations calculated with the arithmetic mean (in Figure 1) and the embedded indicator evaluations calculated using the Individual Indicator Metric and the Group Indicator Metric (in Figure 5).

Figure 1 and the use of the arithmetic mean is a good news story. 19 out of the 21 embedded indicators are evaluated as meeting course expectations with nine of the embedded indicators exceeding course expectations.

For Figure 5, ten out of the 21 embedded indicators do not meet our Group Indicator Metric. Even worse, two of the embedded indicators that in Figure 1 were exceeding course expectations (1Q4 and TQ4) are among those that now are below our desired metric.

Perhaps the best aspect of the Individual Indicator Metric and the Group Indicator Metric, though, is that the faculty conducting the assessment now have multiple indicators that provide truly actionable information on where opportunities for improvement may exist within the course. Although all ten of the embedded indicators that did not meet our goal warrant further careful scrutiny, the NET, 2Q1, 2Q3, 2Q4, TQ1, TQ7, and TQ9 embedded indicators are all somewhat egregious and indicate that our current course materials are not accomplishing our desired goals for all students. While these embedded indicator results are not quite the "bathtub" results that are often associated with the computing discipline, they are certainly an example of why using the arithmetic mean alone for outcome assessment is simply a bad idea.

5. OUTCOME EVALUATION

In this section, we discuss potential evaluations of IT305 Outcome 4 "Apply IT to solve problems and make decisions."

For an outcome evaluation using the arithmetic mean method based on the average of student performance, this particular outcome would have 19 out of the 21 embedded indicators meeting the standard, with many of the indicators exceeding expectations.

For outcome evaluation, one best practice is to have an *a priori* goal for how many of your embedded indicators meet your desired standard. With the mean being used to evaluate the embedded indicators, a goal of as high as 90% of embedded indicator evaluations meeting the standard would still be achieved. Thus, using the mean methodology, this outcome level of attainment would be 19 / 21= 90.5%, which would have likely then evaluated as being met, perhaps even strongly met, with minimal opportunities for improvement identified.

Evaluating the same data, though, using the Individual Indicator Metric and the Group Indicator Metric results in a level of attainment of 11 / 21 = 52.4%, which with almost any reasonable *a priori* embedded indicator achievement goal would result in an outcome evaluation that did not meet desired attainment levels. We consider the more strict results much more accurate and valuable because they show more clearly student capabilities across the full spectrum of desired knowledge and skills. This outcome evaluation technique would also offer numerous insights into where in the curriculum (or in the testing mechanisms) improvements need to be made.

As we look at the two above evaluation techniques, besides the second one offering more accurate and granular evaluations and better opportunities for improvement, it also allows for a better accumulation of longitudinal data. The arithmetic mean technique is almost always undocumented in how the embedded indicators were actually evaluated (how they were graded), and with the level of attainment already being so high, there is little room for improvement. The second technique, on the other hand, provides documented and consistent embedded indicator metrics that when combined with their increased granularity truly do allow for tracking whether improvement is occurring. Therefore, while we do recommend identifying *a priori* an embedded indicator achievement goal for your outcome evaluations, we believe that it is the longitudinal improvement in pursuit of that goal, rather than the actual achievement of the goal itself, that truly represents continuous improvement.

6. INDIRECT ASSESSMENT

Indirect assessment evidence is subjective and opinion-based. For instance, if we gave our students a survey and asked them to identify on a Likert scale how competent they feel they are at applying IT to solve problems and make decisions, the survey results would be indirect evidence. Additionally, if we asked their teacher her opinion of how competent she felt her students were at applying IT to solve problems and make decisions, and she gave her opinion based on a Likert scale, or even just as bullets, that too would be indirect evidence. It is therefore not appropriate to evaluate one's outcomes using only indirect (opinion-based) evidence. However, many organizations that assess using direct evidence (such as we described in Sections 3 through 5) miss the valuable opportunity to triangulate their findings [3-5] by not taking the short amount of time needed to also include indirect evidence in their assessment process.

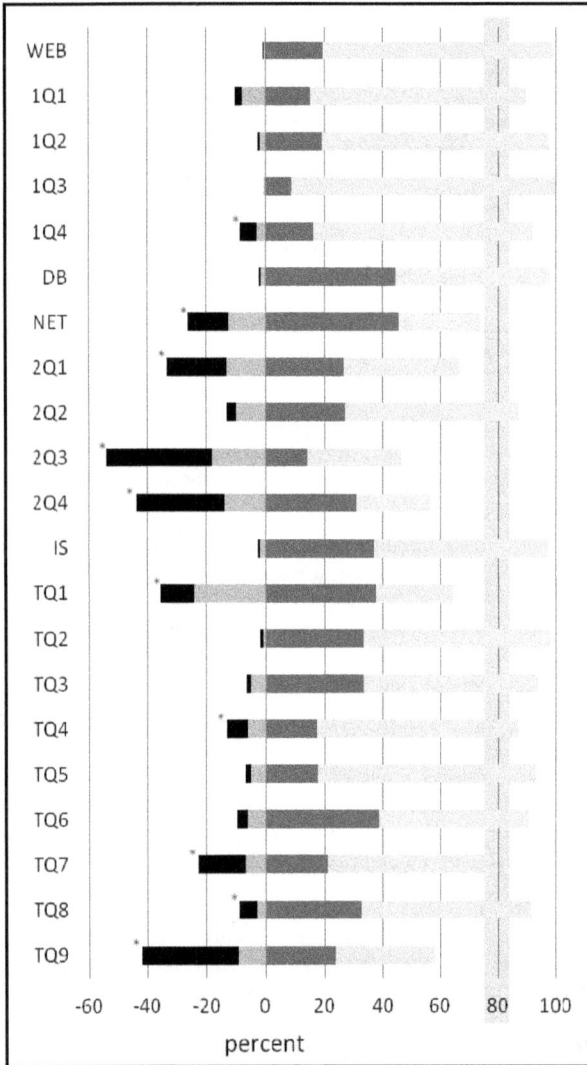

Figure 5. Evaluation of the 21 data sets shown in Figure 1 using the metrics presented in Figure 2 (Individual Indicator Metric) and Figure 4 (Group Indicator Metric). Black depicts student performance in Category 1 (Completely failed to meet the standard), gray depicts student performance in Category 2 (Just barely failed to meet the standard), green depicts student performance in Category 3 (Met the standard), and yellow depicts student performance in Category 4 (Exceeded the standard). Asterisks identify the ten indicators which fail to meet our Group Indicator Metric from Figure 4.

When it comes to the assessment of IT305's course outcomes, our initial indirect efforts involve a very short assessment survey taken by the students at the end of the course. For each of our course outcomes, we asked the students to rate their own abilities with the outcome on a scale of Poor, Fair, Good or Excellent (roughly equivalent to our Individual Indicator Metric levels). Although we kept the student responses anonymous, we did use an ID number for each student that allowed us to correlate their response with their final course grade. Also, in order to ensure we received the most accurate information from the survey, we sometimes adjusted the wording of a course outcome to be more accessible to the students. As an example, for Outcome 4, "Apply IT to solve problems and make decisions," we asked students to rate their "ability to recognize when, where, and to what degree IT can be applied effectively to solve a particular problem." Figure 6 shows the survey results for this survey question.

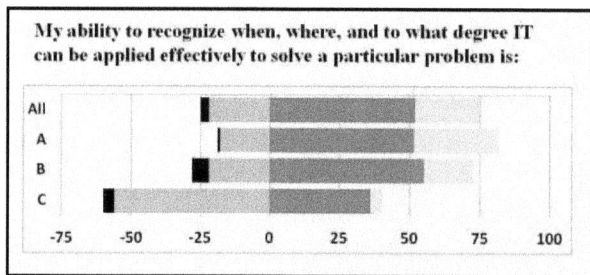

Figure 6. End-of-course survey results (in percentages) from 358 IT305 students whose performance data has been used throughout this paper asking them how well they felt they meet the outcome "Apply IT to solve problems and make decisions." Black is poor, gray is fair, green is good, and yellow is excellent. The chart shows both overall results and results broken out by final course grade.

Interestingly, our students' self evaluation of 75% attainment was near the middle of our two Outcome 4 evaluation technique attainment levels (90.5% for mean only method and 52.4% for the Individual Indicator Metric and Group Indicator Metric method). While this shows the importance of not necessarily putting all trust in opinions, it also was sort of a wakeup call to our faculty as the survey result indicates that one out of four students leaves the class believing they are not fully capable of one of our most important outcomes.

7. CONTINUOUS IMPROVEMENT

In the end, a key driving factor behind assessment is continuous improvement. In the educational domain, we argue that we need to improve the cost-benefit aspect of all the efforts we put into our outcome evaluations.

For the Individual Indicator Metric and Group Indicator Metric method described throughout this paper, we believe we have come much closer to making the cost benefit of outcome assessment be positive. The technique is able to identify several specific parts of the course content in which students are not performing at the level we desire. For these areas, the next question was how to improve? Through our group discussions and personal reflections, we identified several content and pedagogy changes including:

- Significantly revising / adding about twelve 30-minute in class exercises,

- Adding 15-20 very short, check-for-comprehension homework assignments, and

- Revising examination techniques including changing both midterm examinations from open to closed book.

Our next step will be to fully implement these changes and then re-assess.

8. CONCLUSION

In this paper, we presented an assessment methodology that we believe significantly outperforms the standard method of using the average student performance of embedded indicators. We have illustrated our methodology with a case study consisting of data gathered from our intermediate information technology course IT305.

In our case study, the evaluation of IT305 Outcome 4 went from a mean-based "perception" of solidly meeting the outcome with little-to-no areas identified for improvement to application of more beneficial techniques that showed that the course is not meeting the outcome with many areas of weakness identified as well as their associated opportunities for improvement.

We believe in educators, and it has been our experience that teachers care tremendously about their students and their students' level of performance. However, many educators are often frustrated by the effort involved in conducting assessment and the little actual value that is gained from the process.

We hope this paper's recommended techniques will bring both benefit to many assessment efforts as well as foster further debate and discussion on the topic. Assessment is a journey we are all on together. We wish you fruitful travels.

9. REFERENCES

[1] BBC BiteSize. Advantages and disadvantages of mean, median and mode. Available at URL: http://www.bbc.co.uk/schools/gcsebitesize/maths/statistics/measuresofaveragerev6.shtml. Accessed 8 Jun 2014.

[2] National Center for Biotechnology Information. Measures of central tendency: The mean. Available at URL: http://www.ncbi.nlm.nih.gov/pmc/articles/PMC3127352/. Accessed 8 June 2014.

[3] T. Judd and B. Keith. 2012. Student learning outcomes assessment at the program and institutional levels. In C. Secolsky and D. Denison (Eds.) *Handbook on Measurement, Assessment, and Evaluation in Higher Education*, Routledge, 2012.

[4] T. E. Grayson. 2012. Program evaluation in higher education. In C. Secolsky and D. Denison (Eds.) *Handbook on Measurement, Assessment, and Evaluation in Higher Education*, Routledge, 2012.

[5] C. Pondish. 2012. Qualitative evaluation. In C. Secolsky and D. Denison (Eds.) *Handbook on Measurement, Assessment, and Evaluation in Higher Education*, Routledge, 2012.

Formulating Second-Order Logic Conditions in SQL

Jalal Kawash
University of Calgary
2500 University Dr. NW
Calgary, Alberta, Canada
+1 (403) 220 6619
jalal.kawash@ucalgary.ca

ABSTRACT

Researchers continue to find ways by which SQL is better taught. While the language itself is easy, students find it challenging to grasp. This is aggravated with queries that require second-order logic conditions. SQL does not have a construct for universal quantification, which must be done through the negation of SQL's EXISTS construct. This paper describes a tool, RX, that tutors SQL programmers how to formulate SQL queries that require second-order logic conditions. The paper also reports on an experiment that evaluates RX.

Categories and Subject Descriptors

K.3.2 [**Computers and Education**]: Computer and Information Science Education – *Computer science education.*

General Terms

Design, Human Factors, Theory

Keywords

Database education; universal and existential quantifiers; SQL; relational calculus

1. INTRODUCTION

One major limitation of SQL is its lack of a direct support to a universal quantification construct. The *for all* and *every* English phrases can be satisfied in SQL through negating the existential quantifier construct EXISTS.

Harvey et al. [1] found that the number of students that make errors in writing exclusionary queries is very high (about 80%). It is common knowledge to Psycholinguists that negation poses a comprehension problem to students [2, 3]. Coupled with the difficulty introduced by quantification, using the negated forms of existential quantifiers to represent universal quantifiers further complicates comprehension. When universal quantifiers become nested and twisted with each other and with existential quantifiers, translating the English query to SQL can be cumbersome, even for the very experienced. Klein [4] stated that

the combination of negation and quantification "may result in critical loss of information." Kawash [5] argued that the use of universal quantifiers to comprehend and express the *for all* and *every* phrases is more natural and intuitive than negating existential quantifiers. Quantification in SQL is far more complex than joining and grouping. Yet, Resiner [8] reported that users even have some difficulties using the SQL join and group constructs. Date [6] proposed some workaround techniques to avoid the use of quantification in SQL. Nevertheless, these proposed techniques require other constructs that are not supported in many commercial implementations of SQL, as Date himself warned [6]. Thus, the use of quantifiers in SQL is unavoidable.

This paper introduces RX, a tool that aims at helping students develop a systematic method in order to formulate SQL queries that involve second-order logic. The method is based on Kawash's SQL Normal Form (SQLNF) of tuple relational calculus [5]. While the SQLNF method helps students easily translate tuple relational calculus queries to SQL, many students still struggle to formulate complex logic queries in tuple relational calculus. With RX, users formulate English-like (we call it RX-English) queries in a controlled, interactive way, allowing them to build the query only from pre-defined widgets and controls. This substantially limits errors allowing the learner to focus on the core issue: the logic of the query condition. RX interactively generates such English-like query, which is rigorous enough to comprehend its logic without ambiguities, but informal enough to be close to every day's logic. Figure 1 shows an RX screenshot, consisting of an example RX-English query.

The RX-English is translated by the tool to tuple relational calculus. Then, RX utilizes the method proposed by Kawash [5] to translate relational calculus expressions to SQLNF and then to SQL queries. Going back and forth between these different forms allows learners to pin-point logical mistakes and further enhances their learning experience by trial-and-error. RX also shows a step-by-step illustration of normalizing the relational calculus expression to SQLNF, giving the students a hands-on, interactive tutorial to learn the normalization procedure. Finally, the tool generates the SQL query from SQLNF tuple relational calculus, using the systematic method of Kawash [5]. RX serves as a tool to teach learners these translation procedures, which when mastered allow learners to systematically write complex queries, more effectively. The ultimate objective is to eventually allow students formulate complex logic queries without depending on RX.

We evaluated the tool with students who successfully completed introductory database course. The experiments show that students who were trained with the tool outperformed students who did not in a controlled closed-book "mock" exam.

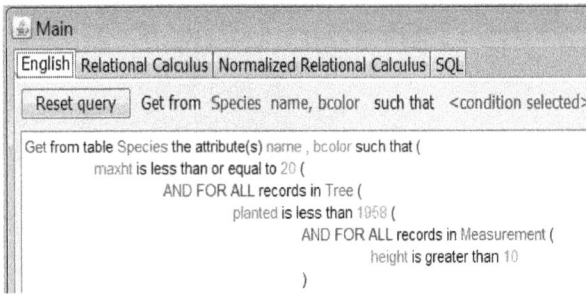

Figure 1. RX English-like query

Education researchers are still studying ways by which SQL and related concepts can be better taught. However, to the best of our knowledge none of these studies is dedicated to teaching second-order logic in SQL. Cembalo et al.'s SAVI tool allows student to visualize basic SQL queries [9]. Similarly, esql is concerned with teaching join and aggregate function queries [10]. Both esql and SAVI are not concerned with second-order logic. Matos et al. focus on teaching outer-joins in SQL queries [11]. Many of the previously developed tools are aimed at evaluating student responses (e.g., AsseSQL[12], SQLator[13] and SQLify [14]). Others are meant for high school students (e.g., eledSQL [15]).

Before introducing the tool in Section 3, required definitions and preliminaries are reviewed in Section 2. Section 4 summarizes the evaluation experiment of RX and concludes the paper.

2. SQLNF

The SQLNF method proposed by Kawash [5] is at the core of RX. This section summarizes the SQLNF approach. SQLNF eliminates universal quantifiers from the relational calculus expression and replaces them with logically equivalent (negated) existential quantifiers. It also replaces implications associated with universal quantifiers with their equivalent disjunctive form [5]. This section gives the definition of SQLNF, and assumes that the reader is familiar with database terminology, relational calculus, and SQL.

The main idea in SQLNF is to eliminate universal quantifiers from the relational calculus expression. The highlighted negation in the formula $(\neg \exists t)\neg(F(t))$ is referred by a *sandwiched negation*.

Definition. A formula F is in *SQLNF* if it does not contain: implication, universal quantification, implication, or sandwiched and double negations.

Each one of these undesired forms can be eliminated as follows. Implications are replaced by their equivalent disjunctive forms $((F_1 \Rightarrow F_2) \Leftrightarrow (\neg F_1 \vee F_2))$. Universal quantifiers are replaced by their existential quantification equivalence $((\forall t)(F(t)) \Leftrightarrow (\neg \exists t)\neg(F(t)))$. Sandwiched negations are removed by applying DeMorgan's laws $(\neg(F_1 \wedge F_2) \Leftrightarrow (\neg F_1 \vee \neg F_2)$ and $\neg(F_1 \vee F_2) \Leftrightarrow (\neg F_1 \wedge \neg F_2)))$. Double negations are simply dropped.

Definition. A tuple relational calculus query

$$\aleph = \{t_1.a_1, t_2.a_2, ..., t_n.a_n | F(t_1, t_2, ..., t_n, t_{n+1}, t_{n+2}, ..., t_{n+m})\}$$

is in *SQLNF* if and only if F is in *SQLNF*.

To normalize the query $\aleph$ to SQLNF, simply eliminate all the undesired forms in the following order: implications, universal quantifiers, sandwiched and double negations.

Given a query $\aleph$ in SQLNF, $\aleph = \{ t_1.a_1, t_2.a_2, ..., t_n.a_n | F(t_1, t_2, ..., t_n, t_{n+1}, t_{n+2}, ..., t_{n+m}) \}$, the translation to SQL is straightforward. The list $t_1.a_1, t_2.a_2, ..., t_n.a_n$ is called the *left part* of $\aleph$ and $F(t_1, t_2, ..., t_n, t_{n+1}, t_{n+2}, ..., t_{n+m})$ is called the *right part* of $\aleph$. Let $R_i(t)$ and $R_j(t)$ denote relations with tuple variable t in F. Translating expressions in SQLNF is accomplished through the following procedure:

1. The SELECT clause consists of the *left part*.

2. The FROM clause consists of each $R_i(t)$ in the *right part*, where $R_i(t)$ is not within the scope of a quantifier.

3. The WHERE clause consists of F translated to SQL constructs, excluding each $R_i(t)$ that is not within the scope of a quantifier. Since F is in SQLNF it must only consist of existential quantifiers and logical operators that exist in SQL. For each occurrence of an $R_j(t)$, we should expect a correlated SQL query having R_j in its FROM clause.

Example: To illustrate this approach, we work out an example query that is based on the partial ERD shown in Figure 2 [7].

English Query: Retrieve the name and bark color for each species with a maximum height not exceeding 20 meters such that every tree of that species that was planted before 1958 has had every measurement showing a height greater than 10 meters.

Tuple Relational Calculus Query:

$\aleph = \{$ s.sname, s.bcolor | Species(s) $\wedge$ s.maxht $\leq$ 20 $\wedge$

$(\forall t)((\text{Tree}(t) \wedge \text{t.sname} = \text{s.sname} \wedge \text{t.planted} < 1958) \Rightarrow$

$(\forall m)((\text{Measurement}(m) \wedge \text{m.tree\#} = \text{t.tree\#}) \Rightarrow \text{m.height} > 10)) \}$

Normalizing $\aleph$:

1. Eliminate implications:

$\aleph = \{$ s.sname, s.bcolor | Species(s) $\wedge$ s.maxht $\leq$ 20 $\wedge$

$(\forall t)(\neg(\text{Tree}(t) \wedge \text{t.sname} = \text{s.sname} \wedge \text{t.planted} < 1958) \vee$

$(\forall m)(\neg(\text{Measurement}(m) \wedge \text{m.tree\#} = \text{t.tree\#}) \vee \text{m.height} > 10))$

$\}$

116

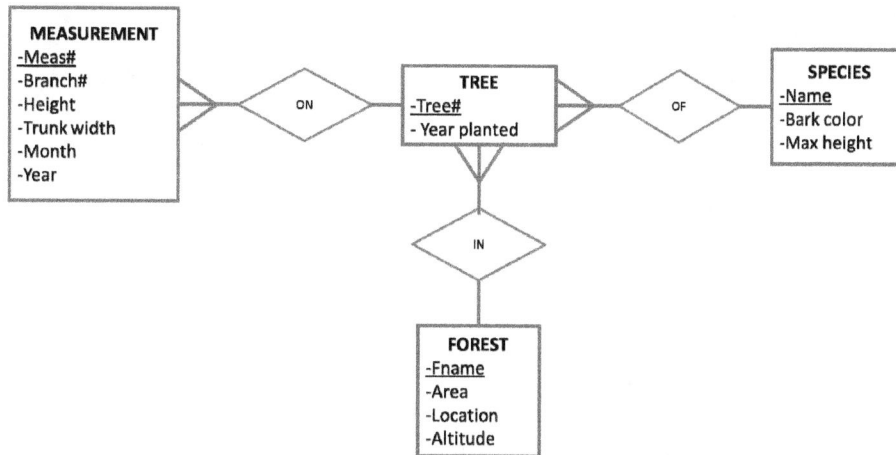

Figure 2. Example ERD

2. Eliminate universal quantifiers:

ℵ = { s.sname, s.bcolor | Species(s) ∧ s.maxht ≤ 20 ∧

(¬∃t)¬(¬(Tree(t) ∧ t.sname = s.sname ∧ t.planted < 1958) ∨
(¬∃m)¬(¬(Measurement(m) ∧ m.tree# = t.tree#) ∨ m.height >
10)) }

3. Eliminate sandwiched and double negation:

ℵ = { s.sname, s.bcolor | Species(s) ∧ s.maxht ≤ 20 ∧

(¬∃t) ((Tree(t) ∧ t.sname = s.sname ∧ t.planted < 1958) ∧

(∃m) ((Measurement(m) ∧ m.tree# = t.tree#) ∧ m.height ≤ 10)) }

Translating ℵ *to SQL:*

ℵ = {	ℵ in SQL
s.sname, s.bcolor |	SELECT s.sname, s.bcolor
Species(s)	FROM Species s
∧ *s.maxht ≤ 20*	WHERE s.maxht ≤ 20
∧ *(¬∃t)*	AND NOT EXISTS
(	(SELECT *
(Tree(t)	FROM TREE t
∧ *t.sname = s.sname*	WHERE t.sname = s.sname
∧ *t.planted < 1958)*	AND t.planted < 1958
∧ *(∃m)*	AND EXISTS
(	(SELECT *
(Measurement(m)	FROM Measurement m
∧ *t.tree# = m.tree#)*	WHERE t.tree# = m.tree#
∧ *m.height ≤ 10))* }	AND m.height ≤ 10) ;

3. TOOL OVERVIEW

Guided by an XML representation of the database schema, RX loads all the related meta-data when a particular database is loaded. The tool aims at assisting the learner to formulate the query condition, which is the most difficult task in query formulation. RX condition window is shown in Figure 3.

The user uses the left panel to formulate the query condition. The *NOT <condition>* checkbox is used to negate an input condition. Three sets of radio buttons are provided. The first allows the user to compare a particular attribute to a constant value. The comparison operator is chosen from a drop-down list and is inferred from the XML metadata, depending on the data type of the chosen attribute. The second and third radio buttons represent the universal and existential quantifiers. The tree structure on the right side of the window contains the condition being formulated by the user, using the left panel. The current focus of condition formulation is preceded by 'Root ==>'. Additions to the condition are added to the current focus point. The root position can be modified by the 'Set as root' button. A branch or leaf of the tree can be deleted by the 'Delete Selection' button. The Add buttons are used to add a sub-condition to an existing condition.

The resulting query is given in RX-English as it is being formulated. A formulated query is given in Figure 1.

The Relational Calculus pane (Figure 4) displays the relational calculus equivalent of the query formulated in the RX-English pane. This is done by choosing the Translate option in the menu bar. Learners can skip the RX-English step, entering the relational calculus query directly in this pane. Color-coding is used in all queries, for easier visualization and better comprehension. Figure 4 shows the translation of the RX-English query of Figure 1 to relational calculus.

The Normalized Relational Calculus pane displays the SQLNF relational calculus expression (Figure 5). The "Show Steps" button shows the steps performed in the normalization procedure (Figure 6). Finally, SQL pane displays the query in SQL (Figure 7).

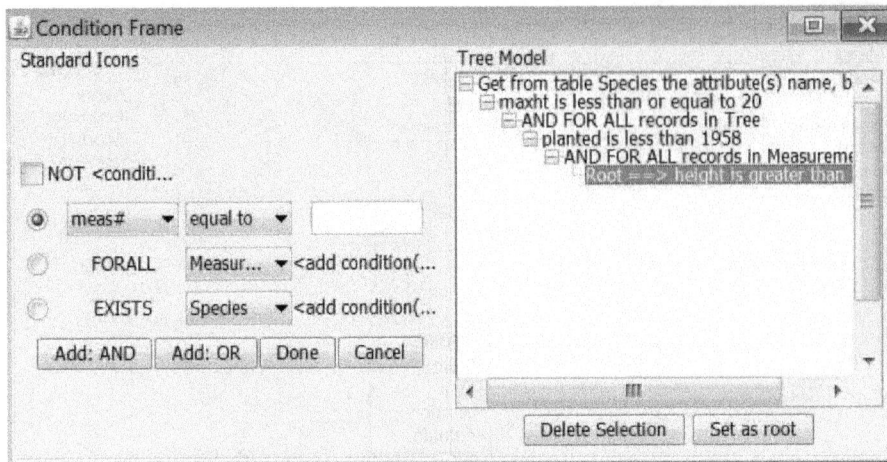

Figure 3. Condition formulation window

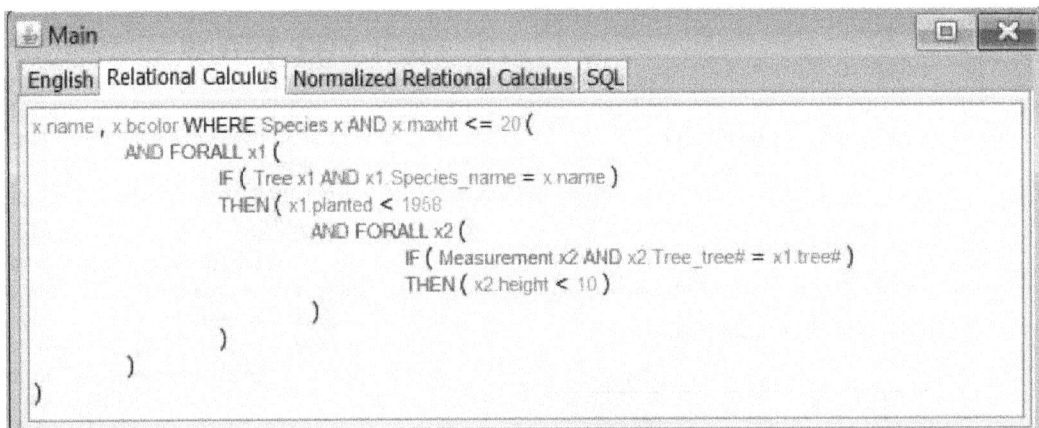

Figure 4. Relational calculus pane

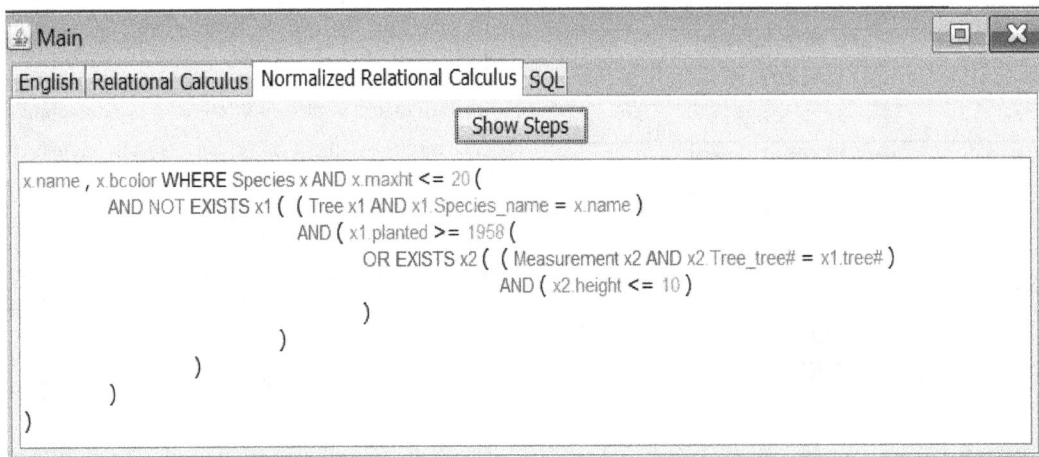

Figure 5. Normalized relational calculus pane

Normalization Procedure □ ⟲ ✕

Eliminate implications:

```
x.name , x.bcolor WHERE Species x AND x.maxht <= 20 (
        AND FORALL x1 ( NOT ( Tree x1 AND x1.Species_name = x.name )
                OR ( x1.planted < 1958 (
                        AND FORALL x2 ( NOT ( Measurement x2 AND x2.Tree_tree# = x1.tree# )
                                OR ( x2.height > 10 )
                        )
                )
        )
    )
)
```

Eliminate universal quantifiers:

```
x.name , x.bcolor WHERE Species x AND x.maxht <= 20 (
        AND NOT EXISTS x1 NOT ( NOT ( Tree x1 AND x1.Species_name = x.name )
                OR ( x1.planted < 1958 (
                        AND NOT EXISTS x2 NOT ( NOT ( Measurement x2 AND x2.Tree_tree# = x1.tree# )
                                OR ( x2.height > 10 )
                        )
                )
        )
    )
)
```

Eliminate sandwiched and double negations:

```
x.name , x.bcolor WHERE Species x AND x.maxht <= 20 (
        AND NOT EXISTS x1 ( ( Tree x1 AND x1.Species_name = x.name )
                AND ( x1.planted >= 1958 (
                        OR EXISTS x2 ( ( Measurement x2 AND x2.Tree_tree# = x1.tree# )
                                AND ( x2.height <= 10 )
                        )
                )
        )
    )
)
```

Close

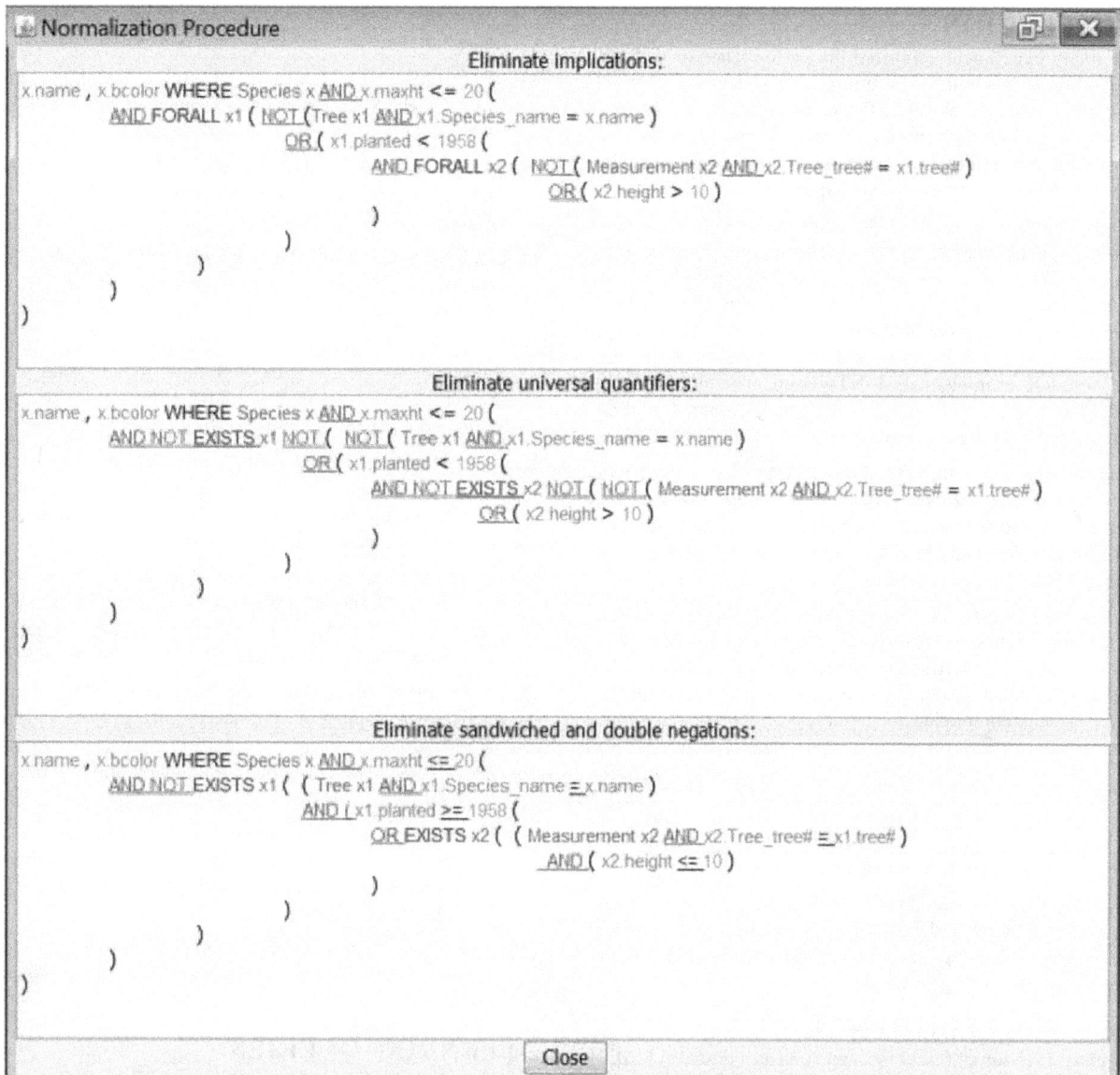

Figure 6. Steps for normalizing a relational calculus query

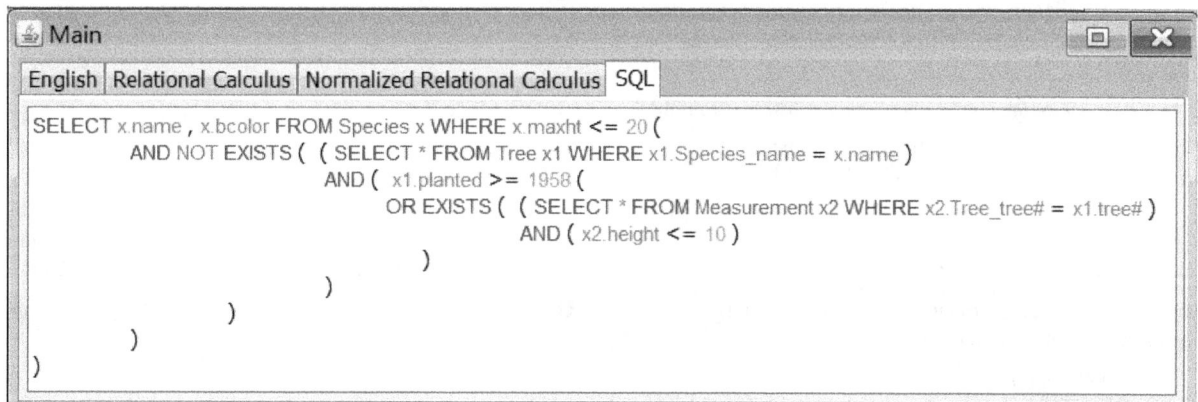

Main □ ✕

| English | Relational Calculus | Normalized Relational Calculus | SQL |

```
SELECT x.name , x.bcolor FROM Species x WHERE x.maxht <= 20 (
        AND NOT EXISTS ( ( SELECT * FROM Tree x1 WHERE x1.Species_name = x.name )
                AND ( x1.planted >= 1958 (
                        OR EXISTS ( ( SELECT * FROM Measurement x2 WHERE x2.Tree_tree# = x1.tree# )
                                AND ( x2.height <= 10 )
                        )
                )
        )
    )
)
```

Figure 7. SQL pane

4. EVALUATION

A preliminary experiment compared the performance of students before and after receiving RX training. It did show a slight increase in the students' ability to formulate complex queries. The main experiment that we report about here is mainly concerned with how RX can improve the understanding of students of the intricacies entailed in formulating such queries.

The study involved a total of 40 students in two semesters, divided equally between the two semesters. The students were chosen so that each must have successfully completed the database course. In each semester, the 20 students were divided into two groups: (1) a group that received extensive RX training, we will call this the **RX-group** and (2) a group that did not receive any RX training, called **NT-group**. The groups were chosen to have mixed levels of students, classified based on their final marks in the database course.

The students were asked to write a "mock" exam that consisted of 4 different queries (reproduced in the Appendix). The queries, numbered from 1 to 4, increase in complexity with query number. So, Q1 is the easiest and Q4 is the most complex. All 4 queries are taken from [5] (queries 2 to 5 in Section 4).

There were no substantial differences in the aggregate data between both semesters. So, we group results from both semesters. Table 1 shows the percentage of students who successfully formulated each query. It does not count the students who were close to completion and deserve partial marks.

Query	1	2	3	4
RX-group	100%	90%	65%	45%
NT-group	85%	65%	30%	15%
Difference	15%	35%	35%	40%

Table 1. Summary of results

Notably, only 15% (3 students) of the NT-group completed Query 4 successfully, while 9 students of the RX group were able to ace it. The benefits of using the tool are obvious, and the more complex the query, the higher the benefits.

5. ACKNOWLEDGMENTS

A preliminary version of this works appeared as a poster in [16].

6. REFERENCES

[1] V. J. Harvey, C. M. Ruzich, J. M. Baugh, B. A. Johnston, and A. J. Grabt. 2003. The challenge of negation in searches and queries. *The review of Business Information Systems* 7(4), 63-75.

[2] H. H. Clark. 1976. *Semantics and Comprehension*. Mouton.

[3] P. Wright P. 1981. The instructions clearly state… Can't people read? *Applied Ergonomics* 12(3), 31-141.

[4] H. J. Klein. 2002. How to modify SQL queries in order to guarantee sure answers. *ACM SIGMOD Record,* 94(9).

[5] J. Kawash. 2004. Complex quantification in Standard Query Language (SQL): A tutorial using relational calculus. *Computers in Math. & Science Teaching 23(2),* 169-190.

[6] C. Date. 2000. *An introduction to database systems,* 7th ed. Addison-Wesley.

[7] J. Bradley. 1982. *File and database techniques*. Holt, Rinehart, and Winston.

[8] P. Resiner. 1981. Human Factor Studies of Database Query Languages: A Survey and Assessment. *ACM Computing Surveys,* 13(1), 13-31.

[9] M. Cembalo, A. De Santis, and U. F. Petrillo. 2011. SAVI: a new system for advanced SQL visualization. In *Proc. SIGITE '11.* ACM, 165-170.

[10] R. Kearns, S. Shead, and A. Fekete. 1997. A teaching system for SQL. In *Proc. of the 2nd Australasian conference on Computer science education* (ACSE '97). ACM, 224-231.

[11] V. Matos, R. Grasser, and P. Jalics. 2006. The case of the missing tuple: teaching the SQL outer-join operator to undergraduate information systems students. *J. Comput. Sci. Coll.* 22, 1 (October 2006), 23-32.

[12] J. Coleman Prior and R. Lister. 2004. The backwash effect on SQL skills grading. In *Proc. of the 9th annual SIGCSE conference on Innovation and technology in computer science education* (ITiCSE '04). ACM, 32-36.

[13] S. Sadiq, M. Orlowska, W. Sadiq, and J. Lin. 2004. SQLator: an online SQL learning workbench. In *Proc. of the 9th annual SIGCSE conference on Innovation and technology in computer science education* (ITiCSE '04). ACM, 223-227.

[14] S. Dekeyser, M. de Raadt, and T. Yu Lee. 2007. Computer assisted assessment of SQL query skills. In *Proc. of the eighteenth conference on Australasian database - Volume 63* (ADC '07), Australian Computer Society, Inc., 53-62.

[15] A. Grillenberger and T. Brinda. 2012. eledSQL: a new web-based learning environment for teaching databases and SQL at secondary school level. In *Proc. of the 7th Workshop in Primary and Secondary Computing Education* (WiPSCE '12). ACM, 101-104.

[16] J. Kawash. 2005. Tutoring Tool for Formulating Database Queries with Complex Quantifiers. *ITNG 2009*. IEEE, 1614-1615.

APPENDIX - QUERIES

These queries [5] assume the ERD in Figure 2.

Query 1: Get the name and location of each forest under 1000 square meters in which *every* tree was planted before 1960 and has had *at least one* measurement showing a height over 20 meters.

Query 2: Get the name and bark color for each species with a maximum height exceeding 30 meters such that *every* tree of that species that was planted before 1960 has had *every* measurement showing a height greater than 15 meters.

Query 3: Get the name and maximum height of each species that occurs in *every* Alberta forest over 1500 meters in altitude and in which there is at least one employee who has been hired in 1993.

Query 4: Get the name and size of each forest in Alberta in which *every* tree was planted before 1960 and has had *all but one* measurements showing a height over 20 meters.

The Practical Application of LEGO® MINDSTORMS® Robotics Kits: Does it Enhance Undergraduate Computing Students' Engagement in Learning the Java Programming Language?

Ethan Tsang
Department of Computing
Edge Hill University
St Helens Road, Ormskirk

ethan.tsang@go.edgehill.ac.uk

Collette Gavan
Department of Computing
Edge Hill University
St Helens Road, Ormskirk
+44 1695657633
gavanc@edgehill.ac.uk

Dr. Mark Anderson
Department of Computing
Edge Hill University
St Helens Road, Ormskirk
+44 1695657634
mark.anderson@edgehill.ac.uk

ABSTRACT

This research investigates the extent to which the practical application of robotics affects undergraduate computing students' engagement in learning the Java programming language. Current literature suggests that the practical application of objects enables students to engage and understand concepts within engineering, robotics and computing disciplines easier than purely theoretical teaching methods. This research measures student engagement based on affective, behavioural, cognitive and performance engagement factors. Questionnaires, interviews and observations were exercised in order to explore the reasons that student engagement is affected. The findings suggest that the LEGO® MINDSTORMS® robotics are positively engaging students to learn the Java programming language at an undergraduate level. Negative aspects, of limitations and non-participation, may be explained through external factors including the structure of the module and peer and social pressure.

Categories and Subject Descriptors

K.3.2 [**Computer and Information Science Education**]: Computer science education

General Terms

Management, Design, Human Factors, Theory

Keywords

Programming; student engagement; teaching

1. INTRODUCTION

This research is important to the subject area as technology is required in order to effectively teach concepts [1][2]. "With the development of the modern educational technology, more and more teachers are looking for efficient methods and creative ideas, both to get their ideas across and to hold the interest of their students" [3]. At the UK university that is the focus of this study, the practical application of robotics have been employed in order to teach undergraduate computing students the Java programming language. Whilst there is evidence to support that such applications have a positive effect on student's learning outcomes including improved grades [4], no current research identifying the engagement factors associated with LEGO® robotics currently exists. Furthermore this research builds upon a study by Gavan & Anderson [4] to determine why engagement is affected and offer recommendations to future developments in academia. The aim of this research is to understand the effects of the practical application of LEGO® MINDSTORMS® robotics on undergraduate computing students' engagement in relation to learning the Java programming language.

2. BACKGROUND

Traditional approaches to education, where concepts are taught mainly by lecture, have many shortcomings which result in a lack of motivation as a result of a lack of active learning [5]. Building on the shortfalls of teacher-focused learning environments and the Socratic Method; the Harkness Method was developed in the early 1930s. The Harkness Method focuses on allowing students to develop their understandings through peer collaborations, instead of trying to understand concepts through lectures and Socratic questions [6]. This teaching method encourages the critical development of ideas, promotes soft skills and builds students' confidence [7].

Student's learning experiences are significantly enhanced by increasing levels of student engagement and the depth of learning afforded by the teaching and learning environment [8]. Therefore educators must alter the teaching environment, away from the traditional approaches, and towards active and experience-based learning in order to promote student learning [9]. Additionally as a result of the significance of technology in modern culture, educators must address expectations of equipping students to handle and understand technology within their future endeavours [10]. To this point two challenges have been identified in academia: the challenge of engaging students learning in the technological era, and implementing technology within academia. This poses challenges for educators in the technological subject areas such as computing and computer programming.

These challenges can be addressed simultaneously. Students' interest and motivation in learning can be stimulated through the use and demonstration of practical applications of computing software within teaching methods [11]. Rais, et al. [12] states that as a result of a lack of previous exposure and experience in programming, learners may struggle to engage with particular programming concepts without the application of practical activities. Furthermore, increasing students' engagement is becoming increasingly essential in education because the experts who develop complex systems are retiring faster than universities are graduating students, which is increasing the need for students to gain exposure to complex systems and concepts [13]. In an attempt to improve students' engagement and understanding of such complex subjects such as programming, higher educational institutions have integrated the practical application of objects to instil a positive effect on the learning experience [14][15].

The inclusion of such objects in education can be viewed as a motivating element allowing for students to develop a motivation for learning, and to develop a deeper interest in the application of concepts [16]. Gassert, et al. [17] observed that when objects were used in education as a learning tool, it is evident that the hands-on experience supports higher-order learning; as a result of opportunities for students' to develop their own representations and concepts of educational theories [18]. Furthermore, Gavan & Anderson [4] concluded that the practical application of robotics in undergraduate computing courses in the UK context has been proven to improve student engagement.

2.1 Student Engagement

There is a common understanding that student engagement is more than visible student participation and behaviour within the course, and that it is a combination of various components that together describe engagement [19][20][21][22][23]. Student engagement has been defined as participation in academia and identification and valuation of academic goals [24][25]; with affective/emotional, behavioural, and cognitive engagement subtypes being related to student engagement [26][27]. It has also been described as a willingness to participate [28], attitude and participatory behaviour [29], and combination of cognitive, intellectual, academic, social, behavioural, participatory and emotional engagement [30].

A study on school engagement by Fredricks, et al. [31] identifies behavioural engagement, emotional engagement and cognitive engagement, as individual factors which determine and define engagement within academia. Handelsman, et al.[32] (see Figure 1), defines four separate engagement factors: skills, emotional, participation/interaction and performance. The skills factor represents students' engagement in terms of practising skills such as "taking good notes in class" and "looking over class notes between classes". The skills factor shares a relation to the NSSE's [33] 'level of academic challenge' which represents the assigned work, complexity of cognitive tasks and student performance evaluation standards. Emotional engagement represents student engagement through the emotional involvement with the class

material, including "Applying course material to my life" and "Thinking about the course between class meetings". Emotional engagement in the academic context can be viewed as an engagement with learning opportunities, and not simply participation and attendance [34]. The third factor labelled participation/interaction draws similarities with the NSSE's [33][35] 'student-faculty interactions'; and measures the student engagement with the course through interactions with faculty members both inside and outside of the module. The final factor, performance engagement, shares similarities with extrinsic motivation and personal performance goals [32][36]. Handelsman, et al [32] reveals that the four engagement factors shared an association with at least one other measure, the factors were clearly distinguishable from each other and supports a multidimensional construct of student engagement which allows student engagement to be measured accurately. This four-dimensional measure of student engagement is appropriate to this study as it has four clearly distinguishable engagement sub-types that can be individually measured.

Figure 1: Student Engagement 4-Dimensional Factors [32]

TABLE 1. Factor Structure of Student Course Engagement Questionnaire

Items	Factor 1 (Skills)	Factor 2 (Emotional)	Factor 3 (Part/int)	Factor 4 (Performance)
Making sure to study on a regular basis	.64			
Putting forth effort	.59			
Doing all the homework problems	.57			
Staying up on the readings	.55			
Looking over class notes between classes to make sure I understand the material	.53			
Being organized	.53			
Taking good notes in class	.53			
Listening carefully in class	.51			
Coming to class every day	.47			
Finding ways to make the course material relevant to my life		.86		
Applying course material to my life		.86		
Finding ways to make the course interesting to me		.54		
Thinking about the course between class meetings		.46		
Really desiring to learn the material		.43		
Raising my hand in class			.82	
Asking questions when I don't understand the instructor			.64	
Having fun in class			.57	
Participating actively in small-group discussions			.55	
Going to the professor's office hours to review assignments or tests or to ask questions			.50	
Helping fellow students			.45	
Getting a good grade				.77
Doing well on the tests				.68
Being confident that I can learn and do well in the class				.64

Note. Part/int = participation/interaction. Factor loadings less than .40 are not displayed.

Whilst in literature there is not a definitive definition or measure of engagement, reoccurring similarities across the definitional variations on the conceptualisation of engagement include identification of affective/emotional engagement, behavioural engagement, and cognitive engagement. Handelsman, et al. [32] discovers that performance engagement was a subtype of engagement that proved to be a relevant and reliable factor in measuring student engagement.

In its simplest form, affective/emotional engagement can be described as the feelings that students have towards learning and the learning environment [37]. In adopting the Handelsman, et al [32] measure of student engagement, affective/emotional engagement was measured based on students' perception that the practical application of LEGO® MINDSTORMS® robotics: causes students to make course material relevant to their lives, generates application of course material to students' lives, results in the desire to make course material specifically interesting to the individual, and produces the desire to learn the material. These measures align with various definitional variations of affective/emotional engagement as they refer to students' positive application of the learning opportunities to a broader context and demonstration of enthusiasm to learn.

Behavioural engagement is a significant factor in measuring student engagement as negative student behaviour causes students to become less engaged in lessons and as a consequence students often perform worse in school [38], which has a direct relation with performance engagement. In adopting the Handelsman, et al [32] measure of student engagement, behavioural engagement will be measured based on students' perception that the practical application of robotics: results in asking questions in class, consequently results in 'fun' learning, results in active participation in small-group discussions, instigates tutor interaction outside of designated seminar time, stimulates peer-to-peer tutoring.

Cognitive engagement refers to the amount of and methods/strategies of processing that students employ in learning [39]; Cognitive engagement differentiates from behavioural engagement as it focuses on a students' mental involvement in academic tasks [40], by incorporating thoughtfulness and willingness to exert the necessary effort to comprehend and master skills[41]. In adopting the Handelsman, et al [32] measure of student engagement, cognitive engagement will be measured based on students' perception that the practical application of robotics: encourages regular study, inspires effort exertion, advocates homework completion, promotes staying up on readings, encourages looking over notes between seminars, sponsors organisation, stimulates taking meaningful notes in class, reinforces careful listening in seminars, and spurs attendance. These measures align with the definitional variations of cognitive engagement as they refer to academic processing tasks that are employed and producing knowledge.

Performance engagement represents student engagement in terms of academic performance and performance goals rather than learning or mastery goals [32]. In adopting the Handelsman, et al [32] measure of student engagement, performance engagement will be measured based on students' perception that the practical application of robotics: will eventuate in the student getting a good grade, will conclude in good test marks, and champions confidence in learning and achieving well in the module. These measures align with the definitional variations of performance engagement as they refer to how students' perceive their engagement in achieving academic success.

This study is looking specifically at how LEGO® MINDSTORMS® robotics affects student engagement in learning Java programming and several of the factors identified by Handelsman, et al. [32] cannot be accurately measured as students interact with other modules and develop skills from a range of different sources.

3. RESULTS

Quantitative primary data was gathered from questionnaires using a Likert scale using the range 1-5 (in which a higher score indicated a more positive response) and qualitative data was gathered from interviews and observations. The subjects of the study consisted of two groups of first year students in programming sessions. These groups contain 50 students between

them. The questionnaires were designed such that the questions aligned with the work of Handelsman et al [32]. Using the responses from the questionnaires, the mean values were calculated to determine a holistic view of the opinions of the subjects. These are presented in table 1 (below).

Table 1: Mean values of questionnaire results

Class	Question	Mean response
Cognitive	Ensure that you study on a regular basis outside of class	3.6
Cognitive	Put effort into the programming activities	4.24
Cognitive	Complete all homework tasks	4.49
Cognitive	Look over course material between classes	3.58
Cognitive	Listen carefully during classes	4.00
Cognitive	Attend every class	4.71
Emotional	Apply what you learn in class to other aspects of your life	3.38
Emotional	Think about the programming module in between classes	3.85
Emotional	Desire to learn the course material	4.00
Emotional	Find ways to make the course more interesting	3.89
Interaction	Ask questions when you do not understand	4.09
Interaction	Have fun in class	4.20
Interaction	Participate in group activities	4.33
Interaction	Contact your tutor outside of class about the programming module	3.11
Interaction	Help fellow students on the programming module	4.04
Performance	Feel like you will get a good grade	3.89
Performance	Feel confident that you can learn and do well in class	4.00

It is possible to determine that the area that benefitted the most from the approach to the study was that related to attending sessions, as students provided very positive opinions. Indeed, the cognitive benefits all rank highly as benefitting by the students, with the cognitive average mean being 4.10 (compared to the overall average of 3.96). The interaction (3.89) and performance (3.95) means are also close to the overall average.

The observations took place over two hour sessions with the same subjects. These were designed to determine the student attendance in a session, whether the non-attendance was authorized, and also how the students participated in sessions. The attendance rate was high (84%), with only 7% of students not requesting permission for absence.

Figure 2: Engagement vs Non-engagement on screen

Engagement vs. Unengagement On Screen

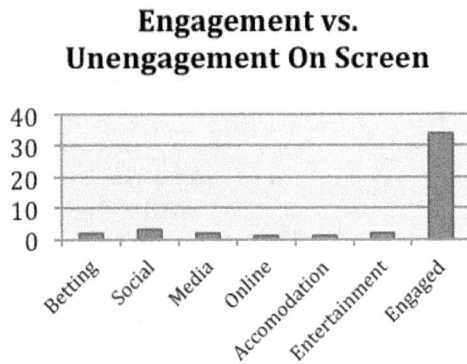

Figure 3: Engagement participation

Participation

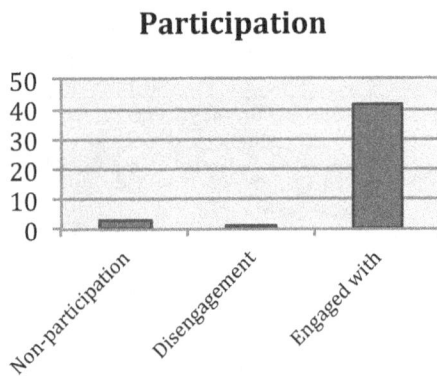

Figure 2 above shows the number of students who showed unengaged activity throughout the scheduled class and those who maintained on-screen engagement throughout the class. This measured student's cognitive engagement and provides results to support rationale for negative emotional engagement. In total there were 11 students who accessed 'un-productive' websites, or otherwise unrelated activities during the class.

This study found the 34 students maintained their engagement with the module throughout the class showing that 75.6% of students engaged with the module throughout the seminar in regards to their on-screen activity.

Figure 3 above shows student engagement and participation within the group during the seminar. This measured student's participation/interaction engagement towards the group exercises. This study found that 4 students did not participate with their groups during the seminars. Of these 4 students, 3 (6.7%) students were otherwise engaged with unproductive on-screen activity as not engaging with the group exercises. 1 (2.2%) student did not engage with their own group and was communicating with another group on an un-related topic to the module.

The aim of the interviews were to identify and explore why and how the practical application of robotics affects student engagement towards learning the Java programming language.

The following list is the terms that respondents described LEGO® MINDSTORMS® robotics:

Physical; Play; Dynamic; Different; Trial and Error; Interesting; Alternative; Creative; Hands-On Experience; Visual Output; Limiting; Deserving.

This suggests that the LEGO® MINDSTORMS® robotics are providing students with a more interesting, dynamic and physical method of learning the Java programming language which contributes positively to student's engagement. The only negative factor is that the robotics were described as limiting to what can be achieved through them, however this support the academic direction of the learning object. The findings of how the robotics impact the learning experiences of students largely aligns with the literature review. However there were few comments on how robotics affected soft skill engagement.

In terms of what engages students to the Java programming language in comparison to lectures that adopt a more Socratic method of learning, the following list includes descriptors that respondents used to describe the comparative impact of robotics to lectures and other learning methods:

"Play rather than sit in front of a PC screen", "Construction and design", "Lectures are more a listening thing", "A more physical thing", "Visual output"

This suggests that students are engaged towards learning Java programming through the LEGO® MINDSTORMS® robotics as a result of the physical and visual outputs. In comparison to lectures and other learning tools students find that the robotics engage them as it is not a simple listening exercise and not just sitting in front of a screen. Whilst students perceive that more can be achieved through Alice in the time given; the physical and constructive elements of robotics engage students to learn Java programming.

Finally, in terms of performance engagement the following list describes how students feel about the impact on their performance as a result of the LEGO® MINDSTORMS® robotics:

- Probably achieve a higher grade;
- More motivated to get a higher grade;
- Feel like you deserve a higher grade;

Therefore it can be interpreted that the robotics have a positive effect on students' perceptions of achieving a higher grade as a result of motivation and sense of deserving a higher grade. However students do identify that the foundations of Alice and Eclipse are required to achieve a higher grade, therefore the module progression is required to engage students to achieve a higher grade.

4. DISCUSSION

Students' perceptions of how the LEGO® MINDSTORMS® robotics are likely to engage students to think about the programming module in between classes resulted in an engagement level of 77%. This figure suggests that students are more likely to consider programming aspects outside of classes and therefore develop ideas in order to apply to future tasks.

Reasons to which students may not engage in this aspect may include that they may not want to continue down the programming pathways, or may not have outstanding work to complete and may concentrate their efforts elsewhere.

In terms of how students are more engaged with the programming module as a result of the of LEGO® MINDSTORMS® robotics students found that they were engaged as a result of the physical, visual, constructive and creative aspects of the of robotics. This gave students an increased interest in the programming module as they were not limited to sitting in front of a computer screen or listening as they would in lectures or other teaching methods. Students were more engaged as a result of the fun aspects, interesting, dynamic, trial and error and different aspects of the of robotics. This therefore led students to perceive the use of robotics as more deserving, rewarding and motivating than other teaching methods. Students also found that the collaborative aspects were engaging allowing them to share ideas, and participate within the module. Furthermore the concept of LEGO® was an engaging factor to students as they could relate to it more.

However students did feel as if there were time pressures as a result of the amount of work expected from them, this might engage students to complete the work but may detract from the learning experiences as the additional pressure may limit their enjoyment. Students also found that Alice was less limiting and more could be achieved through the Alice tool, this suggests that although the of robotics may focus the learning more, they feel more trapped in the structure of the module.

5. CONCLUSIONS

The findings suggest that the LEGO® MINDSTORMS® robotics are positively engaging students to learn the Java programming language at an undergraduate level. To identify the existing application of objects in academia, the concept is currently being applied in various computing and technological fields across various academic levels in different environments. This includes the practical application of robotics which has been applied with positive results to academic achievement. Literature also supports the use of robotics to improve students' learning experiences as they benefit academia through the possible interactivity.

This study then defined student engagement and identified a set of criteria to which student engagement can be measured. It was found that student engagement comprises many different aspects, mainly affective, behavioural and cognitive engagement. This study found that additional engagement factors including performance may also be measured. This study exercised the engagement factors adopted by Handelsman, *et al.* (2005) which used affective, behavioural, cognitive, and performance engagement to define student engagement in the academic context.

To discover the extent of which the practical application of robotics affects student engagement towards learning the Java programming language, was achieved by this study through quantitative research methods. This study found that students were 79.2% likely to engage with learning the Java programming language as a result of the practical application of robotics. Student's cognitive engagement was the most positive engagement factor affected by the robotics.

In identifying and exploring why and how the practical application of robotics affects student engagement towards learning the Java programming language, two qualitative research methods were exercised. Observations revealed that 91% of students attended the sessions; there was 75.6% engagement throughout the seminars and 91.1% of students showed participatory engagement in the seminars. These findings, along with the quantitative research, were explained through the use of interviews. The practical application of robotics affects student engagement as a result of them being perceived as hands-on, dynamic, interesting and creative tool for learning Java. Students expressed a preference for being able to work in groups and see a visual output compared to lectures which students found less interesting and less rewarding. Students perceived the robotics as fun and motivating which provided them with engagement towards the robotics and learning Java programming.

Finally to answer the research aim, to understand the effects of the practical application of robotics on undergraduate computing students' engagement in relation to learning the Java programming language, the effects are largely positive. The negative aspects of limitations and non-participation may be explained through external factors including the structure of the module and peer and social pressure. Overall the robotics has a significantly positive effect on undergraduate computing students' engagement towards learning the Java programming language.

6. ACKNOWLEDGMENTS

Our thanks to the first year students at Edge Hill University, who supported this study and provided the evidential feedback.

7. REFERENCES

[1] Szweda, L., Flotynski, J., Wilusz, D. & Dabrowski, P. (2012) 'Robot simulator facilitating the education of concurrent programming' *2012 Federated Conference on Computer Science and Information Systems (FedCSIS)*. pp. 891 – 896.

[2] Safer, A. H. & Alkhezzi, F. A. (2013) 'Beyond Computer Literacy: Technology Integration and Curriculum Transformation' *College Student Journal*. 47 (4). pp. 614 – 626.

[3] Yu, X. (2012) 'Using LEGO Mindstorms in the undergraduate curriculum of IT' *2012 International Symposium on Information Technology in Medicine and Education (ITME)*. 1. pp. 270 – 273.

[4] Gavan, C. & Anderson, M. (2013) 'Engaging Undergraduate Programming Students: Experiences using Lego Mindstorms NXT' *SIGITE 2013, 23 – 25 October 2013*, Calgary.

[5] Jalali, M., Marti, J. J., Kirchkoff, A. L., Lawrenz, F. & Campbell, S. A. (2012) 'A Low-Cost Hands-On Laboratory to Introduce Lithography Concepts' *IEEE Transactions on Education*. 55 (4). pp. 517 – 524.

[6] Smith, L. A. & Foley, M. (2009) 'Partners in a Human Enterprise: Harkness Teaching in the History Classroom' *History Teacher*. 42 (4). pp. 477 – 496.

[7] Rao, M. S. (2013) 'Exploring "Meka's method" to achieve effective teaching and training outcomes' *Industrial & Commercial Training*. 45 (6). pp. 362 – 368.

[8] Mustafa, B. (2011) 'Modern Computer Architecture Teaching and Learning Support: An Experience in Evaluation' *International Conference on Information Society (i-Society 2011), 27-29 June 2011*, London.

[9] Halvorson, W., Crittenden, V. L. & Pitt, L. (2011) 'Teaching Cases in a Virtual Environment: When the Traditional Case Classroom is Problematic' *Decision Sciences Journal of Innovative Education*. 9 (3). pp. 485 – 492.

[10] Barter, B. (2013) 'Rural Schools and Technology: Connecting for Innovation' *Australian International Journal of Rural Education*. 23 (3). pp. 41 – 55.

[11] Jun, L. & Huiqing, Z. (2012) 'A study on the reform of VB programming teaching methods' *2012 7th International Conference on Computer Science & Education (ICCSE)*. pp. 1768 – 1770.

[12] Rais, A. E., Sulaiman, S. & Syed-Mohamad, S. M. (2011) 'Game-based approach and its feasibility to support the learning of object-oriented concepts and programming' *2011 5th Malaysian Conference in Software Engineering (MySEC)*. pp. 307 – 312

[13] Crenshaw, T. L. A. (2013) 'Using Robots and Contract Learning to Teach Cyber-Physical Systems to Undergraduates' *IEEE Transactions on Education*. 56 (1). pp. 116 – 120.

[14] Behrens, A., Atorf, L., Schwann, R., Neumann, B., Schnitzler, R., Balle, J., Herold, T., Telle, A., Noll, T. G., Hameyer, K. & Aach, T. (2010) 'MATLAB Meets LEGO Mindstorms - A Freshman Introduction Course into Practical Engineering' *IEEE Transactions on Education*. 53 (2). pp. 306 - 317.

[15] Akın, H. L., Meriçli, Ç. & Meriçlia, T (2012) 'Introduction to autonomous mobile robotics using Lego Mindstorms NXT' *Computer Science Education*. 23 (4). pp. 368 – 386.

[16] Aroca, R. V., Gomes, R. B., Tavares, D. M., Souza, A. A. S., Burlamaqui, A. M. F., Caurin, G. A. P. & Goncalves, L. M. G. (2013) 'Increasing Students' Interest With Low-Cost CellBots' *IEEE Transactions on Education*. 56 (1). pp. 3 - 8.

[17] Gassert, R., Metzger, J., Leuenbeger, K., Popp, W. L., Tucker, M. R., Vigaru, B., Zimmermann, R. & Lambercy, O. (2013) 'Physical Student-Robot Interaction With the ETHZ Haptic Paddle' *IEEE Transactions on Education*. 56 (1). pp. 9 - 17.

[18] De Cristoforis, P., Pedre, S., Nitsche, M., Fischer, T., Pessacg, F. & Di Pietro, C. (2013) 'A Behavior-Based Approach for Educational Robotics Activities' *IEEE Transactions on Education*. 56 (1). pp. 61 – 66.

[19] Guthrie, J. T., Anderson, E., Alao, S. & Rinehart, J. (1999) 'Influences of Concept-Orientated Reading Instruction on Strategy Use and Conceptual Learning from Text' *The Elementary School Journal*. 99 (4). pp. 343 – 366.

[20] Baker, L. & Wigfield, A. (1999) 'Dimensions of children's motivation for reading and their relations to reading activity and reading achievement' *Reading Research Quarterly*. 34 (4). pp. 452 – 477.

[21] Harris, L. (2011) 'Secondary teachers' conceptions of student engagement: Engagement in learning or in school?' *Teaching and Teacher Education*. 27 (2). pp. 376 – 386.

[22] Lee, J. (2012) 'The effects of the teacher-student relationship and academic press on student engagement and academic performance' *International Journal of Educational Research*. 53. pp. 330 – 340.

[23] Stroet, K., Opdenakker, M. & Minnaert, A. (2013) 'Effects of need supportive teaching on early adolescents' motivation and engagement: A review of the literature' *Educational Research Review*. 9. pp. 65 – 87.

[24] Audas, R. & Willms, J. D. (2001) 'Engagement and Dropping out of School: A life course perspective. Working paper for the Applied Research Branch, Strategic Policy, Human Resources Development Canada. Quebec: HRDC Publications Centre.

[25] Finn, J. D. & Rock, D. A. (1997) 'Academic Success Among Students at Risk for School Failure' *Journal of Applied Psychology*. 82 (2). pp. 221 – 234.

[26] Connell, J. P. & Wellborn, J. G. (1991) Competence, autonomy, and relatedness: A motivational analysis of self-system processes. In M. Gunnar & L. A. Sroufe (Eds), *Minnesota Symposium on Child Psychology* (Vol 23). Chicago: University of Chicago Press.

[27] Furlong, M. J., Whipple, A. D., St. Jean, G., Simental,J., Soliz, A. & Punthuna, S. (2003) 'Multiple contexts of school engagement: Moving toward a unifying framework for educational research and practice' *California School Psychologist*. 8. pp. 99 – 114.

[28] Chapman, E (2003) 'Alternative approaches to assessing student engagement rates' *Practical assessment, research & evaluation*. 8 (13). Retrieved September 16, 2013 from http://PAREonline.net/getvn.asp?v=8&n=13.

[29] Mosher, R. & McGowan, B. (1985) Assessing student engagement in secondary schools: Alternative conceptions, strategies of assessing and instruments. University of Wisconsin. Research and Development Center (ERIC Document Reproduction Service No. ED 272812).

[30] Yazzie-Mintz, E. (2007). Voices of students on engagement: A report on the 2006 High School Survey of Student Engagement. Bloomington: Center of Evaluation & Education Policy, Indiana University. Retrieved September 16, 2013, from http://files.eric.ed.gov/fulltext/ED495758.pdf.

[31] Fredricks, J. A., Blumenfeld, P. C. & Paris, A. H. (2004) 'School Engagement: Potential of the Concept, State of the Evidence' *Review of Educational Research*. 74 (1). pp. 59 – 109.

[32] Handelsman, M. M., Briggs, W. L., Sullivan, N. & Towler, A. (2005) 'A Measure of College Student Course Engagement' *The Journal of Educational Research*. 98 (3). pp. 184 - 192.

[33] National Survey of Student Engagement. (2000) '*The NSSE report: National benchmarks of effective educational practice*. Bloomington: Indiana University Center for Postsecondary Research and Planning.

[34] Skinner, E. A., Kindermann, T. A. & Furrer, C. J. (2009) 'A Motivational Perspective on Engagement and Disaffection' *Educational and Psychological Measurement*. 69(3). pp.493 –525.

[35] National Survey of Student Engagement. (2002) '2002 Annual Report From Promise to Progress: How Colleges and Universities Are Using Student Engagement Results to Improve Collegiate Quality' Bloomington: Indiana University Center for Postsecondary Research and Planning.

[36] Sansone, C. & Harackiewicz, J. M. (2000) Intrinsic and extrinsic motivation: The search for optimal motivation and performance. San Diego: Academic Press.

[37] Veiga, F. H. (2012) 'Proposal to the PISA of a New Scale of Students' Engagement in School' *4th World Conference on Educational Sciences (WCES-2012) 02-05*. 46. pp. 1224 – 1231.

[38] Brackett, M. A., Reyes, M. R., Rivers, S. E., Elbertson, N. A. & Salovey, P. (2011) 'Classroom Emotional Climate, Teacher Affiliation, and Student Conduct' *Journal of Classroom Interaction*. 46 (1). pp. 27 – 36.

[39] Rastegar, A., Jahromi, R. G., Haghighi, A. S. & Akbari, A. R. (2010) 'The relation of epistemological beliefs and mathematics achievement: the mediating role of achievement goals, mathematics self-efficacy, and cognitive engagement' *Procedia – Social and Behavioural Services*. 5. pp. 791 – 797.

[40] Akiva, T., Cortina, K. S., Eccles, J. S. & Smith, C. (2013) 'Youth belonging and cognitive engagement in organized activities: A large-scale field study' *Journal of Applied Developmental Psychology*. 34 (5). pp. 208 – 218.

[41] Font, S. & Maguire-Jack, K. (2013) 'Academic engagement and performance: Estimating the impact of out-of-home care for maltreated children' *Children and Youth Services Review*. 53 (5). pp. 856 – 864.

Using Android as a Platform for Programming in the IT Curriculum

Michael Halper
Information Technology Department
NJIT
Newark, NJ 07102
1-973-596-5752

michael.halper@njit.edu

ABSTRACT

Mobile devices have become fixtures of our everyday lives. As such, it is sensible to deploy them in the IT curriculum where they can help students attain their core competency in programming. Android has been adopted as the platform for an advanced programming course in which students are using Java (Android's native language) and XML to build apps. Many subtle issues and common pitfalls have been encountered when transitioning this programming course to Android apps from traditional Java programs. Gathered from over a year's experience teaching app development, these issues are discussed, and suggestions and tips beneficial to IT instructors and students for working with Android are presented. Overall, the issues dealt with range from setting up devices and emulators to subtleties in linking Java and XML to quirks of the Eclipse IDE. Accessing the Internet is also covered. Some additional benefits of Android development for the undergraduate IT curriculum are discussed.

Categories and Subject Descriptors

D.2.6 [**Software Engineering**]: Programming Environments – *Integrated environments.*

Keywords

Java Programming; Android; Apps; Android SDK; Eclipse Integrated Development Environment (IDE); Mobile Computing

1. INTRODUCTION

Mobile devices have become ubiquitous. According to a recent article in *The New York Times*, mobile access accounts for 25% of Web use [1]. Walk into any IT classroom, and you will undoubtedly see students armed with an array of such devices. Indeed, IT students (and much of the general populace) have become enthralled with these devices and have become dependent on them for many daily routines. Since students are so engaged with mobile computing, it is reasonable that they would be more excited about programming if the results of their efforts could be seen immediately on these devices. That is, IT students should be developing apps. Moreover, in their apps, students can quickly learn to access the Web, manipulate multimedia data, and do other interesting data processing.

Indeed, mobile computing has been introduced into introductory programming courses [2,3]. In the IT degree program at my university, we have transitioned an advanced programming course over to app development. The Android operating system was chosen as the development platform for a number of reasons. First, it is the most widely used of the current generation of mobile platforms. Second, it is freely available, and there are no costs associated with its app development tools or testing on devices. Moreover, the native language of Android apps is Java, which has the added benefit of being among the most important programming languages in the IT field. Another benefit is the extensive use of XML in app development, particularly in the context of GUIs. This exposure to a popular markup language addresses further core competencies expected of the IT student.

In this paper, I present some of the important logistical issues and potential pitfalls that instructors and students will face when employing Android app development in the classroom. Among other things, these issues pertain to Android devices and emulators, working with Java in the Android setting, the Java-XML linkage, debugging, quirks with the Eclipse IDE, and accessing the Internet via apps. This information has been gleaned from over a year's worth of experience teaching the subject in the context of our IT programming course. A number of suggestions and tips for successful app development are presented throughout. While some basics of app development are introduced, this paper is not meant to be a tutorial for "developing my first app." Those can be found on-line [4] or in various books [5,6]. Some additional benefits of Android development for the IT curriculum are discussed.

2. BACKGROUND

Android is an operating system developed for mobile devices. It was originally built by a team at Android, Inc., which was eventually acquired by Google. Android has gone through a number of versions over the years, each dubbed as an appetizing treat: Froyo, Honeycomb, Ice Cream Sandwich, Jelly Bean, and most recently KitKat. In order to support development of apps written for this platform, Google has built an extensive Software Development Kit (SDK) [4] comprising a large collection of Java classes. The SDK had gone through some major transitions along with the various versions of Android. This made development somewhat unstable and therefore not very amenable to the IT classroom. However, by the time of Jelly Bean (Android 4.2 and 4.3), the SDK had stabilized quite a bit. That is when it was adopted in our IT curriculum.

The primary app development environment currently is the Eclipse IDE. A version of Eclipse coupled with the ADT (Android Developer Tools) is available as a free download from [4]. It is referred to as the "ADT Bundle." In the works is a new environment called "Android Studio." A preview version is downloadable at [4].

An Android app can be viewed as a collection of so-called *activities*. Loosely, an activity is a piece of app functionality that requires its own user interface (UI). So, if some functionality requires a new UI, it would be defined as a new activity in its own right. An activity is modeled as its own Java class, which is defined to be a subclass of the built-in SDK class Activity. As such, it is good for the students to be aware of the subclass (extends) mechanism of Java, though a thorough knowledge is not absolutely necessary. Accompanying each activity class is an XML file defining the UI's layout. There are a number of built-in widgets available. Some of the most useful for basic app development include: EditText (for text input), Button (for invoking activity functionality), TextView (for displaying text to the user), and ImageView (display of images). An excerpt of an XML file for a UI is shown in the following:

```
<EditText    android:id="@+id/edit_number"
             android:layout_width="match_parent"
             android:layout_height="50dp"
             android:inputType="number"
             android:hint="@string/edit_number" />
<Button      android:layout_width="wrap_content"
             android:layout_height="wrap_content"
             android:layout_gravity="center_horizontal"
             android:onClick="displayDouble"
             android:text="@string/button_double" />
<TextView    android:id="@+id/text_answer"
             android:layout_width="match_parent"
             android:layout_height="match_parent"
             android:text="@string/text_answer" />
```

This XML defines three widgets: an EditText, a Button, and a TextView. It will be noted that all the XML entities have a number of attributes that define their appearance and behavior. For example, the EditText and the TextView have the attribute "id" allowing for the designation of an identifier that can be used to access these widgets from within the Java code. The respectively assigned identifiers in this case are *edit_number* and *text_answer*. The value of the EditText's "hint" attribute, denoted "@*string/edit_number*," is a string whose value is defined in a special app resource file named strings.xml. That file contains the predefined strings used throughout the app, such as, in this example, a hint in an input field or a label on a button (see its attribute "text"). The hint in this case is "Enter an integer value." The button's text is "Double It." Assuming these widgets are grouped within an Android vertical "Linear Layout," this XML code would be rendered as shown in Figure 1. Another important attribute of the Button is "onClick" that defines the Java callback method to be invoked on the button press. Here, the method is *displayDouble*. This will be discussed further below.

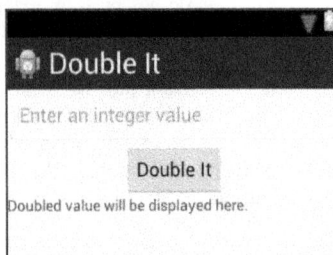

Figure 1. Activity UI including an EditText, Button, and TextView.

The entire collection of files constituting a given app is organized in the "Project File Hierarchy." This is generated automatically by Eclipse on issuing a command to create a new app. Within this hierarchy, one will find a folder for the Java source files, another for the UI XML files, and various others containing app resources (such as predefined values and graphics). An example of a hierarchy of the app named "DoubleIt" is shown in Figure 2.

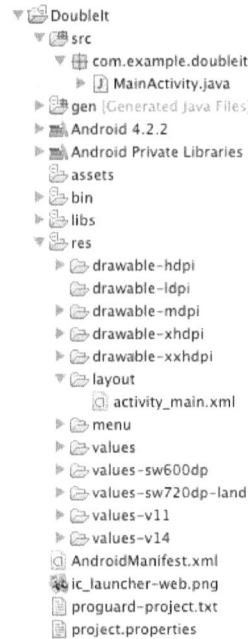

Figure 2. An app ("DoubleIt") project hierarchy in Eclipse.

A very important file is the app's *manifest*, denoted as AndroidManifest.xml, which is an inventory of all the app's components. In it, one will find entries (in XML) that define all the assets of the app. In particular, there are XML entries for each activity as well as others for various app characteristics. The manifest file itself is created automatically by Eclipse, and is most often updated automatically as a result of a development action (e.g., the creation of a new activity). Manual editing of the file is done sparingly.

As a summary, I list the files that a beginning app developer, who is mostly interested in producing basic apps (as might be the case in a lower-level IT course), would need to concern themselves with the most:

- Java files for the activities
- XML files for the activities' UIs
- Android Manifest
- strings.xml

The respective folder locations within the project hierarchy for these are as follows. (See Figure 2 for an example.)

- /src/<*package name*>, where <*package name*> is the Java-style package name associated with the app
- /res/layout
- app's top directory
- /res/values

If the app happens to have only one activity, namely, the main activity, then the only Java file would be MainActivity.java. Its UI would be defined in activity_main.xml. This can be seen with the DoubleIt app in Figure 2.

3. ISSUES WITH APP DEVELOPMENT

In this section, I go through some of the important logistical issues that I have dealt with in my experience using Android with IT programming students. I also cover various pitfalls that have been encountered. Some of these are highly technical in nature, but it is important that they be documented for those embarking on Android app development in their classes. Various suggestions for improving the students' and instructors' experiences with Android are also given.

3.1 Android Devices and Emulators

Eclipse connects relatively seamlessly to actual Android devices, so students can see the products of their work almost immediately in a "real-world" setting. An app can be launched directly from Eclipse and be seen running on a device. However, there is a need for appropriate device drivers to be made available in the operating environment. The Mac OS is probably the simplest as many of the drivers for the most popular devices are provided without the need for further downloads. In a Windows setting on a PC, the student will often have to search out the proper driver and download it. In a laboratory network setting, it is sensible for the instructor to make requests for drivers for popular devices in advance, maybe via a poll of the students.

When connecting to and running apps from Eclipse on an actual device, it is mandatory that "USB debugging" be enabled on the device. This feature can often be found under the device's settings page. Let me note that this was a common source of frustration for students, particularly at the beginning of their studies. They would often be baffled as to why a seemingly correct app would not run.

An easy way to check that a device is properly connected and visible to Eclipse is with the use of the command-line tool adb ("Android Debug Bridge"), distributed with the ADT Bundle. This is a very useful utility that has a variety of applications. To see a list of currently available devices, issue the command:

```
adb devices
```

If an expected device is not shown, it indicates either a lack of an appropriate driver or the fact that USB debugging is disabled.

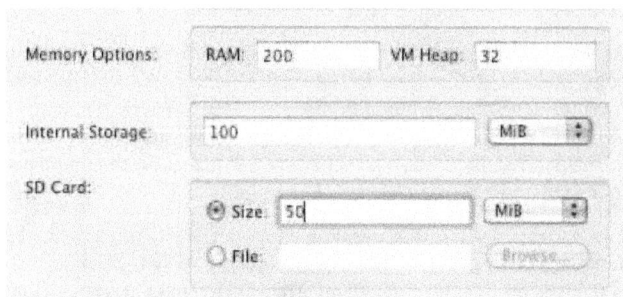

Figure 3. Setting the memory sizes of an emulator.

An alternative to real Android devices is one of the many available software emulators. Students will need to set it up using Eclipse's Android Virtual Device Manager. These emulators are very sophisticated, and mimic the features of the devices very well. For example, they have their own internal file systems that can be navigated using Linux-like commands (with the help of adb). However, due to their complexity, it is widely known that the emulators can be excruciatingly slow, particularly on older model laptops. One suggested way to overcome this problem is to

significantly reduce the emulator's memory requirements. At device setup time, one is asked to specify the sizes of RAM, the VM heap, internal storage, and the SD card. See Figure 3 showing that portion of the setup dialog. Typically, there will be some default values depending on the type of device, like a Nexus 7. On Windows machines, it is important that these figures do not total more than 750 Mbytes or so. Far less than that amount, say, 300 Mbytes, is a better target.

3.2 Manifest Activity Entries

As noted, the manifest contains entries specifying the components of the app. The following shows an example entry for the main activity of an app:

```
<activity
    android:name="com.example.myapp.MainActivity"
    android:label="@string/app_name" >
    <intent-filter>
        <action android:name="android.intent.action.MAIN"/>
        <category
            android:name="android.intent.category.LAUNCHER"/>
    </intent-filter>
</activity>
```

While the details of this entry are not overly important, it is important that the student be aware that such an entry must appear for each activity created. If an entry is not included, then the app will immediately crash when an attempt is made to invoke that activity (from within the Java code of another activity). This situation is often very confusing to the student. And Eclipse does not provide any guidance or alerts in this situation.

The lack of a manifest entry for an activity often arises when the student tries to create a new activity "manually" by directly creating a new Java class in the project instead of using Eclipse's "new activity" mechanism to do it. The former requires that the student manually edit the manifest (and do a considerable amount of additional bookkeeping). Letting Eclipse handle the initial creation of the new activity allows the student to forgo that work and avoid this common pitfall.

3.3 Java in the Android Setting

Working with Java in the Android environment differs somewhat from working with it in more traditional settings. For instance, in an app, there is no "main" method, which oftentimes students are expecting from their previous Java development work. Instead, there is a "main activity" that serves as the primary entry point into the app. It is critical that the main activity, as with all other activities, be created by Eclipse itself, and not manually by the programmer.

Apps do not quit in the sense that traditional, stand-alone Java programs do. In fact, apps are effectively assumed to be running all the time—sometimes, though, they are pushed to the background and enter an idle state. As such, a foundational notion of Android is the activity lifecycle and its management [4,5]. For example, an app developer needs to be concerned with the issue of what happens when an activity is initially created, or when it is restored, or when it ends. Each activity class is defined with an *onCreate* method to deal with the former. This processing modality can be quite unfamiliar to a beginner. And, in general, properly managing the activity lifecycle can be complicated. Luckily, for simple apps in an IT course setting, this topic can be reasonably ignored. For students interested in seriously pursuing app development for commercial production, it is something they must eventually wrap their heads around.

3.4 Java-XML Connection

Android app development has the added benefit of reinforcing the GUI development process and enhancing the student's XML skills. That said, there are some serious pitfalls that the students are liable to encounter in this context. In fact, a seemingly innocent syntax error in an XML UI file will often propagate into mysterious errors in the Java code that are not easy for the students (or their instructor) to pick up on. Errors in the rather simple file strings.xml can also cause unexpected problems throughout the app.

In the following, I examine two major problems that I have seen time and again in my courses.

3.4.1 Missing or Incorrect Callback Methods

In order to link a button widget to the Java code that it is designed to invoke, we use the XML attribute "onClick." From the example presented above, this looks like:

```
android:onClick="displayDouble"
```

In this instance, a user click will invoke (callback) the method *displayDouble* defined as part of the corresponding Java activity class. The signature of this method must be exactly:

```
public void displayDouble(View view)
```

where View is a built-in class SDK class. Deviating from this signature or omitting the method altogether will result in a run-time crash of the app on the button press. A common pitfall is the omission of the View parameter, which must be included even if it is not used. Therefore, students should get into the habit of immediately inserting a stub in their activity class when adding a button widget to their UI.

A related, and perhaps more insidious, problem arises when using the "action bar" UI component introduced as of Android 3.0. The action bar is an important app navigational feature, similar to a menu of action items. From the programmer's perspective, each action item is linked to a callback method that implements the appropriate functionality. Again, the action item defined in XML has an onClick attribute for declaring this linkage. The callback method's signature differs slightly from that of the button callback as can be seen in this example:

```
public void onOption1(MenuItem i)
```

The difference with the action-bar callback mechanism is that an omitted or incorrectly written callback signature will result in an *immediate* crash of the app on startup, not at the time the action item is selected by a user. This can be particularly disconcerting to students and often leaves them unaware as to how to proceed. Here, too, they must be encouraged to define stubs for their callbacks when building their action bar in XML.

Again, it is important to note that Eclipse will not detect these kinds of problems with callback methods before run-time. Arguably, that is a flaw of the environment.

3.4.2 Incorrect Access of Widgets by Id

Simple text input is accomplished using the EditText widget. The related TextView widget provides a convenient means for text output. Both widgets have been used extensively by my students in their app projects. As shown above, these widgets would be included in the UI by writing XML code entries and assigning explicit id's. In order for the Java code (e.g., a callback method) to access these widgets, they must be instantiated as Java objects with the use of the intrinsic SDK method *findViewById*. For the two widgets shown in Section 2, we would write:

```
EditText et = (EditText) findViewById(R.id.edit_number);
TextView tv = (TextView) findViewById(R.id.text_answer);
```

EditText and TextView are built-in classes. The "R.id.*x*" notation is an Android convention for accessing various app resources.

This is a case where Eclipse will aid in the linkage between the Java code and the XML. When typing the Android id, such as *edit_number*, the programmer will see it automatically italicized if Eclipse has successfully located an existing widget with that given id. A failure is immediately apparent and can be corrected easily.

Even with the help of Eclipse, students will on occasion have real problems with this Java-XML linkage. First, the Android id of the widget could be mistyped and not noticed. Worse is the case when students copy code inattentively. In either case, the value of the reference to the widget object may very well end up being null, which would result in an app crash when an access such as the following reading of a value from the EditText is attempted:

```
num = Integer.parseInt(et.getText().toString());
```

Sometimes the students instantiate the EditText independent of *findViewById* and the UI altogether. That is, they create an EditText object that has no connection whatsoever to the declared UI. This leads to an eventual confusing crash.

3.5 "Import android.R" Problem

An issue related to Java-XML connection issues discussed above is what I term the "import android.R" problem. At times, an import statement of the form "import android.R" showed up in an activity class file along with an error message of the form: "R cannot be resolved." This problem would arise for no particular rhyme or reason, and it would not even be consistent for a particular student. Apparently, it is dependent on the version of the platform being used and the version of Android and Eclipse. When this problem occurred, it manifested itself in such a way that none of the Android id's of the UI widgets could be resolved, and errors would propagate throughout the entire app project. The student would be facing a sea of red flags, leaving them totally perplexed and running to the instructor for help.

As some background, R.java is a file generated automatically to help manage references to an app's resources. The on-line Android developer community discusses this problem in a number of different forums (such as [7]). It apparently comes about due to misnamed resource files and other similar mistakes, though many in the community refer to it as a bug in Eclipse.

The way to resolve this problem is to delete all imports in the activity class, generate them anew (using CTRL-SHIFT-O in Windows or CMD-SHIFT-O in Mac OS)—making certain that "import android.R" is no longer present—and then "clean" the app using the command under the "project" menu.

3.6 Permissions

In order for apps to do certain kinds of tasks, such as writing to external SD card storage or accessing data on the Web, the app must be given explicit *permissions*. These are included as XML entries in the manifest. For example, to allow the app to write to the SD card, it needs this permission:

```
<uses-permission
    android:name="android.permission.WRITE_EXTERNAL_STORAGE" />
```

To access the Internet, it requires:

```
<uses-permission android:name="android.permission.INTERNET" />
```

If a necessary permission is omitted, then the app will crash when it attempts the operation. Note that Eclipse is not helpful in regard to permissions as it does not inspect the manifest for you. It is therefore very important that students include the specification of permissions as part of a check-list for their development process.

3.7 Importing and Copying App Projects

With traditional Java programs, it is quite simple to distribute sample programs to a class so that the students can read through them and run them on their own. The distribution is especially easy when the program comprises just a few modules. With an app, the entire project hierarchy has to be distributed. I would typically deliver fully working apps to my classes as zipped archives posted on Moodle. After the students downloaded and unzipped an app, there was still the issue of importing it into their Eclipse workspace, from which it can be run. Eclipse maintains a workspace of app projects. (There can be multiple workspaces, but only one is deemed to be open at a time.) As it happens, the import process does not always work properly. In fact, some students could simply not complete the import process at all. This usually occurred on personal laptops, for unknown reasons. In such cases, they were forced to start new apps from scratch and copy the required code elements in manually.

In other cases, the app would import with certain names altered unexpectedly. In the simplest situation, the app could be renamed ("refactored").

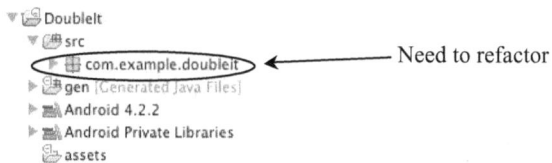

Figure 4. Refactor folder containing Java source files.

A related issue is that of making a copy of an existing app to serve as the basis for a new one. Again, with an app, this requires that an entire project hierarchy be duplicated. Eclipse will do this for you, but there is some bookkeeping that is required after the fact. The steps needed are as follows.

1. Change the package name in the manifest.
2. Refactor (rename) the folder under the folder /src such that its name is now the same as the new package name. This is the folder that holds all of the app's Java source files. (See Figure 4.)
3. Make updates to strings.xml, including changing the app's name to the desired new name.

With regard to (3.), the entry for the app's name in strings.xml will look like:

```
<string name="app_name">Double It</string>
```

3.8 Internet Access

Arguably, one of the most exciting characteristics of apps from a student's perspective is the ability to access data and resources on the Internet and Web. For example, an app might go out and directly open a file at some given URL. I have found this particularly useful in reinforcing the notion of file input.

However, there is a problem with this activity in the context of Android. As of SDK API Level 11 (available with Honeycomb), blocking activities occurring on the main UI thread automatically cause exceptions to be thrown. Such an operation must be moved off the main thread and completed asynchronously. This can be done with the use of standard Java threads [5]. Additionally, the SDK provides a class called AsyncTask that conveniently models the necessary background processing. AsyncTask is a generic that is extended as a private class within the activity class needing its services. See, e.g., [5] (Volume II) for details.

From a pedagogical perspective, writing asynchronous code using AsyncTask, or other means, is probably too advanced for the beginning app developer. I have personally avoided it in my own courses. (It would be quite suitable for an upper-level, advanced treatment of app development.) For non-production apps in a course setting, it makes sense to simply override Android's so-called strict-mode policy and allow apps to do whatever business they need to do on the main thread. Completely overriding this policy is quite straightforward. One simply includes the following two somewhat verbose statements in the *onCreate* method of the app's main activity:

```
StrictMode.ThreadPolicy policy = new
  StrictMode.ThreadPolicy.Builder().permitAll().build();
StrictMode.setThreadPolicy(policy);
```

I have utilized this disabling of the strict-mode policy in most app projects in my courses. On occasion, I will provide students with some complete code demonstrating the use of AsyncTask, such as in Java code for downloading jpeg images from the Web.

I have also found occasion to use it when doing socket programming in the context of client/server topics. I will typically have the students write servers as conventional Java programs and run them on our server machines on campus. The clients are written as Android apps connecting to the servers via the standard Java socket mechanism. However, the strict-mode policy will forbid the blocking accompanying the network communication. To simplify matters, I have the students disable it here, too.

3.9 Debugging

Students will invariably find their apps crashing. This can happen for many reasons, some already documented above. The Eclipse environment is excellent for uncovering syntax errors and guiding students to their correction. However, as noted in places above already, with Android-specific problems, it is much less effective in its assistance. Students must become comfortable with the debugging features that are available to them. It is imperative that they make use of Eclipse's "LogCat," in which various status messages of Eclipse and running apps are displayed. The SDK has a built-in "Log" feature that allows a running app to explicitly post different kinds of messages directly in the LogCat. (Note that the feature is unavailable to apps running directly on Android devices.) Students should get comfortable right from the outset using Log commands within their apps, particularly during the testing phase. Instructors are advised to make these a requirement of assignments early on.

3.10 App Submission and Testing

The rather mundane issue of student project submission and testing can be a major headache for a course instructor. To test an app, one must load it onto a device or emulator. This means having access to an app's entire project hierarchy and being able to import it into your Eclipse workspace. As discussed, the import feature does not always function too well. Moreover, the logistics of having to import all the code and run the apps with sample data is very time-consuming. Often, it is better to arrange lab time during which students can show personal demonstrations. This, of course, is in contrast to traditional Java assignments where it is often possible to set up scripts in, say, a Linux environment that help automate the process of running through and testing submitted projects. Some degree of automation is available with the use of the adb tool, which has the capability of inputting data directly into an app's UI while it is running. For example, to have the string "Hello" placed in a selected EditText, you can use the following command:

```
adb shell input text "Hello"
```

Putting a sequence of such commands into a script can be useful for app testing.

4. DISCUSSION

Android apps have become pervasive, and the well-prepared IT student should be able to program in that environment and be aware of the many issues and pitfalls surrounding such development activities. This paper has addressed and provided guidance in dealing with a number of these, both from an instructor's and a student's perspective.

There are many useful on-line resources that provide guidance to Android developers. One of them is the Android Developers site [4]. Another site that I have encouraged my students to take advantage of is Stack Overflow [7]. In an effort to simplify students' app-specific coding requirements, the Sofia framework [8] has been introduced to hide various details of the Android environment, such as elements of GUI management.

Of course, Android is not the only mobile platform. Apple iOS is very popular but imposes developer fees and restricted access to actual devices like iPhones. Moreover, students will need to learn Objective-C, whose main use today is with Apple. A comparison of Android and iOS can be found in [9]. Windows RT allows developers to choose from a number of languages, including C#, VB, and C++. JavaScript along with HTML/CCS can also be used in Windows RT and in the device-agnostic PhoneGap framework [10]. App Inventor for beginning programmers in Android uses the blocks language [11]. TouchDevelop allows for programming directly on a mobile device without a connected computer [12].

Beyond programming skills, the Android platform is suitable for more advanced studies within the IT curriculum. Android comes with an embedded database engine called SQLite [5], allowing it to serve as a vehicle for the study of DBMSs and DB programming. Moreover, mobile-device security is a critical issue in IT, and knowing Android and app development puts students in a good position to study this topic as well. And there are many opportunities for covering more advanced programming topics in Android, such as inter-activity communication using singleton classes, asynchronous processing using multithreading, managing dialogs using the SDK's "fragment" facility [5], etc.

Eclipse is a widely used IDE that offers many benefits to students. However, it does have some drawbacks that have been discussed above. Furthermore, it is not designed for a multi-system, multi-user environment. An instructor will probably be "leaning" on the system administrator for help with some of its idiosyncrasies and guiding students through assorted setup tasks (e.g., setting environment variables in Windows). It is therefore probably better to have students install Eclipse on their own laptops and have them do their development work there.

5. CONCLUSION

Mobile computing using smartphones and tablets—and eventually watches and other wearable devices—is beginning to dominate the IT field. Students are now entering IT degree programs armed with these devices and a clear understanding of their utility. As such, students are apt to get more excited about programming when they are building apps on devices they can readily relate to. Moreover, they can develop apps that access the Web, manipulate multimedia assets, etc., gaining first-hand experience with the inspiring products programming can achieve.

Android is now being used as the development platform in an IT programming course at my university. In the process of transitioning to Android, many subtle issues and pitfalls have been encountered. These have been documented in this paper, and tips and suggestions have been provided that should make the Android app development experience more successful and that much more rewarding for instructors and students alike. Some additional uses of Android in the IT curriculum were discussed.

6. REFERENCES

[1] V. Goel. Mobile Internet Rising, Report Says. Business Day, The New York Times, p. B7, June 2, 2014.

[2] Q. H. Mahmoud and A. Dyer. Mobile devices in an introductory programming course. Computer, 41(6): 108–107, June 2008.

[3] B. Burd, J. P. Barros, C. Johnson, S. Kurkovsky, A. Rosenbloom, and N. Tillman. Educating for mobile computing: addressing the new challenges. In Proc. ITiCSE-WGR '12, p. 51–63, Haifa, Israel, July 2012.

[4] Android Developers, available at http://developer.android.com. Accessed June 2, 2014.

[5] L. Darcey and S. Conder, Android Wireless Application Development (Volumes I and II), Third Ed., Addison-Wesley, Upper Saddle River, NJ, 2012.

[6] P. J. Deitel, H. M. Deitel, A. Deitel, and M. Morgano, Android for Programmers: An App-Driven Approach, Pearson Education, Upper Saddle River, NJ, 2012.

[7] Stack Overflow, available at http://stackoverflow.com. Accessed June 5, 2014.

[8] S. H. Edwards and A. Allevato. Re-imagining CS1/CS2 with Android using the Sofia framework. J. Comput. Sci. Coll., 29(3): 101, January 2014.

[9] M. H. Goadrich and M. P. Rogers. Smart smartphone development: iOS versus Android. In Proc. SIGCSE '11, p. 607–612, Dallas, TX, March 2011.

[10] PhoneGap, available at http://phonegap.com. Accessed June 6, 2014.

[11] App Inventor, available at http://www.appinventor.org. Accessed June 6, 2014.

[12] N. Tillmann, M. Moskal, J. de Halleux, M. Fahndrich, J. Bishop, A. Samuel, and T. Xie. The future of teaching programming is on mobile devices. In Proc. ITiCSE '12, p. 156–161, Haifa, Israel, July 2012.

Using Mobile Apps to Support Novice Programming Students

Sonal Dekhane
Georgia Gwinnett College
1000 University Center Lane
Lawrenceville, GA 30043
1-678-407-5000
sdekhane@ggc.edu

Cynthia Johnson
Georgia Gwinnett College
1000 University Center Lane
Lawrenceville, GA 30043
1-678-407-5000
cjohns25@ggc.edu

ABSTRACT

The ubiquity of mobile devices and the advancement in mobile technology have enabled teaching and learning to occur outside of traditional teaching spaces. Learning can now occur anytime and anywhere. In this project the authors created and used two mobile apps to support the learning needs of novice programming students enrolled in an introductory programming course. Initial results from surveys and tests indicated positive impact on student learning and engagement.

Categories and Subject Descriptors

K.3.2 [**Computer and Education**]: Computer and Information Science Education – *computer science education, self assessment.*

Keywords

Mobile learning, programming, CS1

1. INTRODUCTION

Mobile learning has been gaining significant ground lately. It is described as any form of learning that is mediated through the use of a mobile device, with an emphasis on "mediated". As smartphones and tablets become an integral part of students' lives, it is imperative that we investigate these platforms from a learning perspective. The ability to provide immediate feedback and rectify any prior misconceptions is a significant advantage of mobile applications. Previous studies have investigated the use of mobile devices to deliver content, conduct polls and quizzes and use scheduling applications to enhance learning (Belanger (2005), Dekhane (2012)). These studies have also indicated that mobile learning should supplement existing learning materials and is not intended to substitute them. Understanding the results of existing studies and realizing that mobile devices can provide a personalized learning platform for the students, the authors focused on creating mobile apps to aid novice programming students' learning and investigating their effectiveness.

2. METHODOLOGY

In the first phase of this project two groups of students enrolled in a junior level software development course consulted with two programming professors and designed and developed two mobile applications. One application focused on the topic of "variables" and the other application focused on "for loops". These applications were targeted at novices and were designed to aid in the understanding of fundamental programming concepts. This was an authentic learning experience for the software development students, as they practiced all phases of SDLC with the programming professors as their clients and programming students as the end users. Software development students participated in client interviews, peer reviews, walkthroughs, prototype demonstrations, usability testing and deployment, among other things.

The completed apps were installed on iPad devices and shared with students enrolled in an introductory programming course. The students in this course used the apps as part of an in-class lab during the time when the relevant topic was covered. The students participated in pre and post-tests and surveys. The post-tests showed a 2 to 3 % increase in understanding of the topics after using the apps. More importantly, pre and post-surveys showed a positive attitude towards the apps and many students commented that the apps were fun and a good addition to the learning process. One comment was "I found that the app as a whole was useful. It was an easy way to study.".

3. FUTURE DIRECTION

The initial results have encouraged us to continue this study. The future plans are to develop more apps covering the fundamental programming topics and using them to meet the learning needs of novice programming students. The authors also plan to make the iPads available for use outside of class. The authors plan to revise the surveys to gather data about students' usage patterns and investigate the impact of that on their class performance, if any.

4. REFERENCES

[1] Belanger, Y. 2005. Center for Instructional Technology, Duke University, viewed 29th May 2014, <http://cit.duke.edu/pdf/reports/ipod_initiative_04_05.pdf>.

[2] Dekhane, S. and Tsoi, M.Y. 2012. Designing a Mobile Application for Conceptual Understanding: Integrating Learning Theory with Organic Chemistry Learning Needs. *International Journal of Mobile and Blended Learning.* 4,3 (2012), 34-52.

Operation Java Blitz: Extracurricular Programming Workshops to Engage IT Students

Evelyn Brannock
Georgia Gwinnett College
1000 University Center Lane
Lawrenceville, GA 30043
ebrannoc@ggc.edu

Nannette Napier
Georgia Gwinnett College
1000 University Center Lane
Lawrenceville, GA 30043
nnapier@ggc.edu

Robert Lutz
Georgia Gwinnett College
1000 University Center Lane
Lawrenceville, GA 30043
rlutz@ggc.edu

ABSTRACT

An engaging context has been shown to improve student motivation and performance in programming courses. Therefore, we incorporated six hands-on, supplementary, voluntary workshops (called Operation Java Blitz, or OJB) on subjects that were not exhaustively included in the current programming curriculum in Spring 2014. The poster will discuss the sessions, the initial results from 34 students, and future plans.

Categories and Subject Descriptors

K.3.2 [**Computers and Information Science Education**]: Computer science education – *curriculum*

Keywords

Programming

1. SIGNIFICANCE OF TOPIC

Information technology (IT) majors at Georgia Gwinnett College are required to take a sequence of at least two Java programming courses. Unfortunately, the pass rates for these programming courses are often a little higher than half of the students who begin the sequence. For example, literature shows that the introductory programming course is often a difficult course for students [1, 2]; in fact, some estimates show that 33% of students either drop or fail their first programming course [3, 4]. Since an engaging context can positively impact student performance [5], we wanted to offer motivational sessions in a low pressure, engaging, practice driven environment outside of the classroom.

2. PURPOSE OF OJB

The purpose of the experiment was to evaluate the effectiveness of a series of programming workshops, named Operation Java Blitz (OJB), offered to all IT students. Bi-monthly informal, instructor-led but interactive, sessions were organized in addition to regularly scheduled classroom time. Each meeting was an hour and 15 minutes in length. Students were encouraged (but not required) to bring their laptops for active and collaborative participation.

SIGITE'14, October 15–18, 2014, Atlanta, Georgia, USA.
ACM 978-1-4503-2711-4/14/10.
http://dx.doi.org/10.1145/2656450.2656486

3. OVERVIEW OF OJB SESSIONS

A total of six sessions, in Spring 2014, were taught outside of regular class time at Georgia Gwinnett College. Instructors volunteered their time to teach. An instructor also acted as the coordinator that scheduled the sessions, reserved space, built promotional materials and gathered volunteers to teach from the faculty. A student IT group volunteered to disperse flyers to advertise. All IT majors were invited (but programming students, especially those thinking of attending competitions, were targeted). The topics included: 1. Advanced Eclipse and Programming Competition Pointers, 2. Regular Expressions, 3. File IO and File Handling, 4. Designing Classes, 5. Eclipse with WindowBuilder, 6. Algorithm and Problem Solving Strategies.

4. RESULTS AND FUTURE WORK

After each session, the students were asked to fill out a short survey. They responded to demographic information on gender, race/ethnicity, and major as well as six attitudinal questions. Since both attendance and the survey were voluntary, the poster will present the preliminary 34 survey responses that were gathered. For example, the question "How would you rate the overall OJB workshop?" garnered a rating of 4.53 out of 5. In future semesters, the authors plan to repeat the sessions (or similar sessions), conducting surveys to gather additional student perspectives on the Operation Java Blitz.

5. REFERENCES

1. Douglas, J., R. McClelland, and J. Davies, The development of a conceptual model of student satisfaction with their experience in higher education. Quality Assurance in Education, 2008. 16(1): p. 19-35.

2. Furnham, A., A. Eracleous, and T. Chamorro-Premuzic, Personality, motivation and job satisfaction: Hertzberg meets the Big Five. Journal of Managerial Psychology, 2009. 24(8): p. 765-779.

3. Bennedsen, J. and M.E. Caspersen, Failure rates in introductory programming. SIGCSE Bulletin, 2007. 39(2): p. 32-36.

4. Bergin, S. and R. Reilly. The influence of motivation and comfort-level on learning to program. in Proceedings of the 17th Annual Workshop of the Psychology of Programming Interest Group (WPPI). 2005.

5. Guzdial, M. and A.E. Tew. Imagineering Inauthentic Legitimate Peripheral Participation: An Instructional Design Approach for Motivating Computing Education. in International Workshop on Computing Education Research 2006. Canterbury, United Kingdom: ACM

ACM Associate-Degree IT Curricular Guidance

Elizabeth K. Hawthorne
Union County College
1033 Springfield Ave
Cranford, NJ USA
+1 908 497 4232
hawthorne@ucc.edu

Cara Tang
Portland Community College
12000 SW 49th Avenue
Portland, OR USA
+1 971 722 4447
cara.tang@pcc.edu

Cindy S. Tucker
Bluegrass Community &
Tech. College
500 Newtown Pike
Lexington, KY USA
+1 859 246 4634
cindy.tucker@kctcs.edu

Robert Campbell
CUNY Graduate Center
365 Fifth Avenue
New York, NY USA
+1 212 817 7350
rcampbell@gc.cuny.edu

ABSTRACT
As directed by the ACM Education Board, the ACM Committee for Computing Education in Community Colleges (CCECC) delivered the final version of its curricular guidance for associate-degree Information Technology (IT) programs consisting of core IT learning outcomes with associated assessment metrics. The competency model is available from www.capspace.org. The CCECC invites institutions to highlight their IT programs by submitting course examples correlated with the core IT learning outcomes contained in the guidance.

Categories and Subject Descriptors
K.3.2 [Computers and Education]: Computer and Information Science Education – *Curriculum*

Keywords
Two-Year College, Community College, Education, Information Technology, Assessment

1. BACKGROUND
The CCECC has now fulfilled the 2011 directive by the ACM Education Board that an associate-degree IT curricular task force be constituted to produce IT curricular guidance which is:

- Built from the ground up on a framework of learning outcomes.
- Constituted by core IT competencies assembled into a competency framework.
- Influenced by the current and future needs of business and industry, by certifications and related curricula, by government and standards bodies, and by new and emerging technology.
- Designed in a manner that provides for staying power, breadth and adaptability.
- Accompanied by meaningful evaluation metrics.

In fulfilling this charge, the CCECC pursued a multiphase process of collaboration and debate among representatives from two-year college faculty, business and industry, and certification/standards bodies, including peer dissemination and public comment on draft results, and oversight by a team of experts in student assessment.

2. RESULT
The final product is a set of well-vetted student learning outcomes that express core IT competencies across all IT-related associate-degree programs representing both the technical and behavioral. The 50 learning outcomes span the first three levels of Bloom's Revised Taxonomy [1]. Each student learning outcome is accompanied by a structured, three-tier assessment rubric, giving further clarity and meaningful evaluation metrics for the outcomes. The assessment rubrics facilitate integration of the learning outcomes into assessment-based curricula which are typical among associate-degree and career-preparatory programs.

To make the collection of student learning outcomes more accessible to various groups, the CCECC has categorized them in accordance with a variety of existing frameworks, including the SIGITE 2008 "Curriculum Guidelines for Undergraduate Degree Programs in Information Technology" [4], the U.S. Department of Labor Competency Model [2], the European e-Competence Framework [3], and Bloom's Revised Taxonomy [1].

Several organizations have championed the guidance, including companies such as Cisco, Google, Intel, Microsoft and IBM; colleges such as Portland Community College and Bluegrass Community and Technical College; and other organizations such as CSSIA, CSTA, and MPICT. Champions appreciate the importance of robust associate-degree IT programs, make a commitment to the academic foundations of IT students, and promote education that meaningfully prepares graduates as future employees and practitioners.

3. FOLLOW-UP OPPORTUNITIES
Examples of courses that align with the ACM core IT learning outcomes are part of a growing repository at capspace.org. As a follow-on to the recent dissemination of the *ACM Associate-degree Curricular Guidance for Information Technology*, the presenters seek additional course examples. Course correlations demonstrate the adaptability of this competency-based curriculum approach to a variety of computing courses, certificates, and degree programs. See capspace.org/correlation/ for more details.

4. REFERENCES
[1] Anderson, Lori, et al. *Taxonomy for Learning, Teaching, and Assessing: A Revision of Bloom's Taxonomy of Educational Objectives.* Boston. Allyn and Bacon, 2000.

[2] Employment and Training Administration, U.S. Department of Labor 2012. *Information Technology Competency Model.*

[3] European Commission Enterprise and Industry CEN. European e-Competence Framework 2.0: A Common European Framework for ICT Professionals in all Industry Sectors. 2010

[4] Lunt, B., et. al. 2008. Information Technology 2008: Curriculum Guidelines for Undergraduate Degree Programs in Information Technology. Special Interest Group for Information Technology Education

Success Factors and Challenges for IT Capstone Projects

Jack Zheng, Chi Zhang, Lei Li
Southern Polytechnic State University
1100 South Marietta Parkway
Marietta, GA 30060
jackzheng@spsu.edu

ABSTRACT

IT capstone projects have become an essential part of the IT curriculum and give students valuable experience to work in a semester long project in a real world context. This paper investigates project success factors and challenges by examining the student feedback data we collected for the past two years. We plan to use a template analysis method to identify the success factors and challenges from the collected student feedback. Then we plan to use a survey method to study the importance of the identified factors and challenges. Our findings will provide an in-depth understanding of IT capstone projects to discover new approaches for better curriculum design and enhanced student learning experience.

Categories and Subject Descriptors

K.3.2 [**Computer and Information Science Education**]: Information systems education

Keywords

IT Capstone Projects, Group Projects, Curriculum Design.

1. INTRODUCTION

To apply IT skills in solving real world problems, students majored in Bachelor of Science in Information Technology (IT) at a public university in southeast of the US are required to complete a capstone group project course in their senior year. Students work in teams to develop or implement a real-world IT solution integrating the knowledge acquired in preceding IT courses. Components emphasized include technical design, development, research, documentation, project management, leadership, team work, and communication skills.

For most students, the capstone project is their biggest project so far with defined real-world objectives. In order to prepare and guide students to successfully complete the project, it is critical for them to understand the success factors and the challenges they may face. So they can better prepare and plan for the projects. This study is guided by two questions: 1) What makes a student capstone project successful and in what ways they have impacts on projects? 2) What are the challenges that the student usually face during the course of the capstone project?

We have done a prior study trying to investigate the issue [2]. Although the investigation has shed some light on the questions,

SIGITE'14, October 15–18, 2014, Atlanta, Georgia, USA.
ACM 978-1-4503-2686-5/14/10.
http://dx.doi.org/10.1145/2656450.2656488

the survey feedback was coming from only four projects in one semester. The results were meaningful but the data was limited for us to have a deeper understanding about each factor. Therefore we plan to conduct an additional study involving 22 student-teams spanning over a two-year period.

2. RESEARCH METHOD

We obtained the data from IT capstone projects for the academic year 2012-2014. There are a total of 20 different projects, 22 student-groups, and 87 students, in four semesters. Each team submitted a project experience summary from the team's perspective as art of the final report. Each student also submitted a self-reflection from an individual perspective.

Our study has two phases. In phase one, we plan to use the template analysis method [1] to investigate the success factors and challenges from student reflections. Our previous study identified three major success factors: communication, leadership, and knowing team member's strengths; and three challenges: group size, time, and documentation. The findings can serve a baseline while additional success factors and challenges may be identified in the qualitative data analysis process. Three coders will analyze the data independently and will get together regularly to compare their findings and reconcile the differences. From this analysis, themes of success factors and challenges will arise and conform. We will also report the mentioning frequency of each theme.

In the next phase after identifying the success factors and challenges, we plan to study the importance of each factor and challenge. A questionnaire will be developed and distributed to the participants at the end of the capstone project. In the survey, the participants will be asked to rate the importance of each factor or challenge. Qualitative data (e.g. students' comments) will also be collected.

3. CONCLUSION

This study intends to gain a complete understanding of the team dynamics and the factors that affect student learning experience in an IT capstone project course. There are unique issues in IT capstone projects that are different from regular course projects, or internships and co-ops. Understanding success factors and challenges the IT students are facing will help us better design the capstone course, select and evaluate capstone projects.

4. REFERENCES

[1] King, N. 2004. Using templates in the thematic analysis of text. *Essential Guide to Qualitative Methods in Organizational Research*. SAGE. 256–270.

[2] Zhang, C. and Wang, J.A. 2011. Effects of Communication, Leadership, and Team Performance on Successful IT Capstone Projects: A Case Study. *Proceedings of the 2011 Conference on Information Technology Education* (New York, NY, USA, 2011), 281–286.

Designing a Graduate Program in Information Security and Analytics

Sathish Alampalayam Kumar
Coastal Carolina University
P.O. Box 261954
Conway, SC, 29528
843-349-2810
skumar@coastal.edu

ABSTRACT

This paper introduces the concept of the Master of Information Security and Analytics (MISA) program for the graduate students with a background in CS, IS and IT. The 10-course graduate level program is benchmarked against existing masters programs in the areas of Information Security and Data Analytics, and an assessment was done on the estimated demand for MISA graduates in the nation. The program outcomes were then mapped against the course objectives to insure the correct mix of courses and topics. The program's admission requirement is also being discussed.

This paper discusses the design process and possible ways to reduce risk in the start-up of a new degree program. How a program is marketed to prospective students and what program graduates will do after program completion is just as important as the initial design of the program. Planning for the administration of the program and the assessment process is an important phase of the initial design.

Categories and Subject Descriptors

K.3.2 [Computers and Education]: Computer and Information Science Education – Information Security Education - Data Analytics Education - Information Technology Education.

General Terms

Degree Programs; Design

Keywords

Information Technology Education; Cybersecurity; Analytics; Assessment; Curriculum Development

1. INTRODUCTION

The proposed MISA program meets the unique needs of individuals seeking advancement in an existing career and /or a course of study, or entry into careers in information security and data analytics. The program will include the theory and principles, as well as the design and development of practical applications that satisfy most users' information security and data analytics needs.

Proposed MISA program will prepare graduates to secure computer information systems and technology and to derive knowledge/decisions from their data to solve problems in business, science, industry, government, and non-profit institutions. Graduates will be prepared to design, implement, manage, and evaluate secure technology systems and infrastructure, as well as to analyze, design and develop analytics infrastructure to discover knowledge and to make decisions. Graduates will also be prepared to pursue doctoral studies in security/analytics or in the various areas where these skills can be applied.

There will be a strong future growth of information industry experts, including security and analytics professionals. Between 2010 and 2020, it is expected that the need for information-related professionals will increase by 20% [9]. While this proposed program is not as broad as the M.S. in Computer Science, students are trained at an advanced level in two high growth areas: (1) Information Security and (2) Data Analytics. They will have a good opportunity for career growth in any one or both of these areas, while further pursuing their academic or industry career. Information Security and Data Analytics concentrations are synergetic. For example, analytics can be used as a tool for improving security and students can use protecting analytical infrastructure as a test bed for their further security training. They can then adapt that skill in protecting production analytics and operations infrastructure in the real world.

By identifying, addressing, and promoting solutions for the issues of information security and data analytics, MISA will serve as an educational foundation for invention, innovation, and entrepreneurship in the global economy, thereby sustaining the vitality of existing and prospective data science and cyber security industries.

2. PROGRAM MOTIVATION

While there is still a need for graduates in CS, IS and IT, there is a critical shortage of information security and analytics professionals who can understand, develop and maintain secure information systems/technology and analyze, evaluate, design and develop the data analytics system to make sense of this information for scientific and business needs. The demand for cyber security and information assurance experts is growing at 3.5 times the pace of the overall IT job market and 12 times the overall job market, due to a worsening barrage of online attacks against businesses and government agencies [12]. Also, it is expected that the cyber security and information assurance related jobs would grow about 22% between 2010 and 2020 [11]. Between 2012 and 2022, the data scientist/information analytics professional career path is projected to increase by more than

20% [9]. An estimated 1.5 million jobs in data analytics need to be filled in the next 5 years to meet the market demand [10].

The MISA degree program addresses these needs by preparing graduates to be qualified as Information Security and Analytics professionals such as Analyst, Engineer, Architect, Manager, Administrator, Chief Information Security Officer (CISO), Consultant/Specialist, Data Scientist and Chief Information Officer among other specializations. Each of these occupations is projected to increase faster than average during the period 2010-2020, with "good" or "excellent" job prospects and preference for master's degrees in the field [9].

The federal government recognizes the importance of the Cybersecurity and information assurance education /research and has created the National Initiative for Cybersecurity Education (NICE) and The National Centers of Academic Excellence, sponsored by National Security Agency (NSA) and the Department of Homeland Security (DHS) to promote higher education and research in Cyber Security and Information Assurance. We have designed such information security related courses to match these curricular recommendations from the NICE and NCAE [22].

The federal government also recognizes the importance of the Informatics analytics/data science and has recently unveiled $200M Big Data R&D Initiative through federal agencies and departments. According to officials of the Federal Office of Science and Technology Policy, "In the same way that past Federal investments in information-technology R&D led to dramatic advances in supercomputing and the creation of the Internet, the initiative we are launching today promises to transform our ability to use Big Data for scientific discovery, environmental and biomedical research, education and national security" [21].

The MISA degree program will prepare graduates to secure the information systems and technology and derive knowledge/decisions from the information to solve problems in business, science, industry, government agencies, and institutions. Graduates will be prepared to design, implement, manage, and evaluate secure technology systems and infrastructure. They will also be able to discover knowledge and utilize information to make decisions. Graduates will also have the ability to pursue research and doctoral studies in information security and analytics.

A benchmarking of similar programs concludes that there are no similar programs in the country and most of the similar programs are either in the concentration of cyber security or analytics but not both. The University of Maryland, Virginia College, Washington Governor's University, Utica College, and New York University offer online master degrees in cyber security [1,2,3,4,5], while George Washington University, University of Washington, New Jersey Institute of Technology, and American University offer it as part of their resident computer science degree [6,7,8]. The following universities North Carolina State University, Louisiana State University, Northwestern University, University of San Francisco, Georgia Institute of Technology, Texas A&M University, Harrisburg University of Science and Technology, University of Chicago, Stevens Institute of Technology, City University of New York, University of Maryland, George Mason University and Johns Hopkins University offers Master's program in analytics [19]. None of

these graduate programs has both the security and the analytics concentration in a single graduate program.

Several indicators suggest the demand for this graduate program will be strong. Overall expected national growth for the Information Security (35%) and the Data Analytics/ Scientist (15%) related occupations during the next decade will attract more students to the study of Information Security and Analytics [9]. The growth in participation rates, combined with the continued growth of the Information Security and Analytics related occupations, supports a future demand for trained individuals in information security and analytics. With the above indicators, the MISA program should see steady enrollments.

3. PROGRAM DESIGN

The MISA program will combine coursework in both the information security and data analytics areas. It is designed to have students from a wide variety of technical backgrounds [13-18]. This program will also help towards the pursuit of an institution's National Security Agency as a Center of Excellence in Information Assurance aspiration. The MISA will expose students to a Common Body of Knowledge in preparation for the Certified Information Systems Security Professional (CISSP) examination and the Certified Analytics Professional (CAP) certification. Upon completion of the program, students should be able meet the program outcomes specified in Table 1.

Table 1. Program Outcomes for the MISA

1. Be able to identify and critically assess issues, threats and concepts related to the protection of information and information systems. Develop and articulate an organization's strategic direction by assessing an organization's security attributes: confidentiality, integrity, and availability. Understand an organization as complex, interdependent system operating in an ever-changing and uncertain environment.
2. Analyze and evaluate proposed or extant information security policies, practices, technologies tools and procedures to provide a secure infrastructure. Provide leadership so that confidentiality, integrity and availability can be protected. Insure an environment of threat reduction is maintained in an organization.
3. Use risk management principles to assess threats, vulnerabilities, countermeasures and impact contributions to risk in information systems. Perform a risk analysis for an environment. Create a management plan for security in an environment. Analyze and diagnose complex organizational problems, design effective solutions, and implement change.
4. Create policies, strategies and standard operating procedures for sourcing and data management process for data analytics including data analytics, cleaning, quality, structure and security of the databases.
5. Apply methods and techniques in data selection and preparation, analytic method selection such as classification and decision trees, and predictive modeling for exploration and knowledge discovery.
6. Analyze and implement processes, methodologies, infrastructure, and current practices used to transform business data into useful information and support business decision-making.

The MISA program is designed to accommodate working adults who are normally working during the day. MISA will consist of ten 3-credit courses of fourteen week durations.

Following are the courses that are planned to the program

Course 1 (C1) Cybersecurity and Information Assurance
Course 2 (C2) Information Security Policy and Risk Management
Course 3 (C3) Network and Internet Security
Course 4 (C4) Mobile and Web Application Security
Course 5 (C5) Secure Cloud Computing
Course 6 (C6) Data Management and Analytics

Course 7 (C7) Data Mining and Knowledge Discovery
Course 8 (C8) Business Intelligence and Analytics
Course 9 (C9) Data Warehousing and Data Visualization
Course 10 (C10) Big Data Analytics

The courses 1 to 5 fall under Information Security category and courses 6 to 10 fall under Analytics category. The student can elect thesis or non-thesis options depending on their needs. Students willing to take thesis option can select 6 credit hours of thesis work in lieu of courses 5 and 10. Courses 5 and 10 would be the special topics courses in security and analytics respectively, which deal with cutting edge topics and the proficiency of the students in these courses would be assessed based on the research skills, critical thinking skills and presentation skills (oral and written), which are on par with the thesis workload.

The courses 1 and 2 are core courses for Information Security category and courses 6 and 7 are core courses for Information analytics category. The core courses need to be completed successfully before the students can enroll in the other courses in that category. Prior to starting the coursework, prospective student should providing evidence of professional experience or undergraduate credits in computer networks/security and application/web development for the security concentration and provide evidence of professional experience or undergraduate credits in Relational databases/SQL development and basic statistics for the analytics concentration.

Course 1 provides an introduction to cyber security and information assurance. It covers the fundamental concepts necessary to understand the threats to security as well as various defenses against those threats. The course includes an understanding of existing threats, planning for security, technology used to defend a computer system and implementing security measures and technology.

Course 2 addresses ethical, legal, risk management and policy frameworks within which information systems and technology lifecycle professionals must practice. Covers ethical, risk management, legal and policy issues related to information and telecommunications systems, such as how they impact privacy, fair information practices and content control.

Course 3 deals with applications and practice of cryptography in securing networks and Internet. Following techniques would be studied: classical systems, symmetric block ciphers, linear and differential cryptanalysis, perfect secrecy, public-key cryptography, algorithms for factoring and discrete algorithms, cryptographic protocols, hash functions, authentication, key management, key exchange, signature schemes and how it can be applied for securing network infrastructure, firewalls, digital right management, and related topics.

Course 4 covers development of security requirements and the design, development and implementation of secure mobile and web applications. Principles of secure design and coding will be covered in depth. Vulnerabilities and countermeasures for computer systems, mobile and web applications are explored. Effects of network, operating systems, database management systems and machine architecture upon application systems will be discussed. This course also covers Secure Development Lifecycle (SDL) needed to understand and apply best practices for development and on-going support to secure software. Course 5 explores the fundamentals of cloud computing and addresses the cloud security related risks, issues and challenges associated with the cloud by exploring the security architectures, cloud software security and cloud networking security tools and techniques.

Course 6 deals with the application of the data management process for analytics including analysis, design, data acquisition, cleaning, quality, structure, and security of the databases. Evaluation of how these data relate and aggregate in analytic databases, data marts, data warehouses, and how they are used by analytical tools will be explored through case studies and projects.

Course 7 will cover the application of methods using techniques in data mining, text mining, and predictive modeling for exploration and knowledge discovery. Design of objectives, data selection and preparation, analytic method selection such as classification and decision trees, and predictive modeling will be used for a variety of case studies and practical applications. Applying data mining techniques using real world data will leverage statistical assessment and interpretation from database information.

Course 8 provides an introduction to business intelligence, including the processes, methodologies, infrastructure, and current practices used to transform business data into useful information and support business decision-making. Business Intelligence requires foundation knowledge in data storage and retrieval, thus this course will review logical data models for both database management systems and data warehouses. Students will learn to extract and manipulate data from these systems and assess security-related issues. Data mining, visualization, and statistical analysis along with reporting options such as management dashboards and balanced scorecards will be covered.

Course 9 deals with the design and development of data fusion and visualization application for data analytics. Topics include distributed data collection, dimensional modeling, ETL (Extraction, Transformation, and Loading) procedures, information access and delivery, as well as the optimization and long-term maintenance of a data fusion application. In addition, this course explores the data visualization tools and concepts to represent the data and insights visually.

Course 10 covers the fundamental concepts of Big Data management and analytics. In addition, course covers the analysis, design and development of the applications that deal with very large volumes of data as well as in proposing scalable solutions for them to aid business intelligence and scientific discovery.

Each of the course objectives can be mapped to the program outcomes to insure a balanced coverage of topics [20]. Figure 1 shows that balance among the courses.

Figure 1. Program Outcomes Mapped to Courses.

Program Outcome\Courses	Information Security					Data Analytics				
	C1	C2	C3	C4	C5	C6	C7	C8	C9	C10
Identifying Threats	I/2	D/2	E/3	E/3	I/2					
Policy of Risk Management	I/2	M/3	D/2	A/2	I/2					
Protection of Infrastructures	I/2	D/2	E/3	E/3	I/2					
Sourcing and Data Management						I/2	D/2	D/1	E/1	M/2
Information Analytics						I/2	E/2	E/2	M/2	D/1
Knowledge Discovery						I/2	E/2	E/2	M/2	I/1

Legend: Student Developmental Level / Instruction Emphasis
Student Developmental Level: I – Introductory, D – Developing
M – Mastery, E- Excel

Instruction Emphasis: 0- No Emphasis, 1 – Some Emphasis
2 – Moderate Emphasis, 3 – Significant Emphasis

Figure 1 maps the course with the program outcome through the student developmental level / instruction emphasis value. The student developmental level represents the developmental level of the student at the end of the course. The different developmental levels are Introductory (I), Developing (D), Mastery (M) and Excel (E). Introductory represent the basic developmental level. Developmental and Mastery level represents more advanced level of the student development at the end of the course. Excel represents the most advanced student development level at the end of the course. The emphasis of the instruction ranges from 0 to 4. Here 0 represents 'No Emphasis' in the instructional level, 1 represents little instructional emphasis, 2 represents moderate instructional emphasis and 3 represents most significant emphasis in the instruction level.

For example, in the Course 1 (C1) - Cybersecurity and Information Assurance – students will be exposed to identifying threats, policy of risk management and protection of infrastructures program outcomes at the introductory developmental level with moderate emphasis in the instruction. While in the Course 10 (C10) – Big Data Analytics, students will be exposed to sourcing and data management program outcome with mastery level of student development and the moderate instructional emphasis. While information analytics program outcome is exposed with developing student development level with little instructional emphasis, knowledge discovery program outcome is exposed with introductory student developmental level and little instructional emphasis

4. ASSESSMENT OF COURSES

4.1 Assessment of C1 Learning Outcomes

Following are the possible ways the Course 1 learning outcomes could be assessed:

- The student's ability to understand the current state of threats and state of art tools, policies, standards and frameworks to defend against the threats could be assessed through quizzes and test questions.
- The student's ability to understand security plan, implement measures and control could be assessed through case study based projects (project reports/presentations) and assignments.

This course should help the students to perform the job responsibilities of Information Security analyst and prepare them towards Information Security Architect.

4.2 Assessment of C2 Learning Outcomes

Following are the possible ways the Course 2 learning outcomes could be assessed:

- The student's ability to understand the current state of ethical, legal issues and its impact on information security risk could be assessed through quizzes and test questions.
- The Student's ability to understand investigate policies, implement policy regulations, management framework, methods and tools could be assessed through case study based projects (project reports/presentations) and assignments.

This course should help the students to perform the job responsibilities of Information Architect and prepare them towards the responsibilities of CISO.

4.3 Assessment of C3 Learning Outcomes

Following are the possible ways the Course 3 learning outcomes could be assessed:

- The student's ability to understand and apply the public key encryption/infrastructure, digital signatures could be assessed through theoretical/practical assignments.
- The student's ability to understand and apply the authentication, key management, and data integrity and non-repudiation functionalities could be assessed through theoretical/practical assignments.
- The student's ability to understand investigate and implement network and Internet security as a layered approach could be assessed through case study based projects (project reports/presentations) and assignments.

These student assessments for this course should help the students to perform the job responsibilities of Network Security Engineer, Information Security Architect and prepare them towards the responsibilities of Chief Information Security Officer (CISO).

4.4 Assessment of C4 Learning Outcomes

Following are the possible ways the Course 4 learning outcomes could be assessed:

- The student's ability to identify and secure database, program, web application and mobile application related vulnerabilities could be assessed through theoretical/practical assignments.
- The student's ability to do review code and perform penetration testing and application security testing could be assessed through practical lab assignments.
- The student's ability to investigate and perform Database/ Mobile/Web application architectural risk analysis and secure development life cycles could be assessed through case study based projects (project reports/presentations) and assignments.

This course should help the students to perform the job responsibilities of Application Security Engineer, Information Security Architect and prepare them towards the responsibilities of CISO.

4.5 Assessment of C5 Learning Outcomes

Following are the possible ways the course 5 learning outcomes could be assessed:

- The student's ability to understand and identify cloud computing related security risks, challenges and fundamentals could be assessed through theoretical/practical assignments.
- The student's ability to analyze, design and implement cloud computing security architecture and secure life cycle development could be assessed through case study based projects and assignments.

This course should help the students to perform the job responsibilities of Cloud Security Engineer, Information Security Architect and prepare them towards the responsibilities of CISO.

4.6 Assessment of C6 Learning Outcomes

Following are the possible ways the Course 6 learning outcomes could be assessed:

- The student's ability to understand and identify methods of data acquisition, access, transformation, and cleaning could be assessed through assignments

- The student's ability to apply analytical techniques and tools for data preparation and analysis could be assessed through theoretical/practical assignments
- The student's ability to analyze, categorize, design and implement different methods of secure data sourcing, transfer and analysis could be assessed through case study based projects (project reports/presentations)

This course should help the students to perform the job responsibilities of Data Analysts and ETL Engineer and prepare them towards the responsibilities of Information Architect.

4.7 Assessment of C7 Learning Outcomes

Following are the possible ways the Course 7 learning outcomes could be assessed:

- The student's ability to assess input data, quality of output as well as the principles and methodologies involved in the data mining could be assessed through theoretical/practical assignments.
- The student's ability to apply, analyze and synthesize different machine learning schemes and data mining algorithms could be assessed through case study based projects (project reports/presentations) and assignments
- The student's ability to construct data-driven discovery and modeling of hidden patterns in large real-world data and text could be assessed through assignments

This course should help the students to perform the job responsibilities of Data Scientist and prepare them towards the responsibilities of Information Architect/CIO.

4.8 Assessment of C8 Learning Outcomes

Following are the possible ways the Course 8 learning outcomes could be assessed:

- The student's ability to design and build data warehouse/data marts and dashboards/scorecards could be assessed through case study based practical assignments.
- The student's ability to understand and apply dimensional modeling, business performance management, operational metrics and key performance indicators could be assessed through quizzes, questions in tests and assignments.
- The student's ability to adapt to the emerging trends in business intelligence and analytics could be assessed through term papers and projects.

This course should help the students to perform the job responsibilities of IT Manager, Business Intelligence professionals, Data Architect and prepare them towards the responsibilities of Chief Information Officer (CIO).

4.9 Assessment of C9 Learning Outcomes

Following are the possible ways the Course 9 learning outcomes could be assessed:

- The student's ability to assess, design and build a distributed data fusion application could be assessed through the case study based practical assignments.
- The student's ability to understand and apply requirements, architectural components, infrastructure, visual representations, visual analysis process, visual analysis, visual analytics, importance of data quality/meta data could be assessed through quizzes, questions in tests and assignments

- The student's ability to explore data visualization tools to obtain insight and knowledge that can directly support situational awareness and decision making could be assessed through the case study based projects

This course should help the students to perform the job responsibilities of Data Scientist/Data Architect and prepare them towards the responsibilities of Chief Information Officer.

4.10 Assessment of C10 Learning Outcomes

Following are the possible ways the Course 10 learning outcomes could be assessed:

- The student's ability to be familiar with the fundamental concepts of Big Data management and analytics could be assessed through quizzes and the questions in tests.
- The student's ability to be competent in handling applications dealing with very large volumes of data as well as in proposing scalable solutions for them could be assessed through case based practical assignments/project.
- The student's ability to research, analyze, design and develop Big Data solutions that impact business intelligence and scientific discovery could be assessed through case based projects.

This course should help the students to perform the job responsibilities of Big Data Scientist/ Big Data Architect and prepare them towards the responsibilities of CIO.

The above student portfolio and their assessments should help the prospective employers to decide if the graduates are qualified to perform the job responsibilities.

5. PROGRAM ADMINISTRATION

The student population entering into the MISA program will likely to have a wide variety of skills and backgrounds, some not necessarily in a science and technology area. To reduce the program risk, the admission requirements need to be in compliant with the Universities' graduate programs and other cybersecurity/analytics graduate programs, and that each entrant should have grounding in CS/IS/IT. Admission requirements to the program is planned to include:

- Bachelor's Degree from a US Institution or equivalent
- Minimum Grade Point Average of 3.0 on a 4.0 scale
- Competitive scores from the Graduate Record Exam
- Fluency with CS/IS/IT

The potential student pool of applicants will come from the alumni of Bachelors of Computer Science, Information Systems and Information Technology program, and from other programs with a background in CS/IS/IT. Working professionals in the public, private, and non-profit sectors, who would be interested in expanding career choices in Cyber Security and Data Analytics are also promising candidates for this program. These individuals desire to learn more about advanced cybersecurity/data analytics concepts, strategies and methods in order to improve their performance in their current job, progress faster in their careers, or transition to a new career field.

The MISA program will require incremental resources in the administration of the program and student advising. This includes (1) Program director to oversee the academic program; and (2) one quarter-time staff person, whose responsibilities will be related to admissions, tracking, maintaining program guidelines, course scheduling, coordinating with the administration and student services staff, students counseling, verifying student requirement fulfillment for graduation and similar tasks. The admission process could be handled by a faculty committee, similar to the current graduate programs.

To assess and mitigate the risks, MISA program would need to have an annual online course and program evaluation survey to assess the program. There will also be group discussions to get feedback on the courses and program. Student course evaluations and classroom assessments (peer evaluations) will also be an integral part of the assessment process. Faculty will consider this information and recommend improvements to the program. Faculty who are teaching MISA courses with an embedded measure of key learning objectives will also discuss results from the prior year, their plans for modifying course assignments based on data and any changes to evaluation criteria used. Additionally, the faculty will discuss what they cover in their MISA courses and how they can better integrate their efforts.

The program leadership will hold focus groups with managers at organizations that employ MISA graduates to garner feedback towards continuous improvement of the program. Similarly, there will be follow-up focus groups with MISA alumni to gather feedback based on their experience and how well the program prepared them for careers in cybersecurity and/or analytics.

6. CONCLUSION

The lack of a graduate program in cybersecurity and data analytics calls for a need that students, employers, and the community desires. Careful research is required prior to launching a new program; else it is doomed to fail. A graduate program needs to be designed from the top-down, so that the courses support the program outcomes. The administration and assessment of the program have to be considered early-on in the design process, because a new program will evolve and grow as it becomes mature. Cybersecurity and data analytics are new areas that encompasses several disciplines. Merging of cybersecurity and data analytics disciplines is an exciting combination with a bright outlook.

This paper proposes a new advancement in the field of Computer Science and Information Technology education by combining the fields of information security and data analytics together into a graduate degree. The idea of a modular design where students will steadily progress into becoming cybersecurity and analytics professionals with an acute business sense makes them very attractive to future employers and can further promote cooperation between business schools and technology programs.

7. ACKNOWLEDGMENTS

Author would like to thank Prof. John Beard, Prof. William Jones Prof. Dodi Hodges and Prof. Crystal Cox for their valuable suggestions and comments.

8. REFERENCES

[1] University of Maryland Cybersecurity Program. Retrieved 05/26/2014 from http://cyber.umd.edu/education/meng-cybersecurity

[2] Virginia College Online Programs. Retrieved May 26, 2014 from htttp://www.vconline.edu/graduate-degrees-online/cyber-security-degree.cfm

[3] Washington Governor's University. Retrieved May 16 2014 from http://washington.wgu.edu/ online_it_degrees/information_security_assurance_degree

[4] Utica College Cyber Security – Intelligence and Forensics. Retrieved May 26, 2014 from http://programs.online.utica.edu/programs/masters-cybersecurity.asp

[5] NJIT MS Cybersecruity Program. Retrieved May 26, 2014 from http://cs.njit.edu/academics/graduate/mscsp.php

[6] Department of Computer Science, George Washington University. Retrieved May 16, 2014 from http://www.cs.gwu.edu/academics/graduate_programs/master/cybersecurity

[7] Master of Science in Cyber Security and Leadership Curriculum UWT. Retrieved May 31, 2014 from https://www.tacoma.uw.edu/institute-technology/master-cybersecurity-leadership-curriculu

[8] Master of Arts in Intelligence Studies, American Military University. Retrieved May 316, 2014 from http://www.amu.apus.edu/academic/programs/degree/1604/master-of-science-in-cybersecurity-studies

[9] Bureau of Labor Statistics, Retrieved May 2014 from http://www.bls.gov/news.release/empsit.nr0.htm

[10] McKinsey Global Institute, Retrieved May 2014 from www.mckinsey.com/insights/americas/us_game_changers

[11] Dept. of Labor Cybersecurity jobs statistics Retrieved April 30, 2014 from http://www.umuc.edu/cybersecurity/careers/

[12] Wall street Journal Report retrieved May 2014 from http://blogs.wsj.com/cio/2013/03/04/demand-for-cyber-security-jobs-is-soaring/

[13] Petrova, K., Kaskenpalo, P., Philpott, A., Buchan, J., Enbedding Information Security Curricula in Existing Programmes. In InforSecCD Conference '04, pages 20-29 Kennesaw GA, USA, 2005. ACM Press.

[14] Bacon, T., Tikekar, R., Experiences With Developing A Computer Security Information Assurance Curriculum, In Consortium for Computing in Small Colleges, 2003, 254-267.

[15] Taylor, C., Ednicott-Popovsky, B., Phillips, A.,Forensics Education: Assessment and Measures of nd Workshop on Systematic Approaches to Digital Forensic Engineering, Seattle WA, USA April 10-12, 2007 IEEE Computer Society

[16] R.H. L. Chiang, P. Goes, and E.A. Stohr, "Business Intelligence and Analytics Education, and Program Development: A Unique Opportunity for the Information Systems Discipline, ACM Transactions on MIS (TMIS), Vol. 3 No.3, Oct 2012.

[17] P.J. Piety, D.T. Hickey and M. J. Bishop, "Educational data sciences: framing emergent practices for analytics of learning, organizations, and systems", Proceedings of the Fourth International Conference on Learning Analytics And Knowledge, March 2014.

[18] P. Anderson, J. Bowring, R. McCauley, G. Pothering and C. Starr, "An undergraduate degree in data science: curriculum and a decade of Implementation experience", Proceedings of the 45th ACM technical symposium on Computer science Education, March 2014.

[19] Survey of Analytics Programs. Retrieved on May 28 2014 from http://analytics.ncsu.edu/?page_id=4184

[20] Suskie, L. "Assessing student learning: A common sense guide". Anker Publishing Company, Inc. Boston, Massachusetts: 2004

[21] Big Data Initiative. Retrieved on May 29 2014 from http://www.whitehouse.gov/blog/2013/04/18/unleashing-power-big-data.

[22] National Centers of Academic Excellence, Retrieved On May 25 2014 from http://niccs.us- cert.gov/education/national-centers-academic-excellence-cae

Design of an Analytic Centric MS Degree in Information Sciences and Technologies

Jai W. Kang
Rochester Institute of Technology
152 Lomb Memorial Drive
Rochester, NY 14623
585-475-5362
jai.kang@rit.edu

Edward P. Holden
Rochester Institute of Technology
152 Lomb Memorial Drive
Rochester, NY 14623
585-475-5361
edward.holden@rit.edu

Qi Yu
Rochester Institute of Technology
152 Lomb Memorial Drive
Rochester, NY 14623
585-475-6929
qi.yu@rit.edu

ABSTRACT
In this paper, we present the design, development, and offering of a new Master of Science (MS) curriculum in Information Sciences and Technologies (IST) at Rochester Institute of Technology (RIT). The new curriculum resulted as we enhanced our original MS curriculum to accommodate to the key technological advances in computing as well as the new demands in IT industry. The new curriculum is featured by its analytic centric foundation that provides students a systematic training in analytical thinking and equips them with a solid skill set to manage and analyze different types of data in scale. A number of concentration tracks are also offered that are build upon the foundation to further advance students' learning and expose them to the state-of-the-art in key computing domains.

Categories and Subject Descriptors
K.3.2 [Computers and Education]: Computer and Information Science Education – curriculum, information systems education.

Keywords
Information sciences and technologies; curriculum; data analytics; database; web technologies

1. INTRODUCTION
Master of Science in Information Technology (MS/IT) degree in Information Sciences and Technologies (IST) at Rochester Institute of Technology (RIT) has provided students with skill sets that no other computing disciplines provide. The skill set developed is an interdisciplinary mix of computing hardware and software technologies, creative mediating tools, data repository strategies, communication technologies, and human performance theory and practices. The MS/IT degree allows each student to develop a personal program of study that suits his or her professional goals within the IT computing discipline.

The IST department continues to update courses and concentrations as technology continue to advance. The technology advancements have often been accompanied by such buzzwords as Information Highway, Web, Cloud Computing, Big Data, BYOD, Analytics, Data Science, Internet of Things, etc. For

SIGITE'14, October 16–18, 2014, Atlanta, GA, USA.
Copyright 2014 ACM 978-1-4503-2686-5/14/10...$15.00.
http://dx.doi.org/10.1145/2656450.2656460

example, Google search returns over 1.9 billion hits for the query "Big Data", over 150 million for "Analytics", and more than 1.7 billion for "Data Science" as of May 2014. It is also hard to miss noticing the buzzwords from major newspapers, magazines or journals. Costello and Prohaska includes BYOD, Cloud and Big Data in 2013 Trends and Strategies [2]. McKinsey Quarterly forecasts business trends for the decade ahead enabled by IT such as Big Data, Advanced Analytics, Cloud among others [1]. Harvard Business Review headlines that the sexiest job of the 21st century is data scientist [3].

As big data and analytics are being discussed everywhere, Morris quotes Rob Bearden, CEO of Hortonworks, saying "The desire on the enterprise side to find truly qualified data scientists has resulted in almost open headcount [7]. It's probably the biggest imbalance of supply and demand that I've ever seen in my career. … The talent pool is, at best, probably 20 percent of the demand." While Zilora, Bogaard, and Leone discuss a new curricular model for teaching IT, the addition of Analytics is proposed as an overarching theme for the BS/IT program at RIT [10].

As RIT converted from its quarter-based academic calendar to a traditional 15-week semester calendar in the Fall of 2013, the IST department renamed the MS/IT program MS/Information Sciences & Technologies (MS/IST). The new program continues to address current IT computing issues and technologies, with the exciting emphasis on Analytics.

This paper begins by comparing the original MS/IT degree with the new Analytic Centric MS/IST degree, followed by discussing differences from other Data Science programs in Section 2. Section 3 describes the curriculum of the MS/IST program including Prerequisite Knowledge, Foundation Courses, and three tracks of concentration. Section 4 discusses how the new program will be assessed before concluding the paper in Section 5.

2. INTEGRATING ANALYTICS INTO THE MS/IST DEGREE

2.1 Differences Between the Original and New MS Degrees
Figures 1 and 2 display degree program curricula of MS/IT and MS/IST respectively, and Table 1 compares them.

Table 1. Original MS/IT Degree vs. New MS/IST Degree

Program Component	MS/IT Quarter Program	MS/IST Semester Program
Foundation Courses	1 course/4 credits	4 courses/12 credits
Concentrations	9 courses/36 credits (2-3 related knowledge areas)	4-5 courses/12-15 credits (1 broad knowledge area)
Elective	1 course/4 credits	0 courses/0 credits
Culminating Experience	Project (4 credits) Thesis (4 credits)	Project (6 credits) Thesis (6 credits) Capstone Course (3 credits)
Total Credits	48 quarter credits	30 semester credits

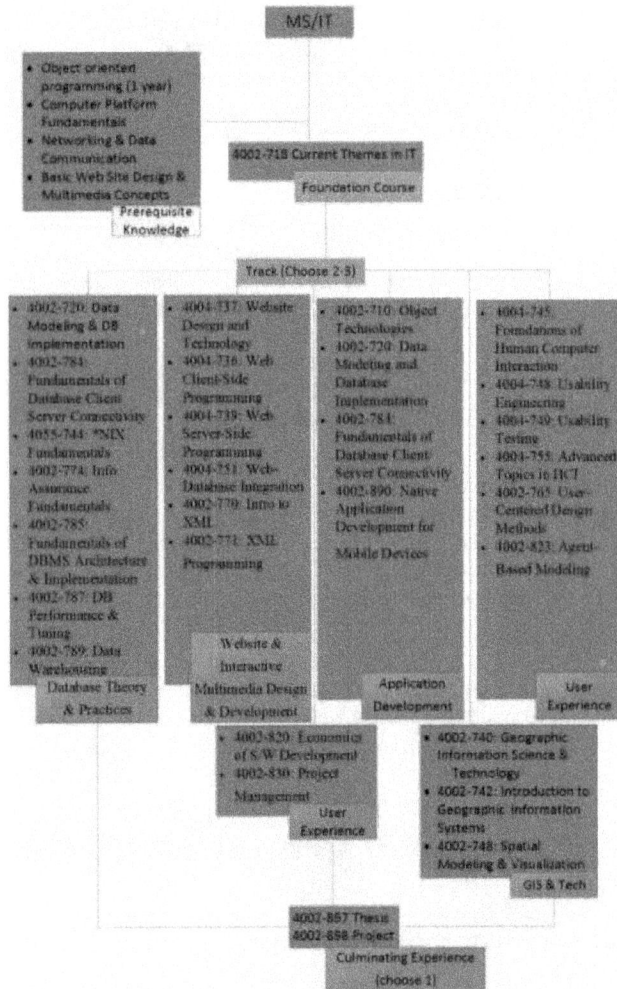

Figure 1. MS/IT Program

2.1.1 Prerequisite Knowledge
The MS/IT & MS/IST admission requirements remain the same, which includes having a solid ability in object-oriented programming and basic Web design and interactive multimedia concepts. However, the other two requirements for MS/IT: knowledge of computer hardware and software architecture and fundamental computer networking theory and concepts has been replaced by database theory and statistics in the new MS/IST degree. This change emphasizes the analytic centric MS degree in Information Sciences and Technologies.

2.1.2 Foundation Courses
MS/IT consists of one course: Current Themes in IT, which exposes students to the breath of opportunity in IT and prepares them for developing a topic for their culminating experience. However, MS/IST needs to prepare students for completing this new analytic centric degree program. The foundation courses therefore, consist of Analytical Thinking, Knowledge Representation Technologies, Knowledge Processing Technologies, and Scholarship in IT. Each course is further described in Section 3.

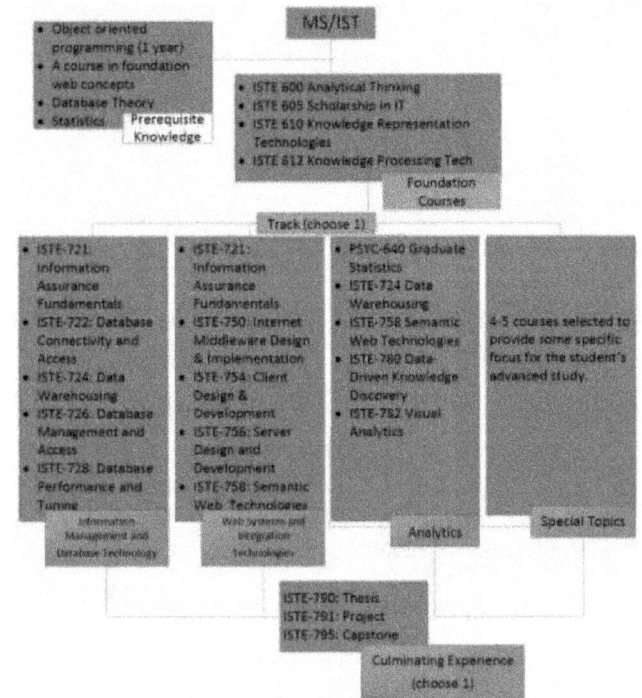

Figure 2. MS/IST Program

2.1.3 Concentrations/Tracks
A concentration in MS/IT is a group of three or more courses that focus on a specific knowledge area and is designed to explore a unique aspect in IT. Each student selects 9 courses in two synergic IT knowledge areas. In MS/IST, the quarter program concentrations are revised into an area of "domain" study that covers the diverse aspects of a given IT knowledge domain. Tracks have been defined to focus students' advanced study in a specific area of study. Section 3 describes the tracks: Information Management & Database Technology, Web Systems & Integration Technologies, and Analytics. Students also have an option to take 4-5 courses differing from the selections from these three tracks to provide specific focus for his or her advanced study.

2.1.4 Elective
In MS/IT, a student may take a course from the concentrations not selected for his or her concentration as the elective. However none are allowed in MS/IST.

2.1.5 Culminating Experience

The purpose of the culminating experience is to allow students to demonstrate their creativity and professional capabilities in one or more of the concentration areas or a specific track studied. Both degree programs offer the Master's thesis and project. A project consists of a nontrivial software development and/or deployment effort and a report discussing it. A thesis deals with a significant question and involves some original insight. Compared to a project, a thesis has much higher level of expectation in terms of background research and justification.

In addition to project and thesis, the MS/IST program offers a capstone course (ISTE-795) option, which is an instructor-guided, team-based, course environment. Students will be grouped into teams, for an integrative system development effort that includes the management, analysis, and/or presentation/visualization of a large dataset(s).

2.2 Difference with Other Data Science Programs

There are quite a few data science programs recently offered across the nation. Most of these programs are research centric with a curriculum focusing on the fundamental theory, algorithmic and architectural support of data management and analytics in scale. The MS/IST degree, on the other side, has a strong career-oriented focus, aiming to equip students with practical skills to handle data management and analysis challenges that arise in their daily work. This degree will fit perfectly into the career-oriented education that RIT has been striving to provide. The career-focused degree will also significantly benefit from one of the world's largest co-op programs at RIT, which brings in practical problems, real-world data, and software tools commonly adopted in industry to enrich our curriculum.

3 THE CURICULUMN
3.1 Prerequisite Knowledge

Since this is a computing program, success in the MS-IST program requires certain prerequisite skills. Students need to be able to write programs, work with basic relational databases and have statistical knowledge used in the analytics portion of the curriculum. A student entering from a BS program in Information Technology, Computer Science or Software Engineering would have this prerequisite knowledge.

Students from other programs may also have this knowledge through minors or other coursework. For those who do not, there is a bridge program, which covers these subject areas. Students may complete some of all of these courses as a requirement for full admission:

- Object oriented programming (1 year)
- A course in foundation web concepts
- Database Theory
- Statistics

These prerequisites ensure that the student can immediately work with the assignments given in their course of study.

3.2 Foundation Courses
3.2.1   ISTE-600: Analytical Thinking

There is mounting evidence of a need to improve the ability of individuals and groups to think thoughtfully and analytically in order to develop appropriate and useful solutions to complex problems. Sources of complexity include human cognitive limitations, uncertainty, system dynamics, and reasoning errors.

This course provides students with frameworks, techniques, methods, and tools to improve analytical, critical thinking and presentation skills. The course goals include 1) increasing students' awareness of the challenges and difficulties related to thinking clearly about complex systems and situations and 2) improving students' skills to analyze data and to use information effectively for complex problem solving.

The Critical Thinking Community [4] defines all thinking by eight elements: "Whenever we think for a purpose within a point of view based on assumptions leading to implications and consequences. We use concepts, ideas and theories to interpret idea, facts, and experiences in order to answer questions, solve problems, and resolve issues. Thinking, then 1) generates Purposes, 2) raises Questions, 3) uses Information, 4) utilizes Concepts, 5) makes Inferences, 6) makes Assumptions, 7) generates Implications and 8) embodies a Point of View."

The Critical Thinking Community [1] also offers an online model to analyze the logic of a problem using the eight elements of thought/reasoning. As a user enters each element to analyze real life problems, the model provides universal intellectual standards to assess it for clarity, accuracy, relevance, fairness, credibility, sufficiency, reliability and practicality as applicable to each element.

The course selects a lecture subject to have the students be equipped with IT content domain knowledge in the area of analytics such as Machine Learning. Students then work in teams on a problem of their choosing that is interesting, significant and relevant to applying data mining algorithms and techniques to some real-world problems. For example, students choose challenging problems by joining the Kaggle [6] for predictive modeling competitions.

Students use the Weka [9] data mining software and the Tableau software [8] for visual analysis and presentations. Student teams construct excellent stories with interactive and dynamic dashboards for their projects with the help of the visual analytics tool.

3.2.2   ISTE-605: Scholarship in IT

This is a typical research methods course and is not unique to our program but the ability to research topics related to the IT industry is becoming increasingly important. This will be used directly throughout their course of study and particularly during their culminating experience.

3.2.3   ISTE-610: Knowledge Representation Technologies

With the proliferation of data and the need to analyze data from disparate sources, there is an increasing need to organize data. The trend toward "big data" emphasizes the need for this organization.

The goal of this course are to provide students with hands-on learning and experience with the information sciences and technologies needed to structure and store, data, information, and knowledge. This course builds on the student's knowledge of programming, basic database skills and web development to manage large datasets in the context of specific problem scenarios.

In this course students will get hands-on experience with using XML to model and organize data and will work with the one of the newer NoSQL databases, initially MongoDB. This will provide a way to view data and data organization in addition to the relational organization, with which they are already familiar.

This information will give them a foundation upon which to build analytical processes.

Student evaluations from the initial offering of this course indicate that effective notes and reading sources helped in understanding the subject and a lot of hands-on assignments, projects and quizzes made the subject interesting. The assignments were a great test of the students' knowledge of the subject.

3.2.4 ISTE-612: Knowledge Processing Technologies

Topics include information processing, modeling, storing, searching, and retrieval technologies, data and text analytics for knowledge extraction, and Internet middleware technologies to access and deliver data and knowledge.

The main objectives of this course is to (1) process, model, store, index, represent, search, and retrieve, modern data collections using fully automatic systems—focusing on information retrieval systems; (2) analyze data by developing algorithms to extract high-level knowledge from it—focusing on data analytics, especially text analytics, including text classification and clustering; and (3) exploit Internet middleware technologies to access external data sources or deliver information to others—focusing on web service technologies.

The major focus of this course is placed on unstructured data, which may be in the form of text, hypertext, or multimedia (e.g., images and videos). Various unstructured data models will be studied, such as Boolean, probabilistic, and vector space models, which are implemented using inverted files, relational thesauri, special hardware, and other approaches. State-of-the-art technologies and research skills of literature analysis, innovation, evaluation of new ideas, and communication are emphasized via lab assignments and projects. Students will get exposed to a broad overview of the research topics, methodologies, major results, open problems, and potential future research directions. More specifically, this course will help students:

- Identify basic theories and analysis tools as they apply to process modern data collections,
- Develop understanding of problems and potentials of current information processing and retrieval systems,
- Learn and appreciate different information processing and retrieval algorithms and systems,
- Apply various modeling, indexing, matching, organizing, and evaluating methods to data processing, retrieval, and analysis problems,
- Become aware of current experimental and theoretical research in the area.

3.3 Tracks of Concentration

3.3.1 Support to the Track Courses from the Foundation

3.3.1.1 ISTE-600: Analytical Thinking

As Elder and Paul (2007) demonstrate the analytical thinking tools to analyze the logic of problems on such subjects as Love, Science, History, Economics, Ecology, etc., this course can connect to not only courses in all tracks in MS/IST but also multi-disciplinary courses.

Offering the course for the first time in the spring semester of 2014, student feedback was quite positive regarding the analytical thinking tools. In general, students felt that the tools helped them solve the problems analytically, in stepwise fashion, and kept them on the right track. The feedback indicates that this analytical thinking approach can be applied to any kind of problems, including research project or even everyday life problems.

3.3.1.2 ISTE-605: Scholarship in IT

Again, this research methods course is not unique to our program, but the ability to do research into new analytical approaches and technologies is critical in all tracks in the MS/IST program. It is also important in gaining domain specific knowledge.

3.3.1.3 ISTE-610: Knowledge Representation Technologies

In most of their database courses, students will have experience with Relational databases but much of the data that needs to be analyzed today is not in a relational database. This course supports the track courses by adding to the relational background, using XML to structure data and a non-relational (NoSQL) database to collect data. This gives the students flexibility in dealing with data from many sources.

3.3.1.4 ISTE-612: Knowledge Processing Technologies

Retrieving information from unstructured data has drawn paramount consideration nowadays, especially with the boom of the World Wide Web. The Web has become a universal information repository by providing a convenient way for the exchange of information. In this regard, the Web can be regarded as a huge database where each Web user can create Web content and share with others. However, unlike the data in the traditional databases that has a rigid structure defined by the database schema, the Web data is typically unstructured textual data. Therefore, the knowledge gained from ISTE-612 will directly benefit students' learning in the track of web system and integration technologies, focusing on developing applications to consume, integrate data on the web or deliver data over the web. The analytics techniques especially text analytics will benefit students choosing the discovery informatics track. In addition to the Web, unstructured textual data is being created anytime, anywhere, and in many different formats. The volume of unstructured data has reached five times larger than the data in databases since 2006 and it keeps growing in a speed that is much faster than database data. In this regard, ISTE-612 provides a much broader treatment of data that goes beyond structured data and relational database, which will better prepare students that choose the information management and database technology track.

3.3.2 Description of the Information Management and Database Technology Track

The Information Management and Database Technology track prepares students for roles working with databases in support of analytics.

3.3.2.1 ISTE-721: Information Assurance Fundamentals

This course provides an introduction to the topic of information assurance as it pertains to an awareness of the risks inherent in protecting digital content in today's networked computing environments. Topics in secure data and information access are explored from the perspectives of software development, software implementation, data storage, system administration and network communications. Current software exploitation issues and techniques for information assurance will be investigated.

3.3.2.2 ISTE-722: Database Connectivity and Access

In this course, students will build applications that interact with databases. Through programming exercises, students will work with multiple databases and programmatically invoke the advanced database processing operations that are integral to contemporary computing applications. Students will examine and evaluate alternative approaches for each of these operations. Topics include the database drivers, the data layer, connectivity operations, security and integrity, and controlling database access.

3.3.2.3 ISTE-724: Data Warehousing

This course covers the purpose, scope, capabilities, and processes used in data warehousing technologies for the management and analysis of data. Students will be introduced to the theory of data warehousing, dimensional data modeling, the extract/transform/load process, warehouse implementation, dimensional data analysis, and summary data management. The basics of data mining and importance of data security will also be discussed. Hands-on exercises include implementing a data warehouse.

3.3.2.4 ISTE-726: Database Management and Access

Students will be introduced to issues in client/server database implementation and administration. Students will configure, test, and establish client-server communication and server-server communication with single and multiple database servers. Topics such as schema implementation, storage allocation and management, user creation and access security, backup and recovery, and performance measurement and enhancement will be presented in lecture and experienced in a laboratory environment. Students will configure and demonstrate successful communication between a database file server and multiple clients.

3.3.2.5 ISTE-728: Database Performance and Tuning

This course covers the fundamental theoretical topics relevant to database performance, and it allows students to apply these concepts to the investigation of real-life issues through the performance monitoring and tuning of one or more databases implemented in enterprise-level database management systems.

Students will explore the theory and application of performance monitoring and tuning techniques as they relate to database systems. Standard topics in DBMS performance will be discussed including: physical and logical design issues, the hardware and software environment, SQL statement execution, and front-end application issues. Techniques in performance monitoring and tuning will be investigated.

3.3.3   Description of the Web Track

The Web Systems and Integration Technologies track offers a comprehensive treatment on the design and development of web based information systems. The three central components of a typical web system, i.e., client, server, and middleware, are covered in detail in three respective track courses. These components are complemented by related key technologies that help protect data and information assets. Preventing unauthorized access or modification is important considering the open web environment. Key advances in web technologies will also be covered to expose students to the state-of-the-art in this area. This track shares one course (ISTE-721) with the Information Management and Database Technology track.

3.3.3.1 ISTE-750: Internet Middleware Design and Implementation

This course provides students with an introduction to the design and implementation of Internet middleware application programming interfaces (APIs) and services. Topics include the blending of interactive and dynamic content from multiple servers and services utilizing data from heterogeneous sources, with a strong design focus on the needs of client software and human users which will utilize those services.

3.3.3.2 ISTE-754: Client Design and Development

This course explores the analysis, design, development, and implementation of client-side programming in the context of Internet technologies, mobile devices, and Web-based client systems. Students will learn to design and build usable and effective interactive systems, clients, and interfaces. Key features addressed will include browser and platform compatibility, object reusability, bandwidth and communications issues, development environments, privacy and security, and related technologies and APIs.

3.3.3.3 ISTE-756: Server Design and Development

This provides students with advanced work in the design & implementation of highly scalable Internet servers, and application programming interfaces (APIs). Topics include the effects of client requirements upon design, creating & blending heterogeneous data for analysis & visualization, and approaches to building highly scalable services. Students will develop dynamic and data centric web systems, as well as building information services systems that are independent of the technologies that use them.

3.3.3.4 ISTE-758: Semantic Web Technologies

This provides students with an in-depth introduction to Semantic Web technologies, utilizing ontologies and relationship metadata. Topics include the creation of data linkage through metadata, practical approaches to the design and implementation of ontologies, server- and client-side parsing and transformation of data and ontologies, and machine interpretation of relationships.

3.3.4   Description of the Analytics Track

The Analytics track advances students' knowledge in data analytics by offering them a systematic training in key analytic techniques, including warehousing, mining, and visualization among others. Students will gain practical skills to handle data analysis challenges that arise in their daily work. This track shares two courses with other tracks, one with the Information Management and Database Technology track (ISTE-724) and the other with the Web track (ISTE-758).

3.3.4.1 PSYC-640: Graduate Statistics

This course is to prepare students to perform data analysis needed for their Master's Thesis and to interpret the statistics presented in research. Students will develop their understanding of: key concepts and methods in descriptive and inferential statistics; hypothesis testing for independent and dependent samples; assumptions underlying statistical analyses; statistical software applications focusing on Statistical Package for the Social Sciences (SPSS); how to select appropriate statistical procedures for specific research problems; best practices in interpreting statistical results; and best practices in writing reports of findings.

3.3.4.2 ISTE-780: Data-Driven Knowledge Discovery

This course is the study and practice of creating new information from existing or newly generated data. Identifying and validating patterns in large datasets are key activities. The goals of this course are to apply available, computer-based techniques and methods to data-intensive problems in a variety of domains. Students will select, prepare, and analyze data, and interpret outcomes of different analyses leading to the discovery of novel information and knowledge.

3.3.4.3 ISTE-782: Visual Analytics

This course introduces students to the science of analytical reasoning facilitated by interactive visual interfaces. Course lectures, reading assignments, and practical lab experiences will cover a mix of theoretical and technical Visual Analytics topics. Topics include analytical reasoning, human cognition and perception of visual information, visual representation and interaction technologies, data representation and transformation, production, presentation, and dissemination of analytic process results, and Visual Analytic case studies and applications. Furthermore, students will learn relevant Visual Analytics research trends such as Space, Time, and Multivariate Analytics and Extreme Scale Visual Analytics.

4 ASSESSMENT

One important aspect of the program is program assessment. The faculty designs assessment criteria and data are collected and reviewed at least every three years, on a rotating basis.

The first three student learning outcomes are assessed from student activities in coursework against a rubric designed for that outcome. The benchmark is that 80% of the students will achieve competence in that outcome. Two of those are assessed using coursework in the core and one from a selected course in the each of the tracks. The last outcome is assessed through successful completion of the culminating experience mentioned earlier, project, thesis or capstone course.

Table 2. Program Assessment

Program Goals	Student Learning Outcomes	Data Source / Measurement
1. Engage with the IST academic or professional communities and contribute to the knowledge bases of the field	Students will write a literature review that is potentially publishable, reviewing theories, models, or professional practice in IT	ISTE-605 *Scholarship in IT:* Rubric used to assess qualities of literature review
2. Apply specialized analytical and technical skills to a domain of work	Students can demonstrate advanced applied skills in an IT concentration area	An advanced project in a student-selected concentration area - Project is assessed via rubric
3. Design information services to enhance the value of information	Students will convey, order, analyze and display complex information using technological means	ISTE-612 *Knowledge Processing Tech:* Rubric used to measure effectiveness of conveying and displaying information
4. Explore and extend creative uses of emerging information technologies	Students will develop innovative technology approaches or solve problems in a new way	Culminating experience - Successful completion of culminating experience

5 CONCLUSION

In this paper, we detail our experience of design, development, and offering of a new Master of Science (MS) curriculum in Information Sciences and Technologies (IST) at Rochester Institute of Technology (RIT). The new curriculum places a strong emphasis on providing students a systematic training in analytics, aiming to achieve workforce readiness in the emerging "Big Data era". The curriculum also inherits the career-oriented focus from our original MS/IT program, aiming to equip students with practical skills. This makes our curriculum different from many data science programs offered by other universities in the country. The very positive student feedback from the first-time offering of the three foundation courses clearly demonstrates that both the topics and delivery of these courses have been well appreciated and received by our students.

6 ACKNOWLEDGMENTS

This curriculum development was a joint effort of all members of the Information Sciences and Technologies Department at RIT. The authors would like to acknowledge the innovation and dedication of their department colleagues.

7 REFERENCES

[1] Bughin, J.,Chul, M. and Manyika, J. 2013. *Ten IT-enabled business trends for the decade ahead.* McKinsey Quarterly. McKinsey & Company.

[2] Costello, T. and Prohaska B. 2013. *2013 Trends and Strategies.* CIO Corner, IEEE IT Pro January/February 2013.

[3] Devonport, T. and Patil, D.S. 2012. *Data Scientist: The Sexiest Job of the 21st Century.* Harvard Business Review (October, 2012).

[4] The Critical Community: Elements and Standards Learning Tool. Retrieved May 12, 2014, from http://www.criticalthinking.org/pages/elements-and-standards-learning-tool/783.

[5] Elder, L. & Paul, R. (2007). The Thinker's Guide to Analytic Thinking. Foundation for Critical Thinking Community.

[6] Kaggle: http://www.kaggle.com

[7] Morris, C. (2014). *The Sexiest Job of the 21st Century: Data Analyst.* Retrieved May 26, 2014, from http://www.cnbc.com/id/100792215

[8] Tableau: http://www.tableausoftware.com/.

[9] Weka: http://www.cs.waikato.ac.nz/ml/weka/.

[10] Zilora, S, Bogaard, S, and Leone, J. 2013. *The Changing Face of Information Technology.* In *Proceedings of the SIGITE Conference on Information Technology Education* (Orlando, Florida, USA, October 10 - 12, 2013). ITE '13. ACM, New York, NY, 29-34. DOI= http://doi.acm.org/10.1145/2512276.2512

Implementing a Living-Learning Community in Information Technology

Sandra Gorka, Matthew Helf, Jacob Miller
Pennsylvania College of Technology
One College Avenue
Williamsport, PA 17701
570-326-3761
sgorka@pct.edu, mch3@pct.edu, jmiller3@pct.edu

ABSTRACT

Living-learning communities (LLCs) have been used as a recruiting and retention tool by colleges and universities since the 1960s. Recently, they have seen resurgence in popularity. In 2010, Pennsylvania College of Technology (Penn College) started developing academically themed residential learning communities and as part of that program, started a LLC for Information Technology in 2011. A fundamental part of these communities is a collection of common activities to engage students both academically and socially. This paper discusses some of the specific activities associated with the Information Technology Living-Learning Community (IT LLC) as well as the observed benefits to academic performance, student interaction and retention.

Categories and Subject Descriptors

K.3.0 [Computing Milieux]: Computers and Education, General
K.3.2 [Computers and Education]: Computer and Information Science Education

General Terms

Human Factors

Keywords

Living-learning community, retention, co-curricular activities, student performance

1. LIVING-LEARNING COMMUNITIES

The different types of living-learning communities (LLC) have been present since the 1960s and have increased in popularity at institutions of higher education [2]. In an effort to increase retention and expand student learning beyond the classroom institutions of higher education are utilizing residential, interest and academically themed, living-learning communities. Residential learning communities allow for students with similar interests or shared academics to be housed in close proximity in the hopes of increasing connections between student participants [10,11]. By also engaging faculty in LLC activities, it is also

hoped that informal connections between faculty and students will develop.

A study conducted by Zhao and Kuh (2004) on learning communities identified several positive links with participating in learning communities [11]. Positive associations with academic performance, engagement with integration activities, college attendance, and satisfaction gains were identified and support much of the literature on learning community programs. Living-learning communities tend to have their own culture advancing cohesiveness, support, interaction, and integration amongst student peers and faculty [9,10].

Current living-learning community models at varying institutions incorporate either academically themed, interest themed, or a mix of both types of programs. Examples of interest based themes include diversity and cultural themes, business, leadership, sustainability, service learning and performing arts [6,7]. Examples of academically themed communities include a broad spectrum of disciplines including agricultural studies, business, science, engineering, communications and humanities majors [3,8]. These programs seem to typically offer educational programs, opportunities for academic support, social activities, career networking and development, skills development, and interactions with faculty [3,6,7,8].

2. LLCs at Penn College

Living-learning communities at Penn College have been a programmatic retention and integration tool since 2010 [4]. These academically themed residential learning communities are initiated by the academic units and supported by the Office of Residence Life to provide informal social and educational co-curricular experiences that increase students' connection with faculty outside of the classroom. Currently these programs are only geared toward first year students at Penn College. Living-learning communities at Penn College include Automotive Technology, Health Sciences, Hospitality, and Information Technology [4].

Development of the Living-learning communities at Penn College has been gradual with experiments in academic themed housing for construction, and aviation as well as interest based housing for first-generation students. Living-learning communities at Penn College follow a program model that includes expectations to provide both educational and social activities each month throughout the fall and spring semester. Assessment for the learning communities is still growing to include a satisfaction survey and program feedback. Resident assistants whose majors are connected to the academic theme for each learning community are hired to support the communities.

A new development for these programs includes the design and hiring of living-learning community mentors. The mentor position is a new leadership experience for students who have persisted beyond the first year and are students of the academic school connected to a learning community. Mentors apply and are selected by the living-learning community faculty to help build programs, support interactions, conduct assessments and guide first year students participating in the learning communities.

The conceptual framework that guides the development and program planning for the living-learning communities at Penn College includes two theories: Astin's Theory of Student Involvement [1] and Tinto's study of student departure [5]. These theories suggest that the level of investment into the academic and social culture of an institution and the outcome of those experiences interfacing with an institution affect a student's decision to stay and the ability to successfully integrate [1,5]. The Information Technology Living-Learning Community at Penn College has been successfully developing programs that are aiding in the retention and integration experiences of first year information technology students.

3. THE IT LLC

The Information Technology Living-Learning Community at Penn College began during the 2011 – 2012 academic year. There have been approximately 18 students participate in the IT LLC in each of the three years. There are currently 17 students who are registered to participate during the 2014 – 2015 academic year.

This section discusses the organization of the IT LLC at Penn College as well as summarizes the IT LLC activities, both social and educational over the past three years.

3.1 Framework for the IT LLC

When we first considered the IT students that may participate in an LLC, two significant needs came to mind:

First, by enabling these students to better adjust to college life we can increase the likelihood they will remain enrolled. A significant obstacle to this for many freshmen and particularly IT freshmen is social interaction. Hence we seek to create social activities that facilitate these students' interaction, with each other, with other students in their major, and with faculty. The objective is to lower the intimidation factor associated with engaging socially in a new community and increase the sense of belonging to that community.

Second, as is true with most disciplines, IT professionals must learn early that scholarly development cannot be confined to the classroom and needs to become a part of everyday life. To that end, we create educational activities that provide opportunities for students to learn new things outside of the academic classroom. These activities typically embrace knowledge or skills that are not part of, but complement, the regular curriculum. We strive to target areas where students already have an interest in learning something that is not part of the regular curriculum.

These two types of activities form the main foundation of the programming for the IT LLC at Penn College. Specific examples of activities in each category are discussed in a later section.

The IT LLC has a team of people who develop programming for the students as well as participate in various activities and events.

For the past three years this team has included a resident assistant (RA) and two faculty members who serve as advisors to the IT LLC. The RA is selected through the usual RA selection process. Once the RAs have been selected, an RA within one of the IT majors is selected to become the RA for the IT LLC. The RA is principally responsible for managing the students in the residence hall. The RA has also been responsible for working with the faculty to plan events for the IT LLC participants.

While this has worked, two issues have arisen that have induced Penn College to change this process. First, the RA currently has split responsibilities between his/her job as an RA and the extra work created planning LLC events. Most RAs do not have any responsibility for an LLC so the work associated with the LLC is simply added on to the RA's current workload. Second, by functioning as both the RA and the student LLC point of contact, this puts the RA in an unenviable Jekyll and Hyde position of being, on the one hand, a trusted friend to help freshmen acclimate to college and on the other, the enforcer of all dormitory rules and regulations. These two roles of the RA are, at times, at odds with one another.

In order to better address both of these issues, beginning in the 2014 – 2015 academic year, the LLC will employ a mentor in addition to the RA. Like the RA, the mentor is an IT major who will focus on the IT LLC programming activities as well as providing an additional support structure for the LLC members. This effectively separates the two roles the RA is currently fulfilling and resolves the issues described above.

The LLC team (faculty advisors, RA and mentor) develops a plan for offering both social and educational activities to LLC members. Generally speaking, the LLC Team tries to plan events in a consistent manner; for example, the second Tuesday of the month is a social event and the fourth Tuesday is an educational event. At times, the team needs to be flexible with its planning. There have been times when a planned event must be rescheduled due to conflicts with other activities such as an exam scheduled for the day following a planned LLC event. Generally these considerations were made regardless of whether the interfering event was an IT specific event or not. For example, whether it is a programming exam or a math exam, the LLC event would be rescheduled.

At the beginning of each semester, LLC members are surveyed to determine the best times for planning LLC activities. To the extent possible, the team tries to avoid conflicts that prevent a group of students from participating in an activity. LLC members are also solicited for areas of interest that will assist with planning social and educational events. In the interest of providing some stability, the team tries to plan out the calendar for the entire year before the start of the academic year. However, we plan for making adjustments in the event the participants find a particular event unappealing.

3.2 Social Activities

Social activities are activities that allow students and faculty to interact on a social level. Social activities are generally planned in the evening to provide both students and other IT faculty the opportunity to participate. Activities are intended to give students the opportunity to interact with faculty in a less formal setting than the classroom or a faculty office.

In addition to the monthly social activities, the IT LLC also offers a weekly IT LLC lunch. The purpose of the IT LLC lunch is to provide the LLC students (or other interested students if they desire) the opportunity to converse with faculty on an informal basis. By having a regularly scheduled time, the student know when the faculty members will be available; by having it over lunch, the intimidation factor is greatly reduced and two tasks can be accomplished at once (provide an informal meeting without sacrificing lunch break).

At the beginning of the semester, student schedules are reviewed and a time selected that allows a majority of students to attend the weekly lunch. The lunch is held in the campus dining hall located in the dormitory that houses the IT LLC. The number of participating students varies each week and generally ranges from one to about eight students. Likewise, the number of participating faculty ranges from two to about five faculty.

Lunch conversation varies. The conversation at the beginning of the year often involves typical get-to-know-you conversations – which major, which classes do you teach, where are you from, etc. As the year progresses, conversations evolve into IT product comparisons, which minors should be taken, which courses should be taken the next semester, etc.

Another important early event is the LLC mixer. This usually takes place in the first few weeks of class in the fall. LLC students get to meet the faculty and administrative staff who will be teaching and advising them throughout their college career. In addition, the LLC team invites representatives from the several IT student clubs to present an overview of each club. This gives students an early exposure to some of the extra- and co-curricular activities available to them.

Other social activities are designed to promote team building skills and provide for some friendly competition. In the fall semester the IT LLC participates in a miniature golf night; in the spring semester the IT LLC participates in a bowling night. Teams for miniature golf and bowling typically consist of a mix of faculty and students to encourage better interaction. Other such events included a Ping-Pong and dodge-ball night at the field house and a day of sand volleyball during a spring barbeque event. During Ping-Pong and dodge-ball night, teams were dynamic as students learned each other's capabilities. Students also have the opportunity to learn that faculty are "people too". That is, in some cases faculty are not any better at physical activities than many IT students are. These activities help the students develop a certain amount of trust in the faculty thereby making it easier for students to interact with faculty on more formal occasions.

Other types of social activities are designed to provide for general interaction where the students have more control of the venue. For example, special dining events and movie night allow for students to select where they would like to go and, to some extent, what they would like to do. This puts them in charge of the event's success. Having faculty participate and enjoy the event gives the students a sense of empowerment and gratification that strengthens the student-faculty bond.

The other social event we have used is more of a tension breaker. Several events have been conducted where the students are allowed the freedom to just hang out for a while with no obligation other than to meet back at the car by a certain time to go home. Our most successful of these events to date was to take the students to a local amusement park for the day the week before spring final exams. It is a reward for participating in the program throughout the year and an opportunity to let loose for an afternoon before the final end-of-year grind. Students have reported that this event provides them with a necessary respite from a student's life and reinvigorates them to begin the push to prepare for finals.

These events are sponsored by the Office of Residence Life. Many of the activities are held off-campus and typically have 14 – 20 combined faculty and students participating. It is necessary to budget for things like movie passes, ride tickets for the park, mileage for school vans, and funds for dinner. However, the total budget is not excessive and the investment is easily offset by retaining only one student that may have otherwise left.

3.3 Educational Activities

Educational activities are typically planned for mid-afternoon during a time when Penn College does not typically schedule classes. Penn College offers majors in System Development & Information Management, Gaming & Simulation, Networking and Information Assurance & Security. As a result, the LLC Team tries to plan a variety of activities that focus on different aspects of IT.

Some educational activities are of a tutorial nature and have included things like using virtualization software, writing Linux scripts to automate port scanning, configuring Cisco routers, terminating fiber optic cable, and programming simple games. The team has included an activity related to organizational behavior and working in teams.

While some of these activities reflect things that may occur later in the various programs, not all content is common to all programs. For example, gaming students have a somewhat limited exposure to networking and do not terminate fiber or program routers. Likewise, networking students seldom program games unless it is for their own purpose. The opportunity to do these things as freshmen exposes the students to the variety of IT, and in some cases, helps students determine which major best suits them.

Other activities are more of a professional awareness nature. We arranged several talks and presentations by professionals in the field including recent graduates. These events are, in part, sponsored by the LLC and open to the IT student population at large. These events give student an early exposure to the working world through the eyes of the people who live in the "real world". In the cases of presentations by recent graduates, the students see these presenters as peers – not too distant future images of themselves. Naturally, these sources have a very high level of credibility with the students even though the message is the same as what we tell them.

Student participation in the educational activities is not always as strong as participation in the social activities. Typically, five to nine students participate in the tutorial activities with attendance at professional talks and presentations being comparable to attendance at the social events.

4. BENEFITS

There have been several benefits associated with the IT LLC at Penn College. Benefits are of both a tangible and intangible nature.

4.1 Tangible Benefits

Tangible benefits are noted with respect to both retention and student performance. Performance and retention data was collected for the IT LLC during the 2012 – 2013 academic year. The data collected was for information technology majors residing in residence halls on the west side of campus. The data was classified as LLC participant versus non-LLC participant.

The fall 2012 to spring 2013 retention rate for students participating in the LLC was 88% whereas the freshman retention rate for non-LLC participants was only 66%. During the fall 2012 semester, LLC members obtained an average GPA of 2.79 out of 4.0 whereas non-LLC members obtained an average GPA of 2.30. During the spring 2013 semester, LLC members had an average GPA of 3.15 and non-LLC members had an average GPA of 2.62. Although both LLC participants and non-LLC participants saw an increase in GPA from the fall to spring semester, LLC students realized a greater increase in GPA.

This result is of course important to college and project administration. However, it is of significant importance to parents. Based on anecdotal feedback, this has been an influential fact in the decision making process for parents encouraging their sons and daughters to enroll in the LLC. Surprisingly, this has also influenced students' decisions to participate in the LLC program as well.

4.2 Intangible Benefits

In addition to the tangible benefits, LLC faculty advisors have noticed several intangible benefits associated with student participation in the IT LLC. The intangible benefits have been noticed both while students are currently involved in the LLC as freshmen as well as when they "graduate" from the LLC and become upperclassmen.

Students who have participated in the LLC seem to be more engaged during class. LLC members tend to be more involved in class activities. This includes both asking and answering questions. They tend to be more apt to completing in-class activities in an efficient manner.

LLC members have a higher likelihood of seeking out their academic advisor when academic issues arise. They have a greater tendency to bring these issues to their academic advisor early on rather than wait. In addition to seeking out their academic advisor, they are also willing to discuss issues with the LLC faculty advisors. There have been situations in which students attend the LLC lunch in order to explicitly discuss academic issues with the faculty at lunch. Over the course of time, these discussions (particularly at the LLC lunch) have headed off many advising, scheduling, attendance, and administrative issues before they could become problems.

Another, somewhat unexpected, benefit of the IT LLC is the parent response. During recruiting efforts such as Penn College's Open House activities and regular on-campus tours, faculty members discuss the IT LLC and the benefits it provides. In addition to appreciating the increase in retention and academic performance, parents often focus on the social benefits of the LLC. Parents like the fact that their son or daughter will be living with other IT students thereby providing a peer support network for classes. Parents seem to especially appreciate that the social activities will get their son or daughter "out from behind a computer monitor" to do something other than play computer games or surf the Internet.

Students appreciate the social activities. Entering a new social environment is emotionally stressful. Add to that the workload of the typical freshman and students can quickly become overwhelmed. Having an environment that is inherently non-threatening allows these students to at least relax on that front and concentrate on the other work at hand.

Many students enrolled in the IT programs at Penn College begin their college career taking developmental mathematics courses. At Penn College students are not allowed to enroll in their IT classes until after they have remediated their mathematics skills. Students who are remediating mathematics and participate in the IT LLC have the opportunity to begin learning more about IT by attending the educational activities. This allows the student to begin learning more about IT even if it is not within their IT classes.

5. LESSONS LEARNED

During the three academic years we have had an IT LLC at Penn College, we have made some observations we would like to pass along:

- One educational event and one social event per month is plenty. More than that and you create too much interference with getting school work done and leave little or no time for the students to be "on their own" once in a while.

- The weekly lunch provides a focal point for students to pass along and get information without appreciably disrupting their normal routine. Since this happens within an already scheduled event (eating lunch) it does not add to their time burden.

- Social activities seem to yield greater benefit with IT students than academic activities. The students and parents both seem to appreciate the social activities more than the educational activities.

- Separate the LLC programming responsibilities from the RA responsibilities.

- Get faculty engaged. Where faculty engagement was lacking, the LLCs were not successful.

- Provide funding for events. It is nearly impossible to provide a selection of interesting and meaningful events without it.

- Give student participants an opportunity to have some say in the programming. Attendance will be much better when the students have provided input into selecting some of the activities.

- Keep a published calendar of events and get it finalized as early in the year as possible. Plan to be flexible, but do not invite chaos by not keeping a calendar.

6. CONCLUSION

Living-learning communities have been increasing in popularity. At Penn College, the Office of Residence Life and the Information Technology Department have worked together to implement a successful living-learning community to support the college's information technology majors. Benefits realized by the IT LLC include an increase in student performance and retention, a more engaged student in the classroom and in their academic performance and as a recruiting tool to put parents more at ease concerning their offspring attending college away from home.

7. ACKNOWLEDGMENTS

Our thanks to the Office of Residence Life at Penn College in supporting the IT LLC, the resident assistants Taylor Lapointe and Derek Teay for smoothing the transition of LLC members from high school to college and the LLC members for providing feedback on LLC activities. We would also like to thank the faculty who regularly participate in social events and have presented educational activities. Finally we would like to extend a special thank you to Brian Walton who, as our then matriculation and retention coordinator, guided the IT LLC through its infancy.

8. REFERENCES

[1] Astin, A.(1984). Student involvement: A developmental theory for higher education. Journal of College Student Development,40 (5), 518-529.

[2] Inkelas, K., Weisman, L.(2003). Different by Design: an Examination of Student Outcomes Among Participants in Three Types of Living-Learning Programs. Journal of College Student Development, 44 (3), 335-368.

[3] Iowa State University.(n.d.). Residential Learning Communities and Theme Houses. Retrieved from http://www.housing.iastate.edu/places/rlc-th

[4] Penn College.(n.d.). Living-Learning Communities. Retrieved from www.pct.edu

[5] Tinto, V.(1993). Leaving College. Rethinking the Causes and Cures of Student Attrition. (2nd ed.). Chicago, IL. The University of Chicago Press

[6] University of California, Davis.(n.d.). Shared Interest Communities. Retrieved from http://www.housing.ucdavis.edu/education/communities/

[7] University of Maryland, Baltimore County.(n.d.). Living-Learning Communities at UMBC. Retrieved at http://www.umbc.edu/reslife/communities/llc.html

[8] University of Rhode Island.(n.d). Living and Learning and Theme Communities at URI. Retrieved from http://housing.uri.edu/info/living-learning-communities.php

[9] Wawrzynski, M., Jessup-Anger, J.(2010). From Expectations to Experiences: Using a Structural Typology to Understand First—Year Student Outcomes in Academically Based Living-Learning Communities. Journal of College Student Development. 51 (2), 201-217.

[10] Wawrzynski, M., Jessup-Anger, J., Stolz, K., Helman, C., Beaulieu, J.(2009). College Student Affairs Journal; 28 (1), 138-158.

[11] Zhao, C., Kuh, G.(2004). Adding Value: Learning Communities and Student Engagement. Journal of Research in Higher Education. 45 (2) 115-138.

Guiding Students to Discover Concepts and Develop Process Skills with POGIL

Clif Kussmaul
Muhlenberg College
2400 Chew St
Allentown, PA 18104
+1-484-664-3352
kussmaul@muhlenberg.edu

ABSTRACT

This workshop introduces **Process-Oriented Guided Inquiry Learning** (**POGIL**). In a POGIL classroom, teams of 3-5 learners work on instructor-facilitated activities. Through scripted inquiry and investigation, learners discover concepts and construct their own knowledge. Using assigned team roles and meta-cognition, learners develop process skills and individual responsibility. Studies show that POGIL can significantly improve student performance. POGIL incorporates practices such as discussion and reflection that are particularly helpful for students from underserved populations.

This workshop is intended for anyone interested in teaching and learning approaches that are described as active, constructivist, or discovery-based. Participants will experience POGIL activities, learn core practices, and draft parts of activities. More information (including sample activities) is available at http://pogil.org and http://cspogil.org.

Categories and Subject Descriptors

K.3.2 [Computers and Education]: Computer and Information Science Education – Computer science education, information systems education, literacy, self-assessment.

General Terms

Management, Design, Experimentation, Theory.

Keywords

Active Learning, Process Skills; Teams

1. INTRODUCTION

To improve learning, enthusiasm, and retention, educators have developed a variety of approaches to engage students, enhance learning, and emphasize attitudes and skills, not just rote knowledge. This workshop introduces one proven approach, Process Oriented Guided Inquiry Learning.

2. BACKGROUND

2.1 POGIL

Process Oriented Guided Inquiry Learning (**POGIL**) is based on learning science (e.g. [6]), and shares characteristics with other forms of active, discovery, and inquiry-based learning (e.g. [1]). As described below, POGIL combines effective learning practices in ways that are synergistic.

In POGIL, teams of learners (typically 3-5) work on scripted inquiry activities and investigations designed to help them construct their own knowledge, often by modeling the original processes of discovery and research [5]. The teams follow processes with specific roles, steps, and reports that help students develop process skills and encourage individual responsibility and meta-cognition. The instructor serves as a facilitator, not a lecturer. POGIL activities and processes are designed to achieve specific learning objectives; typically an activity is designed to focus on 1-2 (disciplinary) concepts and 1-2 process skills. The POGIL Project (http://pogil.org) offers a set of workshops to help faculty learn about POGIL theory and practice, including how to facilitate, evaluate, and develop POGIL activities.

POGIL activities generally follow a 3 phase **learning cycle**. First, students **explore** models or data to look for trends or patterns, and generate and test hypotheses to help understand or explain them. Second, the patterns or hypotheses are used to define or **invent** a new concept or term; ideally, students construct understanding before they learn new terminology. Third, the new concept is **applied** in other situations or contexts to help students generalize its meaning and relevance. Thus, the activity provides information and asks questions to guide students through the learning cycle and help them develop process and learning skills.

Usually, A POGIL activity is organized into sections that address individual topics or sub-topics. Each section contains a series of questions, with data, other information, and/or commentary. The questions in each section generally increase in difficulty, so that the activity leads students to explore new ideas, create techniques and artifacts, and then apply them (in class or for homework).

For example, an activity on project scheduling starts with a simple **model** – using a recipe to bake cookies. To **explore** the model, the team reviews the recipe to identify steps that are missing or implicit, and then organizes the steps in different ways (by ingredient, by tool used, etc.) which leads them to **define** a work breakdown structure (WBS). Next, they take a set of cards labeled with the steps, and arrange them to show the most efficient sequence of steps, including which can be done in parallel, which leads them to **define** a Gantt chart. Next, they **apply** these concepts by creating a WBS and Gantt chart for their own project.

Ideally, a POGIL activity requires little background, and could be adapted to a variety of contexts. For POGIL activities to be readily adopted in other contexts (courses or institutions), it is helpful to: define learning objectives, prerequisites, resources, and vocabulary; provide more complete background information; and package them in a standard format.

2.2 POGIL for Information Technology

POGIL has particular potential for education in information technology and computer science. These are largely team-based, problem-solving disciplines, and POGIL helps students to develop important problem-solving and team process skills. POGIL also encourages students to collaborate and learn from each other rather than focusing on an instructor. In chemistry and other disciplines, effective POGIL activities are often adopted and adapted by other faculty and at other institutions. Thus, POGIL may provide useful models for reusable materials in IT and CS education, where such reuse appears to be a particular challenge.

3. WORKSHOP AGENDA

The agenda for this 3 hour workshop is summarized in Table 1. Participants will receive paper or electronic copies of slides and POGIL materials for a variety of concepts.

Table 1. Workshop agenda with time in minutes.

#	Time	Content
1	5	Introductions, form teams.
2	30	Work through a sample activity.
3	10	Discuss how this approach can benefit students.
4	10	Introduce POGIL theory and core practices.
5	30	Work through meta-activity on POGIL practices.
6	5	Review & discuss outcome data.
7	10	Q&A
8	10	(Break)
9	30	Work through meta-activity on activity structure.
10	15	Assemble activity from pieces.
11	15	Draft questions for an activity.
12	10	Conclude with general discussion.

4. PRESENTER BACKGROUND

Clif Kussmaul, PhD, teaches CS at Muhlenberg College, and has developed POGIL activities for CS1, CS2, software engineering, and AI. He is a member of the POGIL Project Steering Committee, and is the PI for an NSF TUES Type 1 Grant to develop POGIL activities for CS and to foster a community of CS faculty who use and develop such materials. During 2009-2010 Clif was a Visiting Fulbright Scholar at the University of Kerala, India, where he used POGIL and related techniques in graduate courses. Clif's professional interests include active learning, free and open source software, distributed collaboration and knowledge management, and entrepreneurship.

This workshop is based on workshops developed and used extensively by the POGIL Project (http://pogil.org). Clif completed the 2011 POGIL Project facilitator training workshop, and has facilitated or co-facilitated POGIL workshops at SIGCSE 2012, 2013, & 2014, CS&IT 2012 & 2013, IEEE Technology for Education 2012 (Hyderabad, India) (e.g. [2], [3], [4]). Clif has also facilitated or co-facilitated ½ day, full day, and multi-day workshops in the US and in India, for faculty and staff in CS, IT, engineering, and other disciplines.

5. ACKNOWLEDGMENTS

This material is based upon work supported by the National Science Foundation under Grant No. DUE-1044679 (TUES Type I). We also acknowledge the US-India Educational Foundation for a Fulbright-Nehru teaching award, and the National POGIL Office (http://pogil.org) for encouragement and support.

6. REFERENCES

[1] Eberlein, T., Kampmeier, J., Minderhout, V., et al. 2008. Pedagogies of engagement in science. *Biochemistry and Molecular Biology Education*. 36(4):262-273.

[2] Kussmaul, C. 2012. Tutorial: Improving student outcomes through guided inquiry activities. In *Proceedings of the IEEE Int'l Conference on Technology for Education (T4E)*, Hyderabad, India.

[3] Kussmaul, C. 2012. Process oriented guided inquiry learning for computer science & software engineering. In *Proceedings of the ASEE Annual Conference*, San Antonio, TX.

[4] Kussmaul, C. 2012. Process oriented guided inquiry learning (POGIL) for computer science. In *Proceedings of the ACM Technical Symposium on Computer Science Education (SIGCSE '12)*. ACM, New York, NY, USA, 373-378. DOI= http://doi.acm.org/10.1145/2157136.2157246.

[5] Moog, R. S., Spencer, J. N. eds. 2008. *Process-Oriented Guided Inquiry Learning (POGIL)*. Oxford University Press.

[6] Zull, J. 2002. *The Art of Changing the Brain: Enriching the Practice of Teaching by Exploring the Biology of Learning*. 1st ed. Stylus Publishing.

The Experiences and Challenges in Setting up a Mobile Computing Track

Becky Rutherfoord
Southern Polytechnic State University
Marietta, GA USA 30060
(678) 915-7400
brutherf@spsu.edu

Jon A Preston
Southern Polytechnic State University
Marietta, GA USA 30060
(678) 915-4982
jon.preston@acm.org

Jack Zheng
Southern Polytechnic State University
Marietta, GA USA 30060
(678) 915-5036
jackzheng@spsu.edu

Ming Yang
Southern Polytechnic State University
Marietta, GA USA 30060
(678) 915-6869
mingyang@spsu.edu

Categories and Subject Descriptors

K.3.2 [**Computers and Education**]: Computer and Information Science Education

Keywords

Mobile computing; curriculum development

1. SUMMARY

The world of web development has been impacted by the mobile computing, particularly the wide use of smart phones. The rising trend in mobile computing has motivated us to develop a new senior technical track (Bachelor of Science) on Mobile and Web. This panel will discuss the various aspects of setting up new mobile computing courses to be added to the curriculum. IT and other computing faculty must create and deliver these new and exciting mobile computing courses – all while teaching their regular courses. Difficulties arise with not having the correct technology platforms for the students to use, faculty not knowing all of the elements of these new mobile computing courses themselves, and the time element for faculty to create new courses with their heavy workloads.

The panelists will discuss the various aspects of creating a new mobile computing "track" for the BSIT program at SPSU. Each panelist will discuss various aspects of the track and how SPSU went about creating the track and how it will be rolled out. After each panelist speaks, the floor will be open for discussion and sharing between all attendees.

The remainder of the proposal summarizes the experiences of the panel members and their main contributions to the summary points.

SIGITE'14, October 15–18, 2014, Atlanta, Georgia, USA.
ACM 978-1-4503-2686-5/14/10.
http://dx.doi.org/10.1145/2656450.2656483

2. BECKY RUTHERFOORD: Challenges for Setting Up Courses

The original proposal for mobile courses came from the Information Technology Department who was considering an upper level track in this area. After speaking to coordinators from the other computing programs of Computer Science, Computer Game Design and Development and Software Engineering, it was agreed that a general introductory course for mobile computing would be applicable for all of our majors. A small task force made up of faculty from each department was created to come up with the student learning outcomes and course description for this new course. This was presented to each departmental faculty for approval. Once approved by the faculty, the course was sent through the normal approval chain.

The Information Technology Department faculty then worked to create additional courses for the mobile and web track. The courses include various aspects of mobile computing – including platforms, application development, networks and security issues. The following are various descriptions for these areas.

3. JACK ZHENG: Mobile Web Development

Mobile web refers to the access and use of websites and web applications using smart mobile devices (and optimized for these devices) through computer networks. It particularly focuses on user interfaces and interactions but more recently it has begun to impact the application architecture as well.

More and more website visits are coming from mobile devices. The industry has a strong need to upgrade or redesign many websites and applications to be optimized for mobile user experience. Students have also shown a strong interest to gain skills in developing mobile friendly websites and applications. We responded to this trend and develop a new mobile web development course. This course introduces the concepts, practices, and technologies to design, develop, and manage cross-platform web sites and applications running on modern mobile devices.

A particular challenge of designing the course is, as in other IT courses focusing on emerging technologies, the consideration of technology development and adoption. On one hand, the mobile web is still in its early development stage. The industry is still pretty fragmented and lack of strong standards. Newer frameworks and architectures are coming out frequently and the industry is shifting its attention rapidly. On the other hand, even with a lot of uncertainties, many companies has already moved ahead of the industry and began to utilize non-standard tools and technologies. They are in great needs of people with mobile web knowledge and skills. This poses the greatest challenge on course design: what should we include as the most important and relevant practices in this course? How do we select from a large pool of emerging tools and techniques, and do we have access to them? In this panel we want to discuss some questions and some experience in designing our mobile web development course and track.

4. JON PRESTON: Mobile Game Design

Many students have quite a strong interest in game development; having played many games in their youth, students know the context of the domain and feel they have a firm grasp of what it takes to design and develop a strong mobile game. In offering the Mobile Game Design and Development course for the past four years, we have determined that while students have a passion for playing games and have a design to learn how to develop them, the technical aspects of game development remain a challenge as in any computing course.

One of the initial challenges in offering a mobile game development course is selecting the technology that will be used in the class. For the first semester we offered our mobile game development course, we allowed students to select any technology they wanted to use – including iOS, Android, and HTML5/browser. This created a challenge in that no standard content was being discussed in the class itself; only concepts were discussed, and students were left to flounder and determine on their own time how to implement any technical details in the development. For the next two semesters, we adopted Android development; this worked well since students had prior experience with Java (in their CS1 and CS2 courses), and the Android Development Kit (ADK) is both freely-available and is an environment atop the Java language. Standardizing on the Android platform has proven successful in advancing student learning and in lessening the overhead in managing the course.

Finally, students are encourages not only to learn the technical aspects of managing the limited resources (such as battery and input/output) of the mobile platform but also to understand and develop towards the expectations of the mobile game market. As such, we discuss pricing and the difficulty in achieving success in a mobile market but also discuss the low barrier to entry and low distribution costs. The pros and cons of the mobile space are presented to students, and students are encouraged to submit their final game project to a mobile store/marketplace by the end of the semester. Given the time consuming nature and iterative refinement that accompanies the marketplace submission process, this exercise is sometimes not completed before the end of the term, but the experience in beginning this process is invaluable to the students.

5. MING YANG: Mobile Computing and Networking Courses

Smart mobile devices and applications have the unique advantage in the design of computer science course materials such as networking classes, since they create a strong connection between the academic study and the reality of students' everyday lives. This provides an excellent opportunity for the adoption of mobile devices as a motivational tool to stimulate and engage student learning in computer science.

The balance between promoting student learning interests and enhancement of student academic learning has always been a challenge. Computer games have been shown to be a successful learning tool as it leverages students' enthusiasm towards computer games and their social relevance. Introduction of game programming, game development courses, or even entire degree programs has also received a wide attention. However, an issue in stimulating computer science learning with gaming and robotics is its long learning curve: students need to learn extra knowledge that is exclusive to games or robotics, and have little relevance with the degree requirements in computer science program. Today's smart mobile devices and applications can incorporate most of the core subjects in computer science while imposing less extra requirements on students; thereby shortening its learning curve. This makes mobile computing easier for adaptation in the computer science curriculum, such as networking courses. In addition, students will benefit from the instant gratification of mobile application development – they can quickly build a working graphical application and play the resulting application on their mobile devices.

So far, in terms of the integration to networking course, mobile computing has received relatively less attention compared to computer games or robotics. Although the ACM Computing Curriculum Recommendation lists wireless and mobile computing as an elective course under the "Net-Centric Computing" body of knowledge, very few colleges/universities offer a course on mobile computing at the undergraduate level. When it is offered, the focus of such a course is usually on theory of wireless local area networks and protocols. In addition, the integration of mobile computing into networking curriculum should not be limited to the use of mobile devices to promote communication and collaboration; instead, the mobile computing technology should be treated as an essential part of the course itself.

In order to address the above challenges and enhance networking-related course teaching with mobile computing, we proposed to design and develop a labware based on smart phones. The goal is to introduce mobile computing knowledge and practice into the networking curriculum, and thus cover the layered structure of computer networks and a wide range of networking concepts. Since the Android operating system is open-sourced and java-based, and since it is the dominating mobile operating system nowadays (more than 50% market share), we exemplify the labware in Android platform. Our preliminary evaluation shows that students can learn many important concepts in networking and develop experience in mobile application with a shortened learning curve.

An Academic Profile of IT Faculty in the USA

Barry M. Lunt
Brigham Young University
Information Technology
Provo, Utah
luntb@byu.edu

Bill Paterson
Mount Royal University
Computer Science & Information Systems
Calgary, Alberta, Canada
bpaterson@mtroyal.ca

ABSTRACT

A common sentiment at SIGITE conferences is that IT faculty come from a wide variety of disciplines. But is this true? In this paper we present an academic profile of IT faculty that was discovered through examination of credentials reported on the websites of 224 IT programs. The profile shows that the vast majority of IT faculty come from a Computer Science background but there is also evidence of diversity. This information should prove helpful in advising students in their preparation to teach IT.

Categories and Subject Descriptors

K.7.0 [**The Computing Profession**]: The Computing Profession; Occupations; Organizations; Computers and Education.

General Terms

IT Faculty; Academic credentials; Faculty profile.

Keywords

Faculty Profile, Faculty Credentials.

1. INTRODUCTION

This paper presents the results of research into providing a profile of IT (Information Technology) faculty at the 4-year college level in the USA. As with any new discipline, most faculty come from other disciplines. It is this author's experience that many IT faculty wonder where most other IT faculty come from (what their academic and professional background is), and that most data is only anecdotal. This paper is an effort to answer that question with a standard research approach.

2. METHOD

In a previous paper[1], Lunt et al. proposed a method for identifying 4-year IT programs in the USA, and then applied that method to produce a list of 224 4-year IT programs, each with a compliance factor score which was used to describe how closely the curriculum of each IT program aligned with the IT model curriculum[2]. This list of 224 IT programs was used as our starting point.

The websites of each of these 224 IT programs were visited, and data was collected, where available, on the number of faculty teaching in that IT program, the academic qualifications of each

SIGITE'14, October 15–18, 2014, Atlanta, Georgia, USA.
Copyright © 2014 ACM 978-1-4503-2686-5/14/10…$15.00.
http://dx.doi.org/10.1145/2656450.2656455

Parameter	Value
4-Year IT Programs	224
With IT Faculty Data	114
Max # of IT Faculty	37
Min # of IT Faculty	1
Mean # of IT Faculty	8.69
Standard Dev of Mean	7.44
Median # of IT Faculty	6.50

Table 1: Information about the number of IT faculty in IT programs

faculty member, and the professional experience of each faculty member. The specific information being gathered included each IT faculty member's 4-year degrees (BA or BS), and advanced degrees (MA, MS, PhD and other doctoral), professional experience (years working in industry), and academic experience (years working in academia).

It should be pointed out here that here is a great deal of variation in the content of IT program websites, particularly in the individual faculty web pages. Some programs had no information at all about their faculty; others had very spotty information; and still others had quite a bit of information. In all cases, the data gathered was purely from the program's website.

3. RESULTS

The websites of some IT programs included very little information about the faculty, and on only 114 of these 224 programs' websites (50.4%) was sufficient information found to be able to make a reasonable determination how many faculty taught in each IT program. Table 1 summarizes this information.

3.1 Academic Qualifications – Bachelor's Degrees

One of the most common questions in a new academic discipline is what are the academic qualifications and backgrounds of the faculty. Table 2 summarizes the information about the bachelor's (4-year) degrees of the IT faculty for whom this information could be found. There were 981 faculty identified as IT faculty; website information was sufficient to identify academic qualifications for 48.2% (473) of these faculty. By "academic qualifications", we refer specifically to any and all college-level degrees which were earned by these faculty members. Based on the information available on the websites accessed, all but one of these IT faculty had at least one bachelor's degree (472). Additionally, 26 of these 472 faculty had two bachelor's degrees, and two of them had three bachelor's degrees. These bachelor's degrees came in 95 unique majors; the top majors are summarized in Table 3, (shown on right).

Parameter	Value
Total IT Faculty	981
% IT Faculty w/ Bachelor's Degree Info	48.2%
IT Faculty w/ Bachelor's Degree Info	473
IT Faculty w/ 2 Bachelor's Degrees	26
IT Faculty w/ 3 Bachelor's Degrees	2

Table 2: Summary of information about IT faculty bachelor's degrees.

It is interesting to note that the top BS degrees are Computer Science (CS), Math (out of which many CS programs grew in the early years of the CS discipline), Electrical Engineering, and Computer Engineering, all closely related majors. It is also interesting to note that only two IT faculty had a bachelor's degree in IT, a clear sign of the newness of the IT degree.

3.2 Academic Qualifications – Master's Degrees

Most 4-year academic programs require their faculty to have an advanced degree, and this is borne out in the percentage of IT faculty having Master's degrees – nearly 93%. Information about the master's degrees of IT faculty is summarized in Table 4. Information about IT faculty with an MBA degree is also in this table, although most master's degrees are one-year programs, while most MBA degrees are two-year programs. In this analysis, we counted the MBA degree as equivalent to other master's degrees, and this is shown in Table 4. We should also point out that not all faculty provided information on their advanced degrees, which means that we were not always able to ascertain if a faculty member with a bachelor's degree also had any advanced degrees.

These master's degrees came in 91 unique majors; the top majors are summarized in Table 5. As with bachelor's degrees, the most popular major was CS (37.5%), followed by Mathematics and Electrical Engineering.

There are a few surprises among the top majors for bachelor's and master's degrees. Among these are economics, philosophy, and psychology; a total of 28 IT faculty had either a bachelor's or a master's degree in these seemingly unrelated majors.

3.3 Academic Qualifications – Doctoral Degrees

When it comes to doctoral degrees, the mission of an institution is generally what determines if the faculty there are required to have a doctoral degree. Of the 80 institutions in this study with doctoral degree information about their faculty, 46 of them (57.5%) had 100% of their faculty with doctoral degrees. Only three institutions (3.8%) had no faculty with doctoral degrees.

Parameter	Value
Total IT Faculty	981
% IT Faculty w/ Master's Degree Info	48.7%
IT Faculty w/ Master's Degree Info	478
IT Faculty w/ Master's Degree	444
%age IT Faculty w/ Master's Degree	92.9%
IT Faculty w/ 2 Master's Degrees	47
IT Faculty w/ 3 Master's Degrees	2
IT Faculty w/ MBA Degree	50

Table 4: Summary of information about IT faculty master's degrees.

Bachelor's Degree Majors	#
Computer Science (CS)	67
Mathematics (Math)	44
Electrical Engineering (EE)	31
Computer Engineering	14
Business Admininistration	8
CS & Math	8
Economics	8
Chemical Engineering	6
Physics	6
CS Engineering	5
Education (Ed)	5
Mechanical Engineering	5
Computer Information Systems	4
Philosophy	4
Psychology	4
Applied Math	3
English	3
Industrial Engineering	3
Management	3
Management Information Systems	3
Music Ed	3
Software Engineering	3
Accounting	2
Biological Science	2
Business	2
Computer Information Technology	2
Civil Engineering	2
Computer Technology	2
Electrical & Computer Engineering	2
English Literature	2
Information Systems	2
Information Systems Engineering	2
Information Technology	2
Mass Communications	2
Math & Physics	2
Political Science	2

Table 3: Bachelor's degree majors of IT faculty, for those majors with two or more faculty having chosen that major.

This information is summarized in Table 6. As shown in Table 7, the majority of IT faculty in this study, (492 of 628, or 78.3%), do have doctoral degrees. There were even four IT faculty with two doctoral degrees. These doctoral degrees came from a total of 78 different majors; the top majors are summarized in Table 8.

As with the majors of IT faculty for their bachelor's and master's degrees, CS was, by far, the most popular major for a doctoral degree, with 140 (46.8%). And again we see EE among the other more popular majors for doctoral degrees among these IT faculty.

Master's Degree Majors	#
Computer Science (CS)	124
Mathematics (Math)	22
Electrical Engineering (EE)	15
Computer Information Systems	13
Computer Engineering	11
CS Engineering	6
Economics	6
Education (Ed)	6
Biology	5
Information Systems	5
Management Information Systems	5
Industrial Engineering	4
Psychology	4
Applied Math	3
CS & Math	3
EE / CS	3
Engineering	3
Math Ed	3
Technology	3
Applied CS	2
Chemical Engineering	2
Communications	2
Electrical & Computer Engineering	2
Educational Computing	2
Electronic Commerce	2
Finance	2
Information Management	2
Instructional Technology	2
Information Technology Ed	2
Library Science	2
Philosophy	2
Software Engineering	2
Teaching	2
Telecommunications Management	2

Table 5: Master's degree majors of IT faculty, for those majors with two or more faculty having chosen that major.

3.4 Experience – Academic and Professional

The categories of professional and academic experience constituted the data which was generally not available on the websites for the IT programs studied. Of the 981 IT faculty in the study, academic experience information was available for only 169 of these faculty (17.2%); professional experience information was available for only 95 of these faculty (9.7%).

Parameter	Value
IT Programs w/ IT Faculty Data	114
Programs w/ 100% Doctoral	46
Programs w/ 0% Doctoral	3
Programs w/ mixed Doctoral	31
Programs w/o Doctoral Info	34

Table 6: Summary of information about the institutions and their mix of faculty with doctoral degrees.

Parameter	Value
Total IT Faculty	981
% IT Faculty with Doctoral Degree Info	64.0%
IT Faculty w/ Doctoral Degree Info	628
IT Faculty w/ Doctoral Degree	492
%age IT Faculty w/ Doctoral Degree	78.3%
IT Faculty w/ 2 Doctoral Degrees	4

Table 7: Summary of information about IT faculty doctoral degrees.

Table 9 summarizes the information for these two types of experience, for the relatively few faculty who included this information on their website. As might be expected, the years of experience spanned the full range, from zero to 40 years of academic experience, and from zero to 50 years of professional experience, each with a substantial standard deviation (SD).

CONCLUSION

The authors believe the information presented in this paper will prove beneficial in advising students who are interested in preparing for a career in teaching IT. It will also be helpful for IT faculty who are considering further academic preparation and/or more advanced degrees. Finally, it should also be informative for programs as they assess the academic credentials of their faculty and compare those against their institution's academic mission.

The data gathered for this study was limited to that which was available on the websites for each institution and for each faculty member in this study, and was thus not a fully-inclusive study. However, because there is no inherent bias in the availability of the data, it is believed that this is a representative sample.

In academic qualifications, the most popular major for IT faculty is Computer Science, followed at a distance by Mathematics, Electrical Engineering, and Computer Engineering. Among the most unusual majors for IT faculty are Philosophy, Psychology, and Economics.

4. REFERENCES

[1] Lunt, Barry M., Andrew Hansen, Bikalpa Neupane, Richard Ofori, Identifying and Evaluating Information Technology Bachelor's Degree Programs, *Proceedings of SIGITE 2012*, Calgary, Canada, Oct 2012

[2] Lunt, Barry M., Joseph J. Ekstrom, Sandra Gorka, Reza Kamali, Eydie Lawson, Jacob Miller, Han Reichgelt, Computing Curricula: IT Volume,

[3] www.acm.org//education/curricula/IT2008%20Curriculum.pdf

Doctoral Degree Majors	#
Computer Science (CS)	140
CS Engineering	10
Electrical Engineering (EE)	10
Information Systems (IS)	10
Computer Information Systems	8
Business Admininistration	7
Instructional Technology	6
Mathematics (Math)	6
Computer Engineering	5
Education (Ed)	5
Management Information Systems	4
Applied Math	3
Chemical Engineering	3
CS & Math	3
Educational Leadership	3
EE / CS	3
Operations Management	3
Computer & Information Science	2
Communications	2
Doctorate of Business Administration	2
Electrical & Computer Engineering	2
Information	2
Information Operations Management	2
IS & Technology	2
Information Technology	2
Physics	2

Table 8: Doctoral degree majors of IT faculty, for those majors with two or more faculty having chosen that major.

Parameter	Value
Avg # years Academic Exp (SD)	11.8 (9.00)
Median # years Academic Exp	10
Max # years Academic Exp	40
Min # years Academic Exp	0
Avg # years Professional Exp (SD)	19.0 (10.3)
Median # years Professional Exp	17
Max # years Professional Exp	50
Min # years Professional Exp	0

Table 9: Summary of information about the academic and professional experience of the IT faculty in this study.

A Longitudinal Examination of SIGITE Conference Submission Data, 2007-2012

Randy Connolly
Dept. Computer Science & Information
Systems
Mount Royal University
4825 Mount Royal Gate SW, Calgary,
AB, T3E 6K6
403-440-6061
rconnolly@mtroyal.ca

Janet Miller
Dept. Student Counselling
Mount Royal University
4825 Mount Royal Gate SW, Calgary,
AB, T3E 6K6
403-440-6362
jbmiller@mtroyal.ca

Rob Friedman
Institute of Technology
UW Tacoma
1900 Commerce St., Tacoma, WA
98402
253-692-4611
rsfit@u.washington.edu

ABSTRACT

This paper examines submission data for the SIGITE conference between the years 2007-2012 with an emphasis on the reliability and validity of the peer review process. Despite the centrality of peer review to academic endeavor, it is not easy to assess it due to the confidentiality of blind reviewing systems. This paper provides a unique addition to the study of peer review by examining reviews and submissions for a single international computing conference across an extended time period. It examines which external factors (such as nationality and familiarity of the reviewer) and which internal characteristics of the submissions (such as word length, number of references, and readability measures) are related to eventual reviewer ratings. Ramifications of the findings for future authors and conference organizers are also discussed.

Categories and Subject Descriptors

K.3.2 [Computer and Information Science Education]: Information Technology Education

General Terms

Measurement

Keywords

Peer review, validity, reliability, conference submissions.

1. INTRODUCTION

ACM SIGITE annual conferences have been ongoing since the group's instantiation as a special interest group within ACM in 2004. A handful of individuals, representing a small number of academic institutions were the original stakeholders within the SIG's governing body, which then organized and hosted the SIG's main activity, its annual conference. While the early SIGITE conferences mirrored the interests and values of the original

"elders" for the discipline, over time, new faces and voices contributed new ideas to the organization, which reshaped peer review and technical paper coordination practices. In this paper, we present peer review data obtained from six years of SIGITE conferences that respond to questions such as: Does the average number of authors per paper affect acceptance rates? What is the average number of reviewers per paper? Is there a relationship between the number of reviewers and acceptance rates? Does the geographic location of the reviewer influence the review? Can we determine the impact of the peer review process as it pertains to future citation rates and/or download rates from the ACM DL? Answers to these questions yield suggestions for future conference organizers, authors and attendees.

2. RELATED WORK

Peer review is the main quality control mechanism within the academic sciences and is used for assessing the merits of a written work as well as for ensuring the standards of the academic field. Based on a series of surveys across a wide range of disciplines [2], peer review enjoys broad and strong support. Despite this support, peer review has its limitations. It can be distorted by biases such as the academic status of the author (or the author's institution) or by asymmetrical power relations between the author and the reviewer. The usual mechanism for minimizing these biases is to employ either single-blind reviews (SBR), in which authors do not know the identities of the reviewers but the identity of the author is known to the reviewer, or double-blind reviews (DBR), in which neither the author or reviewers know the identity of the other [17]. The SIGITE conference in the period covered in this paper used DBR.

SBR and DBR have been subjected to a variety of critical examinations. Marsh and Ball [11] found *reliability* (defined as the correlation between two independent reviewers of one paper across multiple papers) of journal DBR submissions to be quite low. Examining the record of SBR used in the evaluation of research grants, [8] found that the reliability of peer reviews was also disappointingly low. Some have found support for the contention that peer reviews often also lack *validity* – that is, there is little relationship between the judgments of reviewers and the subsequent judgments of the relevant larger scholarly community as defined by eventual citations [2]. Others, in contrast, have found that there is indeed a "statistically significant association between selection decisions and the applicants' scientific achievements, if quantity and impact of research publications are used as a criterion for scientific achievement" [3].

Despite the centrality of peer review to academic endeavor, it is not easy to assess it due to the confidentiality of DBR and SBR reviewing systems. Most examinations of peer evaluation have occurred in the context of academic journals. Given the importance of conference publishing and peer review within computing disciplines [6, 7, 19], the examination of conference reviewing is especially relevant for those within computing. Walker, Ma, and Mboya [21] performed an important evaluation of peer review from the 2000 SIGCSE conference. They assessed the variability of 1917 different reviews and found that paper ratings do not appear to be influenced by external factors such as gender or nationality. Subsequent examinations of SIGCSE and ITiCSE reviewer data [20] found in contrast that the nationality of reviewers and authors had a small but statistically significant impact on ratings and also acceptance rates. More recently, [13] examined a much larger data set containing over 9000 reviews from ten different conferences in computer science and found quite low reliability and validity measures.

Our study provides a unique addition to this literature. Unlike previous work cited above it assesses reviews and submissions for a single international computing conference across an extended time period (2007-2012). It assesses the reliability of the peer view process at SIGITE by examining both internal and external factors; the combination of these analyses is also unique. This paper also provides some innovation in the measures it uses to assess the validity of the peer review process

3. METHOD
From 2007 to 2012, the ACM SIGITE conference used the same "Grinnell" submission system as the larger SIGCSE and ITiCSE education conferences. This web-based system was used by authors to submit their work, by reviewers to review submissions, and by program committees to evaluate reviews and to organize the eventual conference program. Starting in 2013, SIGITE switched to the openConf system which is organized internally quite differently, so this study only contains the data from the years the conference used the Grinnell system.

3.1 Data Collection
The Grinnell submission system stores the data for a single conference year within a single Microsoft Access database file. As a consequence, our first step in collecting the data was the rather laborious process of merging the relevant data from the six databases into a single data set in Access. This process was complicated by the fact that from 2007-2010, the conference had a two-stage process for submitting papers. In these years, short abstracts were first submitted, reviewed, and then either rejected or the authors were encouraged to submit a full paper (which subsequently went through DBR). For 2011-2012, the abstract submit process was skipped, so that only full papers were submitted and reviewed. The submitted abstracts from 2007-2010 were excluded from the data set as were posters and panels.

For each review, the reviewer supplied a rating between 1 and 6 for five different categories. These review categories were: "technical content", "organization and writing style", "originality", "significance", and "overall rating". The reviewer also supplied a textual comment for each of these categories as well as comments to the author about any eventual presentation and a private comment to the program committee about the paper.

Other relevant data, such as the number of references, citation rates, and download numbers, were also manually gathered from the submitted PDFs for each paper, from Google Scholar, and from the ACM Digital Library. A wide variety of relevant queries were executed, exported to Microsoft Excel where further data manipulation was performed, and then finally imported into SPSS for statistical evaluation.

4. RESULTS
SIGITE is a smaller international conference, and this stature is reflected in the total number of papers submitted. Over the six years, there were 1026 reviews from 192 different reviewers, and 508 authors were involved in submitting a total of 332 papers. The 2010 version of the conference had the lowest number of paper submissions (n=37), while the 2012 had the largest (n=87).

4.1 Author and Paper Information
Papers were submitted by authors from 32 different countries, with the majority of the authors being from the USA (n=378), followed by Canada (n=24), Saudi Arabia (n=14), and Pakistan, Italy, and the United Arab Emirates (each n=8). Of the 332 submitted papers, two were not reviewed. There was an overall acceptance rate of 74.1% (or a 25.9% rejection rate). However, this acceptance figure is not representative of the true acceptance rate of SIGITE, because the review process was altered back in 2011. Recall that from 2007-2010 there was a separate abstract submission stage, which helped reduce the eventual number of rejected papers during those years. Based on data available on the ACM Digital Library, the actual acceptance rates for the years 2007-2012 were 41%, 63%, 68%, 49%, 52%, and 58% respectively. The abstract submission stage was eliminated in 2011 to help reduce the amount of work for reviewers (as well as for the program committee).

On average there were 2.27 authors per paper amongst submissions. Single authored papers accounted for 31% of submissions, 38% were co-authored by two, 15% were submitted by a team of three authors, 8% by teams of four, 7.5% by teams of five and 1% by teams of 6 or 7. Although no statistical analysis was done, it appears that a paper's probability of being accepted is not impacted by the number of authors involved (e.g., 28% of accepted papers had a single author; 39% were co-authored by two; 16% co-authored by three).

4.2 Paper Categories
To situate the peer review data in the context of the SIG and the conferences, we note that several topics and themes have persisted throughout the period under review. Figure 1 represents the trends of paper submissions whose focus is on one of four of the five pillars of IT education: networking, information management, HCI and Web systems.

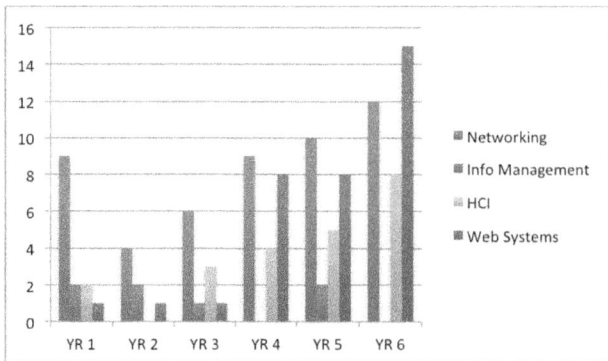

Figure 1. Categories by IT pillars

While Information Management remained quite low in number of submissions, ranging from 0 to 2 across time, and HCI shows an increasing trend (from 2 to 8), Networking dominated this IT Pillar category, ranging from 9 to 12 for four of the six years examined. Web Systems was dormant until 2010 and ended with the highest number of pillar-specific submissions at 15. Papers on programming, the first pillar of the IT curriculum framework, were subsumed into the IT Education category, given the relatively small number of programming-specific submissions.

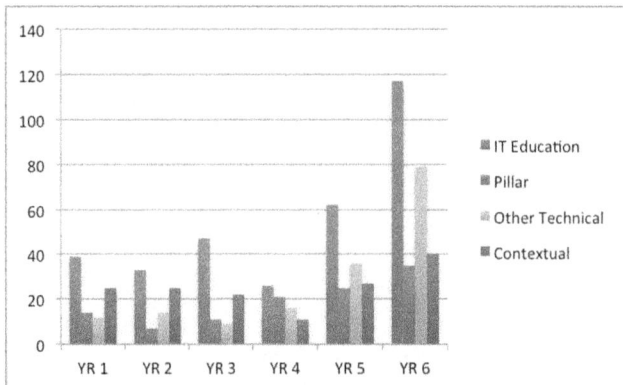

Figure 2. Genre Trends

Figure 2 breaks down all submissions during the study period into four generic categories: IT Education (non-pillar), pillar-related papers, other technical submissions, and contextual, meaning those that deal with non-technical issues and papers that are not specifically IT education in scope. YR 4 (2010) is an anomalous year in that papers related to IT pillars and other technical issues rose, while IT education papers fell by 50% over previous years, as did contextual papers. Otherwise, IT education papers, other technical papers, and pillar papers have been trending upward; while contextual papers have remained relatively flat.

4.3 Reviewer Information

Between 2007 and 2012, there were 192 active reviewers in SIGITE, and together they completed 1026 reviews. The DBR process involved multiple reviews per paper (average or 3.11 reviews per paper), and most papers (70%) were reviewed by three or four reviewers.

As can be seen in Table 1, almost half of our reviewers (91) completed between 1 and 3 reviews during this six-year period, and 27% completed between 4 and 6 reviews. Less than 8% of our reviewers completed more than 10 reviews during timeframe, and most (74%) did six or less.

Table 1. Number of reviews per reviewer

# Reviewers	N	%
Reviewers doing 1-3 reviews	91	47.4
Reviewers doing 4-6 reviews	51	26.6
Reviewers doing 7-9 reviews	22	11.5
Reviewers doing 10-12 reviews	13	6.8
Reviewers doing 13-15 reviews	6	3.1
Reviewers doing >= 16 reviews	9	4.7

Interestingly, the number of reviews a paper had was negatively correlated with its probability of being accepted to the conference. Generally speaking, the more reviews a paper had, the less likely it was of being accepted (F (1, 328) = 5.119, $p<0.024$; and $r=$ -0.124, $p<0.024$).

This led us to question whether the number of reviews a reviewer did in a given year affects how they did their review: that is, was the reviewer who had to do four or more reviews harsher or more lenient than those that had to do less reviews? Our analysis showed that there doesn't appear to be any difference in the reviewing leniency for reviewers doing additional reviews.

4.4 Rating Information

We were especially interested in this data, since it provides the most relevant feedback about the effectiveness of peer review at SIGITE. In the Related Work section, we noted that [21] examined the variability of reviewer scores at SIGCSE 2000 and also explored some of the potential factors that might affect reviewer ratings. We wanted to extend their analysis to not only examine the reliability of our peer review but also its validity.

Recall that for each review, the reviewer supplied a rating between 1 and 6 for five different categories. Table 2 shows the rating definitions and the frequencies for the overall rating category

Table 2. Rating definitions and number received

Overall Rating	Description in review form	N	%
1	Deficient	51	5.0%
2	Below Average	192	18.7%
3	Average	223	21.7%
4	Very Good	254	24.8%
5	Outstanding	267	26.0%
6	Exceptional	39	3.8%
Total		**1026**	**100.0%**

All reviewers provided ratings on four subcategories (technical merit, organization, originality and significance) as well as an overall rating (mean scores 3.62, 3.86, 3.70, 3.75 and 3.60 respectively). These subcategory ratings were significantly correlated ($p<0.00$) with the overall rating (with Pearson correlation results of 0.813, 0.728, 0.778 and 0.812). Further, post-hoc testing using Tukey HSD showed significant relationships between every one of these four factors and every level of overall rating, which suggested strong internal reliability for each of the reviewers (that is, a reviewer was reliable within a single review). It also suggests possible limitations of subcategories scores as a necessary part of the reviewing process.

Central tendency statistics for subcategory ratings (mean, median, standard deviation, etc.) alone are not adequate to capture the variability of reviewer scoring for poor, average, and excellent papers. In an effort to explore this, we looked at the range of scores for each kind of paper (as shown in Table 3). As can be seen, reviewers sometimes agreed with one another (narrow range of rating scores) and at other times disagreed (large range of rating scores). For instance, looking at papers with a minimum overall rating score of 2, we found that 26% of these papers received a maximum score of 2 or 3 by other raters (good reliability) but 49% received ratings between 5 and 6 (substantial variability). While the overall statistics exhibited a strong tendency towards the mean, paper ratings vary considerably and must be reviewed on an individual level. Based on these findings, it is recommended that the program committee individually consider papers where rating scores deviate by 2 or more rating points.

Table 3. Combination of min vs max overall rating

Minimum Values	Maximum Values						
	1	2	3	4	5	6	N
1	2	5	8	10	14	2	41
2		8	23	29	47	10	117
3			11	21	51	5	88
4				16	31	14	61
5					16	5	21
6						2	2
# papers							330

4.5 Factors Affecting Rating

Previous work ([20, 21]) has focused on whether different reviewer characteristics affect ratings and suggest the potential for biases which impact rater reliability. We also looked at these factors, but supplemented them with an examination of textual factors in the submissions themselves.

4.5.1 Reviewer Characteristics

Here we looked at two factors that may impact reviewer ratings: familiarity with the subject being reviewed and regional location. First, looking at familiarity, in each review, reviewers assigned themselves a familiarity rating of low, medium or high with the material covered in the paper being reviewed. Our ANOVA indicated that there were no differences in overall ratings between these groups (F (2,1025)=0.330, p=0.719), which supports the findings of [21] and [20].

What about reviewer location? Walker [21] found that reviewer location did not have a statistically significant impact on SIGCSE reviewer ratings; however in his later study [20], reviewer location was significant. To assess the effect of location on our data, we divided total reviews (1026) into three groups: reviewers from native English speaking countries (n=903), those from Europe (n=53), and those from everywhere else (n=70). We found no differences between regions (F (2,1023) = 1.304, p=0.272).

4.5.2 Textual Characteristics

Ideally, a reviewer bases his or her ratings on the quality of the paper being evaluated. Given the large number of papers in our data set, in this study we did not perform our own qualitative evaluation of each paper and compare that to the reviewers' ratings (as suggested by [16]). Instead, we compared several quantitative textual measures on a subset to see if any of them were related to reviewers' overall ratings. Table 4 indicates the results of our examination.

Table 4. Textual characteristics examined

Characteristic	Significant	Correlation
Total number of words in paper (n=55, M=3152.22)	No	$r = 0.264$ $p = 0.052$
Readability indices of paper (n=55, M=39.33)	No	$r = -0.016$ $p = 0.909$
Readability indices of abstract (n=34, M=30.96)	No	$r = -0.083$ $p = 0.641$
Total # of words in abstract (n=159; M=115.13)	Yes	$r = 0.379$ $p < 0.00$
Number of references in paper (n=159; M=16.47)	Yes	$r = 0.270$ $p = 0.001$

The readability indices that we tested included the following: the percentage of complex words, the Flesh-Kincaid Reading Ease Index, the Gunning Fog Score, the SMOG index, and the Coleman Liau Index. All of these indices are meant to measure the reading difficulty of a block of text [16]. While the usefulness of these types of calculations have been subjected to significant criticism ([5, 15]), one recent study [14] reported that papers winning awards in four academic marketing journals had better readability scores than those that did not. We performed similar readability calculations on a small random subset of our papers (n=34) as a preliminary test. The results reported in Table 4 reflect the Flesh-Kincaid results, but measures using the other instruments listed above were comparable; we found no significant relationship between any of the readability indices and the papers' reviewer ratings.

4.6 Peer Review Validity

Validity refers to the degree to which a reviewer's ratings of a paper are reflective of the paper's actual value. Some have argued that a review process is valid if it selects the best contributions [13]. While this may be the goal of all peer review, it is difficult to measure objectively. Perhaps the easiest way to assess the academic impact and quality of a paper is to examine the paper's eventual citation count. We grouped all the accepted papers (n=245) into four quartiles based on average overall rating. We then took a random sampling of 96 papers from all six years, with an even number from each year and each quartile. For each of these papers, we gathered the number of citations from Google Scholar. We used Google Scholar even though it tends to provide, on average, a higher number of citations than other citation sources [6]. This higher number is thought to be due to Google Scholar's incorporation of citations from conferences [9], which in the field of computing science and IT are an especially important venue for dissemination [19].

Academic citations are only one measure of a paper's impact. The vast majority of the papers at SIGITE are broadly about computing education. There is a practical value to many of the

SIGITE conference's papers and a paper may have an important impact on the wider academic community in that it potentially changes teaching practice. This importance would not be reflected in academic citations. We tried to capture the practical impact of an accepted paper by examining the number of times a paper had been downloaded (in total and in the past year) from the ACM Digital Library. We thereby also recorded these download numbers for our sample of 96 accepted papers

Did the peer review process at SIGITE predict the longer-term impact of the paper? As can be seen in Table 11, we did not find any correlation.

Table 5. Validity measures

Characteristic	Significant	Correlation
Number of Google Scholar citations (n=96; M=4.60)	No	$r = 0.121$ $p = 0.241$
Cumulative ACM DL downloads to date (n=96; M=239.61)	No	$r = 0.096$ $p = 0.351$
Number of ACM DL downloads in past year (n=96; M=37.23))	No	$r = 0.023$ $p = 0.822$

5. LIMITATIONS

This study has several limitations. Our data set contained six years of data for a computing education conference: such conferences arguably have a unique set of reviewers and authors in comparison to "normal" computing conferences. As such, there may be limits to the generalizability of our results. It is also important to recognize that correlations are not the same as causation. For instance, our findings showed that there is a relationship between the abstract's word count and the eventual overall reviewer ratings, but this does not mean that the abstract word count by itself increases or decreases the reviewer rating.

Another important limitation lies in the underlying database system used in the original conference submission system. Since the data for each conference year was contained in its own database, this multi-year information had to be manually combined, which potentially introduced data irregularities. Also, because reviewer and author information was duplicated from year to year, the final data set contained many duplicate author and reviewer records; grouping by last and first name eliminated duplicates but it is possible that some duplicate names still existed in the analyzed data set.

In this study we only evaluated the validity of the peer review process on a subset of the papers, and next we plan to extend our analysis to the entire data set. In the future, we hope also to examine whether reviewer reliability is related to the experience level of the reviewer, and to fine tune our validity analysis by seeing if correlations differ for the top or bottom quartile of papers.

6. DISCUSSION AND CONCLUSION

Peer reviewed conferences are an important and valued venue for the dissemination of knowledge within computing disciplines [19]. As such, it is important to occasionally evaluate what happens "behind the curtain" with peer review at academic computing conferences. This paper adds to this literature. Some of our results are in line with other findings, but some of our results

could be construed as new findings. We briefly discuss each of the key findings below.

We found no difference in acceptance rates between multi-author and single-authored papers. Even though there are perceptions that single authorship (or conversely, multiple authors) results in better papers, our results are similar to what others have found [4, 10]: namely, there is no discernible difference (at least as far as acceptance rates are concerned). We also found that there was significant variability in reviewer ratings, a result similar to [20]. Given that this appears to be constant, future program chairs would be advised to control for this variability by increasing the number of reviewers per paper. For instance, [13] concludes that "3 reviews per paper—i.e., the number generally used in peer review I conferences—give highly confident results … only for conferences with high agreement among reviewers." Our data shows that SIGITE reviewers do not have high agreement, and we therefore recommend having a minimum of four reviewers per paper in the future.

Reviewers for the SIGITE conference in the years of this study gave a ranking between 1 and 6 for five subcategories (technical content, organization and writing, originality, significance, and overall). Ultimately we found that these other categories did not act as significant factors on the key overall ranking subcategory. That is, it might suffice to provide the reviewer with just a single overall ranking. Nonetheless, reviewers might appreciate having these subcategories as they may provide reviewers with a rubric or a series of guidelines that help them construct their overall rating score. It is also worth noting that in the context of a single SIGCSE conference, [21] did find in contrast to our findings that these subcategories were statistically significant factors.

This paper examined two factors external to the paper to see if they played a noticeable role in the eventual ratings. Happily, there was no evidence that the nationality (or whether they were native English speakers) of the reviewer or the author played a statistical significant role in the eventual ratings the paper received. Similarly, the relative familiarity of the reviewer for the technical content of the paper appears to also have no statistically significant impact on the ratings. This may indicate that reviewers generally rate a paper on criteria that are independent of the technical content of the paper, such as organization, writing style, coherence with established research norms, and so on.

We also examined if there was any relationship between different characteristics of the papers themselves and their eventual ratings. Here the results were mixed. We found no relationship between various readability statistics and the papers' ratings. This result appears to confirm the skepticism that some have about the usefulness of these measures [15]. We were quite surprised to find however that the number of words in the abstract was statistically significant. Presumably, reviewers read the abstract particularly carefully (a fact which can be deduced by examining server-records for online scholarly journals [12]). As such, our results show that erring on the side of abstract brevity is usually a mistake. On the contrary, our evidence shows that it is important for authors to make sure the abstract contains sufficient information.

We also found that the number of references was also statistically significant. This should not be surprising result. Education research does not happen in a vacuum, but exists in a conversation with previous work by other scholars. In a recent study of bibliographic references in ACM papers, [19] found that the average number of references per document is 21.26 (median 18). Our average was 16.47 (median 14), which is considerably below that threshold. This appears to indicate that prospective SIGITE authors should endeavor to increase the number of references per paper. Comparisons to mathematics and physics (18.25 and 24.11 references per article respectively) might seem to indicate that reference numbers in SIGITE papers is close to the appropriate range for our discipline [18]. That would be a mistaken assumption. Most of the papers at SIGITE are broadly-speaking educational research papers, and so citation rates within academic computing science or mathematics provides a misleadingly lower benchmark comparison. When compared to the average number of citations per article (34.63) for all disciplines in the Science Citation Index [1], making a concerted effort at increasing citations is likely to improve a paper's ratings with reviewers. It should be emphasized that the number of citations is not the cause of lower or better reviewer ratings; rather, the number of citations is likely a proxy measure for determining if the paper under review is a properly researched paper that is connected to the broader scholarly community.

Finally, this paper addressed the issue of the validity of peer review at SIGITE. This is an especially important area. We did not find any connection between reviewers' ratings of a paper and its subsequent academic impact (measured by citations) or practical impact (measured by ACM Digital Library downloads). This might seem to be a disturbing result. However, other research in this area also found no correlation between reviewer ratings and subsequent academic impact. It is important to remember that, "the aim of the peer review process is not the selection of high impact papers, but is simply to filter junk papers and accept only the ones above a certain quality threshold" [13].

Posteriori evaluation of conference review results is an important way to evaluate and assess disciplinary quality and perspectives. This paper provided some preliminary steps towards this larger goal. In the future, we hope to extend the analysis to include not only more recent years, but also to include more fine-grained examinations of the different factors affecting peer review at the SIGITE conference. Such data can improve not only the reviewing process, but potentially may improve the construction of the papers submitted to this and other conferences.

7. REFERENCES

[1] Biglu, M. H. 2008. The influence of references per paper in the SCI to impact factors and the matthew effect. *Scientometrics* 74(3), pp. 453-470.

[2] Bornmann, L. 2011. Scientific peer review. *Annual Review of Information Science and Technology* 45(1), pp. 197-245.

[3] Bornmann, L., Wallon, G. and Ledin, A. 2008. Does the committee peer review select the best applicants for funding? an investigation of the selection process for two european molecular biology organization programmes. *PLoS One* 3(10), pp. e3480.

[4] Bridgstock, M. 1991. The quality of single and multiple authored papers; an unresolved problem. *Scientometrics* 21(1), pp. 37-48.

[5] Connatser, B. R. 1999. Last rites for readability formulas in technical communication. *Journal of Technical Writing and Communication* 29(3), pp. 271-288.

[6] Franceschet, M. 2010. A comparison of bibliometric indicators for computer science scholars and journals on web of science and google scholar. *Scientometrics* 83(1), pp. 243-258.

[7] Goodrum, A. A., McCain, K. W., Lawrence, S. and Giles, C. Lee. 2001. Scholarly publishing in the internet age: A citation analysis of computer science literature. *Information Processing & Management* 37(5), pp. 661-675. DOI= http://dx.doi.org/10.1016/S0306-4573(00)00047-9.

[8] [8] U. W. Jayasinghe, H. W. Marsh and N. Bond. 2001. Peer review in the funding of research in higher education: The australian experience. *Educational Evaluation and Policy Analysis* 23(4), pp. 343-364.

[9] Kousha, K. and Thelwall, M.. 2007. Google scholar citations and google web/URL citations: A multi-discipline exploratory analysis. *J. Am. Soc. Inf. Sci. Technol.* 58(7), pp. 1055-1065. 2007.

[10] Leimu, R. and Koricheva, J. 2005. Does scientific collaboration increase the impact of ecological articles? *Bioscience* 55(5), pp. 438-443.

[11] Marsh, H. W. and Ball, S. 1991. Reflections on the peer review process. *Behav. Brain Sci.* 14(01), pp. 157-158.

[12] Nicholas, D., Huntington, P., Jamali, H. R. and Watkinson, A. 2006. The information seeking behaviour of the users of digital scholarly journals. *Information Processing & Management* 42(5), pp. 1345-1365.

[13] Ragone, A., Mirylenka, K., Casati, F. and Marchese, M. 2013. On peer review in computer science: Analysis of its effectiveness and suggestions for improvement. *Scientometrics* 97(2), pp. 317-356.

[14] Sawyer, A. G., Laran, J. and Xu, J. 2008. The readability of marketing journals: Are award-winning articles better written? *J. Market.* 72(1), pp. 108-117.

[15] Schriver, K. A. 2000. Readability formulas in the new millennium: What's the use? *ACM Journal of Computer Documentation* 24(3), pp. 138-140.

[16] Schriver, K. A. 1989. Evaluating text quality: The continuum from text-focused to reader-focused methods. *Professional Communication, IEEE Transactions On* 32(4), pp. 238-255.

[17] Snodgrass, R. 2006. Single-versus double-blind reviewing: An analysis of the literature. *ACM Sigmod Record* 35(3), pp. 8-21.

[18] Vieira, E. S. and Gomes, J. A. 2010. Citations to scientific articles: Its distribution and dependence on the article features. *Journal of Informetrics* 4(1), pp. 1-13.

[19] Wainer, J., Przibisczki, H., de Oliveira and Anido, R. 2011. Patterns of bibliographic references in the ACM published papers. *Information Processing & Management* 47(1), pp. 135-142.

[20] Walker, H. M. SIGCSE by the numbers. 2011. *ACM SIGCSE Bulletin* 43(1), pp. 4-5.

[21] Walker, H. M., Ma, W. and Mboya, D. 2002. Variability of referees' ratings of conference papers. *ACM SIGCSE Bulletin* 34 (3).

Factors Affecting School Choice of Computing Students

Rex P. Bringula
University of the East
2219 CM Recto Avenue
Sampaloc, Manila, Philippines 1008
rex_bringula@yahoo.com

John Noel C. Victorino
Ateneo de Manila University
Katipunan Avenue
Quezon City, Philippines 1108
johnnoelvictorino@gmail.com

ABSTRACT

This descriptive study utilized a validated and reliable questionnaire to determine the profile, perception towards the identified eleven institutional image indicators, level of school choice in terms of rank and preference. It was shown that there were two types of students in terms of economic status. Respondents reported that they were informed mostly by those who had close tie relationship with them. They also disclosed that they preferred their school but it was ranked only as their second choice. Overall, they considered institutional image indicators in deciding to enroll in the school. Multiple regression analysis showed that tuition fee and scholarship and grants were the only institutional image indicators that could the influence level of school choice. Thus, the null hypothesis stating that institution image indicators, singly or in combination, do not significantly affect the level of school choice is partially rejected. Implications and further research were also presented.

Categories and Subject Descriptors

K.3.2 [**Computer and Information Science Education**]: Information systems education

General Terms

Management

Keywords

Institutional image; Rank of choice; School choice; Scholarship; Tuition fee

1. INTRODUCTION

Currently, the education system of the Philippines is based on the Education Act of 1982 [8]. This law stated that the elementary education is "the first stage of compulsory, formal education primarily concerned with providing basic education and usually corresponding to six or seven grades, including pre-school programs" while secondary education is "the state of formal education following the elementary level concerned primarily with continuing basic education and expanding it to include the learning of employable gainful skills, usually corresponding to four years of high school." Since then, the Philippine basic and

secondary education had a total of 10 years of schooling – short of two years of schooling in terms of international standard. To cope with other countries, the law was amended under the Republic Act 10533 [15] and two years of schooling were added to the secondary level. The implementation of the current law is commonly called the K-12 system.

The Philippine higher education institutions are now challenged by the adverse effects of the implementation of K-12 in terms of student enrolment by 2016. Its impact on the enrollment in universities will be felt until 2020. Computing education providers have a more pressing concern since the new curriculum will aggravate the present computing education enrollment conditions. The non-enrollment of first year students in 2016 will have a significant impact on the faculty and on the PHEIs such as non-renewal of faculty teaching contracts, teachers' displacement from college to high school level, limited teaching hours translated to lower compensation, and impact on retirement compensation. In short, the new system will greatly change the landscape of computing education.

Philippine higher education institutions (PHEIs) are aware of this situation and they responded to these pressing concerns by formulating different strategies at least to lessen the negative impact of K-12. One of these strategies is to inform possible entrants on what the school can offer [16]. Aggressive marketing strategies are presently employed to attract possible entrants. In order to accomplish successful marketing strategies, it is imperative to determine the considerations in choosing a school of the possible enrollees [16]. However, the computing literature were focused on what influenced students to choose their computing majors (e.g.,[1,3]). Though these studies are important, the academic community still lacks studies that explain the school choice considerations of computing students and the factors that influence such considerations. This study aims to fill in this gap.

Toward this goal, it seeks to answer the following questions. 1) What is the profile of freshmen in terms of degree program, gender, city address, type of house residence in the city address, family monthly income, travel time, mode of transportation, average number of family members, and number of family members studying in the university? 2) Who were the "marketers" that informed the respondents about their chosen school? 3) Who influenced the respondents in choosing their school? 4) What is the level of school choice in terms of rank and level of preference? 5) What is the level of consideration of the respondents in deciding to enroll in the University in terms of institutional image indicators, such as Tuition Fee, Tuition Fee Payment Scheme, Admission Process, Schedule of Classes, Degree Offerings, Facilities, Faculty Profile, Scholarships and Grants, Kinship Patronage, Security in Campus, and Accessibility? 6) Do the institutional image indicators, singly or in combination, affect the level of school choice?

SIGITE'14, October 15–18, 2014, Atlanta, Georgia, USA.
Copyright © 2014 ACM 978-1-4503-2686-5/14/10...$15.00.
http://dx.doi.org/10.1145/2656450.2656467

2. LITERATURE REVIEW

Institutional image is defined as "the organization's portrait made in the mind of a consumer" [13]. It can be viewed either as a functional or an emotional image. The former is tangible in nature and can be measured while the latter can be manifested through feelings and attitudes towards an organization [12]. Dobni and Zinkhan [7] called these components as cognitive (the beliefs) and affective (the feelings).

Institutional image was investigated in different studies. The data from a longitudinal study of postsecondary educational choice of high school students in the state of Indiana showed that tuition fee was directly related to the preference of students in choosing a school [9]. Hu and Hossler [9] further showed that subjective responses of students to tuition costs and financial aid availability were also directly related to student preference for a certain type of postsecondary institution, independent of students' family background and academic characteristics. They concluded that not only the ability to pay but also the willingness to pay played a direct role in student college choice decisions. In particular, a merit-based scholarship tended to increase the enrollment levels in higher education institutions [17].

In the study of Kazoleas et al. [11], institutional or university image was operationalized in terms of personal/demographic variables (e.g., gender, ethnicity, age, income level, and educational level), environmental factors (relative quality, location, financial reasons, comparative admission standards), and organizational factors (building, landscaping, sports facilities, campus size, academic programs, libraries, technical facilities). Three hundred thirty-seven respondents who participated in the telephone survey were given a list of potential sources such as student, family/friends, employee, and media. The researchers were also interested to determine the factors that influenced institutional image. Their study showed that family members and friends who attended the university influenced the image of the university. It was followed by experiences as a student, media, family members and friends who knew about the university, and someone who worked at the university. It was concluded that most respondents' perceptions towards the image of the university were shaped by personal experience or by interpersonal relationships with others who had attended the university. Moreover, using factor analysis, it was disclosed that the seven factors that had an impact on the university image were overall image and images of the programs, teaching emphasis, quality of education, environmental conditions, financial reasons, and sports programs.

Soutar and Turner [16] reported that tertiary education in Australia had become more competitive due to reductions in government funding and higher student fees. As a result, the role of marketing in the universities had grown significantly. Driven by a goal to understand what determined a student's university preference, the researchers conducted an adaptive conjoint analysis on the data gathered from 259 final high school students in Western Australia. The variables investigated were type of university (e.g., new/modern, old/traditional, technological university), ability to transfer (e.g., offers or does not offer ability to articulate/transfer units between technical and further education (TAFE) and university), distance from home (e.g., close to home (less than 10km), moderate distance from home (10-20km), and far from home (over 20km)), academic reputation (e.g., has a poor/average/strong academic reputation), quality of teaching (e.g., has average/very good quality of teaching), job prospects

(e.g., would equip me with qualifications that provide average/good job prospects), family opinion (e.g., is held in good/poor/no opinion by my family), friends (e.g., Is where/not where my friends will be going to the same school), campus atmosphere (e.g., has a very little/great campus atmosphere), and course suitability (e.g., offers a course that is more or less/not really/just what I want). Their findings showed that the four most important determinants of university preference were course suitability, academic reputation, job prospects, and teaching quality.

Arpan et al. [2] investigated the perceptions of two groups of respondents on institutional image indicators of ten universities in the US. Respondents were drawn from two major universities in the United States of America which both ranked in the second tier of national universities examined by U.S. News and World Report's annual college rankings. The first university was a private university located in the northeast of US with enrollment of more than 10,000 undergraduate students. The second university was a public university from the southeast with an enrollment of 20,000 undergraduate students. There were 78 and 177 participants from the northeastern and southeastern university, respectively.

Respondents answered a 20-item instrument with dimensions on perceived commitment to and/or excellence in academics and athletics, perceived social/cultural environment of the university, degree of familiarity with the university achieved via consumption of news coverage regarding the university, peer and family influence, degree of perceived commitment to social responsibility, appearance of campus, and perceived quality of resources available to students. The study revealed that different groups used different criteria when rating ten major (i.e., based U.S. News and World Report's annual college rankings) US universities. Academic factors, athletic factors, and the extent of news coverage of the university were found to predict the overall image of the universities significantly.

Factors considered in choosing a college or university by 196 softball players from the ten (10) National Collegiate Athletic Association (NCAA) Division I member institutions were investigated in the study of Kankey and Quarterman [10]. Availability of a major or academic program, head coach, career opportunities after graduation, social atmosphere of the team, and the amount of financial aid were the most influential factors in selecting a school for softball players. On the other hand, the least influential factors were friends, affiliation of the university (i.e, religion, public, and private), media coverage, softball team website, softball team sponsorships, high school coach, and ethnic or gender ratio of the university.

Bringula and Basa [6] investigated the level of school choice in deciding to enroll in the three Universities in the University Belt in Manila in terms of eleven institutional image indicators. Tuition Fee, Tuition Fee Payment Scheme, Admission Process, Schedule of Classes, Course Offerings, School Facilities, Faculty Profile, Scholarship and Grants, Kinship Patronage, Security in Campus, and Performance in Licensure Exams were the eleven institutional image indicators of the study. It was shown that the three sets of respondents considered five indicators (Course Offerings, School Facilities, Faculty Profile, Scholarship and Grants, and Performance in Licensure Exams) but had different levels of considerations for the rest of indicators. Interestingly, researchers also found that the three sets of respondents did not consider Tuition Fee in choosing their school. The researchers argued that this indicator was considered by their parents, not by the students.

Bringula [4] also examined the school choice of IT freshmen in terms of accessibility of and proximity to school. Using two hundred twenty-seven (227) questionnaire gathered from the respondents, it was revealed that most of the respondents were male, did not have a home province, lived in Manila and Quezon City, belonged to a middle-income class, belonged to a family with five members, spent almost an hour in going to school, and utilized jeepneys and the Light Railway Transit to reach the school. Using regression analysis, it was disclosed that perceived accessibility of the school was the only factor to influence school choice. In a similar study, Bringula [5] also showed that facilities were the only institutional image indicator that predicted the level of school choice of freshmen.

3. DEFINITION OF VARIABLES AND HYPOTHESIS

This study adopted the institutional image indicators of Bringula [4,5] because of two reasons. First, it covered almost all other indicators presented in the literature review. Second, both institutional image indicators were rated by the computing degree programs. There were eleven institutional image indicators in the study that served as the independent variables. These variables were defined as follows:

- Tuition Fee refers to the affordability of tuition and miscellaneous fees.
- Tuition Fee Payment Scheme is the system of the University of collecting fees from students in a flexible, secured, and easy manner.
- Admission Process measures the ease of college admission procedures from the application to the actual enrollment.
- Schedule of Classes is an indicator of convenience and appropriateness of time allotment for classes.
- Degree Offerings refer to the perceived popularity and prestige of the computing degree programs offered by the University. Prestige was contextualized in terms of strong focus on major subjects, local degree programs certifications, and government and private accreditations.
- Facilities are the resources of the University, such as classrooms, laboratories, library, computers, and computing infrastructures that supported students' learning.
- Faculty Profile determines the qualifications of teachers (e.g., educational attainment and certifications) and desirable personal qualities (e.g., strict yet reasonable, friendly yet professional, dedicated, and motivated).
- Scholarship and Grants Scheme refers to the availability of financial aids not only for academically excellent students but also for arts- and sports-inclined students.
- Kinship Patronage signifies the likelihood that the student will enroll in the University because a family member or a friend is an alumnus.
- Security in Campus is the perceived safety of the students within and outside the campus.
- Accessibility refers to time spent in travelling from the home address of the respondents to the school and the subjective perception on the accessibility of the school with respect to good road conditions, availability of different modes of

transportation, convenience in getting to school, and affordability of fare [4].

Level of school choice was used to mean the degree to which the students preferred to enroll in the university [4]. This served as the dependent variable. It was hypothesized that institutional image indicators, singly or in combination, do not affect the level of school choice.

4. METHODOLOGY

The descriptive study was conducted in one university in University Belt in Manila. Third and fourth year students were chosen as respondents because their responses on school choice considerations were more stable than those of first and second year students. While freshmen and sophomores had a higher propensity of transferring to other schools, juniors and seniors might have already proven that they chose the right school for them. Further, institutional image was likely to vary, depending on the groups among whom the image was assessed [2].

There were 594 third and fourth year students during the first semester of school year 2013-2014. Using Sloven's formula ($n = N/(1 + Ne^2)$), where e=0.10, a sample size of 86 was computed. Students were convened in a hall and 210 survey forms were distributed to achieve high return rate. Two hundred forms were retrieved and these were all used in the analysis.

The first part of the questionnaire gathered demographic data such as gender, degree program, provincial address, city home location, type of house ownership, family monthly income, number of family members, number of family members studying in the same university, and travel time. The second part determined the level of school choice of the respondents in terms of rank (e.g., first choice, second choice, third choice, etc.) and level of preference (1 – Not preferred to 5 – Highly preferred). The third part of the questionnaire gathered data as to where the respondents got information about their school and persuaded them to enroll in the university.

The last part of the questionnaire measured the level of consideration in deciding to enroll in the university in terms of eleven institutional image indicators. All questions under each statement begin with "*I decided to enroll in the university because....*" Respondents utilized a five-point scale (1 – Highly disagree to 5 – Highly agree) to answer these questions.

The research instrument was pretested to a one-class section with forty students. They were excluded in the population of the study. Factor analysis and Cronbach's alpha analysis were employed to determine the validity and reliability of the constructs, respectively. A construct with a factor loading (f.l.) of less than 0.50 were discarded and Cronbach's alpha (α) values of at least 0.70 were retained. Initially, there were fifty-three (53) questions. The number of questions was reduced to 46 items.

The statistical tools utilized in the study were frequency counts, percentages, ranking, and means to describe the data. Multiple regression analysis was employed to determine the factors that influenced school choice of computing students. A 5% level of probability with 95% reliability was adopted to determine the degree of significance of the findings.

5. RESULTS AND DISCUSSION

5.1 Profile of the Respondents

Table 1 shows the profile of the respondents. There were more Information Technology (IT) students (f = 179, 90%) than Computer Science students (f = 21, 11%). This is not surprising since more than one-half of the total population (2,000 students) of the college were IT students. It was also revealed that there were more male students (f = 139, 70%) than female students (f = 61, 31%). More than 50% of the respondents were from Manila (f = 72, 36%) and Quezon City (f = 44, 22%). It is worth noting that the University was able to attract students from Rizal (f = 20, 10%) than the rest of the 14 areas of Metro Manila. Rizal is not part of Metro Manila and it is about 45.3 kilometers from Manila.

This can be explained by the fact that the travel time from Rizal to the University is cut short by the presence of Light Railway Transit (LRT) 2. They could reach the University for about an hour through LRT 2. In fact, LRT was the second (f = 85, 43%) most utilized mode of transportation. Further, the travel time of the respondents from their house location to the university was a little over an hour (mean = 60.36).

Majority of the respondents (f = 112, 56%) were living in family-owned houses. They also belonged to a family consisting of five members. In terms of earnings, 58% of the respondents (f = 115) had a family monthly income of no more than Php 50,000 (US $1,200). On the other hand, there were also those who belonged to an income of at least Php50,000 (f = 85, 42%). It must be noted that the tuition fee for a computing degree at the University is about Php50,000 (US $1,200) per semester. This shows that the economic status of the respondents in terms of house residence, number of family members, and monthly income could support a relatively expensive private college education. It also reveals that the financial capabilities of the respondents' family meet the financial requirements of the University. In fact, they could not survive the final years in computing if they were not capable of paying their tuition fees.

Table 1. Profile of the Respondents

Profile	Findings
Degree Program	Information Technology, f = 179, 90% Computer Science, f = 21, 90%
Gender	Male, f = 139, 70% Female, f = 61, 31%
City Address	Manila, f = 72, 36% Quezon City, f = 44, 22% Rizal, f = 20, 10% Other parts of Metro Manila, f = 64, 32%
Type of House Residence	Family-owned, f = 112, 56% Apartment-Rented, f = 48, 24% Others, f = 40, 20%
Family Monthly Income	Php50,000 (US$ 1,200) and below, f =115, 58% Above Php50,000, f = 85, 42%
Average Number of Family Members	5 family members
Average travel time	60.36 minutes
Modes of Transportation	Jeep, f= 146, 73% Light Railway Transit, f = 85, 43% Toyota Tamaraw FX, f = 51, 26%

Moreover, the findings also signal that there were two types of students to whom the University catered. On one hand, there were those who had just enough financial resources for a family with five members. On the other hand, there were those who had more than enough to cover the expenses of the family. This implies that it will be difficult for more than half of the total number of computing students to cope with tuition fee increase. Thus, a stable tuition fee of higher year students will greatly benefit the students, especially those who belong to the lower income. The University is aware of this situation and follows this practice. The findings of the study justified this practice. Consequently, this is also beneficial for parents since they can formulate a long-term financial plan for the college education of their children. Thus, the University could direct their marketing strategies towards parents.

5.2 Marketers and Influencers

Table 2 shows the marketers of the University. "Marketers" refer to the sources of information of the students about the University. As can be seen from Table 2, friends (f = 74, 37%) were the topmost source of information of about the school. It was followed by parents (f = 55, 28%) and relatives (i.e., other parents and siblings) (f = 46, 23%). Meanwhile, Siblings (f = 33, 17%) were fifth in the rank of the marketers. It can be noticed that three out of the five ranks have personal relationship with the respondents. It reveals that the top marketers for possible entrants have personal or close relationship with the respondents. These findings are similar to the findings of Kazoleas et al. [11]. Moreover, these warrant the recommendation that marketing strategies could be directed to parents.

The Internet (f = 42, 21%) also plays an important role for information dissemination about the University. As commented by various researchers [14,18], a website is one of the best media in communicating the brand and mission of academic institutions. The information found in the website of prospective entrants could serve as basis for them to decide to apply in the University [13].

Table 2. Marketers

Marketers	f	%	Rank
Friends	74	37	1
Parents	55	28	2
Relatives	46	23	3
Internet	42	21	4
Siblings	33	17	5
UE Marketing Team	32	16	6
High School Teacher	15	8	7
Television	10	5	8
Neighbor	9	5	8
Newspaper	8	4	9
UAAP	4	2	10

Other marketers such as the University's marketing team (UE Marketing Team), high school teachers, televisions, neighbors, newspaper, and University Athletic Association of the Philippines (UAAP) membership were also found sources of information. Though there were a small number of respondents informed through these information providers, their impact could not be eliminated. It just shows that respondents were informed in various ways.

Meanwhile, Table 3 shows the influencers, that is, those who persuaded the respondents to enroll in the University. It was shown that most of the respondents enrolled in the University because of their own decision (f = 66, 33%). This reveals that students are now empowered to make their own choice in deciding to enroll in a school. However, when taken collectively, the second up to the fifth rank (Parents, f = 54, 27%; Friends, f = 47, 24%; Relatives, f = 35, 18%; and Siblings, f = 22, 11%) of influencers revealed that close tie relationship again played an important role in school selection. It can be concluded that, in this data set, marketers of the school were also the influencers. Thus, conducting information dissemination to the marketers is a good marketing strategy since they do not only inform possible entrants, but they also persuade the latter to enroll at the University.

Table 3. Influencers

Influencers	f	%	Rank
Own Decision	66	33	1
Parents	54	27	2
Friends	47	24	3
Relatives	35	18	4
Siblings	22	11	5

5.3 Computing Students' Perceptions on Institutional Image Indicators and Their Level of School Choice

Overall, the respondents agreed (mean = 3.62) that they considered the eleven indicators in deciding to enroll in the University (See Table 4.). Among the indicators investigated, Scholarship and Grants (mean = 4.13, Agree) got the highest mean rating while Tuition Fee (mean = 2.83, Moderately Agree) got the lowest mean rating. It was shown that respondents agreed that they considered scholarships and grants offered by the school when they enrolled in the University. The result seems to be unusual since the parents of the students could afford the tuition fee of the University. This phenomenon could be explained by two points.

First, scholarship and other financial aid grants scheme offer by the University covers half or even full payment of tuition fee. Thus, this scheme greatly helps the students as well as their parents since the amount given significantly reduces the household cost. Second, being a scholarship grantee adds prestige to the profile of the students and may have consequential impacts on their job-seeking capabilities. Being a scholar also becomes a status symbol which implies that the students are intelligent and are easily capable of acquiring the skills needed for their future jobs.

Table 4. Level of Consideration in Deciding to Enroll in the University

Institutional Image Indicators	Mean	Verbal Interpretation
Tuition Fee	**2.83**	**Moderately agree**
Tuition Fee Payment Scheme	3.76	Agree
Admission Process	3.81	Agree
Schedule of Classes	3.63	Agree
Degree Offerings	3.99	Agree
Facilities	3.62	Agree
Faculty Profile	4.04	Agree
Scholarship and Grants	**4.13**	**Agree**
Kinship Patronage	2.86	Moderately agree
Security in Campus	3.59	Agree
Accessibility	3.52	Agree
OVERALL MEAN	**3.62**	**Agree**
Level of School Choice	**3.80**	**Preferred**
Rating/Range: 1/1.00 – 1.50 = Disagree/Not preferred 2/1.51 – 2.50 = Slightly (agree/preferred) 3/2.51 – 3.50 = Moderately (agree/preferred) 4/3.51 – 4.50 = Agree/Preferred 5/4.51 – 5.00 = Highly (agree/preferred)		

Meanwhile, tuition fee (mean = 2.83, Moderately agree) was considered only to a lesser extent. This was consistent with the

findings of Bringula and Basa [6]. They argued that students had low rating on this indicator because it was their parents that decide whether they could afford to pay their tuition fees. While the students could choose the school they might enroll in, it was their parents who would ultimately decide whether they could afford to pay the tuition fee of that school [6].

The level of school choice of their school was 3.80 with a verbal interpretation of "Preferred." It is an indication that they like the University. However, in terms of rank of choice, most of the respondents reported that the University was only their second choice (f = 81, 41%) (Table is not shown.). This gives a vivid understanding of school choice of the students. Students may have chosen to study in the University but, given a chance, they would choose other Universities. However, it is unclear whether this behavior was the same as that of students of other Universities. It is also unknown as to why they did not opt to enroll in the school of their first choice. Further studies can shed light on this matter.

5.4 Factors Influencing School Choice

As shown in Table 5, Tuition Fee (beta = 0.206, $p < 0.01$) and Scholarship and Grants (beta = 0.203, $p < 0.01$) were the only institutional image indicators that influenced school choice. The small p-values of the predictors show that the results are unlikely to have arisen from sampling error. Interestingly, the beta values of Tuition Fee and Scholarship and Grants were almost equal. The findings suggest that both predictors have almost equal weights on contributing to predicting the level of school choice of the students. The findings confirm the studies of Hu and Hossler [9], Kankey and Quarterman [10], and Stanley and French [17].

Table 5. Regression on School Choice on Institutional Image Indicators

Predictors	Beta	p-value
Tuition Fee	**0.206**	**0.004**
Scholarship and Grants	**0.203**	**0.009**
Tuition Fee Payment Scheme	-0.053	0.530
Admission Process	0.025	0.766
Schedule of Classes	0.019	0.841
Degree Offerings	0.095	0.335
Facilities	0.150	0.065
Faculty Profile	0.012	0.924
Kinship Patronage	0.067	0.317
Security in Campus	-0.038	0.658
Accessibility	-0.004	0.957
F-value = 15.23; Sig. = 0.00; Adj. R^2 = 0.18		

It is observed that the two predictors of school choice are finance-related factors. It must be noted that the parents of the students have the capabilities to pay for their tuition fees. However, students are still seeking ways to receive financial grants from the University. Simply, it can be concluded that not only the ability to pay, but also the willingness to pay played a direct role in student college choice decisions [9]. Furthermore, these factors are accounted to explaining the 18% (Adj. R^2 = 0.18, F-value = 15.23, p-value < 0.01) variation in school choice. There are other variables (e.g., demographic variables, school atmosphere, sports affiliation, and affective institutional image) not included in the study that might predict school choice.

The finding also extended the result of Bringula's study [5] that school facilities predict school choice of first year students. This means that prospective entrants look first at the school facilities in deciding to enroll in the University. However, in the long run, it is the finance-related factors that will determine whether students will continue to enroll in the University. The implications of this finding are twofold. First, it confirms that the institutional policy of the University to freeze tuition fee increase for higher year students is a good marketing strategy. It is suggested that this practice be continued to able to attract possible entrants. Second, the finding has practical value. School marketers are encouraged to include this finding in their marketing strategies information dissemination.

5.5 Conclusion, Recommendations, and Future Research

The implementation of K-12 education in the Philippines prompted higher education institutions to formulate strategies at least to lessen its impending impact. One of these strategies is to attract now as many entrants as possible through marketing efforts. Toward this goal, this study aims to determine the factors that might influence school choice of computing students.

Based on the results of statistical analysis, the null hypothesis stating that institutional image indicators, singly or in combination, do not affect the level of school choice is partially rejected. Only tuition fee and scholarship and grants were the factors that influence level of school choice of computing students. Thus, only finance-related factors contributed to explaining the variation in school choice.

It was also shown that the University catered to two types of computing students in terms of economic status. It was also revealed that though students preferred the University, it was only their second choice. The marketers of the school were also the ones that persuaded the students to enroll in the University. It can be concluded that people with close tie relationship with the students were the sources of information about the University.

It is suggested that the current practice of freeze tuition fee increase for higher year students and the use of different marketing media be continued. It is also recommended that marketing campaign be directed to the parents, relatives, and siblings of the prospective students. In the marketing campaign, it is strongly suggested that facilities, tuition fee, and scholarship and grants of the University be emphasized. Lastly, it is proposed that other variables such as demographics, sports affiliation, and school atmosphere, be included in future studies.

6. ACKNOWLEDGMENTS

The authors are greatly indebted to Dr. Ester A. Garcia, Dr. Linda P. Santiago, Dr. Olivia C. Caoili, Dr. Socorro R. Villamejor, Dean Rodany A. Merida, Dr. Ma. Mercedes T. Rodrigo, Dr. Regina Estuar, Commission on Higher Education, Ateneo Laboratory Learning Sciences, and to all students who participated in the study.

7. REFERENCES

[1] Akbulut, A. Y., and Looney, C. A. 2007. Inspiring students to pursue computing degrees. *Communications of the ACM*, 50, 10 (Oct. 2007), 67-71.

[2] Arpan, L. M., Raney, A. A., and Zivnuska, S. 2003. A cognitive approach to understanding university image. *Corporate communications: An International Journal*, 8, 2, 97-113.

[3] Babin, R., Grant, K. A., and Sawal, L. 2010. Identifying influencers in high school student ICT career choice. *Information Systems Education Journal*, 8, 26 (June 2010), 1-18.

[4] Bringula, R. P. 2012. Influence of Proximity to and Accessibility of School on School Choice of Information Technology Students. In *Proceedings of the 13th ACM-SIGITE Annual Conference on Information Technology Education* (Calgary, Alberta, Canada, October 11-13, 2012). SIGITE 2012. ACM, New York, 19-24. DOI = http://doi.acm.org/10.1145/2380552.2380560.

[5] Bringula, R. P. 2013. Predictors of school choice of Information Technology students. In *Proceedings of the International Research Conference in Higher Education 2013* (Manila, Philippines, October 3-4, 2013). IRCHE 2013. Manila, 65.

[6] Bringula, R. P., and Basa, R. S. 2011. Institutional image indicators of three Universities: Basis for attracting prospectie entrants. *Educational Research for Policy and Practice*, 10, 1 (Feb 2011), 53-72.

[7] Dobni, D., and Zinkhan, G. M. 1990. In search of brand image: A foundation analysis. *Advances in Consumer Research*, 17, 1 (July 1990), 110–119.

[8] Education Act of 1982. Available at http://www.lawcenter.ph/law-library/laws/batas-ambansa/an-act-providing-for-the-establishment-and-maintenance-of-an-integrated-system-of-education/

[9] Hu, S., and Hossler, D. 2000. Willingness to pay and preference for private institutions. *Research in Higher Education*, 41, 6 (Dec 2000), 685–701.

[10] Kankey, K., and Quarterman, J. 2007. Factors influencing the university choice of NCAA Division I softball players. *The Smart Journal*, 3, 2 (Spring 2007), 35-49.

[11] Kazoleas, D., Kim, Y., and Moffit, M. A. 2001. Institutional image: A case study. *Corporate Communications: An International Journal*, 6, 4, 205-216.

[12] Kennedy, S. H. 1977. Nurturing corporate image. *European Journal of Marketing*, 11, 3, 120-164.

[13] Nguyen, N., and LeBlanc, G. 2001. Image and reputation of higher education institutions in students' retention decisions. *The International Journal of Educational Management*, 15, 6, 303-311.

[14] Peterson, K. 2006. Academic web site design and academic templates: Where does the library fit in?. *Information Technology and Libraries*, 25, 4, 217-221.

[15] Republic Act 10533. Available at www.gov.ph/2013/05/15/republic-act-no-10533/

[16] Soutar, G. N., and Turner, J. P. 2002. Students' preferences for university: A conjoint analysis. *The International Journal of Educational Management*, 16, 1, 40-45.

[17] Stanley, R. E., and French, P. E. 2009. Evaluating increased enrollment levels in institutions of higher education: A look at merit-based scholarship programs. *Public Administration Quarterly*, 33, 1 (Spring 2009), 4-36.

[18] Won Jae, S., Green, B., Yong Jae, K., Seunghwan, L., and Schenewark, J. 2007. The effect of web cohesion, web commitment, and attitude toward the website on intentions to use NFL teams' websites. *Sport Management Review (Sport Management Association of Australia & New Zealand)*, 10, 3, 231-252.

Big Data Trends and Evolution: A Human Perspective

Flavio Villanustre
LexisNexis & HPCC Systems
Alpharetta, GA,USA

Abstract

The Big Data revolution has already happened and, through it, organizations started realizing the potential of using data to take better informed decisions, mitigate risks and overall better control their destiny. With all the benefits that Big Data brings, it also creates new challenges; the growing talent gap possibly being the most representative of them all. In order to effectively leverage Big Data, a new profession is emerging: the data scientist. Tasked with understanding the methodologies to process and analyze vast and complex data, this professional must possess knowledge in a broad spectrum of domains, including mathematics (calculus, linear algebra, statistics, probabilities and even possibly category theory), programming languages (Python and R being frequently cited), data processing and analysis expertise (profiling, parsing, cleansing, linking), machine learning techniques (supervised and unsupervised learning, dimensionality reduction, feature selection, etc.) and business domain knowledge. While it is conceivable to identify individuals that can achieve this breadth of knowledge with significant depth, it is unreasonable to expect this to be the norm, so these individuals fall usually far into the upper tail of the population distribution. To make things worse, the current toolsets available to the data scientist tend to be very involved and require considerable amounts of time to develop applications, reducing the overall effectiveness of these experts. The solution to this talent gap is certainly not to try and breed a new step up the evolutionary ladder that can cope with this vast knowledge, but to create radically different abstractions as part of the toolsets that data scientists use, to increase efficiency and reduce the scope of the basic knowledge required to build Big Data applications.

During this presentation we will explore this challenge and provide a new perspective on more efficient toolsets for Big Data applications.

Categories and Subject Descriptors:
I.2.5 Computing Methodologies, ARTIFICIAL INTELLIGENCE, Programming Languages and Software: Expert system tools and techniques

Keywords
Data Science; Data Analysis; Declarative Programming; Dataflow Programming; KEL; ECL; HPCC

Short Bio
Dr. Flavio Villanustre, VP Technology Architecture & Product, for LexisNexis and HPCC Systems. In this position, Flavio is responsible for Information and Physical Security, overall infrastructure strategy and new product development. Prior to 2001, Dr. Villanustre served in different companies in a variety of roles in infrastructure, information security and information technology. In addition, Dr. Villanustre has been involved with the open source community for over 15 years through multiple initiatives. Some of these include founding the first Linux User Group in Buenos Aires (BALUG) in 1994, releasing several pieces of software under different open source licenses, and evangelizing open source to different audiences through conferences, training and education. Prior to his technology career, Dr. Villanustre was a neurosurgeon.

RIIT'14, October 15–18, 2014, Atlanta, Georgia, USA.
ACM 978-1-4503-2711-4/14/10.
http://dx.doi.org/10.1145/2656434.2657486

Author Index

Welcome from the Chair

Welcome to Atlanta!! Southern Polytechnic State University (SPSU) is your host institution for our 15th Annual SIGITE and 3rd Annual RIIT conferences. We are located in Marietta, GA – a bit northwest of downtown Atlanta. We hope your stay before, during and after the conference will allow you to see some of our great venues in and around the city.

Close to SPSU you will find Kennesaw Mountain (for those Civil War buffs), and the "General" Train Museum. For those interested in politics and history we have the President Carter Library, Dr. Martin Luther King memorial, Margaret Mitchell house, the Fernbank Museum of Natural History and the Swam House and Historical Center. In downtown Atlanta you can visit such things as the Atlanta Aquarium, CNN Center, Centennial Olympic Park, and the World of Coca-Cola. Cultural venues include the Fox Theater, High Museum, Atlanta Symphony and Center for Puppetry Arts. You can take a 90-minute Trolley tour around Atlanta to see highlights. Zoo Atlanta and Stone Mountain (with the carving of civil war historical figures – President Jefferson Davis, General Robert E. Lee and General Thomas "Stonewall" Jackson) offer full or half-day experiences. And, of course, the Atlanta Falcons may be playing as well.

Our Conference Hotel is the Atlanta Buckhead Marriott Hotel and Conference Center. Buckhead is located a bit northeast of downtown Atlanta. The hotel is also close to MARTA – our mass transit system. We have wonderful restaurants in Buckhead and downtown Atlanta. We have two lovely malls – Lenox Square and Phipps Plaza - close to the hotel. All in all, Atlanta offers you great cultural, culinary and fun activities. We hope you can take advantage of seeing some of these while you are here.

Our program chairs have done a wonderful job of coordinating our papers and workshops for the conference. We have a busy and active schedule. I wish each of you a great conference and exciting time in Atlanta!!

Becky Rutherfoord
Conference Chair

Program Chairs' Welcome

It is with great pleasure that we welcome you to the *15th Annual Conference on Information Technology Education (SIGITE 2014)* and the *3rd Annual Conference on Research in Information Technology (RIIT 2014)*. The theme this year is "Riding the Wave of Change in Information Technology" and the many quality submissions we received allowed us to assemble one of the strongest programs in the history of the conferences. As in past years, the synergies between research and education in information technology are prevalent, and several themes emerged from the accepted submissions. Networking, security, and development remain popular with researchers, and interest in mobile computing, resource measurement and management, capstone courses, and personalization has grown.

The call for participation attracted 111 submissions, 72 of which were submitted to SIGITE and 39 to RIIT. Both numbers represent a larger pool than in recent years, demonstrating that the conferences are of great interest in the community. Ninety-five of the submissions were papers, with 59 papers submitted to SIGITE and 36 papers submitted to RIIT. SIGITE has 27 papers in its program for an acceptance rate of 46% and RIIT has 14 papers for an acceptance rate of 39%. All of the authors presenting should be congratulated on their excellent work.

A conference cannot happen without the help of its reviewers, and this year was no exception. Fifty-five reviewers worked diligently to ensure that every paper had at least three independent reviews. It was a significant effort to produce the 317 reviews that ended up in the system, and we thank the reviewers from the bottom of our heart. New to the conferences this year was a meta review process, in which 13 diligent meta reviewers together examined all reviews for each submission and reconciled those reviews into a coherent message for each author. We hope the meta review process enabled authors to have more substantive feedback on their work, whether it appears in the final program or not.

The conference runs from Thursday to Saturday and each day offers something of interest to attendees. On Thursday our keynote speaker is Dr. Flavio Villanustre, Vice-President of Technology Architecture & Product for LexisNexis and HPCC Systems. The day continues with a workshop on end-user development activities and paper sessions for both SIGITE and RIIT. Thursday concludes with a reception, which we know will be useful for networking with colleagues old and new. Friday introduces a new presentation format, lightning talks on research in progress, at the conferences. There are also paper sessions for SIGITE and RIIT, a poster session in the afternoon and, of course, more opportunities for networking during lunch and the breaks. Saturday offers a three-hour workshop on process-oriented guided inquiry learning (POGIL) as well as a panel on mobile computing courses and some excellent SIGITE papers. We also hope that you stay for the closing session where we will share our plans for SIGITE/RIIT 2015 in Chicago.

We hope you find the conference presentations interesting and thought-provoking, you reconnect with colleagues you know, you find new collaborators, and you submit the work that results to SIGITE or RIIT next year. The excellence you see at SIGITE/RIIT 2014 depends on your energy and effort, and we thank you for letting us be a part of it.

Amber Settle and Terry Steinbach
SIGITE/RIIT 2014 Program Co-chairs
DePaul University, USA

Table of Contents

RIIT Poster

RIIT Paper Session 5

Session Chair: Richard Helps *(Brigham Young University)*

RIIT 2014 Conference Organization

General Chair: Becky Rutherfoord *(Southern Polytechnic State University, USA)*

Assisting Co-Chairs: Lei Li *(Southern Polytechnic State University, USA)* and Susan VandeVen *(Southern Polytechnic State University, USA)*

Program Co-Chairs: Amber Settle *(DePaul University, USA)* and Terry Steinbach *(DePaul University, USA)*

Logistics Co-Chairs: Jon Preston *(Southern Polytechnic State University, USA)* and Greg Scott *(Southern Polytechnic State University, USA)*

Publicity Co-Chairs: Jack Zheng *(Southern Polytechnic State University, USA)* and Dawn Tatum *(Southern Polytechnic State University, USA)*

Registration Chair: Ashley McClure *(Southern Polytechnic State University, USA)*

Materials Co-Chairs: Marilee McClure *(Southern Polytechnic State University, USA)*, Faith Gonzales *(Southern Polytechnic State University, USA)*, and Jasmine Watkins *(Southern Polytechnic State University, USA)*

Meta-reviewers: *In alphabetical order*
By Last Name
Joseph J. Ekstrom *(Brigham Young University, USA)*
Rob Friedman *(UW Tacoma, USA)*
Derek L. Hansen *(Brigham Young University, USA)*
Richard Helps *(Brigham Young University, USA)*
Rick Homkes *(Purdue College of Technology, USA)*
Jim Leone *(Rochester Institute of Technology, USA)*
Barry M. Lunt *(Brigham Young University, USA)*
Bonnie MacKellar *(St. John's University, USA)*
Craig S. Miller *(DePaul University, USA)*
Mihaela Sabin *(University of New Hampshire, USA)*
Edward Sobiesk *(United States Military Academy, USA)*

Reviewers:

SIGITE RIIT 2014 Sponsor & Supporters

Sponsor:

Supporters:

ORACLE ACADEMY

In
cooperation
with:

Big Data Trends and Evolution: A Human Perspective

Flavio Villanustre
LexisNexis & HPCC Systems
Alpharetta, GA,USA

Abstract

The Big Data revolution has already happened and, through it, organizations started realizing the potential of using data to take better informed decisions, mitigate risks and overall better control their destiny. With all the benefits that Big Data brings, it also creates new challenges; the growing talent gap possibly being the most representative of them all. In order to effectively leverage Big Data, a new profession is emerging: the data scientist. Tasked with understanding the methodologies to process and analyze vast and complex data, this professional must possess knowledge in a broad spectrum of domains, including mathematics (calculus, linear algebra, statistics, probabilities and even possibly category theory), programming languages (Python and R being frequently cited), data processing and analysis expertise (profiling, parsing, cleansing, linking), machine learning techniques (supervised and unsupervised learning, dimensionality reduction, feature selection, etc.) and business domain knowledge. While it is conceivable to identify individuals that can achieve this breadth of knowledge with significant depth, it is unreasonable to expect this to be the norm, so these individuals fall usually far into the upper tail of the population distribution. To make things worse, the current toolsets available to the data scientist tend to be very involved and require considerable amounts of time to develop applications, reducing the overall effectiveness of these experts. The solution to this talent gap is certainly not to try and breed a new step up the evolutionary ladder that can cope with this vast knowledge, but to create radically different abstractions as part of the toolsets that data scientists use, to increase efficiency and reduce the scope of the basic knowledge required to build Big Data applications.

During this presentation we will explore this challenge and provide a new perspective on more efficient toolsets for Big Data applications.

Categories and Subject Descriptors:
I.2.5 Computing Methodologies, ARTIFICIAL INTELLIGENCE, Programming Languages and Software: Expert system tools and techniques

Keywords
Data Science; Data Analysis; Declarative Programming; Dataflow Programming; KEL; ECL; HPCC

Short Bio
Dr. Flavio Villanustre, VP Technology Architecture & Product, for LexisNexis and HPCC Systems. In this position, Flavio is responsible for Information and Physical Security, overall infrastructure strategy and new product development. Prior to 2001, Dr. Villanustre served in different companies in a variety of roles in infrastructure, information security and information technology. In addition, Dr. Villanustre has been involved with the open source community for over 15 years through multiple initiatives. Some of these include founding the first Linux User Group in Buenos Aires (BALUG) in 1994, releasing several pieces of software under different open source licenses, and evangelizing open source to different audiences through conferences, training and education. Prior to his technology career, Dr. Villanustre was a neurosurgeon.

RIIT'14, October 15–18, 2014, Atlanta, Georgia, USA.
ACM 978-1-4503-2711-4/14/10.
http://dx.doi.org/10.1145/2656434.2657486

Eye Tracking Data Understanding for Product Representation Studies

Brandeis H. Marshall[*]
Purdue University
401 N. Grant Street
West Lafayette, Indiana 47907
brandeis@purdue.edu

Shweta Sareen[†]
Purdue University
401 N. Grant Street
West Lafayette, Indiana 47907
ssareen@purdue.edu

John A. Springer
Purdue University
401 N. Grant Street
West Lafayette, Indiana 47907
jaspring@purdue.edu

Tahira Reid
Purdue University
585 Purdue Mall
West Lafayette, Indiana 47907
tahira@purdue.edu

ABSTRACT

Within the mechanical engineering discipline, product representation studies have been used to inform engineers on the suitability of their product designs for prospective customers. However, these studies are mainly based in customers' oral responses leading engineers to modify the product design accordingly. In contrast, we consider the eye tracking data associated with customer judgments of 2D and 3D product representation studies. Eye tracking data contains unforeseen facts and patterns not captured through customers' oral responses. In this research, we conduct data analysis and present a set of features for analyzing similar eye tracking studies. These features include (1) question-based analysis, (2) question and category dependencies, (3) product and category dependencies, (4) gender impact and (5) experiment repeatability situations. In addition, a brief comparison of the 2D and 3D product representation experiments is described for each feature.

Categories and Subject Descriptors

H.1.2 [**User/Machine Systems**]: Human information processing; H.3.3 [**Information Search and Retrieval**]: Information filtering; H.2.1 [**Logical Design**]: Data models

---

[*]Brandeis Marshall is now in the Department of Computer and Information Sciences at Spelman College.

[†]This work is an excerpt of Shweta Sareen's Master's Thesis. She is now employed at Bank Of America Merrill Lynch.

RIIT'14, October 15-18, 2014, Atlanta, Georgia, USA.
Copyright 2014 ACM 978-1-4503-2711-4/14/10 ...$15.00.
http://dx.doi.org/10.1145/2656434.2656439.

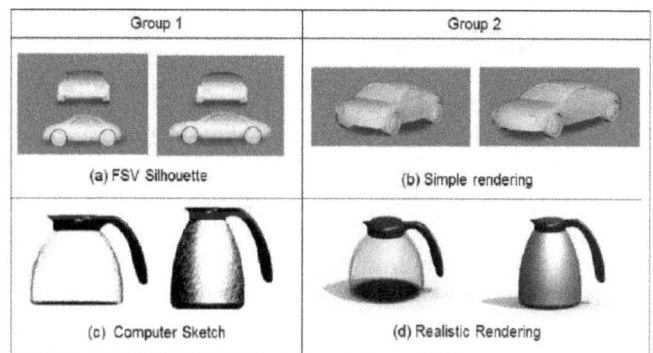

Figure 1: 2D and 3D Product Representation Examples

Keywords

product representations; mind-eye hypothesis; knowledge management

1. INTRODUCTION

This study used eye-tracking data to examine question, category, product and gender differences in subjects' interactions with two and three dimensional product drawings. [2]. These product observations reveal opinions, emotions and preferences through studying an individual's thought process related to what is viewed, which is also called the mind-eye hypothesis [5]. The eye tracking data has the potential to uncover previously hidden commonalities amongst the participants and/or products. It becomes relevant in predicting subjects' understanding and preferences in order to better inform the product design process. The mechanical engineering field is an example discipline that could benefit from this study. As mechanical drawings become complex, it is crucial to not only understand the design but also the design's intended processes. This research's significance lies in laying the groundwork in providing product designers scientific evidence as to how to better interpret participant feedback about products in the designing process.

In this research, we perform preliminary data analysis on two eye tracking product representation studies conducted by Reid et al. [9]. One experiment viewed the FSV silhouettes and computer sketches (2D renderings) and the second experiment viewed the realistic and simplified renderings (3D renderings) as depicted in Figure 1. These studies divided the participants into two randomly-selected groups of 31 subjects each. The participants' demographic information was also collected including their age ranges, educational backgrounds and professions. The product categories are cars, coffee carafes, golf tees and miscellaneous products. Each experiment recorded the participants' product design evaluation through responding to three question categories: (1) opinion, e.g., preference and stylishness, (2) objective evaluation, e.g., width, length and height and (3) inferences, e.g., recyclability, heat retention and fuel efficiency. The resulting eye tracking data consists of scenes with x-y coordinates based on participant, question and product category.

The contributions of this study is to:

- present initial common characteristics for product design that are affiliated with question, product and category elements, and

- showcase a working example of eye tracking data analysis, e.g., data cleaning, data modeling, database design and implementation and finding relevant data patterns.

Section 2 discusses the related work of product representation studies and eye tracking research. Section 3 describes the eye tracking factors of interest to product design evaluations. Section 4 demonstrates the usefulness of these factors through query analysis and results. We conclude and summarize the paper in Section 5.

2. RELATED LITERATURE

2.1 Product Representation Studies

Product representations and its impact on design has been studied not only to capture consumer's choices, opinions, judgments and buying preferences but also to receive design recommendations. HCI researchers often conduct such studies as a part of usability testing. Products presented digitally and their observation leads to uncovering patterns of usability and interest, for both the product and the subject. Lai, Chang and Chang [6] analyze the human affection to a product by using a car and its different representations. Their work will help product designers improve their product design and achieve proximity to target feelings and target specific markets. The consumer's response to the visual domain in product design has been studied in literature [3].

Creusen and Schoormans [2] used product representation to elicit consumer choices, this would help the people manufacturing these products to increase profits as they would be able to design and manufacture products conforming to user's choice. They determined six different roles of product appearance for consumers and then suggested how appearance of a product plays a role in consumer product evaluation and choice and hence this is an example of how product representations are used to determine choices of people that can impact the business of these products. Similar studies [8]. Maeng, Lim and Lee (2012) have also been done to see what captures subject's attention. In Pieters and

Wede [8], advertising had benefitted greatly by using these techniques to increase a product's sale. Maeng et al. [7] proposed user-product interaction concepts to reveal user's needs and functions rather than leveraging technology needs or use cases. The subject better understands her needs as a result of building and using the methods while informing product designers of how to improve the quality of their products.

2.2 Eye Tracking and Eye Fixation Research

Eye fixation research in cognitive psychology dates to the mid 1970's [5], which proposed that "the rapid mental operations of the central processor (active memory) can be revealed by analysis of eye fixation during a task involving visual input and hence it is possible to understand various memory tasks by studying this model" (p.1). This area of research definitely proves that a person's thought processes to a great extent are defined by what they are viewing at that point in time. This piece of research showed possibilities of analysis of eye fixation data in interpreting interesting facts not only about the product being viewed but also the subject viewing it. Just and Carpenter [5] explains that eye fixations can depict thought process and hence prove useful in making many recommendations about the subject. When a subject's verbal responses and eye movements are tracked simultaneously, product designers can better determine what she is looking at exactly. Researchers have also used eye tracking as a tool to determine what the person actually perceives and thinks, which helps make stronger recommendations about the product, its design and usability.

Eye tracking studies draw interesting perspectives to various phenomena. The impact eye movement monitoring [4] has been studied as a process tracing methodology in decision making research. The authors directly relate eye movements to producing a process tracing mathematical model and in turn infer how humans make decisions. The study signifies the new direction of using the eye tracking data for analyzing human thought process along with high end techniques like neuroimaging. Strandvall [11] combines HCI and eye tracking research by devising a system that records the eye movements while a subject is completing a task for example on a web site. By analyzing these eye movements, researchers can record the subject's behavior. The behavioral reactions have been studied and applied to understand usability preferences of people. In contrast to prior eye tracking research, Sahin et al. [10] center on the designers' perspective. It focusses on changes in designer's evaluation with changing media unlike other studies that focus on gathering customer preferences to improve designs rather than understanding the designer's perception.

We use Reid et al.'s work [9] as the testbed of our experimentation since it addresses multiple dimensions of eye tracking research such as opinions (refers to product evaluations for which there is no right or wrong), objective evaluations (product evaluations of a measurable quantity) and inferences (conclusions that cannot be made by observation alone). These dimensions' impact differ based on the products' representation modes. By presenting some factors to consider when analyzing eye tracking data, we can use these findings to better inform similar eye tracking studies. In particular, we are working toward formulating interdependen-

FixIn	Time	FixT	MF_X	MF_Y	Stim	ProdNo	SubjectNo
367	123625	658	439	397	S14	10055.12	SU01

(a) *2D unprocessed data sample*

FixT	X	Y	Scene	Question	Category	Product	SubjectNo
658	439	397	S14	100	55	12	SU01

(b) *2D processed data sample*

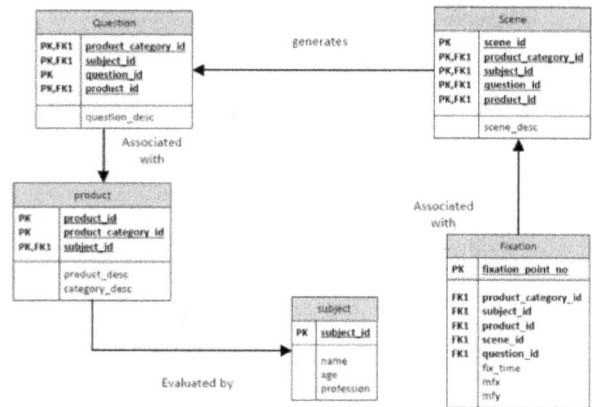

(c) *Entity-Relationship Diagram*

Figure 2: Eye tracking data

cies and correlations amongst subjects, products, questions and designs.

3. DATA FEATURES OF INTEREST

The Tobii eye tracker captures the subject's eye movements while they were taking the 2D and 3D product representation surveys. In Figure 2a, we display a sample of the pre-processed Tobii raw data structure. The first three columns were redundant and not required. The fourth column FixT gives the total fixation time of the subject for the current (x,y) coordinate on the screen in milliseconds. The MF_X and MF_Y features are the (x,y) coordinates of the screen where the subject is fixated for that FixT time. Stim is the scene number. The ProdNo is an number string appending the question, category and product ID(s) to a particular fixation instance. As such, the first three digits are the question ID, the next two digits are the category ID and the digits after the point are product/products identifier depending on if there are one or two digits after the dot. The two digits after the dot depict two separate product identifiers in the scene. The last column is the subject identifier. We proceeded to clean the data (Figure 2b) and structured it for more effective data management. Based on conversations with those who conducted the 2D and 3D product representation studies, we present the database design in Figure 2c. We propagate the subject identifier to each database table subject understanding will be analyzed throughout this study. As such, we identify several data features and feature combinations that are of interest to these studies and would most likely be used in similar eye tracking studies.

3.1 Question Analysis

Question analysis is identifying how subjects' respond to different types of questions over the duration of the experiment. These questions assist product designers in pinpointing the necessary element to the final product design. As a result, the questions impact the product as well as the subject. By collectively analyzing the opinion, objective evaluation and inference questions, researchers can infer impact of certain questions (or group of questions) and/or influence on subjects. Within each question type, a subject's judgement and her behavior may have unexpected interdependence. A particular question type could indicate her increased interest (or the corollary, difficulty) in answering a question.

3.2 Question and Category analysis

The question and category analysis evaluates the correlation between the seven question types and the specific product category. We consider which product category takes more time for each question and then infer a subject's acquaintance with the selected products. For example, between opinion, inferences and objective evaluation, subjects may find it easier to give an opinion about a familiar category like a car but for the same familiar category, they may take more time to objectively evaluate.

3.3 Product and Category Analysis

For the opinion and inference categories, products are viewed in pairs while for the objective evaluation category, single products are displayed. The product and category analysis aims to assess which product/product-pair is more interesting to the subject, product/product pair or its features are difficult to interpret for the subject or which question associated with the product/product-pair was more difficult for the subject to respond. Studies comparing certain day to day products, which belong to separate categories, could use these observations to inform how fixation times vary across categories and whether it depicts patterns of interest. Inferences like which category is familiar and which design makes the category look simpler could be very informative in the design process.

3.4 Gender Analysis

To the best of our knowledge, eye tracking studies have not specifically addressed the role of a subject's gender in contributing to product, category and question evaluations. The familiarity with products and interpretation of questions can vary for subjects and gender can be an important factor in isolating commonalities and differences. By concentrating on a subject's gender, we inquire if eye tracking data is a suitable information source of determining the influence of gender in subjects' judgements. In addition, our initial gender analysis acknowledges the impact of gender on product design selection.

3.5 Repeated Exposure Analysis

Repeated exposure experiments have one unknown variable: the subjects. In our case, the products, category and questions are the control variables so the experiment scenes remain consistent across both 2D and 3D product representation studies. In a prior repeated exposure study and its impacts on choice, "the results suggest that preferences for visually complex product designs tend to increase with repeated exposure, while preferences for visually simple product designs tend to decrease with repeated exposure." [1]. We aim to analyze the changes in opinion of different subjects when they are made to view the same scene. The difference in time and choice patterns may be an indication of changing the the participation population or the product design for the same exact scene.

4. EXPERIMENTAL STUDY

In this section, we describe the experimental evaluation of two product representation studies in which subjects were observed and data was collected using the Tobii Technology. We conducted an initial eye tracking data analysis for product representation studies focussing on the five data features presented in the previous section. We discuss the experimental setup in more depth and the corresponding results.

4.1 Experimental setup

The original experiment [9] surveyed two groups of 31 participants, 15 women and 16 men each. One group viewed 73 scenes and answered questions concerning 2D product representations while the other group viewed 78 scenes and responded to questions about 3D product representations. The 2D and 3D study participant demographics were similar with varying age ranges (18-65) and nearly evenly split between those who were college-educated and those who had degrees beyond college. The opinion (preference and stylishness), objective evaluation (width, length and height) and inference (recyclability, heat retention and fuel efficiency) question types are asked in the same order; however, the actual questions are randomly shown. The cars, coffee carafes, golf tees and miscellaneous product categories are not used for each question type in both studies. Also note that the Tobii eye tracking data collected only included the (x,y) coordinates from the selected area that included the product/product pairs. Single product was shown for objective evaluation and products were shown in pairs for inference and opinion category questions.

4.2 Results

We conducted a series of experiments to showcase the applicability of the five relevant eye tracking data features. We use the average time (per scene) as our performance metric. Due to insignificant representation of participants in each demographic, in particular, educational background, we are unable to conduct an in-depth data analysis e.g., hypothesis testing using a t-test. With more studies, we could perform a comprehensive statistical analysis and provide appropriate supporting evidence. These results are meant to share initial observations. Due to space restrictions, we present a subset of our outcomes from the experimental evaluation.

Question Analysis.

In Figure 3, we display the average time spent per scene per question type for all subjects in the 2D and 3D product representation studies. As expected, the 3D average times of preference questions are slightly elevated due to it being the first question type viewed by all subjects. The width questions are observed as having the highest average time. We hypothesize that the depth perception needed to respond to all objective evaluation questions, and in particular, width, is difficult. Hence, the subjects required more time to render a response. Also, the average time did not vary significantly between the 2D and 3D product representation. Most 3D average times are slightly lower than the 2D average times. Further verification and validation experiments are required to support our claim.

Question ID	2D Avg (sec)	3D Avg (sec)
Preference	7.980	8.240
Stylishness	6.250	5.907
Width	15.764	14.289
Length	14.663	12.651
Height	12.258	11.889
Inference set one	6.997	6.321
Inference set two	6.304	6.578

Figure 3: Average time spent per question for 2D and 3D studies

Question and Category Analysis.

We examine how category selection impact question type and display the results in Figure 4(a)-(c). Building on our observation that objective evaluations have higher average times, we notice that the miscellaneous category takes more time than the other three categories. In subsequent eye tracking studies, we suggest removing this category. Subjects may be too unfamiliar with products and/or product variation implying experimental design bias.

Product and Category Analysis.

We examine how actual 2D and 3D product representations may attribute to the average viewing time of the subjects. There were 33 unique product combinations viewed by the subjects in both the experiments. We show the 2D single product and product pair results in Figure 4(d) and (e). The 3D outcomes were very similar. Single products were viewed for objective evaluation questions to better assess the width, length and heights of the product representations, and thus, the average times are higher than for 2D product pairs. Car image 3, 4 and 9 have higher average times than the other single products using in the study. For 2D product pairs, car images (4, 9) and (2, 5) report higher average times relative to the other combinations. Interestingly, car images (9, 4) did not report a similar average time. To better understand the source and/or cause of this difference, further investigation is warranted. We hypothesize that golf tee image 5 has special characteristics since the average time of golf tee images (2, 4) is nearly 50% of golf tee images (2, 5).

Gender Role Analysis.

The initial evaluation of gender in product representation studies starts with calculated the overall total average time men and women dedicated to completing the surveys. In

	Preference Questions		Stylishness Questions	
Category	2D Avg (sec)	3D Avg (sec)	2D Avg (sec)	3D Avg (sec)
Cars	8.906	8.270	6.980	6.522
Coffee Carafes	6.559	7.496	5.608	5.290
Golf Tees	8.555	7.772	5.724	N/A
Miscellaneous	9.193	11.083	N/A	N/A

(a) 2D and 3D Opinion Questions and Category Results

	Width Questions		Length Questions		Height Questions	
Category	2D Avg (sec)	3D Avg (sec)	2D Avg (sec)	3D Avg (sec)	2D Avg (sec)	3D Avg (sec)
Cars	18.835	14.940	14.663	14.663	11.624	10.680
Coffee Carafes	14.224	12.644	N/A	N/A	12.494	11.944
Golf Tees	12.625	N/A	N/A	N/A	12.773	13.072
Miscellaneous	N/A	14.462	N/A	N/A	N/A	N/A

(b) 2D and 3D Objective Evaluation Questions and Category Results

	Inference Set 1 Questions		Inference Set 2 Questions	
Category	2D Avg (sec)	3D Avg (sec)	2D Avg (sec)	3D Avg (sec)
Cars	6.940	6.065	N/A	N/A
Coffee Carafes	6.878	5.984	6.348	6.459
Golf Tees	7.816	6.500	6.047	6.820
Miscellaneous	7.245	9.354	N/A	N/A

(c) 2D and 3D Inference Questions and Category Results

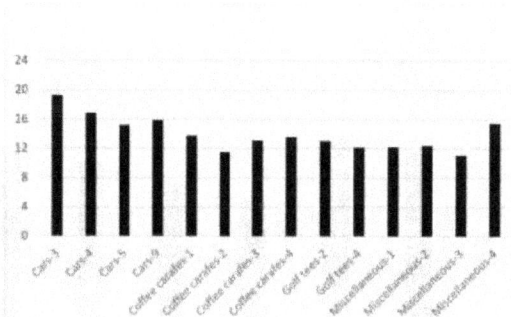

(d) 2D Single Product and Category Results

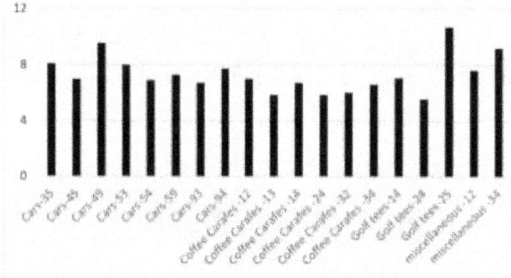

(e) 2D Product Pairs and Category Results

Figure 4: Category Analysis by Question and by Product

our 2D product representation study, men took an average of 613.365 seconds while for women, it was 648.280 seconds. Our 3D product representation study produced the same observation that women took slightly longer with average times of 645.376 and 691.697 seconds, respectively.

We then investigated the role of gender on three product categories as an initial indication of product preference. We are interested in capturing if men or women gravitate to particular categories and if so, whether this tendency (positivity or negatively) motivates their survey responses. More varying and traditionally gender-specific product categories are needed to fully execute this future work. For these two studies, the product categories were not selected with gender analysis as a consideration so the researchers assumed that these categories were equally familiar to men and women.

Figure 5 and 6 denote the average time spent by men and women on product categories for both studies. We observe that men fixate more on the 2D product categories while women fixate more on the 3D product categories. Also, the average times reported between the two studies varied minimally. We are motivated to see if this trend can be generalized as it would have a greater societal impact on business marketing, e.g., women may provide greater yield on 2D marketing campaigns, and curriculum material development, e.g., women may comprehend a product design concept at a different rate than their male counterparts.

Repeated Exposure Analysis.

Within the opinion question type, the same car and coffee carafes were shown for 2D and 3D experiments. Hence, the whole scene remained same (the product, category, question remains the same) and only the design changes. We explore the repeated scene exposure in an effort to see if only the

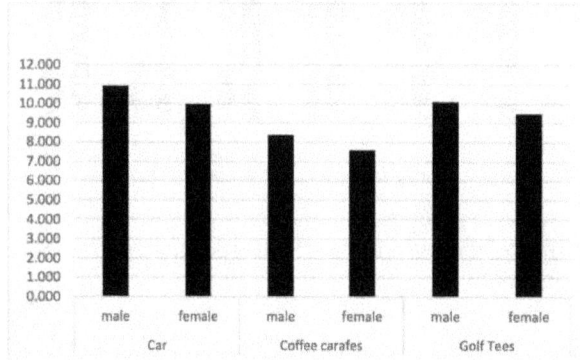

Figure 5: Average time spent on 2D product representation study by gender and category

design change impacts the opinions (preference and stylishness) of the subjects who view them.

In Figure 7 and 8, we show the preference questions results for both cars and coffee carafes. Even though Figure 7's average times are similar for most repeated 2D and 3D scenes, car images (3, 5) and (5, 3) are the exception, in which there is a nearly 2 second differential for the 3D product representation study. Figure 8 shows that consistently subjects took less time 2D repeated scenes in choosing products than for the 3D repeated scenes.

5. CONCLUSIONS

In this research, we make strives to identify general eye tracking data characteristics and test our characteristics on prior product representation studies [9]. The 2D and 3D

7

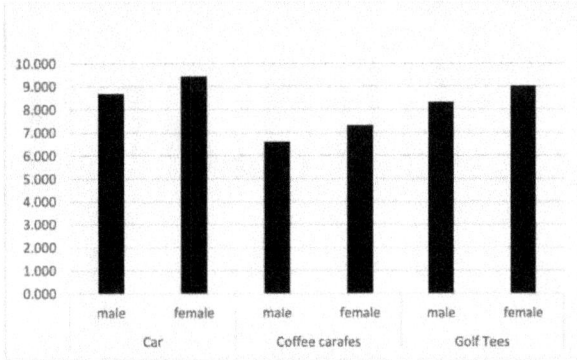

Figure 6: Average time spent on 3D product representation study by gender and category

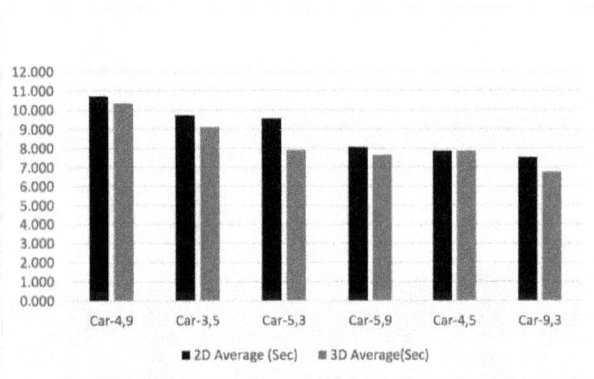

Figure 7: Car scenes with preference questions in 2D and 3D

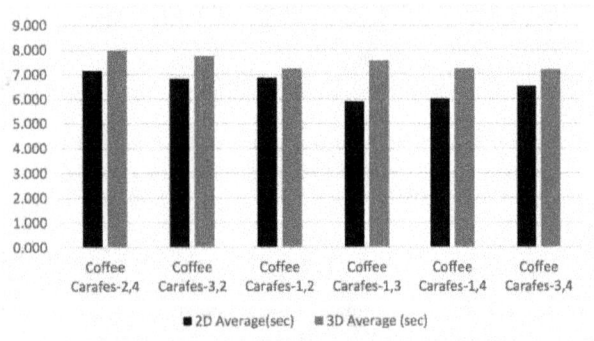

Figure 8: Coffee carafes scenes with preference questions in 2D and 3D

product representation studies consists of a total of 62 male and female participants who varied in age range and educational backgrounds. Each study focused on seven question types across the three question categories and four product categories. This research explored the impact of question, question and category interdependencies, product and category correlations, product judgement differences based on gender and repeated scene exposure for different study participant groups.

By using the average time spent viewing each scene, we observe that objective evaluations (width, length and height question types) are indeed the most time consuming questions while evaluating products. Both 2D and 3D subject groups found it more challenging to gauge width, length and height regardless of product category. As expected, the miscellaneous product category reported the highest average times spent per scene since product familiarity varied amongst the subjects. The role of gender produced a surprising observation: women spent slightly less time (on average) for cars, coffee carafes and golf tees in the 2D study, but slightly more time (on average for the same product categories in the 3D study. For the repeated exposure scenes, we observe some average time consistencies across both experiments. This data evaluation provides a potential template for handling similarly designed eye tracking studies.

6. REFERENCES

[1] D. Cox and A. D. Cox. Beyond first impressions: The effects of repeated exposure on consumer liking of visually complex and simple product designs. *Journal of the Academy of Marketing Science*, 30(2):119–130, 2002.

[2] M. E. Creusen and J. P. Schoormans. The different roles of product appearance in consumer choice. *Journal of Product Innovation Management*, 22(1):68–81, 2005.

[3] N. Crilly, J. Moultrie, and P. J. Clarkson. Seeing things: Consumer response to the visual domain in product design. *Design Studies*, 25(6):557–577, 2004.

[4] M. G. Glaholt and E. M. Reingold. Eye movement monitoring as a process tracing methodology in decision making research. *Journal of Neuroscience Psychology and Economics*, 4(2):125–146, 2011.

[5] M. A. Just and P. A. Carpenter. The role of eye-fixation research in cognitive psychology. *Behavior Research Methods and Instrumentation*, 8(2):139–143, 1976.

[6] H. H. Lai, Y. M. Chang, and H. C. Chang. A robust design approach for enhancing the feeling quality of a product: a car profile case study. *International Journal of Industrial Ergonomics*, 35(5):445–460, 2005.

[7] S. Maeng, Y. K. Lim, and K. Lee. Interaction-driven design: A new approach for interactive product development. In *Proceedings of the Designing Interactive Systems Conference*, pages 448–457, 2012.

[8] R. Pieters and M. Wedel. Attention capture and transfer in advertising: Brand, pictorial, and text-size effects. *Journal of Marketing*, 68(2):36–50, 2004.

[9] T. Reid, E. MacDonald, and P. Du. Impact of product design representation on customer judgment with associated eye gaze patterns. In *ASME International Design Engineering Technical Conference/Design Theory and Methodology*, pages 749–762, 2012.

[10] A. Sahin, M. Boe, J. Terpenny, and J. H. Bohn. A study to understand perceptual discrepancies using visual illusions and data envelopment analysis. *Journal of Mechanical Design*, 129(7):744–752, 2007.

[11] T. Strandvall. Eye tracking in human-computer interaction and usability research. In *Lecture Notes in Computer Science Volume 5727*, pages 936–937, 2012.

Software Architecture Model Driven Reverse Engineering Approach to Open Source Software Development

William Kim
Computer Science & Systems
Institute of Technology
University of Washington
Tacoma, WA, USA
1-253-249-3985
willkim@uw.edu

Sam Chung
School of Info. Sys. & Applied Tech.
College of Applied Arts & Sciences
Southern Illinois University
Carbondale, IL, USA
1-618-453-7279
samchung@siu.edu

Barbara Endicott-Popovsky
Center for Information Assurance &
Cybersecurity
University of Washington
Seattle, WA, USA
1-206-240-0345
endicott@uw.edu

ABSTRACT

Popular Open Source Software (OSS) development platforms like GitHub, Google Code, and Bitbucket take advantage of some best practices of traditional software development like version control and issue tracking. Current major open source software environments, including IDE tools and online code repositories, do not provide support for visual architecture modeling. Research has shown that visual modeling of complex software projects has benefits throughout the software lifecycle. Then why is it that software architecture modeling is so conspicuously missing from popular online open source code repositories? How can including visual documentation improve the overall quality of open source software projects? Our goal is to answer both of these questions and bridge the gap between traditional software engineering best practices and open source development by applying a software architecture documentation methodology using Unified Modeling Language, called 5W1H Re-Doc, on a real open source project for managing identity and access, MITREid Connect. We analyze the effect of a model-driven software engineering approach on collaboration of open source contributors, quality of specification conformance, and state-of-the-art of architecture modeling. Our informal experiment revealed that in some cases, having the visual documentation can significantly increase comprehension of an online OSS project over having only the textual information that currently exists for that project.

Categories and Subject Descriptors

D.2.7 [**Software Engineering**]: Distribution, Maintenance, and Enhancement - *Documentation, Enhancement, Extensibility, Restructuring, reverse engineering, and reengineering*.

Keywords

Open Source Software Development, Software Architecture Documentation, Model-Driven Software Engineering

1. INTRODUCTION

Open Source Software (OSS) development allows for distributed collaboration on software projects that can sometimes compare in the size and scope of traditional enterprise applications. Mainstream online OSS development hubs such as GitHub[1], Google code[2], and Bitbucket[3] have evolved to fit the needs of a globally dispersed population of developers. All three of these sites incorporate an Agile-like iterative development approach with a system of continual code changes using one or more of the major version control systems, allowing for highly flexible change control and release cycles, a necessity in today's constantly changing tech landscape. Project management is performed using a system of issue tracking, tasking, and comment system, which encourages the social angle of the online development process.

The general OSS development pattern may not necessarily map directly to the stages of traditional software development life cycle—requirements, design, implementation, testing, and maintenance. We can see that the common lifecycle of OSS iteration—1) Report bug. 2a) Developer is tasked or 2b) code pull request is submitted. 3) Change is committed to the code base—fits tightly to the highly iterative implementation, testing, and maintenance loop. But what happens further back at the beginning of the engineering process, namely the requirements and the design process?

Currently, the vast majority of design and requirements manifest in the form of developer documentation [1]. These take various forms such as like public wiki pages, getting-started articles, reference documentations, engineering specifications like IETF RFCs, code comments, etc. At this point, we would like to note that this documentation is essentially all textual information and move on to the second key focus of this paper.

It is a foundational principle of software engineering that a good design is critical towards the success of a complex and large software project. Visual modeling of software architecture as part of the design efforts can have significant benefits to the software maintenance process. In particular, Unified Modeling Language (UML), which has become the industry standard for software modeling, has been shown to significantly improve correctness of

---

[1] GitHub, https://github.com/
[2] Google Code, https://code.google.com/
[3] Bitbucket, https://bitbucket.org/

changes by those who used it while adding an insignificant overhead of maintaining the UML documentation [2].

The study referenced above [2] did not deal with the OSS community, which may add other variables such as the technical qualifications of current and potential contributors. However, we assert that having visual documentation in the form of UML models can have a positive impact on OSS development. At the very least, additional meaningful documentation may draw in more newcomers who choose open source projects based strictly on the availability of good starter documentation to break into the project [3].

Despite the opportunity for highly distributed participation, many OSS projects are highly centralized (See Table 1). This reflects a challenging situation where very few people (sometimes a single individual) are managing the development and health of any given large OSS project. Perhaps not surprisingly, the quality of OSS project has been shown to go down as the number of minor contributors (low expertise) goes up [3]. Improvements can be made to increase the effectiveness of distributed development in OSS, both for the managers of such projects and the distributed contributors to those projects.

Table 1. OSS project participation

(*Top three most starred GitHub projects. †Top contributors measured by number of code commits. Data gathered on May 6, 2014.)

Project Name	Total # of Contributors	Top Contributor† % of Commits	Top 3 Contributors % of Commits
twbs/bootstrap*	597	57.6	77.2
jquery/jquery*	223	30.6	49.1
joyent/node*	571	30.5	61.1
openssl/openssl	47	29.9	64.7
mitreid-connect/OpenID-Connect-Java-Spring-Server	18	56.6	82.4

UML is at least part of the answer for development in the traditional enterprise software. Software giant IBM champions its use and develops products for implementing UML processes[4]. However, UML is a massive framework and may not all be appropriate for the fast-paced, iterative development needs of the OSS community. That is why we propose the use of a re-documentation methodology known as 5W1H Re-documentation, based loosely on the journalistic 5 W's and 1 H of Who, What, When, Where, Why, and How [4]. This approach strips down the UML framework to apply the core needs of re-documenting a legacy system. We hope to apply this methodology to the OSS development processes and maintain the benefits observed for more traditional enterprise software endeavors.

2. PREVIOUS WORK

In Table 2, we identify the three key papers that we use as the groundwork of our research.

[4] IBM Rational Unified Modeling Language - UML Resource Center, www.ibm.com/software/rational/uml/. May 2014

Table 2. Key topics in previous work

Paper	OSS Development	UML	Architecture Modeling Best Practices
Dzidek et al. [2]	no	yes	no
Dagenais & Robillard [1]	yes	no	no
Chung et al. [4]	no	yes	yes

The paper by Dzidek et al. [2], which contains an empirical study of the effect of UML on the maintenance of real software projects, is the basis of two aspects of our research. First, it provides the motivation for considering the benefits of using UML and software architecture modeling in general for OSS development. Second, it provides us with a rigorous example of how we can empirically test whether using UML benefits software development. The main conclusion of this paper is that additional overhead of using UML did not have a significant impact on the time it took for software maintenance tasks while having a statistically significant positive impact on the functional correctness of those changes. This clearly shows some benefits to using UML under the conditions set in this paper's experiment. This paper also has the usefulness of demonstrating how the benefits of using UML can be actually tested. One of problems is concerning exactly that, except in the online OSS environment (see Section 3 for exact problem statement).

The paper by Dagenais and Robillard [1] explores various types of documentation (albeit all textual forms of documentation) and their effects on decisions of open source contributors. These decisions include whether or not to contribute to certain projects in the first place, the extent and quality of code contributions, and the amount of effort invested in documentation creation and maintenance. One of the key findings of this paper was how different types of developer documentation had different effects (both positive and negative) on certain factors such as quality of contributions and additional maintenance overhead. Even though all the types of documentation in this study were textual forms, it goes to show how not just the existence and quantity of documentation is important, but the type as well.

As new developers and implementers encounter a new software project or system, there is a need to understand it as quickly and effectively as possible. Visual architecture modeling can be a great asset for the aiding comprehension of a new project. Kruchten's landmark paper on the 4+1 Views architecture modeling in 1995 gave us some high-level guidelines on how architecture of a software project can be abstracted [5]. However, we need more guidelines for best practices on what to do about an existing project that did not have this kind of architectural understanding from the start. This is where re-engineering re-documentation comes in. By taking the perspective of the 5 W's (who, what, when, where, and why) and 1 H (how) and making parallels between those and the different views of the architecture, we can perhaps have clearer understanding of the software itself [4].

3. APPROACH FOR OSS DEVELOPMENT

Based on our literature survey, we identified three main problem areas of our topic. Phrased as questions, they are as follows: 1) Why is software architecture modeling missing from popular online open source code repositories? 2) How can we model complex modern software projects that have multiple components and technologies as part of any given software project? 3) How can including visual documentation improve the overall quality of open source software projects?

One of the goals of our research is to combine the contributions of each of these authors into our own research approach – software architecture model driven reverse engineering approach to open source software development.

4. ARCHITECTURE MODELING

In order to answer the question of why visual architecture modeling is apparently missing from the popular OSS development hubs, we first had to determine that visual architecture and other visual documentation features were in fact not part of the mainstream OSS development process. This was done through a case study of existing documentation features of three of the top online OSS repositories. The results are shown in Table 3. By virtue of being open source code repositories, all three sites offer storage and access to source code and commit history. The major project management mechanism is the issue tracking systems on each repository site. All three sites also host a project home page and "wiki" system for each software project hosted on their site.

Table 3. Open Source Software Repository Names of Links to Features

Repository Name	Home Page	Commit History	Issue Tracker	Wiki	Source Code
GitHub[1]	readme.txt	commits	Issues	Wiki	(default homepage)
Google Code[2]	Project Home	Changes	Issues	Wiki	Source
Bitbucket[3]	Overview	Commits	Issues	Wiki	Source

Altogether, documentation on these three sites exist as a combination of code comments in the source code, messages in the issue tracker and commit history, wiki pages, and the project descriptions on the home page. Not counting links to external resources, this documentation is completely textual.

Finding willing contributors for architecture documentation may not be easy. First, there is a problem of experience. Developers with specific domain experience of the project may not necessarily have architecture development training or experience required to do effective architecture development and those trained in software architecture may not have the appropriate domain knowledge to apply it well [6]. However, at least one benefit is that the type and quality of documentation, such as "Getting Started" articles, can be used as a marketing tool to attract new contributors to the project [1].

A further study of available UML tools shows very little in mature free open source software (FOSS) UML modeling tools. There are some enterprise-level UML tools available for a price, but this goes directly against the spirit of OSS development as the whole technology stack from platform, language, integrated development environments (IDE), version control systems, and repositories all have mature FOSS options.

One of the most popular IDEs for the Java platform is Eclipse. The Eclipse Modeling Project[5] is an effort to promote model-based development and provide a unified set of modeling frameworks, tooling, and standards implementations. Many of the tools support meta-modeling following UML specifications. These meta-models are developed and maintained by via syntactic representations in semi-structured text. An example of this is the Eclipse UML2 plugin[6]. Again, while the models are conceptually architectural in nature, the tangible existing artifact is still textual.

One of the main visual diagramming tools from the above suite of tools and frameworks is known as Papyrus[7]. By their own description, "Papyrus is graphical editing tool for UML2 as defined by OMG." Started in 2008, this project is not in a functional release state. At the time of this writing, the latest release version was 0.10.2.

This cursory analysis of the state of the art of FOSS graphical UML modeling tools with Papyrus as an example may indicate that FOSS options for graphical UML tools for visual architecture modeling may still be in immature stages. This could support the argument that the lack of tool support is one reason for why visual architecture modeling is not prevalent in projects on the major online OSS repositories.

Another reason may be that OSS technologies are evolving faster than the open source UML tool development effort. This claim not validated in this paper and is left as future work. However, in the next section, we discuss the considerations when modeling architecture of modern OSS applications.

5. BEST MODELING PRACTICES

Many modern applications are made up of multiple components and technologies. Any given software project may use many programming languages, especially in the case of web applications where client side and server side functionality have their own suite of platforms and languages. This complexity is a challenge of effectively modeling the software of these composite applications which may not fit neatly to the picture of stand-alone enterprise applications.

Because OSS is often in the category of new, leading edge software using the latest languages and frameworks, we have an increasing need in the open source for best practices of architecture modeling, given the premise that architecture modeling is important to OSS in the first place.

The mix of static and dynamic content from web applications plus the inherently distributed nature of interaction makes web applications not fit neatly into the categories of defined elements of UML. The official OMG UML specification includes extension points with this in mind [7]. Attempting to apply UML to web applications is not new, as a literature survey will reveal suggestions on how to adapt UML to web applications. UML Stereotypes seem like the obvious choice, while other less obvious suggestions may be to reduce the scope of the architecture to just pages, hyperlinks, and dynamic content--such as by modeling each page as its own class (one class for server side page and one for the client side page) [8].

---

[5] Eclipse Modeling Project. http://www.eclipse.org/modeling/

[6] Getting Started with UML2, http://www.eclipse.org/modeling/mdt/uml2/docs/articles/Getting_Started_with_UML2/article.html

[7] Papyrus, http://www.eclipse.org/papyrus/

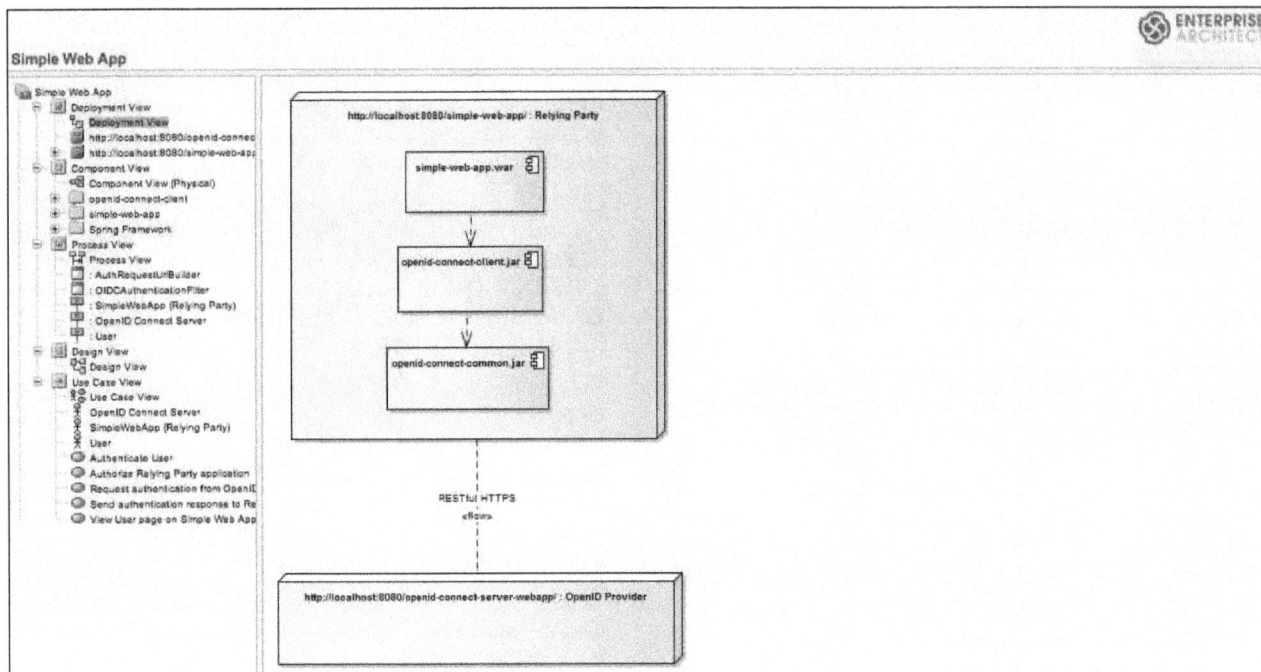

Figure 1. Deployment view

By using the Sparx Enterprise Architect[8] tool, we performed a case study of modeling an OSS project known as MITREid Connect in order to generate our own best practices of visual architecture modeling. MITREid Connect is a reference implementation of a new web authentication protocol called OpenID Connect. There is an active community of developers and implementers for both the OpenID Connect protocol and the OAuth 2.0 protocol it is built on. This means that there is a wealth of textual information on the web about this project.

MITREid Connect was chosen for two reasons: the author's familiarity with the code base and the fact that the project is a combination of both front-end JavaScript and HTML code plus back-end Java code. This is an example of an application with multiple components and different technologies. Because UML is a massive framework requiring expertise of its own to be proficient, we rely on a methodology to simplify and streamline the re-engineering process of the architecture. Using the 5W1H Re-Documentation methodology [4], we developed all 4+1 views in diagrams using Enterprise Architect.

We discovered that despite multiple languages and technologies being used, the Use Case, Component, and Deployment Views were fairly straightforward to diagram. These views do not depend on any specific programming constructs so the fact that multiple languages were used did not affect the difficulty of this part (Figure 1).

Design and Process Views were much more difficult. These views depend on certain assumptions about being able to abstract to classes, object instances, and message exchanges between objects. At the boundaries of where the Java code ends and other parts of the application begin, the ability to diagram the design becomes more challenging.

6. EFFECTIVENESS OF MODELING

The last component of this research was to explore how including visual documentation can improve the overall quality of open source software projects. First, we created a mock site of our UML diagrams (Figure 2). We used the publishing feature of Enterprise Architect tool to generate graphical diagrams viewable as HTML pages continuing to use the MITREid-Connect[9] project as our case study. We then retrofit a local copy of a GitHub project page to include a link to the models, as a thought experiment of the implications of adding such a feature (the link to Models in Figure 1 does not exist on actual GitHub sites). We list a few of our observations below.

As with program documentation of other forms, one of the main challenges that jump out here is the problem of maintaining and updating the documentation. Definitely the socio-technical dynamics of the project group and contributors affect the code contributions, but documentation updates may not be as related to social network effects [3]. In order to improve the social coding benefits of OSS, we propose that OSS diagrams could have a feature for posting comments to parts of the visual models, just as users can post comments on specific lines of code.

6.1 Experiment

As an initial effort to evaluate the effect of including visual documentation on OSS projects, we designed a small-scale experiment using the model diagrams mock site prototype. We used two groups of three university students of various grade levels and taking either an Information Technology or Computer

---

[8] Sparx Systems Enterprise Architect,
   http://www.sparxsystems.com/products/ea/index.html , May 2014.

[9] MITREid Connect, https://github.com/mitreid-connect/

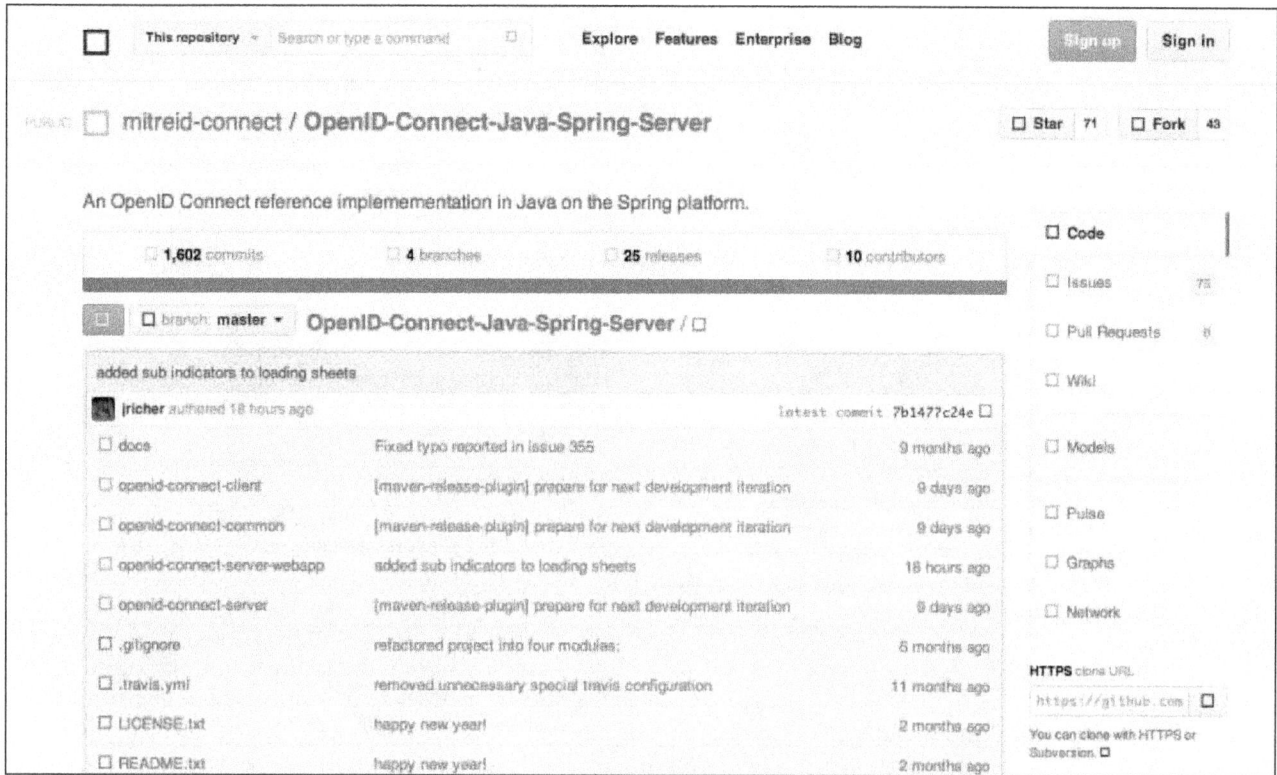

Figure 2. Mock site of modeling functionality

Science major. Their selection was through a voluntary participation upon request to a certain research group at the university. Their task was to answer five questions about relating actual code of the MITREid Connect project to the OpenID Connect specifications it is implementing. The questions were free response answers, but there were explicitly correct answers for each problem. The control group was allowed access to any online resources they can find, including the official OpenID Connect specifications and the source code and documentation on the MITREid-Connect GitHub page. The experimental group had access to same resources plus access to the mock site including the diagrams we developed from earlier part of this research.

This experiment was not intended to be highly rigorous or scientific but should still achieve our goal of bringing to light some issues related to this subject. One very interesting result was that even a question as straightforward as what library dependencies are required by a the web application in question was answered incorrectly by all three participants in the control group while answered correctly by all of the experimental group (see Table 4). The reason was that the experimental group obtained their information from the Deployment View of the diagrams that showed a nested dependency of one library to another that the other group failed to catch from the source code alone. At least in this example, there was a clear benefit to the correctness of developer understanding in the group. Despite having all of the WWW at their fingertips, these kinds of architectural details can be missed, especially without sufficient training in all of the technologies used and under a pressure situation.

Table 4 shows the results of this experiment. The questions are available in Appendix A. In order to be able to score partially

correct answers, each question was scored out of 2 points--2 points for completely correct answer, 1 point for partially correct answer, and 0 points for incorrect answer. All subjects were either Information Technology Systems (ITS) or Computer Science & Systems (CSS) students. The CSS students had significantly more programming related coursework than the ITS students.

Table 4. Experiment results

S	EG/CG	Major	Q1	Q2	Q3	Q3a	Q4
1	CG	IT	1	2	0	2	0
2	CG	IT	1	0	2	2	2
3	CG	CS	1	2	0	0	2
4	EG	CS	2	2	2	2	2
5	EG	CS	2	2	2	2	0
6	EG	CS	2	0	2	0	2

EG: Experimental Group, CG: Controlled Group
IT: Information Technology, CS: Computer Science
Questions:
1. Which of the three libraries from MITREid Connect (openid-connect-client, openid-connect-common, and openid-connect-server) are needed by a Relying Party (or Client) application?
2. Which software components (class, object field, basic data type, etc…) represent the OAuth Access Token in software and what packages are they located in?
3. How does an OIDC client web application (relying party) submit an authorization request to the server? In other words, what sequence of class(es) and method(s) does the program use to do this?
   a. Where does the authorization request URL get built?
4. Where is the client code that processes ID Tokens it receives from the OpenID Server? Show a few lines of code (copy/paste) from the class that shows processing of the ID Token.

13

Based on the feedback from the test subjects, the other questions in the survey proved to be too demanding to be completed in the time frame allowed. The reasons varied from a lack of domain experience, programming experience, or both. The results from the other questions in the survey were highly inconclusive across both groups and therefore omitted from this study. Student #4 outperformed the rest of the group due to having prior knowledge of the MITREid Connect code and should be considered an outlier.

6.2 Experiment Validation

The test subjects were chosen through a voluntary participation request from a student research group. There was no expectation of random sampling and both the sampling group and sampling method has some bias. First, the control group was aware of the additional resources that the experimental group received. This may affect their level of motivation to complete the tasks. The test subjects and the tester are all familiar with each other, introducing other factors of potential bias. The sample questions were designed with the model diagrams in mind. This may limit the evaluation of the results to strictly within the conditions of this experiment.

7. CONCLUSION

In summary, we conclude that the additional overhead of adding a new type of documentation to OSS projects may be justified by the benefits that the existing textual documentation brings for OSS projects. The existence of easily digestible visual diagrams may attract new contributors to a project. And these newcomers can possibly become oriented with the functionality of the software more quickly. We have described some best practices of modeling modern web applications using a case study but discovered many challenges in this work described below. Although our experiment was quite informal and hardly can be considered rigorous, we still see that there is a potential for the quality of code (as measured by lesser number of faults) may increase due to better correctness of understanding by contributors that use models.

We identified some key challenges of including architecture modeling in OSS projects. Mainly, it appears that software development technologies are changing faster than OSS graphical modeling tool support can keep up with. While we can do our best to adapt these new applications to UML using stereotypes and other extension points, how long until next major programming paradigm renders it all obsolete? For instance, we proposed that regardless of the actual programming language at hand, we can design and re-engineer a system in an object oriented way. Already there were new programming paradigms such as aspect-oriented programming that create new issues for this kind of methodology.

Adding additional documentation infrastructure to any kind of project adds additional maintenance costs. Suggested for future work is developing mockups for web-based architecture diagramming with social coding elements, which may inspire more architecture investment in OSS projects. Further rigorous empirical study of the costs and benefits are required in order to validate these claims.

8. ACKNOWLEDGMENTS

This research has been supported by the National Science Foundation (NSF) Division of Undergraduate Education (DUE) Federal Cyber Service: Scholarship for Service (SFS) under Grant No. 091210.

9. REFERENCES

[1] Dagenais, B. and Robillard, M. P. 2010. Creating and Evolving Developer Documentation: Understanding the Decisions of Open Source Contributors. *FSE-18*, November 7–11, 2010, Santa Fe, New Mexico, USA.

[2] Dzidek, W. J., Arisholm, E., and Briand, L. C. 2008. A Realistic Empirical Evaluation of the Costs and Benefits of UML in Software Maintenance. *IEEE Transactions on Software Engineering*, Vol. 34, No. 3, May/June 2008.

[3] Bird, C. 2011. Sociotechnical Coordination and Collaboration in Open Source Software, *27th IEEE International Conference on Software Maintenance*, 2011.

[4] Chung, S., Won, D., Baeg, S. H., and Park, S. 2009. Service-Oriented Reverse Reengineering: 5W1H Model-Driven Re-Documentation and Candidate Services Identification. *2009 IEEE International Conference on Service-Oriented Computing and Applications (SOCA)*, Jan.14-15, 2009.

[5] Kruchten, P.B. 1995. The 4+1 View Model of architecture, *IEEE Software*. Vol. 12, Issue 6, Nov. 1995. p. 42 –50.

[6] Foote, Brian. 1997. Big Ball of Mud, *Fourth Conference on Patterns Languages of Programs* (PLoP '97/EuroPLoP '97). September 1997.

[7] OMG. 2011. Documents Associated With Unified Modeling Language (UML), V2.4.1, August 2011. http://www.omg.org/spec/UML/2.4.1/

[8] Conallen, J. 1999. Modeling Web Application Architectures with UML, *Communications of the ACM*, Vol. 42, No. 10, Pages 63-70, October 1999.

Printer Watermark Obfuscation

Maya Embar
Illinois Institute of Technology
Rice Campus
201 East Loop Road
Wheaton, IL 60189
(630) 788-0841
membar@hawk.iit.edu

Louis McHugh
Illinois Institute of Technology
Rice Campus
201 East Loop Road
Wheaton, IL 60189
(630) 808-9464
lmchughi@iit.edu

William Wesselman
Illinois Institute of Technology
Rice Campus
201 East Loop Road
Wheaton, IL 60189
(630) 540-8957
wwesselm@hawk.iit.edu

ABSTRACT

Most color laser printers manufactured and sold today add "invisible" information to make it easier to determine when a particular document was printed and exactly which printer was used. Some manufacturers have acknowledged the existence of the tracking information in their documentation while others have not. None of them have explained exactly how it works or the scope of the information that is conveyed. There are no laws or regulations that require printer companies to track printer users this way, and none that prevent them from ceasing this practice or providing customers a means to opt out of being tracked.

The tracking information is coded by patterns of yellow dots that the printers add to every page they print. The details of the patterns vary by manufacturer and printer model.

In this document, our team will discuss several obfuscation methods and demonstrate a successful one.

Included in this document is an explanation of the firmware generated yellow dots matrix and answers to the following questions:

1. Which printers produce the dots?
2. How are the dots put on?
3. What is needed for testing?
4. What is the dot size and spacing?
5. Where are the dots located on the page?
6. How can the dots be rendered useless?

Categories and Subject Descriptors

K.6.5 [**Management of Computing and Information Systems**]: Security and Protection – *insurance***, *physical security***

General Terms

Algorithms, Measurement, Documentation, Performance, Design, Reliability, Experimentation, Security, Standardization, Theory, Legal Aspects, Verification

Keywords

Yellow Dots; Obfuscation; Printer; Watermark; Steganography; Tracking; Template; Firmware

1. INTRODUCTION

For almost a decade [1] some color laser printer manufacturers have implemented a system where yellow dots are added to every page printed. These yellow dots are nearly impossible to see with the naked eye, but can be seen with the aid of a high lumen blue or ultraviolet LED light and either a specific background color or a microscope. These dots are not produced by black and white printers or color printers that are not laser. The Electronic Frontier Foundation (EFF) conducted tests to verify the absence of yellow dots on these types of printers. We conducted our own tests to confirm this.

In terms of confidentiality, the presence of yellow (tracking) dots raises the following key issues: What information is being tracked? How can the information be used? Is any personally identifiable information being revealed? We reviewed the findings of multiple sources of information and conducted our own research to address these questions.

2. YELLOW DOTS

2.1 EFF Findings

The Electronic Frontier Foundation (EFF) released this statement regarding printer tracking: "We've found that the dots from at least one line of printers encode the date and time your document was printed, as well as the serial number of the printer." [1]

Since this original statement on the issue, the EFF (with grass roots support) has compiled a list of printers that produce yellow dots. [2]. The EFF has even gone to the next logical step and decoded the yellow tracking dot system implemented on Xerox DocuColor printers.

"So far, we've only broken the code for Xerox DocuColor printers," said EFF Staff Technologist Seth David Schoen, "But we believe that other models from other manufacturers include the same personally identifiable information in their tracking dots." [1]

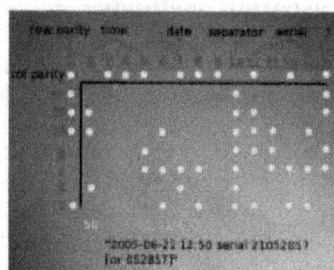

Figure 1. Xerox dot pattern explained

The EFF provided this schematic for decoding: [3]

The topmost row and leftmost column are a parity row and column for error correction. They help verify that the forensic information has been read accurately (and, if a single dot has been read incorrectly, to identify the location of the error). The rows and columns all have odd parity: that is, every column contains an odd number of dots, and every row (except the topmost row) contains an odd number of dots. If any row or column appears to contain an even number of dots, it has been read incorrectly.

Each column shown in Figure 1 is read top-to-bottom as a single byte of seven bits (omitting the first parity bit); the bytes are then read right-to-left. The columns (which we have chosen to number from left to right) have the following meanings:

15: **unknown** (often zero; constant for each individual printer; may convey some non-user-visible fact about the printer's model or configuration)
14, 13, 12, 11: printer **serial number** (in binary-coded-decimal, two digits per byte) (constant for each individual printer; see below)
10: **separator** (typically all ones; does not appear to code information)
9: **unused**
8: **year** that page was printed
(without century; 2005 is coded as 5)
7: **month** that page was printed
6: **day** that page was printed
5: **hour** that page was printed (may be UTC time zone, or set inaccurately within printer)
4, 3: **unused**
2: **minute** that page was printed
1: **row parity bit** (set to guarantee an odd number of dots present per row)

The printer serial number is a decimal number of six or eight digits; these digits are coded two at a time in columns 14, 13, 12, and 11 (or possibly 13, 12, and 11); for instance, the serial number 00654321 would be coded with column values 00, 65, 43, and 21.

The work by the EFF also raises another interesting and troubling thought: How many other technologies and devices have the government and private industries developed to limit or intrude upon our rights and freedoms?

2.2 Obfuscation Methods

One definition of Obfuscation we found was: "Obfuscation (or beclouding) is the hiding of intended meaning in communication, making communication confusing, willfully ambiguous, and harder to interpret." [8] Our team utilized steganographic obfuscation to render the dots meaningless. We have not discovered any way to prevent the tracking dots from printing, and therefore believe this is a beneficial security technique most basic users can implement on their own computer(s).

Some considerations to ensure effective obfuscation:

Halos: Do halos exist, which distort the color around the watermark dots or content color?
Dot layer: Are the yellow dots placed in the foreground or background on the printed document?

The goal of this project was to render the forensic information contained in the yellow dots useless through one of the following obfuscation methodologies: Root Level Bypass, Yellow Block, or Steganographic Obfuscation. Following is a brief overview of each method, and an evaluation of implementation viability.

2.2.1 Root Level Bypass
Our research discovered that the yellow dots are generated at the printer firmware level. This approach involves modifying or overwriting the printer firmware to prevent generation of yellow dots by the printer.

We did not pursue this option due to the lack of available test printers for research and development. Root Level Bypass will void the manufacturer's warranty, and any mistake will likely render the printer unusable.

2.2.2 Yellow Block
Yellow Block is a method that would either print small yellow blocks all over the page, or blanket the sheet with yellow ink.

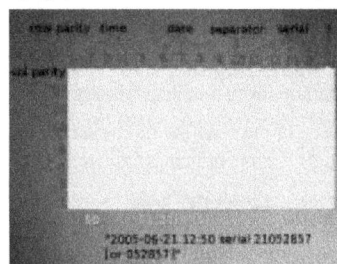

Figure 2. Modified EFF image of Yellow Block Obfuscation

From the outset, this solution seemed unreasonable due to its lack of professionalism, possible distortion of content and excessive consumption of yellow ink. The printers we tested either detected the yellow field and printed white instead of yellow dots, or printed white dots above and below the tracking dots to ensure their detectability in the yellow field (halos).

2.2.3 Steganographic Obfuscation
This method requires determination of the firmware generated yellow dot pattern (size, spacing, color, and distribution) and creation of a fill pattern that obfuscates the yellow dot information.

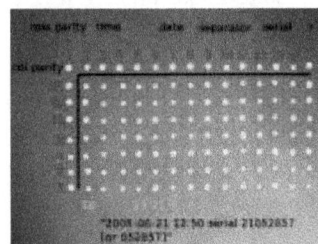

Figure 3. Modified image showing Steganographic Obfuscation

We determined Steganographic Obfuscation was the best choice for the following reasons:

- Yellow block will not work as desired; it is defeated by the printer firmware.
- It has no chance of rendering the printer useless - a distinct advantage over Root Level Bypass.
- It could be implemented simply, and with minimal impact to the appearance of documents.

2.3 Obfuscation Implementation

To implement this method, we created a template in Microsoft Word that blanketed the entire page with yellow dots that are slightly larger than the printer watermark dots. The image created for use in the template was a 600 dpi 8.5 x 11 inch transparent PNG with 1 pixel x 1 pixel yellow dots in a grid pattern. A magnified sample of that image is shown below.

Figure 4. Section from Proof of Concept Template

Figure 4 shows the yellow dot obfuscation pattern on a black background to enhance visibility of the yellow dots. The actual image has a transparent background. We then created a new .dot template using this image as the background. We created a new document using this template, and found the firmware generated yellow dots were obfuscated.

Complete documentation of how to create the obfuscation image as well as how to use that image to create a .dot template can be found in the User Manual available for download. [6]

2.4 Obfuscation Results

2.4.1 Imaging

The following equipment was used by our team to produce the images contained in Appendix 7.1:

- Digital Blue QX7 Microscope: http://www.newegg.com
- Gorilla Glass slides: http://www.shop.gorillascientific.com
- Vinyl Microscope Slide Cover Slips (Figure 5)
- Blue Light: Handmade - parts purchased from Radio Shack
  - Battery Pack
  - Switch
  - Blue LED
  - Battery

Type of Printer	Model
Konica-Minolta bizhub	C452
HP LaserJet Pro Color	M251nw
HP LaserJet Pro Color	M451nw
HP LaserJet Pro Color	M451dn

Table 1. Tested Color Laser Printers

The printers listed in Table 1 were selected because of their availability for use and testing at our campus. The microscope was used to capture magnified images of the yellow dots produced by the tested color laser printers. We determined that a blue LED light and magnification of 10x or greater makes the yellow dots visible.

2.4.2 Image Refinement

Some of the images in Appendix 7.1 have been altered in either exposure or color to enhance the yellow dots produced by the printer. In no case were any dots added or deleted, and in all cases the type of modification that was made is included in the image caption.

2.4.3 Yellow Dot Template

The Yellow Dot .dot template is available for download. [6]

3. Research and Analysis

3.1 Research

3.1.1 EFF updates

The EFF has a list of printers that do or not display tracking dots [2]. There are different printers in the list now than when we began our research in 2013. The Konica-Minolta C452 printer used for testing in 2013 is no longer on the list of printers which have been verified as yellow-dot producing. The three HP LaserJet Pros that our campus recently acquired are not on the EFF list either. These omissions contradict our analyses, because all four printers did in fact produce yellow dots on all color pages that we printed. We contacted the EFF regarding these omissions.

3.1.2 Analysis

The four printers that were tested all displayed the yellow dots. Images of these results appear in the Appendix.

We used cover slips gridded with 0.5mm squares in a 20x20 pattern (Figure 5) as overlays on the printed samples to quantify the size and spacing of the dot patterns. The microscope, set to 60x magnification, was used to capture images of the samples. The resulting images were then imported into AutoCAD. The cover slip grid was used as a reference distance of 0.5mm to determine all other observed distances (see the Appendix for images).

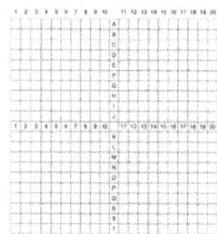

Figure 5. 0.5mm Gridded Cover Slip

3.1.2.1 Grid Spacing

The HP LaserJet Pro Color printers all used 0.8 mm Grid-Spacing. The Konica-Minolta printer used 0.5 mm Grid-Spacing.

This implies that there will be no way to make a universal steganographic template that will work for all printers. A separate template must be created for each specific grid spacing layout.

3.1.2.2 Dot Size

Three of the printers (Konica-Minolta C452, HP M451nw, and HP M251nw) all appear to use dots approximately 0.19mm in diameter.

The HP 451dn uses dashes (0.06mm x 0.14mm) rather than dots.

This implies that for best results the least observable steganographic dot should be customized for each printer according to the dot size it is embedding on the document.

3.1.2.3 Yellow Field Treatment

All of the tested printers were found to have a method for dealing with printing a yellow field (Yellow Block obfuscation).

The Konica-Minolta C452 leaves white/negative space where the Yellow Dot would be expected to appear.

The HP printers all printed the Yellow Dot (or dash) where it would be expected to appear in the yellow field, but created negative space above and below the dot.

3.1.2.4 Steganographic Template Results

There is a small offset to the tracking dots that varies by printer. The obfuscation grid layer, not individual dots, must be moved to compensate for this offset for each individual printer. Once this offset has been made, the obfuscation grid overlays the pattern of the tracking dots and renders them useless.

4. CONCLUSIONS

There are multiple discussions about the yellow dots and their potential impact on privacy (see references), including requests to at least one manufacturer [4] and a Freedom of Information Act request to the US Secret Service. [5]

None of these discussions about the yellow dots has explored what can be done about them. The only "solution" has been to discourage the purchase of printers that appear on the "known to produce dots" list maintained by the EFF.

To the best of our knowledge, the steganographic obfuscation technique developed by our team is the first time anyone has taken direct action to render the printer firmware generated yellow dots useless.

As a proof of concept, we have succeeded in showing that the dots can be effectively and unobtrusively obfuscated by filling the page with a grid pattern of yellow dots that are slightly larger than those generated by the printer.

We encourage the development of printer model-specific templates to obfuscate Yellow Dots.

Further development of this project could incorporate Root Level Bypass as described in Section 2.2.1.

User Manuals and the Yellow Dot Template that was created by our team can be found online in our Google Drive. [6] The Images generated using the QX7 microscope can be found in a separate folder. [7]

5. ACKNOWLEDGMENTS

Steganographix would like to thank Professor William Lidinsky, his Teaching Assistant Ben Khodja, and the staff and faculty at Illinois Institute of Technology Rice Campus for their contributions of testing materials, equipment, time, and guidance.

We would also like to thank Samuel (Stephen) Martin, a member of the initial team (TH2). Mr. Martin came up with the concept of obfuscation that Steganographix is utilizing in our research. Due to scheduling conflicts, Mr. Martin was unable to continue participating, however we would like it to be noted that he will always be considered a member of our team.

6. REFERENCES

[1] Schoen, S. October 16, 2005. Secret code in color printers lets government track you. Electronic Frontier Foundation. Retrieved November 3, 2013 from https://www.eff.org/press/archives/2005/10/16

[2] EFF. List of printers which do or do not display tracking dots. Electronic Frontier Foundation. Retrieved September 22, 2013 from https://www.eff.org/pages/list-printers-which-do-or-do-not-display-tracking-dots

[3] EFF. DocuColor Tracking Dot Decoding Guide. Electronic Frontier Foundation. Retrieved September 22, 2013 from https://w2.eff.org/Privacy/printers/docucolor/

[4] Neufeld, B. 2008 – 2012. FOIA request nets list of manufacturers. Brahm's Yellow Dots. Retrieved September 22, 2013 from http://brahmsyellowdots.blogspot.com/

[5] Prewitt, K. 2012. Freedom of information act appeal – file no. 20100517. U.S. Department of Homeland Security United States Secret Service. Retrieved September 22, 2013 from http://www.scribd.com/doc/94599181/FOIA-release-names-spy-printers

[6] Steganographix, 2013-2014. Steganographix Documentation Retrieved May 20, 2014 from https://drive.google.com/folderview?id=0B9ZrovajUPg2NFEtNXZKUi02Tjg&usp=sharing

[7] Steganographix, 2013-2014. Steganographix Images Retrieved May 20, 2014 from https://drive.google.com/folderview?id=0B9ZrovajUPg2U3Z2Ul9WSXI0b1U&usp=sharing

[8] Wikipedia. The Free Encyclopedia. Retrieved September 22, 2013 from http://en.wikipedia.org/wiki/Obfuscation

7. APPENDICES *

7.1 Images produced from documents printed from HP Color Laser Jet Pro printers

7.1.1 HP LaserJet Pro Color M251nw

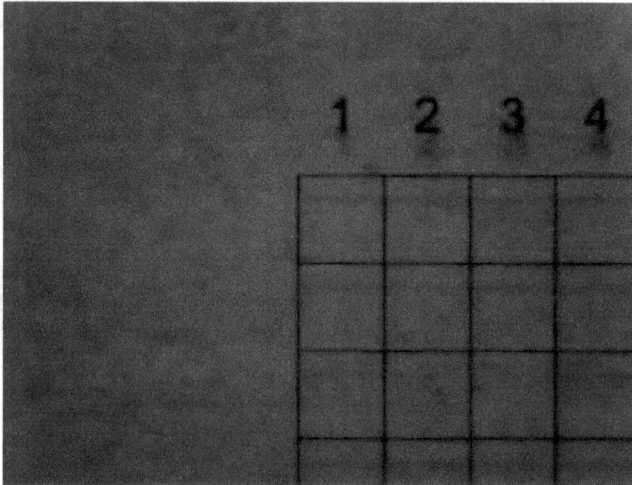

Image 1 (Blue lit, 60x mag.)
Original - No Modification

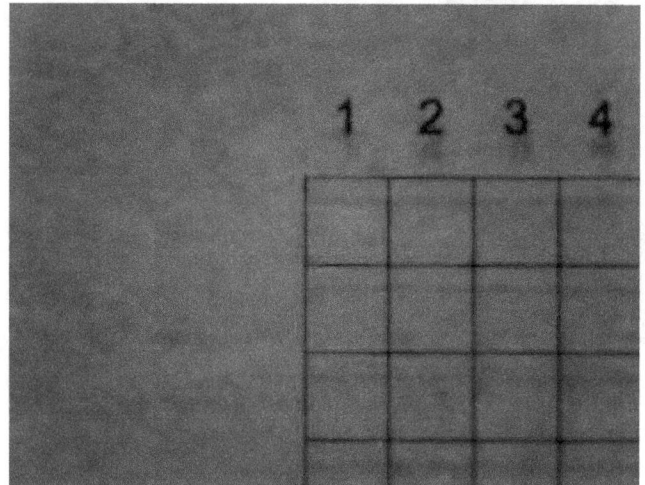

Image 2
Enhanced to showcase yellow dots

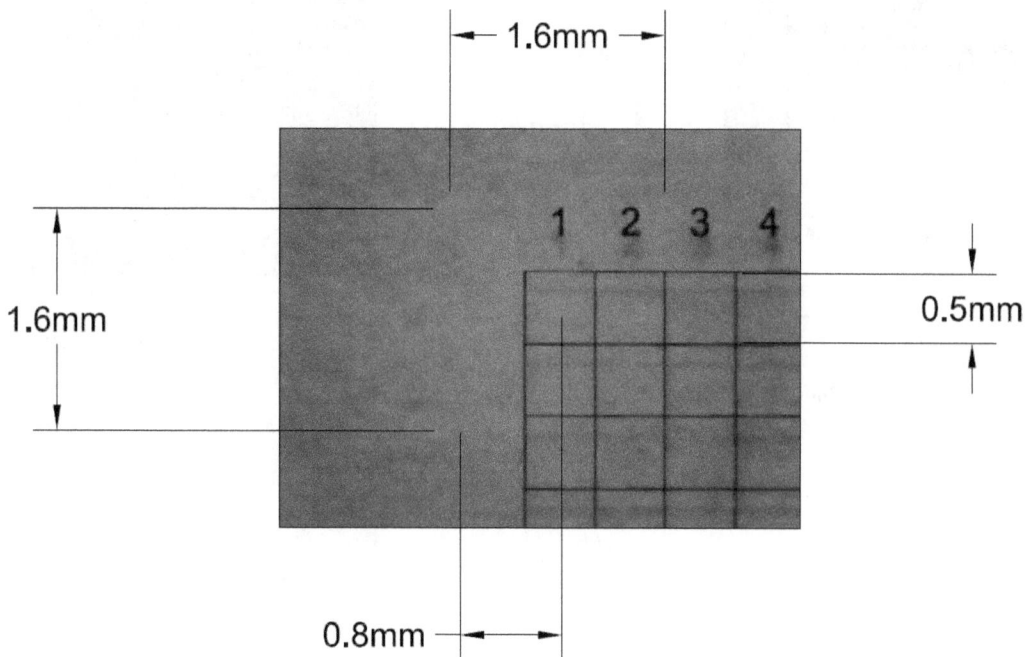

Image 3
Image 2 yellow dot spacing measured with .5mm cover slip

7.1.2 HP LaserJet Pro Color M451dn

Image 4 (Blue lit, 60x mag.)
Original - No Modification

Image 5
Enhanced to showcase yellow dots

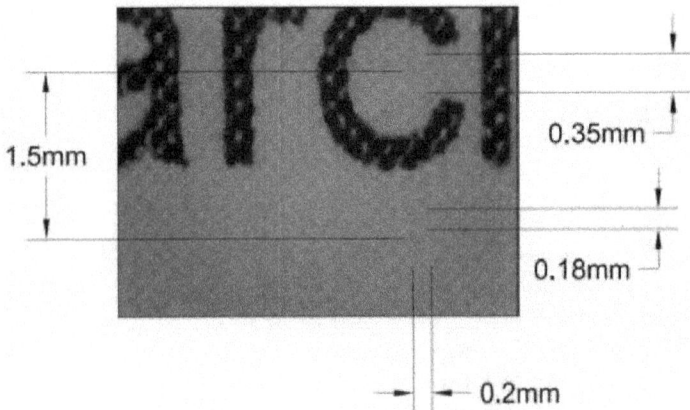

1.5mm

0.35mm

0.18mm

0.2mm

Image 6
Image 4 measured with .5mm cover slip

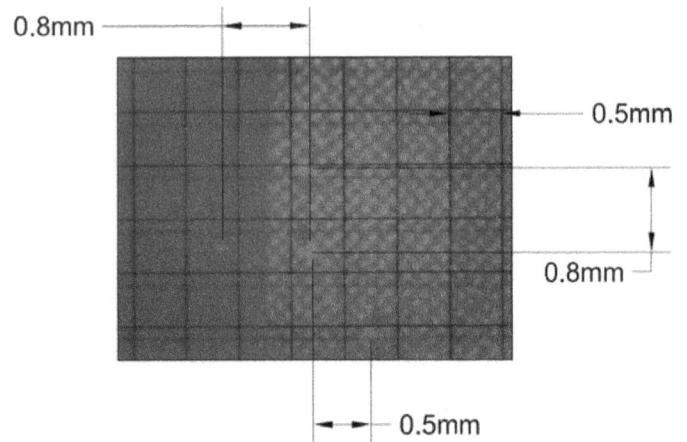

0.8mm

0.5mm

0.8mm

0.5mm

Image 7
Image 5 measured with .5mm cover slip

Probabilistically Detecting Steganography within MP3 Files

Ben Khodja
School of Applied Technology
Illinois Institute of Technology
201 East Loop Road
Wheaton, IL 60189
+1 (630) 815-9149
bkhodja@hawk.iit.edu

ABSTRACT

A powerful application named MP3Stegazaurus was recently created by Illinois Institute of Technology (IIT) student Mikhail Zaturenskiy which exploits a not-so-well-known feature present in MP3 files. [8] By overwriting areas that are either skipped or ignored by MP3 playing and decoding applications, MP3Stegazaurus can use any MP3 file to safely store covert information in a manner that is difficult, if not impossible, for the average user to detect. This is especially true since it leaves an MP3 file's audio information untouched.

As a result of research and work which took place during the first half of a student project, the author developed MP3StegDetector; an application which examines the interesting, non-audio-information-containing portions of MP3 files in order to determine and report whether, and where, steganography may be present. In addition to detecting the potential presence of steganography, MP3StegDetector extracts and outputs the information contained within each of the interesting portions of a given MP3 file. If a complete file such as a JPEG image, PDF document, or AES-encrypted file is identified within this extracted information, MP3StegDetector will extract and recompose it.

In order to determine exactly where in MP3 files these interesting portions exist, the author carried out extensive research on the MP3 file's post-encoding format. This research is included in this document along with details of how MP3StegDetector's various scanning functions and features have been implemented.

Categories and Subject Descriptors

H.5.5 [Sound and Music Computing], E.3 [DATA ENCRYPTION]

General Terms

Algorithms, Measurement, Documentation, Experimentation, Security, Theory, Verification

Keywords

Steganography, Steganalysis, MP3, Anomaly Detection, Secret Writing, Hidden Information, Blind Detection

1. INTRODUCTION

The MPEG-1, Layer 3 (MP3) audio encoding format is perceptual, taking into account the ability of humans to perceive certain frequencies of sound in order to intelligently compress digital audio information. Both lossy and lossless forms of compression take place during the MP3 encoding process. [2]

During the MP3 encoding process, the original, uncompressed audio signal is broken into independent portions called frames which contain audio information that is a fraction of a second in duration; much like the many frames of a film strip which compose a motion picture. First, the original audio signal is analyzed and broken into subbands using algorithms to calculate and determine the best distribution of bits for the pieces of audio signal which fall within the spectrum of frequencies determined to be perceivable by humans. Taking the encoding bitrate (the number of bits per second devoted to storing the audio information) into account, the maximum number of bits that can be included in each frame is calculated which ultimately determines how much of the original audio information is to be kept and how much of it is to be removed.

Using mathematical models of human psychoacoustics included within the MP3 encoding format, the frequency spread of the signal in each frame is analyzed. This process determines the frequencies within each frame that are to be rendered with the most precision as they will be perceivable. It also determines which frequencies are to be rendered with less precision by being given a fewer number of bits as they will not be perceived well thereby ridding each frame of audio information likely to be unperceivable. [2]

The collection of frames is then run through Huffman coding which acts like a traditional lossless form of compression. It compresses the redundant data found throughout the collection of frames and allows for the storage of that same data within a smaller amount of space (20% less space on average when compared to an MP3 file not compressed with Huffman coding). [6]

Lastly, the collection of frames is assembled into a complete MP3 file where each frame is prepended with a header portion, an optional CRC portion, and a side information portion. The header and side information portions contain metadata about the audio information contained within the frame as well as metadata about the frame itself.

2. MP3 FILE FORMAT

Because every frame within an MP3 file, regardless of its bit rate and sampling frequency, contains exactly 26 milliseconds worth of audio information, the number of frames that exist within an MP3 file is directly proportional to the duration of all of the audio information contained within it. [6] The size in bytes of each frame is dependent upon the bitrate and sampling frequency specified and used by the MP3 encoder during the encoding process. As an example, an MP3 file encoded using a specified constant bitrate of 128kbps and sampling frequency of 44,100 Hz will have a frame size of 417 bytes and sometimes 418 bytes when padding must be applied to maintain the exact average bitrate throughout the entire MP3 file. An MP3 file encoded using a specified constant bitrate of 192kbps and sampling frequency of 44,100 Hz will have a frame size of 626 bytes. Optionally, each frame may contain a 2-byte CRC value and the entire MP3 file may begin with an ID3v2 tag or end with an ID3v1 tag. The following figure illustrates the components that make up a complete MP3 file as well as how they are organized.

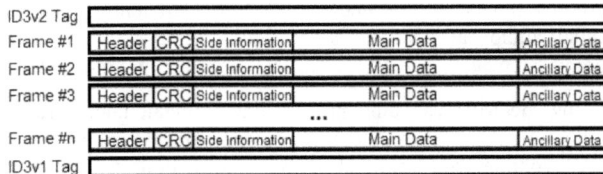

Figure 1. Structure of a complete MP3 file.
Note: ID3 Tag components and CRC portions are optional.

2.1 Frame Header

The first 32 bits (four bytes) of every frame compose the frame's header. This portion contains metadata related to the frame itself including bitrate and sampling frequency values. While the author's project is dependent upon the values contained within all of the fields present in the header portion of every frame in an MP3 file, the ones that are truly interesting include the Private, Copyright, Original, and Emphasis fields. These fields can safely be overwritten in order to store covert information since they are skipped and ignored by MP3 playing and decoding applications. [8]

If the use of CRC protection was specified during the MP3 encoding process, the Protection field within every frame's header portion will contain a value of zero and the 16 bits (two bytes) following every frame's header portion will compose the frame's CRC value. The algorithm used to calculate the CRC value is CRC16. The last 16 bits (two bytes) of the header portion along with the entire side information portion are used as inputs to the CRC16 algorithm. [8] This means whenever the interesting fields within a frame's header and/or side information portion are overwritten in order to store covert information, a new CRC value must be calculated and used to overwrite the original CRC value for that frame. Frames that contain Protection field values that specify the use of CRC values and have missing or incorrect CRC values will be skipped by MP3 playing and decoding applications. [6]

2.2 Side Information

The side information portion, which exists in every frame, contains the metadata needed to decode the audio information contained within every frame's main data portion. The size of the side information portion is dependent upon the channel mode specified during the MP3 encoding process. For MP3 files encoded using the single channel mode, the 17 bytes following a frame's header portion (or CRC value, if one exists) will compose the frame's side information portion. For MP3 files encoded using the dual channel, stereo, or joint stereo mode, the 32 bytes following a frame's header portion (or CRC value, if one exists) will compose the frame's side information portion. [5]

The author's project depends upon the information contained within several of the fields of the side information portion of every frame, however the only field that is of true concern is the padding_bits (or private_bits) field. This field contains a number of bits (five bits for MP3 files encoded using the single channel mode and three bits for MP3 files encoded using the dual channel, stereo, or joint stereo mode) and its only purpose is to round the side information portion up to an integer number of bytes. This field can therefore be safely overwritten in order to store covert information as it is skipped and ignored by MP3 playing and decoding applications. [8]

2.3 Main Data

The main data portion present within every frame contains the audio information. The size of a frame's main data portion is dependent upon the values of the bitrate and sampling frequency fields present in the frame's header portion. It consists of two granule components, Granule 0 and Granule 1, which are further divided into left and right channel portions for MP3 files encoded using the dual channel, stereo, or joint stereo mode. Channel portions are composed of scale factors and Huffman Code bits.

It is important to note the audio information referenced by a particular frame's header and side information portions may actually exist within the main data portion of one or more preceding frames. It is possible for audio information to not exist at all in the main data portion of the frame in which it is referenced; this is due to a space saving feature of the MP3 encoding format known as the bit reservoir. The bit reservoir feature allows frames to share unused main data portion space with any number of frames that follow. As an example, a frame may be allocated 500 bytes of main data portion space based on its bitrate and sampling frequency field values. If only 300 of those bytes are used to store audio information referenced by that frame's header and side information portions, the frame that follows will store the audio information referenced by its header and side information portions starting with the first unused byte of the preceding frame's main data portion (the 301st byte in this case). This ensures that no unused space exists within the main data portion of a frame and results in overall MP3 file size decrease. [6]

2.4 Ancillary Data

Following a frame's main data portion, there may exist a number of bits composing the ancillary data portion. The number of bits within the ancillary data portion usually ranges from one to seven (if it exists) depending on the number of bits left over in the last incomplete byte present in a frame's main data portion. In some cases, the author found the number of bits in a frame's ancillary data portion to exceed seven bits. This was especially true for frames containing a partially empty main data portion, usually found toward the end of an MP3 file. The purpose of ancillary data is mainly to round a frame's main data portion up to an integer number of bytes. It is skipped and ignored by MP3 playing and decoding applications and can safely be overwritten in order to store covert information. [8] The author's project, therefore, is concerned with the ancillary data portions that may exist within the frames of an MP3 file.

3. MP3STEGAZAURUS

MP3Stegazaurus is a powerful MP3 steganography application recently developed by Mikhail Zaturenskiy, a former IIT student. It injects covert information into MP3 files by overwriting the fields within the previously mentioned non-audio-information-containing portions of interest that MP3 playing and decoding applications skip or ignore. It can also retrieve previously-injected covert information as long as a user is aware of and is able to specify exactly which method was used to inject it and which file type extension is to be appended to it. Finally, it cleans potential carrier MP3 files of all previously-injected covert information by using a version of the injection method that overwrites the fields within the specified portions of interest with a repeating zero value.

4. MP3STEGDETECTOR

MP3StegDetector is a steganalysis application developed by the author which examines the interesting, non-audio-information-containing portions of MP3 files where covert information can be safely be stored without affecting playback in order to report whether, and where, steganography may exist. In addition to detecting the presence of steganography, MP3StegDetector extracts and outputs the information contained within each of the portions of interest to files which represent the extracted information in human-readable bit and byte formats. If complete files such as JPEG images or PDF documents are identified within this extracted information, MP3StegDetector extracts and recomposes them. In addition to its scanning features, an added feature called the MP3 Frame Viewer provides a user with detailed information contained within the specified frames of an MP3 file.

Currently, MP3StegDetector is a Java application which can be used from both a Graphical User Interface and an operating system's command line interface (assuming the Java Runtime Environment is installed and appropriately configured). Single and dual channel MP3 files that use constant or variable bitrates are supported as are MP3 files that use any combination of bitrate and sampling frequency values. For testing purposes, the author had access to a training set consisting of 200 clean, unaltered MP3 files retrieved from various sources including Microsoft, Amazon, iTunes, Audacity, GoldWave, FreeCorder, BladeEnc, and Hulkshare.

4.1 Unused Header Bit Scanning

The four fields of interest present within the header portion of a frame include the one-bit Private field, the one-bit Copyright field, the one-bit Original field, and the two-bit Emphasis field. After examining the frames within several single channel and dual channel MP3 files available in his training set, the author observed the values of these four fields remained the same throughout every frame of a clean, unaltered MP3 file. The Unused Header Bit scanning function of MP3StegDetector therefore examines the values of these four fields for every frame within an MP3 file and tracks the number of value changes that occur from one frame to the next.

The scanning process begins by locating the first frame within the MP3 file to be scanned. Once located, several fields within the frame's header portion are examined in order to determine the frame's characteristics. These characteristics include channel mode, bitrate, and sampling frequency as well as whether the frame has its Padding field value set to 1. These characteristics are used to determine the frame's length in bytes. Next, the values of the frame's Private, Copyright, Original, and Emphasis fields are located and stored so they can be compared later with the values of the same fields in the frame that follows. In order to locate the following frame, a number of bytes equal to the current frame's length is skipped and a check is performed to ensure the next valid frame has been accurately located. Again, several fields in this frame's header portion are examined in order to determine its characteristics and determine its length in bytes. The values of this frame's Private, Copyright, Original, and Emphasis fields are then stored separate from those of the previous frame.

The stored values of these two frames' Private, Copyright, Original, and Emphasis fields are then compared. If the values do not match, then a counter that keeps track of the number of value changes for a particular field is incremented by 1. Once the comparison of the field values for these two frames has completed, the next valid MP3 frame is located by skipping ahead a number of bytes equal to the length of the frame that was last examined. This process repeats until the last valid frame in the MP3 file has been reached.

If zero header portion field value changes are counted in a particular MP3 file, it is determined the probability of steganography being present within the header portions of the MP3 file's frames is equal to zero. If one or more header portion field value changes are counted, a percentage value is derived by dividing the total number of header portion field value changes by the total number of interesting header portion field bits present in the MP3 file (this second value is found by multiplying the total number of frames in the MP3 file by five). This anomalous header portion bit percentage value is then interpreted by a user in order to determine whether steganography exists within the header portions of the MP3 file.

Additionally, by examining the bit and byte representations of the information extracted from the interesting header portion fields of an MP3 file's frames, a user is able to independently determine whether patterns or signatures not properly identified by MP3StegDetector may be present.

4.2 Side Information Padding Bit Scanning

The side information portion of a frame contains a Padding (padding_bits, private_bits) field which, according to Martin Ruckert, serves no purpose other than to round the side information portion up to an integer number of bytes. In single channel MP3 files, the Padding field is five bits in length while in dual channel MP3 files, it is three bits in length. After examining the frames within several single channel and dual channel MP3 files available in his training set, the author observed the value of the Padding field was equal to zero in every frame of a clean, unaltered MP3 file. The Side Information Padding Bit scanning function of MP3StegDetector therefore examines the value of the Padding field within every frame of an MP3 file and tracks the number of bits which have non-zero values.

The scanning process begins by locating the first frame within the MP3 file to be scanned and calculating its length in bytes by using the same techniques implemented by the Unused Header Bit Scanning function. Once located, the value of the Padding field within the frame's side information portion is examined. If the value of this field is found not to be zero, the number of bits within it which have non-zero values is counted. In order to locate the following frame, a number of bytes equal to the current frame's length is skipped and a check is performed to ensure the next valid frame has been accurately located. Again, this frame's length in bytes is determined by using the same technique implemented by the Unused Header Bit Scanning method. The value of this frame's Padding field is located and examined in order to count the number of bits with non-zero values. This process repeats until the last valid frame in the MP3 file has been reached.

If zero bits within the Padding fields of an MP3 file's frames are found to have non-zero values, it is determined the probability of steganography being present within the side information portions of the MP3 file's frames is equal to zero. If one or more bits within the Padding field of an MP3 file's frames were found to have non-zero values, a percentage value is derived by dividing the total number of bits found to have non-zero values by the total number of side information portion Padding field bits present in the MP3 file (this second value is found by multiplying the total number of frames in the MP3 file by five for a single channel MP3 file or by three for a dual channel MP3 file). This anomalous side information Padding field bit percentage value is then interpreted by a user in order to determine whether steganography exists within the side information portions of the MP3 file.

Additionally, as with the Unused Header Bit scanning function, by examining the bit and byte representations of the information extracted from the side information portion Padding field of an MP3 file's frames, a user is able to independently determine whether patterns or signatures not properly identified by MP3StegDetector may be present.

4.3 Empty Frame Scanning

Some MP3 files contain a number of "empty frames" which are usually located toward the beginning and/or the end of an MP3 file. [8] Empty frames are just like regular frames except their main data portions contain no audio information. Because of this, the main data portions of empty frames can safely be overwritten in order to store covert information. In order to determine whether a particular frame can be considered empty, one needs to look only at the big_values and table_select fields present within its side information portion. [8] If the value for each of these fields is equal to zero, then it can be determined the frame's main data portion contains no audio information. It is important to keep in mind that because of the bit reservoir feature the MP3 encoding format makes use of, the beginning of the information within an empty frame's main data portion may actually exist in one or several of the preceding frames' main data portions.

After examining the empty frames present within several single channel and dual channel MP3 files available in his training set, the author determined that MP3 encoding applications treat empty frames differently. Some MP3 insert differing types of information into empty frames while others insert no information at all. Because of this, no clear and unique patterns could be used as a basis for determining whether anomalous information exists within the main data portion of an empty frame. However, the information within the main data portions of empty frames is still extracted by MP3StegDetector for independent examination by a user.

The extraction process begins by locating the first frame within the MP3 file to be scanned and calculating its length in bytes by using the same techniques implemented by the previously

mentioned scanning functions. The value of every frame's big_values and table_select fields present in its side information portion is examined in order to determine whether its main data portion contains audio information. If it is determined the main data portion of a frame contains no audio information, the value of the frame's main_data_begin field present in its side information portion is examined in order to determine where in the bit reservoir the frame's main data portion begins. If the value of the main_data_begin field is zero, then the frame's main data portion begins right after its own side information portion. If instead the value of the main_data_begin field is greater than zero, then the frame's main data portion begins within the main data portion of one of the preceding frames.

A non-zero main_data_begin field value is a negative offset representing the beginning location of a frame's main data portion, and it does not account for the sizes of previous frames' header, optional CRC, and side information portions. As an example, if the value of a frame's main_data_begin field is 500, then its main data portion begins 500 bytes ahead of its own header portion, not including the sizes of the previous frames' header portion (always four bytes), optional CRC portion (always two bytes, if it exists), and side information portion (17 bytes for single channel MP3 files, 32 bytes for dual channel MP3 files). [5]

After locating the beginning location of an empty frame's main data portion, the length in bits of the empty frame's main data portion is determined by examining each of the part2_3_length fields contained within its side information portion. All of the information contained within the empty frame's main data portion is then extracted. The next frame within the MP3 file is then located and the process mentioned above is repeated in order to determine whether its main data portion contains audio information. If it is determined the frame does not contain audio information, the beginning location and length in bits of the frame's main data portion are determined in order to extract the information contained within. This process repeats until the last valid frame in the MP3 file has been reached.

4.4 Ancillary Data Bit Scanning

The length of a frame's ancillary data portion varies depending on how many bits are left over in the last incomplete byte of its main data portion. The main purpose of these bits is to round a frame's main data portion up to an integer number of bytes which means the ancillary data portion is usually one to seven bits in length, though in some cases it may be longer. It is possible for a frame not to have an ancillary data portion at all, as is the case when there exists a full eight bits in the last byte of a frame's main data portion. After examining the ancillary data portions present within several single channel and dual channel MP3 files available in his training set, the author observed MP3 encoding applications set the values of the bits within ancillary data portions to a repeating 00, a repeating 11, a repeating 01, or a repeating 10 pattern. The Ancillary Data Bit scanning function of MP3StegDetector therefore examines the values of all of the bits extracted from the ancillary data portion of each frame (if one exists) within an MP3 file and tracks the number of occurrences where a particular bit does not follow one of the four observed patterns.

The scanning process begins by locating the first frame within the MP3 file to be scanned and calculating its length in bytes by using the same techniques implemented by the previously mentioned scanning functions. Next, the beginning location of this frame's main data portion is determined in addition to the beginning location of the following frame's main data portion by examining the main_data_begin field within each frame's side information portion. The values of each of the first frame's part2_3_length fields are examined in order to determine the length in bits of only its main data portion. The number of ancillary bits that exist in-between these two frames' main data portions is then calculated by doing the following: First, the number of bits in the first frame's main data portion is added to the value of the second frame's main_data_begin field (which must first be multiplied by eight since its value represents an integer number of bytes). Then, the length in bits of the first frame is determined. Finally, the number of bits found during the first step is subtracted from the number of bits found during the second step. Using this number of ancillary data portion bits now known to exist in the first frame, a length of information which begins directly after the end of the first frame's main data portion is extracted and examined.

In order to locate and examine the ancillary data portion bits of the frame that follows (if they exist), a number of bytes equal to the current frame's length are skipped and a check is performed to ensure the next valid frame has been accurately located. Again, this frame's length in bytes is determined by using the same technique implemented by the Unused Header Bit Scanning method. This process repeats until the last valid frame in the MP3 file has been reached.

If zero bits within the ancillary data portion of every frame are found to not follow one of the four patterns observed in clean, unaltered MP3 files, it is determined the probability of steganography being present within the ancillary data portions of the MP3 file's frames is equal to zero. If one or more bits within the ancillary data portion of an MP3 file's frames are found to not follow one of the four patterns observed in clean, unaltered MP3 files, a percentage value is derived by dividing the total number of bits found to not follow one of the four patterns observed in clean, unaltered MP3 files by the total number of bits present in the ancillary data portions of the MP3 file. This anomalous ancillary data portion bit percentage value is then interpreted by a user in order to determine whether steganography exists within the ancillary data portions of the MP3 file.

Additionally, as with the previously mentioned scanning functions, by examining the bit and byte representations of the information that is extracted from the ancillary data portions of an MP3 file's frames, a user is able to independently determine whether patterns or signatures not properly identified by MP3StegDetector may be present.

4.5 MP3 Frame Viewer

The MP3 Frame Viewer feature of MP3StegDetector allows for the retrieval and viewing of detailed information regarding any user-specified frames within an MP3 file. The following information retrieved from a frame's header portion is displayed: MPEG audio version, layer value, Protection field state, bitrate value, sampling frequency value, Padding field state, channel mode, mode extension, emphasis type, Private field state, Copyright field state, Original field state, reported length value in bytes, and actual length value in bytes. The following information retrieved from a frame's side information portion is displayed: main_data_begin field value in bytes and Padding field value in bit format, as well as the values of the part2_3_length, big_values,

and table_select fields of all of the granule and channel portions contained within a frame's main data portion. Finally, the length in bytes of the main data portion is displayed along with the information contained within in human-readable bit and byte formats.

Although the author did not intend to include this feature in MP3StegDetector, it was decided it should be after realizing it could be a useful tool for independently detecting steganography and other anomalies at a low level, as well as be useful in other MP3-related applications.

4.6 Testing

The process of testing MP3StegDetector consisted of gathering clean, unaltered MP3 files from various online sources in order to create a training set consisting of 25 MP3 files retrieved from each source for a total of 200 MP3 files. This training set consisted of MP3 files of single and dual channel mode types making use of varying bitrate and sampling frequency values. Once a complete training set of clean, unaltered MP3 files had been gathered, a copy of it was created. MP3Stegazaurus was then used to inject varying types of test information into the interesting portions of the MP3 files within the training set copy. In the end, the author had access to two training sets consisting of clean, unaltered MP3 files and MP3 files carrying covert information of various known types in varying portions of interest.

Using the training set of carrier MP3 files, the author began to take note of the results produced by MP3StegDetector as each file was scanned in order to see whether it was properly determining values related to the probability of steganography and whether it was properly extracting information from the portions of interest. Once satisfied with the results MP3StegDetector was producing after scanning MP3 files from the carrier training set, the author began to scan the MP3 files from the clean training set in order to take note of the universal patterns observed in the information extracted from the MP3 files' portions of interest. It is these observed patterns that the detecting algorithms implemented by MP3StegDetector's scanning functions use in order to track the number of anomalies present and determine a value related to the probability of steganography within a particular MP3 file's portions of interest.

The author intends to eventually implement statistical methods into MP3StegDetector including regression analysis and/or linear discriminant analysis which may offer a solution for reporting values related to the probability of steganography present within the main data portions of empty frames. Other future functionality includes the ability for MP3StegDetector to detect and scan partially empty frames and custom frames potentially created and inserted by other MP3 steganography tools.

5. CONCLUSIONS

Using the patterns found to exist within the interesting portions of the 200 clean, unaltered MP3 files gathered by the author, a tool named MP3StegDetector was created which scans the interesting portions of MP3 files and reports values related to the probability of steganography present within those interesting portions. The patterns found to exist within the interesting portions of clean, unaltered MP3 files include the following:

Header Portion – The values of the Private, Copyright, Original, and Emphasis fields remain constant throughout every frame.

Side Information Portion – The values of the bits within the Padding field are equal to zero throughout every frame.

Ancillary Data Portion – The values of all of the bits within a frame's ancillary data portion follow a repeating 00, 11, 01, or 10 pattern. This is true for every frame where an ancillary data portion exists.

Empty Frame Main Data Portion – No universal patterns were found to exist. The values of the bits within an empty frame's main data portion may follow a repeating 00, 11, 01, or 10 pattern. These bits may also contain information related to the software or device used to encode and create a particular MP3 file.

6. ACKNOWLEDGEMENTS

The author would like to acknowledge the contributions made to this project by Erfan Setork, Kbrom Tewoldu, and Zach Wagner. The author would also like to thank Professor Bill Lidinsky for encouraging him to take on this project and for providing him with guidance and direction. Finally, the author would like to thank Mikhail Zaturenskiy for his work in developing MP3Stegazaurus and for taking the time to help the author understand how certain aspects of the MP3 encoding and decoding processes work.

7. REFERENCES

[1] Bosi, Marina, and Richard E. Goldberg. Introduction to Digital Audio Coding and Standards. Boston: Kluwer Academic, 2003. Print.

[2] Hacker, Scot. MP3: The Definitive Guide. Sebastopol: O'Reilly Media, 2000. Print.

[3] Maciak, Lukasz G., Michael A. Ponniah, and Renu Sharma. MP3 Steganography: Applying Steganography to Music Captioning.

[4] Nilsson, Martin, "ID3 tag version 2.3.0", 1999 ID3, http://www.id3.org/id3v2.3.0

[5] Raissi, Rassol. The Theory Behind MP3.

[6] Ruckert, Martin. Understanding MP3: Syntax, Semantics, Mathematics, and Algorithms. Wiesbaden: Vieweg, 2005. Print.

[7] Supurovic, Predrag, "MPEG Audio Frame Header", 1999 DataVoyage, http://www.datavoyage.com/mpgscript/mpeghdr.htm

[8] Zaturenskiy, Mikhail. "MP3 Files as a Steganography Medium." Illinois Institute of Technology, 2013.

Passive Warden Using Statistical Steganalysis

David Stacey
School of Applied Technology
Illinois Institute of Technology
201 East Loop Road
Wheaton, IL 60189
dstacey@hawk.iit.edu

ABSTRACT

This paper examines the statistical techniques used in blind steganalysis of JPEG images. Blind steganalysis attempts to detect the presence of covert data without knowing the particular steganographic algorithm used. This paper begins by discussing steganography and steganalysis in general with a focus on common techniques. JPEG images are then introduced with a detailed discussion of their format and how they are created. Once the details of JPEG images are understood, common JPEG steganographic algorithms are explained. These algorithms are available in programs like JSteg, Outguess, and F5. This paper focuses on the Calibration Technique and associated features developed by Fridrich [2].

The goal is to develop an application that detects covert data hidden in JPEG images by common steganographic algorithms. The output from this application is an indicator of whether or not the image contains covert data.

Categories and Subject Descriptors

I.4 [**Image Processing and Computer Vision**]: Miscellaneous

Keywords

JPEG; Steganography; Steganalysis

1. INTRODUCTION

This project implements a Passive Warden application, with the goal of detecting the presence of hidden messages in JPEG images. The roots of the Passive Warden comes from an article by G. Simmons entitled "Prisoners' problem and the subliminal channel" [8], which is an illustrated story of Alice, Bob, and Wendy. Alice and Bob are prisoners and Wendy is their warden. Like all prisoners, Alice and Bob are planning to escape. Unfortunately, the warden must approve all communications between prisoners. In order to plan their escape, they need to communicate details of their

RIIT'14, October 15–18, 2014, Atlanta, Georgia, USA.
Copyright is held by the owner/author(s). Publication rights licensed to ACM.
ACM 978-1-4503-2711-4/14/10 ...$15.00.
http://dx.doi.org/10.1145/2656434.2659756.

plan to each other, without Warden Wendy finding out. To do this, Alice hides her message in a document, which she passes to Bob, who extracts the message. Warden Wendy acts passively and only examines the document to determine if it contains a hidden message. Technically, Alice and Bob are using steganography to hide and extract the message while Wendy uses steganalysis to determine if a message has been hidden.

2. STEGANOGRAPHY

Steganography is defined as the art and science of writing hidden messages. It comes from the Greek words *steganos* meaning "covered" and *graphei* meaning "writing." It has been in use, in one form or another, for thousands of years, particularly during wartime. Recently, the suspected use of the Internet by drug dealers and terrorists has sparked a renewed interest in steganography, which some believe is used for covert communications.

In steganography, there are two types of objects: carrier and hidden. Carrier or overt is the host or where the data is hidden. Hidden or covert is the source or the data that is hidden. The goal is embedding the covert data into the carrier in such a way that the embedding is not obvious to visual observation of the carrier or to the application that processes the carrier.

There are three common techniques used in steganography: insertion, substitution, and generation.

2.1 Insertion

The insertion technique hides the message in a location that the application ignores. Two locations used by the insertion technique are comment fields and the area after the end of file (EOF) marker. The key point is the application ignores any data in these two locations. While the rendering application may ignore the embedded data, this technique is susceptible to discovery by visual inspection. The most obvious is the file size increases based on the amount of data embedded. A HTML file that is 5MB in size would be suspicious, to say the least.

2.2 Substitution

The substitution technique replaces insignificant bits of the carrier file content with the message. The goal is to do this with minimal distortion of the carrier. Unlike the insertion technique, visual inspection doesn't work, since the file size normally doesn't change. The unwillingness to increase the file size does limit the amount of data that can be embedded.

The most common substitution technique is Least Significant Bit (LSB) substitution. JSteg, StegHide, and EzStego are JPEG steganographic tools that use LSB substitution. These tools select a sequence of data from the covert file either by some predetermined sequence or by using a pseudorandom number generator to determine the sequence. The LSB of the selected data is substituted by a bit from the overt data.

Gary Kessler [3] gives an example of LSB substitution, where the letter 'G' is "hidden" across the following eight bytes of a carrier file (the least significant bits are underlined):

1001010<u>1</u> 0000110<u>1</u> 1100100<u>1</u> 1001011<u>0</u>
0000111<u>1</u> 1100101<u>1</u> 1001111<u>1</u> 0001000<u>0</u>

In ASCII, the letter 'G' is represented in binary as 01000111. These eight bits are "written" to the least significant bit of each of the eight carrier bytes as follows:

1001010**<u>0</u>** 0000110<u>1</u> 1100100**<u>0</u>** 1001011<u>0</u>
0000111**<u>0</u>** 1100101<u>1</u> 1001111<u>1</u> 0001000**<u>1</u>**

In the example above, only half of the least significant bits were actually changed (shown in bold).

2.3 Generation

The generation technique uses an algorithmic scheme to create an overt file from a covert file. An example of this technique is creating a fractal image from the covert file. Both the insertion and substitution techniques require an overt file, while this technique does not. This means the generation technique is immune to comparison tests, which compare the modified file with an unmodified version of the same file.

3. STEGANALYSIS

Steganalysis is defined as the art and science of detecting hidden messages. This section examines the techniques used for steganalysis. Similar to steganography, where different techniques are used to hide messages, steganalysis uses different techniques to detect those messages. These techniques can be broken down into three broad categories; knowledge of the steganography tool or algorithm used, presence of structural changes to the file, and analysis of statistical properties of the image.

3.1 Steganographic Tool Knowledge

Steganalysis based on knowledge of the steganography tool or embedding algorithm used is called specific or targeted steganalysis. Kumar [4] states if the steganalyst knows the embedding algorithm and its statistical signature then this type of steganalysis is very effective. This approach is similar to how anti-virus software works by looking for a specific signature, in this case a statistical signature. As with anti-virus software, targeted steganalysis doesn't perform well with new or unknown embedding algorithms.

3.2 Structural Changes

Some steganographic algorithms alter the structure of the image. These algorithms primarily use the insertion steganographic file technique where covert data is hidden in areas ignored by the application, such as comment fields and after the end of file. By examining the structure of an image and comparing it to the structure of clean images, steganalysis can determine if covert data is present.

3.3 Statistical Analysis

Current techniques in steganalysis focus on statistical analysis and form the basis of universal or blind steganalysis. Blind steganalysis is agnostic with regard to the steganographic tool or algorithm used to hide data within an image. This approach allows it to detect new steganographic algorithms. Most statistical analysis focuses on how images with hidden data deviates statistically from clean images. As an example, consider two steganographic tools, JSteg and OutGuess.

JSteg is an older steganographic tool and one of the first to do JPEG steganography. It uses Least Significant Bit (LSB) substitution using a simple algorithm to select the bits to modify. This makes it susceptible to detection by statistical analysis, particularly by using the Chi-square test. Westfeld and Pfitzmann [9] developed the use of the Chi-square test for detecting embedded data. They discovered when data is embedded using LSB substitution, it causes adjacent values to change. The Chi-square test measures "goodness of fit" or how an observed distribution differs from a theoretical distribution. Westfeld and Pfitzmann measured the value of adjacent pixels. They calculated a theoretical value by averaging the adjacent pixels and comparing that to the observed value.

OutGuess (www.outguess.org) was developed by Niels Provos in 2001. Like JSteg, OutGuess identifies redundant bits in the carrier and replaces them with bits from the hidden message. Provos [7] wanted to develop a steganographic algorithm for JPEG images that would not be susceptible to statistical analysis, like the Chi-square test. To do this, OutGuess applies additional transforms in order to correct statistical deviations as a result of hiding the message. The resulting carrier image is statistically the same as the clean image.

4. JPEG FORMAT

This project focuses on JPEG images, which are the most common image format found on the Internet. The JPEG format was developed by the Joint Photographic Experts Group and became an approved standard in 1992. The JPEG standard specifies how an image is converted into a stream of compressed bytes and how it is decompressed back into an image. However, JPEG is not a file format. There are two standard file formats for JPEG-compressed images; Exit and JFIF.

In order to understand the approach taken by this project, it is necessary to understand some of the technical details of JPEG images. Figure 1 is a Block Diagram of the JPEG Conversion Process.

This project is interested in the quantized DCT (Discrete Cosine Transform) coefficients that result from the conversion process. The DCT converts an 8x8 pixel block from the spatial to the frequency domain. This means the RGB color model is converted to the YC_bC_r color space where Y represents luminance or brightness and C_bC_r represents chrominance or color. The DCT equation is shown in Figure 2.

To clarify the JPEG conversion process, Figure 3 shows the intermediate results from each step of the conversion

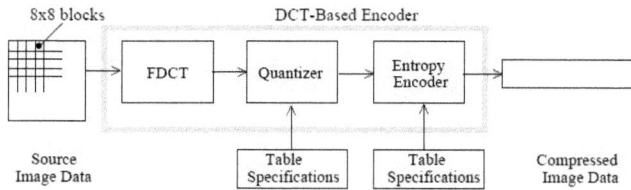

Figure 1: JPEG Conversion Block Diagram [5]

$$F(u,v) = \frac{c(u)c(v)}{4} \sum_{i=0}^{7} \sum_{j=0}^{7} \cos\left(\frac{(2i+1)u\pi}{16}\right) \cos\left(\frac{(2j+1)v\pi}{16}\right) f(i,j),$$

$$c(e) = \begin{cases} \frac{1}{\sqrt{2}}, & \text{if } e = 0, \\ 1, & \text{if } e \neq 0. \end{cases}$$

Figure 2: Discrete Cosine Transform (DCT) [1]

process. The process begins with an 8x8 block of source data (a), which is then converted from the spatial to the frequency domain using the DCT (Figure 2). The result of this transform is the forward DCT coefficients (b). Next, a quantization table (c) is used to normalize the DCT coefficients (d). The element at index [1,1] of d is called the DC coefficient; the others are called AC coefficients. It is these normalized quantized AC DCT coefficients this project is interested in. Steps e and f are the results of the reverse process and are not used by this project. The quantization table is specified by the JPEG standard and determines the level of compression applied to the image.

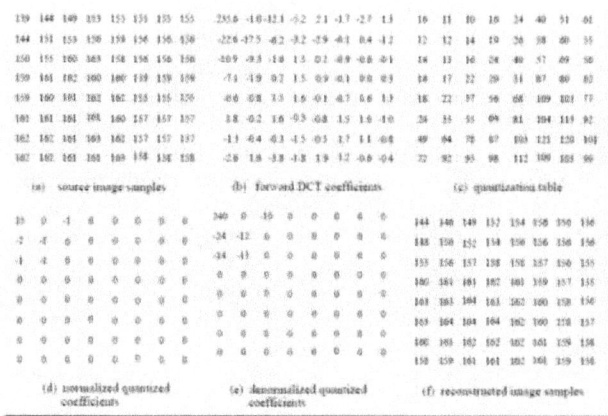

Figure 3: Example JPEG Conversion [5]

5. APPROACH

The approach taken by this project uses the Calibration Technique and associated features developed by Fridrich[2].

The Calibration Technique attempts to create the statistical equivalent of the clean image from the stego image. It does this by decompressing the stego image to the spatial domain, cropping by 4 pixels in each direction, and then recompressing using the same quantization table as the original stego image. Fridrich says this approach should "produce a 'calibrated' image with most macroscopic features similar to the original cover image." [2] The reasoning be-

hind this approach is the cropped stego image is "similar to cover image and thus its DCT coefficients should have approximately the same statistical properties as the cover image." The choice of 4 pixels is important because of its relationship to the 8x8 grid. Fridrich explains that during recompression new DCT coefficients are calculated that have not been influenced by the previous compression and potential embedding in the DCT domain. This results in two images, the original stego image (J_1) and the calibrated image (J_2). Fridrich calculates a calibrated form of feature f which is the difference using $f(J_1) - f(J_2)$.

5.1 First Order Statistics or Features

The histogram of DCT coefficients is the primary first order statistic or feature. Fridrich's assumption is that DCT coefficients are independent and identically distributed (iid) random variables. This means each DCT coefficient has the same probability distribution as the others and all are mutually independent. Fridrich concludes, "their complete statistical description can be captured using their probability mass function." [2]

The following features are derived from the sample probability mass function (pmf) computed from the DCT coefficients.

5.1.1 Kronecker Delta

The Kronecker Delta is used in many steganalysis formulas. It returns a 1 when the value of x is 0 and a 0 when the value of x is not equal to 0. Typically, x is the difference of two values, so the Kronecker Delta is used to determine if the two values are equal and to count how many times the value occurs. The formula for the Kronecker Delta is shown below:

$$\delta_{ij} = \begin{cases} 0 & \text{if } i \neq j \\ 1 & \text{if } i = j \end{cases}$$

5.1.2 Global Histogram

The Global Histogram is considered a normalized histogram (i.e., displays relative frequencies) of all luminance (Y) DCT coefficients. It returns a D-dimensional vector as shown by its formula (1). The range is $-5 \leq r \leq 5$, which produces 11 features. Most of the features described use a limited range. Fridrich explains that without a limited range the feature space dimensionality would be too large and larger values of r exhibit fluctuations that are of little value. [2]

$$H[r] = \frac{1}{64 x N_B} \sum_{k,l=0}^{7} \sum_{b=1}^{N_B} \delta(r - D[k,l,b]) \quad (1)$$

This project focused primarily on the Global Histogram. Table 1 shows the calculations using Fridrich's Calibration Technique. The first row (r) represents the range used in the calculations. J_1 is the original image. J_2 is the cropped image. The third row is the difference between the original and cropped images. Fridrich specified the use of the difference between the two images [2]. This project extended Fridrich's technique by using the absolute value of the difference as shown in the fourth row. A single value per image was calculated by adding the absolute values of the difference. For the sample calculation in Table 1, that value was 0.02174.

r	-5	-4	-3
Image(J_1)	0.01096	0.01555	0.02458
Cropped(J_2)	0.01154	0.01559	0.02534
$J_1 - J_2$	-0.00058	-0.00004	-0.00076
$|J_1 - J_2|$	0.00058	0.00004	0.00076
r	-2	-1	0
Image(J_1)	0.04727	0.12242	0.39056
Cropped(J_2)	0.04930	0.12700	0.38188
$J_1 - J_2$	-0.00203	-0.00458	0.00868
$|J_1 - J_2|$	0.00203	0.00458	0.00868
r	1	2	3
Image(J_1)	0.12587	0.04642	0.02332
Cropped(J_2)	0.12749	0.04628	0.02512
$J_1 - J_2$	-0.00162	0.00014	-0.00180
$|J_1 - J_2|$	0.00162	0.00014	0.00180
r	4	5	$\sum |J_1 - J_2|$
Image(J_1)	0.01524	0.01131	
Cropped(J_2)	0.01591	0.01047	
$J_1 - J_2$	-0.00067	0.00084	
$|J_1 - J_2|$	0.00067	0.00084	*0.02174*

Table 1: Global Histogram Calculation using Fridrich's Calibration Technique

Using the Global Histogram calculation described above, this project calculated values for clean images, JSteg embedded images, and F5 embedded images. A sample of the results is shown in Table 2. The sample shows a very distinct range for each type of image. However, the sample is somewhat misleading and when all images were compared, there existed some overlap that contributes to the results obtained.

Image #	Clean	JSteg	F5
1	0.02174	0.10527	0.06304
2	0.02437	0.13497	0.08288
3	0.02196	0.13561	0.06497
4	0.02093	0.10148	0.07639
5	0.02702	0.11471	0.07781

Table 2: Global Histogram Results Sample

5.1.3 AC Histogram

The AC Histogram is also considered a normalized histogram. It is a histogram of individual DCT modes. Fridrich says, "it is possible to consider the coefficients as 64 parallel iid channels, each corresponding to one DCT mode." [2] While some steganographic tools preserve the Global Histogram, not all preserve the histogram of individual DCT modes. Analysis of the AC Histogram may allow detection of embedding from the use of these tools.

The range is $-5 \le r \le 5$ and $0 < k + 1 \le 2$, which produces 11 x 5 (55) features. The AC Histogram limits the indices examined to the first five AC DCT coefficients in "zigzag" order. The formula for AC Histogram is shown in 2.

$$h^{(kl)}[r] = \frac{1}{N_B} \sum_{b=1}^{N_B} \delta(r - D[k,l,b]) \qquad (2)$$

5.1.4 Dual Histogram

The Dual Histogram returns an 8x8 matrix and determines "how many times the value r occurs as the (k,l)th DCT coefficient." [2] Fridrich states that "it captures the distribution of a given coefficient value r among different DCT modes." [2]

The range is $-5 \le r \le 5$ and $0 < k + 1 \le 3$, which produces 11 x 9 (99) features. The Dual Histogram limits indices examined to the first nine AC DCT coefficients in "zigzag" order. The formula for Dual Histogram is shown in 3.

$$g^{(r)}[k,l] = \frac{1}{N_B(r)} \sum_{b=1}^{N_B} \delta(r - D[k,l,b]) \qquad (3)$$

5.2 Inter-Block or Second Order Features

Fridrich [2] explains an Inter-block feature by saying "that natural images exhibit dependencies over distances larger than the block size."

5.2.1 Variation

The Variation feature is based on Ueli Maurer's "Universal Statistical Test for Random Bit Generators" [6] and Niels Provos [7] application of Maurer's research to JPEG steganalysis.

Provos [7] discovered images with hidden data have higher entropy than those without. He used Maurer's test to measure entropy and found the expected result from a truly random source is 7.184. Fridrich adds, "most steganographic techniques in some sense add entropy to the array of quantized DCT coefficients and thus increase the difference between dependent coefficients across blocks." [2] The dependencies are measured mathematically using a quantity called variation. Fridrich developed the formula shown in 4 for measuring variation. An interesting aside, the Variation Technique produces a single result, unlike the other techniques examined by this project.

$$V = \frac{\sum_{i=1}^{8\lceil \frac{M}{8} \rceil - 8} \sum_{j=1}^{8\lceil \frac{N}{8} \rceil} \left| \mathbf{D}[i,j] - \mathbf{D}[i+8,j] \right|}{64(\lceil M/8 \rceil - 1)\lceil N/8 \rceil} + \\ \frac{\sum_{i=1}^{8\lceil \frac{M}{8} \rceil} \sum_{j=1}^{8\lceil \frac{N}{8} \rceil - 8} \left| \mathbf{D}[i,j] - \mathbf{D}[i,j+8] \right|}{64\lceil M/8 \rceil(\lceil N/8 \rceil - 1)} \qquad (4)$$

5.2.2 Blockiness

Fridrich [2] defines Blockiness as "the sum of discontinuities along the 8x8 block boundaries in the *spatial domain*." Notice this feature is the only feature that works in the spatial domain. There are two blockiness measures for $\gamma = 1$ and $\gamma = 2$. The formula for Blockiness is shown in 5.

$$B_\gamma = \frac{\sum_{i=1}^{\lfloor \frac{M-1}{8} \rfloor} \sum_{j=1}^{N} \left| x[8i,j] - x[8i+1,j] \right|^\gamma}{N \lfloor (M-1)/8 \rfloor + M \lfloor (N-1)/8 \rfloor} +$$

$$\frac{\sum_{i=1}^{M} \sum_{j=1}^{\lfloor \frac{N-1}{8} \rfloor} \left| x[i,8j] - x[i,8j+1] \right|^\gamma}{N \lfloor (M-1)/8 \rfloor + M \lfloor (N-1)/8 \rfloor} \tag{5}$$

5.2.3 Co-occurrence Matrix

Fridrich [2] defines the Co-occurrence Matrix as the "distribution of pairs of neighboring DCT coefficients." It is actually the average of two matrices, one in the horizontal direction and one in the vertical direction. The range is $-2 \leq s, t \leq 2$, which produces 25 features. The Co-occurrence Matrix formula is shown in 6.

$$C[s,t] = \frac{\sum_{i=1}^{8\lceil \frac{M}{8} \rceil - 8} \sum_{j=1}^{8\lceil \frac{N}{8} \rceil} \delta(s - D[i,j])\delta(t - D[i+8,j])}{64(\lceil M/8 \rceil - 1)\lceil N/8 \rceil} +$$

$$\frac{\sum_{i=1}^{8\lceil \frac{M}{8} \rceil} \sum_{j=1}^{8\lceil \frac{N}{8} \rceil - 8} \delta(s - D[i,j])\delta(t - D[i,j+8])}{64\lceil M/8 \rceil(\lceil N/8 \rceil - 1)} \tag{6}$$

5.3 Intra-Block Features

Intra-block features such as the Average Markov matrix measure dependencies within one 8x8 block. This project did not examine Intra-block features, but is including this section for completeness so the reader is aware they exist and how they are used. Fridrich [2] goes into great detail explaining the concepts and mathematics of Average Markov matrices and their applicability to JPEG steganalysis.

6. RESULTS

The results of using Global Histogram for Blind Steganalysis are presented below.

This project examined 600 images, 300 were used for training and 300 for testing Blind Steganalysis. Each group of 300 was divided into three sets of 100 each. The first set was clean, the second embedded using JSteg, and the third embedded using F5. For the 100 clean images, an average plus 2σ (standard deviation) was calculated. The average represents the sum of the absolute values of the difference in the Global Histogram of the original and cropped images. The 300 training images were then evaluated against this value. The results of the training session are shown in Table 3.

Image Type	Correct
Clean	94%
JSteg	91%
F5	64%

Table 3: Training Results

A second group of 300 images was used for testing Blind Steganalysis. Like the ones used for training, the 300 were divided into three sets of 100 each. The first set was clean, the second embedded using JSteg, and the third embedded using F5. These images were evaluated against the same value (average + 2σ) as the training session. The results of the Blind Steganalysis session are shown in Table 4.

Image Type	Correct
Clean	98%
JSteg	99%
F5	74%

Table 4: Blind Results

7. CONCLUSION

Based on this project, three conclusions can be drawn. First, Global Histogram is a better differentiator than the other features evaluated. Considering a single value was calculated from the 11 Global Histogram features, the Blind Steganalysis results are very encouraging. Admittedly, the sample set is small; it does indicate this approach is viable. Future work would be to analyze thousands of images to determine if consistent results are obtained.

Second, the Variation Technique is not as good a differentiator as originally hypothesized. This project's initial premise was that Variation would be a very good differentiator. This was based on the fact that embedding causes an increase in the entropy or randomness in an image. Since Variation is a measure of entropy, the assumption was any embedding would cause a noticeable change in the Variation feature. Future work is planned in this area because the theory behind Variation still has merit and deserves further investigation.

Third, the combination of features should increase predictive accuracy. Most statistical steganalysis techniques use multiple features, sometimes hundreds of features, to increase accuracy. An extension of this project would be to combine multiple features to determine if the predictive accuracy increased and by how much relative to the additional computational complexity.

8. ACKNOWLEDGMENTS

I would like to acknowledge the contributions to this project made by Stephen Felix, Abel Zerazion, and Phil Shriner.

9. REFERENCES

[1] C.-C. Chang, C.-C. Lin, C.-S. Tseng, and W.-L. Tai. Reversible hiding in dct-based compressed images. *Information Sciences*, 177(13):2768–2786, 2007.

[2] J. Fridrich. *Steganography in Digital Media: Principles, Algorithms, and Applications*. Cambridge University Press, 2010.

[3] G. C. Kessler. An overview of steganography for the computer forensics examiner. *Forensic Science Communications*, 6(3):1–27, 2004.

[4] M. Kumar. *Steganography and Steganalysis of JPEG Images: A Statistical Approach to Information Hiding and Detection*. LAP LAMBERT Academic Publishing, 2011.

[5] F. Liu. Jpeg standard - a tutorial based on analysis of sample picture - part 1. coding of a 8x8 block, August 2011.

[6] U. M. Maurer. A universal statistical test for random bit generators. *Journal of cryptology*, 5(2):89–105, 1992.

[7] N. Provos. Defending against statistical steganalysis. In *Usenix Security Symposium*, volume 10, pages 323–336, 2001.

[8] G. J. Simmons. The prisoners' problem and the subliminal channel. In *Advances in Cryptology*, pages 51–67. Springer, 1984.

[9] A. Westfeld and A. Pfitzmann. Attacks on steganographic systems. In *Information Hiding*, pages 61–76. Springer, 2000.

Detecting Subtle Port Scans Through Characteristics Based on Interactive Visualization

Weijie Wang
Department of Computer and
Information Technology
Purdue University
wang2056@purdue.edu

Baijian Yang
Department of Computer and
Information Technology
Purdue University
byang@purdue.edu

Yingjie Victor Chen
Department of Computer Graphics
Technology
Purdue University
victorchen@purdue.edu

ABSTRACT

Port-scan detection is essentially vital to enterprise networks, since many intrusions start with scanning. A port scan can be obvious or subtle in terms of the volume of network traffic. In this paper, we propose a creative approach by combining the characteristic-based method and visual analytics to detect those hard-to-find subtle scans as well as obvious scans in an enterprise environment. The goal of designing this system is to provide useful information and implications about port-scan attackers and benign hosts to a network security team in a simple and efficient manner. The major components of the system consist of three different semantic level visualizations. Through several use cases, we illustrate how the system can detect both obvious and subtle port-scanning activities. The analysis approach proposed in this study proves to be effective by identifying all the port-scan attackers in the data sets.

Categories and Subject Descriptors

D.4.6 [**Security and Protection**]: Information flow controls; I.3.8 [**Computer Graphics**]: Application—; H.5.2 [**Information Interfaces and Presentation**]: User Interfaces—

General Terms

Security, Design

Keywords

port scan; security visualization; characteristic based; interactive visualization

1. INTRODUCTION

Enterprise network infrastructures are often complex, dynamic and massive, consisting of tens of thousands of hosts spreading over multiple geographic locations. Numerous attacks targeting enterprise networks occur on a daily basis, attempting to compromise servers and client hosts to steal confidential information. Protecting the security of such networks is vital to any organization and a daunting task for security analysts.

Port scanning is a method of probing a network host for open ports, determining whether particular services are available on a host or a network by observing responses to connection attempts

RIIT'14, October 15–18, 2014, Atlanta, GA, USA.
Copyright © 2014 ACM 978-1-4503-2711-4/14/10...$15.00.
http://dx.doi.org/10.1145/2656434.2656441

[15]. Scanning a network is very common, probably the initial step in a network intrusion attempt. By analyzing the response information from port scanning, attackers could unearth vulnerabilities of network hosts and launch targeted attacks by exploiting the vulnerabilities found in the network scans. Port scanning by itself is typically not an immediate security threat; however, a security team could greatly benefit from the early detection of such events and be prepared for future attacks.

To penetrate security defenses established at the perimeters of enterprise networks, malicious attacks often conceal themselves in legitimate traffic flows by going low and slow. This is especially challenging when the amount of network traffic is huge. How to effectively and efficiently detect such subtle attacks has intrigued many researchers.

In the past few years, various approaches have been proposed and studied to detect port scanning. Bhuyan et al. divided the detection methodologies into several categories: algorithmic, soft computing-based, rule-based, threshold-based, and visual [2]. Algorithmic approach uses probabilistic models or statistical tests to analyze network traffic [9]. Soft computing incorporates methods and schemes to exploit tolerance for imprecision and uncertainty in real life [17]. Rule-based applies various rules and policies to detect the abnormal traffic [10]. The threshold-based approach is a common and intuitive technique to examine events of interest X across a Y-sized time window to detect port-scan attacks above certain thresholds [5]. However, it's not easy to set a proper detection threshold: if the threshold is set too low, it would then mislabel normal traffic flow; whereas a relatively high threshold would fail to identify some malicious scans, especially those deliberately launched slow scans [12]. Another popular approach is the visualization method. This is especially suitable for monitoring enterprise networks since administrators can perceive the trends and patterns from network traffic and be able to identify suspicious activities in an efficient manner. Visualization tools usually provide interactive components that allow investigators to examine detailed, multilayer network information of any suspicious events [6]. But visualization tools may not be effective to detect subtle threats since the abnormal traffic is too small to be detected visually.

To accurately and more efficiently identify subtle port scans from massive network data, we constructed an innovative approach in this paper by leveraging the advantages of both a threshold-based method and a visual analytics approach. Potential port scans, whether obvious or subtle, will be highlighted in our hosts' overview visualization for further investigation. Security professionals can quickly identify suspicious network events and determine if the events are false alarms. The details of the events can also help to discover who the attackers are; what servers/hosts are the targets; and other implications about the attacks. Additionally, security professionals can fine-tune the value of threshold and thus make the visualization tool more accurately reflect the situation of a given enterprise network environment.

The remainder of this paper is organized as follows: Section 2 describes related work and the motivation of the system design. Section 3 provides information about data sets and details of the system components followed by case studies in Section 4. Section 5 discusses the performance of the system and highlights the pros and cons of this approach. Section 6 draws conclusions on this work and describes future work to extend the system.

2. RELATED WORK AND MOTIVATIONS

Visualization systems and tools have been substantially designed and implemented to detect port scanning and other network intrusions in the past decade [1, 3, 7, 8, 11, 13]. One popular approach is to visualize network connections to identify port-scan patterns. Conti and Abdullah visualized the packet information such as IP and port with parallel coordinate plots to identify port scanning [3]. Similarly, Jiawan et al. used traffic activities among hosts and mapped the collected datagram to graphs that emphasize port-scan patterns [8]. However, the port-scan traffic in these two approaches may be obscured by high-volume normal traffic, and therefore the corresponding patterns cannot be effectively shown on the screen and then detected by the human eye. To effectively hide noises and signify actual attacks in the visual presentations, Yin et al. proposed a set of filtering techniques that includes port filtering, protocol filtering, transfer-rate filtering and packet-size filtering [16]. The downside of such a filtering approach is that it entails an extensive manual process that must be conducted carefully in a manual fashion. Another popular visual approach is port based. Abdullah et al. provided a port-based overview of network activity using stacked histograms of aggregate port activity, with the ability to drill down for investigating small, but important, details without being obscured by large usual traffic [1]. McPherson et al. developed a tool called PortVis, which visualized summarized information of the activities on each TCP port during a time period to uncover network and port scans. Visualizing activities on all the ports is not a trivial task, and PortVis's interface contained a 256 x 256 grid where each point represents one of the possible 65,536 port numbers [11].

There were also some interesting works related to port-scanning detection in the submissions for VAST Challenge 2013: Mini-Challenge 3, which is to design a situation-awareness system to detect network attacks for an enterprise network [14]. Zhao et al. designed a port-matrix view for the source and destination ports to detect abnormal port activities, and all possible ports were divided into four groups: user-customized import ports, well-known ports, registered ports, and uncommon ports [18]. Fischer et al. incorporated several interactive visualization views in the system, including a tree map to highlight the most active ports and an interactive node-link diagram to analyze the aggregated connections between hosts and ports [4]. Even though these approaches are capable of identifying the most obvious port-scan attacks, they have all met some difficulties in uncovering subtle ones from the vast network traffic.

Many existing approaches use snapshots of network systems within certain time window to identify anomalous patterns and activities, on an hourly or daily basis [1, 11]. As a result, network administrators or security analysts need to sift through all the related timeline data on hosts and ports: a considerably heavy task if the investigation involves a long period. In addition, vast volume of normal traffic is quite likely to obscure port-scanning traffic, which is generally few in number.

Therefore we tackle this problem from a different angle: instead of visualizing the network activities, we visualize and highlight the characteristics of network port scans. The overview phase of the analyses employs an approach that is similar to the threshold-based detection. This will enable security investigators to exclude the most benign and legitimate traffic and hosts Next, during the phase of on-demand zoom in, detailed information regarding suspicious hosts and traffic will be presented to the investigators to gain deeper understanding about the nature of the events. Results and discussions in Section 4 and Section 5 demonstrated that the proposed work can effectively and efficiently identify subtle port scans in the presence of a large amount of network traffic. Note that the framework we proposed in this paper can be further expanded to fight network attacks on a much larger scale by integrating other methods, including, but not limited to, data modeling, data mining, and big-data analytics.

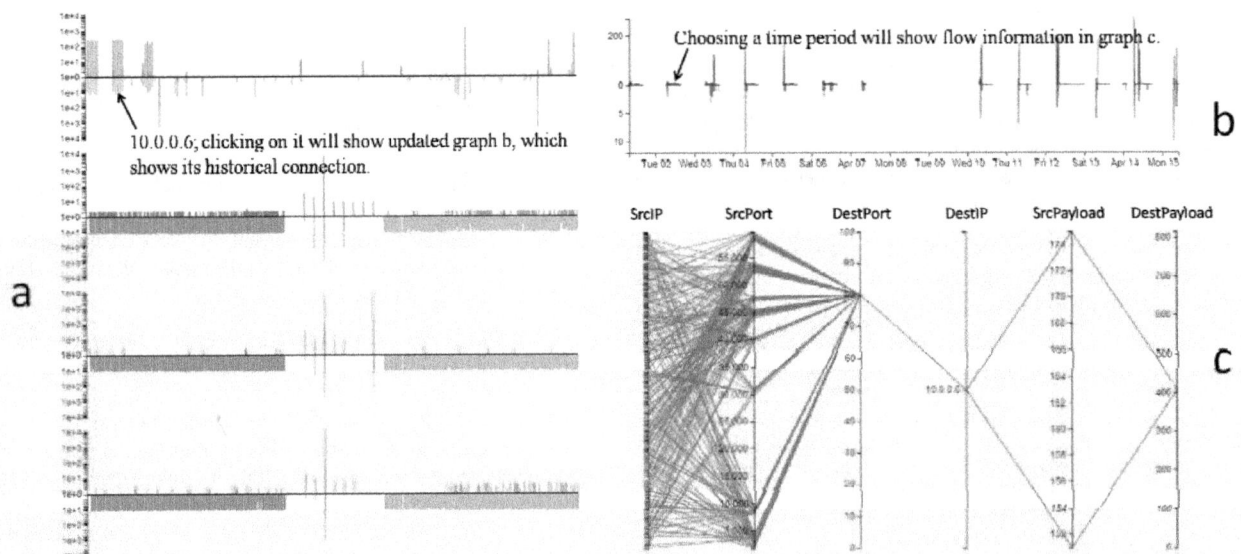

Figure 1. Overview of Interactive System Components.

3. SYSTEM DESIGN AND COMPONETS

3.1 Available Data Sets

Meaningful security data that reflects typical attacks in an enterprise environment is a must-have for any security studies using the data-driven approach. Instead of collecting data in a simulated research environment, where attacks are more or less artificial, we used the data sets provided in the 2013 VAST Challenge, Mini-Challenge 3 [14]. The data sets were normalized and preprocessed so that sensitive and private information was removed, yet the characteristics of some typical network attacks are preserved. A two-week period of network flow data of "Big Marketing" was published, dating from April 1 to 15, 2013. The network infrastructure includes three sites, each containing 400 hosts and a handful of Web servers and e-mail servers. The network flow was captured at the boundary of the organization's network where the firewall was set up. Any transactions that leave or enter the boundary of "Big Marketing" were recorded. The data available for analyses is at per-flow level and the sets contain approximately 70 million entries. Each network flow contains the following information: time stamp, source, and destination IP addresses; source and destination port numbers; size of payloads; and similar. Notably, according to the data-set descriptions, the designation of source and destination IP addresses are not guaranteed to be correct. In a situation where the flow collector did not catch the initial transaction in a flow and captured the response as the first transaction, the destination IP may be labeled as the source IP, and vice versa. After the competition was completed, the VAST 2013 committee released the ground truth to the research teams that participated in the challenges. Having the answer key for network attacks greatly helped us to evaluate the correctness and the efficiency of the proposed approach.

3.2 Design Philosophy

Considering the extremely high volume of traffic data for enterprise networks, the system's overview should display suspicious port-scan activities and potential attackers in a more succinct and efficient manner without losing preciseness. The first question we asked ourselves is this: what do we want to visualize in the overview? Most existing approaches use the timeline chart to show network connections established among different hosts. The results are often disappointing: a small number of security events get easily buried by the huge amount of normal traffic. Therefore our design philosophy is to present aggregated, attack-specific information in a simplified manner and leave the detailed information in the next stage of visualization. Specifically, our overview design is significantly different from most published work in that (1) the overview highlights only the potential attackers without including information of potential victims; (2) overview focuses on visualizing the characteristics of the attacks rather than network traffic; and (3) overview reveals the likelihood of an external host attacking the network over a specified period without the need to be presented in timeline charts. Once a potential attack is identified from the overview, an on-demand zoom-in phase will present related information of potential attackers and victims in detail. Since the key characteristics of port scanning is related to how many different IP addresses and port numbers are contacted by a certain host during a given time, we visualize these characteristics by drawing the maximum number of distinct destinations per unit of time that each host contacts and is being contacted. Since port-scan attackers very likely have a larger maximum value than benign hosts, they can be easily spotted from the overview. The on-demand zoom-in phase will then allow security analysts to extrapolate back and forth in low-level timeline to discover full details of the potential attacks.

In characteristic-based approaches, proper thresholds are often difficult to be established because the network baselines vary in different networks. Therefore a mere maximum number of distinct destinations per unit time is not enough to differentiate the malicious and benign hosts. We also visualize the maximum number of unique IP address and port number combinations that are connecting to each host. The logic behind this is intuitive: a host with very many outbound connections, but very few inbound connections, per unit time is very likely to be malicious. Furthermore, for the maximum number of distinct connections per unit time, an average number of distinct connections for each host is also visualized for comparison.

3.3 System Components

The visualization system consists of three semantic-level views as displayed in Fig. 1. View (a) provides the overall information based on host connections. Users can select a host of interests to drill down in view (b), which provides the time-series activity for suspicious hosts. Users then specify a specific period, and view (c) visualizes connections at a detailed level with the flow information, such as port number and payloads. Multiple views are simultaneously presented to users; thus users can switch between high-level overview and low-level details without losing the context. Each system component is described in detail in the following sections.

3.3.1 Host-MaxConn View

Host-MaxConn View depicts the overall hosts' maximum number of connections per unit of time (e.g.. one second, one minute, or one hour) for external as well as the entire Big Marketing network, as shown in Figure 1(a). In this scenario, the top chart represents external hosts, and the other three represent three internal network sites. The horizontal coordinate represents IP addresses. In the given scenario, there are over 4 billion possible external IP addresses, but a significant amount of them are not active. In our design, we plotted only active IP addresses and automatically place them evenly. Big Marketing's two-weeks of data contains only about 215 active external IP addresses. If there are too many active external ones for the space, a scroll bar can be used to allow all the information to be visible on one screen. For the three Internal network sites, each site has only about 400 hosts at each site, containing domain controllers, Web servers, mail servers, and personal workstations. Because the servers are more active and need more attention, they are placed in the central part and have more space; the workstations are placed at the two ends evenly. The vertical axis represents maximum and average numbers of outbound and inbound distinct connections per unit of time (second, minute, hour, or user-specific) within the time period (two weeks in this situation), with downward representing an outbound direction and upward inbound. A distinct connection is a traffic flow to the host with a unique IP address and port-number combination. Different time scales can benefit in various situations; second or minute is capable of detecting fast-scans, and hour or a longer time unit is more suited for slow scans. Average value is colored in green, and maximum value is stacked, colored in blue (outbound direction) or red (inbound). To accommodate a wide numbered range of connections, the log scale is adopted for a vertical axis. Take an external host (IP address: 10.0.0.6) for instance; the host marked by an arrow in Figure 1(a) has a maximum of 12 outbound connections and 270 inbound connections per second: indicating that the host was contacted significantly during some specific time by the internal hosts and that it's possibly an external server.

3.3.2 Host-TimelineConn View

The second semantic level, as shown in Figure 1(b) is the Host-TimelineConn View, which visualizes time series data for outbound and inbound distinct connection numbers of a selected host from Host-MaxConn View. The horizontal axis corresponds to time; the upward vertical axis corresponds to inbound connection numbers (in red) and the downward vertical axis corresponds to outbound connection (in blue). By default, the horizontal axis covers the entire period of data sets (two weeks), but the user is allowed to select any time span to display information at a finer temporal resolution. Figure 1(b) displays the external host (IP address: 10.0.0.6) activities during the two weeks. We can see periodic connections from internal hosts (red spikes) to this host except on April 8 and 9. According to the released ground truth, Big Marketing took down the network in those two days to investigate security issues and to install an IPS (Please spell out). The inbound periodical connections are normal, with most occurring during the day. This further indicates that this host is quite likely an external server frequently visited by internal hosts. In contrast, host outbound connections are much less comparing to inbound connections. Because of a probability that source and destination IP addresses are mixed up, the outbound connection numbers are reasonable. Host-TimelineConn View often reveals trends and patterns of external hosts and could be beneficial for network administrators to identify active benign external hosts and potential abnormal activities.

3.3.3 Host-Flow View

The third semantic level is the visualization of traffic flows between two groups of IP addresses, which is Host-Flow View as shown in Figure 1(c). Parallel coordinates are used in here since flow-level data contain multidimensional information, including IP addresses, port numbers and flow payloads (in bytes). In Host-TimelineConn View in Figure 1(b), we suspected that the external host (IP address: 10.0.0.6) may be an external server because it's contacted by the internal hosts periodically. To verify our suspicion, we randomly choose a period, such as April 02, 12:00 to 12:02, and visualize the two-minute network traffic to the host (10.0.0.6 as the destination IP address). Figure 1(c) gives the traffic information in details. Clearly, in the two-minute window, many internal hosts are connected to this external host. Although the source port numbers vary, the destination port numbers are all 80. Also, the traffic flows have normal-size payloads. Through the Host-Flow View, we are assured that 10.0.0.6 is indeed an external Web server. Notably, even though we draw only a two-minute period, the number of traffic flows to the host is significantly large. This explains why we need the first two views for necessary filtering and that directly visualizing all traffic flows can reveal no meaningful patterns.

4. CASE STUDIES

In the released ground truth, port-scan attacks are categorized into "obvious" and "subtle," respectively. Generally, "obvious" attacks involved more scanned ports and a larger number of scanning

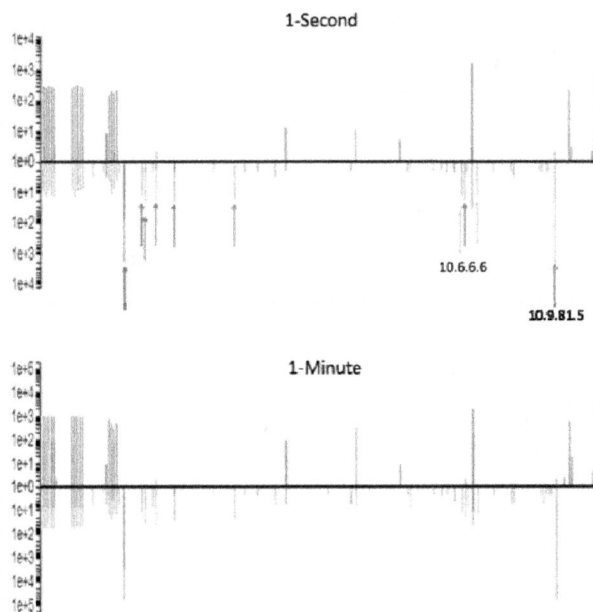

Figure 2. External host connections (per second and per minute) with obvious attackers are marked by red arrows, subtle attackers by orange.

network flows than "subtle" attacks did. During the two-week period are a total of 9 obvious and 3 subtle port-scanning attacks from 10 external attackers. Most of the attacks are single-source port scanning, though a certain attacker may be involved in multiple attacks. In this section, we will demonstrate how obvious and subtle attacks can be detected by using our system.

4.1 Obvious Port-Scan Attacks

As discussed above, a host with a significantly high number of outbound distinct connections per unit of time as well as a low number of inbound distinct connections per unit is a potential port-scan attacker. Figure 2 provides external host maximum and average distinct connection numbers per second as well as per minute. "Obvious" attackers are marked by red arrows, and "subtle" attackers by yellow arrows. Interestingly, a one-second host view identifies all the 10 port-scan attackers, meaning most of the attacks are fast scans.

In the one-second Host-MaxConn View as shown in Fig. 2, two hosts stand out with very high distinct outbound (downward direction) connection numbers per second (10.10.11.15 with 1646 and 10.9.81.5 with 1841). Notably, these two numbers are connections to the internal unique IP address and port number combinations within a second. Meanwhile, these two external hosts have very few inbound connections (upward direction) from internal hosts, and it's almost certain that they launch network scanning or port scanning to internal networks sometime during the two weeks. Apart from these two significant outliers, the other six obvious attackers are also easy to identify in Figure 2. They all

Table 1. Background and attack traffic information for the two port-scan events

Timestamp	Duration (mins)	External attackers	Number of scanned hosts	Background traffic rate (flow/s)	Scanning traffic rate (flow/s)
April 6, 11:10	100	10.9.81.5	8	447.14	270.18
April 1, 11:03	5	10.6.6.6	6	20.75	0.60

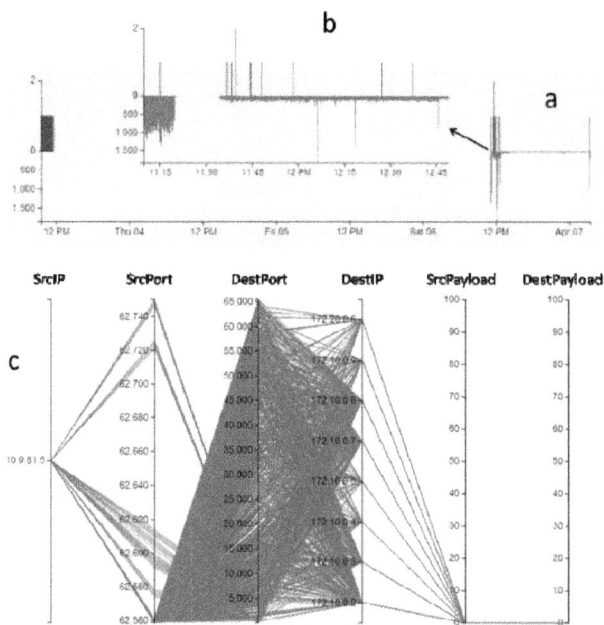

Figure 3. Analyses of an obvious port-scan attack launched by external host 10.9.81.5. Graph (a) is the overall timeline activities for the host; (b) is a zoom-in view of the attack; and (c) is the flow-information visualization.

have relatively high-maximum outbound distinct connections (11~18) with very few inbound distinct connections (only one). Although the disparities are much less than those two spikes, they are still very suspicious. In contrast, there are a few external hosts (most reside on left side in Figure 2) with similar high-maximum outbound distinct connections, but their maximum and average inbound connections (upward direction) from internal networks are also significantly high, indicating that they may be external servers instead of port-scan attackers, as we discussed in the previous section. In fact, a significant character of benign servers is that they have notable average inbound distinct connections (upward direction, in green) in a one-minute view of Figure 2, meaning that they are frequently contacted by internal hosts.

Here we drill down to one of the obvious attackers with IP address 10.9.81.5. Host-TimelineConn View in Figure 3 reveals that this host was active for only very short periods during April 3, 6, and 7. Furthermore, on April 6 at about 12 PM, outbound distinct connections per second to internal hosts reached 1841 with very few simultaneous inbound connections, indicating a network or port scanning. A closer view (Figure 3 b) shows that the attack started at 11:10 AM, and lasted for approximately 100 minutes. The scanning traffic was fairly intensive in the first 10 minutes. Host-Flow View (Figure 3 c) provides more information on this port-scan attack. Note that we use only a very small portion of scanning traffic, since it will be overwhelming to visualize all traffic flows at once. Clearly, the targets of this scan attack were 8 hosts with IP address 172.10.0.x, which were servers in the Big Marketing network. Furthermore, the destination ports covered almost all possible ports, indicating that this was a very aggressive scanning. The destination payloads were all 0 bytes in size, since there were no responses from the server. It's an "obvious" per-scan attack on internal servers, considering the extremely vast amount of traffic flows and scanned ports.

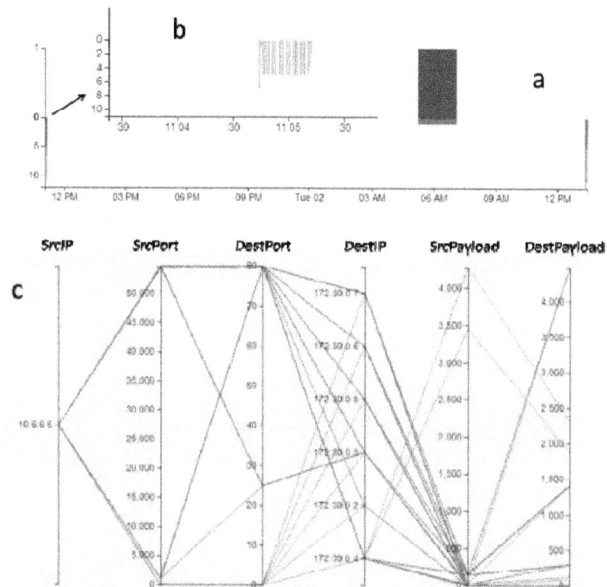

Figure 4. Analyses of a subtle port-scan attack launched by external host 10.6.6.6. Graph (a) is the overall timeline activities for the host; (b) is a zoom-in view for the attack event, and (c) is the flow-information visualization.

4.2 Subtle Port-Scan Attacks

Three subtle port-scan attacks involved two external attackers (yellow arrows in Figure 2). Notably, from the one-second Host-MaxConn View, almost no visual difference is obvious between "subtle" and "obvious" attackers. Further investigation will reveal that their scan rates are actually similar, and only "subtle" scanning has fewer scanned ports.

Here we select the host with IP address 10.6.6.6 for further investigation. Similar to host 10.9.81.5, this host was active only during two-day short periods. Its outbound distinct connection per second reached peak (approximately 12) on April 1 at, 11 AM and on April 2 at 1 PM, as shown in Fig. 4 a. A closer observation on April 1 activity shows that the scanning was beginning at 11:03 and lasted only 5 minutes (Fig. 4 b). Host-Flow View in Fig. 4 c visualizes all the network flow involved in this attack. Internal servers with IP address 172.30.0.x were scanned, but only on ports 25 and 80. This is uncommon because usually port-scan attacks would not scan only these two ports. The unusual port-scanning behavior was due to the firewall blocking of traffic flows to internal servers if the destination port number was not 25 or 80. Thus this port-scan attack is categorized as "subtle" because only two ports were involved and the firewall blocked most of the scanning traffic. More interesting was the uncommon continuous connections of 6 AM on April 2, lasting approximately 2 hours. This is actually a denial of service attack to an internal server. Since 80 is the attacking port of one host, an outbound distinct connection number would be the same one constantly.

5. DISCUSSIONS

5.1 Evaluations

When compared with the ground truth provided by the challenge committee, our visualization detection system was found to be accurate and effective in detecting all the port-scan events hidden in the data set. We successfully identified all 9 port-scan attackers, including both obvious and subtle attacks involved in the two weeks of data. In contrast, none of the teams competing VAST 2013 Challenges could detect all the subtle port scans, and most failed to detect any subtle port scans. The false alarm rate was also very well controlled in our approach. Only three or four activities in non-port scanning activities stand out in the overview, but they were easily filtered out when zoomed in for details. Considering the volume of the data sets (70 million network flow records), we believe this detection system is effective to deal with large volumes of data at enterprise networks. Table 1 displays some scanning and background network traffic statistics about two attacks we discussed in previous section. The obvious attack on April 6 has a fairly high-scanning traffic rate. It reached 270.18 flow per second, and lasted about 100 minutes. Thus it is easy to detect such notable port scans. In contrast, the subtle attack's scanning traffic rate was only 0.60 flow per second and lasted only 5 minutes. Filtering out the normal traffic and unearthing such subtle scans are indeed challenging.

5.2 Limitations

Even though the system is capable of detecting all port scanning attacks in the Big Marketing's data sets, limitations still remain in our study. First, all the port-scan attacks in the data sets are very likely to be fast scans. Even though our design is capable of detecting slow scans by adjusting the length of per-unit time, we were unable to prove it with the given testing data set. In general, a slow scan should be more difficult to detect because of the increased volume of traffic per time unit diluting the characteristics of slow attacks. Second, the system is designed to identify suspicious hosts. It is more effective in detecting single-source port scannings in a one-to-one or one-to-many form. Distributed collusive attacks that have a pattern of many-to-one or many-to-many need more efforts to uncover. Third, we assumed in this study that an external host is likely to be benign if it is contacted frequently by many different internal hosts. This is usually true, but if the external host is compromised and launches port-scan attacks to internal networks, it will be much more difficult to detect.

6. Conclusion and Future Work[1]

This paper proposed an innovative characteristics-based visualization method to detect subtle port scanning in enterprise networks. In the visualization phase, data are first aggregated and preprocessed. A carefully selected set of parameters that reflects the key characteristics of network attacks is shown in the overview. When suspicious network activities become noticeable in the overview, detailed information can be drawn on demand for further investigation. The data sets we examined proved that this approach is highly effective and accurate in identifying all the "obvious" and "subtle" port scans.

Our future work will focus on following directions. We would like to test and evaluate our system on other data sets and optimize it for slow scans and distributed scans. Furthermore, it would be better to incorporate a more-automated process to the system, thus identifying suspicious activities in a more intelligent way. Extending the system to detecting other types of network attacks would also be of interest.

[1] This work is partially funded by the research seed grant of COT, Purdue University

7. REFERENCES

[1] Abdullah, K. et al. 2005. Visualizing network data for intrusion detection. *Information Assurance Workshop, 2005. IAW '05. Proceedings from the Sixth Annual IEEE SMC* (Jun. 2005), 100–108.

[2] Bhuyan, M.H. et al. 2011. Surveying Port Scans and Their Detection Methodologies. *The Computer Journal.* 54, 10 (Oct. 2011), 1565–1581.

[3] Conti, G. and Abdullah, K. 2004. Passive Visual Fingerprinting of Network Attack Tools. *Proceedings of the 2004 ACM Workshop on Visualization and Data Mining for Computer Security* (New York, NY, USA, 2004), 45–54.

[4] Fischer, F. and Keim, D.A. VACS: Visual Analytics Suite for Cyber Security.

[5] Gates, C. 2006. *Co-ordinated Port Scans: A Model, a Detector and an Evaluation Methodology.* Dalhousie University.

[6] Itoh, T. et al. 2006. Hierarchical visualization of network intrusion detection data. *IEEE Computer Graphics and Applications.* 26, 2 (Mar. 2006), 40–47.

[7] Janies, J. 2008. Existence Plots: A Low-Resolution Time Series for Port Behavior Analysis. *Visualization for Computer Security.* J.R. Goodall et al., eds. Springer Berlin Heidelberg. 161–168.

[8] Jiawan, Z. et al. 2008. A Novel Visualization Approach for Efficient Network Scans Detection. *International Conference on Security Technology, 2008. SECTECH '08* (Dec. 2008), 23–26.

[9] Jung, J. et al. 2004. Fast portscan detection using sequential hypothesis testing. *2004 IEEE Symposium on Security and Privacy, 2004. Proceedings* (May 2004), 211–225.

[10] Kim, J. and Lee, J.-H. 2008. A slow port scan attack detection mechanism based on fuzzy logic and a stepwise p1olicy. *2008 IET 4th International Conference on Intelligent Environments* (Jul. 2008), 1–5.

[11] McPherson, J. et al. 2004. PortVis: A Tool for Port-based Detection of Security Events. *Proceedings of the 2004 ACM Workshop on Visualization and Data Mining for Computer Security* (New York, NY, USA, 2004), 73–81.

[12] Paxson, V. 1999. Bro: a system for detecting network intruders in real-time. *Computer Networks.* 31, 23–24 (Dec. 1999), 2435–2463.

[13] Taylor, T. et al. 2008. NetBytes Viewer: An Entity-Based NetFlow Visualization Utility for Identifying Intrusive Behavior. *VizSEC 2007.* J.R. Goodall et al., eds. Springer Berlin Heidelberg. 101–114.

[14] VAST Challenge 2013: Mini-Challenge 3: *http://vacommunity.org/VAST+Challenge+2013%3A+Mini-Challenge+3.* Accessed: 2014-06-07.

[15] De Vivo, M. et al. 1999. A Review of Port Scanning Techniques. *SIGCOMM Comput. Commun. Rev.* 29, 2 (Apr. 1999), 41–48.

[16] Yin, X. et al. 2004. VisFlowConnect: Netflow Visualizations of Link Relationships for Security Situational Awareness. *Proceedings of the 2004 ACM Workshop on Visualization and Data Mining for Computer Security* (New York, NY, USA, 2004), 26–34.

[17] Zadeh, L.A. 1994. Fuzzy Logic, Neural Networks, and Soft Computing. *Commun. ACM.* 37, 3 (Mar. 1994), 77–84.

[18] Zhao, Y. et al. MVSec: A Novel Multi-view Visualization System for Network Security.

Using Time-Series Analysis to Provide Long-Term CPU Utilization Prediction

Daniel W. Yoas

Industrial, Computing and Engineering Technology

Pennsylvania College of Technology

Williamsport, PA 17701

dyoas@pct.edu

Greg Simco

Graduate School of Computer and Information Sciences

Nova Southeastern University

Ft. Lauderdale, FL 33314

greg@nova.edu

ABSTRACT

Time-series analysis has been a recognized method of prediction for years. In computing, prediction has revolved around scheduling problems and is used in computing time to manage resources in the short-term. Long-term prediction using these methods has proven to be problematic and of little use. However, with the rise of Information Technology (IT) and the need to manage resources in a business atmosphere, the need to provide long-term resource management remains a difficult problem without a good solution. At this time, IT professionals use experience and their best judgment to manage equipment and frequently purchase systems based on maximum requirements. The need to take the knowledge gained by computer science in scheduling now needs to be expanded into the realm of IT to facilitate a more economical use of resource availability. This work is just the first step and provides one path to accomplishing long-term prediction in computing.

Categories and Subject Descriptors

D.4.8 [**Performance**]: Measurements, Modeling and Prediction, Monitors;

General Terms

Design, Experimentation, Human Factors, Management, Measurement, Performance, Reliability, Security, Theory.

Keywords

Prediction methods; Demand forecasting.

1. Introduction

Defining areas of research within Information Technology has been a difficult task. The IT 2008 documentation [1] answers part of the question by recommending that IT is founded on programming, networking, database, web development, and Human Computer Interaction, with security woven throughout. In each of these areas, industry demands the support of the IT professional and, for that support to occur, those professionals must have the skills and tools to support industry.

Computer Science (CS) took interest in improving the scheduling routines as part of the operating system functionality for process management and load balancing for distributing process loads with multiple systems. Computer Science, historically, has been focused on the efficiency of the systems. Information Technology has worked to understand how these systems are to be used to optimize business functionality. Research in Information technology should begin developing tools that will help IT professionals increase the efficiency of the functional systems.

A wide variety of systems in use today rely on the expertise of the IT professional to balance their use including virtual machines (VM), web services, distributed system, and network servers. For years, the balance of processes has been maintained through scheduling to keep the systems running. Beyond that the IT professional has used resource logging to estimate long-term resource needs, often looking at the maximum utilization and building systems to meet the highest demand. This has the effect of wasting resources when those systems are not under a full load. With the exception of virtual machines, idle resources have a cost impact for the industry owner.

Within the arena of virtual machines, multiple systems can be combined together to reduce the amount of time resources are idle, as long as the IT professional is able to map how the resource utilization of multiple VMs with complimentary utilization can be combined together on the same system. However, when multiple VMs are placed on a single physical system, there is the risk that the multiple services could result in ongoing exhaustion of a resource, causing the VM services to perform poorly. To prevent poor matching, the IT professional must know not only the maximum utilization of each resource, but also when that utilization peaks. The IT professional needs to evaluate the combination of those systems which don't have the same resource utilization profile once that information for each individual system is known. While two VM systems prove difficult enough to balance, modern virtual systems like vSphere 5.5 [2] can handle and balance up to 512 virtual machines on a single physical unit.

2. Related Work

In recent work with memory allocation for virtual machines [14], the authors used a least recently used (LRU) memory scheduling algorithm to better balance the memory demands of the VMs. In this case, the memory utilization was monitored and adjusted five times each minute, based on the last reading. Additional testing was conducted to help determine how much overhead was required to manage the memory allocation changes. One result the authors [14] determined was that, as they increased the complexity of the system, the prediction mechanism began to take an unreasonable amount of resources, as predicted by [4, 6].

Andreolini, Casolari, and Colajanni [6] also determined that the use of complex prediction algorithms was not appropriate for real-time prediction, while Al-Ghamdi, Chester, and Jarvis [4] were able to establish that the basic time-series analysis techniques showed dramatic improvement in completion time of the prediction with similar accuracy of that prediction. In both cases [4, 6] the authors investigated real-time prediction of resource utilization to improve the performance of web systems. In Andreolini et al. [6] predictions were made in one-second and five-second intervals from recent history. To provide an effective process, a framework was developed for evaluating various time-series

Researchers have also been interested in understanding network load on systems [10, 12]. The network weather service consisted of a series of tools developed by Wolski et al. [12] to provide dynamic resource utilization information in a manner that wouldn't impede performance when gathering the data or evaluating it. The focus of providing the sampling and prediction of the network weather system was on predicting short-term performance. Krithikaivasan et al. [10] considered improving quality of service for network traffic by aggregating samples into fifteen-minute utilization levels, and then used Auto Regressive Conditional Heteroskedasticity and confidence intervals of 50%. The authors [10] determined that the use of the 50% confidence interval provided a better result in determining how provision bandwidth than the higher level of 90%.

Researchers [3] have also looked at the use of a prediction range, instead of attempting to identify the exact level of utilization of a resource. By using a range, Abusina et al. [3] were attempting to address both the predictability of human interaction with the network and the realization that a snapshot of the current utilization would always look like it was chaotic and unpredictable. By using the range and aggregating the data, the authors [3] were able to consider "normal" traffic and the cyclical nature of how the resource was used over time.

3. Experiment Setup

Researchers have looked at the problem of predicting resource utilization in a long-term framework [5, 9] by extending existing CS scheduling methods only to discover that predictions were unreliable. Using those traditional methods, samples of resource utilization were gathered and complex algorithms were used to predict the results multiple steps into the future. The difficulty with this method is two-fold. First, scheduling within a computer is an activity that is repeated many times each second. While this time frame is important to CS, it has little relevance for business functionality and, in turn, IT. Second, because the predictions were extended from CS methods, the predictions frequently only looked up to five minutes into the future. By using what just happened to look into the near future, trends could be identified, but the cycle of computing use over weeks and months was never considered. But, for IT that long range planning is an important part of business functionality that researchers need to address [7].

This work used the prediction methods, [Naive, simple moving average (SMA), and exponential moving average (EMA)], previously used in a simulated environment [13], and extends them to evaluate the effectiveness of predicting long-term resource utilization with trace data from a live system. Data was collected for six months from a live web site. Six resources were selected for data gathering; these included the CPU utilization, memory currently committed to the system functionality, the amount of data received and sent over the Internet connection, and the amount of data read from and written to the local disk. This report will provide results for the CPU utilization and the accuracy of those predictions.

Samples were taken from the server every ten seconds over the collection period. Each data point was then aggregated into one-minute, fifteen-minute, and sixty-minute utilization averages. Each average was used for the hourly, daily, and weekly predictions respectively. The collection time and evaluation are critical to the success of the process [8, 12]. If the times take too long, a live prediction system would never be feasible. Review of the resource utilization for the collection of the data appeared to place less than 0.01% demand on the system. Since a valid method of evaluation and improvement for the system has not yet been determined, the cost in resources remains unknown at this time.

The data processed using SAS to aggregate, calculate, and analyze the accuracy of the naïve, SMA, and EMA predictions. SAS was also used to calculate the Mean Average Percentage Error (MAPE) and the confidence interval of 80% for each prediction. MAPE was selected as the error gauge, since it reports the degree of the error, which is easily compared to the results of the prediction and the actual utilization. Consideration of the confidence interval was included, since understanding of when a system is behaving normally is an important element for IT administrative needs [3], and was later reaffirmed in a parallel study [7].

An 80% confidence interval was selected for this work, since businesses have found in practice that there is frequently an 80/20 split for many of their objectives. The other consideration is that the use of confidence intervals was intended to help identify normal usage. In the end, this will be dependent upon the IT administrator, but for this study, a lower level was selected to help identify the 20% of the time when the system wasn't within the prescribed normal use of resource utilization. This should then theoretically provide time for a system to react to the abnormal event [13].

What makes this study different from previous work is that instead of relying on the previous contiguous events to provide the prediction, the input for the prediction is based on the cycle being reviewed. For example, if the cycle is hourly, then what occurs during the fifth minute will repeat each hour. The issue is that previous work uses minutes one through four to determine what will happen during minute five, instead of what has happened during the last four "minute fives" in the previous four hours. This research uses that basic understanding of cyclical behavior to look back to the previous thirteen cycles to predict the next one. For a system evaluating an upcoming prediction, the information can be stored in an array until needed to compare against the actual results.

4. Results

1.7 million data points were collected every ten seconds over a period of six months. Those data points were aggregated into values to be used to generate the naïve, SMA, and EMA predictions for the hourly, daily, and weekly cycles. The hourly cycles had prediction points every minute, for a total of sixty predictions each hour. When the results of the predictions were examined, the SMA predictions were the worst, with the Naïve and EMA with an error rate within 10% of each other (see Figure 1). Overall, the mean error rate was around 140% of the actual reading with a standard deviation around 22.5%. The difficulty with considering the system every minute is that, over a 24 hour period, CPU utilization can fluctuate greatly. IT professionals understand that the utilization for web and network services is very different during the 3am hour and the 3pm hour.

Live Web Server Forecasting Statistics			Results by Minute within an Hour									Summary	
			Minimum Mean/STD		~-STD Mean/STD		~Mean Mean/STD		~+STD Mean/STD		Maximum Mean/STD		Mean	STD
CPU	Naïve	MAPE	97.74		113.99		138.27		161.10		206.92		138.19	23.89
		Utilization	3.28	3.41	2.10	2.71	2.12	2.30	2.48	3.52	2.04	2.40		
		Cycle	0		32		8		36		58			
	MA	MAPE	98.75		152.15		176.34		201.12		225.78		176.45	24.28
		Utilization	3.28	3.41	2.02	2.31	2.26	2.38	2.30	3.10	2.31	2.80		
		Cycle	0		30		46		38		55			
	EMA	MAPE	100.00		120.39		142.90		161.74		197.17		141.40	21.86
		Utilization	3.28	3.41	2.16	2.46	2.20	2.63	2.27	2.86	2.16	2.27		
		Cycle	0		45		10		35		1			

Figure 1: Prediction Results for the Hourly Cycle

When the results are processed through a box plot (see Figure 2), it is easy to see that the web servers had CPU utilization commonly between 1% and 6% over the 60 periods. The predictions can also be reviewed as a line chart as seen in Figure 3 and, as expected; the EMA prediction slightly trails the actual results. It should also be noted that the CPU sometimes climbed as high as 18%.

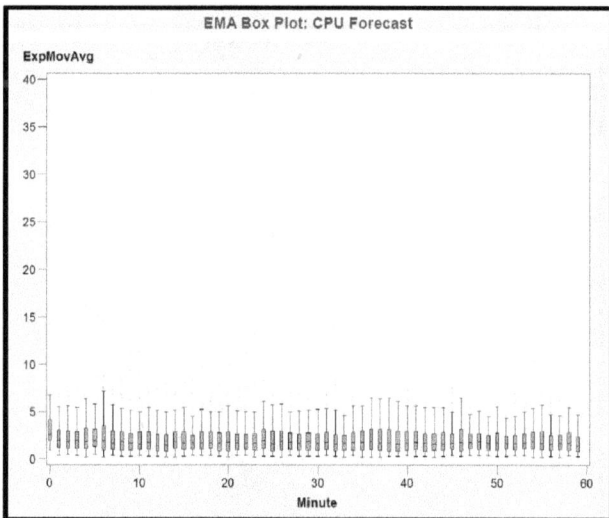

Figure 2: Box Plot for Hourly Predictions

While the mean error rate ran between 138% and 175% for the hourly predictions, the daily mean error rates ran from 62% to 78%. Both the SMA and EMA predictions were greatly improved over the naïve prediction (see Figure 4). For the daily cycle SMA prediction proved to be the best even under the worst prediction set, where the SMA rate of error 266% compared to 446% error rate for EMA and 601% error rate for naïve predictions. Despite the high maximum error rate, the error rates remained reasonable through the first standard deviation where the naïve prediction was 146% and the lowest was 95% for SMA. This is a clear indication that the daily cycle is more closely matched to system utilization patterns than the hourly cycle.

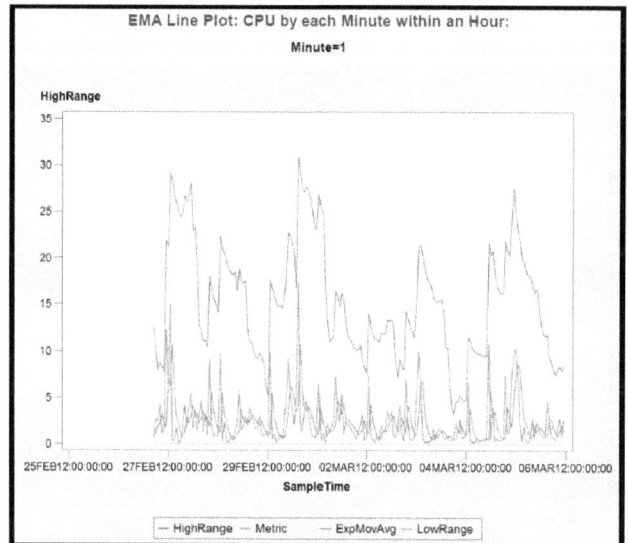

Figure 3: EMA Prediction for Minute 01 of Hourly Cycle

Live Web Server Forecasting Statistics			Results by 15 Minutes within a Day									Summary	
			Minimum Mean/STD		~-STD Mean/STD		~Mean Mean/STD		~+STD Mean/STD		Maximum Mean/STD		Mean	STD
CPU	Naïve	MAPE	16.13				77.21		146.56		601.24		77.33	80.39
		Utilization	3.12	0.52			1.68	1.27	1.67	1.98	2.91	4.28		
		Cycle	4				86		95		93			
	MA	MAPE	11.52		26.54		62.59		95.78		266.29		62.43	37.94
		Utilization	3.12	0.52	1.32	0.39	2.26	2.39	1.84	2.02	2.91	4.28		
		Cycle	4		74		57		2		93			
	EMA	MAPE	14.13				68.48		130.28		446.02		68.19	59.99
		Utilization	3.12	0.52			2.34	2.00	1.85	2.53	2.91	4.28		
		Cycle	4				55		1		93			

Figure 4: Prediction Results for the Daily Cycle

Each hourly time slice represented a single minute but, with the daily cycle, each time slice is represented by fifteen minutes. As with the hourly review, a box chart was created to get a better view of any patterns that might exist on a daily basis (see Figure 5). Unlike the results of the hourly box plot which showed the little of the cyclical nature of the CPU utilization, a clear distinction of overnight use each day shows low CPU use while midday utilization is higher. One interesting aspect of the results is a tightening of the range of CPU utilization between cycle 68 and 79, which represents the time slots between 5:00pm and 8:00pm each evening. A line chart for cycle 71 (see Figure 6), which represents each day between 5:45pm and 6:00pm between May 30th and July 17th 2012, shows a level CPU utilization over the eight week period. The first two weeks were used in the "training" and the remaining six weeks are displayed.

This study was conducted with trace data but the authors envision a time when IT professionals have implemented the statistical analysis in a live format. Once implemented, the ability to flag abnormal usage can begin and results like the CPU utilization shown at the end of the line chart (see Figure 6) could notify the administrator, or other systems, that additional attention is needed. For some reason, the requirements of the CPU jumped on July 17th around 6:00pm from a normal range between 1% and 3% to 10%. While an increase in CPU use to 10% might not stop services, it is this type of change that could: overload a resource, cause delayed service response, indicate a denial of service attack, or be a precursor to a failing piece of software. It is this type of information that remains elusive but is desired by system managers [7].

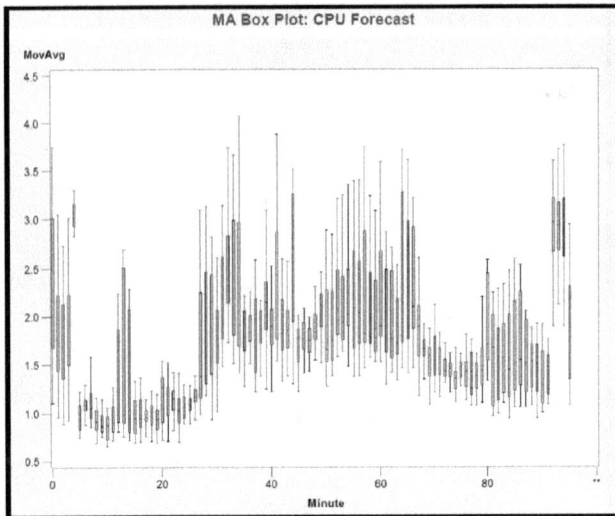
Figure 5: Box Plot for Daily Predictions

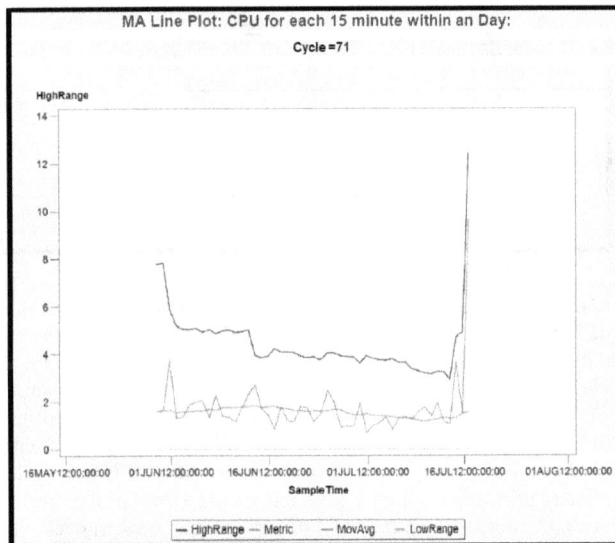
Figure 6: SMA Prediction for Cycle 71 of Daily Cycle

Another set of graphs generated from the live trace data were distribution graphs for CPU utilization for all three cycles reviewed. In Figure 7 the CPU utilization for cycle 71 is displayed. Interestingly, the distribution views show that nearly all distributions, when pulled from a cycle that mimics human utilization, have nearly 90% of the readings fall into limited ranges. In this case, nearly 55% of the 15 minute averages fell around 0.75% CPU utilization. Another 40% clustered around 2.25%. The remaining two blocks were around 3.75% and 9.75%, with nothing between the two lending to the notion that the 9.75% utilization level might not be normal [13].

The weekly cycle aggregated the raw data into one hour blocks for a total of 168 time slices over the week. Again, the SMA and EMA normally performed better that the naïve prediction: both in the MAPE and the standard deviation of the prediction. When the chart for box and whiskers is generated from the aggregate data the seven day pattern of utilization becomes obvious (see Figure 8). The first large peak at hour 72 represents Sunday morning at 1:00am and, according to the owners of the system, is the start of the weekly full backup of the system. Each day

can be seen progressing from an overnight low in usage to the midday starting on Friday and ending on Thursday.

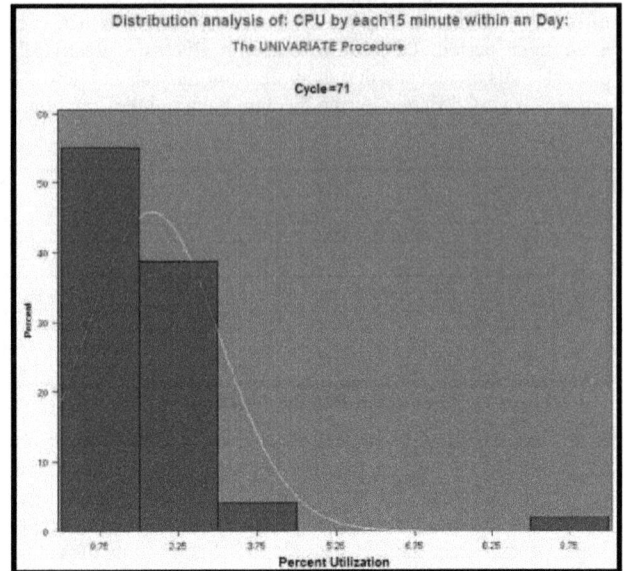
Figure 7: CPU Utilization Distribution at 6:45pm

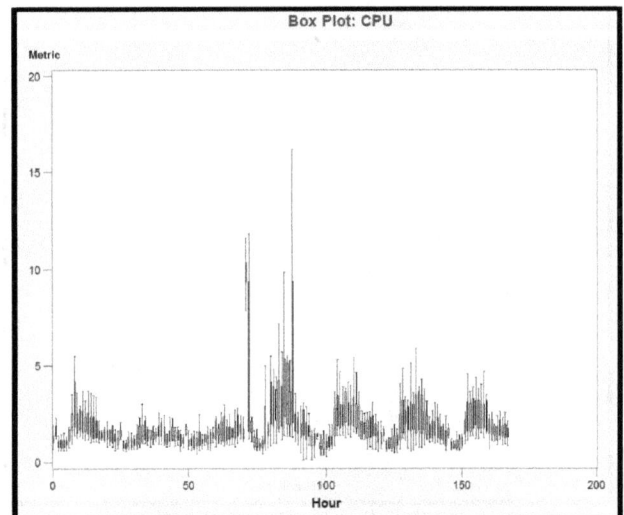
Figure 8: Box Plot for Weekly CPU Utilization

Another tool that was used to evaluate the prediction process was to generate a linear regression chart (see Figure 9). While this is useful for off-line evaluation, it would never be used as part of a real-time evaluation of the system state, due to the amount of time it takes to generate the chart. Even with a range of about 0.5% to 12% representing an 80% confidence level at this time, it would be easy to identify a situation that shoots the CPU utilization well outside the normal usage. While the hour aggregate is too granular for that type of determination, there is no reason that the time slice could be reduced to one minute, allowing the same process to occur but with 10,080 time slices instead of 168.

A second linear regression for hour 150 (Wednesday at 6:00am) is included for comparison. In this case, the confidence interval of 80% binds the usage between 0% and 2.5% (See Figure 10). One of the difficulties with a low and small range is that the

MAPE errors were commonly around 50%, with 40% to 60% as a standard deviation. So with a CPU average around 1.5%, a 50% error still leaves the CPU between 0.75% and 2.25%. For IT professionals looking to understand cyclical resource utilization, this range of 1.5% will not reduce the ability to identify abnormal behavior in the system.

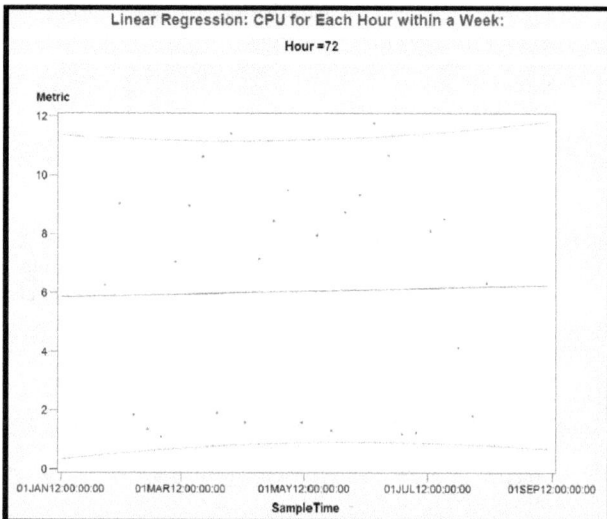

Figure 9: Linear Regression for Sunday 1:00am

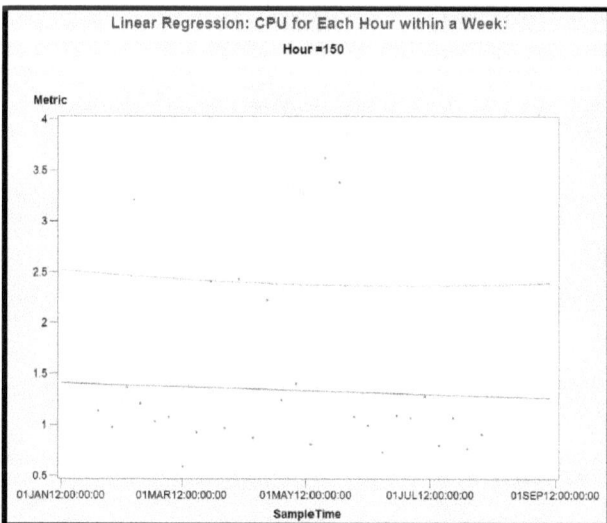

Figure 10: Linear Regression for Wednesday at 6:00am

5. Conclusions and Future Research

Several studies should be considered from the current information gathered in this study. The first is to look at the length of history used for the prediction. While this may eventually be part of tuning for individual systems, it is important to learn if fewer historic points do as well as more points. A second area of additional research will be to look at varying the aggregate time-slice. The hour aggregate may be just fine for the weekly cycle, but a fifteen-minute time slice might be more appropriate as a reaction time, when the system behaves abnormally. A third area of research could also be conducted by identifying the probability of the system exiting normal use of the resource. These values could then be incorporated into a

Markov chain, incorporating a normal, abnormal, and failed state. Finally, once a long-term monitoring system is incorporated into the system a feedback process can be implemented for continuous improvement.

Further into the future, research could begin to address issues of resource utilization for distributed systems. By building a process capable of distinguishing between normal resource utilization and abnormal utilization, the distributed system would be able to adjust its behavior within the collective system. This could include waving off new jobs until the system returns to normal. For virtual systems, a long-term utilization monitor could provide feedback to various virtual machines so they can collaborate in the use of resources and systems with opposite needs could function more effectively on the same hardware. In the realm of graceful degradation, the predictions could provide advanced warning of a system failure or even abnormal behavior, giving the system more time to protect its information in case of failure. For security professionals, system attacks frequently leave footprints but the change in resource utilization could provide an intrusion detection system an additional alert. Finally, systems like web services could be sized based on common need instead of maximum need. Future systems could use this information to dynamically instantiate additional services from the cloud during peak usage and then debrief those systems once that need has passed, bringing a philosophy of "just in time" to the computing environment.

Each area of future research focuses on tasks currently done by IT professionals. These tasks take varying lengths of time and some are not possible, because the information needed to accomplish the tasks isn't easily available. While the information contained here may be considered futuristic, a mechanism to provide long-term prediction has the possibility of allowing these ideas to become a reality.

When a system is working with a scheduling issue, it is imperative to find a good balance between determining what is to be done next and efficiency of selecting the next appropriate task [4, 6]. Operating systems and distributed systems have had a long history of research into optimizing [8, 9, 11], and those techniques don't directly translate into long-term resource utilization predictions [5, 9]. Without a basis to know if long-term prediction for resource utilization was possible, a new way of looking at the problem was needed. And while more complex time-series analysis methods are available, the first step was to show that the prediction of resources over hours, days, and weeks is feasible.

The basic methods of time-series analysis, SMA and EMA, were used to prove that resource utilization prediction was possible. They were also selected since the time for calculating the prediction is very quick and is unlikely to create an issue by disrupting the system resources needed to complete its assigned tasks. This study also used a variety of tools, various plots, which are not suitable for real-time evaluation but support the original premise of resource predictability. For IT professionals that currently review logs and use their experience to determine the resource sizing of the systems, a basic predictive system will provide a set of additional information for making those choices. At this time long-term prediction beyond a few hours is not being actively perused as research topic. This work has shown that long-term prediction is feasible and a desirable area for IT research because of the support information it can generate for system management.

6. References

[1] *Information Technology 2008: Curriculum Guidelines for Undergraduate Degree Programs in Information Technology.* (2008). Retrived, from http://www.acm.org//education/curricula/IT2008%20Curriculum.pdf.

[2] *Configuration Maximums: VMware vSphere 5.5.* (2014). Retrived June 6, 2014, from http://www.vmware.com/pdf/vsphere5/r55/vsphere-55-configuration-maximums.pdf.

[3] Abusina, Z.U.M., S.M.S. Zabir, A. Ashir, D. Chakraborty, T. Suganuma, and N. Shiratori (2005) *An engineering approach to dynamic prediction of network performance from application logs.* Int. J. Netw. Manag. **15**, 151-162 DOI: 10.1002/nem.554.

[4] Al-Ghamdi, M., A.P. Chester, and S.A. Jarvis (2010) *Predictive and Dynamic Resource Allocation for Enterprise Applications.* 10th IEEE International Conference on Computer and Information Technology (CIT 2010) **0**, 2776-2783 DOI: 10.1109/CIT.2010.463.

[5] Andreolini, M. and S. Casolari (2006) *Load prediction models in web-based systems.* Proceedings of the 1st international conference on Performance evaluation methodolgies and tools, 27 DOI: 10.1145/1190095.1190129.

[6] Andreolini, M., S. Casolari, and M. Colajanni (2008) *Models and framework for supporting runtime decisions in Web-based systems.* ACM Trans. Web **2**, 1-43 DOI: 10.1145/1377488.1377491.

[7] Davis, I.J., H. Hemmati, R.C. Holt, M.W. Godfrey, D.M. Neuse, and S. Mankovskii, *Regression-based utilization prediction algorithms: an empirical investigation*, in *Proceedings of the 2013 Conference of the Center for Advanced Studies on Collaborative Research.* 2013, IBM Corp.: Ontario, Canada. p. 106-120.

[8] Dinda, P.A. (2002) *A Prediction-Based Real-Time Scheduling Advisor.* International Parallel and Distributed Processing Symposium (IPDPS'02) **1**, 0010b-0010b DOI: 10.1109/IPDPS.2002.1015480.

[9] Istin, M., A. Visan, F. Pop, and V. Cristea (2010) *Decomposition Based Algorithm for State Prediction in Large Scale Distributed Systems.* Ninth International Symposium on Parallel and Distributed Computing **0**, 17-24 DOI: 10.1109/ISPDC.2010.13.

[10] Krithikaivasan, B., Y. Zeng, K. Deka, and D. Medhi (2007) *ARCH-based traffic forecasting and dynamic bandwidth provisioning for periodically measured nonstationary traffic.* IEEE/ACM Trans. Netw. **15**, 683-696 DOI: 10.1109/tnet.2007.893217.

[11] Rood, B. and M.J. Lewis (2010) *Availability Prediction Based Replication Strategies for Grid Environments.* 10th IEEE/ACM International Conference on Cluster, Cloud and Grid Computing **0**, 25-33 DOI: 10.1109/CCGRID.2010.121

[12] Wolski, R., N.T. Spring, and J. Hayes (1999) *The network weather service: a distributed resource performance forecasting service for metacomputing.* Future Gener. Comput. Syst. **15**, 757-768 DOI: 10.1016/s0167-739x(99)00025-4.

[13] Yoas, D.W. and G. Simco, *Resource utilization prediction: a proposal for information technology research*, in *Proceedings of the 1st Annual conference on Research in information technology.* 2012, ACM: Calgary, Alberta, Canada. p. 25-30.

[14] Zhao, W. and Z. Wang, *Dynamic memory balancing for virtual machines*, in *Proceedings of the 2009 ACM SIGPLAN/SIGOPS international conference on Virtual execution environments.* 2009, ACM: Washington, DC, USA. p. 21-30.

Three-Dimensional Wireless Heat Mapping and Security Assessment using Multi-Rotor Aerial Drones

Scott J. Pack
Brigham Young University
School of Technology
Brigham Young University, Provo, UT
scottjpack@gmail.com

Dale C. Rowe Ph.D.
Brigham Young University
School of Technology
Brigham Young University, Provo, UT
dale_rowe@byu.edu

ABSTRACT

Wireless networks are well known to be at risk a variety of attacks and/or monitoring by malicious users. Much effort has been put into developing encryption and authentication protocols for these networks, yet time has shown that weaknesses are frequently found in their implementation. For this reason, many organizations conduct site surveys to measure signal strength at various locations surrounding the premises. In this paper, we show how a multi-rotor aerial drone can effectively and quickly perform a 3D site assessment. 3D site assessments, unlike traditional assessments measure signal strength at varying altitudes that might otherwise be overlooked. We demonstrate a low-cost platform that can perform these surveys and demonstrate how it can also be used in finding other security concerns such as rogue access points within an organization. We also analyze a number of ways to visualize the results.

Categories and Subject Descriptors

K.6.5 [**Security and Protection**]: Authentication, Insurance, Invasive Software, Physical Security, and Unauthorized Access.

C.2.m [**Computer-Communications Networks**]: Miscellaneous

General Terms

Security

Keywords

Information Assurance; Mechatronics; Security; UAV's; Wireless Surveys

1. INTRODUCTION

A wireless site survey is the process of inspecting the geographic area around a wireless access point (WAP) to determine the signal strength of a network at different points in a target area. In deploying a WAP a survey is used to determine spectrum usage by neighboring or overlapping wireless networks [3]. This is traditionally performed by loading software on a laptop including a map of the area, roaming the area on foot or with a cart while taking received signal strength indication (RSSI) measurements, clicking on the map to associate the reading with the appropriate location to generating a coverage "heat-map." [2] Some tools are

RIIT'14, October 15–18, 2014, Atlanta, Georgia, USA.
Copyright © 2014 ACM 978-1-4503-2711-4/14/10...$15.00.
http://dx.doi.org/10.1145/2656434.2656447

capable of using Global Positioning Systems (GPS) receivers to geolocate the receiver in outdoor installations. This approach can be effective, but is time consuming and is limited to areas accessible by an individual with a laptop, typically only on the ground plane.

In recent years unmanned aerial vehicles (UAVs) have increased in capability and dropped significantly in price, and research is being performed to the end of using both fixed-wing and rotary UAVs as a network attack platform, creating a new attack method of "war-flying." [6] Additional work has been done to use UAVs in providing a covert transmission channel for command and control [4] and performing de-authentication attacks [5]. This makes it important for high security installations to be aware of wireless coverage areas not only on the ground, but also in areas not accessible to most human actors, such as balconies, roof tops, and the airspace surrounding buildings.

This paper explores the creation and use of a multi-rotor and a data collection module for performing three dimensional 802.11 wireless site surveys, and puts forward a few methods of visualizing this data in potentially valuable ways. This allows an individual or organization to gain awareness and visualize the extent of their coverage area above ground level.

Research Objective

The objective of this research is to determine the capability of a multi-rotor aircraft as a transportation platform for an 802.11 data collection module.

2. APPROACH

To perform this research, a multi-rotor and separate data collection module were built. The suitability of the multi-rotor as a transportation platform for the data collection module was assessed in terms of flight time and the impact of radio emanations associated with the multi-rotor upon the data collection module. Once the interaction between the multi-rotor and the data collection module was determined, a series of flights were conducted to test the multi-rotors ability to collect data in a variety of situations, including flights in approximate linear, planar, and volumetric patterns. Flights were performed in open airspace, and in the vicinity of buildings. An access point (AP) was placed within the flight pattern for sampling. Collected data was interpolated across a three dimensional matrix, and visualized in altitude "slices," as grid points and contours in Keyhole Markup Language (KML) for viewing in other applications.

2.1 Multi Rotor

The flight controller that was used for the multi-rotor was the Ardupilot [1] APM 2.5, an open-source controller manufactured by 3DR with an attached uBlox NEO-6M GPS and RCTimer 433 MHz telemetry unit. Motors were the Turnigy 2826 1200KV controlled by Turnigy 30A Plush Electronic Speed Controllers (ESCs). This equipment was mounted on a glass fiber 450mm frame with 8.5x4.5 propellers in a quad-X configuration, and powered by a Zippy 4000Mah 4-cell 12.6v lithium polymer battery.

2.2 Data Collection Module

The data collection module was based on the Raspberry Pi Model B, a small single-board computer, running a modified version of Debian Linux, named Raspbian. The Alfa Networks AWUS036-NHA USB 802.11 Wireless Network Card was used for collecting Link Quality data, and the uBlox CN-06 GPS was used for geolocation.

A power regulator was installed to permit the Raspberry Pi to use the same 12.6V lithium polymer battery already in use by the multi-rotor.

Python scripts were written to do the following: enable the required hardware at boot time, calibrate the barometer, place the wireless card in monitor mode, and initiate a serial connection to the GPS receiver after waiting an amount of time to obtain a GPS lock. The script then enters an infinite loop during which it scans the 802.11 2.4GHz channels for broadcast Service Set Identifiers (SSIDs). The SSID, Media Access Control (MAC) address, channel, Relative Signal Strength Indicator (RSSI), link quality, and geolocation information are saved to a numbered log file on a removable storage card for later retrieval and analysis. Access points were scanned and recorded approximately once per second.

3. RESULTS

Initial testing showed the flight configuration to be slightly more powerful than the default build which was made manifest in 10Hz oscillations of approximately five degrees off normal in pitch and roll axes. As a result, an amount of tuning was required in the proportional figure of the control loop to reduce these oscillations. Once this tuning was completed, the multi-rotor performed reliably and stably. With competent piloting skills, it was possible for the multi-rotor to perform vertical takeoff, maintain a loose hands-off loiter, be flown within a given area, and be flown in the vicinity of buildings. In the absence of strong winds, an experienced pilot can maneuver the multi-rotor safely within 2-3 meters of walls, trees, and other obstacles.

With the 4000Mah battery and attached data collection module, the multi-rotor was capable of maintaining a low speed velocity for an average of eight minutes and forty-four seconds prior to initiating the fail-safe descent. It was determined that to prevent loss of power while airborne, flights would be limited to under six minutes.

Initially, stability issues were present with the USB wireless network card, the cause of which was traced to insufficient current being provided through the USB interface. A modification was done to bypass the polyfuse restricting current supply to the USB interfaces which permitted an increased current draw and has not as yet shown any negative results.

Standalone data collection module testing took place by allowing two minutes to acquire satellites, and walking the module around a perimeter block with some known access points, and inspecting the results. Initial testing showed the altitude as determined by the GPS receiver to have wildly erroneous altitude changes, showing a range of over 30 meters while in a static location. As a result a barometer was included to determine altitude. This decreased the altitude range to 2.26 meters and a standard deviation of 0.52 meters.

The combined standard deviation of the latitude and longitude provided by the GPS receiver on the data collection module at a static location over a five minute period came to .24 meters. When mounted to the restrained multi-rotor and in close proximity to noise generated by the radio equipment, ESCs and motors at hover throttle, the standard deviation increased to 0.63 meters, maintaining sub-meter precision. It is worth noting that again in these tests, two minutes elapsed between providing power to the GPS receiver and taking readings to allow for satellite acquisition.

Assessment flights increased in complexity. The first flight plans consisted of a single line at a low altitude (1-3 meters) in an open area above an access point. The second set of flight plans were planar perimeter flights, followed by multi-plane perimeter flights. Finally building exterior assessments were performed.

4. DATA VISUALIZATION

Several different approaches were made at visualizing the data. 1. Logs were parsed directly into a KML format, using coordinate information to place a point and link quality to determine the color of the point. Points were broken into folders, allowing a given SSID to be enabled or disabled in a KML viewer such as Google Earth. 2. Recorded points were interpolated across the surveyed grid and selected slices rendered. 3. Recorded points for three dimensional flights were interpolated across the surveyed grid and exported as coordinates to a KML.

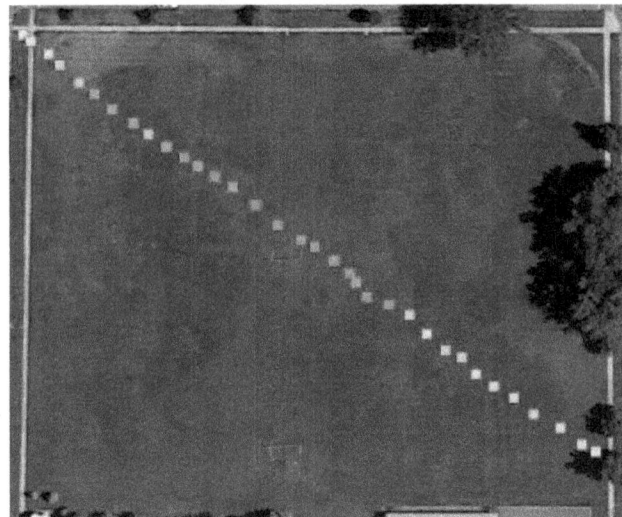

Figure 1 - Linear KML

4.1 Linear Flight Visualization

An access point was placed centrally in this area, and the multi-rotor was flown at an altitude of approximately two meters. The results show that, as could be expected, link quality was higher at positions closer to the AP. (See Figure 1 and Figure 2).

4.2 Planar Flight Visualization

The multi-rotor was flown around the perimeter of the area, with a central access point. The corners of the flight have a lower signal quality, as they are at a greater distance from the centrally located AP. Greater signal strength in one area near the north (top) of the figure suggests that the antenna may be directionally focused. Resulting coordinate and link quality data was interpolated across the grid area, and used to generate a planar contour plot. (See Figure 3 and Figure 4).

Figure 2 - Linear Contour

4.3 Multi-Plane Flight Visualization

A multi-planar flight was performed over a quarter of the anticipated coverage area of the placed access point. During the flight altitude was changed to collect readings from multiple heights.

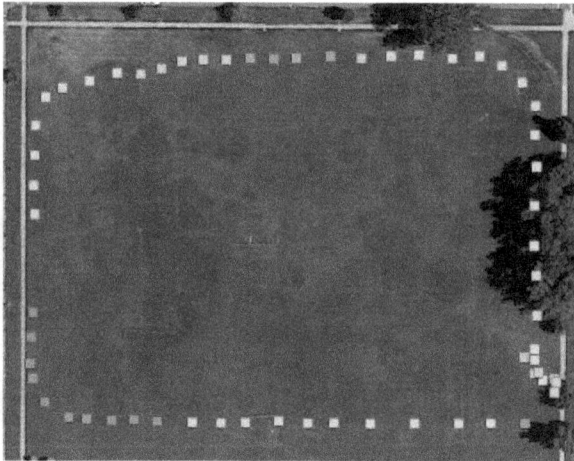

Figure 3 - Planar KML

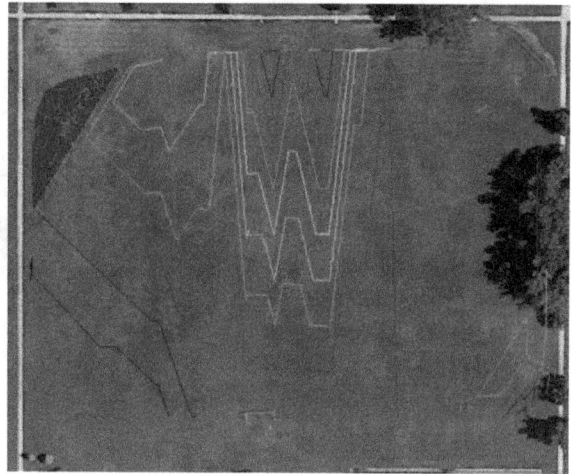

Figure 4 - Planar Contour

The interpolated results suggest that at a given distance from the access point, a better connection may be had at 10 meters above ground compared to five meters above ground. Figure 5 displays the collected data, and Figure 6 displays a selection of the interpolated values.

Planes from the interpolated data were selected at five and ten meters, and used to generate contour maps. This illustrates one method of visualizing layer by layer the data collected. (See Figure 7 and Figure 8)

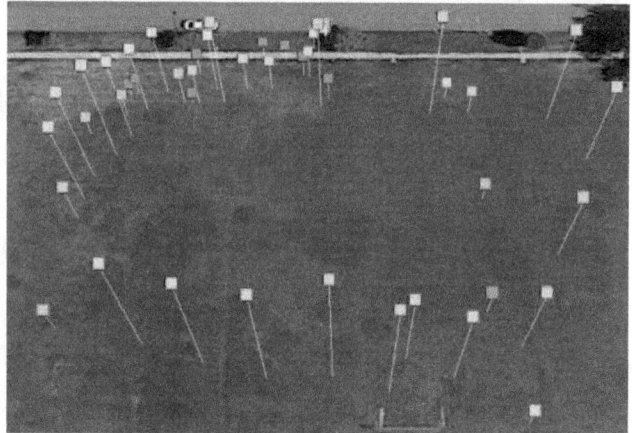

Figure 5 - Volumetric KML

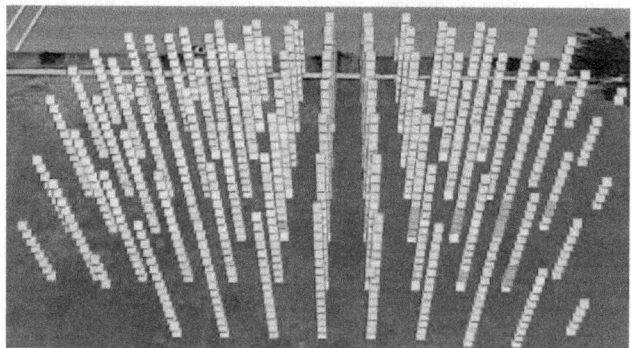

Figure 6 - Interpolated KML (Flight 19)

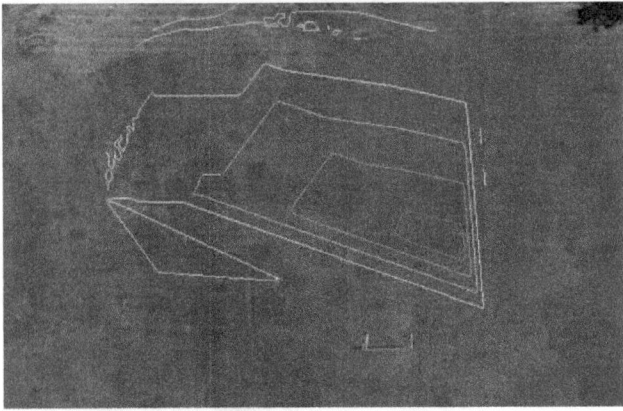

Figure 7 - Contour at 5m

4.4 Structure Flight Visualization

Having established a reasonably stable flight platform and a functional data collection unit, structure assessments were started. Two flights were made on the south and west sides of an eight story building and their logs combined. Almost 300 access points were detected and mapped, but Figure 9 and Figure 10 illustrate only a select access point, placed within the building on the southeast side, appearing closest the camera. This access point was placed by campus technology and was intended to provide internet to those on the east side of the ground floor.

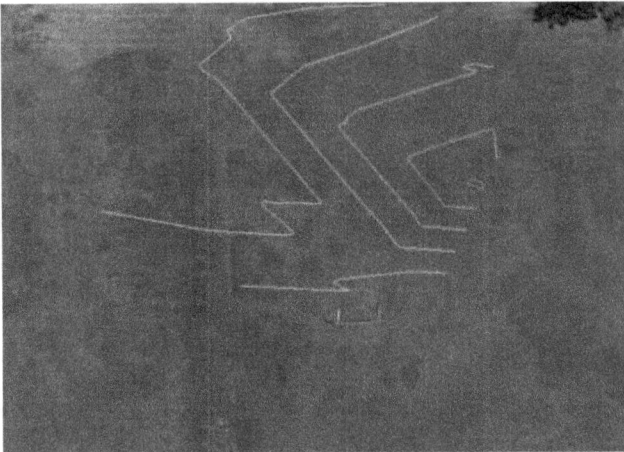

Figure 8 - Contour at 10m

In the duration of the structure flight, several access points were identified which were not placed by campus technology. Figure 11 and Figure 12 illustrate a rogue access point, not authorized for placement, also representing a potential security risk to the campus network. The interpolated contour plot suggests that link quality is strongest near the north-west corner of the building on the fourth and fifth floors. This rogue access point was later identified in the building in the estimated area.

Figure 9 - Structure Assessment KML

5. CONCLUSIONS

A multi-rotor appears to be a suitable platform for performing three-dimensional wireless data collection over small areas. Current lightweight GPS receivers, even in the presence of interference generated by the multi-rotor, provide sufficient accuracy and precision to geolocate collected data. The flight time limitation of 6-7 minutes makes the platform useful only for short flights, which results in the need to perform multiple flights for most assessments. This understood, the low ground velocity, vertical maneuverability, positioning precision, and degree of control afforded by a rotary-wing aircraft allows for access to areas which would otherwise be very difficult to access.

Figure 10 - Structure Assessment Multi-Layer Contour

Three-dimensional heat-maps of the type generated by this platform and data collection module can be of use in identifying and approximating the location of rogue access points, performing channel usage analysis for site surveys in wireless deployments, and determining the coverage area of wireless access points in high-security installations.

Figure 11 - Rogue AP (Interpolated)

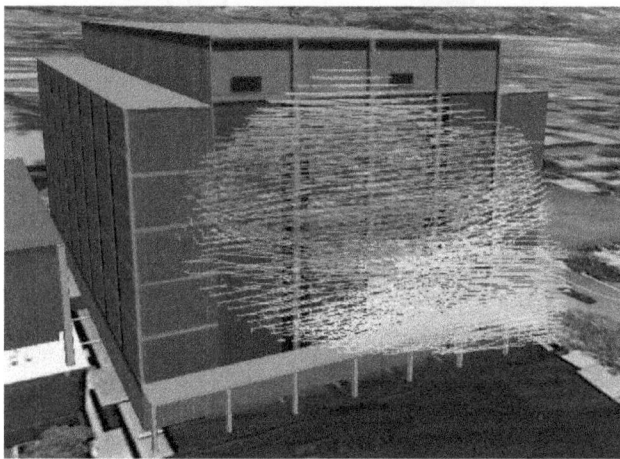

Figure 12 - Rogue AP Multi-Layer Contour

6. FUTURE RESEARCH

Further work planned in this topic includes increasing the performance and flight-time of the multi-rotor, implementing automated flight planning and collision avoidance, and performing spectrum analysis in ranges other than 2.4GHz. Increasing the frequency of access-point sampling rate, and making real-time changes to navigation velocity in response to a high delta in link quality to capture more dynamic networks may also be explored.

7. REFERENCES

[1] ArduCopter: 2013. *https://code.google.com/p/arducopter/*. Accessed: 2013-08-12.

[2] Hills, A. and Schlegel, J. 2004. Rollabout: a wireless design tool. *IEEE Communications Magazine*. 42, 2 (Feb. 2004), 132–138.

[3] Prasad, A.R. et al. 2001. Performance Evaluation, System Design and Network Deployment of IEEE 802.11. *Wireless Personal Communications: An International Journal*. 19, 1 (Oct. 2001), 57–79.

[4] Reed, T. et al. 2011. SkyNET: a 3G-enabled mobile attack drone and stealth botmaster. *Proceedings of the 5th USENIX Conference on Offensive Technologies (WOOT'11)* (San Francisco, CA, Aug. 2011), 4.

[5] SkyJack - autonomous drone hacking: 2013. *http://samy.pl/skyjack/*. Accessed: 2013-08-12.

[6] Tassey, M. and Perkins, R. 2009. WASP: Wireless Aerial Surveillance Platform. *DEFCON 19* (2009).

Analysis of Mobile Malware Based on User Awareness

Youngho Kim
Electronics and Telecommunications
Research Institute (ETRI)
Daejeon, Korea
wtowto@etri.re.kr

Bill Stackpole
Rochester Institute of Technology
(RIT)
Rochester, New York
bill.stackpole@rit.edu

Tae Oh
Rochester Institute of Technology
(RIT)
Rochester, New York
thoics@rit.edu

ABSTRACT

The number of mobile device malware has been increasing drastically last several years. When attempting to detect malware within a device, it is difficult to draw a clear line between malicious and normal activities. Even useful applications naturally result in data transfer from a mobile device to a remote server and a malware detection mechanism based solely on information flow might consider this as data leakage. Therefore one should also consider the surrounding context of an application to make a better decision on whether it is malicious or not. In this current research, a dynamic analysis approach is taken which monitors and measures the runtime behavior and logs from the mobile application. In particular, a concept of user awareness (UA) is proposed which represents a degree of intent with which an application tries to hide its activities from a user. This extended analysis measurement, combined with dataflow-based analysis, will help make a more accurate decision with less false positives.

Categories and Subject Descriptors

K.6.5 [**Management of Computing and Information Systems**]: Security and Protection – *invasive software, unauthorized access*.

Keywords

Mobile; Malware Analysis; Emulation; User Awareness

1. MAIN IDEA

To this end, we adopt a dynamic analysis approach in which the runtime behavior and data generated from the application should be monitored while it is running. The main objective is to track all activity that takes place and process the gathered information afterwards. In general, the data leakage analysis approach gets a log of the traces on the data flow which allows for the identification of data leakage [1]. In addition to explicit data flow analysis, the paper proposes the concept of user awareness (UA). This value represents the degree of user interaction with the application in order to gauge the evasiveness of the application from the user's perception in reverse. This extended analysis will help the existing approaches on data leakage detection make more accurate detection decisions with less false positives.

Since users are willing to send private or sensitive data to a remote server in exchange for useful service(s), it is often difficult to define a specific situation when information leakage really occurs. For example, Foursquare, a popular mobile application, helps people to find places of interest nearby by exposing the user's GPS location. It is hard to discern how or whether the data exfiltration of the GPS location might be harmful to the user. To make things worse, the information leakage continues to occur – even when the phone is believed to be inactive. Most of the time, the device infected with mobile botnet malware can be activated and controlled by a remote "bot master", but not by the device owner [2]. Thus, indication of what seems to be data exfiltration in a certain period of time stems from the rough definition of data leakage. The best way to learn the original intention that allowed outgoing data flow would be to ask the user what is going to happen and check if that would be permissible with them. However, getting the intention from a user is not viable in the real world system. Instead, we decide to analyze the intention of the application experiencing outbound data flow, in terms of its hiding efforts in preventing the user from being aware of its internal activity.

In general, recent user-friendly applications comprise multiple instances of view objects and view layers to implement Graphic User Interface (GUI). Moreover, the event-driven application framework provides an independent execution unit like activity in the case of the Android mobile platform. The UA analyzer records all activities of an application in question while user input is generated and then monitors any additional activities even after there is no more input. Most of internal activities respond to a user input generated by an input generator immediately and others run after a short or long while. The UA analyzer measures those differences and calculates a value to assign as the degree of user consciousness on the application. This will provide a better understanding of the hiding efforts the application intends to conceal inside.

2. ACKNOWLEDGMENTS

This work was supported by the ICT R&D program of MSIP/IITP. [13-912-06-901, Development of the security technology for MTM-based mobile devices and next generation wireless LAN]

3. REFERENCES

[1] W. Enck, P. Gilbert, B.-G. Chun, L. P. Cox, J. Jung, P. McDaniel, and A. N. Sheth. 2010. TaintDroid: an information-flow tracking system for realtime privacy monitoring on smartphones. USENIX OSDI, 1-6.

[2] C. Xiang, F. Binxing, Y. Lihua, L. Xiaoyi, and Z. Tianning. 2011. Andbot: Towards Advanced Mobile Botnets. USENIX Conference on Large-scale Exploits and Emergent Threats.

Insider Hacking: Applying Situational Crime Prevention to a New White-Collar Crime

Mark Stockman
University of Cincinnati
Cincinnati, OH 45221
(513) 556-4227
mark.stockman@uc.edu

ABSTRACT

Insider hacking consists of cybercrimes against entities initiated by individuals who hold a legitimate trust relationship with that entity. The responsibility of preventing insider hacking falls to information technology (IT) or information security departments staffed by computing professionals. The same can be said about research into the prevention of insider hacking, computing centric academics/professionals do the work. While this seems logical, established behavioral methods for reducing crime have largely been ignored. In this paper, the author places insider hacking into the context of the white-collar criminology literature then pulls from crime science, applying a situational crime prevention model to inform future research on insider hacking.

Categories and Subject Descriptors

K.6.5 [**Management of Computing and Information Systems**]: Security and Protection – *authentication, physical security, unauthorized access.*

General Terms

Management, Measurement, Experimentation, Security, Human Factors, Legal Aspects.

Keywords

Insider Hacking; Situational Crime Prevention; White-Collar Crime; Criminology; Cybercrime; Crime Science; Cybersecurity.

1. INTRODUCTION

While insider hacking does not represent the majority of cyberattacks, its threat exists and the potential outcome is often perceived as more damaging than hacking incidents coming from outside. The 2011 CyberSecurity Watch Survey reports that of the cybercrimes where offenders could be identified, 21% were insiders. Of the more than 600 survey respondents (business and government executives, professionals and consultants), 46% thought the damage caused by insiders was more severe than damage from outside attacks. 43% of respondents experienced at least one insider hack in the past year [11].

Prevention of such incidents is imperative for the cybersecurity

professional and researcher. In this paper the author lays out a groundwork to advance insider cybercrime prevention using traditional (non-cyber) criminological methodologies. While the issue of cybersecurity, including insider hacking, has been at the forefront of computing practice and research over the past few decades, very little has been done to apply established criminological theory to the problem.

First, insider hacking is addressed at from a white-collar crime perspective. White-collar crimes differ in the offenders' motivation and techniques, and therefore prevention strategies also will differ. Next, from crime science, insider hacking is investigated from the lens of situational crime prevention. This methodology has been used successfully for the prevention of street crime, applying it to insider hacking may provide additional insight to cybersecurity.

2. CRIMINOLOGICAL CONTEXT

2.1 White-Collar Crime

Is hacking a white-collar crime? By looking at the definitions historically attributed to white-collar crime, prior research can be applied to this relatively new form of criminal activity, hacking.

Sutherland [12] uses an offender-based definition for white-collar crime, "crime committed by a person of respectability and high social status in the course of his occupation." Edelhertz [6] instead defines white-collar crime based on the crime rather than the offender, "an illegal act or series of illegal acts committed by nonphysical means and by concealment or guile, to obtain money or property, to avoid the payment or loss of money or property, or to obtain business or personal advantage." Felson [8], too using a crime-based definition, focuses on the idea of studying crimes of specialized access. Benson and Simpson [1] extend this saying that what distinguishes white-collar crime are offenders who have legitimate access, are spatially separate from their target, and exhibit a superficial appearance of legitimacy.

Sutherland's broad offender-based definition of white-collar crime is not useful for cybercrime prevention; the offence-based definitions have the benefit of allowing analysts to conceive targeted crime prevention strategies for the crimes. Traditionally conceived cybercrime (hacking by outsiders) does not easily fit into the definitions put forth by Felson or by Benson and Simpson. Most cybercriminals would not expect to have legitimate access to their target.

Hacking in its traditional form falls under the broad Edelhertz definition, non-physical acts using guile. Insider hacking fits most offence-based definitions of white-collar crime well, offenders having legitimate access to their target. An insider in this context is someone who holds a legitimate trust relationship with an organization primarily employees, but more broadly other individuals such as contract workers, vendors, and customers.

2.2 Situational Crime Prevention

Ronald Clarke [3] wrote that to best prevent crime from occurring, research should focus on the crime itself rather than the offender. The work requires an in-depth understanding of how, and in what situations, specific crimes are committed. This practical activity of preventing crime by limiting opportunity he calls situational crime prevention.

Later Clarke [4] went on to categorize situational crime prevention techniques into five common categories of techniques to reduce the likelihood of a crime being committed; increasing perceived effort, increasing perceived risks, reducing anticipated rewards, reducing provocations, and removing excuses. This focus on the crime requires the development of specific prevention techniques for each offence type under the situational crime prevention framework.

Willison and Siponen rightly argue that information security should apply traditional criminological theories like this one in their work. They detail an explanation of situational crime prevention and begin to apply it to "employee computer crime" [13].

The following sections dig into the specifics of insider hacking and how offenders carry out their actions. This will enable an application of situational crime prevention to insider hacking.

3. CATEGORIZING INSIDER HACKING
3.1 Computer Crime

Carnegie Mellon's Software Engineering Institute (SEI) publishes a report every three years detailing insider cybercrime, the most recent one in 2012, Common Sense Guide to Mitigating Insider Threats [11]. In these reports, the authors categorize insider cybercrimes. The 2009 report [2] included cybercrimes of IT (information technology) sabotage, theft or modification for financial gain, theft or modification for business advantage, and miscellaneous. In 2012 [11], they altered the categories to IT sabotage, fraud, intellectual property (IP) theft, and miscellaneous.

Insider cybercrimes can more generally be categorized into just two types; computer crimes and computer-enabled crimes. Computer crimes are new offence types created because of the existence of computers and networks, the specific act of hacking computer systems or networks. Computer-enabled crimes, on the other hand, represent a new vector for committing existing white-collar crimes.

Looking at SEIs categories again, only IT sabotage can be labeled a computer/cyber crime rather than a computer-enable crime. The others just use a computer to carry out traditional white-collar crimes such as fraud, embezzlement, securities, espionage, etc. The SEI studies show that non-IT sabotage (computer-enabled) offenders exhibit similar patterns to traditional white-collar criminals. Generally these offenders were not technical in nature, but because of their position had legitimate access to systems and data for their job. They used this specialized access (their own log-in accounts) 75% of the time to carry out the crimes. The offenders modified data to get money for themselves or family, colluded with others in the offence, carried out the crime during normal working hours, and 50 percent of the offenders were female [2]. These computer-enabled offenders were not what we typically think of as hackers at all. Because of their connection to traditional white-collar crimes, crime prevention techniques

associated with corresponding white-collar crime should remain effective.

3.2 Legal Definitions

Even using the perspective of law, these computer-enabled insider activities may indeed be illegal, but do not fall under the umbrella of cybercrime. The Computer Fraud and Abuse Act [5] applies to insiders only when the offender acts with "intentional conduct" defined as "knowingly transmitting a program, information, code, or command resulting in damage to a protected computer." Damage is met when victims spend at least $5,000 to investigate and/or remedy an incident (a low bar when you factor in the cost of IT personnel). One definition of a protected computer, "affects interstate or foreign commerce or communication of the United States," can be interpreted as any computer connected to the Internet. This law would not apply to computer-enabled crime.

The Computer Fraud and Abuse Act applies only to outside hackers for simple unauthorized access to data or systems, called reckless or negligent conduct by the law. Insiders are exempt from crimes of unauthorized access. Unable to rely on any legal deterrents or law enforcement for investigations and punishment, organizations must take its own steps to prevent unauthorized insider access to sensitive organizational information.

3.3 Insider Hacking = IT Sabotage

The IT sabotage crimes represent a new kind of white-collar crime. SEI defines IT sabotage as "an insider's use of IT to direct specific harm at an organization or an individual" [2]. Specific actions of IT sabotage include deleting files, locking individuals or groups of individuals out of systems/files, publishing sensitive information (customer data, corporate communications, etc.), planting viruses, disabling services/devices, and defacing webpages. IT sabotage represented 45% of the insider computer based crimes on the SEI survey in 2009 [9], and 29% in 2012 [11]. This drop likely represents an application of some easy prevention methods by organizations over the previous three years. Throughout the rest of this paper, IT sabotage will be referred to as insider hacking.

The data from SEI and PERSEREC show relatively consistent demographics of insider hacking attacks [2, 9]. These data can be used to influence crime prevention strategies. Offenders are primarily male, hold technical positions within the organization, and work without co-conspirators. The PERSEREC studies note that offenders often "knew a great deal more about computer systems than was required by their job" and spent their free time engaged in legitimate computing or outside hacking activities. The data often show insider hackers as former employees; the attacks took place after the individual no longer worked for the organization.

In the majority of cases (70%), offenders did not use their own accounts instead hacking others' accounts, creating new accounts, or using shared accounts (generic accounts for which multiple individuals know the credentials). Most offenders took steps to conceal their actions (beyond not using their own accounts), like deleting or modifying log files. Log files are automatically created text files documenting successful and failed access, changes to those systems, and by whom. The attacks generally took place outside of working hours and originated remotely rather than onsite.

In most cases, insider hackers showed other signs of trouble. There were conflicts in the workplace, a decline in work performance, tardiness, and absenteeism. Management often ignored problems; in some cases employees were sanctioned for problems in the workplace and subsequently increased their hacking activity.

4. APPLICATION OF SITUATIONAL CRIME PREVENTION

4.1 Difficulties
Applying situational crime prevention strategies can be difficult with white-collar crime because the offenders have legitimate specialized access to their victim or target. Additionally, research shows that white-collar criminals often take steps to conceal their crimes; sometimes it is hard to determine if a crime has been committed [1]. This bears true for insider hackers as well.

IT personnel have legitimate and elevated access to the organization's network, systems, data, and user accounts making the detection of illegitimate activities difficult. For example, the data show that instead of using their own accounts for their cyberattacks, insider hackers use shared administrative accounts, creating new accounts, and changing existing accounts. This user account activity is part of the typical duties of many IT employees; they have legitimate access. Additionally, because IT personnel are tasked with fixing computers and systems throughout the organization, they have legitimate physical access that other employees do not. This physical access provides them with more opportunities for traditional white-collar crimes in addition to cybercrimes.

Insider hackers also conceal their actions altering log files on systems. They use the knowledge that systems are prone to break or crash. The causes for such incidents can be hacking, but often are triggered by other problems like technical malfunctions or user mistakes. The outcome of an insider hack can easily be mistaken for one of these other causes.

Methodologies exist for mitigating these difficulties however. In the following sections describe techniques to prevent insider hacking using the principals of situational crime prevention. For insider hacking, most techniques fall under increasing effort to offend, increasing risk of detection, and reducing offender provocations.

4.2 Increase Effort
Many of the offenders studied by SEI were no longer employed by the organization at the time of the attack. Organizations can easily eliminate most of these former-employee attacks. Promptly deactivating accounts of former-employees, scanning for custom created accounts, checking for technical backdoors planted, and changing the passwords to all shared accounts for which the former-employee had access to accomplishes this level of prevention. While the report does not say so specifically, a presumption is that the decrease in IT sabotage cases studied by SEI from 2009 to 2012 [2, 11] represents an implementation of such IT employee termination policies.

For those still employed as IT professionals in the organization, prevention becomes more difficult. Because of their legitimate access to the network, data, and systems to carry out their job duties, increasing the effort required for cyberoffending can also lead to increased effort required for legitimate work activities. That being said, organizations can be more granular in their access rights without hindering legitimate activities. The

legitimate work duties can be studied for each IT employee to target which systems and data they are required to have access. Also, organizations should refrain from giving any one person full access of every system in the network. With small organizations this might prove difficult because of the size of their IT staff and need to employ an IT "jack of all trades."

Noting that most of the insider hacking events occur outside of work hours and offsite, careful consideration should be paid to remote access policies. Again, limiting remote access to systems may delay some IT response time necessary for legitimate work, but a user-by-user and system-by-system review should be performed to fine-tune the remote access policies. There may be some systems and data for which it is decided no remote access is granted. Forcing IT personnel onsite may deter some potential offenders from taking that step to hacking. Such a policy, once technically implemented, would have an added benefit of strengthening those systems further against outsider hackers.

Since most offenders use others' accounts for their attacks, organizations could implement multifactor authentication into their environments. This involves using more than just a username and password for access; biological scans and one time passwords sent as text messages to cell phones are a few examples. Of course, again this may slow the legitimate work of users in their day-to-day activities.

4.3 Increase Risk of Detection
Judging by the fact that insider hackers refrain from using their own accounts, perform their hacks off work time, and alter log files; offenders are sensitive to the risks of detection and are aware of the ability of systems and networks to track the activities its users. Taking steps here then might too prevent cybercrimes by insiders.

Several organizations monitor log files in a haphazard manner, potential insider hackers presumably know this. Log aggregation software should be installed with easy to scan/view dashboards by management. Such software gathers log data from disparate systems and devices on a network and present the information together in an easy to read dashboard display highlighting abnormalities. Knowing that management has such a tool at its disposal, regularly checks the system, and is given alerts for certain activities may deter potential offenders. Any anomalous activity should result in a rational given by IT personnel.

Any deletion/modification of log files should not be allowed in the organization. Deletion should require approval by multiple levels of staff. Any modification presents a definite red flag of inappropriate behavior.

4.4 Reduce Provocations
The data all suggest that much of the insider hacking activities were preceded by other personnel problems in the workplace; conflicts, performance, tardiness, absenteeism. As such, these indicators should be watched closely for IT staff. Noticing any of these behaviors should result in increased monitoring of their activities on the systems. While such action may seem to infringe on the privacy rights of employees, corporate ownership of the computing resources and network use policies follow the law to allow monitoring. The Electronic Communications Privacy Act [7], while covering the privacy of users' stored network activity, only applies to internet providers not employers. The wiretap statute of the Omnibus Crime Control and Safe Streets Act [10] covers live network traffic but employer network use policy acts

as a consent exception to the law. Both federal laws also allow for monitoring to protect an organization's "rights or property." In this case an organization's property would be data or computing resources, monitoring high-risk employees would amount to protection.

IT management should be trained to assure they are sensitive to the needs of their staff. HR should be pulled in to deal with issues, avoiding punishments that might provoke insider hacking. It may be necessary to terminate IT staff more quickly than traditional staff, then revoking system/network access perhaps even prior to giving them official termination notice.

5. DISCUSSION

In the first published attempt to apply situational crime prevention to insider hacking, Willison and Siponen detail the situational crime prevention framework [13]. They begin documenting some techniques for preventing computer crime by insiders. What is missing is a specific definition of employee computer crime. The piece also lacks detail about the acts of insider hacking; such detail is necessary to correctly apply situational crime prevention to a crime.

The reports published by SEI every three years go a long way towards providing best practices for the prevention of what they call insider threats [11, 2]. The reports give excellent advice to practitioners; describing specific steps (technical and managerial) organizations should take. This work, along with the PERSEREC studies [9], contributes in-depth research reporting the criminal techniques used by insider hackers. The reports lack, however, a theoretical basis for their crime prevention recommendations and do not distinguish which techniques should be used for computer crimes verses computer-enabled crimes.

Recognizing the difference between computer crime and computer-enabled crime could go a long way towards advancing the prevention of insider hacking. The computer-enabled crime should parallel crime prevention techniques for their associated non-cyber white-collar crimes instead of being lumped in with insider hacking. A more granular look at computer crimes will advance the study of the prevention of insider hacking.

6. ACKNOWLEDGEMENTS

Thanks to Michael Benson from the University of Cincinnati, School of Criminal Justice for the inspiration to investigate the application of situational crime prevention to white-collar crime and providing notes for the text of this paper.

7. REFERENCES

[1] Benson, M. L., & Simpson, S. S. 2009. *White-Collar Crime: An Opportunity Perspective*. New York, NY: Routledge.

[2] Cappelli, D., & Shimeall, T. J. 2009. *Common Sense Guide to Prevention and Detection of Insider Threats 3rd Edition*. Pittsburgh, PA.

[3] Clarke, R. V. 1980. "Situational" crime prevention: Theory and practice. *British Journal of Criminology*, (20), 136–147.

[4] Clarke, R. V. 1997. *Situational Crime Prevention: Successful Case Studies*. Guilderland, NY: Harrow and Heston.

[5] Computer Fraud and Abuse Act (CFAA) (1986). Pub. L. No. 99-474, 100 Stat. 1213 (Oct. 16, 1986), codified at 18 U.S.C. §1030

[6] Edelhertz, H. 1970. The Nature, Impact, and Prosecution of White-Collar Crime. Washington, DC: U.S. Department of Justice.

[7] Electronic Communications Privacy Act (ECPA) (1986). Pub. L. No. 99-508, 100 Stat. 1848 (Oct. 21, 1986), codified at 18 U.S.C. §3121

[8] Felson, M. 2002. *Crime and Everyday Life*. Thousand Oaks, CA: Pine Forge Press.

[9] Fischer, L. F. (2003). Characterizing information systems insider offenders. In *Proceedings of the 45th Annual Conference of the International Military Testing Association* (Pensacola, FL, November 03-06, 2003). IMTA, Seoul, South Korea, 289–296.

[10] Omnibus Crime Control and Safe Streets Act (1968). Pub. L. 90-351, 82 Stat. 197 (June 19, 1968), codified at 42 U.S.C. §3711

[11] Silowash, G., & Shimeall, T. J. 2012. Common Sense Guide to Mitigating Insider Threats 4th Edition. Pittsburgh, PA.

[12] Sutherland, E. H. 1940. White-collar criminality. *American Sociological Review*, 5(1), 1–12.

[13] Willison, R., & Siponen, M. 2009. Overcoming the insider: reducing employee computer crime through Situational Crime Prevention. *Communications of the ACM*, 52(9), 133-137.

A Survey of Security Vulnerabilities in Social Networking Media – The Case of Facebook

Elizabeth Fokes
Department of Information Technology
Southern Polytechnic State University
1100 South Marietta Pkwy
Marietta GA 30060
01-678-915-4292
efokes@spsu.edu

Lei Li
Department of Information Technology
Southern Polytechnic State University
1100 South Marietta Pkwy
Marietta GA 30060
01-678-915-3915
lli3@spsu.edu

ABSTRACT

This paper conducted a survey study on the security vulnerabilities in one of most popular social networking site, Facebook. We divide the vulnerabilities into two main categories: platform-related and user-related. For each vulnerability, we present its origin, description and remedy if there is any. Our work not only increases users' awareness of those vulnerabilities, but also provides a comprehensive view to the researchers who are interested in improving security measures of social media services.

Categories and Subject Descriptors

A.1 [**General Literature**]: Introductory and Survey.

General Terms

Documentation, Security

Keywords

Security; Vulnerability; Facebook; Social Media.

1. INTRODUCTION

The statistics regarding use of social networking media are staggering. According to Statistic Brain in 2012, 58% of the population in US used any social network; 56% used Facebook; 14% used Linked in, 11% used Twitter; 9% used Google+. [18] Social media has also become a platform for a very large number of businesses. In 2011, 77% of Fortune Global 100 Companies use Twitter, and 61% have a Facebook page. [15]

Social media sites, in particular are the focus of vulnerabilities, because of their large user base and the instant attention that is brought about by the attack. Social networking sites have databases of user activities, their email addresses, potentially financial information, ISP addressing information, and some have authorized location tracking. These are all items that can be potentially utilized for great harm against users.

RIIT'14, October 15–18, 2014, Atlanta, Georgia, USA.
Copyright © 2014 ACM 978-1-4503-2711-4/14/10…$15.00.
http://dx.doi.org/10.1145/2656434.2656444

There are many different types of vulnerabilities that users may encounter. Vulnerabilities cause a disruption in the integrity, confidentiality and availability of services. Some are seen directly, and others are not seen at all by the user. Attacks can be launched against users and against the social networking media services individually. There are many motivations behind attacks: financial gain, social hacking, activism, or intentional harm against someone or a company that the attackers do not like. Attackers go after a user's account for financial gain, social hacking, activism, and intentional harm against someone or a company that the attackers do not like to name a few.

The rest of the paper is organized as follows: section two describes the research method used. Section three presents the security vulnerabilities specific to Facebook. Section four concludes the paper.

2. RESEARCH METHOD

We conducted extensive literature search on the vulnerabilities of Facebook. We collected information not only from academic sources but also Internet sources due to the topic our paper. We then created a categorization scheme to sort the sources into different categories and sub categories. For each source, we recorded the description of the vulnerability and potential remedy to it if there is any.

There are two major categories for vulnerabilities: platform-related and user-related. The platform-related vulnerability is divided into four sub categories: SMS verification, social authentication, applications, and general web-based vulnerabilities. For user-related category, there are three sub categories: fake profile, Sybil-type vulnerability, identify theft and access to user account.

The detail of each security vulnerability is described in the next section.

3. FACEBOOK SECURITY VULNERABILITIES

3.1 Technical Background of Facebook

Facebook has an extremely large user base. The company has had to come up with solutions to handle data at a rapid pace and to be able to keep up with the demands. As part of that initiative, in 2012, the company built Presto (a distributed SQL query engine that supports ANSI SQL) that would enables the system to work at a "petabyte scale." This system is implemented in Java, as

Facebook has used Java for the rest of the data infrastructure. Hive/HDFS and Scribe (log server) are on the backend. [19]

3.2 Vulnerabilities Relating Specifically to the Facebook Platform

As with other websites, Facebook has a user interface and the supporting infrastructure which handles requests, databases, and user services. Some weaknesses seen on the Facebook platform include issues with SMS Verification, Social Authentication, vulnerabilities that come through Applications, and Puppetnets. What is special about these types of attacks is that they are not affiliated with what a user does, but rather has to do with the programming that has been done by the service, and manipulates that code which is on the server(s). The issues that come from the vulnerabilities in this section cannot be solved by the user, but rather the company has to solve them. In some cases, companies like Facebook will offer large rewards for finding the coding vulnerabilities.

3.2.1 SMS Verification Weaknesses

SMS stands for "Short Message System." When a user signs onto a user has the option of having additional verification of their identity via the use of SMS verification. SMS verification is a great resource for a user who utilizes multiple computers to access Facebook and doesn't want to accidentally leave his or her account exposed for others to access, or for a user who feels that an additional layer of security is preferable for any other reason. Facebook offers SMS for secondary verification of account ownership, and for sending updates to profiles. This is a second layer to account verification in addition to the password on the account. The goal of this is to be able to make an account more secure because of the second layer of verification that the user has input. The process is simple for a user to follow. When someone chooses to sign on to Facebook and has the SMS option for secondary verification chosen on the account, a code is sent to the user's phone or to an email that the user assigns for verification purposes. When the user receives the code, he or she then inputs the code into a screen that comes up on Facebook that requests the code.

In June of 2013, Jack Whitten, a security researcher won an award from Facebook in the amount of $20,000 for finding a very serious flaw on Facebook. This flaw would allow a user's account to be taken over by a hacker through the exploitation of a weakness in SMS verification of user accounts. Facebook's system for SMS had a flaw in it wherein a hacker could modify the information that is input into the "profile_id" field to the identification of another user, thereby attaching the victim's account to the attacker. By doing this, the attacker could then request a password reset on the victim's account and the verification information would then be sent to the attacker's phone instead of the user's phone. The attacker could then reset the password without the user being aware of it, and the user is locked out of his or her account. "We enter this code into the form, choose a new password, and we're done. The account is ours[2]

The good news with this vulnerability is that this SMS bug was reported to Facebook on May 12, 2013. It was fixed on May 28, 2013. Facebook disabled the profile_id parameter from users in order to protect their users from this vulnerability.

3.2.2 Social Authentication

In response to Mark Zuckerberg's account having been hacked, Facebook added authorization features. Like SMS, social authentication was created as a type of two-factor authentication (where a user will have to provide two pieces of information for authentication). In Facebook, social authentication utilizes the use of a selection of photos belonging to friends in order to prove identity. "Facebook is the largest storage for photos with approximately 1 billion uploaded photos." [3]

The use of social authentication was put in place in Facebook to help an account holder retrieve his or her account when a password has been lost or stolen. Should Facebook determine that there is the possibility that an account has been stolen, the photos of friends will be posted for a user to say whether or not they know the people and who they are. Facebook questions suspicious logins if a user logs in from a different location than normal, or if the user is logging in for the first time to the account from a device that is not recognized as being affiliated with the user's account. The social authentication layer that Facebook put in place utilizes photos that the user must identify in order to access the account. It is important to note that until recently, one could not keep others from accessing the photos on their account. It was easy to copy the photos without a user's permission.

When the social authentication protocol responds, the first item that is presented is a CAPTCHA that has to be solved before the challenges are presented. While this is not something that computer can easily solve, a person can. It does, however, serve the purpose of slowing down a potential attacker. Next come the social authentication challenges. Specifically, there are seven challenges presented, which must be completed within 5 minutes. Each "challenge is comprised of 3 photos of an online friend; the names of 6 people from the user's social circle are listed and he has to select the one depicted. The user is allowed to fail in 2 challenges, or skip them, but must correctly identify the people of at last 5 to pass." [4] The average Facebook user has 190 friends, with the allowable upper limit of 5000.

When Polakis and friends looked at Facebook initially, they thought that the vulnerability would only attack those users who had their photos and friends lists publicly visible. However, they discovered that by 47% of users did not secure their photos and friends lists. When someone "friended" one of the users, there was a 90% success rate in matching friends with photos. [4] This brought the overall percentages of Facebook users who were vulnerable to 84%. It was also found that 71% of Facebook users have at least one photo album accessible publicly.[4] When tested, the research group was able to access a user's account within a minute with the use of a software program designed for facial recognition.

The reason that the testers were able to access user accounts was partially due to the "tagging" option related to photos on Facebook. "Tagging" refers to the option to click on an image and say who the person or people are, individually on a photo. If that person is a Facebook user, it will attach to the user's account. One does have the option to be notified when someone "tags" a user, and there is the ability to refuse the "tag." However, many users do not have the protocol set up to be notified and refuse the tagging. Also, when a user has open "friending" allowed on the account, an attacker can easily access the information that the user cares to share, whether it be photo albums or other pertinent information. Users who do not allow themselves to be tagged, and do not have public profiles or photo albums are the ones who are not as easily accessed, however other users can compromise this should they tag or share information about the user.

In testing the vulnerability, the researchers found that they were able to issue a large number of friend requests to users, and many would passively accept the requests. They collected photos and the associated URLs from the targets via screen scraping methods, and they stored the metadata, comprised of URL of the individual users, UID of the owner, tags, and coordinates. [4] They then scanned the downloaded photos from photo albums and used a face detection classifier. They were able to label the photos with the UIDs of the user associated with them. Next, the researchers assigned the user names with the photos. Through the short range of user names that are presented in the challenge, the attackers were able to lower the scope of matching photo with user name.

There are ways to make sure that an account is secure against such attempts of social authentication attacks. Users can have a message sent to a trusted device to alert them that their account is experiencing an attempt for access. That feature is set up in the security settings on Facebook. The user would simply receive the notification and verify or deny that they are trying to access the account. The message has a security token sent and they can input the information into the account. Of course, if an attacker has access to that device, he or she can get around the extra layer of protection. If the challenge is failed in an attempt, the account moves to a security page that notifies the user (or attacker) that the authentication has failed. If the attacker is successful, there will be no notification sent to the user. Another possible solution is for the account to automatically notify a user whenever the account is accessed from any location. This is typically sent to the user's email account. As long as the attacker does not have access to the email, the user can respond. If the email is accessible, the attacker will still have access until such time as he or she is able to change the password on the account.

Specifically in relation to photos, a user can use one of the following solutions: lock a photo when it is being uploaded to their account, stop the use of print screen and use of snipping tool, remove the right click option on the locked photo, and remove the feature of photo share on a locked photo. [5]

3.2.3 Vulnerabilities from Applications
Facebook offers applications (apps) to enhance the user experience. These applications come from third party vendors who host them on remote sites, which are accessed via the Facebook platform. Applications offer music, games, horoscopes, and puzzles. "Facebook provides developers an API that facilitates app integration into the Facebook user-experience. There are 500K apps available on Facebook, and on average, 20M apps are installed every day. Furthermore, many apps have acquired and maintain a large user-base. For instance, FarmVille and CityVille apps have 26.5M and 42.8M users to date." [6] Many apps ask for far more information from user accounts than they truly need. This information can be leaked to third parties. It only costs $25 to put an app on Facebook. [6] Before an app is added to a user account, he or she needs to authorize it (Facebook uses OAuth 2.0 for authentication and authorization of third-party applications). By default, basic information is provided once the user authorizes an application access to his or her account. [7] Some applications have extended permissions, and will post on user accounts, access posting information, gain the user's birthday information, email address, and access user's messages to other users. They can even access information from the user's friends' accounts.[7] In 2012, the App Center was introduced to Facebook. Applications found here are considered to be of higher quality than others, and only contains a few thousand applications in the list.

Hackers are particularly interested in using apps, because it can be financially rewarding. Through malicious apps, personal information about users can be obtained, apps can suggest use of other apps (reproduction), and can spread to a large number of users via spam generated from friends lists. There is really no way to know if an app is malicious or not from the user end, and therefore, they can easily spread from one user to another. Instead of concentrating on malicious apps, Facebook has concentrated on spam and malicious posts.

3.2.4 Puppetnets
"Puppetnets exploit the design principles of World Wide Web. Web pages can contain links to pages hosted at different domains, other than the one they are hosted at. A malicious user can craft special pages that contain thousands of links pointing at a victim site. When an unsuspecting user visits that page, her browser starts downloading elements from the victim site and thus consuming its bandwidth." [8] Basically, "Puppetnets rely on web sites to coerce web browsers to (unknowingly) participate in malicious activities. Such activities include distributed denial of service, worm propagation, and reconnaissance probing, and can be engineered to be carried out in stealth, without any observable impact on an otherwise innocent-looking website." [9] Users come into contact with this vulnerability, because Facebook hosts applications for games and other "fun" activities for users. These applications are very popular on Facebook, and they insist on inviting friends on playing the games, either by automatically posting on user accounts or causing "better play" through invitation of friends. When a designer of an application wants it to be hosted by Facebook, he or she registers with Facebook and then submits it through Facebook's developer application. The developer application requires information on the Canvas page (the main page of the application) URL and the Canvas callback URL (the address of the web server where it is actually being hosted on). One can write a malicious application and have hidden documents that the victim then hosts and unknowingly shares (for instance, self-executing files). [8]

"An adversary can take full advantage of popular social utilities, to emit a high amount of traffic towards a victim host. However, apart from launching a DDOS attack on third parties, there are other possible misuses in the fashion of Puppetnets" [8] They can be host scanning, where an application can identify open ports through HTTP requests, malware propagation ("Every user that interacts with the application will propagate the attack" [8]) attacking cookie-based mechanisms, embedded self-signed Java applets, personal information leakage, URL scanner cloaking, and collection of sensitive information. A collection of web browsers can be transformed into a distributed system that an attacker can control, hence the term "puppetnet." "Puppetnets expose a deeper problem in the design of the web. The problem is that the security model is focused most exclusively on protecting browsers and their host environment from malicious web servers, as well as servers from malicious browsers. As a result, the model ignores the potential of attacks against third parties." [9] Puppetnets exploit the architecture of a site that allows dynamic content and then amplifies vulnerabilities, which can cause significant damage to a website. It is tough to eliminate because site functionality will be eliminated in doing so.

In order to protect against puppetnets, disabling Javascript would cause a reduction of this threat, but it would not eliminate it. Of course, on Facebook, if one disables Javascript, one cannot access the applications that are the potential source of the issue. In actuality, puppetnets can still work with Javascript disabled, but it the effectiveness of the attacks would be less. On the server side,

"one way for doing this is for servers to use the "Referer" tag of HTTP requests to determine whether a particular request is legitimate or compliant... the server could consult the appropriate access policy and decide whether to honor a request. This approach would protect servers against wasting their egress bandwidth, but does not allow the server to exercise any control over incoming traffic." [9]

Another way to utilize the "Referer" tag is to shut down the controlling website by tracing the source of the attack. This process is time consuming, as it is done by people and not machines. Once the controlling website no longer has access, it can still take up to an hour for all of the puppet browsers to become pointed elsewhere. [9]

3.3 Vulnerabilities Relating Directly to the Facebook User

These vulnerabilities are affiliated with the users, because they do not attack the servers, and they do not involve third-party applications. Instead, these vulnerabilities involve the actions of other users, which can be thwarted by the users themselves. Users, for the most part are aware when these types of attacks happen, unlike those affiliated with the service and with applications. On an emotional and psychological level, the user can be gravely impacted, because of the social aspect of social media. Like chat rooms of the past, where users would become emotionally attached, social networking sites have the same emotional draw. Part of this is due to the fact that real life friends and family interact directly with the user through this platform. In this section, fake profiles, identity cloning, cyberbullying, and injection attacks will be considered.

3.3.1 Fake Profiles
Fake profiles have been used by sexual offenders, people meaning to defame or harm other users, and others who wish to launch attacks. [10] "The personal risk associated with these types of attacks includes kidnappings, child molestation, sexual abuse, defamation and other forms of harassment and indecency." [10] Because of these types of activities, fake profiles are a risk that can be very serious. As mentioned previously, users can put whatever information they want when an account is set up. There is no authentication other than checking to see if the email address affiliated with the account is real. The other aspects of the user profile are not checked.

Users are asked if they would like to add a friend to their friends list. While many users do check to see if they truly know a person who would like to connect, others do not properly scrutinize the invitation and will accept anyone who wants to be a friend. This opens the user up to the possibility that the friend requesting acceptance could be malicious. This is a trust relationship between the user and the person asking to be added as a friend. "Trust can be defined as the willingness of an individual to be vulnerable to the actions of another individual, based on the expectation that the other will perform a particular action. This acceptance of vulnerability and risk is irrespective of the ability to

monitor or control the behavior exhibited by the other party involved. Another view defines trust as a mental phenomenon that occurs within social contexts and applies to both online and offline environments." [10] Based on the profile presented to the user, trust will determined by what information is presented regarding the person wishing to be added to the friends list.

Users feel a confidence in the system, because of the following elements: Users also trust that their posted information is honest. Users have a strong perception that their information is safe and that they will encounter honesty from other users. They not only trust other users, but they trust the system[10] There are controls available to user regarding what is seen by other users, and this can limit who sees what is posted by the user. This adds to user confidence. When a person is trusted, less controls put into place by the user. There are also controls available if another user needs to be removed from a friends list, or if a user is upset by something that another user posts.

When an attacker decides to harm another user with a fake profile, there are many things that they can do. Harm can come to a user via psychological harm. There have been reports of users who have been bullied by other users who intentionally joined the service under a fake profile for this sole purpose. Due to the psychological harm of bullying, there can be physical and emotional implications. One can identify a problem user to the service for investigation. While the offending user profile can be blocked by the service, there is nothing in place to keep the malicious user from creating a new profile and resume the malicious activities against the victim. This makes the blocking of users ineffective.

3.3.2 Sybil
This type of attack is most often found in peer-to-peer networks, which Facebook, as a social networking platform, can be described as a model of. In this type of attack, the reputation system is forced to make decisions that benefit an adversary by being provided false or biased information under a number of identities. [11] In a Sybil attack, "a single faulty entity can present multiple identities, it can control a substantial fraction of the system, thereby undermining this redundancy. [12] "Our third example comes from a Facebook voting application. If an adversary maliciously creates many identities, she can easily change the overall popularity of an option by providing plenty of false praise, or bad-mouthing of the option through Sybil ids." [11] Sybil attacks can look a great deal like identity cloning. However, in a Sybil attack, the attacker is not stealing the identity of another user; he or she is making multiple profiles instead. Each identity that a Sybil attack creates has a direct node attached to it. By having the multiple profiles, one can "influence the choices made by victims' friends using the trust built in friendships. [13] An attacker can use the identities to launch malicious messages and spam other users.

One way to mitigate the issue of a Sybil attack on distributed hash tables is use a product called X-Vine, which is "resilient to denial of service attacks, and in fact the first Sybil defense that requires only a logarithmic amount of state per node, making it suitable for large-scale and dynamic settings. X-vine also helps protect the privacy of users social network contacts and keeps their IP addresses hidden from those outside of their social circle, providing a basis for pseudonymous communication." [14]

3.3.3 Identity Theft

As mentioned when discussing fake profiles, users merely need a working email address to create an account on Facebook. Web-based email accounts are accepted as proper identification of a user on the Facebook platform. Some users allow their web-based email accounts to expire, due to inactivity, while they are user of Facebook. "some users may decide to delete their own email accounts, without realizing the security threats that this action entails. Such threats arise from the fact that the same web-based email services allow any other willing user to *reactivate* and use the *same* email address which had previously expired, when they sign up." [16]

In relation to identity theft, it has been found that one can take a photo that is unlocked of a user, and the user name to create a new account (with an email address) and post it into the details of the account. By doing so, the account will show the name of a user and the associated photo. An attacker can then accumulate friends associated with the user name, because they are none the wiser. This effectively is another route for identity theft. Users need to be careful when adding someone by verifying with their friend before adding an additional account with their name and photo attached to it.

The researchers found that they were able to access a user's account if they were aware that the user was using a web-based email that had expired. This was relatively simple. "Once we have acquired control of a previously expired email address, which had once been used to open up a Facebook account, we can visit Facebook on the web and claim to the user in question and have forgotten our password. Facebook then promptly sends an email to our reactivated Hotmail email address, which contains a code that allows us to reset the password for the Facebook account in question." [16] Once the researchers have access to the account, they can look at the friends list and see the email addresses affiliated with those who share personal information. They can then test the email addresses to determine which ones have expired web-based email and take over the newly exposed accounts. In testing, the researchers found that out of 760 friends, 4 were susceptible to the exploit. From there, they were able to get to 15 accounts, and subsequently they attempted their attack on 2000 friends to find that 23 were vulnerable. [16]The fault of this issue is not Facebook's alone, but also Hotmail's fault, because Hotmail did not delete inactive accounts. While the researchers chose Hotmail as the attack vector, there are other web-based email services that may have the same level of laxity on account deletion. Researchers noted that, "techniques such as IP spoofing, using a proxy server, or using a public workstation would significantly reduce the risk of tracing the attack back to its origin."[16]

There are limitations to this kind of attack. First of all, the attackers were unable to target a specific user. An attack has to be initiated from the friends list, which the user has imported from his or her Hotmail address. "Hotmail and Windows Live user are currently susceptible to this kind of attack." [16]

Recommended ways for users to protect themselves from the vulnerability of identity theft are simple. Users could use an email address that is not from a web-based service, and can make sure that the email is active. The user can also add SMS authentication to their account as an additional layer of security. While SMS is not a solution on its own, it can be used in addition to other security choices.

3.3.4 Accessing User Accounts Even When Blocked

In 2008, penetration tester Byron Ng discovered a way to clone an account on Facebook the use of a user's ID number. The vulnerability works even on accounts that have the attacker blocked, as long as there has been some level of correspondence between the victim and the attacker. Every user account on Facebook has a number and it can be found just after the "profile.php?id=" part of the URL for a user's account. In testing, he got the number and then clicked a link that would send a message to the victim. Obtaining the number is pretty simple. One merely needs to find a tagged photo. The identification number in the tag is the album's owner's number. Upon obtaining the ID number, it is easy to access the user's account. An attacker would then do a search on the ID number. Even if an error message pops up, it will autocorrect to the pid number that the user was most recently tagged in. "From there, you'd take the given URL and delete the entire &id portion, leaving just &subj=####### as the end of the URL. Hit enter, and *voila*! Instant access to the last photograph the target was tagged in, and access to the entire album of pictures from which that one image resides, whether you're the friend of the individual who created it or not." [17]

With a little Firefox extension called Firebug, a user can open up web pages to "tweak" them. For instance, some applications have the option to "send gifts" to other users. The attacker simply needs to go to the gift sending page and enter the name of your friend in the **to:** field. "Right click on the Send Gift button and click Inspect Element. Then click on the Dom tab at the top of Firebug's little window. Scroll down – you're looking for the To field. When you find it, you'll see a number. Guess what? It is the Facebook ID number of the person you entered in the To: field! Click on the number and Firebug will open up a large list of other options. Scroll down until you've found the "Value" field – it should be right below the "Type: Hidden" option. Double click on the ID number and enter the target's Facebook ID in quotes. Hit enter, then turn your attention to the Free Gifts sending page and hit Send. Blam. One anonymous gift to someone who isn't your friend/has blocked you/ whatever." [17]

4. DISCUSSIONS

This paper surveyed security vulnerabilities in one of most popular social networking sites, Facebook. We hope our research not only increase users' awareness of those vulnerabilities, but also provide a comprehensive view to the researchers who are interested in improving security measures of social media services.

5. REFERENCES

[1] Bowman, M., Debray, S. K., and Peterson, L. L. 1993. Reasoning about naming systems. *ACM Trans. Program. Lang. Syst.* 15, 5 (Nov. 1993), 795-825. DOI= http://doi.acm.org/10.1145/161468.16147.

[2] Kirk, J. (2013, July 27). *Researcher nets @20K for finding serious Facebook flaw*. Retrieved September 25, 2013, from CSO: http://www.cso.com.au/article/466029/researcher_nets_20k_finding_serious_facebook_flaw/

[3] Albesher, A., & Alhussain, T. (2013). Privacy and Security Issues in Social Networks: An Evaluation of Facebook. *ISDOC '13 Proceedings of the 2013 International*

Conference on Information Systems and Design of Communication (pp. 7-10). New York: ACM.

[4] Polakis, I., Lancini, M., Kontaxis, G., Maggi, F., Ioannidis, S., Keromytis, A. D., et al. (2012). All Your Face Are Belong to Us: Breaking Faceook's Social Authentication. *Annual Computer Security Applications Conference* (p. 399). Orlando: ACSAC.

[5] Sharma, R., Jain, A., & Rastogi, R. (2013). A new face to photo security of Facebook. *2013 Sixth International Conference on Contemporary Computing (IC3)* (pp. 415-420). Noida: IEEE.

[6] Rahman, M. S., Huang, T.-K., Madhyastha, H. V., & Faloutsos, M. (2012). FRAppE: Detecting Malicious Facebook Applications. *CoNEXT 2012 Proceedings of the 8th International Conference on Emerging Network Experiments and Technologies* (pp. 313-324). New York: ACM.

[7] Huber, M., Mulazzani, M., Schrittwieser, S., & Weippi, E. (2013). AppInspect: Large-scale Evaluation of Social Networking Apps. *ACM COSN Proceedings of the First ACM Conference on Online Social Networks* (pp. 143-154). Boston: ACM.

[8] Jagnere, P. (2012). Vulnerabilities in Social Networking Sites. *2nd IEEE International Conference on Parallel Distributed and Grid Computing (PDGC)* (pp. 463-468). Solan: IEEE.

[9] Lam, V. T., Antonatos, S., Akritidis, P., & Anagnostakis, K. G. (2006). Puppetnets: Misusing Web Browsers as a Distributed Attack Infrastructure. *ACM Conference on Computer and Communications Security. 12.* New York: ACM.

[10] Galpin, R., & Flowerday, S. V. (2011). Online Social Networks: Enhancing User Trust Through Effective Controls and Identity Management. *Information Security South Africa (ISSA)*, 1-8.

[11] Chang, W., & Wu, J. (n.d). *A Survey of Sybil Attacks in Networks.* Temple University, Computer and Information Sciences. Philadelphia: Temple University.

[12] Douceur, J. R., & Donath, J. S. (2002). The Sybil Attack. *International Workshop on Peer-to-Peer Systems* (pp. 251-260). Cambridge, MA: IPTPS.

[13] Jin, L., Long, X., Takabi, H., & Joshi, J. B. (n.d). *Sybil Attacks VS Identity Clone Attacks in Online Social Networks.* Pittsburgh: University of Pittsburgh.

[14] Mittal, P., Caesar, M., & Borisov, N. (2010). Facebook under attack on all fronts. *Network Security, 5*, 1-2.

[15] McNaughton, M. (2012). *77% of Fortune Global 100 Companies Use Twitter.* Retrieved November 20, 2013, from The Realtime Report: http://therealtimereport.com/2011/03/18/77-of-fortune-global-100-companies-use-twitter/

[16] Parwani, T., Kholoussi, R., & Karras, P. (2013). How To Hack Into Facebook Without Being A Hacker. *WWW '13 Proceedings of the 22nd International Conference on World Wide Web Companion*, 751-754.

[17] Murphy, D. (2008, March 27). The Tip of the Facebook Exploit Iceberg. *MaximumPC*.

[18] *Social Networking Statistics.* (2013, August 12). Retrieved November 5, 2013, from Statistic Brain: http://www.statisticbrain.com/social-networking-statistics/

[19] Traverso, M. (2013, November 6). *Presto: Interating with petabytes of data at Facebook.* Retrieved February 4, 2014, from Facebook Engineering: https://www.facebook.com/notes/facebook-engineering/presto-interacting-with-petabytes-of-data-at-facebook/10151786197628920

A Taxonomy of Privacy-protecting Tools to Browse the World Wide Web

Kelley Misata
Department of Computer and
Information Technology
Purdue University
kmisata@purdue.edu

Raymond A. Hansen
Department of Computer and
Information Technology
Purdue University
hensenr@purdue.edu

Baijian Yang
Department of Computer and
Information Technology
Purdue University
byang@purdue.edu

ABSTRACT

There is a growing public concern regarding big data and intelligence surveillance on unsuspecting Internet users, and an increase in public conversation around what does privacy really mean in the digital realm. Although technologies have been developed to help generate public protect their privacy, average users found the tools complex and difficult to decipher. This research aims to weed through some of these complexities by reviewing 6 publicly recognized technologies promoted to help users protect their privacy while browsing the web. The scope will be broad in order to touch on the important aspects each technology including promises, privacy realities, technical construct, ease of use and drawbacks average users should be aware of before using.

Categories and Subject Descriptors

K.4.1 [**Computers and Society**]: Public Policy Issues – *Privacy, Anonymity, User/abuse of Power*

Keywords: Privacy; Privacy-protecting; anonymity; pseudonymity; web browsing

1. INTRODUCTION

There is little argument that global awareness regarding digital privacy has increased significantly over the past few months. People of all skill levels are looking to experts in cyber security to identify solutions which will help protect privacy through anonymity or the perception of anonymity. But do average users know to translate their need for privacy and anonymity on the Internet to a technology solution?

The mass collection of user data from the Internet is nothing new. Most of the over 2.7 billion Internet users online today [1] [15] blatantly disregard the amount of information they give up every day to Internet providers, social media, marketers, and potentially malicious actors. It is not until something horrific happens that users take notice and begin thinking about their online privacy in a whole new light. Users are now asking important questions including: who is using the data which is being collected, what potential threads or assumptions can be drawn about an individual as result of what is being collected, and how are the new breaches in data security going to affect users in the long run? All these questions and more are raising public awareness and the demand for technology solutions which can help protect them. Before evaluating any possible solutions, users need to first define what privacy means to them in the digital space.

- Clarification is necessary between these often interchangeably used terms. *Anonymity* and *privacy* are not equivalent terms; nor are *anonymity* and *security*. These terms are technically distinct and have specific definitions. Additionally, the inclusion of *pseudonymity* further confuses many, especially the non-technical users of technology.

- Privacy is the ability to control what personal information is shared with another party, when that information is shared, and in what context. For this paper, privacy will be narrowed to deal with the control of information being shared over the Internet, intentionally or unintentionally.

- Security, in a broad definition, is the resistance to undesired loss. Again, focusing on this paper, security is narrowed to pertain to resisting undesired loss of personal identifying information.

- Anonymity is "nameless", and has been used to mean unidentifiable. Pseudonymity is similar, but distinct, meaning the use of a false or fictitious name. Typically, real information is shared under a distinct pseudonym, such as a user name or other unique identifier that is not a person's specific name. For this paper, anonymity is desired and is the state of being completely indistinguishable from any other party on the Internet, while pseudonymity provides a measure of privacy while, potentially, not degrading anonymity.

Navigating through what level of anonymity is needed, what solutions are available, how they work technically, and what the potential risks in using them can be daunting even to experienced technologists. Technologies which are user friendly and protect the identity of users through their web traffic or content are becoming increasingly essential. Demand for these technologies is increasing as the use of anonymity technologies is moving from hackers, dissidents, and security experts to average users now more aware of how vulnerable and easily collectable all of their online activities are. Six popular technologies which promote anonymous web browsing are identified in this study and the results of this research is summarized in Table 5. The tools analyzed in this study are: Steganos Online Shield™, Hideme™, Guardster™, HTTPS Everywhere, DuckDuckGo™, and Ixquick™. For each organization, its mission and privacy policies and technology constructs are analyzed to help answer the following research questions:

R1: What technologies are available to protect privacy by anonymizing user identities and web browsing traffic?

R2: What are the advantages and drawbacks of each technology in this study?

R3: What are the features and promises made by the technologies company?

This paper is organized in sections consistent with answer the above research questions. Section 2 and 3 describes the concepts and terms related to anonymity and privacy followed by the detailed analyses of privacy-protecting tools in Section 4. Section 5 provides the overall summary of the previous sections and final analysis based on the research. At last in Section 6, conclusion of this study and future work are described.

2. WHAT DOES ANONYMITY REALLY MEAN?

The recent influx of data breaches, invasions of digital privacy, and stories around national surveillance puts security on top of mind for many Internet users. However, first question users should ask themselves is: what does anonymity really mean? A term once reserved only for hackers, criminals, and terrorists, anonymity has become the topic of conversation for the general Internet user, as well as, enterprises around the world.

Rooted in the Greek word ανώνυμος (pronounced anonymous), to be anonymous means to be without a name, or nameless [2]. It is "the state of not being identifiable within a set of subjects, the anonymity set." [3] Different in context and definition is pseudonymity, which many users often mean when discussing anonymity. Pseudonymity is the use of a false name. Often going in hand in hand, it is important in the context of this research to keep these two important terms separated.

As mentioned, privacy, anonymity, pseudonymity are all related yet vastly different when looking through the lens of technology. The criteria taken under consideration during the initial phase of this research evaluates anonymity-providing vs. pseudonymity-providing, internal and external traceability, obfuscation, communication channels including client, server, proxy, and path, and ease of use for average Internet users. Further, in-depth research and usability testing is required, however, for the purpose of this paper the first criteria is summarized in Table 1.

Table 1. Types of Anonymity and Pseudonymity [4]

Traceable Anonymity	A system that leaves the identifying components of the sender in the hands of an intermediary.
Untraceable Anonymity	A system in which the author of the message is not discoverable.
Untraceable Pseudonymity	A system in which the author is known, but the author's real Identity is concealed.
Traceable Pseudonymity	A system which creates the link between a user's "fake name" and real identity.

In order to understand privacy protecting technology it is important to dissect anonymity and build an understanding of the components of communication. Communicating nodes, communication channels, and traffic policies all contribute to the privacy-preserving aspects of the web browsing need to be assessed. Security professionals strive to ensure all aspects of the user interface with technology is safe and secure. This is typically accomplished in a variety of manners; encryption, hashes, and the development of private and open source promising secure web browsing. A topic for further research would be to examine how increase demand for anonymity and pseudonymity tools pose difficult ethical challenges relating to who should be allowed to hide in plain sight with these tools? Always bearing in mind that the ease of use, availability, and successfully functionality of technology solutions outlined in this research can be also used for malicious actors.

3. DIGITAL CRUMBS USERS LEAVE BEHIND

Understanding the digital crumbs left by users is important groundwork before analyzing the privacy-protecting tools in this study. Users both knowingly and unknowingly surrender email address, age, gender, location, religious preferences, sexual orientation, bank, job, type of products bought on the Internet, period of holidays, political orientation, lifestyle, or social network. Search engines openly collect keywords and history of the sites users click on. This sharing of personal information is referred to as "search leakage." For example, when a user's searches for sensitive medial information, they are sharing that private search not only with the search engine, but also with all the sites they clicked on during the search session. Ultimately, each search engine query and the subsequent web-surging leaves countless crumbs of personal data in key word searches, timestamps, websites visited, IP address, trackers, and cookies.

Recent world events spotlighting government and industry surveillance tact on a large scale of Internet users has required many users to stand up and take notice. Many are now beginning to comprehend the enormity of traces their online behaviors are leaving behind. Traces threat actors may just be waiting for in order to launch an attack; some motivated by malicious intentions and others by profit and greed. In fairness many honorable businesses are built on the mining of user data to improver user experience and build new products. Users need to evaluate the landscape of threat actors who may be targeting them. This is not necessarily an exercise to thwart these threat actors, as there is doubt this is even possible; but any means to provide additional points of context for users to have when assessing privacy-protecting tools. Understanding the motives of these potential threat actors (Table 2) provides key insight into where privacy-protecting tools may or may not fit within the security architecture average users want or need.

Part of this process of identifying privacy-protecting tools is to subvert the mountains of data being collected on them through searches — which is sold to their partner or other 3rd parties and is stored for potential future use. Search engines collect search terms, date and times, links users click on, IP addresses, and user cookies which identify the users.

4. PRIVACY-PROTECTING TOOLS FOR WEB TRAFFIC

Four types of information may expose the privacy of an Internet user. They are 'who', 'what', 'where', and 'when'. Since the location information can often be inferred from the 'who' information by using technologies such as IP Geolocation, and there is really not much users can do to hide when the communication occurs, most privacy-protecting tools therefore focus on protecting the 'who' and 'what'. These two privacy related information can be mapped to the structure of IP packets as follows. It should be noted that *all* user communications over modern networks (in general) and the Internet (specifically) utilize this structure for communications between two parties.

As discussed above, a host with significantly high number of outbound distinct connection per unit time as well as low number of inbound distinct connection per unit time is a potential port scan attacker. In figure 2, external hosts' maximum and average distinct connection numbers per second as well as per minute are provided. "Obvious" attackers are marked by red arrows, and "subtle" attackers are marked by yellow arrows. Interestingly, 1-second host view identifies all the 10 port scan attackers, meaning most of the attacks are fast-scans.

Shown in Figure 1, the IP packet header reveals the network identities of the communication parties, because it includes both the source and destination IP addresses. Unless it is a raw IP packet, upper layer protocol header is followed by the IP header.

Table 2. Threat Actors		
Threat Source	**Motive**	**Access Threatening Anonymity**
Individuals	Intelligence gathering, target attacks (stalking), tracking.	Email, chat rooms, message boards, social media, etc. — users sharing too much information
Corporate Websites	Intelligence gathering, patterns of user behaviors.	Logging pages, cookies, Java or Java-script, prompts at launch for user information — User browsing histories and patterns.
Internet Service Providers (ISPs)	Intelligence gathering, surveillance, patterns of user behavior	Eavesdropping on emails, data, browsing, contents, sender and receiver details — tampering is possible.
Hackers & Network Attackers	Hacktivistm, Disruption, Notoriety, Bribery	Disrupting traffic on the Internet, using "rootkits" to break into user computers — making private and confidential information vulnerable and the availability of the services not reliable.
Corporation	Intelligence gathering, patterns of user behaviors.	System hackers hired to obtain big company data and secrets.
Law Enforcement	Tracking criminals, Tracing Identities, and Surveillance	Wiretapping gives them network monitoring capabilities comparable to ISPs, with a willingness to use those capabilities not shared by the networking companies.
Governments & State Actors	National Defense, Intelligence	Regimes where there is conflict or little respect for human rights extracting information is not illegal.

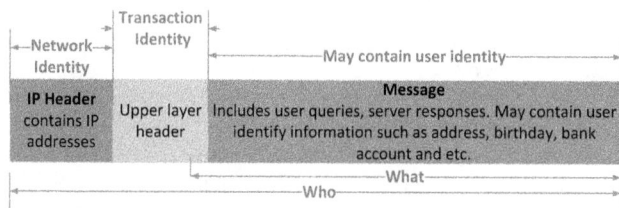

Figure 1. IP Packet Structure and Privacy Information in Typical Web Traffic

Communication type, source and the destination port number are typically presents in the upper layer protocol header. These information are related to a session of communication, or the identity of a specific web transaction. The actual message is the remaining part of an IP packet. It may contain user generated query message, or even highly sensitive user information, such as name, birthdate, address, financial account information, or even social security number. Therefore, while 'who' information are often found in packet headers, it may also include the messages themselves. In contract, the 'what' information often presents only in the body of the message. The detailed protocol formatting and interactions are not critical to this paper, and will not be covered in additional depth, except where specifically necessary. Three primary privacy related methods are proposed and widely adopted in today's Internet. They are proxies, cryptography, and mix networks.

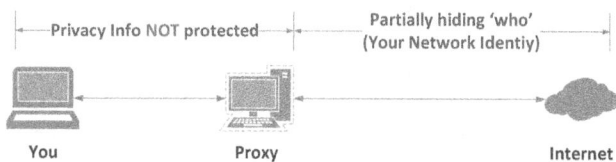

Figure 2. Proxies

First, proxies are one of the most common and easy to understand services for a general users. A secondary function of a proxy services is to maintain privacy on the Internet. The proxy server acts as the middle point providing a layer between the user and the Internet. (Figure 2) The user sends a request to a location on the Internet. The proxy service intercepts this request, modifies the

packet header, and then forwards the modified request on behalf of the user. The response to the modified request is then sent to the proxy service, which then forwards the response to the user. As seen from Figure 2, proxies can provide some level of privacy protection once the message left from the proxy and being transmitted over the Internet. However, before the message reaches the proxy, there is no additional protection between the client and the proxy server.

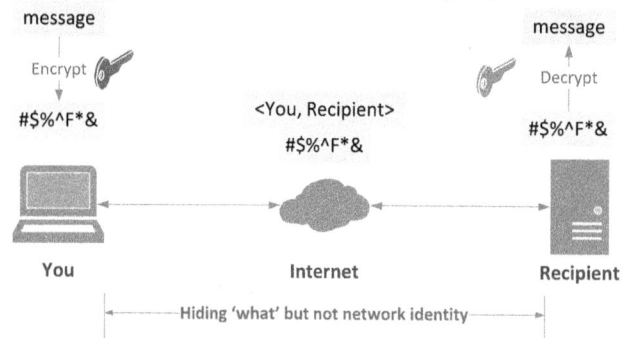

Figure 3. Cryptography

The second aspect of privacy-protection is cryptography. The most popular implementation of cryptography is encryption where a message becomes unintelligible ciphertext unless the secret is known to convert it back to the original message. Some protocols in use on the Internet natively include or support encryption services, such as HTTPS. However, these protocols are not necessarily required to be implemented by sites or services. As a result, user generated web traffic (both the header and the message) can be easily monitored by sniffing tools. As shown in Figure 3, privacy related information is partially protected by encrypting the message when transmission on the Internet. Most cryptography solutions however, does not encrypt IP headers and may still expose the client network identify on the Internet.

Last, mix networks take advantage of existing networks and overlays a second order network on top of the existing network. (Figure 4) This creates a hard-to-trace communications by using a chain of servers known as mixes which take in messages from multiple senders, potentially shuffle the data packets in random order, and then forward them to the next destination which can possibly be another mix node.

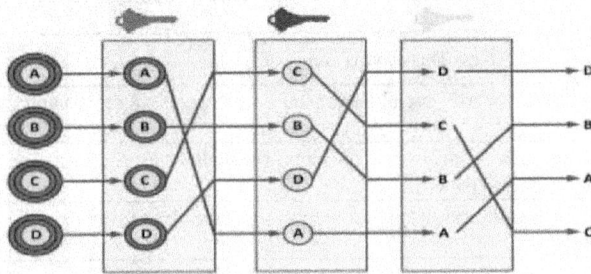

Figure 4. Mix Networks

Mix network is a much stronger anonymity approach than proxy and cryptography because 1) the 'what' information is encrypted; 2) the 'who' information in an 'end-to-end' communication is broken into many hard to trace steps where only the network identities of two neighboring nodes are exposed; and 3) the 'who' and 'what' information is further obfuscated by chopping a message into pieces of same sizes with each piece flowing through different routes in the overlay.

4.1 Steganos Online Shield™

The focus for this research study is Online Shield™ 365 as the promises to users to "locks hackers out reliably and secures you online when you shop, browse or download - 365 days a year." Online Shield™ 365 uses encryption OpenVPN, where all inbound and outbound traffic is encoded using a secure SSL Keys. Available to users in free and paid versions — $99.95 USD. As with other standard VPN technologies, Steganos Online Shield™ 365 redirects users Internet traffic across different regions. "User can conceal their IP address from media services and encrypt their data traffic." [25] Additionally, Steganos offers: a) Internet Anonym™ VPN - "Become invisible in the Internet. Surf and work anonymously at the click of a button"; b) Privacy Suite™ 15 - "Simple secure files and passwords."; c) Safe™ 15 - "Protects data from hackers, thieves and loss."; d) Password Manager™ 15 - "Protects your passwords from hackers." [25]

Over the course of this research several questions and drawbacks rose to the surface. For example, when users simply click on the table Free Version of the Online Shield™ 365 from the website it automatically downloads on the user's computer. No warning. No option to opt out. No confirmation. Online Shield™ 365 is also only available on Windows. Under their policy regarding forwarding data to 3rd party users. Steganos Online Shield™ 365 does not share user info to third parties unless — the user has explicitly and willingly agreed to do so, or there is a legal obligation to do so. What users should be aware of is that when forced from law enforcement or others, Steganos will divulge user information. Additionally as they state on their website, they save user data on especially protected severs — the access is only made available to a small number of people. Who are this small number of people? What access do they have? What if there is an insider breach? The paid version of Online Shield™ 365 collects user information even if a pseudonym is used, the potential for tracing back does exist. Online Shield™ 365, users should also be made aware that as a VPN the technology only protects the flow of traffic and does not protect files which leave a computer or other file transport system. Last, in 2007, users reported that passwords were stored in clear text providing an open vulnerability [23].

4.2 HideMe™

Another recognized anonymizing technology is HideMe proxy services. A company based in Belgium, HideMe touts "Free proxy and anonymous surfing. Hide your Internet history from your boss, partner, or kids and protect your privacy online." [13]. The primary objective of this technology is to unblock websites, hide Internet history, and changes users IP address to HideMe identifier so eavesdroppers are unable to see the identity of the user. As a general user, HideMe, appears to offer very easy to use services as offered on the home page of the website.

Several drawbacks and questions discovered throughout this research. First, when users click on the "My IP Address" tab HideMe immediately provides current users IP information raising the question where this information is now being stored and/or tracked by the HideMe servers. Additionally, video performance was weak. Special formatted media files such as videos on CNN.com, CNTV.cn, were not able to be played at all. Videos on YouTube.com were redirected to their own video player with no way to change the resolutions.

HideMe does not "guarantee" anonymity. They caution users that the way the technology is structured that it may reference other resource which user browsers may automatically download. HideMe also stresses that users should exercise caution when sharing confidential information even through secure connections. In an effort to promote greater security HideMe recommends that users visit WooVPN..

4.3 Guardster™

Guardster™ 's mission is to protect user privacy rights whenever they access the Internet [12]. To accomplish this, Guardster™ states that their technology provides tools and the knowledge to help users preserve and protect their privacy through their free proxy services and other technology solutions.

Guardster™'s ecosystem includes three primary services both free and paid versions. Guardster™'s technology works to protect users through these possible solutions, each with expanded technology expectations. In fact, Guardster™ cautions users who are not familiar with SSH tunnels or SOCK proxies not to use this product. Guardster™ blocks cookies, stops JavaScript, blocks advertisements, encrypts data streams, and hides images all to protect users. The technology uses an encrypted SSL proxy subscription and allows access across encrypted sites.

Limitations exist that SSL sites will not function with the free version of Guardster™. In addition, though they do not collect user information, they do collect keywords to sell to advertisers. Beyond the free web proxy, Guardster™ payment options include check, money order or PayPal in US currency only — raising questions regarding where payment details are again being stored and can they be tracked back to users? As with other technologies included in this research, Guardster™ makes it clear that if pushed by law enforcement, they will release any user information they have access to through their servers or payment systems.

4.4 HTTPS Everywhere

Most user have been oblivious to what URL's appear in their browser, never mind if it is using a secure communication channels. The Electronic Frontier Foundation sought to change this by promoting the free, downloadable technology of HTTPS Everywhere. [8]. Produced in partnership with The Tor Project. The technology makes is easy for users to browse safety through Firefox, Chrome, and Opera extensions. Browsing major websites becomes more secure and Fire-sheep protection. Users accessing websites via HTTPS encrypts the session using a digital certificates. Requests are encrypted from Firefox to the websites users choose. Configuring preferences is as simple as checking the box.

Easily installed, using HTTPS users are reducing eavesdropping and potential hijacking of critical information. However, HTTPS Everywhere does not mask patterns of user behaviors which are still visible beyond HTTPS. Though on the forefront of the open source security community and linked with The Tor Project, HTTPS is the closest users can get to some layer of privacy almost without even having to think about it.

4.5. DuckDuckGo™

The open source tool DuckDuckGo was founded in 2008 by Gabriel Weinberg from Pennsylvania. According to their website, DuckDuckGo is a "general purpose search engine." Their promise to users is to provide more "instant answers, way less spam, and real privacy." [6]. A positive and effective user experience as much a part of their mission as security. DuckDuckGo's technology is geared toward preventing search leakages — discussed above — by routing user traffic either encrypted or un-encrypted. It takes out the eyes of the middle man, the Internet Service Provider and when it's DuckDuckGo..

Through the encrypted version, they will automatically route users to the HTTPS Everywhere versions of major websites. DuckDuckGo also offers users HTTP POST requests which don't show search results in the browser or send potentially private header data to other sites, as HTTP GET requests might reveal. This must be turned on manually: it's not default. The browser back buttons often fail and it prevents users from copying and pasting from the Web browser's address bar. It is recommended to use DuckDuckGo

plus Tor. DuckDuck Go is proud to announce they run a Tor exit enclave assuring users that by using the two services together they get both anonymous and encrypted searching.

4.6. Ixquick™

Ixquick™ offers users free proxy services, holds no records of user IP addresses, no cookies, and doesn't sell any user data to 3rd parties. To begin using Ixquick™, users type in the website they want to visit. User's traffic is then routed through SSL encryption. The search engine offers advance searching features, setting options — which have some elements of technical jargon which may be confusing to average users, but overall the layout is friendly.

Offering HTTPS/SSL, Ixquick™ claims to be "the world's most private search engine." [16]. Built from community of supporters, Ixquick™ and its sister company, Startpage, have been on progressive positive growth pattern.

Ixquick™'s position protecting user privacies includes:

- Users have a right to privacy.
- User search data should never fall into the wrong hands by quickly deleting user data or not storing them.
- Since January 2009, users' IP addresses were not stored.
- User personal data are not shared with any third party.

As stated above, Ixquick™'s technology holds no records of users' IP addresses, no cookies, no collection of personal data, no sharing of personal data with third parties, offering HTTPS/SSL, and a free proxy service — only since 2005. In June 2006, Ixquick™ deleted

Table 3. Research findings

Tool	Anonymity vs. Pseudonymity	Traceability	Security Channels	Ease of Use
Steganos Online Shield™ 365	Provides both anonymity and some pseudonymity features in their suite of tools and paid version. Free versions provide basic anonymity.	Users are not 100% untraceable in any of the tools but the mere factor that the company will divulge user information if required to do so. Additionally they admittedly sell user data to 3rd parties.	Security is provided through proxy services and VPN services using Steganos Online Shield™ 365. Other products provide additional channels of security.	The free version is almost too easy to use as it downloads without warning. Paid versions are less user friendly.
HideMe	Provides basic anonymity to users with IP address being traced back to HideMe. As a free service creating a pseudonym is possible.	Users are untraceable from the outside world, however, HideMe technology is capturing user data making the links back possible.	Security is provided through VPN and proxy services	Almost too easy for users therefore caution should be taken.
Guardster™	Provides both anonymity and pseudomyity at varying degrees through their suite of technologies.	Traceability is reduced as users move up the suite of options. The free version appears weakest in traceability.	Security is provided through proxy services, HTTPS and SSL Tunnels	Less user friendly especially as users move into the paid VPN, SOCKS and SSL configurations.
HTTPS Everywhere	Provide privacy-protecting anonymity only.	Users are protected from eavesdroppers tracing back.	Security is provided through proxy services, HTTPS and SSL	Extremely user friendly with EFF's community to help users. Also HTTPS is now default for many browser including Google - however it is not enough
DuckDuckGo	Provide private browsing it is up to the user to hide their own identities.	In combination with Tor it is untraceable, without using Tor with DuckDuckGo there are traces of users data left behind.	Security is provided through proxy services, HTTPS and SSL	Designed to be highly user friendly, DuckDuckGo achieves this — combined with Tor is gets more complicated for users.
Ixquick	Provide private browsing it is up to the user to hide their own identities.	At first glance it does not appear traceably technologically — however further research is needed.	Security is provided through proxy services, HTTPS and SSL	Provides users an instantly available search engine with promises privacy.

all stored search data and IP addresses of users. However, it wasn't until 2009 that they stopped recording any IP addresses at all. Leaving users to wondering what was happening during those three years?

5. FINDINGS AND FUTURE RESEARCH

Further, in-depth research is certainly warranted, however, the focus of this research was to look at these privacy-protecting tools from the perspective of the Internet population who is not technically savvy or advanced. With the most secure technology in the world, there are other points of vulnerability when addressing concerns of anonymity. Humans in the system continue to challenge technologists and researchers in creating tools which reduce the amount of human error. Trust is also a factor — trust in the people creating the technology, trust in the people sending/receiving, trust that the middle whatever that is (IP, anonymity network, technology) is providing the layers of security required. Future research: How many malicious actors are need to bring an anonymity network to its knees?

6. CONCLUSION

The bulk of this research is documented in the early sections of this paper with the findings summarized in Table 5 in accordance with the criteria for the taxonomy discussed at the beginning. Further, in-depth research is warranted, however, the focus of this research was to look at popular privacy-protecting tools from the perspective of the Internet population who is not technologically advanced. With more than 2.7 billion Internet users online [15] sharing and leaking immeasurable amounts of information about themselves, even if they are using the anonymity tools included in this paper is an overwhelming undertaking to research. Who is talking with whom, the contents of what they are talking about, and patterns of communications will continue to be challenging to circumvent and far too easy to profile users. We have shown six tools that can be used in a significant number of cases to provide privacy-protecting capabilities. Based on this research, the first step for users to take in this process is deciding what information they are willing to put at risk in the Internet and what they need to secure beyond all costs. Many of the tools reviewed do offer immediate security at some level — the point of caution to users is to be aware of every step they take engage with these technologies. . Such as, if someone uses their personal credit card to purchase Steganos Online Shield™, they are surrendering private information from the start; maybe not to 3rd party eavesdroppers, but certainly to the organization managing the technology.

In closing, the conversations surrounding anonymity and privacy are not going to stop anytime soon. Also, there is no magic button by which average Internet users will be able to protect their privacy. Beyond just using the technology, as evident in this research, digging deeper into policy and technical constructs is the critical next step in understanding fully the ways to help protect the privacy of Internet users around the world.

REFERENCES

1. Anjum, U. (2011, July 11). 10 Privacy Tools To Browse The Web Anonymously. Retrieved from http://www.smashingapps.com/2011/07/11/10-privacy-tools-to-browse-the-web-anonymously.html.
2. Baggili, I. (2009). *GRADUATE SCHOOL* (Doctoral dissertation, Purdue University).
3. Bai, X., Zhang, Y., & Niu, X. (2008, November). Traffic identification of tor and web-mix. In *Intelligent Systems Design and Applications, 2008. ISDA'08. Eighth International Conference on* (Vol. 1, pp. 548-551). IEEE.
4. Collins, H. (July 2013). Little known search engine that refuses to store data on users doubles web traffic amid NSA tapping scandal. *MailOnline*. Retrieved from http://www.dailymail.co.uk/news/article-2360059/DuckDuckGo-little-known-search-engine-refuses-store-data-users-doubles-web-traffic-amid-NSA-tapping-scandal.html.
5. Diaz, C. (2005). Anonymity and privacy in electronic services. Heverlee: Katholieke Universiteit Leuven. Faculteit Ingenieurswetenschappen.
6. DuckDuckGo. (2014). Home, about, Settings, and Privacy. Retrieved from https://duckduckgo.com.
7. DSL Reports. (2003). Guardster warning…NO PRIVACY AT ALL!!!. Retrieved from http://www.dslreports.com/forum/r8024528-Guardster-warning.NO-PRIVACY-AT-ALL-.
8. Electronic Frontier Foundation. (2014). Home, FAQ, and Deploying. Retrieved from https://www.eff.org/https-everywhere.
9. Froomkin, A. M. (1995). Flood control on the information ocean: Living with anonymity, digital cash, and distributed databases. *JL & Com., 15*, 395.
10. Google Images. (n.d. c). Mix Networks. https://www.google.com/search?q=proxies&source=lnms&tbm=isch&sa=X&ei=ZGJrU-SyNIGFyQHs4YHQCw&ved=0CAcQ_AUoAg&biw=1047&bih=633#q=Mix+Networks&tbm=isch.
11. Goth, G. (2011). Privacy Gets a New Round of Prominence. *Internet Computing, IEEE, 15*(1), 13-15.
12. Guardster. (2014). Home, about, Privacy, Terms, and etc. Retrieved from http://www.guardster.com.
13. Hideme. (2014). Home, email, IP, tips, faq, and disclaimer. Retrieved from http://www.hideme.be.
14. High Scalability. (January 2013). DuckDuckGo Architecture - 1 Million Deep Searches A Day And Growing. Retrieved from http://highscalability.com/blog/2013/1/28/duckduckgo-architecture-1-million-deep-searches-a-day-and-gr.html.
15. Internet Users. (n.d.) Retrieved April 2014 from http://www.internetlivestats.com/internet-users/.
16. Ixquick. (2014). Background, and traffic. Retrieved from https://ixquick.com/eng/company-background.html.
17. Kim, B., Laas, C., O'Gilvie, S., & Yip, A. (2001). Anonymity Tools for the Internet. Retrieved from http://www.swiss.ai.mit.edu/6.805/student-papers/spring01-papers/anonymity.pdf.
18. Kuiper, M. (n.d.). 20 Proxy sites to browse the net anonymously. Retrieved from http://www.marcofolio.net/tools/20_proxy_sites_to_browse_the_net_anonymously.html.
19. Loshin, P. (2013). Practical Anonymity: Hiding in Plain Sight Online. Newnes.
20. Love, D. (2013). How Totally Paranoid People Stay Safe Online. *Business Insider*. Retrieved from http://www.businessinsider.com/the-best-online-privacy-tools-2013-1?op=1.
21. Merriam-Webster. (n.d.). Dictionary - Privacy. Retrieved from http://www.merriam-webster.com/dictionary/privacy.
22. Pfitzman, A. & Kohntopp, M. (2001). Anonymity, Unobservability and Pseudonymity - A proposal for Terminology. In Hanns Federath (Ed), *Designing Privacy Enhancing Technologies,* Lecture Notes in Computer Scient, LNCS 2009, pp. 1-9, Springer-Verlag.
23. Rizzo, F. (2007). Security Advisory: Steganos Encrypted Safe NOT so safe. Retrieved from http://securityvulns.com/Qdocument686.html.
24. Rubenking, N. (2014, February 16). How to browse the web anonymously. ITProPortal. Retrieved from http://www.itproportal.com/2014/02/16/how-to-browse-the-web-anonymously/.
25. Steganos. (2014). Profile, online Shield, and etc.. Retrieved from https://www.steganos.com/
26. Sweeney, L. (2002). k-anonymity: A model for protecting privacy. International Journal of Uncertainty, Fuzziness and Knowledge-Based Systems, 10(05), 557-570.
27. Wolinsky, D. I., & Ford, B. (2013). WiNoN-Plugging the Leaky Boat of Web Anonymity. *arXiv preprint arXiv:1312.3665*.

Comparing Public and Private IaaS Cloud Models

Matthew LaPointe
Michigan Tech University
Houghton, MI 49931, USA
malapoin@mtu.edu

Lucas Walker
Michigan Tech University
Houghton, MI 49931, USA
lwwalker@mtu.edu

Matthew Nelson
Michigan Tech University
Houghton, MI 49931, USA
matthewn@mtu.edu

Justin Shananaquet
Michigan Tech University
Houghton, MI 49931, USA
jjshanan@mtu.edu

Xinli Wang[*]
Michigan Tech University
Houghton, MI 49931, USA
xinlwang@mtu.edu

ABSTRACT

To better understand the advantages and disadvantages of deploying a private cloud or employing a public cloud for computing resources, a fully featured private cloud of infrastructure as a service (IaaS) was built from bare metal servers using Xen Server and featured mobile device compatibility. Amazon Elastic Compute Cloud (EC2) was experimented as an example of public clouds. In this work, configurations are discussed. Costs, reliability, and usefulness of private and public clouds are examined.

Categories and Subject Descriptors

H.3.4 [**Information Systems**]: Systems and Software—
Performance evaluation (efficiency and effectiveness)

General Terms

Experimentation

Keywords

Cloud Computing; Infrastructure as a Service; IaaS

1. EXECUTIVE SUMMARY

In order to determine whether building a private cloud or outsourcing a public cloud to meet the computing needs of an organization, we need to gain in-depth understanding of the advantages and drawbacks of them. This project is designed to comprehensively assess private cloud deployment *versus* public cloud utilization in the perspective of IT management and system administration.

In this study, a fully functional IaaS private cloud was built from bare metal servers by using Xen Server as the hyper-visor, Xen Center as a management GUI for clients,

*Corresponding author: Phone: 906-487-1873

RIIT'14, October 15–18, 2014, Atlanta, Georgia, USA.
ACM 978-1-4503-2711-4/14/10.
http://dx.doi.org/10.1145/2656434.2656449.

and Xen Orchestra as a ubiquitous web management server. Amazon EC2 was experimented as a public IaaS cloud. Advantages and disadvantages of them were examined based on hands-on experiences and first-hand data.

- **Advantages of Deploying a Private Cloud:** The fact that the user owns the hardware enables the user to define what exactly each part does and how to secure it. Private clouds offer more customization in VM templates as well as more configurable VMs in general.

- **Disadvantages of Deploying a Private Cloud:** The cost is higher in general because the user must provide, house and maintain all of the hardware components needed for holding and operating the private cloud. A team with technical knowledge and background of cloud computing is also necessary, since there may be a lot of in-depth configurations to be made.

- **Advantages of Using a Public Cloud:** In addition to lower startup and maintenance costs, it is easy to expand your business globally as well as consolidate acquired computing resources into a central location since most cloud providers allow international access. The availability of well trained professionals from cloud providers provides users with fast and professional services while needed. Reliability is another advantage of using a public cloud due to the sufficient redundancy established by the cloud providers.

- **Disadvantages of Using a Public Cloud:** The main issue brought up with using a public cloud stems from the fact that the end users do not own the hardware components or the data stored in the cloud. In this condition, security is the major concern while a public cloud is employed. Data could be lost. In addition, we noticed that the performance of one instance might be negatively impacted by other's utilization of resources in the same region. Finally, the user's reputation is in the hands of the cloud provider. If the reputation of the provider is thought of negatively, the user may receive the same reputation as well.

During this year-long project a lot of hands-on experience has been gained both with building a full-featured private cloud from bare metal to full functionality, and with using a public cloud provider to achieve the same tasks. The free tier offer from Amazon Web Services helped us conduct this study without extra costs.

Modeling of Class Imbalance using an Empirical Approach with Spambase Dataset and Random Forest Classification

Kiranmayi Kotipalli
Computer Science
University of North Carolina at Greensboro
Greensboro, North Carolina, USA
k_kotipa@uncg.edu

Shan Suthaharan
Computer Science
University of North Carolina at Greensboro
Greensboro, North Carolina, USA
s_suthah@uncg.edu

ABSTRACT

Classification of imbalanced data is an important research problem as most of the data encountered in real world systems is imbalanced. Recently a representation learning technique called Synthetic Minority Over-sampling Technique (SMOTE) has been proposed to handle imbalanced data problem. Random Forest (RF) algorithm with SMOTE has been previously used to improve classification performance in minority class over majority class. Although RF with SMOTE demonstrates improved classification performance, the relationship between the classification performance and the imbalanced ratio between the majority and minority classes is not well defined. Therefore mathematical models that describe this relationship is useful especially in the big data environment which suffers from imbalanced data.

In this paper, we proposed a mathematical model using an empirical approach applied to the well known Spambase dataset and Random Forest classification approach including its adoption with SMOTE representation learning technique. We have presented a linear model which describes the relationship between true positive classification rate and the imbalanced ratio between the majority and minority classes. This model can help IT researchers to develop better spam filter algorithms.

Categories and Subject Descriptors

I.6.1 [**Simulation Theory**]: Model classification

General Terms

Design, Experimentation, Measurement and Performance

Keywords

Random forest; SMOTE; Imbalanced data; Classification; Machine learning

1. INTRODUCTION

Many real world applications including network intrusion detection, document classification, Spam filtering, fraud detection and drug discovery, suffer from imbalanced data problems consistently.

In these applications, the class that is of interest is under represented, and thus the accurate classification of the minority class than the majority class becomes difficult. For instance, in intrusion detection systems, attack patterns or malicious activities can be classified by monitoring the network where the number of instances of attacks is comparatively much smaller than the regular network traffic. It is therefore extremely challenging to classify such imbalanced data with machine learning techniques that in general learn from the characteristics of the majority class.

Figure 1 shows a representation of imbalanced data using two classes plotted against two attributes (x-axis and y-axis). The minority class is denoted by circles and the majority class denoted by crosses. In this case, the data points of the minority class may be treated as outliers and anomaly detection algorithms may be applied. However, the classification algorithms require balance between the classes and hence it is challenging to derive optimal classifiers when the dataset is imbalanced.

There are two forms of class imbalance problems in machine learning areas [8]: between-class imbalance data (a commonly occurring problem where the majority class samples out represent the minority class), and within-class imbalance data (it occurs when there exist small clusters of data within a class that are under represented).

When classification algorithm such as C4.5 or any learner in general is applied on imbalanced data, it is more likely to classify the minority class as the majority class [13]. Thus machine learning algorithms like Random Forest (RF) [10], Support Vector Machine (SVM) [1], Deep Learning (DL) [9] may also be biased to majority class. This is because these algorithms are first trained on the class data which has fewer samples of minority data and therefore will be more biased to the majority class. Also, since the data is divided into training and test samples, the probability of bias to the majority class can be even higher. Foster Provost [11] attributed this problem to the assumptions made by the machine learning algorithms.

To handle the imbalanced data problem in classification, a representation learning technique called Synthetic Minority Oversampling Technique (SMOTE) [5], which can be adopted with a classification technique like RF, has recently been proposed in machine learning. The effectiveness of RF

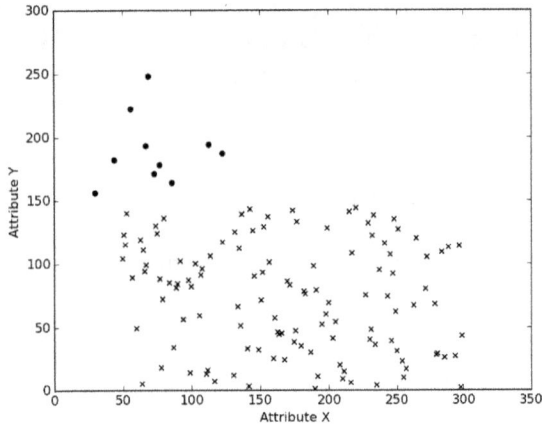

Figure 1: Imbalanced data with two classes

Table 1: Spambase dataset summary

Table 1: Spambase dataset summary

$Number of classes$	2
$Number of Instances$	4601
$Number of Spam mails (Class 1)$	1813
$Number of Non-spam mails (Class 0)$	2788
$Number of Attributes$	57

combined with SMOTE has been reported in machine learning, but modeling of class imbalance and its effect on the performance of RF or RF with SMOTE is still required. Such models will be useful to address big data problems and develop automated tools for information technology.

In this paper we conducted an empirical research using RF, RF with SMOTE and Spambase dataset (available at UCI repository) [2], and modeled the relationship between the variability in minority and majority classes, and the true positive classification rate. The model derived is linear and hence it is useful for automating big data classifiers to handle imbalanced data problems.

2. RANDOM FOREST AND SMOTE

Random Forest is a machine learning algorithm that uses an ensemble approach by combining many decision tree models. To grow these decision trees, firstly different subsets of data are randomly generated from the original dataset with replacement. This is called *bootstrap aggregation* or *bagging*. These subsets of data are then fed to individual decision trees that classify the data by selecting a random subset of the features at each split. The best split at each node is selected using the GINI impurity. Each tree then casts its vote on a class. Random forest then uses the majority vote among all trees to classify the data. In this way each individual tree acts as a weak classifier and combines with all other trees in the forest to become a strong classifier [3]. When a subset of data is used to train a decision tree, the remaining data which is called the out-of-bag sample is used to estimate error and variable importance [4].

Many techniques and algorithms have been proposed to improve the original Random Forest algorithm on imbalanced data. Some of these methods include modifying the imbalanced dataset to balance the data (sampling technique) and associating high cost for misclassification of minority class (cost-sensitive learning) [6]. Oversampling and undersampling are some of the commonly used sampling techniques. Oversampling involves duplicating randomly selected minority class samples, while undersampling involves selecting a small random subset of the majority class for training. Both these techniques balance the data and are simple to implement. However oversampling introduces the problem

of overfitting and undersampling results in loss of information of the majority class. Many of these algorithms have been tested on imbalanced data where the class distribution of minority class may range from 1% to 50%. There is no benchmark on what is the percentage of class distribution that really makes a class imbalanced for classification, and this is the focus of our research presented in this paper.

SMOTE is an oversampling approach in which the minority class is oversampled by creating synthetic or artificial samples instead of oversampling with replacement. It is based on the idea that the samples closer to the minority class also belong to the minority class. This is achieved by introducing new samples along the line segment joining the k-nearest neighbor minority class which are selected based on the Euclidean distances. Based on the amount of oversampling the nearest neighbors are chosen randomly. After choosing the nearest neighbor, the difference between its feature vector with the current sample is computed and multiplied with a random number between 0 and 1. This value is then added to the feature vector space, thus creating a new feature. This way a new sample is created along the line segment between two specific features.

The default implementation uses five nearest neighbors. So, in order to achieve 100% oversampling, one neighbor among the five nearest neighbors is chosen randomly and a new sample is generated in that direction. Using SMOTE, the decision region of the minority class becomes less specific as it is increased by encompassing the nearest neighbors. This is a better approach than the oversampling with replacement technique because mere data replication creates specific decision regions leading to over fitting problem.

3. SPAMBASE DATA SET

For this experiment the spambase dataset from the UCI repository is considered which was donated by George Forman from Hewlett-Packard laboratories, Palo Alto, California [2]. This dataset contains a collection of mails containing regular and spam mails. Spam mails include unsolicited commercial mail with advertisements, schemes for making money, chain letters etc. Table 1 provides a summary of this dataset.

The dataset was created to build a spam filter to distinguish between regular and spam mail. The data for this dataset is collected by the postmaster and individuals filing spam mail. Most of the attributes indicate whether a particular word or character was frequently occurring in email.

For example, word_freq_money indicates the number of times the word money occurs in a mail. This is given as a percentage of words in the e-mail that match the word money. Table 2 shows the percentages for some of the words. Occurrence of words like George, hp (company name) and 650 (area code) indicate genuine mails while words like free, money and the character ! indicate spam mail. Some of the attributes look for uninterrupted characters.

Table 2: Statistics of words in spambase

	free	!	money	george	hp	650
spam	0.52	0.51	0.21	0	0.02	0.02
legitimate	0.07	0.11	0.017	1.27	0.9	0.19

Table 3: Confusion matrix of imbalanced binary class

Class	Predicted (Minority)	Predicted (Majority)
Actual(Minority)	True Positive	False Negative
Actual(Majority)	False Positive	True Negative

Similarly, capital_run_length_longest is the length of longest uninterrupted sequences of capital letters. The last attribute type indicates the class: Class 0 indicates legitimate or regular mail and class 1 indicates spam mail.

This dataset is an example of imbalanced data as the ratio of spam to legitimate email is approximately 0.65. The minority class is the spam email and the majority class is the legitimate email.

4. SETTINGS FOR EXPERIMENT

We have used the Random Forest implementation of the WEKA tool [7] to classify the data. WEKA is a Java package which contains machine learning algorithms for data mining tasks. We first converted the spambase data to .arff format that is supported by WEKA. In order to create different degrees of imbalance characteristics in the dataset, we first fixed the number of minority class instances and then varied the majority class instances in intervals of 100. All the instances are chosen randomly. As shown in Table 1 the spambase dataset has 1813 minority (spam) and 2788 majority (legitimate) class instances and we prepared different subsets of training data as follows: firstly fix the number of minority class instances to 100 and varied the number of majority class instances in intervals of 100 as (100, 100), (100, 200)...(100, 2400) so on. Then incremented the number of minority class instances to 200 repeating the first step as (200, 200)...(200, 2400) so on (1800, 1800), (1800, 1900)..(1800, 2400). This process is followed with minority class instances 300, 400, ... and so on. We generated these samples so that we could create 18 models. Some of these choices can bee seen in the graphs presented in Figure 2.

We also used a ten fold cross validation on training data for Random Forest. Using SMOTE we chose 100% increase of minority data and selecting the default neighbors as 5.

5. PERFORMANCE METRICS

In machine learning confusion matrix has been used significantly as a performance measure of classification algorithms. Confusion matrix shows the relationship between the actual class and the predicted class. It has four parameters true positive (TP), true negative (TN), false positive (FP), and false negative (FN). Table 3 shows the confusion matrix defined for two classes in an imbalanced dataset. TP indicates the number of samples classified as true while they are true. True negative indicates the number of samples classified as false while they are false. False positive indicates the number of samples classified as true while they are false. False negative indicates the number of samples classified as false while they are true. Hence the measures FP and FN give the number of misclassified samples [12].

From the confusion matrix four performance metrics can be derived: accuracy, sensitivity, specificity, and precision. Accuracy gives the percentage of correctly classified instances. For imbalanced data since the minority class is the class of interest it is represented as the positive class and the true

positive rate is equal to the sensitivity. True negative rate or the accuracy of the majority class is equal to the specificity. For the experiment we plotted the graphs for the true positive rates computed using equation 1 [13]. For imbalanced data it is desirable to have a high true positive rate while maintaining reasonable true negative rates.

$$TP\ rate = \frac{TP}{TP + FN} \qquad (1)$$

The true positive rate effects the majority of these measures directly: accuracy and precision and hence the proposed model considers the effect of imbalance data on the true positive rate.

6. MODELING PARAMETERS

We modeled the relationship between the classification rate (true positive rate) using equation 1 and the ratio of minority class size (m_1 and majority class size m_2. Hence m_1 and m_2 are part of the set of modeling parameters. In this set up, we generated several linear models ($y = mx + c$) that are defined by the slope parameter m and the intercept parameter c.

7. RESULTS AND FINDINGS

We plotted the true positive rates using both Random Forest with and without SMOTE by varying the degree of class imbalance in the dataset. These plots are presented in Figure 2 and in these plots the number of majority class instances are plotted in X axis and the true positive rate for the corresponding majority class instances is plotted in Y axis. Each figure belongs to a fixed minority class. For example, Figure 2(a) is for the minority class with 100 instances, Figure 2(b) is for the minority class with 300 instances and so on. In these plots, thick-lines represent the results of Random Forest and dashed-lines represent the results of Random Forest with SMOTE. In addition, the blue lines represent the results of majority class and red lines represent the results of minority class. From these plots, we noted the point of intersection or the breakpoint where both the minority and majority classes show the same true positive rates. The majority classes instances corresponding to these points of intersections are listed in second column (RF) and fourth column (RF with SMOTE) of Table 4 respectively. We also listed the ratio between the minority and majority classes at that instances in third column (RF) and fifth column (RF with SMOTE)) of this table. We can observe that the average ratio of minority to majority class instances is 0.8 for Random Forest and 0.42 for RF with SMOTE. This shows that SMOTE performs significantly better than Random Forest for imbalanced data as expected. It helps our modeling objectives.

We modeled the true positive curves for each minority class as a straight line that describes the relationship between the true positive rate and the majority class instances

Table 4: Breakpoints of True positive rates using Random forest with and without using SMOTE for spambase dataset

Minority class instances	Majority class instances - TP breakpoint using RF	Ratio of minority to majority class	Majority class instances - TP breakpoint using RF and SMOTE	Ratio of minority to majority class
100	151	0.662251656	263	0.380228137
200	273	0.732600733	480	0.416666667
300	373	0.804289544	725	0.413793103
400	445	0.898876404	1006	0.397614314
500	635	0.787401575	1132	0.441696113
600	715	0.839160839	1276	0.470219436
700	913	0.766703176	1580	0.443037975
800	962	0.831600832	1830	0.43715847
900	1046	0.86042065	2100	0.428571429
1000	1195	0.836820084	2400	0.416666667
1100	1390	0.791366906	No breakpoint	
1200	1432	0.837988827	No breakpoint	
1300	1708	0.761124122	No breakpoint	
1400	1855	0.754716981	No breakpoint	
1500	1775	0.845070423	No breakpoint	
1600	1975	0.810126582	No breakpoint	
1700	2098	0.81029552	No breakpoint	
1800	2340	0.769230769	No breakpoint	

Table 5: True positive line coefficient and intercepts for spambase dataset

Slope when RF is used	Intercept when RF is used	Slope when RF and SMOTE are used	Intercept when RF and SMOTE are used
-0.00013813	0.82057971	-7.08E-05	0.926758893
-0.000104447	0.912737154	-4.91E-05	0.963136646
-7.59E-05	0.935910032	-4.00E-05	0.976982684
-5.36E-05	0.931593074	-2.78E-05	0.975990602
-4.12E-05	0.938344361	-2.10E-05	0.977394737
-3.92E-05	0.951798246	-2.07E-05	0.983096549
-3.69E-05	0.961879208	-1.45E-05	0.98012605
-3.81E-05	0.971397059	-1.82E-05	0.989161765
-3.35E-05	0.971326797	-1.47E-05	0.98751918
-2.58E-05	0.971035714	-1.66E-05	0.993857143
-2.56E-05	0.973786214	-1.33E-05	0.992842158
-1.66E-05	0.96010989	-9.19E-06	0.986555458
-2.54E-05	0.982854581	-1.34E-05	0.996566434
-1.54E-05	0.969435065	-7.99E-06	0.988253247
-2.12E-05	0.981951515	-1.76E-05	1.008555556
-2.70E-05	0.997708333	-6.21E-06	0.988478423
-1.39E-05	0.973865546	-1.40E-05	1.003665966
-1.61E-05	0.983511905	-2.30E-06	0.982772487

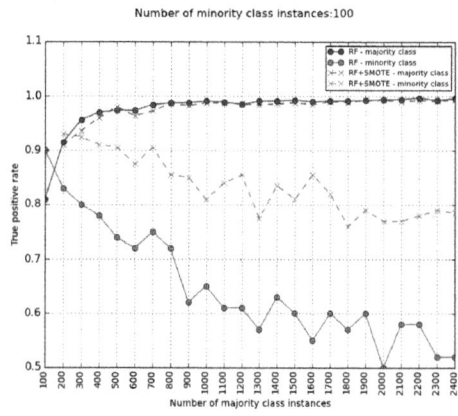

(a) 100

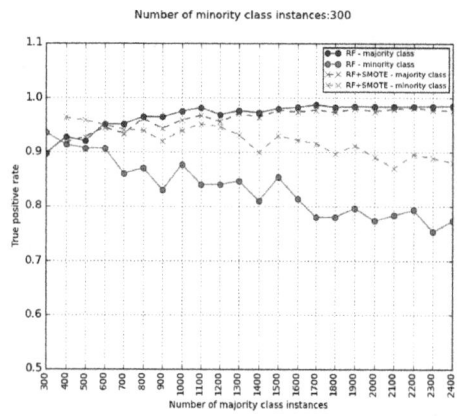

(b) 300

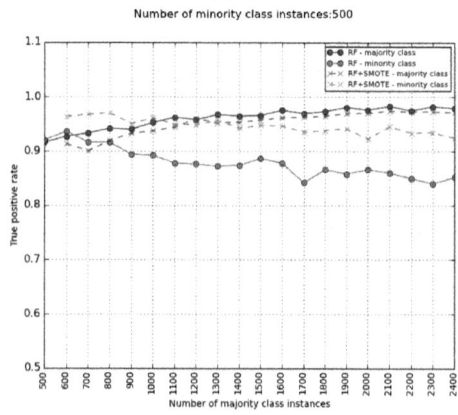

(c) 500

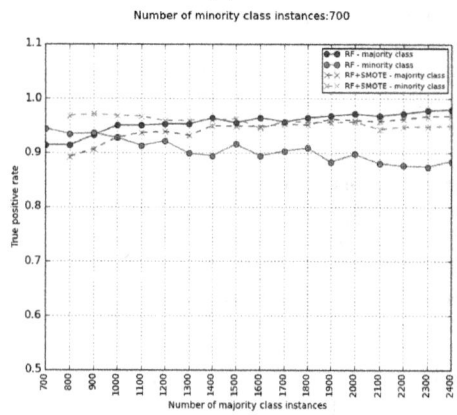

(d) 700

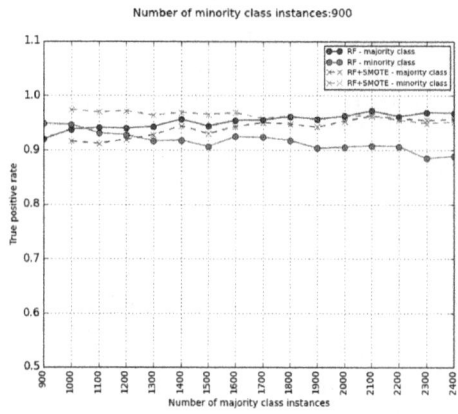

(e) 900

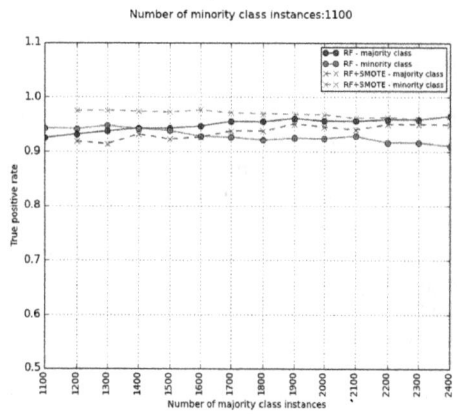

(f) 1100

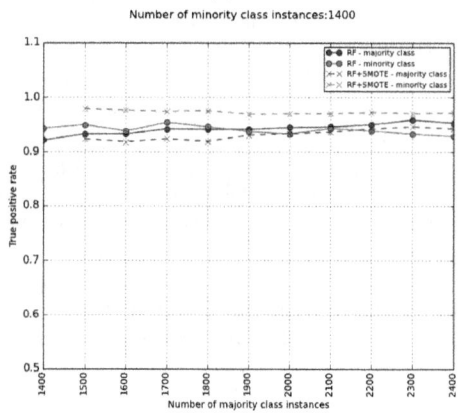

(g) 1400

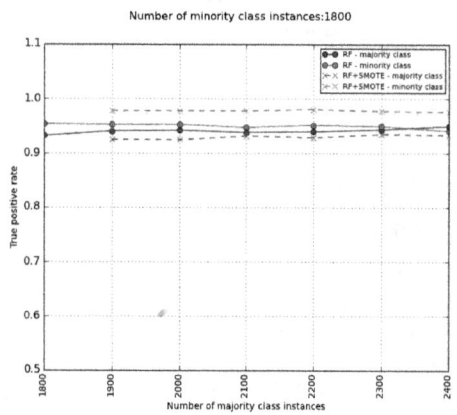

(h) 1800

Figure 2: True positive curve for spambase dataset with different degrees of imbalance

corresponding to a minority class. The slopes (m) and intercepts (c) are in the first and the second columns for RF and the third and the fourth columns for RF with SMOTE respectively. We found that the average slope of the line using RF is -0.0000415 and the average y intercept is 0.954 whereas for RF with SMOTE it is -0.000021 and 0.983 respectively. The slope of the line indicates that SMOTE is consistent with varying degrees of imbalances, the y intercept indicates that the true positive rate is higher when using SMOTE. It is also observed that the true positive rates of the majority class is slightly lesser when using SMOTE compared to random forest without SMOTE. This is natural as using SMOTE the number of instances of minority class is doubled so the classifier is more biased towards minority class if the majority class instances is fewer. Also as the number of minority class instances is increased the gap between the performance of RF with and without SMOTE is reduced. We plotted these average models for RF and RF with SMOTE in Figure 3 where the red line corresponds to the model associated with RF and blue line corresponds to the model associated with RF with SMOTE. The x-axis in this figure represents the ratio between majority and minority classes. This model is useful for predicting true positive rates when RF and RF with SMOTE are applied to big data classification where the imbalanced data is problematic.

Figure 3, for example, provides the following information: when the imbalanced ratio between majority and minority classes in $u : u$, where u is large, then the true positive rate is about 0.95 for RF and 0.98 for RF with SMOTE; when this imbalanced ratio is $3000u : u$, the true positive rate is about 0.84 for RF and 0.93 for RF with SMOTE; and when the ratio is $8000u : u$, the true positive rate is 0.63 for RF and 0.82 for RF with SMOTE.

8. CONCLUSION

This research work shows that linear models that describe the relationship between true positive classification rate and the imbalanced ratio between the majority and minority classes can be generated using an empirical study with imbalanced datasets and classification techniques. In addition, an average linear model can be generated as a predictor to estimate the true positive classification rate for a particular imbalanced class ratio. The linear models that we fit can help in the development of new spam filter algorithms. Although the empirical study is conducted with spambase dataset, RF, and RF with SMOTE, it can be applied to other imbalanced datasets and classification techniques with SMOTE to develop linear models. The parameters of the model will further be studied in future to understand under which conditions the linear model works better. Finally, the proposed models can be used to determine the domain size when multi-domain classification techniques are explored for a big data classification.

9. REFERENCES

[1] R. Akbani, S. Kwek, and N. Japkowicz. "Applying support vector machines to imbalanced datasets." Machine Learning: ECML 2004. Springer Berlin Heidelberg, pp. 39-50, 2004.

[2] K. Bache, and M. Lichman. UCI machine learning repository. http://archive.ics.uci.edu/ml, 2013.

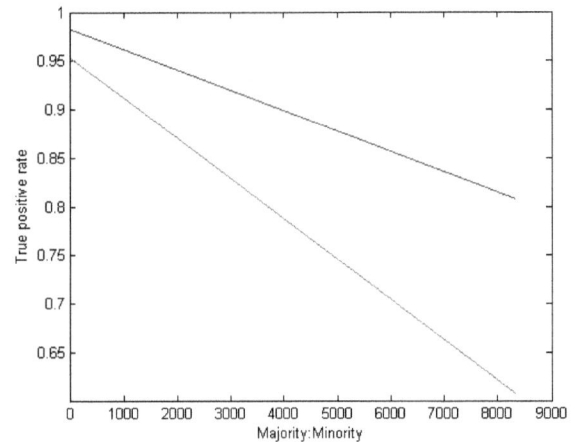

Figure 3: Imbalanced data with two classes

[3] D. Benyamin. "A gentle introduction to random forests, ensembles, and performance metrics in a commercial system." http://citizennet.com/blog/2012/11/10/random-forests-ensembles-and-performance-metrics.

[4] L. Breiman. "Random forests." Machine Learning, vol, 45, no. 1, pp. 5-32, 2001.

[5] N. V. Chawla, K. W. Bowyer, L. O. Hall, and W. P. Kegelmeyer. "SMOTE: synthetic minority oversampling technique." arXiv preprint arXiv:1106.1813, 2011.

[6] C. Chen, A. Liaw, and L. Breiman. "Using random forest to learn imbalanced data," University of California, Berkeley, 2004.

[7] M. Hall, E. Frank, G. Holmes, B. Pfahringer, P. Reutemann, and I. H. Witten. "The WEKA data mining software: an update." ACM SIGKDD explorations newsletter, vol. 11, no. 1, pp. 10-18, 2009.

[8] H. He, and E. A. Garcia. "Learning from imbalanced data." IEEE Transactions on Knowledge and Data Engineering, vol. 21, no. 9, pp.1263-1284, 2009.

[9] G. E. Hinton, S. Osindero, and Y. W. Teh. "A fast learning algorithm for deep belief nets." Neural computation, vol.18, no. 7, pp. 1527-1554, 2006.

[10] T. M. Khoshgoftaar, M. Golawala, and J. V. Hulse. "An empirical study of learning from imbalanced data using random forest." 19th IEEE International Conference on Tools with Artificial Intelligence, 2007, vol. 2, pp. 310-317, 2007.

[11] F. Provost. "Machine learning from imbalanced data sets 101." in Proceedings of the AAAI'2000 workshop on imbalanced data sets, pp. 1-3, 2000.

[12] D. Yao, Dengju, J. Yang, and X. Zhan. "An Improved Random Forest Algorithm for Class-Imbalanced Data Classification and its Application in PAD Risk Factors Analysis." Open Electrical and Electronic Engineering Journal, vol. 7, no. 1, pp. 62-70, 2013.

[13] Weiss, Gary M., and Foster Provost. "The effect of class distribution on classifier learning: an empirical study." Rutgers Univ (2001).

Termediator II: Measuring Term Polysemy using Semantic Clustering

Owen Riley
Brigham Young University
owen.g.riley@gmail.com

Jessica Richards
Brigham Young University
jessicamsrichards@gmail.com

Joseph J. Ekstrom
Brigham Young University
jekstrom@byu.edu

Kevin Tew
Brigham Young University
kevin_tew@byu.edu

ABSTRACT

We report on Termediator II, an application designed to identify potentially confusing terms. Termediator I focused on identifying synonymous terms whereas this work, Termediator II, focuses on identifying polysemous terms. Using an expanded collection of 399 glossaries, we combine hierarchical clustering algorithms and text similarity measures to assign each terms a numeric value indicating its degree of polysemy. Cosine, latent semantic indexing (LSI), and latent Dirichlet allocation (LDA) text similarity measures are evaluated using hierarchical agglomerative clustering with complete and average linkage types. To improve results, we combined bodies of knowledge (BOKs) with the glossaries to create an enhanced training corpus for LSI and LDA. We introduce the convergence value as a new generic metric of polysemy. Polysemous terms are identified by sorting the glossaries by cluster quantity at the convergence value. The similarity measure and linkage type combinations produced slightly different but effective lists of highly polysemous terms.

Categories and Subject Descriptors
H.4.3 [**Communications Applications**]

General Terms
Languages, Measurement, Standardization, Theory

Keywords
Communication; terminology; glossary; XML; processes

1. INTRODUCTION
Rapidly evolving technical vocabularies can cause cross-disciplinary terminological confusion [4]. The term "interface" for example can be defined as: a point where two components meet, the visual layout of a web page or application, the act of communicating with a machine, or the act of communicating between any two entities. Identifying terms with a high potential to cause confusion motivated a project called Termediator I [8].

RIIT'14, October 15 – 18, 2014, Atlanta, GA, USA
Copyright is held by the owner/author(s). Publication rights licensed to ACM.
ACM 978-1-4503-2711-4/14/10…$15.00.
http://dx.doi.org/10.1145/2656434.2656443

The source data for Termediator's analysis comes from technical glossaries. Glossaries, like dictionaries, contain lists of terms that are defined using concepts or definitions. Despite this similarity, glossaries are different from dictionaries in a few fundamental ways that affect our research. Dictionaries start with terms and produce hierarchies of definitions across all domains. In contrast, glossaries start with concepts and produce terms to represent the concepts. Typically, experts author glossaries for use within a particular domain. We can address interdisciplinary terminological confusion at the domain level using glossaries.

To illustrate the problem of "confusing" terms, we introduce two nomenclature definitions: text concepts and abstract concepts. The distinction between a text concept and an abstract concept is important. Text concepts are the text we read when we look up a term in a glossary. For example, a text concept of the term "computer" is "a general-purpose tool for communication and control as well as computation". An abstract concept is the semantic meaning or Platonic "Form" the text concept is trying to represent. Any attempt to represent the abstract concept using text simply creates another text concept. The idea of an abstract concept cannot be concretized. It simply gives us a name for the Platonic ideal that humans attempt to represent with text concept.

The Termediator work focuses on two sources of confusion that occur in communication: synonymy and polysemy. We define synonymous terms as having text concepts associated with the same abstract concept as shown in figure 1. Confusion arises when a person communicates a specific abstract concept using an unfamiliar term to a listener who attaches that abstract concept to another term. The listener can resolve synonymous concept confusion by recognizing a term as unknown and asking follow up questions to resolve the confusion. Termediator I attempted to identify synonymous terms using a cosine distance metric between text concepts [8].

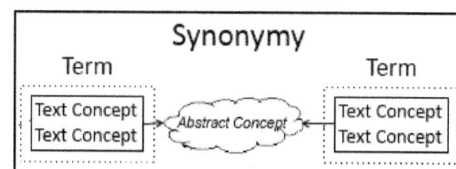

Figure 1. Synonymy Model

Polysemy, meaning "many signs", refers to a term with text concepts that belong to different abstract concepts (figure 2). Confusion arises when someone uses a polysemous term intending one abstract concept but the listener interprets the term as another abstract concept. Confusion from polysemy is more complex than synonymy because both parties use the same term for different abstract concepts and are unaware a miscommunication has taken place. The second revision of our tool, Termediator 2, focuses on identifying and measuring term polysemy.

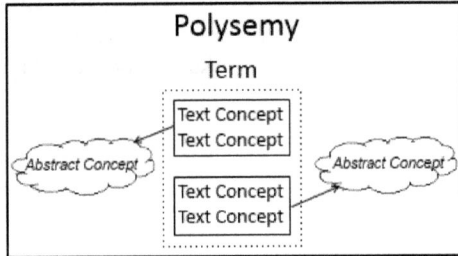

Figure 2. Polysemy Model

We began our investigation into term polysemy with the *sevocab* collection that contained 124 software and system engineering glossaries edited by the IEEE computer society. The IEEE editing process excluded terms that were "considered parochial to one group or organization" or "whose meanings could be inferred from the definitions of the component words" or "whose meaning in the IT field could be directly inferred from their common English meaning" [6].

The number of text concepts associated with each term in the *sevocab* collection initially correlated with the degree of polysemy of that term. In other words, terms that had the most concepts seemed to be the most polysemous as well. We hypothesized that sorting the terms in our compendium by their quantity of text concepts would identify the most potentially confusing terms [5]. Initial results confirmed this hypothesis, placing polysemous terms like "constraint", "process", and "entity" at the top of the list.

As more glossaries were added, the correlation between quantity of text concepts and polysemy deteriorated. Adding 36 glossaries that were not edited by the IEEE introduced some noise into the results such as the term "Gantt Chart" ranking as the 9th most polysemous term in the collection. With 399 glossaries, conceptually simple terms, such as HTML and GIF, had the highest concept frequencies [8]. Terms identified earlier as highly polysemous fell off the resulting lists entirely.

Table 1. Previous Termediator Polysemy Results

124 Glossaries		160 Glossaries		399 Glossaries	
Term	**# Concepts**	**Term**	**# Concepts**	**Term**	**# Concepts**
Constraint	14	Process	22	Bandwidth	54
Process	13	Activity	18	HTML	53
Entity	10	Task	17	Firewall	50
Measure	10	Baseline	15	Browser	49
Function	10	Constraint	14	Software	49
Baseline	9	Stakeholder	14	Internet	47
Implementation	9	Risk	13	URL	46
Input	9	C(A)	12	GIF	44
Activity	9	Gantt Chart	12	Download	43
System	9	Software	12	Virus	43

The new glossaries added to the original collection introduced a new problem: abstract concept duplication. Our initial metric of polysemy, text concept quantity, was premised on the idea that each text concept represented a different abstract concept. *sevocab's* editing process by the IEEE produced a glossary collection that erroneously validated this premise by combining similar text concepts together. Many terms had multiple text concepts communicating the exact same idea after the unedited glossaries were added which rendered text concept quantity ineffective. It should have been obvious that very commonly used terms might be in a lot of glossaries, and that concept quantity was not a sufficient measure of term polysemy. We needed metrics of polysemy that could cut through the commonly used terms introduced by independently generated glossaries.

2. HIERARCHICAL CLUSTERING

We address commonly used terms by combining semantically similar text concepts using clustering. Each term has its associated text concepts semantically clustered so that each cluster represents an approximation of a different abstract concept, or collection of semantically similar text concepts. We will then count the clusters associated with terms exactly like we counted the filtered concepts in *sevocab* with a significantly better result: accurately identifying term polysemy independent of how common a term may be.

Clustering text concepts clears the noise and identifies highly polysemous terms. We hypothesized that if each term's text concepts were semantically clustered together, the most polysemous terms would have the highest number of associated clusters.

A variety of clustering techniques exist which require the number of resulting clusters to be predetermined. There are over 40,000 distinct terms currently in the collection and we have no way of knowing how many clusters to form for each one. As a result, Termediator II employs hierarchical agglomerative clustering (HAC) which produces cluster quantities based on the data and not from a predetermined value. HAC initially places each text concept into its own cluster. Next, HAC systematically combines clusters together hierarchically using an associated proximity matrix starting with the two closest text concepts. The proximity matrix contains semantic distances between each of the text concepts as measured by different algorithms. HAC results are often represented using a dendrogram (figure 3).

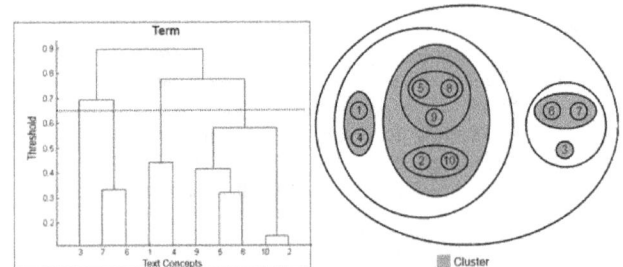

Figure 3. Sample Dendrogram (left) and Alternative Representation (right) with Threshold = .65

The data in the dendrogram can be reduced to a single metric of polysemy by establishing a threshold value. This value takes a horizontal slice of the dendrogram, identifying a cluster for each line it intersects. The number of clusters identified ranges from a single cluster at very high thresholds to N clusters at very low thresholds where N is the number of text concepts being clustered.

Constructing the proximity matrix for text concepts is the first step to performing semantic clustering.

To establish a sense of text concept distance, we chose to use text similarity measures. Highly similar texts would be considered close together while dissimilar texts would be considered distant. We selected three different text similarity measures to evaluate together: cosine similarity, latent semantic indexing, and latent Dirichlet allocation.

Cosine similarity is a simple vector based approach that transforms each text concept into a numerical vector [9]. Vectors consist of a dimension for each unique word found in the corpus. Each dimension is often weighted by a function of the index word's frequency. The idea behind cosine similarity is that similar texts will point in similar directions. Each text concept is transformed into a vector that points in a direction based on the words found within. Similarity is measured by taking the cosine of the two text concept vectors. Cosine similarity relies solely on word occurrence, so two text concepts, no matter how semantically related, will have no similarity if there are no shared words between them.

Latent semantic indexing (LSI), also called latent semantic analysis (LSA), premised on the assumption that words used in similar contexts indicate similar meaning [3]. Using singular value decomposition, LSI can identify similarity between texts even if they don't share the exact same words.

The last similarity measure we evaluated is latent Dirichlet allocation (LDA) that identifies topics, or distributions over words that are found within a particular corpus [1]. LDA measures similarity between texts based on the degree to which they share the identified topics. Like LSI, this allows LDA to detect similarity in texts that don't share the exact words.

LSI and LDA both require training before they can be used to evaluate text similarity. Initially, the compendium was the training corpus with the assumption that the text concepts would contain enough information to generate effective models. Training LSI and LDA requires a predetermined number of topics to be identified. Prior research into the topic quantity parameter by Roger Bradford revealed that an ideal number of topics to create for any sufficiently large corpus is between 300 and 500, and that any value chosen outside this range results in "significant distortions" [2]. We chose to generate 400 topics based on that information.

All three of the similarity measures produce values between zero and one with higher values indicating greater similarity. Taking the complement of the similarity values by subtracting them from one will convert similarity to distance, causing highly similar values to approach a distance of zero and dissimilar values to approach a distance of one. Each term will have a different proximity matrix that is the collection of the distance values generated from the complemented similarity measures between each pair of text concepts.

HAC linkage types play an important role when measuring the proximity of clusters containing more than one member. The proximity matrix generated earlier handles individual text concept proximity, but it does not handle how to determine the proximity of clusters of text concepts. What is the distance between two clusters that each have two text concepts? We initially looked at three main linkage types to evaluate: single, complete, and average. Single linkage compares the two closest points of the clusters, which in our data is the two most similar text concepts from both clusters. We chose not to evaluate single linkage

because prior research has shown that it "generally gives results that are far inferior to those obtainable when the other hierarchic agglomerative methods are used" [10]. Complete linkage compares the two furthest points, or the two most dissimilar text concepts between two clusters. Average linkage compares the centroids of the two clusters. Both complete and average linkages were evaluated to compare their effectiveness.

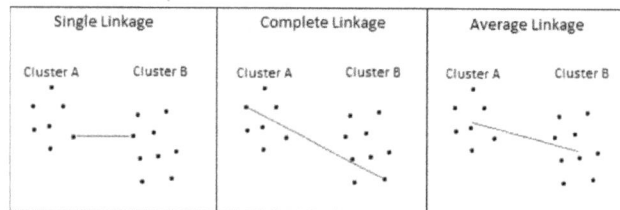

Figure 4. Cluster Linkage Types

The clustering threshold determines where each term's dendrogram would be sliced. The HAC process repeatedly combines the nearest two clusters until the closest two are further apart than the threshold. A candidate clustering threshold would result in the majority of terms having their text concepts semantically clustered properly, with each cluster representing a single abstract concept. We attempted to obtain data leading to a candidate threshold through crowdsourcing because of the subjectivity of determining when a term's text concepts are "properly" clustered. We hoped a larger representative sample would eliminate any individual biases. A web application that visually displayed clusters for a set of sample terms allowing users to manually adjust the threshold until the clusters appeared "right" was created. It was expected that the submitted thresholds would create a regular distribution that we could take the mean from as our chosen clustering threshold.

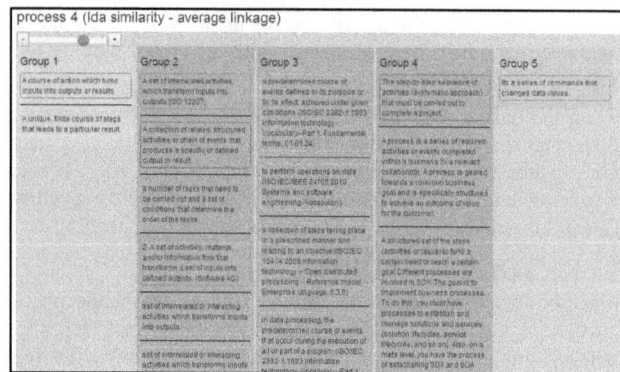

Figure 5. Crowdsourcing Tool Interface

The interface shown in figure 4 allowed users to pick a term and then adjust a threshold slider shown in the upper left which would instantly adjust the resulting clusters accordingly. Sliding it to the right would result in fewer clusters, essentially sliding the threshold line shown in figure 2 upward. Once each group contained text concepts that all discussed the same idea according to the user, the threshold was recorded.

The amount of text that needed to be visually processed and the complexity of the semantic clustering concept proved to be too overwhelming for users resulting in little valid data being collected. Despite this setback, the crowdsourcing tool's visual representation of the clusters illuminated a new potential measure of complexity. Adjusting the thresholds of various terms in the tool revealed that terms converged into a single cluster at different thresholds. Terms we considered to be complex converged at higher thresholds than terms we considered to be simple. For each similarity measure and linkage type, we collected the threshold value when the last two clusters converged for every term, calling these convergence values. Graphing them all at the same time revealed a similar trend regardless of the similarity measure or linkage type used (figure 5).

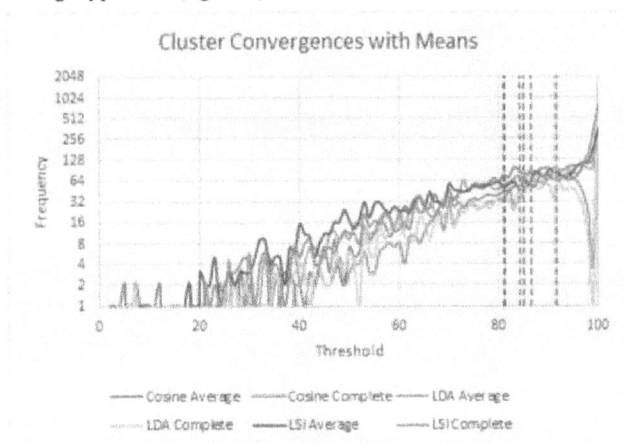

Figure 6. Convergence Values with Means

The failure of the crowdsourcing app to generate a candidate threshold led to the discovery of convergence values. Since the convergence values appeared to be a general indicator of term polysemy, we chose to use them in place of the data generated by crowdsourcing. To generate our chosen threshold, we took the mean of the convergence values for each combination of similarity measure and linkage type. Each mean convergence value was located in the last quartile of the possible thresholds in the same range that the experiments with the crowdsourcing tool revealed as being ideal.

Using the cosine, LSI, and LDA similarity measures along with the complete and average linkage types with their associated mean convergence value, we performed hierarchical clustering on each term in the compendium and sorted the results by cluster quantity. This produced six different lists of terms shown in appendix A.

3. RESULT ANALYSIS

Semantic clustering uses the actual text of text concepts to calculate a numerical degree of polysemy for terms. Our prior methods in Termediator I only counted the number of text concepts. By letting the text play a role in determining term polysemy, our semantic clustering tool is able to determine term polysemy much more effectively.

Many of the polysemous terms identified in our early prototypes are found in each of the new lists. These terms include constraint, process, and entity. Alternatively, many of the less polysemous terms identified in later prototypes like HTML and GIF have completely disappeared. Terms in the resulting lists shown in Appendix A contain anywhere from 7 to 67 text concepts. Comparing the number of clusters with the number of text concepts reveals that there is no direct correlation meaning terms with high numbers of text concepts are not guaranteed to be highly polysemous.

Our Termediator II tool mitigates the noise of terms with many associated text concepts. Due to the subjective nature of polysemy, it is difficult to objectively rank the six lists generated by semantic clustering. We cannot mathematically state which list is "best", but we can say that all six are comparable and filled with highly polysemous terms. The measure of cluster quantity we have identified in this paper appears to be a general indicator of polysemy.

Some slightly polysemous terms like "kilobyte" still managed to appear near the top of our results despite our efforts to remove them. We attribute the noise to the short text problem of lacking adequate contextual information within text concepts. For example, take the following three text concepts obtained from the term "byte":

- Eight bits is equal to 1 byte.
- The representation of a character.
- A unit of measure of computer memory.

Each of the three text concepts takes a different approach to describing the same fundamental idea. Short length prevents text concepts from being easily clustered together even with advanced similarity techniques. We set out to improve our results despite facing this fundamental short text problem by improving the training corpus used by LSI and LDA. LSI and LDA are both capable of overcoming the vocabulary mismatch problem, which is when different words are used to describe the same idea. The training process for both LSI and LDA identifies words that co-occur often, so words like "computer" and "desktop" can have high similarity. Improving the training corpus may strengthen these relationships and better deal with vocabulary mismatch resulting in better clustering and better polysemy detection overall.

4. IMPROVING TRAINING CORPORA

We wanted to try to improve the effectiveness of the training corpus used in both LSI and LDA by using a collection of bodies of knowledge (BOKs). Bodies of knowledge are official domain specific documents produced by academic and professional expert groups which outline topics of study. A collection of bodies of knowledge from various domains is an ideal choice for expanding the training corpus for both LSI and LDA because each BOK already contains lists of topics chosen by consensus within academic and professional circles. The word relationships and patterns found in the bodies of knowledge are much stronger and higher quality than those found in the glossaries due to having been generated through the consensus of specialists.

We obtained 16 different bodies of knowledge from several different domains and converted them into a standard XML format. We evaluated the bodies of knowledge effectiveness as a training corpus by looking at the topics generated with LSI because, unlike LDA, LSI produces topics ordered by prevalence. The bodies of knowledge alone generated poor topics that consisted of unrelated words. The topics generated by the compendium were much more related and stronger as a result.

We evaluated whether or not adding the bodies of knowledge to the compendium for the training would further increase the topic quality. The topics themselves were too similar to determine the stronger corpus so we performed semantic clustering using both corpora and compared the results. Training with the compendium with the bodies of knowledge appeared to produce lists of more polysemous terms than training on the compendium alone. For example, the term "Workstation" dropped significantly in one of the LDA lists which allowed terms we considered to be more polysemous to rise up as shown in table 2.

Table 2. Top 5 Polysemous Terms (LDA-Complete)

RANK	WITHOUT BOKS	WITH BOKS
1	Data	Interface
2	Interface	Risk
3	Workstation	Object
4	Firewall	Function
5	Baseline	Firewall

The poor quality of the topics generated from the bodies of knowledge alone was surprising considering all the points made previously. One reason for the bodies of knowledge inability to stand up as a training corpus is likely due to its small size. Compared to the compendium, the body of knowledge collection has about ¼ the number of entries. The poor topic quality is also likely due to the number of topics generated, which we chose to be 400. For the size of the bodies of knowledge, 400 may have been too high.

5. METRICS OF TERM POLYSEMY

From our research, we were able to identify two metrics that indicate the polysemy of a term. The first measure was the convergence value, or the threshold value when every text concept becomes a member of a single parent cluster. Through experimentation with the crowdsourcing tool, we discovered that conceptually simpler terms had lower convergence values than polysemous terms. We showed that no matter what combination of similarity measure and linkage type we used, they all produced convergence values that followed a similar trend.

The second polysemy metric is cluster quantity which cannot be obtained without first determining a clustering threshold. We planned on taking the mean of the thresholds collected using the crowdsourcing tool but replaced those thresholds with the convergence values when little crowd sourced data was obtained. Using a similarity measure to determine text concept proximity, a linkage type for establishing standard cluster proximity, and the threshold for knowing when to cease clustering from the mean convergence value, we clustered the text concepts for every term in the glossaries. Each cluster within a term indicates a different key idea leading to the conclusion that terms with higher cluster frequencies have higher polysemy.

We used the first metric, convergence value, to calculate the second more powerful metric, cluster quantity. The metrics were used to generate all new lists showing the most polysemous terms for each of the similarity measure and linkage type combinations. There are ten terms found in every one of the six generated lists which summarize the effectiveness of semantic clustering. This list is a clear improvements over the previous list generated using concept quantity as the sole metric of polysemy (table 3). Conceptually simple terms, regardless of the number of text concepts found in the glossaries, have much lower cluster frequencies and drop down in the term rankings when using our methods.

Table 3. Top 10 terms by Polysemy Metric Alphabetized

Old Metric _# of Concepts_	New Metric _Semantic Clustering_
Bandwidth	Design
Browser	Function
Download	Interface
Firewall	Object
GIF	Risk
HTML	Signature
Internet	System
Software	Task
URL	Template
Virus	User

6. CONCLUSION

Searching for a candidate threshold for the semantic clustering led us to key findings. First, we learned that our crowdsourcing application was too complex for users despite our attempts at simplifying the process. The tool itself gave us a new perspective on visualizing the clusters which was previously unavailable. Using the tool, along with our attempts to find an initialized threshold in the interface, revealed a new generic measure of term complexity that we call the convergence value. We noticed that simpler terms tended to converge into a single cluster earlier than more complex terms. Experimentation showed that taking the mean convergence value for the whole compendium gave us values around the same thresholds that the crowdsourcing tool showed were ideal for accurately semantically clustering a term's text concepts.

Comparing the resulting lists of polysemous terms is difficult because all six contain complex terms and no clear winner emerges. Despite that, the semantic clustering techniques are generally effective regardless of the similarity measure and linkage type used and are far superior to our initial metric of term polysemy: concept quantity.

REFERENCES

[1] Blei, DM, AY Ng, and MI Jordan. "Latent Dirichlet Allocation." _the Journal of machine Learning research_ (2003).

[2] Bradford, Roger B. "An Empirical Study of Required Dimensionality for Large-Scale Latent Semantic Indexing Applications." _Proceeding of the 17th ACM conference on Information and knowledge mining - CIKM '08_ (2008): 153.

[3] Deerwester, Scott, ST Dumais, and TK Landauer. "Indexing by Latent Semantic Analysis." _JASIS_ (1990).

[4] Ekstrom, JJ, and BM Lunt. "Academic IT and Adjacent Disciplines 2010." _Proceedings of the 2010 ACM conference on ..._ (2010).

[5] Ekstrom, JJ. "Experience with a Cross-Disciplinary Aggregated Glossary of Technical Terms." _Proceedings of the 13th annual conference on ..._ (2012).

[6] ISO/IEC 24765 (SEVocab), http://pascal.computer.org/sev_display/24765-2010.pdf

[7] Metzler, Donald, Susan Dumais, and Christopher Meek. "Similarity Measures for Short Segments of Text." Advances in Information Retrieval (2007)

[8] Richards, Jessica, Owen Riley, Joseph J Ekstrom, and Kevin Tew. "Termediator□: Early Studies in Terminological Mediation Between Disciplines." _Proceedings of the 2013 ACM conference on Information technology research_ (2013).

[9] Salton, G, A Wong, and CS Yang. "A Vector Space Model for Automatic Indexing." _Communications of the ACM_ 18, no. 11 (1975)

[10] Willett, Peter. "Recent Trends in Hierarchic Document Clustering: A Critical Review." _Information Processing & Management_ 24, no. 5 (January 1988): 577–597

Appendix A

COSINE						LSI						LDA					
AVERAGE			COMPLETE			AVERAGE			COMPLETE			AVERAGE			COMPLETE		
Term	# Clusters	# Concepts	Term	# Clusters	# Concepts	Term	# Clusters	# Concepts	Term	# Clusters	# Concepts	Term	# Clusters	# Concepts	Term	# Clusters	# Concepts
Function	11	25	Interface	10	42	Interface	13	42	Interface	14	42	Interface	10	42	Interface	12	42
User	8	34	Firewall	10	67	Function	10	25	Function	11	25	Risk	9	30	Risk	10	30
Risk	8	30	User	9	34	Template	9	28	Bandwidth	11	64	Function	9	25	Object	10	32
Resource	8	12	Spam	9	53	Signature	9	31	User	10	34	Signature	8	31	Function	10	25
Process	8	36	Risk	9	30	Object	9	32	Risk	10	30	Scope	8	17	Firewall	10	67
Object	8	32	Function	9	25	Unit	8	13	Object	10	32	Policy	8	13	Template	9	28
Interface	8	42	Design	9	23	Stakeholder	8	19	Firewall	10	67	Object	8	32	Encryption	9	46
Entity	8	18	Data	9	41	Scope	8	17	Signature	9	31	Design	8	23	Baseline	9	42
Cc	8	13	Baseline	9	42	Process	8	36	Node	9	31	CC	8	13	Authentication	9	36
Case	8	15	Bandwidth	9	64	Feedback	8	15	Network	9	47	Baseline	8	42	User	8	34
Unit	7	13	Signature	8	31	Design	8	23	Header	9	24	AI	8	14	Signature	8	31
Template	7	28	Object	8	32	Constraint	8	21	Domain	9	32	User	7	34	Scope	8	17
Task	7	29	Node	8	31	CC	8	13	Design	9	23	Template	7	28	Path	8	20
State	7	12	Encryption	8	46	Baseline	8	42	Constraint	9	21	Standard	7	13	Design	8	23
Spoofing	7	20	Domain	8	32	Spoofing	7	20	Bot	9	21	Padding	7	10	Database	8	44
Signature	7	31	Cc	8	13	Risk	7	30	Baseline	9	42	Lol	7	11	Class	8	23
Set	7	10	Bot	8	21	Resource	7	12	Authentication	9	36	Firewall	7	67	CC	8	13
Scope	7	17	Virus	7	61	Queue	7	18	Stakeholder	8	19	Class	7	23	AI	8	14
Robot	7	15	Terminal	7	25	Pi	7	8	Scope	8	17	Worm	6	43	Worm	7	43
Project	7	16	Template	7	28	Parameter	7	13	Protocol	8	48	Tos	6	13	Terminal	7	25
Policy	7	13	Task	7	29	Lol	7	11	Process	8	36	Testing	6	17	Task	7	29
Non-Repudiation	7	15	System	7	20	Link	7	23	Gateway	8	30	Task	6	29	System	7	20
Feedback	7	15	Phishing	7	35	Header	7	24	Flash	8	30	System	6	20	Standard	7	13
Domain	7	32	Link	7	23	Error	7	15	Encryption	8	46	State	6	12	Spoofing	7	20
Design	7	23	Input	7	23	Entity	7	18	Data	8	41	Spoofing	6	20	Node	7	31
Data	7	41	Header	7	24	Domain	7	32	Cut	8	11	Simulation	6	21	Measure	7	17
Constraint	7	21	Feedback	7	15	Data	7	41	Client	8	37	Resource	6	12	Lol	7	11
Class	7	23	Entity	7	18	Cut	7	11	CC	8	13	Queue	6	18	Link	7	23
Bot	7	21	Database	7	44	Case	7	15	Thread	7	18	Process	6	36	Kilobyte	7	25
Authentication	7	36	Client	7	37	Bot	7	21	Terminal	7	25	Paradigm	6	7	Header	7	24

Author Index

www.ingramcontent.com/pod-product-compliance
Lightning Source LLC
Chambersburg PA
CBHW061350210326

41598CB00035B/5945